Communicable Disease Control

THE MACMILLAN COMPANY
NEW YORK · CHICAGO
DALLAS · ATLANTA · SAN FRANCISCO
LONDON · MANILA

BRETT-MACMILLAN LTD.
TORONTO

Communicable Disease Control

A Volume for the Health Officer and Public Health Nurse

THIRD EDITION

BY

GAYLORD W. ANDERSON, M.D., Dr. P.H.

Mayo Professor and Director, School of Public Health, University
of Minnesota; Formerly Director, Medical Intelligence Division,
Office of The Surgeon General, War Department; Formerly
Deputy Commissioner and Director of the Division of Communicable Diseases, Massachusetts Department of Public Health

AND

MARGARET G. ARNSTEIN, R.N., M.P.H., Sc.D. (Hon.)

Chief, Division of Nursing Resources, United States Public Health
Service; Formerly Consultant in Communicable Disease Division,
New York State Department of Health; Formerly Associate Professor of Preventive Medicine and Public Health and Director of
the Course in Public Health Nursing, University of Minnesota

New York, 1957   THE MACMILLAN COMPANY

Printed in the United States of America

Preface to the Third Edition

In preparing a third edition of this volume, *Communicable Disease Control,* the authors have realized that they were faced with a dual task —modernization and perspective. The first of these is the usual problem of any revision. It has involved incorporation of new knowledge and removal of that which is outdated. While the developments of the past five years have been somewhat less striking than were those of the years of World War II, the advances have nevertheless been so far reaching that many of the practices acceptable in 1948 are today obsolete. New antigens and drugs have been developed, new uses found for old products. New concepts of pathogenesis have been advanced, with resultant changes in administrative practices. As the work of revision has progressed, the authors have been increasingly impressed with the progress and changes of the years that have elapsed since the earlier revision. In accordance with the policy followed in the earlier editions, historical developments— including recent concepts and practices that have been superseded as a result of new discoveries—are discussed only to the extent necessary for an understanding of present-day thought and practice.

The second task, change in perspective, has been more difficult. As public health problems and causes of death, the communicable diseases have declined in importance. At the turn of the century they accounted for 31 per cent of all deaths in the registration states. The first quarter of the twentieth century saw such striking reductions in the death rates that public health workers justly prided themselves on their accomplishments. None could foresee, however, the almost phenomenal changes that lay ahead in the second quarter of the century. Antibiotics, chemotherapy, insecticides, new antigens, improved case-finding procedures—these are but a few of the significant developments that have brought about an unprecedented decline in the toll of infectious disease. Today these diseases are responsible for less than 7 per cent of the deaths in the United States, and several of the infections that were rampant a few years ago are now medical curiosities. The concept of "eradication" has appeared more and more in the literature.

All of this necessitates a change in perspective. No longer can the health department program be built around the communicable diseases.

Death Rates for Certain Diseases
U.S. Registration Area
Deaths per 100,000 Population

	1900	1925	1950
Diphtheria	40.3	7.8	0.3
Malaria	6.2	2.0	0.1
Measles	13.3	2.3	0.3
Pneumonia (and influenza)	202.2	121.7	27.0
Scarlet fever	9.6	2.7	0.2
Tuberculosis	194.4	84.8	22.6
Typhoid fever	31.3	7.8	0.1
Whooping cough	12.2	6.7	0.7

No longer can the prospect of lower rates from typhoid fever, malaria, hookworm, or diphtheria be used to persuade a community of the need for a full-time health department. No longer must the health officer budget so heavily for the care of infectious disease, nor does the community need to plan so generously for hospitalization for these conditions. As a group, the communicable diseases have been brought under control, and each year sees even more striking reduction. The health officer must put these conditions in their proper relationship to the other needs of his community health program. He must analyze critically those procedures that are worth while and eliminate those that are unproductive, however much they may be hallowed by tradition.

Yet the successes of which public health is so proud must neither blind us to the problems that remain nor lull us into a sense of complacency. There are still many unknowns in the infectious diseases, much still to be accomplished in applying that which is already known. Poliomyelitis and encephalitis have not been controlled. Tuberculosis still causes over 30,000 deaths a year. Children still die from diphtheria and whooping cough. Brucellosis is widespread, and the common cold is as common as ever. Rheumatic fever is still uncontrolled; each year it leaves thousands of children or young adults with seriously damaged hearts. In many parts of the world intestinal infections still rank as a major cause of death, and malaria is far from eradicated. Jungle yellow fever is a constant threat; and cholera, plague, and typhus may at any time escape their bounds. The virulence of many of the infections has declined, but there is no assurance that this decline is permanent nor that present control measures will be equally effective if virulent strains of organisms reappear. The incidence of some infections may actually be increasing. While we may take just pride in past accomplishments in control of infectious disease, we must be equally on our guard lest this pride turns into complacence. "Pride cometh before a fall."

In preparing this revision the authors have tried to recognize this change in perspective without losing sight of the need for continued watchfulness. An attempt has been made to evaluate control procedures, eliminating wherever possible those which cannot be shown to be of value. Opinions will doubtless differ as to certain details, for there are many difficulties and hazards in trying to sail the narrow channel between the Scylla of overcaution and the Charybdis of neglect. To the extent that the procedures and ideas here presented are progressive and modern yet at the same time not dangerously radical, the authors will have succeeded in their task.

Three new chapters have been added. One of these deals with the control of communicable diseases in the school. Such a chapter seems indicated as the schools present many special administrative problems. For ease of reference, much of the school material that appeared under other headings in the first two editions has been brought together in this new chapter. The other new chapters deal with hepatitis and Q fever, problems of growing importance to health departments.

As in earlier editions, we have been aided greatly by our associates, friends, and critics who have made invaluable suggestions. To all of these we present our sincere thanks, even though we may have failed to concur with all of them. We alone accept full responsibility for the ideas here expressed. In no way should they be interpreted as official pronouncements or expressions of opinion of the agencies with which we are now or have formerly been connected.

GAYLORD W. ANDERSON
MARGARET G. ARNSTEIN

Preface to the Second Edition

The seven years which have elapsed since the publication of the first edition of this volume have probably witnessed more important changes in communicable disease control practice than has any comparable period of history. It has been a period of war in which scientific and technical developments, rather than brute strength, have been deciding forces. As in former years, infectious disease has often been a dominant element in determining the success or failure of military ventures. At one period infection, uncontrolled, threatened the entire success of the Pacific campaign.

During this period, the threat of disease has been met with research which has provided new weapons of communicable disease control far superior to any previously possessed. One needs merely mention the advent of penicillin, DDT, new antimalarials, and new antigens to realize the strides that medical progress has taken during this era. Many other discoveries, such as the sulfonamides, tetanus toxoid, and typhus and yellow fever vaccines which were relatively new and untried at the outbreak of war, have been subjected to severe field tests and found to measure up to the most optimistic predictions as to their efficacy. Many other fields of research have been actively pursued and valuable, though somewhat less spectacular, additions made to our armamentarium of disease prevention. Military necessity has been the spur and has often provided the facilities for much of this progress, but no one should lose sight of the fact that this progress rested on long and tedious fundamental research during the years of peace. Without this background, the rich harvest of war research could never have been reaped.

Although these new developments have greatly altered many of the details of disease control and opened many new vistas, they have not altered the fundamental principles. These remain unchanged and even strengthened. The student who has a firm grasp of these fundamentals has the framework on which he can hang new details as they become available.

In preparing this revision, the authors have therefore made no change in the fundamental pattern but have attempted to incorporate the many developments of the past seven years. The full impact of many of these is still not clear. Much is still even in the realm of controversy. Whenever possible we have attempted to indicate these elements of uncertainty, yet have felt impelled to assist the reader by some sort of temporary appraisal. It should be recognized, however, that such appraisals are hazardous and may be upset by subsequent experience and research. An open mind in such matters is an essential attribute of every intelligent reader.

As in the first edition, the bibliography has been prepared as a guide to the reader who wishes to study a given topic more extensively but does not have access to a comprehensive metropolitan library. So far as possible, therefore, references have been given to the most readily accessible journals and to review articles even though this has often meant the deliberate omission of excellent articles in less accessible journals and of many articles to which historical priority is doubtless due. The reader who wishes to make an exhaustive review of any topic will obviously pursue his readings far beyond the few references that can be appended to any chapter.

In the preparation of this review, the authors are again indebted to their colleagues and friends who assisted with many helpful criticisms of the first edition and suggestions for the second.

GAYLORD W. ANDERSON
MARGARET G. ARNSTEIN

Preface to the First Edition

Communicable disease control presents two rather distinct problems, protection of the individual and protection of the community. While it is true that the community is merely the sum of its individual members, nevertheless the problems of protection are not simply the mass application of personal prophylaxis. The community presents a complex mixture of social, political, and economic influences that may either facilitate or impede the spread of disease. These same influences affect the control measures that may be developed. Just as the test-tube methods of the chemical research laboratory must be modified for adaptation to large-scale, industrial production—even though the basic reaction is unchanged—so must individual disease control measures be patterned according to community needs. Procedures that are effective in protecting the individual are often too expensive or cumbersome to apply en masse, whereas other measures of only partial personal value may yield real community protection if they reach a large enough group.

This volume is written principally from the standpoint of the community. While personal protection has not been neglected, emphasis has been placed on those procedures which are designed to protect the population as a group rather than merely the individual. In preparing the manuscript we have had in mind the problems that confront the health departments, the schools, the visiting nurse associations, and other community agencies. An attempt has been made to evaluate the various control measures as to their relative effectiveness and to outline programs that will yield the greatest return in terms of necessary expenditure. The public or private agency knows its problem is that of giving the greatest degree of protection for the greatest number of persons from the money made available through the appropriating agencies. It is therefore essential that funds not be wasted on control practices that yield too few returns; often expenditure of this money elsewhere in the public health program will give more health protection to the taxpayers. We have therefore attempted to appraise the practical value of various control measures and have been led to discard or minimize the importance of many as yielding too few returns in terms of the severity of the problem and the expense involved.

We have limited our discussion of control measures to those that are applicable under the conditions which confront the health department. No attempt has been made to consider details or techniques included in hospital care; patients so treated pass from the jurisdiction of the health department to that of the hospital authorities. Home care is always a community problem and often a health department's responsibility; it has therefore been included. The role of the sanitary officer and the principles governing his work have been pointed out; for the details of method and procedure the reader should consult the standard references on community sanitation. In the selection of diseases to be discussed, we have been governed by a desire to include those of major interest in most communities. Some diseases of great importance in other parts of the world have been given scant attention, because they are of such limited or local concern in the United States under present conditions.

Experience has taught us that a clearer concept of the epidemiology and control of the infectious diseases is obtained if an orderly pattern of thought is followed. The several diseases have therefore been considered under a set pattern that has been found to be useful for the student. The reader will note many repetitions. The pattern that has been followed makes these inevitable, but they have been retained to give a reasonable completeness to the several units of thought. No attempt has been made to include an exhaustive discussion of the epidemiology of the individual diseases; rather have we limited ourselves to those few facts essential to an understanding of the control program.

The references at the end of each chapter are intended as a guide to the student who wishes to supplement the material here presented. A conscious effort has been made to select books and periodicals to which the average reader will find easy access. Especially have we drawn upon review articles which summarize investigations within a rather broad field and which are supplemented by more extensive bibliographies. It is believed that these will be of more value to most workers than will exhaustive references to original data, though the serious and inquisitive student will, of course, wish to examine the facts upon which reviews are based. References presenting both sides of controversial matters have been included, regardless of our personal convictions as to the merits of the case. The reader should draw his own conclusions.

In the preparation of this volume we have had immeasurable aid from our associates and friends. In particular we are indebted to Dr. Wilson G. Smillie, who advised with us on the chapters on malaria and hookworm disease; to Dr. J. Arthur Myers, who read the chapter on tuberculosis; to Dr. Nels A. Nelson, for assistance with the chapter on gonorrhea and syphilis; to Professor Theodore Olson, for help with the chapters on diseases spread through arthropods; to Miss Ida McDonald, for advice with respect to the nursing sections; and to Miss Jean Hirsch, for the diagrams. These friends cannot be held responsible for the views here expressed. This responsibility we alone must assume, with full regret and apologies if we have failed to profit from the counsel given us. The New York State Health Department kindly consented to extensive use, and at times virtual copy of certain sections of its manual on communicable disease nursing, for the preparation of which the junior author had been largely responsible. The members of our respective families and our colleagues on whom we have tried out various parts of the volume deserve special credit for their patience, understanding, and friendly advice.

In preparing this volume, it is our hope that it may be of value to other communicable disease control workers who, like ourselves, have often wished that the wealth of material in current periodicals might be abstracted and appraised as to its applicability to community problems.

GAYLORD W. ANDERSON
MARGARET G. ARNSTEIN

Contents

List of Tables

Part One

1. Historical Considerations

Communicable disease control practices of any era depend upon the prevailing concepts as to the cause of these conditions and the manner of their spread. These concepts have varied from period to period under the changing influence of human thought and the degree to which man has placed a correct and practical interpretation upon his observations. These observations as to the circumstances under which illness occurs have therefore been the foundation upon which theories of the cause and prevention of communicable diseases have been built. Man observed that plagues and pestilences appeared under certain conditions as to season, weather, movements of people, floods, heat, and other variables and associated these observations with his current philosophy regarding these variables. Many of the theories that he evolved to explain these circumstances seem naïve and grotesque today; yet others represented correct observations of essential facts, though the explanations are inadequate and unsound in the light of modern bacteriology. An understanding of the growth of knowledge in this field is essential to a clear conception of present practices, for unfortunately much of the lore and mysticism of earlier philosophies persists in the public mind and hampers the application of modern scientific methods.

ERA OF RELIGION

A philosophy of life that we call religion is one of the basic characteristics of all mankind. The most primitive man observes some form of worship, though the object of his reverence may vary from a tangible deity associated with his everyday life to the invisible spirit of higher religions. Coincidental with the recognition of a good spirit, the deity, has been the concept of an evil force equally associated with tangible objects or vague spirits. To the former have been attributed those events and occurrences that exerted a favorable influence on human affairs; upon the latter have been blamed the unfavorable happenings. Primitive religion was a balance between these forces, and the success or prosperity of a tribe was believed to depend upon whether the good or the evil spirit prevailed.

The most primitive tribe of man unquestionably recognized that from time to time plague and pestilence appeared within its midst, involving large numbers of persons and killing many of them. As this operated to the detriment of the tribe, it was naturally attributed to the evil spirit, who was taking this means of wreaking destruction upon mankind. The reasoning was simple. If other harmful influences such as famine, drought, and storm were but manifestations of the working of the evil spirit, so was disease. If disease involved but one person, he was believed to be under the spell of the devil. The ravings of the maniac were attributed to the fact that he was possessed of a devil. An epidemic involving many persons was evidence of the operation of this spirit upon the tribe rather than the individual. In either case the remedy was the same—appeasement of the evil spirit or driving the devil out of the afflicted. Which course might be followed depended upon man's estimate of his power over this spirit. The remedy was in any case some sort of dealing with this evil spirit and was, therefore, within the hands of the tribal priest. Some peoples believed in appeasement through offerings of human wealth, others through sacrifice, which at times involved human beings. These measures were our earliest and most primitive form of disease control. They were surrounded with the mysticism of this type of religion, and their execution was entrusted to the religious officer of the tribe. Thus evolved the association between the medicine man and the priest.

As man's religious thinking developed from this primitive form to a somewhat higher stage, he still associated disease with his religion but, quaintly enough, transferred the responsibility from the evil to the good spirit. Under such a philosophy one conceived of disease as the punishment for sin. Plague and pestilence were the punishment that an offended deity meted out to sinful men, who had transgressed the divine laws. When David, inspired by Satan, offended Jehovah through numbering the children of Israel, his people suffered through pestilence; and in three days "there fell of Israel seventy thousand men" (I Chron. 21:14). Early historic records abound with such explanations of epidemic disease. Obviously these are records of facts, for recurrent waves of disease did occur. The explanation as to their cause was in each instance based upon the existent belief that they were the act of an offended deity, who either inflicted his punishment directly or permitted an evil spirit to prevail temporarily. The remedy was, however, the same as before. Through the religious officer, man sought to appease the offended deity by making such offerings or atonements as his religious rituals prescribed.

Although these explanations of the cause of pestilence were commonly accepted by the primitive tribes, it should not be inferred that their influence ceased with civilization. The recurrent waves of plague, smallpox, and cholera that swept over Europe during the Middle Ages were described as punishment for mankind's sins. Days of prayer, of fasting, and of sacrifice were set aside as control measures. Peoples who had discarded the former doctrines instinctively drifted back to them when, faced with pestilence that raged uncontrolled through the application of current measures, they found themselves helplessly in the grip of a veritable conflagration of disease. In Colonial times when smallpox raged in Boston, days of prayer were set aside, though at the same time the General Court prudently moved across the bay to Charlestown to avoid the infection. Cotton Mather preached that the disease was the avenging whip of God, yet in the next breath urged inoculation upon his parishioners. When yellow fever ravished Philadelphia in 1793, the idea of an avenging God was revived. In 1832 President Jackson was petitioned to set aside a day of national prayer and fasting as a precaution against the spread of cholera, which had made its appearance on the North Atlantic seaboard. Even in the present biological era (that is, the period since the discovery of bacteria), we find many persons who sincerely believe that spiritual and not material forces condition the development of epidemic diseases.

ERA OF PHYSICAL FORCES

The beginnings of a physical philosophy as to the spread of disease appeared long before the discard of the religious theories. Man observed that the occurrence of these illnesses was associated with certain physical states of the environment. Out of these observations he evolved complicated and often grotesque theories as to the causation. One of the first of these variables to be studied carefully was the motion of the stars and planets. Astrology ascribed all happenings on this earth to the relative position of the heavenly bodies. Wars and famines were so explained; naturally plague and pestilence were considered in the same light. Other theories attributed these conditions to earthquakes or other terrestrial phenomena. Grotesque as these notions may appear today, they exerted great influence over certain peoples. That they have not fallen entirely into popular discard even at the present time is attested by the recurrent vogue of modern-day astrologists.

Certain correlations between disease and environment were based on sounder observations and therefore contained elements of truth, though the theories advanced to explain these phenomena were essentially unsound. Even primitive man had noted variations of disease with season as well as association with climate, temperature, moisture, overcrowding, and filth. From these observations certain physical theories evolved. Foremost among these was that of toxic miasmata and vapors, a theory that dated from the writings of Hippocrates in the pre-Christian era and was further advanced by the teachings of the early Christian period and the Middle Ages. According to these doctrines disease was caused by hypothetical poisonous substances that rose up from the earth and might be spread through the winds. Those who lived near swamps showed a high incidence of fevers, thought to be due to the poisonous gases emanating from the marshes. Thus the surrounding air was made bad, and the fever came to be known as malaria (*mal aria,* bad air). Here obviously was a correct observation as to the association between a definite disease entity and environmental influences. As marshes were known to generate gas, it was logical to attribute the disease to this pollution of the air. It was not until the end of the nineteenth century that the role of the mosquito in the spread of malaria offered a better explanation of this centuries-old observation.

This doctrine of miasmata and vapors held sway until the end of the nineteenth century. It apparently explained many facts in the occurrence of certain diseases, even though it was frequently stretched to rather extreme limits to fit other diseases. The crowding of people into cities resulted in conditions of extreme filth, especially in the poorer sections. Here were to be found the highest disease rates; plague and pestilence wrought their greatest havoc in these areas. It was but natural to attribute these diseases to the toxic emanations of decaying filth and to overlook the now obvious fact that the overcrowding favored the transmission of infection from person to person. The rapid spread of cholera in squalid, congested tenements was attributed to the filth among which the victims had lived, an explanation with a certain element of truth, though it failed to recognize the communicability of the disease.

So dominant was this doctrine of toxic vapors, often thought to be due to decaying animal and vegetable matters, that rather fantastic theories as to the cause of certain epidemics were advanced. Thus in 1793 Benjamin Rush ascribed the outbreak of yellow fever in Philadelphia to the decay of coffee that had been piled upon the wharves. Diphtheria was attributed to sewer gas, typhoid to decaying filth and somewhat later to the emanations of defective house drains. It was only after long years of bitter dispute that house sewage was admitted to the London sewers which had been built originally as street drains. In other cities it was also held to be dangerous to contaminate these drains with human waste lest the gas from these sewers pollute the air. In Munich, Pettenkofer advanced a theory of typhoid that explained outbreaks as due to the rise and fall of the level of the ground water.

Current practices for the control of epidemics were naturally built upon these theories. Among the most spectacular of these measures were the firing of a cannon [1] and the building of huge fires to purify the polluted air. Fumigation was used to purify the air of houses where disease had occurred. A wrecked ship on which cholera patients had traveled was punctured in order to let out the poisonous air and later burned. Even houses were burned. Programs to remove filth were instituted. A Massachusetts statute dating back to 1797 empowered boards of health to regulate "dangerous and noisome odors"; later these boards were instructed to control "sources of filth and causes of disease." Philadelphia attempted to ward off the invasion of cholera in 1832 by a program of municipal cleanliness. The nuisance-regulating powers at present quite generally vested in boards of health are vestiges of this doctrine of the relationship between filth and disease.

The theory did much to advance community sanitation, even though it offered an incorrect explanation of the true origin of communicable diseases. Upon it were erected the forerunners of our modern health departments. Without it, sanitation, municipal cleanliness, and public health might have been greatly retarded. Although the theory has been pushed aside in the light of modern bacteriological knowledge, its influence remains. It still colors much popular thinking that fails to differentiate between decay and specific infectious disease germs. Man is slow to discard the doctrines of past generations, especially when the doctrines brought about such tangible improvements as municipal sanitation. It need occasion little surprise, therefore, that the filth-miasmatic theory of disease should linger in the popular mind, since it was barely seventy years ago that bacteriology began to show how untenable were some of its doctrines.

EARLY GROWTH OF THEORY OF COMMUNICABILITY

Although the religious and miasmatic theories of disease held sway until the end of the nineteenth century, there were many indications of a growing belief in the communicability of these conditions from one person to another. The Mosaic law as set forth in the Old Testament contains

[1] As late as the end of the nineteenth century, cannons were occasionally fired in the hope of stopping an epidemic of yellow fever. History does not record that many mosquitoes were hit.

public health regulations that recognized the importance of human contacts as well as environmental factors in the spread of disease. The children of Israel were forbidden to eat pork or shellfish and were instructed in the safe disposal of human wastes and in avoidance of contact with lepers. Certain passages have been interpreted as referring to the communicability of gonorrhea. The incorporation of these public health regulations as an integral part of a religious code was but a reflection of the current ideas of the association between disease and morals. Violations of these sanitary principles were considered sins, offensive to the deity, and accordingly punishable by the development of disease.

Many of the early medical writers likewise recognized the possibility that disease might spread from person to person. Travelers from afflicted areas were frequently detained lest they be bringing disease with them. The trail of sickness in the wake of the crusades and the diffusion of disease by those who returned are frequently recorded. When syphilis spread over Europe in the early sixteenth century, its conveyance from one person to another was recognized. In the midst of the panic that prevailed during the various epidemics of plague, smallpox, and yellow fever, the sick were carefully shunned and even cruelly left unattended in their illness. Even the well were at times avoided. Segregation of lepers was observed with a fervor that amounted to little less than persecution.

Thus in the midst of the prevailing theories of miasmata and toxic emanations from decaying filth, there was constant evidence of an expressed belief that disease might spread from person to person. This was even extended to conditions such as yellow fever, now recognized as noncommunicable through direct association. Although medical teaching might vigorously deny the communicability of these conditions, the public instinctively gave expression to a contrary belief, at the same time accepting the miasmatic theory. Thus the public was in some measure prepared to receive the teachings of bacteriology at the end of the nineteenth century.

BACTERIOLOGICAL ERA

Just as other theories of the spread of disease were intermingled with one another, so may the evolution of the bacteriological concepts be traced from rather primitive beginnings several centuries before the work of Pasteur. The studies of Anton van Leeuwenhoek in Holland in 1676 had shown the existence of microscopic forms of life. It had even been suggested that these might be of pathogenic significance, though this suggestion was not taken seriously. Between this time and that of Pasteur, there had been a slowly growing attention to this realm of microscopic organisms.

The investigations of Pasteur in the latter half of the nineteenth century may, however, be considered as the beginning of the bacteriological era, as this earlier work did nothing to influence medical thought or action. Pasteur proved beyond doubt that certain diseases were due to microscopic forms of life. Many of these he was able to recognize and to grow outside the body. When the organisms were transferred to animals, disease ensued. In other cases the communicability of these diseases could be demonstrated even though the causative agent could not be isolated and identified under the microscope. He further showed that these bacteria did not arise spontaneously from decaying vegetable or animal matter but were in all instances the offspring of pre-existing bacteria of the same character. These findings were rapidly confirmed and extended by his associates in France, by Koch and his pupils in Germany, and by a rapidly growing number of students in all parts of the world.

The recognition of the role of microscopic organisms gave rise to entirely new concepts in disease prevention. Whereas these plagues and pestilences had heretofore been considered more or less spontaneous in origin, due to environmental factors, their communicability was now clearly proved and logically explained. Previously infected persons were recognized as the foci from which disease might spread. Environmental influences dwindled to mere secondary factors which might facilitate the spread of disease but could not possibly originate it and which were important only to the extent that certain environments permitted the germs to survive outside of the body long enough to pass from one host to another.

It should not be inferred, however, that the miasmatic theories were lightly discarded in favor of the newer ideas regarding the bacterial origin of certain diseases. The discoveries of Pasteur were the subject of frequent and, at times, acrimonious attack by the medical and public health leaders of the period. The filth-borne theory offered a more obvious and readily understood explanation of certain conditions than did the supposition of germs too small to be seen by the naked eye. Many physicians vehemently denied the communicability of these diseases. To some it seemed fantastic to believe that such minute objects could be of significance to human beings. Further, in only a few of the diseases could specific bacteria be demonstrated. As the idea of healthy carriers had not yet been advanced, there were apparent inconsistencies in rejecting the idea of spontaneous generation yet in accepting the idea of bacteria as a cause of disease.

In spite of an almost militant opposition, the germ concept of disease was firmly established by the end of the nineteenth century. The factual evidence upon which it was based was incontrovertible, whereas the filth theory was highly speculative. Each decade brought startling discoveries in bacteriology, and new diseases were added to the list of those shown to be so spread. The discovery of the role of insects as vectors opened new vistas and cleared up certain troublesome problems that had held back ready acceptance of the new ideas. The further recognition of animals as sources from which certain diseases might spread to man clarified other problems. Although there were and still are those who persisted in denying the evidence of the bacteriological laboratory, the germ concept has by now become no longer mere theory but rests on solid factual foundations.

The bacteriological explanations opened up new avenues of disease control. Since the sources from which infection spread might now be recognized, segregation to avoid the dissemination of the disease and even complete control and eradication were envisioned as possibilities. Isolation and quarantine found full justification and were advocated with an ardor that made it difficult to accept what was later learned as to their limitations. Fumigation and disinfection were pursued with enthusiasm in the hope of destroying the germs as they passed from host to victim. Cleanliness found new champions. The attention devoted to inanimate objects during the miasmatic era was even intensified, though made more specific. Such attention was fixed upon inanimate objects of the environment, not as spontaneous breeders of disease, but as vectors of specific infection. It was not until after the turn of the century that concern for material objects as vectors began to be replaced by consideration of human beings as primary sources. The discovery of carriers and the work of the late Dr. Charles V. Chapin in Providence, Rhode Island, in showing the relatively greater importance of persons than of things as spreaders of disease marked the end of the teachings of the miasmatic-filth era.

Coincident with the growth of knowledge concerning microorganisms as the cause of communicable disease, there evolved a sister or companion science, immunology. It had been known for centuries that certain diseases rarely attacked the same individual more than once. So long as the miasmatic theories persisted, there could be no satisfactory explanation of these observations. Even less satisfactory could be the theories advanced in explanation of artificial protection acquired against smallpox through vaccination. Edward Jenner's discovery of vaccination had antedated the germ concept of disease by approximately three-quarters of a century, and inoculation against smallpox had been known much longer. Neither could be explained satisfactorily on the basis of spontaneous origin of disease through decaying filth. They had to await the advent of the science of bacteriology before a satisfactory explanation was forthcoming. Pasteur's early work with anthrax and later his work with rabies opened up new possibilities in disease prevention through increasing the resistance of the potential new host.

Thus bacteriology introduced not only a new concept as to the origin and mode of spread of infectious disease but coincidentally ushered in a new era of prevention through specific control measures and artificial immunization. It wiped out unsound ideas based upon unsupported hypothesis and theory and replaced these with new concepts which rest upon proven fact. It permitted accurate analysis of older theories so as to retain what ideas and procedures were basically sound and coupled these with new concepts to give us the present methods of communicable disease control. This is the era in which we now live—an era rich in heritage but equally abounding in new ideas only recently developed through exploring the secrets of nature.

One is at times inclined to wonder that there should have been opposition to the teachings of the bacteriological school. Likewise, one may be tempted to impatience at the slowness of the public to discard the outmoded and disproven doctrines of the miasmatic-filth theories. It seems hard to understand that ideas shown to be so fallacious should color current thinking on the part of the public and should still retard the application of modern methods of disease prevention. Yet on second thought we can perhaps wonder that the present-day knowledge has been so rapidly accepted in view of the heritage of misconceptions that had to be discarded. The thinking of the public does not change rapidly, except perhaps on political subjects. It took centuries for the world to accept the mathematical and astronomical teachings as to the shape of the earth. No one has ever seen a ghost, and our sober sense tells us that such apparitions do not exist; yet how many can truthfully deny a sense of uneasiness when in situations suggestive of the dead? How many still persist in believing that thirteen is an unlucky number? Who is there who does not have some favorite remedy for certain forms of indisposition, even though there is no basis of fact to support the use of this form of treatment?

The human mind does not change its ideas rapidly. We have been brought up by parents reared in an era when the miasmatic theories were still popular. Our grandparents did not hear about germs until long after their formal schooling. It is not surprising, therefore, that many vestiges of these theories of yesterday should persist. They have been written into legislation, have set precedents for board of health procedure, and are ingrained in the subconscious thoughts of the people. The public health worker must not expect these ideas to disappear in a single generation. He should be grateful that they have faded as rapidly as they have and must exercise patience when his path of progress is rendered difficult by their survival.

SUGGESTED READINGS

Chambers, J. S.: *The Conquest of Cholera: America's Greatest Scourge.* New York: Macmillan Co., 1938.

Chapin, Charles V.: *The Sources and Modes of Infection,* 2nd ed. New York: John Wiley & Sons, 1912.

Greenwood, Major: *Epidemiology, Historical and Experimental.* Baltimore: Johns Hopkins Press, 1932, pp. 1–25.

————: *Epidemics and Crowd-Diseases: An Introduction to the Study of Epidemiology.* London: Williams & Newgate, Ltd., 1935, pp. 15–67.

Hirsch, A.: *Handbook of Geographical and Historical Pathology.* Translated by Charles Creighton. London: The New Sydenham Society, 1883–86.

Newman, Sir George: *The Rise of Preventive Medicine.* London: Oxford University Press, 1932.

Newsholme, Sir Arthur: *Evolution of Preventive Medicine.* Baltimore: Williams & Wilkins Co., 1927.

————: *The Story of Modern Preventive Medicine: Being a Continuation of the Evolution of Preventive Medicine.* Baltimore: Williams & Wilkins Co., 1929.

Winslow, Charles-Edward Albert: *The Conquest of Epidemic Disease.* Princeton: Princeton University Press, 1943.

Winslow, Charles-Edward Albert; Smillie, Wilson G.; Doull, James A.; and Gordon, John E.: *The History of American Epidemiology.* St. Louis: C. V. Mosby Co., 1952.

Zinsser, Hans: *Rats, Lice and History.* New York: Little, Brown & Co., 1935.

2. The Infectious Process

Epidemiology is the science of the occurence of disease. The late Dr. William H. Welch expressed the same concept when he defined it as the study of the natural history of disease. The word is derived from two Greek words: *epi,* upon, and *demos,* people. It thus refers to what descends upon the people and was originally restricted to the study of those diseases that occur in epidemic proportion. Even though the philologist might maintain that this should still be its proper use, custom has broadened the concept of the word to embrace not only the occurrence of disease in explosive outbreaks but also the existence of disease in any form or degree of prevalence. Occasionally, one finds persons who restrict the use of the word to refer to the infectious conditions. While this may have certain etymological support, current usage has extended the term to apply to all forms of disease regardless of cause. Thus we may study the epidemiological aspects of cancer or pellagra or pernicious anemia just as we may study the factors leading to the occurrence of measles or typhoid fever.

The study of epidemiology embraces consideration of all factors that condition the occurrence of disease. It considers the specific cause, be it bacteriological, physiological, or chemical. Of equal interest or importance are the many secondary factors which favor the development of disease when the primary etiological force is operative. These secondary factors may be economic, sociological, political, even religious. It likewise considers the problem of treatment, inasmuch as prompt and effective care in the early stages may either lessen the spread of infection or reduce the likelihood of development of permanent damage to the body. Thus epidemiology is catholic in its interests, attempting to consider all the factors that may directly or indirectly cause or favor the development of disease either in the individual or the community.

Epidemiology is the backbone of disease prevention. It is obvious that, in order to control a disease effectively, we must know under what conditions it exists and what factors favor its development. Unless we have this knowledge, we cannot hope to achieve effective control; with this information, we may so organize our efforts as to strike the disease at its most vulnerable spot. We do not attempt to correct or control every factor leading up to the development of the condition. Such would be obviously impossible and certainly inefficient even if it were possible. Rather do we study the epidemiology of the disease to learn the etiological or predisposing factors and then direct our energies at those that can be controlled the most readily. This process of control directed by epidemiological study is particularly effective in dealing with the communicable diseases, which concern us in this book.

Every case of infectious disease represents the result of the operation of a series of factors, all of which lead up to the final result, the case. Each step depends upon the successful completion of the preceding one. There is thus a chain of events, the completion of which is necessary if disease is to ensue. If this chain is broken in any of its many links, disease will not develop. The common remark that a chain is no stronger than its weakest link is amply illustrated by the infectious diseases. Epidemiological study of these diseases is, therefore, directed particularly to the search for the weak links. These are the spots where we may direct our control energies with full assurance that, if we can but break the chain at one spot, we need not worry over the integrity of the other links. As diseases differ from one another in the location and nature of these weak spots, the measures effective in the control of one disease may be very different from those useful in the prevention of another. Only through a study of epidemiology can we understand the principles of disease control.

THE NATURE OF THE INFECTIOUS DISEASE PROCESS

The term "infection" implies that an organism capable of causing disease is present and multiplying within the body. Strictly speaking, the word might refer to the presence of any organism regardless of its disease-producing potentialities, but convention restricts the term to those organisms which may, under favorable circumstances, bring about illness. The term also implies that the body responds in some way to defend itself against the invader even though the evidence of this response may not be readily visible. As inanimate objects, such as food and water, cannot respond, the presence of microorganisms in or on them is usually referred to as "contamination" rather than "infection." It is well to recognize, however, that the term "infected" is used very commonly (and by the dictionaries) to refer to the presence of pathogens in or on inanimate substances as well as in the body. Thus reference is commonly made to "infected" milk or food, even though the purist will insist on use of the word "contaminated." [1]

The term "disease," on the other hand, implies visible interaction between the organisms and the body that is infected. Whenever infection of the animal body occurs, a struggle between the invading organisms and the body ensues. Each is vying for supremacy over the other. The visible evidence of this struggle we label "disease." This interaction may be manifested by symptoms such as fever, rash, malaise, nausea, diarrhea, and so forth. Lacking these signs or symptoms, we have no simple way of recognizing this struggle and may overlook the fact that it is going on. Thus, the border line between the broad concept of infection and that portion of it that we conventionally call disease is very indistinct and depends on our diagnostic acumen. The same process or struggle may be going on within the body in both instances; but, in the case of disease, it reaches the level of our consciousness.

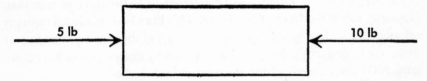

FIG. I.   *Forces acting on a block.*

A simple analogy may assist in the development of a sound understanding of infectious disease processes. In the physics laboratory, the student has observed the effect of forces acting upon a block which rested on a hypothetical frictionless plane. He has found that, if a force of 10 lb operating to the left is opposed by a force of 5 lb operating to the right (Fig. I), the block will be moved to the left with a force of 5 lb. This result has been reached by determining the difference between the two opposing forces. When several forces are exerted at each end of the block and they are directed toward it at varying angles, it is necessary to resolve these forces into a single resultant force, the magnitude and angle of application of which depend upon the magnitude and angles of application of the components. The student of physics learns simple methods of measuring these resultant forces and can determine exactly what will happen to the block under any circumstances.

---

[1] The distinction seems to the authors to be rather strained and unnecessary. Furthermore, it leads to highly illogical terminology, for the term "disinfection" is limited to refer only to inanimate objects. Thus objects which by definition cannot be infected can nevertheless be disinfected, while persons and animals which can be infected are never referred to as being disinfected. The reader may well find this illogical but such is convention. The authors have felt bound to follow this convention even though they do not approve of it.

If we were to replace this block by the animal body and replace these mechanical forces by the specific forces of infection and resistance, we should have a picture of what happens when infection occurs. The body is acted upon by two opposing forces, those of infection and those of resistance (Fig. II). The infecting forces are made up of many compo-

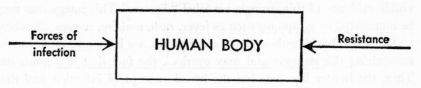

FIG. II. *Forces of infection and resistance.*

nents, such as the type of infecting organism, its quantity, virulence, and capacity for multiplication and invasion. All of these act to the detriment of the body. Their resultant may be referred to as the force of infection. Opposing this is the force of resistance. This likewise is made up of many components, such as specific antibodies and all of those nonspecific factors that serve to protect the body against invasion by disease-producing organisms. All of these together form the resistance of the body.

What happens to this body under such circumstances will depend upon the difference in magnitude between these two opposing forces. If the infecting forces are sufficiently greater than the resisting forces, we have the development of disease, possibly even a fatal attack if the difference is large. If the difference is slight, we may have a very mild form of the disease, so mild in fact that it escapes unrecognized; if the forces are equal, the so-called "carrier condition" (see p. 23) may develop. On the other hand, if the resistive forces are sufficiently greater than the infecting forces, no infection will occur. The relative magnitude of these forces may vary from time to time during an infectious disease.

The relative severities of the infectious process may be expressed graphically in the form of a spectrum of infection. Everyone has seen a spectrum of light. It is easy to see that the colors vary from one end of this band to the other but difficult to determine just where one color ceases and another begins. The spectrum of infection (Fig. III) is very comparable. At one end we have the fatal cases; at the other, cases so mild that they cannot be detected except by special bacteriological procedure. The severe cases merge imperceptibly into the moderately severe, and these into the mild cases. The difference in magnitude of the infecting and resisting forces determines the place which an infected body will occupy in this spectrum of disease at any particular moment.

This concept of variable severity of infection is fundamental to the establishment of effective control measures. The student who reads the conventional description of an infectious disease is likely to forget that this portrays the symptoms and findings which most commonly occur in a moderately severe attack. He is apt to gather the impression that the

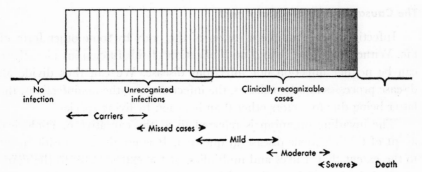

FIG. III.   *Spectrum of disease.*

infectious process is a clean-cut entity and that a person either has a disease or has not. Many physicians assume too quickly that an infection is not present simply because the symptoms described in the textbook are absent. These symptoms are present only in the severe half of the spectrum; they are frequently absent in the milder half and completely lacking in the zone of invisible infection. Yet infection exists in all these cases, and the possibility of conveying it to a second person is equal in all parts of the spectrum. As we shall see later, the risk of spread is actually greater from cases in the milder end simply because these cases are usually overlooked and no precautions taken to guard against such spread.

THE DEVELOPMENT OF THE INFECTIOUS DISEASE PROCESS

For the development of the infectious disease process, six factors are essential:

1. A causative or etiological agent
2. A reservoir or source of the causative agent
3. A mode of escape from the reservoir
4. A mode of transmission from the reservoir to the potential new host
5. A mode of entry into the new host
6. A susceptible host

These represent a logical sequence of factors or links of a chain, all of which are essential to the development of the infectious disease process.

If any one of these links is lacking, disease will not ensue even though the remaining five factors may be present. It is desirable at this point to consider the general nature of these components. In the second part of this book, the individual diseases will be considered from these several standpoints.

The Causative or Etiological Agent

Infection represents the invasion of the body by some other form of life. Without the growth and multiplication of this foreign invader, there can be neither infection nor infectious disease. We can thus divide all disease processes into two classes, the infectious and the noninfectious, the latter being due to factors other than invasion by living species.

The invading organism is referred to as the causative or etiological agent of the infectious disease in question. It is usually a parasitic agent to the extent that it lives and multiplies, at the expense and to the detriment of the host. In occasional instances, there may be so satisfactory a balance between the invader and the host that temporarily, at least, no ill effects are noticeable, as in the case of certain carrier conditions or in the case of the colon bacillus (*Escherichia coli*), which is harmless so long as it is confined to the lumen of the intestinal tract. Such a relationship, if truly harmless to the host, is referred to as a commensal or symbiotic relationship. The border line between parasitism and symbiosis is, however, rather vague and indistinct, as it is often difficult to determine whether or not the foreign species is really harmful to the host. Thus, although we may not be aware of damage to the body due to the carrier condition, careful pathological study may show that a local disease process is operative but is so mild as to be overlooked when judged by the conventional criteria. There are many reasons to believe that a carrier condition never occurs without some local reaction to some degree detrimental to the host. The only true symbiotic invaders of the human body are the bacteria that naturally inhabit the intestine; yet these can be pathogenic if they escape into other tissues.

Types of Infecting Organisms. This is not the place for a detailed classification of organisms that can invade the animal or human body. The student of bacteriology and parasitology is familiar with such groupings. For our purpose, a very simple classification is adequate.

Animal Parasites. These are members of the animal kingdom that can attack the human body through invasion. Collectively they are often referred to as the "parasites" to distinguish them from other types of invaders. By the same token, the study of them is frequently referred to as "parasitology." Invasion of the body by these parasites was formerly referred to as "infestation" in contradistinction to "infection," which was reserved as a term for invasion by other pathogens.[2] Currently the term "infestation" is being restricted to refer to the presence of parasites on the surface of the body, while the term "infection" has been broadened to include the invasion of the tissues by animal parasites.[3]

The animal parasites may be simply grouped into:

1. *Protozoa.* These are one-celled animal forms, such as the amebae, trypanosomes, and plasmodia.

2. *Metazoa.* These are animals of more than one cell. Those of special significance to human beings are the various worms.

Bacteria. Although there are many subdivisions of bacteria, we are not concerned with classification here. Of the many known, only a few can attack the human body; such are referred to as "pathogenic" bacteria.

Viruses. The viruses, formerly referred to as "filtrable viruses," represent an ultramicroscopical form of life. As they present certain differences from the bacteria and possess many characteristics peculiar to their own group, it seems warranted to classify them separately. Biologically, the most important difference between viruses and bacteria is that viruses invade the living tissue cells and multiply within them whereas the bacteria do not invade the cells of the host which they parasitize. Thus viruses are often referred to as obligatory intracellular parasites. Knowledge of viruses is advancing rapidly but has not yet shed clear light upon their true nature. They are recognized by the effects which they produce upon the body rather than by our ability to separate them out and look at them. Epidemiologically, the diseases which they cause present certain characteristics distinguishing them from bacterial infections. Among the common diseases due to viruses are measles, mumps, smallpox, rabies, and poliomyelitis.

Rickettsiae are so closely related to viruses that the two are frequently classed together. They resemble bacteria in that they are visible under the microscope and resemble viruses in that they are found within tissue cells. Biologically, they act like the viruses. Among diseases caused by rickettsiae are typhus fever and Rocky Mountain spotted fever.

Plant Parasites. A few members of the plant kingdom may attack the human body and thus set up disease processes. The best examples of these are certain fungi and molds, producing such conditions as epidermophytosis and coccidioidomycosis.

Specificity of Infecting Organisms. So far as is known, each form of life represents a specific entity, capable of reproduction and giving rise to

[2] A pathogen is an organism, of whatever type, that is capable of producing disease.
[3] *J. Parasit.*, 23:325–26, 1937.

offspring which are identical with, or closely resembling, the parent. Conversely, each form of life is derived from a parent form of the same character. This principle of specificity of species was a point of major dispute during the nineteenth century. Many at that time believed in spontaneous generation, a concept according to which life might spring *de novo* from other organic though nonliving material. It was supposed that flies might come from manure, worms from vinegar or water, and bacteria from decaying filth. The work of Pasteur showed conclusively that there is no form of life without pre-existing life and that each species is derived from previous generations of the same species; these concepts, therefore, have now become axiomatic in biology. They are of major importance to the student of infectious disease, for upon this concept rest all our attempts at control. Typhoid bacilli are derived only from pre-existing typhoid bacilli; diphtheria bacilli, from diphtheria bacilli. Were this not so, our control measures could not be directed at the specific sources of these bacteria.

Although the concept of specificity means that diphtheria bacilli always give rise to diphtheria bacilli and never to typhoid or scarlet fever organisms, it does not, however, imply that this new generation will be identical in every minor detail with the parent generation. We know that, through growth and reproduction under special circumstances, certain characteristics of these organisms may be altered. These changes may not be seen in a single generation but may appear or become noticeable after repeated generations. The organisms are still diphtheria bacilli, capable of causing no disease other than diphtheria; but they may differ in certain respects. This variation in properties of successive generations is frequently encountered in the viruses. It does not, however, affect the fundamental concepts of the specificity of organisms and the dependence of life upon pre-existing life.

Mode of Action of Parasitic Organisms. The invading organisms may attack the host either through (1) processes of direct invasion or (2) the production of toxins which poison the body. The former implies the establishment of an inflammatory process with resultant tissue destruction followed by repair if recovery occurs. In some instances, the parasite may actually invade the body cells (viruses, rickettsiae, and malaria parasites) and bring about cellular changes and possibly destruction. Action through toxins is more characteristic of certain bacteria. These toxins are poisonous substances released during the life or destruction of the bacterial cell. They may produce a local irritation or be absorbed and carried by the blood stream to distant parts of the body. Thus the damage to the body may occur at parts far distant from the site of entry or growth of the bacteria, for example, in tetanus, in which the toxin produced by the bacteria growing at the site of the wound is carried by the blood stream to the central nervous system.

The Reservoir of Infection

Since life cannot be derived from other than pre-existing life, it is obvious that all infecting organisms must, for their perpetuation, have certain places where they can live and multiply. Lacking these, they would die out. These places of usual growth and multiplication are referred to as the reservoirs of infection. Whenever a person is infected with a communicable disease, it means that he has received organisms either directly or indirectly from such a reservoir.

With one or two possible exceptions, all organisms pathogenic for man are incapable of prolonged growth and multiplication under natural conditions outside the living body [4] and are, therefore, derived from human or animal sources. Thus the animal kingdom represents the principal reservoir for pathogens attacking man. For purposes of discussion we can divide this reservoir into several groups.

Human Reservoirs. Most of the infectious diseases to which man is heir are more or less specific to, or characteristic of, man and, therefore, derived from some other infected person. The human being is thus the most important reservoir of these diseases. Human reservoirs may be subdivided into:

Frank cases are those who are obviously ill with the disease in question. They represent the cases at the severe end of the spectrum (Fig. III) of disease. So long as the infecting organisms have an avenue of escape from the body, these persons may transmit their infection to other persons with whom they may be associated. Thus the nurse who contracts typhoid fever while caring for a patient is infected by a frank case. A severe case of a disease is obviously of greater danger to the sick individual than is a mild case, but it is not necessarily of equally greater danger to the community. On the contrary, the more severe cases are generally less dangerous to the community than are the mild ones. The sicker the patient, the greater the certainty that he will go out of circulation and, therefore, expose fewer persons in the community. Even if the diagnosis is not made and suitable control measures instituted, the patient who is severely ill is likely to be confined to his bed and thus has fewer opportunities for exposing others. Furthermore, the severer the illness, the greater the likelihood

---

[4] The reader will immediately recognize that many bacteria have been cultivated on artificial laboratory media for years but that this is not a natural condition. These bacteria would soon die if they were not transferred frequently to fresh media. Their natural habitat is the animal kingdom, where they perpetuate their species by spreading from animal to animal.

of seeking medical attention, and the easier the diagnosis. These in turn
mean the possibility of establishing control measures to minimize spread
of infection. It is thus apparent that, in general, the severer the case, the
less the likelihood of spread because of the reduced opportunity for the case
to come in contact with other persons. From the point of view of the
infected patient, however, the greater severity constitutes an added hazard.

Subclinical Infections (Missed Cases, Abortive Cases, Walking
Cases). Just as the severe case of infection is of reduced community hazard
because the severity of the disease lessens the likelihood of circulating in
the community, so the infections mild enough to escape recognition constitute an increased hazard. These latter are the cases in which the symptoms
are so vague and apparently so insignificant that the patient fails to seek
medical attention or in which the physician overlooks the true nature of
the condition because of the absence of the findings usually associated with
the disease. These are the infections in the less severe end of the spectrum.
The case of "walking typhoid" may feel little more than lassitude or easy
fatigability, with or without transient intestinal symptoms and headache.
He may pay little attention to the condition, especially if it disappears after
a few days or a couple of weeks. If he takes any notice of it, he fails to
consider its potential seriousness, as the symptoms are not characteristic
and might be attributed to a score of diverse conditions. He may, therefore, continue at his normal occupation, with resultant spread to other
persons if he is engaged in food handling. Similarly, the mother who permits her child to return to school after a day of slight indisposition and
fleeting rash is not intentionally sending a subclinical case of scarlet fever
to school. Had the symptoms continued, she might have sought medical
advice; but, since they do not, she dismisses the incident as a "food rash"
and the child returns to school. By this time, since there are no signs or
symptoms by which the infection may be recognized, the child circulates
freely and exposes other children. Obviously, while the condition in the
first child may not be serious, the risk to the community is far greater
than in the case of a seriously ill child who automatically goes out of circulation. Even though the number of organisms present in unit quantity of
nasal or throat secretion of the seriously ill may be greater than in the subclinical case, the latter comes into contact with so many more persons as
to constitute a more serious risk from the point of view of spread.

What may be the numerical relationship between the number of severe
and of mild or subclinical infections in any disease is not known. The ratio
varies for different diseases and probably from time to time for the same
disease. In many conditions, such as dysentery, typhoid, and the prevailing
form of scarlet fever, the mild or subclinical infections undoubtedly con-

stitute a large fraction of the total cases, often outnumbering those that are recognized. In other instances, such as smallpox, cholera, and measles, the abortive cases are the exception rather than the rule.

Carriers. The carriers represent that zone at the milder end of the spectrum of infection beyond the realm of visibility. They are usually unaware of their condition since it does not give rise to any symptoms and there is no way of recognizing it other than through bacteriological methods. It is, therefore, inevitable that most carriers should circulate freely in the community and constitute the same menace as do the subclinical, unrecognized cases. In fact, the carrier may well constitute a greater menace because the condition is usually of longer duration, sometimes lasting the remainder of the person's life. Taken collectively, the subclinical cases and carriers constitute the ultimate reservoir responsible for the greater portion of the spread and for the perpetuation of certain human diseases.

Carriers are frequently classified according to various criteria. When considered from the standpoint of time, they may be divided into: (1) convalescent carriers who continue to harbor and shed the organisms for a variable period of time following recovery from the disease; (2) chronic or permanent carriers who harbor the organisms for a long period of time, usually the duration of life; and (3) transient carriers who, without a recognized attack of the disease, harbor the organisms for a short period of time. In other instances, carriers may be classified according to the site of growth of the organism (biliary, intestinal, nasal, or faucial carriers) or according to the vehicle of exit from the body (fecal and urinary carriers).

Animal Reservoirs. The second largest reservoir of organisms capable of infecting man is the remainder of the animal kingdom. Although this remainder is a huge group, only a few species harbor important pathogens harmful to man, while others harbor organisms that only under unusual circumstances may invade man. The principal animal reservoirs are our domestic animals and rodents. In both cases we are dealing with species that are in close association with man or in which the gap between them and man may be bridged very readily by insect vectors.

The relationship between man and these animal reservoirs is a most interesting one, the study of which has opened up many new avenues of investigation. We are dealing here with organisms capable of parasitizing widely varying species of the animal kingdom.[5] In general, these are infections of species of animals other than man; when seen in man, they repre-

[5] Most of the animal reservoirs at present recognized are mammals, though the existence of salmonellae in poultry and isolation of the viruses of psittacosis and equine encephalomyelitis from wild birds show that species other than mammals may be concerned.

sent an accidental escape from the animal host and an equally accidental invasion of the human body. Thus, many of these conditions may be highly communicable within the animal species of which they are characteristic, whereas in man they are very slightly if at all communicable. Each infection is usually derived directly from the animal and is not further transmitted from man to man.

Other Reservoirs. So far as is known at present, these are of minor importance and of infrequent occurrence. The pathogenic animal parasites, bacteria, and viruses do not multiply outside the animal host. The only important nonanimal reservoir is that of the pathogenic plant forms, the fungi and the molds. These are capable of independent growth in and around the soil, whence they spread to man.

Escape of Organisms from Reservoir

The mere existence of a reservoir of infection is not sufficient to bring about the spread of infectious disease since, before they may attack a new host, the organisms must find an avenue of escape. Some reservoirs may, therefore, be of no public health significance merely through the inability of the organisms to escape. Thus the human being who is infected with trichinosis is no menace to his associates, even though he may have living trichinae within his body. So long as man refrains from cannibalism, the trichinae find no avenue of escape from the host or of transfer to a new victim. Similarly, a patient with malaria is incapable of infecting his associates unless some of his blood containing the plasmodia is withdrawn through the medium of a mosquito or hypodermic needle.

The avenue of escape from the reservoir is dependent upon the site of parasitic growth within the body of the host. For the sake of convenience, we may divide these avenues into the following groups:

The respiratory tract is the most common and, at the same time, the most dangerous channel of escape when viewed from the standpoint of ease of spread. Anatomically it consists of the nose, nasal sinuses, nasopharynx, larynx, trachea, bronchial tree, and lungs. Many organisms grow along the various parts of this tract and are carried out with the exhalations. From the epidemiological standpoint, we may be justified in including the mouth in the respiratory tract, for much of our exhalation is through the mouth. Speaking, coughing, sneezing, and expectoration involve the mouth but carry out of the body the secretions of both mouth and respiratory passages.

It is common knowledge that exhalation is accompanied by a certain degree of moisture in the form of droplets of varying size. The respiratory passages (including the mouth) are normally moist; in the presence of infection, this moisture is usually increased in amount. Consequently, whenever the individual exhales, he expels droplets containing the infecting organisms. These are literally driven from the body by means of the bellows-like action of the lungs. If this is in the form of a cough or a sneeze, the droplets may be driven many feet from the body and possibly carried even farther by air currents. The act of normal conversation will drive the droplets several feet.

Another factor complicating the control of organisms escaping from the respiratory tract is the fact that departures from normal occasioned by infection are so slight as to be frequently overlooked. As the surfaces are normally moist, it is frequently difficult to recognize the slight variations in degree of moisture due to infection. On the contrary, an open sore on the body surface or a "running ear" is an obvious departure from the normal; and, consequently, its existence will be observed and suitable precautions taken to care for the discharge.

Finally, it must be remembered that the respiratory mechanism is a constant physiological process which can be neither interrupted nor obstructed. Man breathes several times each minute. Wherever he goes, he breathes and, consequently, if suffering from a respiratory tract infection, will exhale infected droplets into his environment. The intestinal and urinary discharges, on the contrary, are intermittent and, therefore, subject to more ready control. A discharging sore or draining sinus may be covered with a dressing that catches the pus; the respiratory tract cannot be obstructed effectively without risk to life or great personal inconvenience. For these several reasons, the control of diseases in which the escape from the reservoir is through the medium of the respiratory tract is vastly more difficult than the control of those escaping through other avenues.

The Intestinal Tract. The principal avenue of escape of infected material from the intestinal tract is through discharge with the feces. Discharge through the mouth by expectoration is, epidemiologically speaking, a part of respiratory escape, while vomiting plays relatively little part in the escape of pathogenic organisms. The feces, however, are made up in large part of bacteria. Usually these are not pathogenic; but in the case of typhoid, dysentery, cholera, and other intestinal diseases, the feces may carry the causative agents in large numbers. While the presence of these organisms may frequently cause symptoms such as diarrhea, this is by no means invariable. As in the case of the respiratory tract, the discharge of infecting organisms may be without any signs or symptoms which would lead the infected person to be aware of his potential danger to others.

Fortunately, defecation is an intermittent rather than a constant physiological function. Furthermore, our social habits are such as to provide for disposal of these wastes so as to avoid creating offense. This does not hold, however, in all parts of the world or for all species of animals; nor are the measures for disposal invariably perfect where they are carried out. Infected material discharged through the intestinal wastes may all too frequently find its way to new hosts.

Urinary Tract. Aside from the fact that man is, in general, less meticulous in the disposal of urinary discharges, the epidemiological aspects of escape of infection from the urinary tract are identical with those of escape from the intestinal tract.

Open Lesions. When infection is accompanied by the existence of open sores or discharges on the surface of the body, the causative agents find little difficulty in escaping from the reservoir. All barriers that may have obstructed escape are broken down when open lesions develop. Thus, a tuberculous infection of the joint may be of no danger to other persons; but, if an abcess develops and ruptures on the surface, the infecting organisms find a ready means of escape, and the patient enters into a communicable stage. Fundamentally one may think of all infectious cases as having open lesions which discharge either directly upon the surface of the body or upon the membranes lining the cavities connected in turn with the normal outlets of the body. The lesions that discharge directly upon the body surfaces differ from the others only in their comparative obviousness and the lack of some propulsive force or vehicle to carry the organisms away from the body from which such organisms are escaping.

Mechanical Escape. By this term is meant the liberation of organisms through the intervention of processes inherent in neither the host nor the invading organism. Some external force is brought into play to liberate the infecting agents from the tissues in which they are living. Most frequently this is some biting or sucking insect that draws out the infected blood and is thus capable of transmitting the infection to others. Neither yellow fever nor malaria can be spread directly from person to person, simply because the infecting organisms have no means of escape. Were it not for the insects, many of our most important infectious diseases would die out. In those diseases in which a biological change in an insect host is not essential, the transfer of blood by hypodermic syringe or transfusion has at times brought about the escape of organisms from a body not normally in a communicable stage. Both malaria and syphilis have at times been so spread. Some of the parasitic worms, such as the trichinae, present similar examples of infection that cannot escape until released by mechanical methods—in this case, the eating of the infected flesh.

Transfer of Infection from Reservoir to New Host

After the infecting organism has escaped from the host, it can cause new infection only if it finds its way to a new host. Transmission may be divided into two types, direct and indirect.

Direct transmission is the simpler and more obvious of the two. The organisms pass from one person to another without the intervention of intermediate objects. Such a direct transfer implies a fairly intimate association of persons, though not necessarily actual physical contact. Thus the spread of infectious diseases through inhalation of the organisms breathed out by another person is a form of direct transmission. Most of the cases of diseases in which the organisms enter and leave the body through the respiratory tract are probably so spread. The crowding of people into small areas where they are forced to breathe and too often to cough and sneeze into each other's faces favors the spread of such infections, as it increases the likelihood of the organisms finding a new host and reduces the distance which they must travel between hosts. In other types of direct transfer, there is an actual physical contact, as in the spread of gonorrhea and syphilis.

Indirect transmission means transfer of infection without close relationship between the reservoir and new host. In order that indirect transmission may occur, it is essential that (1) the organisms be capable of survival for a period of time outside the body and (2) there be some vehicle which will transmit the organisms from one place to another.

The inability of certain organisms to survive for any period of time outside the host is a factor of considerable importance in reducing the likelihood of indirect spread. Thus the spirochete of syphilis, the gonococcus, and the meningococcus are relatively fragile organisms, which die rapidly when removed from the body and subjected to adverse conditions. It is, therefore, extremely unusual for infection with these organisms to be spread by other than direct contact. On the other hand, typhoid bacilli can survive for long periods of time outside the body if in reasonably moist environments that are not too acid; in some cases, they can even multiply. There is thus a far greater likelihood of indirect transfer of typhoid than of gonorrhea or of meningococcus infection. Some organisms, notably tetanus and anthrax bacilli, have the capacity to surround themselves with a hard, protective shell to form a spore, which will resist unfavorable environmental factors and permit them to remain viable for years, thus effecting an indirect transmission long after escape from the host. Fortunately, most of the organisms that infect man are not capable of spore formation; if removed from the body, they die in a relatively short period of time, varying from a few minutes to a few months. Each type of organism has its own peculiar characteristics upon which hinges the likelihood of indirect transfer.

Classification of Vehicles. Of equal importance with the viability of the organism is the nature of the vehicle. Vehicles may be classified into two types, animate and inanimate.

Animate vehicles, referred to as vectors, include the various insects capable of conveying infection from one host to another. As already pointed out, these may serve the triple role of liberating the organisms from the reservoir, transferring them to a new host, and injecting them into the victim. Such, in fact, is their usual role. In such instances, the insect is usually itself infected with the organisms, at times without apparent detriment to the insect (yellow fever and malaria) and at other times causing its illness and even death (plague and typhus). Care must be taken to avoid confusing the reservoir of the infection and the insect vector. The term "reservoir" refers to the ultimate source of the infection; the term "vector" to the insect that bridges the gap from reservoir to victim. Man is the reservoir of malaria, the anopheline mosquito the vector.[6] Occasionally one finds the terms "definitive host" used to refer to man and "intermediate host" to refer to the mosquito in such a situation. This again is a matter of point of view. This usage is biologically incorrect as applied to malaria, as the term "definitive host" is correctly applied to the host in which the sexual phase of reproduction of the parasite occurs, while the term "intermediate host" is reserved for that which harbors the asexual phase. On this basis, man would be the intermediate host of malaria, and the mosquito the definitive. While this latter usage is biologically correct, we are so inclined to look at such matters from the selfish standpoint of mankind that we frequently, though incorrectly, refer to any insect vector as an "intermediate host."

Insect vectors may cause transfer of infection either through harboring the unaltered organisms or through effecting a biological change in them. The first type is exemplified by the housefly that picks up typhoid bacilli on its body hairs or feet, if it finds access to infected feces, and later deposits these organisms on food over which it may walk. In other instances, an insect may carry the infecting organisms in its intestinal tract and deposit them on or in the body at the time of defecation or feeding. Thus the plague-infected flea has an infection of the intestinal tract with the result that in the early stages the organisms may escape from its body with

[6] In a certain sense, the distinction between reservoir and vector is an arbitrary one, depending upon the point of view. As human beings, we look at the problem from the standpoint of mankind; yet, if the mosquito were capable of having a point of view, it might reverse the role and consider itself the host, and man the vector.

the feces. As the infection progresses, an obstruction of the proventriculus develops which causes regurgitation of infected material into the wound whenever the flea attempts to feed. In all such cases, the insect, whether diseased or merely mechanically infected, transmits the infecting organism unchanged.

Other organisms are not only carried from one place to another by the insect but also undergo a biological change during their sojourn in the insect's body. The malaria plasmodium undergoes sexual reproduction in the *Anopheles* mosquito; the yellow fever virus while in the *Aëdes* mosquito acquires a capacity to infect a new victim, a power that is lacking at the time of its withdrawal from the host. See Chapter 35 for a further discussion of insects as vectors.

Inanimate vehicles include all nonliving objects that may be contaminated and so transfer infection from one person to another. In order that any substance may serve as an effective vehicle, it must permit survival of the organisms long enough for the transfer to be accomplished. As this time interval varies for different organisms, obviously few general rules can be laid down as to the type of substances that may serve as vehicles. In general it can be said, however, that moisture and a fairly bland environment prolong the survival of organisms in inanimate vehicles. The following substances may serve as vehicles for the transmission of infection.

1. *Water.* If polluted by specifically contaminated sewage, water may transmit the organisms of certain intestinal diseases. The almost universal consumption of water in fairly large quantities serves to bring about a fairly wide spread of infection if the supply is polluted. As a result of modern water supply practices, water is a less frequent vehicle of infection than in former years. In countries where community sanitation remains defective water is still, however, an important mode of spread of intestinal pathogens. Surface supplies are obviously more likely to be polluted than are ground waters. In all cases, the source is human excreta, which have found their way into the water. In general, pathogenic organisms do not multiply in water.

2. *Milk.* Like water, milk is an article of almost universal consumption. Hence, its contamination brings about a fairly widespread infection affecting primarily the children, as they are the principal consumers. The infecting organisms may multiply in the milk and thus bring a more massive dose to the consumer than was originally introduced. Contamination of milk may be of three types:

a. Contamination within the udder by organisms of a bovine disease from which the cow is suffering; for example, bovine tuberculosis, brucellosis.

b. Infection within the udder by organisms of a human disease that have been accidentally introduced into the udder; for example, streptococcal infections, such as scarlet fever and septic sore throat.

c. Direct contamination of the milk after it has left the cow; for example, typhoid fever and dysentery. Such contaminations are always caused by carelessness in the handling of the milk.

3. *Other Foods.* The list of other foods that may at times serve as vehicles of infection is long and under certain circumstances might include any substance eaten. The most important ones are those that are consumed with little or no cooking after preparation, have a reasonable degree of moisture, are not too strongly acid, and are intimately handled during the course of preparation. The source of contamination of food may be:

a. Direct contamination by food handlers due either to coughing or to touching with contaminated hands. This is one of the most important sources.

b. Contamination during growth as in the case of shellfish and of certain vegetables in countries where human excreta are used for fertilizer.

c. Derivation from an infected animal, as in the case of trichinosis or tapeworm.

It is frequently assumed that cooking is an adequate protection against infection through food. This would be true if, in the process of cooking, the heat were to penetrate all parts. Unfortunately, food is such a poor conductor of heat that the interior of the food mass may be barely incubated even though the surface may be burned.

4. *Air* was formerly considered an important vehicle of respiratory infections. Later studies failed to adduce evidence that any substantial number of cases were so transmitted, and it was consequently assumed that such spread could not occur. The studies of Wells have shown, however, that exhaled droplets do not fall to the ground as rapidly as was formerly supposed but may actually remain suspended in the air for many hours. Experience has shown that spread of certain diseases, notably measles and chickenpox, cannot be effectively prevented within a hospital by the usual aseptic nursing technique but that disinfection of air through the use of barriers of ultraviolet irradiation will reduce such spread. Furthermore certain outbreaks of virus and rickettsial infections within buildings have spread in a manner that could be explained on no hypothesis other than the assumption that air had served as a vehicle. Although these facts bring one to the conclusion that air can serve as a vehicle of infection, it does not follow that it is an important vehicle in the spread of all or even many respiratory diseases. Within a closed and carefully regulated

environment in which direct respiratory association can be eliminated or controlled, as in a hospital ward, air may well be an important mode of spread, as shown by the reduction of respiratory infections through use of aerosols or ultraviolet irradiation. On the other hand, the failure of such measures to effect a substantial reduction of infection in a school, industry or barracks or in any group of persons who move freely throughout the community suggests that the number of cases of infection spread through the medium of contaminated air is small as contrasted with the large number due to direct spread from person to person through inhalation of contaminated droplets immediately after exhalation by the person already infected.

5. *Fomites* include all inanimate vehicles other than water, milk, food, and air. The term embraces such articles as clothes, bed linen, books, toys, and the like. Even streetcar straps and doorknobs have been accused as serving as vehicles, though the evidence is lacking. In former years, prior to the recognition of the significance of carriers and subclinical cases, a great deal of attention was directed to the supposedly important role that fomites might play in the spread of infections, as fomites seemed to offer the only possible explanation for many cases. While at the present time none would deny the theoretical possibility that fomites might serve to transmit infection under certain circumstances, few would agree that they play such an important role. The number of cases so transmitted is at most very small as compared with the large number due either to direct spread or to indirect spread by water, food, milk, and insects. Thus the likelihood of contracting scarlet fever through a library book used previously by an unrecognized case is insignificant as compared with the much greater risk of exposure in the crowds in schools, streetcars, motion picture theaters, and other public places.[7] In general, pathogenic organisms do not live long away from the animal body and are readily destroyed by drying and sunlight. The amount of disease that may be spread by fomites is, therefore, relatively small and, as compared with the total, is too small a portion to warrant many of the conventional regulations, if these precautions are observed to the neglect of those more important precautions dealing with the source of the infection.

6. *Soil.* Under certain conditions, soil may serve as a vehicle of pathogenic organisms. The germs of tetanus, anthrax, and certain wound infections may live for many years in soil because of their ability to form spores. Similarly, hookworm eggs and larvae may live for many months

[7] Similarly, no one would wish to minimize the aesthetic value of hand-washing prior to meals; yet, it seems hard to believe that such procedures will appreciably alter the incidence of respiratory diseases among school children in view of the far greater likelihood of spread through direct breathing and coughing into each other's faces.

in certain types of ground. In general, however, the soil, while heavily laden with bacteria, does not carry human pathogens that are spread from one person to another.

Entry of Organisms into New Hosts

The mere arrival of pathogenic microorganisms at the new victim does not, however, suffice to set up a disease process. It is necessary that the organisms find entry into the host. Arrival and entry are not synonymous, for the body possesses certain barriers that must be passed before the eventual struggle for supremacy begins within the new host.

The mode of entry corresponds roughly with the mode of exit from the reservoir and with the parts of the body to be first affected. There are, however, so many exceptions to this general rule that the reader should be cautious about too wide generalization.

Just as certain infections present more than one portal of exit (for example, respiratory tract and skin lesions in smallpox), so also there may be multiple sites of entry. In general, however, there is one site most commonly utilized, entry through this channel resulting in infection as we are accustomed to encounter it. Yet under certain circumstances, the organisms may be introduced through abnormal channels. In such instances, the disease may present an altered form, as in the case of smallpox induced by artificial infection through the skin with material from the variolous pustules, thereby resulting in a milder form of infection than that transmitted through the respiratory tract.

The portals of entry correspond to the avenues of escape. They are:

Respiratory Tract. Entry is effected through breathing the fine droplets exhaled by infected persons. Just as it is physiologically impossible to interrupt the body processes of exhalation, so is it equally impossible to curb inhalation. Comparatively little is known about the local defense mechanisms in the respiratory passages, mechanisms that might protect the body against invasion. It seems generally agreed, however, that diseased conditions of the membranes and of the lymphoid tissues of the nose and throat favor establishment of local infection. The exact role of diseased tonsils as predisposing factors in certain communicable diseases is not, however, definitely understood. Nor is there general agreement as to the exact portion of the mucous membranes where invasion occurs. For many reasons one would suspect this to be, in some instances, by way of the lymphatic drainage of the lymphoid tissue; in other instances there may be direct invasion of the lungs. Also necessary to remember is that the respiratory and alimentary tracts have one part in common, the pharynx. Thus certain organisms breathed in may be swallowed; and, conversely, bacteria entering through the mouth with the food may find their way to parts of the respiratory passages.

Gastrointestinal Tract. The normal direction of flow through this part of the body is from the upper end downward. Infection entering through this system is, therefore, usually introduced through the mouth, principally with food or drink. Although the saliva has some bacteria-killing power, the duration of stay in the mouth is so short that little real destruction occurs. In the stomach, however, a certain degree of destruction occurs, owing to the presence of hydrochloric acid. It is important to remember that entry of pathogenic organisms into the intestine does not always result in infection. Physiologically speaking, the contents of the intestine are not yet absorbed into the body. Thus tetanus spores may exist there without harm. The colon bacillus is capable of great harm if it escapes from the intestine into the tissues, but normally there is no effective escape. Even in the case of organisms capable of penetrating the intestinal wall, there is a defense mechanism in the form of vomiting and diarrhea. If either of these processes occurs because of inflammation, a large number of pathogenic organisms may be cast off, thus reducing the number that penetrate into the system. The same mechanism is, of course, operative in ridding the body of certain poisonous substances that may be ingested. It should not be forgotten, however, that under special circumstances infections may enter through the rectum. Cases of typhoid are on record as being due to infection through enema tips and rectal tubes inadequately sterilized after use on a previous case or carrier. A similar hazard probably holds in the case of dysentery. Gonococcal infection of the rectum (proctitis) has been spread in nurseries through improper sterilization of rectal thermometers; proctitis is not uncommon in the female infected with gonorrhea (especially the child with vulvovaginitis), because of direct infection from pus passing over the perineum and the anus.

Direct infection of membranes is best represented by the usual gonorrheal involvement. The infecting organisms are brought in direct contact with the body surfaces that are to be involved. There are no barriers or local defense mechanisms to be passed other than the natural degree of moisture or acidity.

Percutaneous infection implies passage of infecting organisms through the skin. When intact, the skin and, to a lesser degree, certain other epithelial surfaces prevent the passage and invasion of pathogenic organisms. It is common knowledge that disease-producing bacteria may and do exist on the skin without causing illness but that, when a break occurs, infection may ensue. The ordinary infection through a cut is a simple example of this type of invasion. Any trauma that causes a break in the integument may open the avenue for infection. Most frequently this is a cut or an abrasion; in the case of rabies it may be a bite or saliva-contaminated scratch. The mode of entry of most insect-borne diseases is through the skin, which is punctured by the bite of the insect. The importance of insects in the spread of infectious diseases is in large part due to this capacity to break the skin at the time of biting, thus withdrawing infection from the reservoir and later injecting it into the new host or depositing it on the skin.

The question is frequently raised as to the ability of certain pathogens to penetrate the unbroken skin or mucous membranes. It appears certain that hookworm larvae can penetrate some parts of the intact skin, as for example between the toes or the back of the hand. Similarly, it would appears that the spirochete of syphilis might penetrate the unbroken genital and mucous membranes. This question is largely an academic one as there exist many minute abrasions of which the person is usually unaware yet which are large enough to permit the entry of pathogenic organisms.

Resistance of the New Host

Even though the pathogenic organisms may reach and penetrate the body of the host, infection or disease may not ensue, as the body possesses certain defense mechanisms which may protect it against the harmful effects of the invaders and may aid in the latter's destruction. To these defense mechanisms we give the name "resistance." If it is sufficiently great, we call it "immunity."

It is essential that the reader have a clear understanding of the difference between resistance and immunity. The public usually uses the terms interchangeably, and the professional worker sins almost as frequently as do his lay brethren. The term "immunity" implies absolute protection, an "all-or-none" connotation. Strictly speaking, if a person is "immune" to a disease, he cannot contract it under any circumstance. The very term gives no intimation of relative degrees of protection or of resistance to varying degrees of exposure. In actual practice, absolute immunity is a vary rare thing, best illustrated by the natural resistance of certain forms of life to attack by organisms highly pathogenic for other species. Yet absolute immunity following an attack of a specific disease is unusual and probably never occurs except in the case of a few infections, such as yellow fever. In general, the protection is merely a relative resistance.

"Resistance," on the other hand, is a relative term, which conveys the idea of different degrees of protection. Some persons may be highly resistant to a disease while others have very little resistance. When we speak of a person as being "immune" to a disease, we do not imply that he possesses absolute protection under all circumstances but rather that he has sufficient resistance to protect him against the average infecting dose of the invader. If this same "immune" person is exposed to an overwhelming dose, infection may ensue. Thus a person with a low level of resistance may be effectively protected against a small dose of infection; yet at the same time another person with a higher level contracts the disease because of a heavy dose. The latter might have been labeled resistant on the basis of immunity tests yet not be protected against this large dose. The usual classification of persons into susceptibles and immunes is a purely artificial and inexact one which expresses merely what will happen in the majority of cases. In other words, it attempts to determine whether or not the individual has enough resistance to guard him against the average vicissitudes of life so far as concerns a certain infecting organism. It does not imply protection under all circumstances.

Failure to understand the true import of the terms "resistance" and "immunity" has led to a great deal of confusion in both lay and professional circles. If a child who has a negative Schick test contracts diphtheria, the critical public sees evidence of the lack of value of such tests; the professional worker feels constrained to apologize for error of performance. While such errors may occur, neither apology nor misunderstanding is necessary if it is only remembered that these are tests for a certain degree of resistance and not for absolute immunity.

Under such circumstances, we might logically discontinue the use of the term "immunity" and substitute for it the term "resistance." This would be satisfactory if we had a simple term or phrase to describe that degree of resistance which is adequate to protect the body against the average infecting dose. Unfortunately, no such term exists, so we continue to use the term "immunity" to refer to this particular level of resistance. Similarly we have no simple term to express the concept of increasing the degree of resistance, so we continue to use the word "immunize" to convey this idea. There need be no confusion if we keep clearly in mind the limitations of these terms.

The nature of resistance is not clearly understood. The reader interested in the details of this subject should consult the standard works on immunology. For practical understanding of communicable disease control practices, it suffices to think of resistance as those properties of the body which enable it to ward off the invasion of pathogenic organisms. This broad definition might include certain of the local defense mechanisms already discussed above as limiting the penetration of the body by the invading organisms. In a certain sense, these are forces of resistance and are quite important. Yet, in common usage, the term "resistance" is limited to refer to the defense mechanisms which are called into play after invasion has occurred and which enable the body to kill off the invader and to combat its ill effects.

The factors of resistance may be classed as nonspecific and specific. Under the former heading are included the white blood cells which serve to engulf and destroy any foreign body. They are referred to as "nonspecific factors" because they are normally present in the body and operate against any foreign substance. The specific factors, on the other hand, are not normal [8] and essential constituents of the body but are produced only in response to definite stimulation by invading organisms or the products of these organisms. Such factors are therefore highly specific for the organisms against which they are produced. Thus a body may have a high level of resistance against diphtheria yet little or none against scarlet fever.

Autarcesis. This term, introduced by Aycock, refers to nonspecific physiological factors that govern the individual's response to an invading organism. It has long been recognized that persons differ in their capacity to produce antibodies and that antibodies and white blood cells are not the only factors that govern the response of the body to infection. These other factors probably represent physiological variations between persons or within an individual at different periods of time and under different circumstances. The diet of the individual certainly influences his ability to produce antibodies and to withstand infection. Racial and climatological differences may be factors governing the comparative absence of clinically recognizable diphtheria in the tropics even though the diphtheria bacilli may be found and the native population becomes Schick negative through processes of latent immunization (see p. 38). Familial tendencies to develop rheumatic fever or poliomyelitis are also apparent. It is the physiological variants of this type that are referred to as autarceological factors. The nature of these factors is very poorly understood. The entire phenomenon of autarcesis has been largely ignored by investigators of infectious diseases, yet appears to hold the key to an understanding of the epidemiology of many infections. Although the phenomenon is well recognized, the term "autarcesis" has found little acceptance and is little encountered outside of the literature of poliomyelitis. Yet no other term has been proposed to describe these highly important physiological factors.

---

[8] This does not mean that the presence of antibodies is abnormal in the usual sense of the word but rather that they do not appear in the absence of definite stimuli, which in turn may or may not exist in the normal course of human life. Thus, during the sixty-five years when measles was absent from the Faroe Islands, no specific antimeasles resistance developed in the persons born in the interim; yet these individuals were perfectly normal beings.

The specific factors may be divided into humoral and tissue resistance. The former is made up of the antibodies that occur in the blood and tissue fluids. Some of these are definite chemical substances that neutralize the harmful effects of the bacteria; others are properties that the blood acquires to enable it to combat and destroy the invaders. The term "tissue immunity" is frequently used to refer to the capacity of the body to produce these antibodies.[9] Examination of the blood of many persons may reveal low concentrations of antibodies; yet the individual may be effectively protected because the tissues have the capacity to produce antibodies in large quantities in a short period of time when the demand arises. This capacity is more highly developed in a person whose antibody-production mechanism has been previously stimulated and is, therefore, on edge, ready to respond to minor stimuli. A good example of this mechanism is seen in the rapid increase in diphtheria antitoxin in response to a Schick test applied to a previously immunized person; if the person has not been previously immunized, there is little response.

Active and Passive Immunity. It has already been pointed out that infection with certain organisms brings about the development of increased resistance through the production of antibodies. The factor in the invading organism that stimulates the system to produce these antibodies is referred to as an "antigen," which is merely a contraction of the cumbersome term "antibody-generator." In some instances, this antigen is a specific substance secreted by the bacteria, for example, diphtheria toxin. In other instances, the product of the organism that acts as the antigen cannot be isolated, and we therefore refer to the organism itself as the antigen.

When the antigen is introduced into the human or animal body, it stimulates the body to the production of the antidote or antibody. If these are produced in sufficient quantity, the body becomes immune. In such an instance the body is said to possess "active immunity," because this resistance was created through an active process of the body protected. In other words, the body has produced its own antibodies and thereby has acquired a new characteristic, that of production of these specific protective elements. Active immunity is, therefore, of comparatively long duration.

If we were to withdraw some blood from the actively immunized body and inject it into a susceptible person, we would be placing in the latter's body a definite quantity of antibodies. If this quantity were sufficiently large, this person might be temporarily immune; but, since his body had taken no part in the production of these antibodies, this would be referred

---

[9] The term is also used to refer to the resistance of the cells to parasitic invasion, as, e.g., by viruses.

to as a "passive immunity." In other words, it was acquired without direct participation on the part of the recipient. These antibodies would be present as mere foreign substances and, therefore, destroyed fairly rapidly. Nor would they be replaced, since the body of the recipient had had no part in their production and would be incapable of manufacturing them. Passive immunity is therefore of short duration. One student very aptly compared it to a magazine subscription which runs out and is not automatically renewed.

Development of Resistance. When a child is born, it usually has a high degree of resistance for certain diseases, dependent in part upon the mother's resistance. That this is due to factors other than placental transmission of antibodies is attested by the resistance to scarlet fever found in the newborn infant even though the mother may be susceptible, as shown by the existence of puerperal scarlet fever infection. Whatever may be the factors causing this resistance, it is completely lost by about six months of age or shortly thereafter. The child then begins to acquire resistance to infection gradually, either through actual attacks or through subclinical or latent immunization.

Let us suppose that a particular infant, after losing all his birth resistance, is infected with a single diphtheria bacillus. It is improbable that a single organism would be able to multiply with sufficient rapidity to produce disease. The infant body would be able to dispose of, and destroy, this one bacillus. A few days later it is exposed to two bacilli. From its prior experience the body has acquired a certain facility for dealing with diphtheria bacilli and, therefore, disposes of the two. At short intervals, it is later exposed to four, then eight, sixteen, thirty-two, sixty-four, and so forth. Each time the body, profiting from its earlier experience, is able to destroy the increasingly large dose and each time acquires an increased resistance. Ultimately it is able to combat a dose large enough to have caused illness or even death if introduced into a body that had never had any contact with diphtheria bacilli. Thus through its experience with small doses, the body acquires a protection which we call resistance. As there has at no time been any evidence of this process, we are unaware of its existence and, unless a test is made, may not realize that the body has been so protected. This process is, therefore, referred to as "latent immunization." [10] Of course actual practice has no such simple geometric pro-

[10] This is often referred to as "natural immunization," and the resistance so acquired as "natural immunity." The authors have preferred to follow the current English usage of designating this process as "latent immunization" and reserving the term "natural immunity" for the absolute insusceptibility of various species of animal life to a certain disease. This usage is appearing more and more in the American epidemiological literature.

gression of doses; the above example shows merely an ideally simple process. Yet, the phenomenon of latent immunization is constantly going on in accord with the general principle of protection through exposure to repeated small doses. If at any time during the process a large dose is encountered, disease ensues. The cases of diphtheria occur in those persons who were exposed to a larger dose of infection than they were prepared to combat at the particular moment.

This phenomenon of latent immunization does not occur for all diseases. There is very little evidence of resistance against some, even with repeated exposure or attacks, as, for example, the common cold or pneumonia. In other instances there is apparently no protection until a clinical attack has occurred. Thus a person is susceptible to smallpox until he has had the disease or been vaccinated.[11] This may be due to the fact that minimal doses of infection will bring about the disease or that in the case of virus diseases no resistance exists until cellular changes incidental to the disease have occurred.

The natural development of resistance occurs either through processes of latent immunization or through actual attack of disease in clinically recognizable form. (Artificial immunization will be discussed in the chapter, "Control Measures.") In either case the resistance is due to experience with the infecting organisms. Therefore, the greater the likelihood that the individual may have had exposure to these, the greater the probability that he is resistant or immune. This likelihood of exposure is conditioned by three factors: age, incidence of the disease in the community, and opportunities for spread.

Age. The longer a persons lives, the more opportunities he will have had to come in contact with certain microorganisms. Therefore we should logically find an increasing resistance with increasing age.

Incidence of the Disease in the Community. The higher the prevalence of the disease, the greater the opportunities for exposure. Thus, twenty years ago when diphtheria was more prevalent than now, the percentage of children of a given age who were resistant to diphtheria was distinctly higher than in a group of comparable age tested today. Similarly, with a higher incidence of typhoid fever in the Southern states than in the North, an inevitably higher percentage of persons in the South will have had an attack of the disease. The reservoir of infection is greater and consequently also the risk of infection. Yet, in both North and South, the incidence of typhoid is lower today than it was a generation or two ago;

---

[11] Natural immunity is often claimed by some persons, but its existence has been denied by most authorities. It may well be due to prior occurrence of a mild and therefore unrecognized attack.

and, therefore, the likelihood of resistance through prior exposure is decreased.

Opportunities for Spread. This includes physical factors of the environment, such as sanitation, and personal factors, such as crowding. The spread of respiratory diseases is especially favored by crowding, as this brings within a given area more persons who will be breathing into each other's faces and thus exchanging pathogenic organisms.[12] Many of those exposed will contract the disease; others will be latently immunized. In either case, the more crowded the community, the higher the percentage of immunes at any given age level. Thus, in large cities, measles is rarely encountered in the teen age because the children brought up in this crowded environment have already been exposed and had the disease. Yet, during World War I, the training camps that received conscripts from the rural areas had a serious problem in caring for the measles that developed. The exposures on the farm had been so few that these youths were still susceptible. A similar difference is found in communities of different economic status: those children brought up in the crowded poorer sections are more resistant than those brought up in the well-to-do residential suburbs, while those reared in luxury are the most likely to be susceptible.

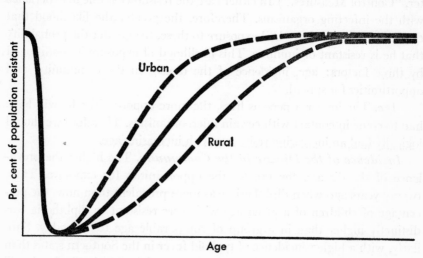

FIG. IV. *Normal development of resistance through latent immunization.*

These several factors are illustrated by Figure IV, showing the normal development of resistance to a given disease within a community. The height of the line during the first few months of life is an expression of the resistance, at birth, to certain diseases. After this has disappeared, there is

[12] It has been said that man lives in a state of "salivary communism."

a gradual increase in the percentage of individuals who are resistant, this number increasing with age. The actual shape of this curve varies for the several diseases, and for a given disease it varies with the incidence of the conditions and the character of the community. As shown by the dotted lines, the rate of development of resistance is usually higher in the urban than in the rural community.

SUMMARY

The development of an infectious disease represents a succession of events or circumstances. There must be a reservoir of the specific etiological agent; this organism must find escape from the reservoir and be transmitted to a new host which it must penetrate; and the host must be susceptible. There are thus several events that must happen in logical sequence. If a single link in this chain should be broken, the remainder will collapse, and infection will not ensue even though all the other events in the chain may occur. It is the task of epidemiology to test the strength of these various links. The public health officer may then adapt his control measures to concentrate his forces upon the weakest link in the chain.

SUGGESTED READINGS

Aycock, W. Lloyd, and Foley, George E.: "Serologic Types of Bacteria as an Epidemiologic Principle," *Am. J. M. Sc.,* 211:350–73, (Mar.) 1946.

Burnet, F. M.: *Biological Aspects of Infectious Diseases.* New York: Macmillan Co., 1940.

———: "Epidemiology Today," *M. J. Australia,* 2:825–30, (Dec. 14) 1946.

Chapin, Charles V.: *The Sources and Modes of Infection,* 2nd ed. New York: John Wiley & Sons, Inc., 1912.

Downes, Jean: "Control of Acute Respiratory Illness by Ultra-Violet Lights," *Am. J. Pub. Health,* 40:1512–20, (Dec.) 1950.

Dudley, S. F.: "On the Biological Approach to the Study of Epidemiology," *Proc. Roy. Soc. Med.,* 29:1–14, (Oct. 25) 1935–36.

———: "The Ecological Outlook on Epidemiology," *ibid.,* 30:57–70, (Oct. 23) 1936–37.

Findlay, G. M.: "Discussion on the Routes of Infection and Paths of Transmission of Viruses," *Proc. Roy. Soc. Med.,* 29:563–70, (Jan. 22) 1935–36.

Frost, Wade Hampton: Papers of: *An Exposition of the Epidemiological Method,* edited by Kenneth F. Maxcy. New York: Commonwealth Fund, 1941.

Gordon, John E.: *Epidemiologic Problems in Virus Diseases. Harvard School of Public Health Symposium on Virus and Rickettsial Diseases.* Cambridge: Harvard University Press, 1940, pp. 3–64.

Greenwood, Major: *Epidemics and Crowd Diseases: An Introduction to the Study of Epidemiology.* London: Williams & Norgate, Ltd., 1935.

Maxcy, Kenneth F.: "Principles of Epidemiology," Chapter 36 of Dubos, Réné J.: *Bacterial and Mycotic Infections of Man,* 2nd ed. Philadelphia: J. B. Lippincott Co., 1952, pp. 776–804.

———: "Epidemiology," Chapter 7 of Rivers, Thomas M.: *Viral and Rickettsial Infections of Man,* 2nd ed. Philadelphia: J. B. Lippincott Co., 1952, pp. 141–60.

Meyer, K. F.: "Latent Infections," *J. Bact.,* 31:109–35, (Feb.) 1936.

Smith, Theobald: *Parasitism and Disease.* Princeton: Princeton University Press, 1934.

3. Control Measures

Although many measures may be used for the control of communicable diseases, all of them may be classified under three headings:

1. Preventing spread
2. Increasing the resistance of the new host
3. Minimizing the ill effects of cases that have not been prevented

Each of these measures is largely complementary to the other two; an intelligent combination of them constitutes the usual control program as applied to any specific disease.

PREVENTING SPREAD

This is obviously the most desirable and, in theory at least, the simplest type of control procedure. As no one can develop an infectious disease unless the causative organisms have escaped from the reservoir and found their way to a new host, effective disease control will have been achieved if suitable barriers can be built around this reservoir. These barriers may be established in several different ways.

Reservoir Eradication

The most desirable and permanently successful form of infectious disease control is to eliminate the reservoir of infection, for without such a focus spread may not occur. In dealing with animal reservoirs this is the method of choice. As soon as infected animals are discovered, they are promptly slaughtered. Such were the measures used so effectively in the program for eradication of bovine tuberculosis, the tuberculin test being used to discover infected cattle.

Slaughter is of course applicable only in dealing with animal reservoirs; it has no place in human disease control. Yet in certain instances it is possible through surgical or chemotherapeutic means to eliminate focuses of infection, thus curing the human carrier. Removal of the gallbladder frequently cures the biliary typhoid carrier, and removal of the tonsils may eliminate the carrier condition in diphtheria and streptococcal infections. Though such procedures are extremely effective, they are of limited applicability, as any surgical operation entails some risk to the patient. The carrier is, of course, benefited by removal of foci which might ultimately produce symptoms and even further damage, yet this threat of future trouble often seems to the patient to be insignificant in comparison with the risk of operation. It is not surprising, therefore, that the possibility of surgical cure is not always received with enthusiasm by the carrier, who is, for the moment, free of any symptoms referable to his infection.

The recent development of drugs which have the capacity to kill microorganisms within the body without seriously damaging the individual has opened the way for nonsurgical elimination of reservoirs of infection. The sulfonamide derivatives and antibiotics, such as penicillin, are highly specific for certain bacteria; there is reason to expect that even more potent antibiotics will be developed in the near future. Through the proper use of these drugs, infected persons, both cases and carriers, can frequently be cured of their infection within a very short period of time. Marked success has been achieved in the treatment of gonorrhea, syphilis, bacillary dysentery, and infections with meningococci, pneumococci, and hemolytic streptococci. Use of these chemotherapeutic agents constitutes a highly valuable control measure; their use has brought about more rapid cures of certain cases and carriers than was formerly possible. Indiscriminate use is contraindicated, however, as the drugs, especially the sulfonamides, are potentially toxic, and their widespread use may result in the development of strains of organisms that are resistant to their effects. The sulfonamides may also affect the blood-producing mechanisms of the body, resulting in the development of serious or even fatal anemia. The patient receiving sulfonamides must, therefore, be kept under good medical observation to detect the earliest sign of toxic effects. The development of strains of organisms that are resistant to these drugs means that as such strains become dominant within the community the effectiveness of the drugs declines, with the result that a patient infected with one of these strains cannot benefit from treatment with the drugs in question. It is important therefore that the sulfonamides and antibiotics be used only when definitely indicated and not be administered indiscriminately. Fortunately, the reactions to the antibiotics are less common or severe than are those to the sulfonamides, and there is less tendency toward development of resistant strains. Nevertheless it is important that neither group of drugs be administered indiscriminately; they should be used only when definitely indicated.

Reducing Communicability

Adequate treatment may in other instances keep the patient from spreading his infection, even though he is not immediately cured. A few injections of arsenicals may render the syphilitic patient noninfectious even through sexual contacts, while collapse therapy may convert an open case of tuberculosis into a closed one and thus reduce the likelihood of spread. Neither of these procedures effects an immediate cure; failure to continue them may result in a relapse into a communicable stage. So long, however, as treatment is actively pursued, the infected person may be maintained in a noncommunicable condition. Adequate treatment therefore serves the dual purpose of benefiting the patient and the community alike. In the case of syphilis, it is our most effective control measure. Under such circumstances it seems hardly fitting to question the propriety of governmental participation in the treatment of these conditions. In fact one might question the wisdom of a government in failing to provide lavish treatment of conditions in which the duration of communicability is so dependent upon the adequacy of therapy.

Segregation of the Reservoir

This implies that the infected person or animal is so separated from the community that the organisms, even though escaping from the body, cannot reach other persons. The oldest and simplest form of this type of control is found in isolation and quarantine procedures.

Isolation refers to the infected person or animal and connotes segregation until all danger of conveying the infection shall have passed. Such at least is the goal toward which all isolation regulations are directed. That they may at times fall short of their purpose is due to several factors, including the impossibility of determining in all instances the duration of the infectious state.

Wherever possible, bacteriological methods are used to determine the necessary period of isolation, samples of secretions or excretions being obtained and submitted to the laboratory for examination. These samples, colloquially though incorrectly referred to as "cultures," are taken from the materials by which the organisms leave the body. Specimens of sputum may be examined for tubercle bacilli, feces and urine for typhoid organisms, and the moisture of the nose and throat for diphtheria germs. Obviously, however, in making such tests only small samples of the entire excretion are selected. Furthermore, in the laboratory only a small fraction of this sample is usually examined. Therefore, the report of the laboratory tells merely what was or was not found in the relatively minute portion subjected to bacteriological examination.

Laboratory findings must consequently be interpreted with proper precaution. A "positive" report, indicating that the organisms in question were found, is clear evidence that the person who was "cultured" was shedding the organisms at the time the cultures were taken and, therefore, a potential source of infection. A "negative" report, on the other hand, merely indicates that the laboratory failed to find the organisms in the particular particle of specimen studied. It does not prove that the person was not infected, for the organisms might possibly have been found had further search of additional material been made or had better methods for examination been available.[1] It is apparent, therefore, that a positive laboratory finding is of far greater significance than is a negative report. Consequently most isolation requirements based upon "cultures" provide for release only after a series of negative reports.

Although we recognize these limitations, we must acknowledge that the cultural method, where applicable, is the best, as it individualizes the period of isolation to the needs of the case in question. Unfortunately it is applicable in only a limited number of diseases, because of a lack of suitable methods. In order to use cultural methods, laboratory procedures must be reasonably accurate, yet at the same time neither too costly nor time consuming. Many methods are not practicable in public health work because of the expense or the time necessary for their completion.

The second method of determining the period of isolation is through selection of an arbitrary time period which experience or study of representative samples shows to be satisfactory in most cases. It is known that after a certain length of time the patient is no longer capable of transmitting, or is extremely unlikely to transmit, the infection to others. Consequently all patients are segregated for this period, even though some have unquestionably ceased to harbor the organisms some time before this period has elapsed. This method makes no provision for individualization. In fact it might appear to presume that up to a certain moment the patient was infectious and after that moment was not. In reality no such assumption is made, the time being determined merely by general experience.

This method is highly satisfactory in diseases such as measles or chickenpox, in which the period of communicability is short and in which there is no evidence of a convalescent carrier condition. If, however, the

---

[1] It must also be remembered that laboratories differ greatly in the skill of their personnel. So long as so many states fail to exercise any jurisdiction over public health laboratories, some laboratories will be less reliable than others, and little credence can be placed upon their findings.

period is long and carriers do exist but cannot be routinely detected, we must recognize the fact that, no matter what the period, certain infected individuals will be released to spread the disease to others. Thus in scarlet fever occasional persons may harbor the organisms for many weeks or even months. As there is no suitable routine method for their detection, we might isolate all scarlet fever patients for several months in order to be on the safe side; yet this would hardly be fair to the majority of the patients, who cease to harbor the bacteria fairly quickly.

We attempt to select a period that will give as few failures as possible and at the same time will not work an undue hardship on those recovering from the disease. The longer the period, the greater the margin of safety and at the same time the greater the risk of injustice to those entitled to earlier release. Until we have better methods of laboratory examination, we must attempt to sail that difficult course between too great a risk to the community and too great an injustice to the patients. Lucky is the health officer who can avoid both Scylla and Charybdis.

Quarantine refers to the measures exercised with respect to those who have been in contact with an infected person. Such an association will obviously have created certain risk of developing either an attack of the disease or a carrier condition. In some instances the associate, referred to as a "contact," may be the source from whom the patient has acquired his infection. In either case, it may be desirable to exercise some restraint over this "contact" until we are certain that infection does not exist or is not developing. These measures are referred to as "quarantine."

The period of quarantine may be based either on laboratory findings or on the length of the usual incubation period or on both. The former are carried out in a manner identical with that used for determining isolation of a case. They attempt to determine whether or not the contact is infected; if so, a new source of infection has been found and must be isolated. It must be remembered, however, that in addition to the precautions normally used in interpreting negative findings, additional caution must be exercised in the case of contacts, because the findings indicate merely the conditions present at the moment the specimens were taken. A contact with a negative culture might still be incubating the disease, and additional cultures a few days later might be positive. If we recognize these limitations, we have in the cultural method an extremely valuable procedure for detecting infected contacts who should be placed in isolation. Most quarantine regulations provide for culturing of intimate contacts if suitable laboratory methods are available and further provide for isolation of all "positives" until a suitable number of negative cultures have been obtained.

The other factor to be considered in determining the duration of quarantine is the incubation period of the disease in question. A contact not infectious at the moment may, if susceptible, contract the disease and be in a highly communicable stage in a few days. By segregating him until the incubation period has elapsed, we may avoid the risk of his transmitting the infection to others during the prodromal period, before the condition has been recognized. Consequently many quarantine regulations provide for segregation of susceptible contacts until the end of the maximum incubation period. Those immune on the basis of a previous attack or as shown by a recognized test are usually exempt from this provision, though still subject to culturing for possible carriers.

Current quarantine practice embraces a combination of these two methods. Laboratory search for carriers is done wherever practicable, and susceptibles are segregated during the incubation period. If the person is neither susceptible nor a carrier, he is usually permitted to resume his normal activities, provided all contact with the case shall cease. In certain instances, special precautions are observed with respect to food handlers and those whose occupation brings them into intimate contact with children. If the incubation period is long, as in measles or chickenpox, the quarantine may be held in abeyance until the final few days when infectiousness begins, thus avoiding an undue loss of time without increasing the hazard of spread. Frequently no attempt is made to quarantine contacts to certain of the less serious diseases, as the results obtained do not justify the interference with normal life.

Variability of Isolation and Quarantine Procedures. It is common knowledge that isolation and quarantine regulations differ from community to community. All states have some provision for a minimum code,[2] and yet no two codes are exactly alike. To a certain degree this represents lack of precise knowledge as to periods of communicability. More frequently it represents variations in the margin of safety considered desirable. Obviously, more reliance can be placed on two negative cultures than on one, and more on three than on two, yet no number can be selected that yields infallible results. Similarly, in the use of the arbitrary time periods, great variation occurs in the duration of isolation and quarantine, simply because different communities have allowed varying margins of safety. These variations are at times confusing to the public and profession alike, who see in them evidence of lack of precise knowledge. The engineer who builds a bridge always provides a margin of safety in excess of the maximum load that the bridge will be called upon to carry.

[2] Certain large cities determining their own regulations may be exempted from this code.

The health officer does the same with his isolation and quarantine regulations. It must be confessed, however, that occasionally archaic requirements still clutter the statute books. Attempts to enforce regulations that are unreasonable and not supported by scientific fact may serve only to cast all regulations into disrepute. Isolation and quarantine requirements must be constantly revised in the light of advancing knowledge. The American Public Health Association, through the reports of its Subcommittee on Control of Communicable Diseases, has done much to standardize isolation and quarantine practices and to persuade health departments to eliminate the excessively long periods that formerly prevailed.

Procedures for Isolation and Quarantine.[3] The power of boards of health to institute isolation and quarantine is an expression of their "police power" or, in other words, their right to regulate the conduct of the individual for the benefit of the group. The state board of health is empowered to establish minimum standards; the local communities may be more, though not less, stringent. In some instances, placards may be attached to the premises to indicate the restrictions applied to the inhabitants of that house and to warn all visitors away from contact with those so restricted. While these signs undoubtedly serve as warnings to visitors and may have a certain restraining effect on the inhabitants, the present tendency is away from the indiscriminate use of the gaudy placards of former years. Frequently they serve little useful purpose other than questionable decoration of the house, and at times they may even create popular panic and apprehension. Certainly all isolation and quarantine procedures, including placarding, must be reasonable if public cooperation is to be expected. If they become unreasonably stringent, there is a tendency to hide cases in order to avoid unpleasant and seemingly unnecessary restrictions upon personal freedom. This is especially true when it is common knowledge that many mild cases are escaping recognition and therefore are not being segregated.

Under certain circumstances isolation and quarantine restrictions may be greatly modified to accomplish their purpose without too great interference with normal activities of life. There is no need of placarding an entire apartment house just because of a case of communicable disease on the third floor, nor is it always necessary to restrict all the contacts, provided the infected individual in the family may be effectively segregated. Wage earners may frequently be permitted to come and go, provided they avoid association with the patient and are not engaged in certain occupa-

[3] Detailed procedures within the home are a part of the nursing care and are discussed in Chapter 8.

tions. The restrictions which prevent the employment of typhoid carriers as food handlers but permit their free circulation in the community are only modifications of the isolation and quarantine principles. Only those special precautions necessary to prevent spread of the infection are required. Experience shows that many of our former rigid measures can be reasonably modified without hazard to the community.

Limitations of Isolation and Quarantine Procedures. Unquestionably, isolation and quarantine confer some degree of individual and community protection, for they segregate certain individuals who might otherwise spread the infection. On the other hand these measures can be applied only to recognized cases and their contacts. In order to achieve absolute control through isolation and quarantine, it would be necessary to find all infectious individuals at the beginning of their period of communicability. Delayed or inadequate recognition of infectious persons must mean that isolation and quarantine procedures would be applied to only a fraction of the total reservoir and would therefore achieve a very incomplete success.

Experience shows that all sources of infection are not found. The factors that limit the effectiveness of isolation and quarantine procedures are, therefore:

Hidden Cases. Unfortunately some parents and even, occasionally, physicians deliberately fail to report infectious diseases so as to avoid the embarrassment of isolation and quarantine restrictions. This represents a selfish disregard of the rights of others and a lack of a sense of community responsibility. While laws provide a penalty for such neglect, enforcement of these laws is difficult.

Missed Cases. It has already been pointed out that a very substantial number of cases of infectious disease may be so mild as to be overlooked. In fact there is reason for believing that in certain diseases the number of subclinical unrecognized infections equals or exceeds the number diagnosed. In some instances the physician may not recognize the condition; more frequently the patient is so slightly ill that medical aid is not sought. Yet these cases circulate freely in the community and are just as capable of transmitting the infection as are the more acutely ill.

Carriers. It has been remarked that if all carriers were dyed indigo, we might envision the eradication of many diseases. Unfortunately, from the standpoint of disease control, they are not dyed indigo, nor have they any other distinguishing mark. They are, therefore, usually not discovered and continue to spread their infection. A community-wide search for them is not practicable.

Infectiousness during the Prodromal Stage. The communicability of the patient is greater in the early stages of certain diseases than it is after the appearance of the characteristic signs and symptoms by which the diagnosis is made. During this prodromal period the patient may have a very vague indisposition, the symptoms being suggestive of a wide variety of less serious conditions. In measles the child may have what is apparently merely a head cold, the characteristic rash not appearing until the third day. Yet during this period the child is in a highly communicable stage. Similarly, the spasmodic cough by which the diagnosis of whooping cough is usually made does not appear until the child has been coughing for a couple of weeks, and in many cases it never appears. Bacteriological studies show that during this preparoxysmal stage the pertussis organisms are found more frequently and in greater abundance than after the "whooping" has commenced. Since isolation is not instituted until after the diagnosis has been made, so much spread has already occurred that we can hope for little effective control through isolation procedures. It is veritably locking the stabledoor after the horse has been stolen.

Value of Isolation and Quarantine Procedures. It should not be inferred that isolation and quarantine are of no value. Such would be contrary to fact, for in their proper sphere they are of unquestioned merit, especially in those conditions, such as tuberculosis or typhoid carriers, in which the infectious period is of long duration. In the acute communicable diseases, however, they are of greater personal than community protection. If one of two children who are playmates should develop scarlet fever, the well one will not acquire the infection from the other if isolation is instituted early enough; but isolation of the sick child will not prevent the other from contracting the disease from the missed case who is attending school and who was responsible for the original infection. In many respects the chief value of such measures lies in the protection that the isolated patient receives against acquiring a secondary infection from a visitor. Respiratory complications constitute the chief hazard of some infectious diseases, notably influenza, measles, and whooping cough. Often these complications are due to organisms acquired from contacts. Isolation, through reducing the number of contacts, may be of greater value to the patient than to the community.

Isolation and quarantine procedures are actually of very limited community value because they can be applied to only a fraction of the total reservoir of infection. To this extent they almost penalize the victim so unfortunate as to have a moderately severe and therefore recognizable infection while they spare the mild case. It is doubtful if they have greatly affected the community prevalence of acute communicable disease or will ever provide control of any infection unless supplemented by other methods. This does not mean that they are of no value, but rather that they are merely one of the many weapons in our disease-control armamentarium. So long as we recognize their limitations, we are sound in applying these measures. If, however, we believe that complete control can be achieved through mere isolation and quarantine, we are bound for disappointment. Similarly, it is essential that we recognize these limitations lest we devote too much of our energy and budget to these measures to the neglect of other practices of equal or greater value. The present-day trend is toward more liberal isolation and quarantine measures; in some communities all restrictions have been removed from certain diseases inasmuch as experience has shown that the standard measures were mere irritants, could not be enforced, and did not produce effective control. There is no doubt that the next few years will see even greater liberalization of isolation and quarantine practices. Such liberalization is long overdue.

Environmental Sanitation

Environmental sanitation seeks to prevent spread by regulating those objects by which pathogens may be transferred from a reservoir to a new host. It assumes not only that the organisms have escaped from the reservoir but also that they are living for a variable period of time in the environment. Unless a period of viability outside the body exists, there is obviously no need for concern as to vehicles. Vehicle control therefore serves as a barrier applied to the environment, just as isolation constitutes a barrier built around the reservoir.

Types of Environmental Sanitation. The measures used aim either at killing the organisms as they are encountered outside the body or at destroying or controlling the vehicle itself.

Disinfection [4] refers to the destruction of pathogenic organisms on inanimate objects which may have become contaminated. It can be brought about through the use of either physical or chemical forces. Of the former, burning is by far the most effective and is used wherever possible. It is of very limited application, however, for it usually necessitates destruction not only of the pathogen but also of the substance contaminated. At times this is desirable, as in the disposal of sputum, bandages, and other material of no value. If, however, the contaminated object has real value, as in the case of books or clothing, burning is a wasteful and

---

[4] Disinfection conveys the idea of destruction of pathogenic organisms but does not imply that all forms of life are destroyed. The term "sterilization" refers to the latter.

usually unnecessary procedure. Heat, drying, and exposure to sunlight or other sources of ultraviolet rays constitute effective though less rapid methods and are frequently used where burning is not applicable. The degree of heat or the duration of drying or irradiation necessary to kill microorganisms varies with different species. Moist heat in the form of steam or of hot or boiling water is the most commonly used method of disinfection of inanimate objects that are of any intrinsic value, but can obviously not be applied to books, furniture, or other articles that are damaged by moisture. Fortunately such articles require little if any treatment for their role in the spread of disease is insignificant if not actually nonexistent.

Chemical methods of disinfection are frequently more convenient than physical measures. They rely upon the destructive action of various chemicals if applied in proper strength, the concentrations required varying for different substances and for different bacteria. As in the case of physical methods, it is necessary to remember that in every instance two variables must be considered, namely, the intensity of the force (concentration of chemical, degree of heat, and so forth) and the duration of exposure. The greater the intensity, the shorter the period required for destruction; as the intensity decreases, the time must be longer, until an intensity is ultimately reached at which destruction will not occur in any reasonable time period or at which growth may even be favored. Specific methods of disinfecting various articles in the home are considered in Chapter 8.

Fumigation implies disinfection through the use of gases or fumes. The practice had its origin in the early concepts of miasmata and noxious vapors. Diffusion of various toxic gases was supposed to purify the atmosphere. With the discovery that microorganisms, not miasmata, were the cause of these diseases, gaseous disinfection seemed even more logical, for gases poisonous to men were assumed to be equally destructive to germs. Unfortunately, experience shows little correlation between the toxicity of gases for bacterial and for animal life. We know today that bacteria and viruses may survive concentrations of gas capable of killing men, rodents, or insects. The striking work of Chapin in Providence demonstrated that fumigation of a home where a case of communicable disease had occurred did not affect the incidence of secondary cases; conversely, failure to fumigate the home did not increase the risk of further spread. Fumigation has therefore fallen into disrepute as a means of disinfection except in those situations in which destruction of animal life is sought. It is still used as a means of destroying rodents and insects, as in the disinfection of a ship coming from a plague-infested port. Unfortunately, popular practices usually lag at least a generation behind scientific knowledge, with the result that health officers are at times still urged by the public to fumigate homes or schools where infection has occurred. Although it must occasionally be done in order to allay popular apprehension—in other words, for psychological reasons—it is a waste of both time and money. It is veritably burning incense to false gods.

The need for disinfection is at times very hard to determine, as it depends on the potential survival of the organisms outside the host and on the relative importance of indirect, as contrasted with direct, spread of the infection. Whenever organisms are known to exist, to attempt to destroy them is logical if feasible. Thus there can be no argument as to the burning of the sputum of the tuberculous, disinfecting the stools of the typhoid patient, or washing the hands of the attendant upon any communicable disease. Similarly logical is disinfection of water with chlorine to kill bacteria that may have contaminated it and pasteurization of milk to destroy any pathogenic organisms that may have passed the usual sanitary barriers. On the other hand, disinfection can be carried to ridiculous extremes, with resultant waste of time and effort. The traditional example of this is the mother who boils the baby's toys, while at the same time she permits him to creep on the floor or be fondled by relatives. An article potentially soiled with the organisms of a communicable disease certainly merits some attention, but it should be remembered that most of the communicable diseases, especially those carried by the respiratory tract, are spread by direct contact more frequently that by fomites. We must not expect to control these diseases by disinfection so long as missed cases and carriers exist. Undue attention to disinfection may at times serve to create false notions about the usual mode of spread and to direct attention toward the minor, rather than the major, hazards. Too many school children have been taught that, if they wash their hands before meals, they will be reducing the risk of many diseases; yet it is doubtful if the organisms commonly found on a child's hands are an important source of infection when introduced into the mouth. The aesthetic value of personal cleanliness warrants training in hand-washing; there is no need of justifying cleanliness by creating false fears as to what might happen if it were neglected. Undue or improper emphasis on such matters merely directs attention away from the really important sources of infection, namely, the carriers and missed cases circulating freely in the community.

Control of insect vectors is based upon efforts directed either at destruction of the insects after they are grown or at prevention of their breeding. The former is best exemplified by the delousing processes used in the control of typhus; the latter, by mosquito control in the prevention of malaria or yellow fever. Destruction of the adult insect has a double value, in that it cuts down multiplication and destroys insects that have bitten infected persons and are thus already infectious or will be infectious in a few days after completion of the period of extrinsic incubation. Since insects acquire infection as adults, every adult that is destroyed reduces the risk of spread of disease, even though breeding has occurred. Yet prevention of breeding is obviously more effective for, if carried out over a period of time, it may result in extermination of an insect vector from a particular locality. If this insect is essential for the transmission of the disease from person to person, this measure alone may break the chain of events leading to the occurrence of the disease and thereby bring about effective control. Methods of destruction of insects and their breeding places will be discussed in Chapter 35. At times it is simpler to direct attention to the animal that harbors the insect, the vector of a vector, as in the case of plague control through eradication of rats. In this instance the attack upon the rat brings about simultaneous destruction of both reservoir and vector.

Sewage Disposal. Aside from the aesthetic offense created by the faulty disposal of sewage, real danger exists if the fecal and urinary excretions contain certain microorganisms, notably those of typhoid, paratyphoid, the dysenteries, hookworm, or cholera. Therefore these wastes must be so disposed of that they cannot find their way into food and drink. Ideally this means treatment of human excreta to destroy all pathogenic organisms by processes of digestion, filtration, chlorination, or burning. In municipalities this may be possible, but in the average rural area reliance must be placed on disposal into sites from which there is no possible access to water or food supplies. Under such conditions the biological processes that occur in the soil and the excreta ultimately bring about destruction of the bacteria, so that these pathogens do not accumulate.

Protection and Purification of Water Supplies. As water, if polluted, may be the means of wide dispersion of certain organisms, the incidence of some diseases may be strikingly reduced by sanitation of these supplies. Wherever possible, water is obtained from sources free of pollution. As the crowding of civilization has frequently made this impossible, resort must be had to methods of destroying any pathogens that may have found their way into the supply through inadequate or improper sewage disposal. Water purification includes storage, sedimentation, filtration, and chlorination. Due attention must also be paid to methods of distribution to avoid risk of pollution after treatment.

Milk Sanitation. Milk cannot be produced and marketed without risk of contamination with extraneous material, including pathogenic bacteria. Milk sanitation has as its object the application of methods which will reduce this possibility of contamination to a minimum. As these methods depend on human cleanliness—and the human factor is always an uncertain quantity—it is necessary to superimpose pasteurization to guard against slips in technique and against those dangers which cannot be completely avoided through sanitation, notably direct contamination from carriers. Thus pasteurization does for milk what chlorination does for water. Neither takes the place of cleanliness of source or handling, but each superimposes an additional factor of safety by destruction of those pathogens that may have slipped through the best of sanitary barriers.

Food sanitation serves to reduce the risk of spread of disease through food. The measures are diverse, depending upon the food in question and the specific organisms involved. In general they embrace cleanliness of sources and processing, protection of animals used as sources of food, and heating to destroy pathogens. Disinfection of dishes is an integral part of food sanitation.

Disinfection of Air. The recent work of Wells has shown that, under certain conditions, air may serve as a vehicle for the dissemination of human pathogens. This has given rise to the suggestion that measures of disinfection comparable to those used in water and milk treatment should be applied to air. Although ultraviolet irradiating devices have been shown to be capable of accomplishing this disinfection, they have had but little application except in the surgical operating room or the hospital nursery because the bulk of the respiratory infections are apparently spread through direct droplet infection rather than through the air. Use of ultraviolet lamps in military barracks appears to have brought about a slight reduction in the incidence of the nonspecific upper respiratory tract infections but not of influenza or of streptococcal infections. Although some studies have suggested that use of such lamps within schoolrooms or offices might result in a slight reduction of communicable disease, other carefully controlled studies have shown no such reduction. One may safely conclude that the value of ultraviolet lamps in such situations has not been proved. Use of disinfectant mists (aerosols), usually in the form of diethylene glycol, likewise reduces the bacterial content of air, but has similarly effected little if any reduction in the incidence of respiratory infections. Until we can avoid spreading disease through breathing, talking, coughing, and sneezing into each other's face, there seems but little value in disinfecting devices applied to air-conditioning apparatus or installed in living or working quarters. At best it can disinfect only a small portion of the air that we breathe.

Closely allied with air disinfection are measures to reduce the number of bacteria that are dispersed into the air. Sweeping of floors and making of beds cause a marked increase in the number of bacteria suspended in the air. The oiling of the floors and impregnation of the sheets and blankets with oil [5] markedly reduce the degree of air contamination, but unfortunately there is no satisfactory evidence that such measures cause a significant reduction of respiratory diseases even in crowded military barracks. One must conclude that the contamination of the air incidental to sweeping or bedmaking is of little significance so far as concerns spread of respiratory tract infections. Oiling appears therefore to be a factor in maintenance of general cleanliness but not a disease control measure.

Factors Limiting the Applicability of Environmental Sanitation. In the control of certain diseases, environmental sanitation has been remarkably effective, in others a great disappointment. Thus the remarkable decline in typhoid can be attributed in major part to better sanitation of water, milk, and food supplies, supplemented by safer methods of excreta disposal. The elimination of yellow fever from urban districts is due to eradication of certain mosquitoes. Malaria may be controlled by preventing the breeding of certain species of anophelines. Yet in spite of improved community sanitation, there has been no decline in measles, scarlet fever, or whooping cough. Diphtheria and smallpox have been attacked by immunization rather than by attention to vectors. Sanitation has, therefore, a definite sphere within which it will produce results; in other fields it is ineffective.

Environmental sanitation is particularly effective in the control of intestinal diseases. Both the intake and escape of the organisms are associated with intermittent physiological functions of the human body. It is therefore possible to erect barriers for the protection of water and food and to provide for safe excreta disposal. Neither would be possible if these functions of intake and excretion were being constantly performed without interruption, as in the case of respiration. Furthermore, a definite period of time elapses between the escape from the reservoir and intake into the new victim, thus affording opportunity for destruction of the organisms.

In the control of respiratory diseases, on the other hand, sanitation has been disappointing and offers little promise of success. The process of respiration, by which the organisms both enter and leave the body, is a function that cannot be interrupted for more than a few seconds. We cannot breathe a tank of air and then suspend respiration for several hours before further inhaling, yet this is exactly what we do with respect to food intake. We are constantly breathing in and out and perform these functions wherever we go. The crowding of human beings means that we often inhale droplets just exhaled by our associates. There is little reason to

[5] Oil impregnation, if properly done, does not alter the appearance, feel, or odor of sheets or blankets nor does it constitute a fire hazard.

hope, therefore, that environmental sanitation can effectively control diseases spread by respiration. Attention to vehicles of infection cannot be expected to control a disease in which they play a very minor role.

INCREASING RESISTANCE OF NEW HOST

As shown above, the barriers that can be expected to prevent the spread of certain pathogens are relatively inadequate. In spite of the most rigorous precautions, some organisms will reach other persons and produce further disease if the new host is susceptible. If, however, this new host is resistant, the seeds fall on barren soil and illness does not follow. While, ideally, we may strive to prevent spread of infection, we must recognize our failures and therefore direct attention at measures which will increase the resistance of the new hosts.

Passive Immunization

If it is known that a person has been exposed to infection, increased resistance may be conferred quickly through administration of definite quantities of antibodies, that is, passive immunization. This has definite value in certain cases, as it makes possible the rapid protection of the susceptible individual. Inasmuch as exposure has already occurred, there is no time for the slower development of active immunity.[6] Passive immunization is therefore an emergency measure designed to carry the individual through a limited period of increased hazard. As the duration of this immunity is short, usually two to four weeks, the person so protected is just as susceptible as formerly after the temporary protection has worn off. The method is applicable only in cases of known exposure, for renewal of such protection every few weeks of a person's life is obviously impractical. A resistance that is inherent in the body and will be automatically called into action when need arises through unrecognized exposure to infection is by far preferable. Passive immunization has a further disadvantage that, if achieved through use of a serum obtained from some other animal species, there is a definite risk of serum reactions. Even if these do not occur, the individual may be left sensitive to the foreign protein so introduced. While this may be of no immediate concern, it may prove embarrassing and distressing if therapeutic use of such serum is later necessary. In view of these limitations and disadvantages, passive immunization has found limited application in disease control; when used, it has been on an individual, rather than a community, basis.

[6] Protection against rabies through antirabic vaccine is an exception to this general principle but is possible only because of the long incubation period of the disease.

Modification of disease is an attempt to confer a partial passive protection, adequate to modify the course of the illness but not sufficient to confer complete immunity. It is based on the assumption that, if a certain level of resistance can be achieved promptly after a known exposure, the illness will be relatively mild and therefore free of complications but will at the same time stimulate the body to the natural production of antibodies. Under such circumstances, the individual will acquire the same degree of permanent resistance that would have developed from a normal attack of the disease. Modification is therefore a combination of passive immunity and normal infection. To achieve modification, the individual who has been exposed to infection is given a limited amount of antibodies. If too much is given, complete passive protection will result, and the body will still be susceptible when this has disappeared; if too little, no effective protection will be achieved. Because of our limited ability to measure the amount of antibodies that are present in any serum and because of our obvious lack of knowledge concerning the quantity of infection in any individual case, it is often difficult to gauge the proper amount of serum needed to achieve the degree of partial immunity that will bring about modification.

A few examples will illustrate the sphere of usefulness of passive immunization and modification. During World War I all wounds were potentially infected with tetanus spores as the fighting was very largely over fields heavily contaminated because of years of agricultural fertilization. In the early days of the war, tetanus therefore exacted a heavy toll. As there was at the time no known method of active immunization, administration of tetanus antitoxin to all wounded men was necessary to give them a passive immunity. The results of such methods were dramatically successful in reducing the incidence of the disease because the risk of tetanus was confined to a few days immediately following the wound— an exposure of which the individual was of course aware. Immunity could be withheld until the need arose and then achieved rapidly and temporarily.

In the control of diphtheria, however, active immunization is better, for there is usually no knowledge of exposure. Yet if a case develops in a family of susceptible children, the siblings are exposed to a special risk against which they may be protected by passive immunization. In former years, this was done almost routinely. Today it is usually used only in those instances in which it is impossible to keep these exposed children under observation; if frequent observation is possible, one may withhold passive immunization and rely on the use of massive therapeutic doses as soon as symptoms develop. Thus is avoided the risk of serum reactions and sensitization of children who, as shown by experience, have less than one chance in five of developing the disease.

In the case of measles, however, we have no known serum or drug to alter the severity of the illness after it has developed. Furthermore, the attack rate among the susceptible family contacts is about 100 per cent. As the disease is particularly serious for children under the age of three, especially if they are in a debilitated condition, one may seek either passive immunity or modification. The former, chosen if the child is very small or debilitated, will confer a purely temporary resistance; the latter will achieve a lasting protection and will, therefore, be selected if the condition of the child is such that he can withstand a mild attack without undue risk.

Methods Used for Passive Immunization or Modification. Any substance that contains antibodies may be given to confer passive immunity, the degree of resistance depending upon the ultimate concentration of antibody in the blood stream. An adult, having more blood than a child, requires a larger quantity to achieve the same degree of protection. Several different sources of antibodies are used:

Specific therapeutic serum is usually derived from a horse actively immunized against the disease in question, though occasionally the serum of other animals may be used. Specific serum has the advantage that its antibody content is large, can be measured with relatively high degree of accuracy, and that such serum can be produced in any quantity needed. On the other hand, it has the disadvantage of containing a protein foreign to the human body. It may, therefore, produce serum reactions (rarely anaphylactic reactions) in persons allergic to this protein and may so sensitize others that they later react if given further doses. In some cases the serum reaction may be comparable in severity to the infection against which protection is desired. Such is the case with respect to the present mild form of scarlet fever.

Hyperimmune serum differs from the usual specific therapeutic serums in the fact that it is derived from humans rather than other animals. It is prepared from the blood of persons whose resistance has been raised to unusually high levels by frequent injections of suitable antigens; the concentration of antibodies is thus much higher than is usually achieved through conventional measures of immunization. Actually all therapeutic sera can be described as "hyperimmune" for they are derived from animals that have been given very intensive immunization, which has been repeatedly reinforced by booster doses of antigen. In common parlance the term "hyperimmune serum" is restricted to human serum; the only one of present practical importance is that for whooping cough. Hyperimmune serum has the special advantage of containing no foreign protein.

Convalescent serum is blood serum from a person who has recently recovered from the disease in question. The term "recently" is an indefinite one; it has been variously interpreted as ranging from a few weeks to several years, depending perhaps upon the current need for the serum. Convalescent serum owes its effectiveness to the antibodies produced by a person in recovering from a specific infection. As the concentration of these is probably greater shortly after recovery than after the lapse of several years, the best results will usually be obtained with serum drawn as early as possible after recovery. Convalescent serum has the advantage of containing no foreign proteins and is, therefore, not likely to produce serum reactions or to sensitize. It may contain a variety of antibodies against a particular infection, whereas the therapeutic serum is usually confined to a single type of antibody. On the other hand, convalescent serum has a very limited application because of the difficulty of obtaining an adequate supply. Most of the victims of the acute infectious diseases for which convalescent serum can be used are children. The amount of blood that can be safely withdrawn from a child, even if permission can be obtained, is very limited, and the number of adults who are "recently" convalescent is small. Consequently, the supply of convalescent serum is very limited. It could never be adequate to meet the real needs of a community if it were used in all applicable cases. The expense entailed frequently prevents its use in the situations where it is most needed. Furthermore, the antibody content of convalescent serum may be low as compared with that of horse serum, is extremely variable, and is difficult to measure. Through pooling of the blood from several donors, a more nearly uniform concentration of antibodies may be obtained, but there is still variation depending upon the interpretation of the word "recently."

Adult serum, little used in this country, is merely blood serum of adults selected at random from the general population. Its use depends on the assumption (usually correct) that the donors have developed a resistance, due either to an earlier frank attack of the disease or to latent immunization. A weaker form of convalescent serum, it has the sole advantage of being obtainable in larger and, within limitations, in any desired quantity.

Parental Whole Blood. Using injections of whole blood from one of the parents of the child to be protected depends on the same assumption as in the case of adult serum. Rather than obtaining the blood in advance and extracting the serum which contains the antibodies, the blood is drawn as needed and injected immediately. In a certain sense, this is a wasteful procedure, as the serum constitutes only half the blood; the corpuscles containing hemoglobin are of little value since they are broken up. Blood typing is not needed as in transfusions, inasmuch as the blood is not injected into the veins of the child but into the muscles or subcutaneous tissues. The sole advantage of this method is that the supply is almost unlimited and is usually available when needed. There are so many disadvantages, however, that the method has not been popular: large quantities (20 to 40 cc) must be injected because of the low concentration of antibodies; the level of antibodies is extremely variable and cannot be averaged as in pools of convalescent or adult serum; the technique is at times cumbersome; destruction of the red corpuscles in the tissues of the recipient leaves an area of soreness; and the parent may be reluctant to permit the withdrawal of the blood. There is also a risk of transmitting an infection, such as syphilis or malaria, from the parent to the child. This danger may be reduced, though not eliminated, by suitable tests upon the donor, provided time and facilities are available. The use of parental whole blood has been found to be practical only with respect to measles and even here has been of only limited application.

Placental extract ("immune globulin human") is obtained from the normal human placenta. As this is embryonic tissue, the blood in it has the same concentration of antibodies as is found in the infant at birth. Placental extract has the following advantages: it is relatively cheap, as it represents the use of a previously wasted substance; the supply is commensurate with the community demand; and it can be prepared in adequate quantities. Through pooling of the extracts of many placentae, its antibody content can be kept fairly uniform. Experience has shown the material to be effective, though its use has been somewhat curtailed by occasional reactions not encountered with convalescent serum.

Gamma Globulin (human immune serum globulin). The antibodies in any human serum are contained in that part of the blood serum protein referred to as the gamma globulin fraction. This fraction, which can be separated from the rest of the blood, contains, therefore, a very high concentration of antibodies which are free of many of the immunologically inert parts of the blood to be found in convalescent or adult serum or in whole blood and from certain tissue extracts contained in placental extract. It represents the most highly refined and purified source of human antibodies. Fortunately the gamma globulin is one of the fractions that is discarded in the preparation of blood serum for transfusion purposes. Thus the blood serum program of World War II produced a large quantity of gamma globulin which, so far as the blood program was concerned, was a waste product. This has been further refined and made available by the Red Cross for use as an antibody. The gamma globulin is available as a dried powder which is readily dissolved in salt solution to prepare it for injection. The availability of gamma globulin after exhaustion of the current wartime stock is still problematical.

Active Immunization

Active immunization aims to give the individual a lasting protection, to guard against potential future exposures. It is obviously preferable to passive immunization for we are usually unaware of exposure to infections, especially those entering through the intestinal and respiratory tracts. Furthermore, it has an element of permanence lacking in passive protection.

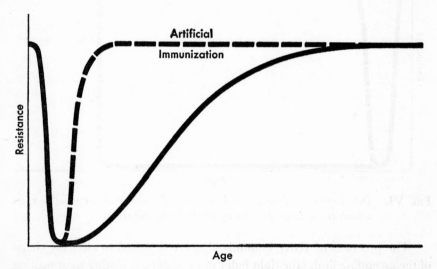

FIG. V. *Development of active resistance by artificial as contrasted with latent immunization.*

Experience shows that, if a program of active immunization is vigorously pursued, a disease may disappear from the community. Active immunization, if applied to a large enough fraction of a population and extended to new generations as they come into the community, gives a more lasting protection than any other method except certain types of environmental control, such as water sanitation and insect eradication.

Nature of Active Immunization. It was shown in the previous chapter (p. 38) that latent immunization against certain diseases occurs as a result of exposure to subinfecting doses. The development of this resistance was shown in Figure IV and is further portrayed by the solid line in Figure V. The high part of the curve on the left indicates the resistance which is so frequently present at birth and which disappears at about six months of age. The level of resistance then gradually increases, the exact shape of the curve depending upon the frequency and severity of the subclinical infections. In some diseases, such as measles and smallpox, there is no latent immunization, so that the resistance stays at a minimum until actual infection raises it to a satisfactory level (see Fig. VI). To what extent the ultimate resistance will remain high or may fall to lower levels depends on many complex factors. It is drawn here as though there were no fall.

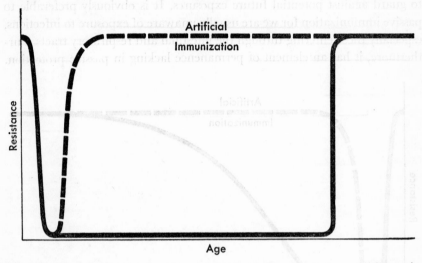

FIG. VI.   *Development of active resistance to disease, such as smallpox, in which there is no process of latent immunization.*

The processes of active immunization are designed to alter the shape of the ascending limb (the right half) of these curves. Rather than waiting for natural exposure and infection to stimulate the body to produce antibodies, definite quantities of antigen are introduced, thus bringing about a rapid development of antibody. If the antigen used is the same as that produced by the organisms under conditions of natural infection, the antibody produced will be similar. Active immunization thus aims to accomplish in a short period of time and without risk of disease the same effects achieved more slowly and with greater risk under natural conditions. This is portrayed in the dotted lines of the graphs, it being assumed that active immunization has been undertaken as soon as the resistance at birth has disappeared.

Duration of Active Immunity. Examination of these graphs gives some answers to the question of the duration of active immunity. The level of resistance has been raised rapidly by artificial methods, but the individual is still subject to the subclinical exposures that bring about latent immunization of the susceptibles. These exposures serve to reinforce the artificially acquired resistance. It is, therefore, impossible to determine to what extent the duration of the resistance is due to the immunizing process or to this subclinical reinforcement. In general, however, the artificially acquired resistance is quite comparable to that which comes from an attack of the disease or from latent immunization. Second attacks of almost all diseases except yellow fever have been described. It is not surprising, therefore, that artificially induced resistance sometimes fails to persist. If the disease in question is one in which the likelihood of subclinical exposure after immunization is slight, one may logically expect a more rapid falling-off of the antibodies and, therefore, a need for more frequent restimulation through repeated injections than if exposure to infection is frequent. Thus we might expect that diphtheria and scarlet fever immunization would be relatively lasting because of the existence of carriers spreading the organisms through their respiratory secretions. On the other hand, since smallpox carriers rarely if ever occur, we should anticipate a more rapid decline in resistance in areas where smallpox is absent and reinforcement through frequent exposure to cases is impossible. Similarly, we should expect a decline in typhoid resistance in a person who lived in a well-protected community and thus had no opportunity to come in contact with the bacilli through water, milk, or food. General experience bears out these expectations. The often repeated rule of three-year duration for typhoid immunization and seven-year duration for smallpox is only a crude approximation based on scant evidence and had best be forgotten, as it implies a degree of exactness not warranted by experience and ignores the question of reinforcement through exposure to unrecognized cases or carriers of infection.

In former years artificially induced active immunity tended to persist longer than it does today. This was not because the antigens then in use were superior to those currently employed. On the contrary the present antigens are much improved. The greater duration of resistance was due to the fact that the diseases were more common and therefore the immunized person had more exposures to help maintain the resistance which had been artificially established. The total effect of extensive immunization programs has been to reduce the incidence of these diseases and therefore to reduce the number of exposures to so low a point that the resistance produced by antigen injections tends to disappear. This has introduced a need for additional injections to reinforce the declining resistance. These are referred to as "booster" injections.

Booster injections are a practical application of what is referred to as the "anamnestic response." If a child that has never been actively immunized is given a very small dose of antigen, e.g., as much diphtheria toxin as contained in a Schick test, no demonstrable production of antibodies results. A great many such small doses can be given without apparent rise in the concentration of antibodies. On the other hand, if this person has been previously immunized but the antibody level has fallen, injection of a very small quantity of antigen will cause a very rapid rise in the level of antibodies. This rise may be to a level even higher than that originally attained. This rise is an expression of the fact that the antibody-production mechanism, which has previously "learned" to produce a given type of antibody, responds to a very minute subsequent stimulus. This rise is referred to as an "anamnestic response," [7] and the injection as the "booster dose." This dose is usually no greater than one of the original injections. If given intradermally, a smaller dose is required than if given subcutaneously, but owing to the greater difficulty of intradermal techniques, the subcutaneous injection is more commonly used.

The need for booster doses depends on the rate of disappearance of antibodies. This in turn depends on the frequency of restimulation through community exposures. These latter vary with the incidence of the disease and the extent to which the child is exposed to other persons. Thus current practices with respect to booster injections against diphtheria may be adequate at the moment but not suitable in future years when diphtheria will probably be less common and more boosters required to maintain a satisfactory level of resistance. Similarly the booster practices of one country may not necessarily be the same as those of another in which the diphtheria rate is different. Likewise the physician who is dealing with private patients drawn largely from a segment of the population with a minimum of human exposures may need to provide for more frequent booster injections than does a public clinic with a clientele drawn from a congested section of the city in which the exposure rate is high. There can obviously be no generally applicable standard for booster injections. What is needed is a program best suited to the needs of the situation, this program to be based on a sound understanding of the principles involved.

Applicability of Active Immunization. It is possible at present to immunize against a wide variety of infections; future research may add other diseases to the list of those against which we may be so protected. Yet, in practice, we seek protection against only a few. Several factors enter into the decision as to the desirability of attempting active immunization.

1. *Existence of a Suitable Antigen.* It has already been seen that active immunization depends upon the use of an antigen which stimulates the body to produce its own antibodies. The method may be applied, there-

---

[7] The French very descriptively call this the "réaction de rappel"—reaction of recall.

fore, only if there is a suitable immunizing agent. The general requirements of an antigen are as follows:

a. *Protection.* The antigen shall be capable of conferring a reasonable degree of protection comparable to that which comes from a natural attack of the disease. The ideal antigen would be one that produces a sufficiently high resistance in all cases to guard against any possible dose of infection. Obviously no such antigen exists. Yet, unless an antigen stimulates the body to produce a sufficient quantity of antibodies for at least a reasonable degree of protection, its use would be futile. Individual opinion may differ as to what may be considered a reasonable degree of protection. To some extent it varies with the severity of the disease. It might be hardly worth while to immunize against a disease which is usually mild, unless we could expect a reasonably complete protection in all except the occasional instance. On the other hand, if the disease were severe and often fatal and the risk of attack great, we might gladly accept an immunization which gave only partial protection, thus reducing the severity and risk of death from the disease; or we might accept a protection effective only in certain persons, each of us hoping, of course, that he would be the one to be protected. Unless the risk of the disease is great, there is little use for an antigen that gives a poor degree of protection.

b. *Risk.* The danger attendant upon the use of the antigen should be less than that of the disease under natural or epidemic conditions. As the purpose of immunization is to protect against illness, nothing is gained by using an antigen which entails a risk equal to, or greater than, that of the disease in question. Methods are available whereby we might immunize against many more infections than we do; yet in some cases the procedure, though effective, is attended with a risk out of all proportion to that of the disease. Such antigens have no practical value. In dealing with human beings, we seek an antigen devoid of all risk. Yet in former years when many of our diseases were more serious than at present, it was reasonable to accept some risk so long as it was less than that of the disease against which it protected. Smallpox inoculation, the forerunner of vaccination, was attended with a definite risk but became popular because this risk was so much less than that of the prevailing malignant smallpox. With the advent of the safer method of vaccination, inoculation fell into discard and was ultimately outlawed.

c. *Reaction.* The reaction from the antigen must be less than that of the prevailing form of the disease. The use of certain antigens, while perfectly safe, may be attended with reactions out of all proportion to the severity of the condition against which they protect. One might logically hesitate to accept such an antigen, however effective it might be in conferring protection. This of course varies with the personal evaluation of the relation between reaction and the disease. To the professional person who knows the potential severity and complications of a disease, the dread of uncomfortable, though not serious, reactions seems a poor excuse for withholding immunization. One cannot, however, overlook the fact that public acceptance of an antigen is conditioned as much upon its likelihood to produce reactions as upon its effectiveness.

d. *Number of Injections.* The number of injections required must not be too great. To a large degree, the number required will depend upon the level of protection desired. The fewer the injections needed to reach the level which will protect most persons against the average dose, the more readily will the use of the antigen be accepted. The obvious ideal is to concentrate all the needed antigen into one dose, for experience shows that as the number increases, popular acceptance decreases. The general public has shown little acceptance of more than three injections. While it may be argued that this is due to lack of public education, one cannot overlook the desirability of keeping the number of injections to the lowest figure consistent with effective results. Yet caution is needed, lest in our desire to reduce the doses we unduly sacrifice efficiency and durability of the resultant resistance.

2. *Need for Immunization.* The mere existence of a suitable antigen does not imply that its use is desirable for all the population or even for many individuals. The risk of the disease must be considered by both the individual and the health officer. There would obviously be little sense in widespread use of yellow fever vaccines for the residents of the United States, especially in the northern part, as the country is free of the disease at the moment and the risk of infection is, therefore, infinitesimal. Yet the traveler to the infected areas of South America or Africa may well decide in favor of immunization, and the health officials of these areas may reasonably consider the desirability of mass immunization programs. In other instances, one may recommend that the individual seek such protection for his own benefit, even though the health department may not logically foster a community program. Thus in the northern tier of states, the incidence of typhoid fever is so low that it would be necessary to immunize many thousands each year in order to prevent a single case. Under such circumstances, health departments might well be criticized for spending their limited budgets on such a program, though in areas of higher typhoid incidence such procedures would be highly desirable. Yet even in these areas of low typhoid risk, the individual may reasonably desire to obtain such protection, even though the chance of infection is remote. Furthermore, regardless of the general community prevalence, it must always be

considered expedient to immunize those persons exposed to a special risk. In the above example, this would include physicians, nurses, laboratory workers, contacts with a typhoid case or carrier, and other persons whose mode of living is such as to expose them to a special risk of infection.

3. *Seriousness of a Disease.* Apart from its prevalence, the seriousness of the disease must likewise be taken into account in deciding as to immunization. Chickenpox, for example, is so mild, even though common, that little community benefit would accrue from immunizing against it, even if an ideal antigen were to be discovered. The money required to administer it would do more good elsewhere in the public health program.

From the foregoing paragraphs it is apparent that no detailed rules can be laid down to determine whether active immunization procedures should be utilized in a given situation. The decision must be based upon a thorough knowledge of the disease in question and the needs of the community.

Types of Antigens. As has already been pointed out, any substance stimulating the body to produce its own antibodies is called an antigen, which is merely an abbreviation for the more cumbersome term "antibody-generator." For a full discussion of the nature of antigens, the reader is referred to a standard text of bacteriology or immunology. A simple description will suffice for a clearer understanding of the proper use of active immunization procedures. Antigens may be grouped as follows:

Living antigens are organisms that, during the process of infecting the body, stimulate it to the production of antibodies. Such a process occurs whenever a person is ill with an infectious disease. Were it not for the risk entailed, one might therefore attempt immunization through deliberate infection. Though such a suggestion may appear grotesque, everyday experience shows it to be followed in too many instances. The mother who exposes all of her children to the one with measles and justifies her procedure on the ground of "getting it over with at one time" is following the practice of immunization with virulent organisms, which bring about a normal attack of the disease. Such a procedure is usually attended with too great a risk to be looked upon with favor, even though it is effective. Living organisms may, however, be used if their virulence has been so reduced that they are unable to cause serious disease though they still possess antigenic properties. Such organisms are said to be "attenuated." Many of the antigens used in the prevention of diseases of animals are of this character. Though extremely effective, they are less frequently employed in human immunization, as it is obviously preferable to use an antigen which has no capacity for multiplication. Furthermore, the preparation, storage, and determination of dosage of living antigens are more difficult. The only living antigen commonly used in human beings is small-pox vaccine; yellow fever vaccine, the original Pasteur antirabic vaccine, and the recently developed influenza vaccine fall into this same group.

Nonliving antigens are derived from microorganisms. To a large degree, they are the active antigenic principle by which these organisms stimulate the body to produce antibodies during the course of infection. As they cannot multiply, their dosage can be measured with greater precision than in the case of living antigens. Similarly, the storage of these products is simpler, as there is nothing to be kept alive. Nonliving antigens are of two types.

1. *Bacterial Extracts.* Some bacteria during growth secrete antigenic substances which may be separated by filtration. Although these may be injected in their original form, they are usually purified or modified in the chemical laboratory before use. The diphtheria antigens furnish an excellent example of these procedures. Diphtheria bacilli, during growth in a suitable medium, produce a toxin, the same as that which develops in the course of the disease. If injected into the body, it would cause the production of antibodies and might therefore be used as an immunizing agent. Yet its poisonous effects are such that only minute quantities could be given safely. Consequently, this toxin is subjected to formalin treatment, which virtually eliminates the poisonous properties though at the same time permitting retention of the ability to stimulate the production of antibodies. It is therefore still antigenic, though relatively nontoxic, and can be safely given in large enough quantities to produce a high level of resistance. As it is a modified toxin, it is referred to as a "toxoid."

2. *Dead Organisms.* In some cases it is not possible to separate any active component from the living organisms; yet a suspension of killed organisms is found to be antigenic. In such cases, the antigen consists of the dead organisms. Typhoid and whooping cough vaccines are of this type.

Antigens versus Vaccines. Considerable confusion exists in the minds of many persons as to the difference between a vaccine and an antigen. The difficulty is due to careless use of the terms and a tendency on the part of many to consider them as interchangeable. An antigen is any substance capable of stimulating the body to produce antibodies. It is thus a general and very inclusive term. A "vaccine," on the other hand, is that type of antigen which consists of either living or dead organisms. Originally the term was used to refer only to smallpox vaccine, but it has been broadened to its present usage. Although some persons use it as synonymous with the term "antigen," it does not correctly include bacterial extracts or their derivatives. Thus, a streptococcus vaccine is a suspension of killed streptococci and contains the dead cell bodies as well as any intracellular substances released by the breaking up of these bodies. Streptococcal toxin, on the other hand, is a substance secreted by the streptococci during their life and does not contain any cell bodies, either living or dead. A vaccine is thus a type of antigen, but the term does not include either the toxins or toxoids.

Multiple Antigens. Until recent years, the various antigens have been administered separately. This has necessitated a long series of injections if the child was to be protected against several diseases. Since World War II, there has been a rapid shift toward multiple antigens, i.e., a mixture of two or more antigens. In such a mixture each of the antigens retains its full immunizing power; actually some increase in this power is often observed. The reactions may be slightly greater but not sufficiently severe to contraindicate their use. The most commonly used multiple antigen is the mixture of diphtheria and tetanus toxoids with pertussis vaccine (DPT). Besides reducing the number of injections, this preparation has the advantage of including an antigen (tetanus toxoid) which, because of the rarity of the disease, would probably be little used if it required a separate course of injections. Although tetanus is rare, there is a real advantage in having a child actively immunized so that subsequent injuries entailing a risk of tetanus can be treated with a booster dose of toxoid rather than a prophylactic dose of tetanus serum.

Whom to Immunize. Assuming the existence of a suitable antigen, and a population exposed to a sufficient risk to warrant immunization, all susceptible persons must be protected if we are to gain absolute control over the disease. This group may be determined in two ways.

Susceptibility tests are designed to determine whether or not a person has sufficient resistance to withstand the average infecting dose. Such tests are thus measures of a definite level of resistance, not of absolute immunity; yet they give a fairly accurate indication of what may be the experience of the individual in the presence of infection. If we remember their limitations, we can use these tests in determining the need for immunization of an individual and in checking the effectiveness of immunizing procedures.

Susceptibility may be measured either by injecting a definite quantity of test material into the skin and observing the reaction or by withdrawing a sample of blood and testing the serum for the presence of antibodies. These tests determine the quantity of circulating antibody but give very little indication of the capacity of the body to produce further antibody in response to the stimulus of infection. This latter can be measured only by repeated tests after graduated stimuli. It should be emphasized that susceptibility tests are not immunizing injections.

Selection by Probable Risks. Testing of each individual prior to immunization is cumbersome and expensive; nor is it devoid of errors of technique whereby one might incorrectly assume a person to be immune who is actually susceptible. Consequently, testing is often omitted and immunization extended to all persons who fall in the age groups at which susceptibility is high. Extensive testing has shown definite variations in resistance at different ages, varying somewhat according to the likelihood of exposure within the community (see Chap. 2). Thus one may reasonably estimate the approximate proportion of a group in need of immunization. If a large majority is susceptible, little is gained by performing elaborate tests in order to eliminate the small resistant fraction. In such situations, immunization is commonly extended to all of the group without preliminary test, thus saving both time and expense. Those who did not need the immunization are not harmed; in fact they are helped, in that they are given an even higher level of protection than they formerly had. This procedure of immunization without prior testing is commonly followed at present with respect to diphtheria, even though there is a susceptibility test, the Schick test. If there is no suitable test readily performed, as in the case of typhoid fever or smallpox, one must assume that all persons who have not previously had the disease or been successfully immunized earlier are susceptible. Particular consideration should be given to persons, such as nurses and physicians, whose occupation exposes them to a special risk.

Control through Immunization

Complete control of a disease through immunization can be achieved only if all susceptibles are protected. For many reasons this is neither possible nor practicable except in selected groups. It is, therefore, desirable to determine the extent to which a disease may be controlled through protection of a fraction of the susceptible population.

Let us assume that we are dealing with a hypothetical disease, each case of which transmits infection to two other persons; that all individuals in the community are susceptible; and that one attack confers a lasting resistance. If we start with one case, this will give rise to two additional cases. Each of these will infect two others, so that the next generation of cases will be four. Each of these in turn will infect two others with eight resultant cases, and so forth. The spread of the infection through such a community will be shown by a simple geometrical progression as follows:

1   2   4   8   16   32   64   • • •   • • •

Ultimately some of the persons who are exposed will be those previously attacked and will not therefore be reinfected. As these become more frequent, the exposures will be less effective, and the disease will die out for lack of susceptibles.

Now let us assume that, before the infection is introduced into this community, half the population has been immunized and that an immunized person may not serve as a carrier. The first case will expose two others, but only one of these will be susceptible, while the other is immune and therefore not capable of transmitting the infection. Only one infecting case will result rather than two. This one will expose two others, but again only one will be susceptible; thus the third generation of cases will still be one instead of the four that occurred in the completely susceptible community. This one case will again expose two persons, only one of whom will be susceptible, so that the next generation is still one. Under such hypothetical conditions each generation of cases will be but one, as shown:

1   1   1   1   1   1   1   1   . . .

Thus through the simple procedure of immunizing only half the susceptible population, this particular disease has been reduced from one which spreads rapidly through the community to one which spreads slowly but is not completely eradicated. Although the residual infection has not been wiped out, the disease has been reduced from epidemic to endemic proportions.

In the above examples, we have of course made certain assumptions for the sake of clarity. In reality no disease behaves so simply, for certain cases infect no contacts while others may spread infection to many susceptibles. Furthermore, an immune person may be a carrier of certain diseases. Yet the basic principle set forth above holds in field experience, namely, that immunization of a substantial fraction of a community results in a greater reduction in incidence of a communicable disease than is expressed by the proportion of the susceptibles protected. In other words, those who are not actually immunized derive some protection from the reduction in the number of susceptibles.

A great mass of factual data might be presented to support this generality. One need only call attention to a few simple examples. Thus we find that immunization of approximately 50 per cent of the child population (provided this 50 per cent is reasonably distributed among the various age groups) brings about effective diphtheria control, even though occasional cases may occur. Similarly, the reduction in the incidence of smallpox has been out of proportion to the percentage of the population vaccinated, though a close parallelism exists between the incidence and the vaccination rate of any particular state.

It has at times been argued that immunization of only a fraction of the susceptible population might constitute a menace to the nonprotected group, owing to a hypothetical increase in the number of carriers. This argument has been based on the assumption that persons who were immunized were more likely to become carriers than were those not so protected. In other words, a susceptible person would probably develop a clinically manifest attack of a disease and therefore be segregated from the community; whereas the immunized person might have enough resistance to guard against a severe, and therefore recognizable, infection yet might develop a mild attack or the carrier condition. The mild case or carrier would circulate freely in the community, thus increasing the hazard to the nonprotected susceptibles. It has been argued, therefore, that immunization is hazardous unless it reaches all the susceptibles.

No one would deny the possibility of such a situation in individual instances, for an immunized person can unquestionably acquire either a mild infection or a carrier state. Yet there is no evidence to show that on a community-wide basis the incidence of carriers or mild cases is increased by immunization. Within isolated institutional groups, this increase has been shown; yet repeated studies of the prevalence of carriers of diphtheria show them to be less, rather than more, numerous today than in the era prior to immunization. There are unquestionably many factors other than immunization that determine the carrier rate, yet so far no evidence exists to show that immunization has increased the prevalence of carriers in the general population.

Furthermore, at least in diphtheria and scarlet fever, there is good evidence to indicate that the individual risk of infection from exposure to a carrier is much less than that due to exposure to a clinical case. Thus a substantial increase in the number of carriers would be more than offset by the reduction in cases. Finally, we must recognize that at present the incidence of subclinical cases and carriers of some diseases is so great that the magnitude of the reservoir would be little affected by the addition of even a large number of carriers. Thus it is doubtful if we recognize more than half our scarlet fever infections. There need be little concern, then, if this number of subclinical cases and carriers is increased by immunization, provided at the same time there is a better protection to those immunized. Even if one were to agree with all these doubts as to community value, one must still decide in favor of immunization on the basis of results so far achieved.

MINIMIZING ILL EFFECTS OF CASES THAT HAVE NOT BEEN PREVENTED

The mere existence of communicable disease does not in itself warrant extensive control measures. The real importance of these conditions lies in their killing power or the damage that they may inflict upon the body. It is, therefore, important that measures be taken to minimize these ill effects even if the diseases cannot be completely prevented. In this way, it is possible to salvage some of the wreckage of our failure to prevent spread or to increase body resistance.

The prevention of death or of permanent damage implies medical and nursing care. While to a very large degree this is a matter of individual rather than public responsibility, many aspects of the proper care of these conditions require the utilization of community resources, even in a society in which medical care of all is not a state function. It must be recognized, however, that, even under the present conditions of medical practice, the community has the responsibility of caring for those financially unable to provide for themselves. The degree to which a community, through its public health agencies, may be called upon to furnish aid in the care of cases caused by these diseases will, therefore, depend upon local and personal circumstances and may vary all the way from nothing to complete medical and nursing care, including hospitalization.

The forms of community participation designed to minimize the ill effects of communicable disease may be divided into several categories.

Aids to Diagnosis

Prompt and early diagnosis serves a dual purpose: the establishment of control measures to minimize the risk of spread and the institution of effective treatment to reduce the likelihood of death or complications. The former is of prime benefit to the community, the latter to the patient. The availability of these diagnostic aids is a real help to the physician in the better treatment of his patient.

Laboratory Service. The furnishing of bacteriological and serological laboratory service to aid in the diagnosis of infectious diseases is a well-recognized function of public health agencies. Obviously the average physician cannot be expected to provide, in his own office, facilities for bacteriological study of suspected infectious cases. Such tasks may be required so infrequently in the experience of any one physician as to make the cost prohibitive, or they may be so complicated as to be impossible of accurate performance by a person who does not carry them out almost daily. For such tests to be performed correctly and with reasonable economy, it is necessary that they be carried out in laboratories equipped for this purpose and staffed with personnel especially trained in this field. While obviously these might be (and often are) organized on a private basis, the patient paying all costs on the basis of service rendered, experience shows that under such a plan the decision as to the use of such tests will be based too often on the patient's capacity to pay rather than upon his medical needs. Lavish use of laboratory tests is important for diagnosis. Consequently, the community, through its health agencies, furnishes such services. This is, of course, a form of socialization of medicine, for the ready availability of such laboratory services reduces the demands made upon privately conducted laboratories. Yet few persons today question the propriety of government's conduct of such laboratories, as they are obviously in the public interest. Besides rendering diagnostic aid, the laboratory serves in a disease control capacity, for it performs those bacteriological tests needed to determine the period of isolation or to detect carriers among contacts with cases. It should be emphasized that the laboratory does not make diagnoses but merely performs tests for the physician to assist him in arriving at a correct diagnosis. Laboratory tests supplement, but do not take the place of, clinical skill and acumen.

Clinical Diagnostic Service. This implies direct examination of the patient by a person with special skill in the clinical manifestations of the infectious diseases. It is essentially a consultation service offered at government expense. This service may be rendered in three forms:

Field consultation implies a clinical consultation at the request of the attending physician. It may be rendered either by a physician on the staff of the health department or by a specialist whose services have been engaged for this particular function. In either case, however, this is purely a consultation service, no patient being seen except on special request of the attending physician and in conjunction with him. This type of service is frequently rendered by the health officer in establishing the diagnosis in a questionable case of the commoner infectious diseases, thus transferring to the official agency the responsibility for determining the need for isolation precautions. In the case of the less common infectious diseases and especially such conditions as poliomyelitis and meningitis, in which bedside surgical procedures are required for diagnosis, special consultants are sometimes furnished by the public health agency.

Clinic Service. The function of a clinic is twofold—diagnosis and treatment of ambulatory patients. Persons may come to the clinic either upon their own initiative (open clinic) or upon referral by a physician, the findings being reported to the physician rather than to the patient (consultation clinic). Clinics may be organized upon either a free or a part-pay basis. In the control of the infectious diseases, they have been most extensively developed for the diagnosis and treatment of tuberculosis and the venereal diseases. Such clinics may be supported either through public funds or by private social agencies.

Community diagnostic surveys are programs for the examination of entire community groups in hope of finding incipient and unrecognized infections. They depend usually upon the application of technical diagnostic procedures (x-rays for tuberculosis, serological tests for syphilis, and so forth) to all persons who may be persuaded to submit to examination. Clinical examination is given to those persons who are selected for further study as a result of the tests. Unquestionably, mass surveys of this character bring to light many unsuspected cases that otherwise might not have been discovered; yet they are the most expensive form of case-finding, as the number of infections discovered is usually very small for the amount of money required. Such procedures are, therefore, of limited application. They are most suitable for research purposes and as a case-finding measure applicable to a group in which the rate of infection is known to be relatively high.

Aids to Treatment

Treatment of the patient serves two purposes—it reduces the likelihood of death or permanent physical damage, and it may shorten the period of communicability. The second of these serves to reduce the likelihood of spread of infection and has been discussed above (p. 45). The former is essentially for the sake of the patient, the community benefiting only to the extent that the welfare of the group is the sum of the welfares of the individuals comprising the group. As the prime purpose of government is to further the well-being of its citizens, it is logical that the state should render such services as will reduce the risk of death or permanent physical impairment. This is particularly true since the state has the responsibility for support of those who may be left destitute by the death or debility of the wage earner. As the state is faced by this ultimate responsibility, it is reasonable—and certainly it is good business—to render such assistance as will reduce the likelihood that the need for such payments will arise. Government, therefore, very logically has a direct interest in the treatment of the case. The degree to which it may actually participate in the treatment depends very largely upon the laws and practices of the community in question.

The cost of care of patients in either the home or hospital, when furnished by the community, may be charged against the health or welfare department, depending upon the local laws. There is often provision for sharing of such costs by both the local community and some larger governmental unit, such as the county or the state.

Public health participation in treatment may be divided into four types:

Hospitalization. Although much of the value of hospitalization lies in the breaking of contacts and, therefore, reduction of spread, the patient also derives real benefit. The decision as to the hospitalization of a patient must take both factors into consideration. The patient with laryngeal diphtheria is in obvious need of care in an institution with facilities and personnel for intubation or tracheotomy if needed. The patient with measles complicated by pneumonia may require the medical and nursing care to be found only in a hospital. Yet there are situations in which hospitalization may be a distinct hazard to the patient, in view of the possibility of contracting a secondary infection. Experience shows that routine institutional care of influenza and measles may be undesirable, as it brings the patient in contact with others and thus increases the risk of pneumonia. This risk of complications, while small, must be considered in any decision as to hospitalization. Hospitals for the reception of infectious diseases are usually conducted by government—either the health department or the institutional or welfare agency.

Home Care. Even though removal to a hospital may be unnecessary or even undesirable, there may still be need for assistance in home care. In some cases, this means medical and nursing care as well as public support, if the financial circumstances of the home prevent adequate care without such assistance. In other instances, the public health or visiting nurse may instruct the mother in the nursing care of the patient or give such direct nursing care as can be rendered during the course of such a visit.

Clinics. The use of clinics for the treatment of infectious diseases is confined very largely to the care of tuberculosis, syphilis, gonorrhea, and the aftereffects of poliomyelitis. In the first three, the treatment serves to keep the patient in a noninfectious condition, so that this activity might be considered as primarily designed to reduce spread. The orthopedic care of those crippled by poliomyelitis is, however, almost exclusively for the benefit of the patient, the community profiting only to the extent that the treatment serves to reduce the risk of permanent invalidism which may affect the patient's ultimate capacity for self-support. Though this service may well be considered a form of socialization of medicine, few would challenge the statement that without this assistance many children, who might be benefited, would be doomed to unnecessarily crippled lives.

Distribution of specific therapeutic agents is a well-accepted public health procedure, which unquestionably contributes to the better treatment of infectious diseases. Under this heading may be included various sera as well as those chemical agents which are used so extensively in the treatment of the venereal diseases. Future policy may add many new substances to the list. In some states these products are manufactured by the government; [8] in others, the health department purchases them from the commercial manufacturers at a wholesale rate. The distribution practices vary considerably in different states. Some provide for lavish free distribution to all alike; others resell them at reduced cost to those otherwise unable to pay and limit free distribution only to the recognized indigent. The present tendency is toward more widespread free distribution, thus providing for more lavish use in those situations in which the proper care of the patient depends on such products.

There can be no question that free distribution of these therapeutic agents, as well as vaccines, represents a socialistic form of competition with business. State manufacture is competition with the large manufacturing drug houses; state distribution is competition with the retail pharmacist. Yet there can likewise be no question of the benefit that accrues to the public health from making adequate treatment agents available in such cases. These products are uniformly expensive yet must be used in relatively large quantity. It is not in the interest of the patient that his capacity to pay for such drugs should take precedence over medical judgment in determining the dosage. Yet unless there is some provision for free or reduced-cost distribution, in many cases the use of these drugs will be inevitably curtailed to a level below that which medical science finds advisable. The physician, who is too often not even paid for his services, cannot be expected to furnish expensive therapeutic agents as a personal charity, nor can the patient wait until a social worker has determined the question of indigency. If the decision as to free distribution is to await careful investigation of the family's financial competence, the treatment may often be delayed until it is too late to yield maximum benefit. It is, therefore, in the interests of better public health for the government to defray the costs of such products and to simplify the methods of their distribution as far as possible in order to avoid unnecessary delay. It must be remembered, however, that such products are expensive and that careless use of them by medical and public health agencies is an indefensible waste of public money.

[8] Massachusettts, Michigan, New York, and New York City maintain extensive establishments for the production of biological products. Certain of the other states manufacture some of the simpler products.

COMMUNITY EDUCATION

One very important, though often neglected, factor in the control of communicable diseases is that of community education. This is fundamental to the application of all other control measures. It is too easy to forget that the enforcement of isolation and quarantine and the protection of water, food, and milk supplies all depend upon public acceptance of the regulatory authority of government. The health officer whose enthusiasm to apply regulatory measures outruns popular opinion as to the need for such measures will find that he is replaced in office by a successor who may be less solicitous in the performance of his duty. The public will tolerate and support measures of reasonable regulation only if it can see the need for them.

Education is equally essential in the promotion of any program of control through service to the individual. The person to be immunized (or his parents) must be informed of the need for such protection. Reasonable doubt and hesitancy are inevitable, as the immediate risk from the disease may be apparently very slight. In too many instances, the parent has been made apprehensive as to immunization because of reports of untoward reactions and failures. Such reports are too often the result of gossip, with its inevitable exaggeration and distortion as it passes from one person to another; yet to the individual they seem like very real objections. It must be constantly remembered that, in promoting immunization, we are asking individuals to submit to potentially uncomfortable procedures that may appear to them to be of scant importance. Education is essential if we are to expect the public to utilize these measures. The very best antigen may be of no practical value if it is not utilized, and the most elaborate program will accomplish nothing unless individuals present themselves for immunization. Similarly, the mere provision of diagnostic, therapeutic, or nursing facilities will do little unless there is a real desire on the part of the public and the medical profession to make use of them. The health department too often assumes that it has merely to provide certain services and forgets to give adequate attention to the education of the public as to the need for utilizing these facilities.

Funds will not be available for any service or even regulatory program unless the appropriating body has been made aware of the need for such expenditures. The community that does not understand the need of milk sanitation will not engage the services of a suitable inspector; unless it appreciates the value of a school health service or a nursing program, it will not allocate funds to either purpose. The authors recall a town board that rejected an appropriation of $150 for diphtheria immunization, only to be faced during the next two years with a bill of $1800 for the care of about forty diphtheria cases (and no sum of money could restore to life the five children who had died). Since then there has been no question of the annual appropriation for diphtheria immunization. Education in this instance was costly in both cash and life. Had it been carried out effectively prior to the original request for funds, the lesson might have been learned at less sacrifice.

Discussion of the detailed methods of health education is beyond the scope of this volume. The reader will find several suitable references at the end of the chapter. The well-balanced program will make use of all channels for the dissemination of information, notably the personal visit, public meeting, formal class, newspaper, pamphlet, exhibit, and radio. The health officer and all of his staff must seize every opportunity to carry on this educational work. If they fail to create informed public opinion, their efforts to apply specific measures will too often come to nought.

APPLICATION OF CONTROL MEASURES

In the foregoing pages we have examined various forms of communicable disease control measures. Obviously not all of these are applicable to each disease, nor would it be logical to attempt to apply, on a community basis, all that could be utilized in dealing with an individual case. Each measure has its particular field of usefulness. A sound community program of disease control is based upon careful epidemiological study to determine those points in the spread of the disease at which these various measures may be applied with hope of success. The usual program is a combination of these various measures with special emphasis on the one or two which will yield the greatest return for a given expenditure of money and effort. It must be remembered that all administrative public health programs are limited by the available funds. The health officer must distribute these funds so as to obtain the greatest protection for the greatest number of persons from a given expenditure of money. In some instances it may be desirable to lay principal stress upon attempts to prevent spread through environmental sanitation; in other situations, to ignore these measures and concentrate on increasing the resistance. Local conditions may be such as to make particularly applicable a measure which in some other community would not be suitable. It is imperative, therefore, that the health officer have a thorough epidemiological knowledge of these diseases and that he attempt to assess the value and special fields of applicability of the various control measures. Only in this way can he spend his limited budget most wisely.

SUGGESTED READINGS

Adams, H. S.: *Milk and Food Sanitation Practices.* New York: Commonwealth Fund, 1947.

American Academy of Pediatrics: *Report of the Committee on Immunization and Therapeutic Procedures for Acute Infectious Diseases.* Chicago: the Academy, 1951.

Chapin, Charles V.: Papers of: *A Review of Public Health Realities,* edited by Clarence L. Scamman. New York: Commonwealth Fund, 1934. See especially pp. 65–115.

Commission on Acute Respiratory Diseases and the Commission on Air-Borne Infections, U.S. Army Epidemiological Board: "A Study of the Effect of Oiled Floors and Bedding on the Incidence of Respiratory Disease in New Recruits," *Am. J. Hyg.,* 43:120–44, (Mar.) 1946.

Control of the Common Fevers. By twenty-one contributors arranged with the help of Dr. Robert Cruickshank by the editor of *The Lancet.* London: The Lancet, Ltd., 1942.

The Control of Communicable Diseases, 7th ed. Report of the Sub-Committee on Communicable Disease Control of the Committee on Research and Standards. New York: American Public Health Association, 1950.

Downes, Jean: "Control of Acute Respiratory Illness by Ultra-Violet Lights," *Am. J. Pub. Health,* 40:1512–20, (Dec.) 1950.

Edsall, Geoffrey: "Active Immunization," *New England J. Med.,* 241:18–26, 60–70, 99–107, (July 7, 14, 21) 1949.

Forsbeck, Filip C.: "An Outfit for Group Immunization, Including an Automatic Syringe and a Needle Rack," *Am. J. Pub. Health,* 18:1407–9, (Nov.) 1928.

Fowler, William: "The Reportable Diseases. Diseases and Conditions Required to be Reported in the Several States," *Pub. Health Rep.,* 59:317–40, (Mar. 10) 1944.

"Insecticides and Rodenticides, 1952. Recommendations for Use," *Pub. Health Rep.,* 67:455–58, (May) 1952.

McGuinness, Aims C.: "Review of Current Trends in Active and Passive Immunization," *J.A.M.A.,* 148:261–66, (Jan. 26) 1952.

Maxcy, Kenneth F.: *Rosenau's Preventive Medicine and Hygiene,* 7th ed. New York: Appleton-Century-Crofts, Inc., 1951.

Mustard, Harry S.: *Rural Health Practices.* New York: Commonwealth Fund, 1936, pp. 354–438.

Parish, Henry James: *Bacterial and Virus Diseases. Antisera, Toxoids, Vaccines and Tuberculins in Prophylaxis and Treatment,* 2nd ed. Baltimore: Williams & Wilkins Co., 1951.

"The Present Status of the Control of Air-borne Infections," Report of the Subcommittee for the Evaluation of Methods to Control Air-borne Infections, Committee on Research and Standards, American Public Health Association. *Am. J. Pub. Health,* 37:13–22, (Jan.) 1947.

"Recent Studies on Disinfection of Air in Military Establishments," Report of Committee on Sanitary Engineering, National Research Council, Division of Medical Sciences. *Am. J. Pub. Health,* 37:189–98, (Feb.) 1947.

Top, Franklin H.: *Handbook of Communicable Diseases,* 2nd ed. St. Louis: C. V. Mosby Co., 1947.

Volk, V. K.: "Observations on the Safety of Multiple Antigen Preparations," *Am. J. Hyg.,* 47:53–63, (Jan.) 1948.

Horvat: *Studies on Humidity and Air in Military Establishments*, Report of Committee on Sanitary Engineering, National Research Council, Division of Medical Sciences. *Am. J. Pub. Health*, 37:189-98, (Feb.) 1947.
Top, Franklin H.: *Handbook of Communicable Diseases*, 2nd ed., St. Louis, C. V. Mosby Co.
Volk, V. K.: *Safety in the Sale of Multiple Antigen Preparations.* *Am. J. Pub. Health*, 6:35, (Jan.) 1946.

4. The Legal Basis of
Communicable Disease Control

Liberty consists in the power of doing that which is permitted by law.
CICERO

It is a generally accepted doctrine that government has the duty and responsibility of protecting the welfare and health of its citizens. One of the earliest formal expressions of this doctrine was the enactment of legislation to guard against the introduction and spread of communicable diseases within a community. As these infections may be transmitted from one person to another and as the unbridled actions of an infected individual may endanger his associates, some code of action that all must follow is necessary to minimize the risk of spread. This code is known as the public health law.[1]

NATURE OF THE REGULATORY AUTHORITY

Public health law is an expression of the "police power" of government. Police power means the right to regulate the conduct of the individual for the benefit of the many. Obviously, organized society could not exist if every individual had unlimited right to do whatsoever he chose regardless of the consequences of his actions upon the interests of others. Were there no restrictions, chaos would follow. Yet these restrictions unquestionably limit man's freedom, in that they compel him to comply with a certain code of conduct. This broad power to regulate the actions of the individual is referred to as "police power." It finds its expression in all spheres of human activity; in public health it is the basis of all regulatory activity.

[1] Although a large portion of the public health law is concerned with communicable diseases, it must be remembered that it encompasses other matters pertaining to the health of the citizens.

Police power is not to be confused with the power of a police department. The police department is merely an administrative agency created to maintain order and to enforce compliance with the laws of the community. The term "police power" is far broader, implying the right of the people to adopt regulations as well as to enforce them. It is expressed by a legislative body when it makes laws and by any administrative agency when it enforces them.

Public health laws are of two types, statutory laws and regulations. American government is based on a division of power among three branches—the legislative, the administrative, and the judicial. The former makes laws, the second administers them, and the last dispenses justice in their enforcement. Consequently the legislative body is empowered to enact laws relating to the public health. In states these are passed by the state legislature, in cities by the city council or board of aldermen.[2] Congress enacts the very limited federal public health law. All of these enactments of the legally constituted legislative body become the law of the community over which this particular body has jurisdiction, subject only to judgment by the proper courts as to their compliance with the intent of the state and federal constitutions and lack of conflict with higher authority. They are enforceable by whatever executive agency is empowered to administer them. In the case of the public health laws, this is usually the health department, though at times the police or some other department may be entrusted with some measure of enforcement.

Although enactment of laws by the properly constituted representative body is a true form of legislation by the people through their delegates and therefore a democratic form of government, it is at times an unwieldy and inefficient mode of government in dealing with highly technical matters or emergency situations. The legislative representatives of the people may properly decide the principles that find expression in health laws, but they cannot be expected to possess sufficient technical knowledge to determine details. A legislative assembly should not be expected to weigh the evidence as to the relative merits of a three-week or four-week isolation for scarlet fever or to determine the bacterial count of water in which oysters may be safely grown. It can do little more than be guided by the technical evidence of experts. This would mean that the administrative body was virtually drafting the laws for the legislative body to adopt or reject. While this is frequently done, especially in those cities where all proposed board of health regulations must be ratified by the city council, the procedure is often cumbersome and ineffective, since the legislative body is not in

[2] Local laws are usually referred to as "ordinances," the term "law" referring more frequently to state or federal enactments.

constant session. The legislature may, therefore, vest the administrative agencies with the right to adopt reasonable regulations. This is referred to as "quasi-logislative power." In other words, an executive body is empowered to adopt regulations which have the full force of law.

While this may at first sight appear to be a breaking down of the principle of separation of powers, such is hardly the case as the executive branch is merely exercising a delegated power. The legislative branch may at any time modify or revoke this delegation of power, thus reducing the likelihood that the administrative agency will act in too arbitrary a fashion. While some have shaken their heads over the rapid growth of quasi-legislative powers, it would seem that the legislative authority to revoke or curtail these powers constitutes adequate safeguard against too great bureaucracy.

CONTROL OF COMMUNICABLE DISEASE THROUGH REGULATION

Although a Utopian society would need no restrictive laws, in real life we know that we cannot count on every person's doing the right thing. In any communal society, the acts of the individual may affect the welfare of his associates. While from a personal point of view there may be no hazard from unrestricted liberty for a mild case or a carrier of infectious disease, this freedom of movement may result in spread of disease to others. Improper discharge of sewage may pollute another person's drinking water; improper handling of milk or food, endanger the consumer. Regulation therefore plays a very important part in communicable disease control, a role more important than in any other field of public health. These laws and regulations cover many phases of control practices.

Compulsory Examination

Many state laws and local ordinances provide for compulsory physical examination or inspection of certain persons. The usual purpose of these examinations is to detect infections that would otherwise pass unrecognized. In general these regulations apply only to persons who, because of their occupations, are likely to infect many other persons if their own infections are not discovered. Certain boards of education have wisely required schoolteachers to submit to pre-employment and periodic chest examinations to detect active tuberculosis which, if unrecognized, may spread to the pupils. Compulsory examination of food handlers is based on the premise of finding persons who might spread infection through the medium of food; while sound in theory and legally valid, such regulations usually fail to yield results commensurate with the expense of their enforcement. The compulsory physical examination of school children is usually designed to detect physical defects but may also reveal infectious disease; the more cursory but more frequent inspections by the teacher or school nurse are, however, intended to detect infections which may warrant the temporary exclusion of the child from school attendance. Most states have laws requiring examination for syphilis prior to the issuance of a marriage license, while many states require the physician to obtain a serologic test in all cases of pregnancy. Certain states provide that persons arrested on certain types of charges may be required to submit to examination for detection of venereal disease. Other states have general provisions whereby the board of health may, under special circumstances, require the examination of any person who is suspected of being infected. Such broad provisions are generally emergency measures to be used only under extreme necessity; too frequent invocation of this right may result in its curtailment by an outraged public which sees undue infringement of its personal liberties. In general there is no provision for compulsory examination of all members of a community, though one state in a still untested law has provided for blood testing of the entire population.

Reporting

"No health department, state or local, can effectively prevent or control disease without knowledge of when, where, and under what conditions cases are occurring." This statement, which formerly appeared at the head of the weekly listing of the current prevalence of communicable diseases published by the United States Public Health Service, is a truism of public health administration. The health officer must know of the occurrence of cases if he is to institute measures to limit further spread. A system of reporting is therefore necessary.

All states require the reporting of communicable diseases.[3] In some instances, the law may specify those diseases which are reportable; more frequently, the state health department is granted authority to decide which conditions must be reported. Under these circumstances, no uniformity of practice exists as to the list of reportable conditions, diseases included in one state being omitted in another. The dictum of Chapin is an excellent rule to follow, namely, that a health department should require notification of only those conditions about which it can do or plans to do something. It must be remembered, however, that while little effec-

[3] In some states this is so broad as to include all "diseases dangerous to the public health." Under this provision reporting of cancer, pellagra, and other noninfectious diseases may be required.

tive use can be made of certain individual reports, yet great value often lies in collective reports as a measure or indication of a community problem. Reporting of gonorrhea and syphilis by number or initial and date of birth will not permit the establishment of restrictions on the individual patient, but the total of reports received during a year sheds light on the nature of the problem and permits intelligent planning of the control program. It must also be remembered that certain conditions about which a health department can do little are reportable because of possible confusion with other more serious conditions. Little official cognizance is taken of chickenpox reports; yet the occurrence of a series of adult infections immediately creates suspicion of possible confusion with mild smallpox.

Responsibility for making a report rests upon the medical attendant. Inasmuch as some cases of infection are not brought to medical attention, there is usually a further responsibility for reporting by the householder or even other persons who may have knowledge of the disease.[4] The same diagnostic acumen is, of course, not expected of a nonmedically trained individual, yet even this person may be aware that the child is ill with a presumably communicable condition. Often the diagnosis can hardly be questioned, as in the instance of a case of measles secondary to an attack in an older brother or sister. The medical practice laws usually include diagnosis as a part of medical practice, thus preventing the nurse or schoolteacher from making a report, inasmuch as reporting implies earlier diagnosis. The laws do not, however, forbid the teacher or nurse from notifying the board of health that a child appears to be suffering from a communicable disease and is therefore being excluded from school until seen by a physician or until apparently well. In fact, some state laws require the school authorities to exclude all children who are in ill-health or suffering from what may be a communicable disease and to notify the board of health of such exclusion. So far as concerns school children, there is thus adequate provision for reporting by nurses or teachers without technical infringement of the medical practice laws. Preschool children and adults may often escape detection because they do not come within the sphere of activity of any official agency. If the family does not choose to obtain medical aid (and such is their right), there is no opportunity for diagnosis and, hence, of reporting.

Most reporting laws require notification by mail within a certain period of time after the diagnosis has been established. While a report signed by the physician has certain advantages, the inevitable delay of

---

[4] A Massachusetts law provides that any person having charge of a newborn baby whose eyes show any abnormal discharge or condition of redness during the first two weeks of life shall report the facts immediately to the local board of health.

having such material pass through the postal system often limits the effectiveness of the report. A 24-hour period between the mailing of the notice and its reception in the board of health office can be expected; over week ends and holidays, even longer. Yet during these intervening hours the patient may be highly infectious and other persons may be exposed. If the control measures are to be effective, they must be instituted at once, not two or three days later. Hence there is much to be said for telephone notification, even though the laws do not always provide for it. This may be made in harmony with the written law by having the board of health clerk make out a report to which she affixes the signature of the physician in the same manner as might his office secretary or nurse. A post card to the physician notifying him that the report in question has been made out assures him that it has been entered properly; it costs no more than the stamped post cards usually furnished to the physician for reporting. Certainly every effort should be made to avoid unnecessary delay in making reports if they are to fulfill their maximum usefulness.

Isolation and Quarantine

Isolation and quarantine are important parts of the regulatory control and are applied after reporting has indicated when and where they should be used. State laws usually make some provision for establishment of isolation and quarantine and prescribe penalties for violations of these restrictions. Usually the state health department is empowered to adopt a code which has the force of law and is applicable to all communities within the state. This code is a minimum standard, each community having the right to adopt more stringent measures if deemed advisable. Specific provision is usually made for only the commonest of the conditions. Unusual situations are covered by a general clause of the code or of the state law empowering boards of health to take such measures as are considered necessary to protect the health of the community. The tendency of the courts has been to interpret such powers, either expressed or implied, as a proper exercise of the basic police power, even though the board of health has exceeded the written regulations formally adopted.

The enforcement of the isolation and quarantine regulations is usually the responsibility of the local health authorities. This is logical as most of the problems are of purely local concern until such time as the disease threatens to spread to other communities. Transfer of a patient from one place to another may introduce intercommunity problems with which the state or even federal authorities must deal. The latter have jurisdiction over interstate matters and must also exercise maritime quarantine to guard against introduction of infection from foreign ports. The measures to be adopted obviously vary with the disease in question and the type of quarantine that is being attempted. See Chapter 3 for a consideration of the mode of determining isolation and quarantine procedures and the factors limiting effectiveness of these measures.

Hospitalization

While isolation of the patient is usually provided for in the home, there are situations in which satisfactory care and isolation can be provided only in hospitals. The law usually empowers a local board of health to require the transfer of a patient to a hospital or other suitable place of reception, provided it can be done without endangering his well-being. This transfer is only a partial measure unless equal provision is made for the retention of the patient until such time as his continued hospitalization is no longer necessary for protection of his associates. The power of boards of health to require prolonged restriction is quite variable.

Compulsory Treatment

A few states have laws requiring persons infected with certain diseases, notably syphilis, to take a certain amount of treatment. Although at first thought this might appear to be an undue interference with personal liberty and the freedom to select or reject medical care of the patient's choosing, further thought will show that this is essentially a means of reducing the possibility of spread. So long as the patient stays under treatment there will be no open lesions and little likelihood of spread. The benefit to the patient through enhancing his chances of cure is of secondary importance, the measure being justified as a control procedure. Such laws are unquestionably desirable but have limited applicability in a country that prides itself on individual liberty.

Regulation of Vehicles of Infection

The laws and regulations that have been enacted to prevent contamination or promote disinfection of vehicles of infection are almost unlimited. They range from the now largely outmoded fumigation requirements to provisions for the compulsory pasteurization of milk. All are included under the term "environmental sanitation." These measures have been very consistently upheld by the courts of review as valid exercise of the police power, even though at times they have inconvenienced certain persons. The courts have recognized the fact that liberty does not entitle the individual to live his life or conduct his business in a manner which will jeopardize the health, safety, and welfare of others. The regulations must, however, be reasonable, must not be discriminatory, and must be designed to protect the public health. There is no excuse for regulations or laws which confer special economic advantages upon certain individuals or industries under the guise of thereby protecting the public against hypothetical hazards. Health is so popular that many commercial interests have tried to hang to its coattails.

Compulsory Immunization

Most health laws and regulations specify what the individual may or may not do. They prohibit certain actions that may endanger others. A few, however, require individuals to perform certain acts. In other words, they provide for compulsory active participation in the program for disease prevention. The statutes regarding compulsory vaccination are of this type.

These laws usually require the vaccination [5] of children as a prerequisite to school attendance. Ten states [6] have laws of this general character, differing somewhat as to the scope of application. Other states permit local boards of health or education to make such regulations. In addition, boards of health in certain states may require the vaccination of all persons when smallpox is present in the community.[7] Other states make no provision for compulsory vaccination, while a "select" few forbid the adoption of any vaccination requirement as a prerequisite to regular school attendance.

Laws for compulsory vaccination clearly require the submission of an individual to a particular procedure for which he may have no desire. He may be willing to accept the hazards of smallpox and forego the protection which comes from vaccination. To require him to submit to vaccination may therefore appear to be infringing his right to "life, liberty, and the pursuit of happiness" (or of smallpox). Such statutes have been the subject of repeated court decisions which have consistently upheld the right of the community to require vaccination. It has been pointed out in this connection that, however willing the individual may be to undergo the hazards of smallpox, his infection with the disease may endanger the health and welfare of the community. The disease may spread to others; if he dies, the community may be left with the responsibility for the care of his dependents. He does not have an unrestricted right to exercise individual liberty if this may jeopardize others. In this connection, the United

[5] The term "vaccination" as used in these laws has been uniformly interpreted by the courts to refer to vaccination against smallpox and not against other diseases.

[6] Kentucky, Maryland, Massachusetts, New Hampshire, New Mexico, New York, Pennsylvania, Rhode Island, South Carolina, and West Virginia.

[7] These laws are not to be confused with those which empower exclusion from school of an unvaccinated child only when smallpox exists in the community. The latter are modifications of the isolation and quarantine laws.

States Supreme Court in the now famous decision upholding the constitutionality of the Massachusetts compulsory vaccination law ruled as follows:

There is, of course, a sphere within which the individual may assert the supremacy of his own will, and rightfully dispute the authority of any human government, especially of any free government existing under a written constitution, to interfere with the exercise of that will. But it is equally true that in every well-ordered society charged with the duty of conserving the safety of its members the rights of the individual in respect of his liberty may at times, under the pressure of great dangers, be subjected to such restraint, to be enforced by reasonable regulations, as the safety of the general public may demand. . . . It is not, therefore, true that the power of the public to guard itself against imminent danger depends in every case involving the control of one's body upon his willingness to submit to reasonable regulations established by the constituted authorities, under the sanction of the state, for the purpose of protecting the public collectively against such danger.[8]

In view of this definitely established right of the people to require vaccination against smallpox, one may logically inquire why the idea of compulsion should not be extended to include other equally successful immunizing procedures. In a few places, such laws have been enacted, such as the 1939 French law for diphtheria immunization before the age of two. Two or three states in the United States have extended the school vaccination law to include diphtheria prevention, though it is questionable whether or not it is being thoroughly enforced. Cities have experimented with compulsory immunization of dogs against rabies.

Although introduction of the element of compulsion in the application of other immunizations would unquestionably increase their use and thus further reduce the incidence of certain diseases, most public health officials have looked with little favor upon such regulations, even though defending compulsory vaccination. They have felt that the element of compulsion should be used as sparingly as possible and should be reserved for those situations that are of major potential danger and controllable through no other procedures. Malignant smallpox may kill 25 per cent of those whom it attacks; it has killed as high as 10 per cent of the population of cities so attacked, disrupting all normal community life and activity. Diphtheria at its worst has not been a community calamity, even though in the preantitoxin era it wiped out whole families of children and ranked high among the causes of death. For smallpox there is no specific treatment once the disease has developed; for diphtheria we have antitoxin. No development of resistance against smallpox occurs without an

[8] *Jacobson v. The Commonwealth of Massachusetts* (1905), 197 **U.S.** 11, 25 **S. Ct.** 358, 49 L. Ed. 643, 3 Ann. Cas. 765.

attack of the disease or vaccination; against diphtheria a gradual acquisition of a high level of resistance occurs through repeated unrecognized exposures.

The problem of smallpox and diphtheria prevention are thus greatly different when viewed from the community standpoint. Recognizing a very general desire to interfere with personal liberty as little as possible consistent with the community welfare, we may logically hesitate to extend the principle of compulsory immunization unless experience shows no other way of combating a potentially serious situation. Experience has shown the need for it in smallpox control. Except in institutions and other relatively limited groups, notably military forces, this need has not been shown in the case of diphtheria or other infections, and compulsion has not therefore been extensively used. Effective control of diphtheria has been achieved through voluntary immunization; control of typhoid in civil populations, through environmental sanitation. There can be no doubt as to the essential soundness of the principle of compulsory immunization, provided it is applied judiciously; yet ill-advised use may threaten it with disrepute and destruction. Wise is the health officer who knows when not to use compulsion.

SUGGESTED READINGS

Graham, George A., and Reining, Henry, Jr.: *Regulatory Administration.* New York: John Wiley & Sons, Inc., 1943, pp. 61–90.

Hanlon, John J.: *Principles of Public Health Administration.* St. Louis: C. V. Mosby Co., 1950.

Tobey, James A.: *Public Health Law,* 3rd ed. New York: Commonwealth Fund, 1947.

5. Administrative Agencies

Control of communicable diseases is a fundamental responsibility of government and is therefore the function of the official health agency. Health departments were originally created for the express purpose of preventing the spread of these diseases, as it was obvious that no one, merely by his own efforts, could satisfactorily protect himself against the menace of infection. So long as persons live in close association with one another and engage in travel and commerce with other people, there is danger of the spread of infection from one to another. Factors beyond the control of the individual facilitate this spread. Some form of organized community activity is essential to protect the people against this menace. As the function of government is to further the interests of the citizens, measures for the control of the spread of communicable diseases are logically entrusted to official agencies. This concept of official responsibility is fundamental to the establishment of any control program and to an understanding of the parts that any particular agency may play in this program.

FEDERAL, STATE, AND LOCAL RELATIONSHIPS

The roles played by various official agencies depend upon the relative powers granted to them under the American form of government.[1] The United States is a union of forty-eight independent states which have, by the federal constitution, granted certain rights to the national government. The federal government is thus a creation of the states. It has only such powers and duties as the states have seen fit to give it and cannot take for itself rights not so delegated under the prevailing interpretation of the constitution by the Supreme Court. The only way in which this distribu-

[1] Although operating under quite different forms of government, the same general relationships between dominion, provincial, and local governments exist in Canada.

tion of power between federal and state agencies may be altered is through constitutional amendment duly approved by three-fourths of the states.

The states retain for themselves all rights not specifically delegated to the federal government. They are thus the ultimate repository of power. Each state is governed by its duly elected or appointed officials—legislative, executive, and judicial. The legislative branch enacts the state laws, subject to the provisions of the state constitution. Among the many powers of the state is the right to provide for local government. This may be carried out either through constitutional provision or by legislative act or both. In any case, the people of the state, acting as a political unit, decide the general form of local government and what shall be the distribution of powers between the state and local governments. They may decide to retain certain powers to be administered by the state government and to delegate others to the local units. As each state determines its own policy, one may find certain states in which the major power is delegated to local governmental units, while in others the central state government retains the greater part of the power.

Whatever may be the distribution of power within any particular state, it is essential to remember that the local units of government are the creations of the state. They came into existence only by the grace of the state and may be changed if the people of the state so desire. The people, either through constitutional amendment or through legislative enactment, may at any time alter the form of local government or redistribute the power between the local and state governments. Every legislative session sees some change in this distribution of power. Granting power upward to the federal government and downward to the local government, the state thus becomes the essential unit of American government. If federal government is bad, the states as a whole are to blame; if local government is bad, both the local community and the state must share the responsibility—the local unit for abusing its power, and the state for permitting the local unit to retain power which is obviously abused.

FEDERAL HEALTH AGENCIES

Although the federal agencies have very limited powers, they must be considered first, as they exercise a broader control than do either the state or local units. The Constitution of the United States makes no mention of health. Consequently the federal government has no specifically prescribed duties in the control of communicable diseases. Yet by interpretation of the constitution, very important functions are assigned to it.

Special Duties of Federal Agencies

Three particular duties which involve public health are detailed to the federal government,[2] namely, (1) regulation of commerce with foreign nations; (2) regulation of commerce between states; and (3) provision for the "general welfare of the United States." Both the terms "commerce" and "general welfare" are very broad in their implications and frequently cover problems of communicable disease control.

Regulation of Commerce with Other Nations. This includes supervision of both persons and things that may introduce infectious diseases into the United States. Obviously this must be a federal function. The border states and cities should not be burdened with the responsibility of protecting the nation against the introduction of disease, nor would the inland states have any opportunity of protecting themselves if the border states were negligent. The introduction of cholera in 1833, either through the port of New York or along the upper Hudson valley from Canada, was not a problem solely of interest to New York or the Atlantic seaboard, as the disease spread throughout the nation and exacted heavy toll. Such matters are of national, not merely local, consequence and are therefore entrusted to the jurisdiction of the federal government, which is created by the people to serve the entire country.

International quarantine was formerly carried out by requiring ships from foreign countries to anchor in the harbor of the port of arrival until a federal officer had made inspection of both persons and cargo to make certain that these were not harboring infection. In practice, little attention was given to many diseases, the procedures being designed essentially to prevent the entrance of cholera, plague, leprosy, smallpox, yellow fever, and typhus. Attention was paid especially to vessels sailing from ports known to be infected with these diseases. Today much of the delay occasioned by these quarantine inspections has been avoided by a system of radio pratique, whereby the ship's surgeon radios ahead as to health conditions on board the ship. If these are satisfactory, the ship may be allowed to dock without delay for inspection. If, however, the ship has come from certain ports, notably those known to be infected with plague or typhus, it may be detained for fumigation to destroy all insect or rodent vectors. In recent years federal quarantine activities have been extended to cover international airplane traffic. Provision is made for destruction of mosquitoes that may be harbored in planes from areas where malaria and yellow fever are serious problems. Attention is also given to passengers

[2] The Constitution of the United States of America, Art. 1, Sec. 8.

coming from areas where diseases foreign to the United States may be prevalent.

Regulation of Commerce between States. Just as the federal government should protect the nation from invasion of disease from without, so is it also the logical agency to act to prevent interstate spread. No state has any jurisdiction beyond its own borders. If threatened with invasion of disease from other states, it must wait until the infection arrives at the border before it can take effective action. This is always less satisfactory than attack on the disease at its source. Local negligence or carelessness in the supervision of an article of commerce may endanger all other states into which this commodity is shipped. The only effective individual protection the other states might have would be to search for and interrupt all incoming shipments, an obviously cumbersome and difficult task. The situation is more effectively handled by a federal agency, which may impose and enforce an embargo against the shipment of this product out of the state in question. The federal government can prevent interstate shipment under its constitutional authority to regulate commerce between the states, even though it has no power to regulate the sale of the article within the state where produced. This latter is a function solely of the state and local governments. Power to regulate interstate commerce is applied in many fields of public health. In the control of communicable diseases, it is limited largely to regulation of (1) travel by infected persons,[3] (2) shipment of infected animals, (3) shipment of infected articles, notably meats, and (4) shipment of sera and vaccines.

Promotion of General Welfare. The meaning of this term is so broad that its interpretation has varied from generation to generation. It has embraced federal subsidies for the promotion of public health work—including the control of communicable diseases—programs of health education, research in the prevention of infectious diseases, and assistance to state and local agencies in their control programs. The activities carried out under this heading have, in general, been of a promotional and service nature rather than regulatory in character.

Federal Agencies Interested in Communicable Disease Control

The chief federal health agency is the United States Public Health Service. Located originally in the Treasury Department, it was transferred in 1939 to the newly created Federal Security Agency, which in 1953 became the Department of Health, Education, and Welfare. To the Public Health Service are entrusted all of the federal activities of international

[3] This power is rarely used at the present time.

and interstate quarantine, so far as they affect persons, and some of the jurisdiction over interstate commerce in goods. Its research staff in the National Institute of Health and in the field has conducted important and fruitful investigations of certain diseases, notably tularemia, plague, psittacosis, endemic typhus, Rocky Mountain spotted fever, undulant fever, meningococcus infections, and Q fever. Its staff has also assisted local agencies in the formulation of disease control programs, especially for syphilis and malaria. An active program of assistance in tuberculosis control has recently been developed. The establishment of the Communicable Disease Center in Atlanta, Georgia, has provided greatly expanded facilities for laboratory research and field studies, as well as staff to aid health departments in epidemiologic investigations and problems of infectious disease control.

Other federal agencies active in the control of the spread of infectious diseases include the Department of Agriculture and the Department of Defense. The former exercises jurisdiction over the importation and interstate sale of animals and meats. The several components of the latter—Army, Navy, and Air Force—have jurisdiction over their respective military personnel.

STATE HEALTH AGENCIES

The state health agency is more active in communicable disease control than the federal, inasmuch as it usually has more direct responsibility for the proper health protection of the people within its jurisdiction. As the state exercises ultimate supervisory control over local government, the state health department is empowered to promote and often to supervise local health service. In addition, it usually has jurisdiction over intercommunity problems comparable to that of the federal government over interstate commerce, though this power is usually not so clearly set forth in the authority given to the state health agency as it is in the federal constitution. In each state, however, the existence of some agency with authority to deal with intercommunity problems is just as important, for health is no longer a matter of purely local concern. The development of methods of rapid transportation has brought distant communities together but at the same time has forced them to share many health problems formerly only local. This has necessitated the assumption of more responsibility by larger units of government, namely, the state and the federal.

The authority of the state to regulate local problems of communicable disease control is best exemplified by the powers possessed by the state health department to adopt a minimum isolation and quarantine code, as well as other sanitary measures. The rules and regulations enacted under this authority must be observed in all communities within the state.[4] These regulations represent a minimum standard of protection guaranteed to all residents of the state. They must be carried out by the local health agencies, but the state is usually empowered to take over their enforcement if the local officials are negligent. The existence of this code does not deprive the local communities of the right to make more stringent ordinances. These may not, however, be less stringent without infringing the state code. In general, the state code is followed very closely, thus giving a high degree of uniformity within a state. No similar uniformity exists with respect to the regulations of different states, as the federal government lacks the power to regulate matters of purely state or local concern. Throughout the country, most of the laws and regulations governing communicable disease control are adopted by the state, either by legislative enactment or by the state health agency under its quasi-legislative power. Covered by these enactments are such subjects as isolation and quarantine, vaccination, reporting of communicable diseases, hospitalization, examination of school children and exclusion of those who are infected, disposal of wastes, sale of potentially contaminated foods, and treatment of syphilitics. The American Public Health Association's report on communicable disease control practices, originally prepared in 1917, and now in its seventh edition, has profoundly affected the regulations adopted by state and local health departments and has brought about an increasing degree of uniformity of practice.

The service functions of the state agencies are matters of growing importance today, even though it is generally considered desirable that direct service by government should be rendered by the smallest unit consistent with efficiency. This is true, but as the functions become more and more technical, their transfer to larger units of government, usually the state, is imperative. The best example of this is to be found in the bacteriological diagnostic laboratory. Such laboratories cannot be operated efficiently by small units of government; for economical and efficient functioning they require a large number of specimens. Except in the larger cities, they are too expensive for local operation. The most economical and best quality of service can often be given by a state agency covering a larger territory than the usual unit of local government.[5] Other types of service functions frequently operated by the state agencies include tuber-

---

[4] Some states exempt certain of the larger cities from these regulations, e.g., the New York State Sanitary Code does not apply within New York City.

[5] Even branch state laboratories frequently fail of economical operation unless they are located to conform with centers for the handling of mail. If a specimen is mailed, it may frequently reach a distant postal center quicker than it will arrive at a city that is only a few miles away but is not a postal center.

culosis hospitals, specialized consultant diagnostic service, consultation clinics, and case-finding surveys. The state is also in a position to carry on the impersonal forms of health education, such as radio and newspaper publicity and pamphlet preparation, more efficiently than can most local departments.

A third type of activity, properly the function of the state, is the program of assistance to the local agencies. The smaller the unit of government, the less able it is to employ personnel skilled in the general field of public health or its technical branches. The board of health of the small community may be composed purely of laymen, who often assume health responsibilities only as a side line to the other duties imposed on their shoulders. The state must obviously be prepared to assist these boards in the proper investigation and control of communicable disease problems. It must furnish technical advice and assistance and may often even have to suggest to the local board the adoption of new measures. Were it not for this advisory and promotional service of the state, it would be impossible to continue local health administration in an era of rapidly developing technical progress.

Organization of State Health Work

Every state has some official public health agency, usually organized as a separate department of the government though occasionally made a branch of a larger welfare department. The plans of organization differ widely. Usually there is a board or council appointed by the governor and serving as a policy-determining body. The state health officer may be named either by the governor or by this board. In the former case, he is usually a member of the board as well as its executive officer; in the latter case, he is essentially an employee of the board and is responsible for carrying out its policies and plans. A few states dispense with the board or relegate it to a merely advisory capacity, thus delegating to the health officer the powers that other states vest in the boards.

The communicable disease control work of the state health department may be concentrated in a single office or distributed through several bureaus. There is usually a division of communicable diseases.[6] In former years this was one of the major divisions of the department. With the recent trend toward consolidation of the many separate divisions into five

---

[6] Some states refer to this as a division of preventable diseases. This seems hardly suitable, as other diseases such as simple goiter, rickets, and scurvy are equally preventable yet are handled by other divisions, notably the child hygiene group. Furthermore the term "preventable" implies a false degree of possible accomplishment. Certain of the communicable diseases can be prevented; yet others, such as poliomyelitis and rubella, can hardly be prevented at the present time.

or six larger units, many states have placed the communicable disease bureau as part of a larger division of medical services. The tuberculosis and venereal disease programs may be part of the communicable disease bureau or may be assigned to separate bureaus. The diagnostic laboratory is usually part of a general division of laboratories, though some states entrust it to the supervision of the communicable disease bureau. There is much to be said for both plans. While these various offices exercise general control over the communicable disease program, it should not be forgotten that other bureaus are also important. The division of environmental sanitation supervises the water and milk supplies and sewage disposal plants; that of nursing helps in the development of the communicable disease nursing; the school hygiene bureau may promote immunization; and the bureau of health education may carry knowledge of disease prevention and control into the home.

LOCAL HEALTH AGENCIES

The purpose of the local health agency is to protect the health of the people under its jurisdiction. It has an immediate responsibility to guard against the spread of communicable diseases, though its authority is obviously limited to the confines of the local community. While this authority which it possesses is in reality delegated to it by the state, yet in practice it is extremely broad, often broader than that delegated by the legislature to the state health department. Essentially the first line of official defense, the local agency is responsible for the local enforcement of state laws and regulations and for rendering most of the direct service. Among the many duties delegated to it are reporting, isolation and quarantine, hospitalization, immunization, case investigation, nursing assistance, and home instruction. In carrying out these several activities, the local board of health is usually following the general plan and regulations laid down by the state. It may turn to the state and, through the state, to the federal agency for assistance, guidance, and advice.

The form of local health organization is more varied than that of the state. In the northeastern and north central portions of the country, local government is usually organized on a town basis; in the South and West, on counties. In both areas, cities may be and usually are somewhat independent of the township or county in which they are located, though there is a current trend to establish city-county health units under which the city and rural parts of the county combine their health activities into one organization under direction of the county government. The local health agency in the larger communities, notably cities, is usually a separate board, appointed or elected for this specific purpose. In the smaller political areas, the duties are more frequently entrusted to the general governing body, such as the board of township trustees or selectmen, board of aldermen, county commissioners, county court, or whatever may be the name applied to the local body. Obviously under such circumstances the members of the board are not selected because of any special knowledge of, or interest in, public health but rather on the same basis as determines election to any political office. The members may even be hostile to public health work. In any case, they may look upon their health duties merely as an extra function loaded upon an already overworked board. Unless they are able to afford a specially trained executive health officer—and smaller communities usually cannot—they must rely very largely upon the guidance and assistance of the state for the proper conduct of their duties, including communicable disease control.

Although the essential responsibility for the protection of the community against the spread of communicable disease rests with the board of health, it should not be inferred that other branches of the local government are disinterested or play no part in the program. In reality they play very important roles. In many communities the school health service is under the auspices of the board of education rather than the board of health. Under such circumstances, the school department is responsible for examining the children for the detection of unrecognized cases of communicable disease and exclusion of those who are, or are suspected of being, infected. The school board may even adopt rules pertaining to the readmission of such children to school. In general, it is better practice for such measures to be concentrated under board of health auspices. Otherwise, there arises the anomalous situation in which the school authorities exercise control over a part of the population for a few hours of the school days, whereas the board of health has jurisdiction over these same children at other times and over the rest of the community at all times. Communicable disease involves preschool as well as school children, occurs during vacations, holidays, week ends, and at night when the school is not in session, and equally attacks children attending private schools. It would seem preferable to concentrate the control practices in the hands of a single agency whose sole responsibility is that of protecting the health of the community. Otherwise, confusion and conflict of authority are likely to ensue, with resultant detriment to the service.

Even though this authority is concentrated in the hands of the board of health, this board obviously cannot carry out its program to the disregard of the schools or of other interested agencies. Isolation of cases and quarantine of contacts must be reasonable, for every day lost from school interferes in some measure with the education of the child. Too long exclusion may even jeopardize the chances of the child's promotion to the next succeeding grade, a personal loss to the child and a financial loss to the community through need of repetition of classes.[7] The aggregation of children within the schools offers easily accessible groups for case-finding and immunization programs and for the distribution of health information into the homes, where many preschool children are to be found. Finally, the schools offer the best medium of health education, which, if properly carried out, should have both an immediate and a long-term effect. Unquestionably the schools are most important in the communicable disease control program, but their proper sphere is education rather than as supplementary or independent health departments.

The control of communicable disease also involves many other governmental agencies at the local level. Provision for hospitalization is usually a function of the institutional or welfare agency, though occasionally boards of health are given jurisdiction over communicable disease and tuberculosis hospitals. It is self-evident, however, that only the larger local units can operate such institutions; the smaller ones must buy such service from the larger. The furnishing of safe water and the proper disposal of sewage are usually under the jurisdiction of the municipal engineer or a separate board of water or sewer commissioners, though the board of health retains regulatory control over private facilities. The welfare department may be involved in the control of communicable diseases because of the need of rendering aid in homes where the presence of infection involves special costs or affects the wage earner. Even the police department enters into the picture in those rare cases in which it is necessary to invoke the legal jurisdiction of the community with respect to such infections.[8] No local program of control can be caried out effectively and smoothly without cooperation between all the units of government.

ROLE OF THE NONOFFICIAL AGENCY

That the control of communicable diseases is a fundamental responsibility of government has already been pointed out. The nonofficial agencies therefore occupy a very limited role in this field, as they are not or

[7] Loss of school days also means a financial loss to the school system in those states in which subsidy is based on attendance rather than enrollment.

[8] In former years the police department carried on all isolation and quarantine procedures. The practice is occasionally encountered even today, a police officer being detailed to the health department to serve as quarantine officer. This practice is disappearing, as quarantine through sympathetic instruction of the mother by public health nurses is replacing the "big stick" of the law in all except the incorrigible cases. In many of the most progressive health departments, all of the quarantine visits, including the placarding, are made by the nurse.

should not be vested with regulatory authority. Regulation is a responsibility of government and should not be delegated to any agency not directly responsible to the people through their legally elected representatives and officials. The nonofficial agencies should therefore limit their programs to service and educational activities.

There may even be serious question as to the extent to which a private, nongovernmental agency should permanently offer service in the control of communicable diseases. The purpose of the service is to limit spread or to protect the individual. If the activity is soundly conceived, it should be rendered by the responsible governmental bureau. A private agency ought not to be expected to bear the responsibility for a diagnostic laboratory or a consultation clinic. Case-finding surveys may be initiated by voluntary agencies as a demonstration but should not be supported indefinitely by private funds. If valuable, they should be taken over as an essential part of the public program. Hospitalization and treatment should be supplied to the needy by the community rather than through private philanthropy,[9] as these are essential parts of the program to reduce spread and minimize ill-effects. Even immunization is better supported by public than by private funds, as it serves to reduce the incidence of the disease. However much the community may appreciate the willingness of certain philanthropies to shoulder some of the load of these programs, it is a very questionable policy to permit them to do so permanently, as it tends to create a sense of dependence and leads to the danger of the community's shifting its official burdens and responsibilities to other shoulders.

The true role of the nonofficial agency is in the field of promotion and education. The former implies the furtherance of an idea that may, if proved sound, be ultimately taken over by the official agency. Government, depending upon tax support, is frequently unable to experiment with new ideas, however sound they may be in theory. The voluntary agency may very suitably carry on such experiment until the soundness of the idea is proved and until government can be convinced of the desirability of incorporating this plan into its official program. In the early days of diphtheria immunization, the costs were properly borne by philanthropies in many communities; today the measure is of such established value that costs incidental to these programs should be borne by the budget of the official agency.

---

[9] This statement is contrary to the philosophy of a few private agencies, such as the National Foundation for Infantile Paralysis, which has held for many years to the belief that "no state, federal or other governmental funds should be spent for the medical care of infantile paralysis patients until all monies in the hands of the Chapter have been exhausted." The authors cannot agree with this philosophy, though they recognize the tremendous value of the supplemental aid that can be given.

The educational work of the nonofficial agency is so important and has accomplished so much that its value and suitability cannot be overstressed. No matter how great its legal authority, no health department can function properly, even in the field of communicable disease control, without the support of informed and interested public opinion. The tuberculosis control program owes much to the educational work of the National Tuberculosis Association; the program for the control of syphilis and gonorrhea, to the American Social Hygiene Association. There is still need for private agencies to promote better understanding of these and other infectious diseases, thus resulting in more effective control.

It must be remembered, however, that the work of the nonofficial agency must always be harmonized with that of the official. The latter, alone, has been vested by the voters with the duty of health protection. The voluntary agency should not, therefore, attempt a program in conflict with that of the official. If differences of opinion arise, the voluntary agency cannot properly proceed in opposition to the wishes of the health department. It can only withdraw from the active scene, even though it is convinced of the soundness of the proposed program. The solution here is found in an attempt to persuade the official agency to alter its decision, but the nonofficial agency should never carry on its program in open conflict with the official. If it attempts to do so, confusion and waste will result; and the public, which it aims to serve, will be the ultimate loser. This principle is so soundly conceived that it is recognized and observed by all well-functioning nonofficial agencies.

INTERNATIONAL AGENCIES

There is no international health agency with actual authority with respect to the spread of disease from one country to another, though quarantine agreements have long existed between specific nations or groups of nations. For many years the Office International d'Hygiene Publique served as an international clearing house for problems of disease spread and attempted to promote uniform standards of quarantine. Later the Health Section of the League of Nations performed this function. The work of both agencies has now been taken over by the World Health Organization (WHO) of the United Nations. Within the Western Hemisphere, the Pan-American Sanitary Bureau has brought about agreements among the respective nations and today serves as the regional office of WHO.

In 1951 the World Health Organization adopted an international sanitary code governing international travel. This code is effective only to the extent that it is ratified by the various nations. In such ratification, a nation may, however, make reservations with respect to certain sections about which it may hold a different opinion. Thus some of the provisions with respect to yellow fever are acceptable to the Western Hemisphere, Europe, and Africa but not acceptable to the Asiatic nations. The disease has never appeared in Asia, and these countries are naturally so fearful of the consequences of its invasion of the continent that they insist upon extrastringent precautions with respect to persons who have traveled through infected areas.

The World Health Organization also aids in establishing international standards and promoting demonstration programs of disease control. It (and its forerunner, the Health Section of the League of Nations) has done much to standardize biologic products on the basis of international units. Centers for the identification of influenza virus and typing of salmonella and dysentery strains have been established. Extensive studies of BCG vaccine and of brucellosis have been inaugurated, and malaria control programs fostered in areas where the problem is greatest. Similar programs are aimed at demonstrating control methods for cholera, typhus, yaws, syphilis, rabies and trachoma.

Also a part of the United Nations but operating independently is the United Nations International Children's Emergency Fund (UNICEF). Although its program covers all phases of child health, special attention has been given to the promotion of immunization programs in certain countries.

Although devoid of governmental support, no agency has played a more important role in the international control of infectious disease than has the International Health Division of the Rockefeller Foundation. Its program has been aimed at laboratory research and field studies. Notable among its accomplishments have been the development of yellow fever vaccine, the discovery of jungle yellow fever, control of *Anopheles gambiae* in Brazil, and studies of malaria in the Mediterranean basin and in Ceylon.

SUGGESTED READINGS

Emerson, Haven: *Administrative Medicine.* New York: Thomas Nelson & Sons, 1951, pp. 287–471.

Folks, Homer: "Citizen Support in Syphilis Control," *Ven. Dis. Inform.,* 18:355–60, (Oct.) 1937.

Goodman, Neville M.: *International Health Organizations and Their Work.* Philadelphia: Blakiston Co., 1952.

Gunn, Selskar M., and Platt, Philip S.: *Voluntary Health Agencies.* New York: Ronald Press, 1945.

Hanlon, John J.: *Principles of Public Health Administration.* St. Louis: C. V. Mosby Co., 1950.

Hiscock, Ira V.: *Community Health Organization,* 4th ed. New York: Commonwealth Fund, 1950.

Mustard, Harry S.: *Rural Health Practice.* New York: Commonwealth Fund, 1936.

———: *Government in Public Health.* New York: Commonwealth Fund, 1945.

Smillie, Wilson G.: *Public Health Administration in the United States,* 3rd ed. New York: Macmillan Co., 1947.

6. School Problems

Among the most difficult problems of communicable disease control is its occurrence in schools. Every school represents a gathering of children, many of whom would have no contact with one another were it not for their school attendance. In the classroom, children meet for the first time in fairly large groups and are closely associated with many other children in a relatively small enclosed space—conditions which are ideal for the spread of infection. The children thus brought together, especially in the lower grades, represent that fraction of the population which has one of the highest levels of susceptibility and, consequently, one of the highest rates of communicable disease. Moreover, the school is in session during the season of maximum prevalence of most of the common acute communicable diseases.[1] Parents are often right, therefore, when they say their children are infected in school, but they are not usually justified when they attempt to affix "blame." As most of these diseases are transmitted before any symptoms are apparent, their spread cannot be prevented, no matter how careful the school authorities may be.

Good attendance is one of the school's objectives which is influenced by the occurrence of communicable diseases. In most places schools strive for good attendance, partly because it is used as a measure of health status, partly because broken attendance and many days of absence interfere with the child's educational progress, and in some instances because the financial support of the school is based upon attendance records. This latter is perhaps the strongest incentive in a few schools. In some cases,

[1] There is a popular notion that the seasonal distribution of these diseases may be dependent upon the gathering of children in schools. For this there is no valid epidemiological evidence. Each of the infections has its own characteristic seasonal pattern, and there is no uniformity among these patterns. Thus in the United States, diphtheria is usually at its peak in November, at which time whooping cough is about at its minimum, whereas the seasonal peak for chickenpox is quite regularly in December and January, for scarlet fever in March, and that for measles most commonly in April or May. Such variations do not support the idea that the school is a factor in determining the rise or the fall of the acute infections.

unfortunately, the authorities have quite forgotten why they are striving for good attendance and are merely trying to compete with other schools for a "prize." Too often so much pressure is put on students to achieve this goal that children come to school when they are feeling ill. In this condition they learn little, possibly in the end prolong the number of days of absence, and may injure their own health, thereby defeating all the original objectives of good attendance. Most important, if the illness is a communicable disease, they may spread it throughout the school and tremendously increase the total absenteeism.

A further difficulty in the control of communicable diseases in schools arises from divided jurisdiction over children of school age. Although in theory the board of health is responsible for the protection of the health of the community and therefore for the control of communicable diseases, in practice most communities have delegated to the board of education a high degree of responsibility for the health of the children in the public schools. While the school must abide by the health regulations of the state, county, village, or city of which it is a part, the school board frequently makes additional regulations governing exclusion from, or return to, school. Thus the board of education assumes control of communicable diseases among a portion of the child population for a portion of certain days in the year, whereas the board of health is responsible for these same children for the rest of the time, and for the rest of the population at all times. The rest of the population includes the younger brothers and sisters of the school children as well as their parents, and all children attending nonpublic schools. It is inevitable that conflicts of policies and practices should arise when separate agencies share jurisdiction over the same families.

The situation is aggravated by the fact that the board of education is concerned primarily with education, not with health, and thus in its thinking as well as in the background of its personnel is usually less well prepared to cope with the problems of communicable diseases. While some school health leaders are well aware of the changing conditions in the communicable disease field and their implications for the school, the majority of the school superintendents have had no adequate training in public health. It is not surprising, therefore, that antiquated methods are often perpetuated in school programs long after they have been discarded by the board of health. This results in ineffective control, waste of money, and public confusion. If the regulations of the school board require a longer period of exclusion than do those of the board of health, there is usually much confusion in the parents' minds. Nor are these additional measures likely to be very helpful in controlling spread, as the child will be playing with other school children on the street as soon as he is released by the board of health. If still infectious, he might transmit the disease at this time even though he is not in the classroom. Many a mother has logically wondered why the periods of isolation and quarantine of the school child should be different from those of the preschool sibling who contracted the disease from the same source. This is not easy for the health department to explain without appearing to criticize another part of the municipal government.

ORIGIN OF PROGRAMS

School health programs in the United States had their origin in attempts to control communicable diseases and to find physical defects which would interfere with the child's capacity to learn. Even the former objective was approached largely from the educational standpoint. The board of education was not concerned so much with the basic problem of disease control as with an attempt to minimize loss of school time through absence due to infection. Inevitably the practices which were developed were those aimed at protecting the school child rather than controlling disease on a community-wide basis. Many of the outmoded practices so commonly followed by the schools today are the residuals of methods that were logical at their inception as they were based on concepts that were at one time considered sound. Today they can no longer be defended, yet have become so thoroughly ingrained in school health tradition that they are retained by the boards of education and often demanded by the public.

SCHOOL INSPECTIONS

One of the oldest and most widely practiced communicable disease control measures in the schools has been that of inspection of the children to locate those who are infected and should therefore be excluded. The method is sound and effective only to the extent that it actually locates a source of infection. Every child so discovered and excluded reduces the likelihood of further spread. The method is ineffective, however, to the extent that, no matter how carefully carried out, it fails to discover all carriers or subclinical infections, or even to recognize all clinical cases at the onset of their period of communicability. At best, the procedure only reduces the number of infections but has never provided lasting and complete control. It is therefore a method of very limited effectiveness, often not worth all of the time and money devoted to it to the exclusion of activities that are more productive of over-all health protection.

The details of the inspection of school children vary considerably in different school systems. There is wide variation in the responsibilities assigned to the teacher, principal, school nurse, and school physician. The most common practice is to require the teacher to observe each child at the beginning of the morning session. This usually consists of observing the pupil for signs of illness as he comes in the classroom or seats himself. Some few schools require the pupils to pass in single file before the teacher for her inspection. The signs suggestive of a beginning infection of the respiratory tract include a watery nasal discharge ("running nose"), inflamed eyes, coughing, rash, or general appearance of malaise. The temperature is usually not taken, nor is any direct inspection made of the throat.[2] Much reliance must be placed on those indefinite factors that go under the heading of "the child looks and acts sick."

Even if the teacher carries out the most thorough type of early morning inspection, she must remain alert for signs or symptoms occurring during the day which were not present at the beginning, for children of this age may often feel perfectly well on arrival at school yet be definitely ill before the end of the day. In such instances much reliance will be placed upon symptoms of which the child may complain. These include malaise, headache, sore throat, nausea, vomiting, chills and a feeling of feverishness; these are often accompanied by a flushed appearance of the face.

In schools where the services of a school nurse are always available at the beginning of the morning session it is common practice for the teacher to send all suspected children to the nurse's office, frequently referred to as the "health room." The school nurse is supposed to examine the child further, possibly take the temperature, and in some school systems a throat culture, and then exclude from the school all those who have evidences of a beginning infectious disease. Thus the nurse does little more than confirm the suspicions of the teacher, for under this system she sees only those who have been screened by the teacher. Children overlooked by the teacher because of less obvious evidences of illness escape detection. There is thus so little real value to this additional inspection by the nurse, that her routine presence in the school building at the beginning of every morning session cannot be justified, nor could one justify the employment of a nurse for every school building simply as a communicable disease control measure.

Actually, most school systems do not have enough nurses so that one can be present in each building at the beginning of the morning even

---

[2] At times one sees schools that require throat inspection of all children arriving at the building, though this is the exception today. This is usually made without the use of a tongue depressor. Under such circumstances it would reveal nothing, even to a competent physician.

though daily visits are made to all buildings. In such instances the children referred to the "health room" [3] because of signs or symptoms suggestive of a communicable disease may wait one or two hours for the arrival of the nurse. During this time they too often swap infection with each other, a situation that could be avoided if the child had been excluded on the suspicion of the teacher rather than waiting for the confirmation of the nurse. If exclusion is worth anything (and it is), it should be carried out promptly and with a minimum of further exposure to other children and especially to other children who are also sick. Secondary infections are often more serious than the primary. Referral to the school nurse and exclusion by her accomplishes so little that cannot be achieved by direct exclusion by the teacher that many of the more progressive schools have placed the basic responsibility on the teacher. The time that the nurse spends in checking over the children selected by the teacher is little more than wasted time and interferes with more profitable activities in the form of home visits and conferences with parents and teachers.

In rural areas and in most cities there is not a nurse who can visit each school building daily; in most rural areas it would not be sensible even to attempt this. Under such circumstances the teacher or principal must assume full responsibility for exclusion. In rural areas, however, much of the damage has already been done inasmuch as the infected child has been brought to school on the school bus which is often crowded, and not infrequently somewhat disorderly, with the result that the other children on the bus have been thoroughly exposed before coming under the observation of the teacher. Ideally, the bus driver as well as the teacher should be instructed as to signs and symptoms that should arouse suspicion, and should be alert to exclude children with such manifestations. In practice, such alertness is rarely found in the bus driver and not infrequently is missing also in the teacher, especially if she has not been carefully instructed as to her responsibility in this connection.

EXCLUSION OF CHILDREN

When it has been determined to exclude a child because of suspicion of communicable disease, three responsibilities remain to the school health authorities: (1) getting the child home; (2) notifying the board of health; and (3) observing the contacts for evidence of spread.

The safe return of the child to its home presents an immediate problem. If the child is not particularly ill and lives in an urban area where he walks to school, he may be safely sent home alone provided there is assur-

[3] "Disease room" would be a better designation under such circumstances.

ance that someone is home to receive him; if more acutely ill, he must be called for or taken home. In rural areas where children come by school bus, exclusion presents special problems, but even in these areas a member of the family can often come to call for the child. In no case should he go home in the bus. The extension of telephones into the rural areas and the degree to which the rural population has acquired automobiles usually means that contact can be made with a home where there are facilities to fetch the child. Of course this is not always true, especially in certain states where the economic condition of many farm families is quite poor.

Each situation must be solved according to its peculiar needs. There is no general rule that will cover all situations except that the school record of each child should show whom to notify if exclusion is imperative. Some person in the school system should know in advance what will be done with any child that must be excluded. Failure to make advance provisions for this is inexcusable. If the plan breaks down and no contact can be made with a suitable person to receive the child, the school has no alternative other than to retain him, even if sick, until suitable arrangements for his return can be made. A sick or potentially sick child must not be turned out on the street without a proper place to go.

As soon as a child has been excluded because of a suspected communicable disease, a report of such action should be made to the board of health. In some states this report is required by statute; whether legally required or not, it is a moral responsibility of the school system. The child is being excluded because he is suspected of having a communicable disease. The board of health has a legal responsibility for control of such infections within the community and has therefore a right to know of such action by the schools. To be of maximum value, such report should be by telephone, so that all necessary action can be taken immediately.

In making such a report diagnosis is not necessary. Neither the teacher nor the school nurse has a legal right to make a diagnosis; to do so would usually be a violation of the medical practice law. Thus even though either may have a strong suspicion as to diagnosis (and the suspicion is often correct, especially if a disease such as measles is currently widespread in the community), the report should be merely that a certain child has been excluded because of signs or symptoms suggestive of a communicable disease.

The third responsibility of the schools incidental to exclusion is that of subsequent observation of other children who may have been exposed. The details of such measures will obviously depend on the disease in question. To carry them out effectively the school should know what is actually wrong with the child. Ideally, every child excluded should be referred to the family physician, and either the board of health or the school nurse should determine from him or the family whether or not a diagnosis of a communicable disease has been made. It is common knowledge, however, that many of the children excluded turn out to have only common colds which are not reportable and that even a high proportion of the cases of reportable illness are not brought to medical attention. Neither the board of health nor the school can therefore assume that a diagnosis will be made. So far as feasible, contact should be made with the home to learn the diagnosis, or, if no physician is in attendance, to attempt to establish a presumption upon which to base readmission of the child and further inspection of school contacts. This check with the home can often be made by telephone, to be followed by home visits if such seem indicated.

Whether this check is to be made by a school nurse or a board of health nurse will vary from one community to another. The essential thing is that whichever agency makes this contact, the other is to be informed. It is the belief of the authors that the board of health is better suited for such check, because it is more likely to concern itself with the preschool siblings. In some diseases, such as measles or whooping cough, the real seriousness of the situation arises from the fact that the school child introduces the infection into the home where it spreads to younger brothers and sisters. Although these diseases are rarely serious for children of school age, they are always serious for those below three and especially those below one.[4] A home visit by a school nurse loses much of its potential effectiveness if she does not discuss with the mother the more important problem of protection of the younger children.

After the nature of the illness has been established, there remains the problem of restrictions upon school contacts. In former years very stringent quarantine practices were commonly observed. These often involved exclusion of certain contacts and strict quarantine until the end of the incubation period. Today, however, far less reliance is placed upon quarantine, for such measures have yielded very little in the form of real control. Consequently, school contacts are rarely excluded except in response to urgent public demand. The teacher should, however, be more alert than usual in observing the other children for signs or symptoms of the disease in question. Since these are not very specific, this observation can be performed even without knowledge of the diagnosis. Such knowledge is desirable but not if it requires excessive expenditures of time or money. The teacher need only be more alert than usual in detecting children that are "sick" and should therefore be excluded.

---

[4] There is an immunity to measles up to six months of age if the mother has had the disease, but no such resistance to whooping cough.

RETURN OF CHILDREN AFTER COMMUNICABLE DISEASE

The readmission to school of children who have been absent because of communicable disease introduces problems that are often more embarrassing than the exclusion even though the procedures are commonly specified by state laws or regulations. There are five methods that may be used alone or in combination:

1. **Certification by the Board of Health.** A certificate is issued at the termination of the isolation period of the case and the quarantine period of contacts. Such certificates can be issued only if the case has been properly diagnosed and reported and are of value only if the board of health and the school board observe identical isolation and quarantine periods. They produce nothing but confusion if the board of education excludes a child for a period longer than that required by the board of health. Such situations existed more commonly in former years than at present. Every reasonable attempt should be made to arrive at uniform action on this point. In general, a child that can safely be released from isolation or quarantine can equally safely return to school. In some communities both boards have agreed to require a margin of safety of a few extra days after release from isolation before the child is permitted to return to school. This is usually of little value. The important aspect is not whether this is or is not required but that both boards agree as to duration of isolation and exclusion.

2. **Certification by the Attending Physician.** In many communities, and especially those without full-time health departments, the physician is deputized by the board of health to issue certificates of release from isolation and quarantine. He can be equally well deputized to issue certificates of readmission to school if such are desired. These have all the limitations and entail the same potential difficulties as do those issued by the board of health. The system works well, however, if there is mutual understanding.

3. **Certification by the School Physician.** This works well where school physicians are available, but unfortunately such situations are so rare that the method is rarely used. It presupposes that the school physician has examined the child who has been absent and has determined that there are no residual evidences of communicability. Where used, the system is theoretically ideal in dealing with children who, during absence from school, have not been under medical care. Actually its effectiveness is limited by the fact that after the subsidence of signs and symptoms, diagnosis cannot be made, and probable infectiousness often cannot be even guessed. The physician can merely certify that he can find no evidence of residual infection.

4. **Referral to the School Nurse.** Many schools require that all children returning to school after an absence be referred to a school nurse if one is available. This often means that if a nurse is not immediately available the child must await her arrival and too often this is in the same "health room" with those awaiting exclusion. If the child has a certificate from the board of health, attending physician, or school physician, the nurse usually does little more than file the certificate and direct the child to its room. Obviously such certificate could have been equally well accepted by the teacher, saving time of the nurse and avoiding delay and possible re-exposure for the pupil. If the child has no certificate, the nurse is supposed to make the necessary inspection to determine if there is evidence of residual infection. This frequently involves taking the temperature and inspecting the nose and throat for evidences of inflammation. A normal temperature is, unfortunately, not a reliable evidence of absence of infection, as in the case of convalescent carriers. Actually the nurse must place her chief reliance on signs of respiratory involvement, criteria often as easily determined by the teacher. Reliance upon the nurse has the further limitation that so many schools do not have her services each day and in too many instances are still completely lacking any type of nursing services. It may take so much time that there is inadequate time for more important duties.

5. **Inspection by the Teacher.** This procedure is actually one of the most extensively used because so many schools still lack nursing service. All applicable methods of detecting evidences of residual infection have so many limitations and defects that the examination by the teacher, if she is alert, is probably as satisfactory as any. The authors know of no study showing that communicable diseases have been more effectively controlled through readmission examinations by a nurse than by a teacher. Probably both are equally ineffective in dealing with doubtful cases or unrecognized convalescent carrier conditions. Under the circumstances this method, with all its obvious imperfections, is usually as satisfactory as is referral to a nurse. Assigning this function to the teacher leaves the nurse free for the more important home visits which are so often neglected because of the amount of time devoted to exclusion and readmission routines.

ROUTINE CULTURES

A generation ago many schools took nose and throat cultures quite extensively in an attempt to locate carriers who could not be recognized by clinical inspection. These cultures were frequently taken by the nurse when children were referred for possible exclusion. At other times the school physician or health department attempted to stop an outbreak by culturing all the pupils of the building or at least those in rooms where cases developed. While the theory was good and quite simple, viz., to locate and exclude otherwise unsuspected sources of infection, the results were very unsatisfactory.

One difficulty arose from the fact that practical methods of carrier detection are available only for diphtheria, meningococcus meningitis, and streptococcal infections. Methods of detection are not uniformly reliable. Although the bacteriologic procedures have been greatly improved, very little reliance can be placed on a single negative finding. Second or third cultures taken on succeeding days may reveal carriers missed on the initial examination. Furthermore, there is often no higher proportion of carriers of streptococci or meningococci in rooms where the disease is occurring than in rooms or even school buildings entirely free of clinically recognizable cases. Thus there is serious doubt as to the epidemiological importance of carriers as contrasted with mild cases that show, nevertheless, demonstrable evidence of infection and are much more likely to spread infection to their associates.

A further imperfection in the theory of control through routine culturing of school contacts comes from the impossibility of keeping the children separated until the laboratory results have been obtained. This often requires at least 48 hours, during which the children have mingled freely, permitting those not originally infected to acquire infection in the interim. Thus by the time the results are known and isolation measures applied, the distribution of carriers may have radically changed.

Because of the above shortcomings and technical laboratory difficulties, routine culturing of school contacts has never found much favor in control of either meningococcus infections or scarlet fever. It was at one time quite popular and widely used in dealing with diphtheria, as the laboratory procedures for diagnosis of this disease are far simpler. Even in the control of diphtheria, however, routine school culturing has fallen into disrepute and been almost entirely abandoned as immunization has come into prominence with a concurrent decline in the number of cases and carriers. Where used today, culturing is little more than a historical remnant of former practices that have been generally discarded because of lack of demonstrable value. The expenditure of time and money on routine culturing of schools can no longer be justified.

CLOSING OF SCHOOLS

The closing of schools in the presence of communicable disease is a time-tried method of control that appeals to the public imagination. Though the method is almost always without value, it is often forced upon the school or health authorities by a popular demand that "something be done." At the present time this demand is more commonly seen with respect to poliomyelitis than for other diseases.

The thought underlying the demand for the closing of schools (or delaying their opening if they are not yet in session) is very simple. It is assumed that schools must facilitate the exchange of infections since they represent a bringing together of many children who would otherwise have little contact with one another. If the schools are not in session such contacts will supposedly be fewer and therefore exchange of infections be less. Under certain circumstances this theory may be correct, but most commonly the closure of the schools has no effect on the total incidence of the disease. Three types of situations may be encountered, each with its specific problems:

1. **Urban or Semi-rural Schools.** Closing of such schools is without any demonstrable effect and often may even increase the hazard of spread. There is no justification for the assumption that because a school or a schoolroom is closed the children will have no further contact with one another. The movies, Sunday schools, and other places of congregation are usually not closed. The children gather in the streets and playgrounds. At times the closing of schools has even been a signal for a round of children's parties or out-of-town trips. Even if schools have not yet opened, the majority of the children are already in the community and making their usual daily contacts. Although the range of these contacts may be somewhat more limited than in school, it is doubtful if the intimacy is less, for during the school session the children are more or less spaced at their respective desks. Thus the actual effect of closing (or failing to open) the schools is not always a substantial reduction in effective contacts; at times it may even increase the contacts. If there are preschool siblings, the latter (for whom the disease is usually more serious) are often more exposed than if the older child was at school.

If the schools are open the discovery of early and mild infections is actually facilitated. An alert teacher will often detect cases that are overlooked by parents.[5] If the school is in session, many of these cases can be detected and appropriately isolated; if it is not, they go unrecognized and cause more extensive spread. In certain diseases, as in poliomyelitis or diphtheria, early recognition is also of vital importance in proper treatment.

In most instances in which a school is closed, the period of closure is

[5] This idea is hard for the average parent to accept as it offends a natural ego, but experience shows it to be true in too many instances. Every mother thinks she would be more alert than the teacher, and doubtless many are, but too many children still come to school with conditions for which they should be kept home.

too short to be of even theoretical value. The closure should obviously exceed the maximum incubation period. Schools are usually closed for one week, which is definitely too short in all but scarlet fever, diphtheria, and meningococcus meningitis. For all other diseases children exposed and infected before the closure would develop the disease after the reopening. Even in the three above-mentioned diseases which have incubation periods of less than a week, exposures while the schools are closed will result in infections which appear as soon as schools have reopened, thus immediately nullifying whatever good, if any, may have come from the closure. Furthermore, mild cases that have gone unrecognized during the closure will still be infective after reopening and will rekindle the outbreak. Experience has too often shown that within a week or two after schools have reopened the situation is identical with that which prompted the closing except that the children now have a week or more of work to make up, often by curtailing subsequent vacations or prolonging school in the spring.

Delay in opening of schools in the fall, most commonly on account of poliomyelitis, is based on the presumption of delay until the outbreak is over or definitely subsiding. It may give temporary protection to a few children who are away for the summer and whose return to the city is thus postponed, but the bulk of the children in the average public school are already present in the community and may better be in school than on the streets. The usual postponement is for one or two weeks, rarely longer. This satisfies the public that "something is being done." What the public does not realize is that the average urban outbreak of poliomyelitis lasts for 14 to 20 weeks and that the peak is often in September and not infrequently in October.[6] Thus a delay of one or two weeks does not cover the duration of the outbreak. In many instances there are as many new cases the week school finally opens as in the week it was scheduled to open. If the peak has been reached in the interim, the public feels well satisfied, for interest and fear quickly wane after the peak has passed, though the actual number of cases after the peak is usually greater than is the number before.[7]

Although there is a complete absence of any suggestion that delay in opening schools has had the slightest effect on a poliomyelitis outbreak, public hysteria is such that the school or health authorities may feel compelled to take some action to prevent further fear. In many instances this may take the form of a delay, preferably for as short a period as is necessary to satisfy the public. In other instances schools have been opened

---

[6] The peak in southern states tends to come a bit earlier than in northern states, most commonly in July and at times as early as June.

[7] The weekly incidence curve of poliomyelitis is usually skewed to the right.

though without any attempt to enforce the attendance laws. Under such circumstances the schools usually open with about half attendance, but more children appear each day until attendance is practically normal by the end of the second week. Although this irregular return of the children produces difficulties for the teacher, the method does get the children off the streets and back under supervision. Since compulsion has been removed the public is satisfied. At the same time the authorities are relieved of any charge of responsibility for cases that may develop after the schools have reopened. Whether schools are in session or not, further cases in school children can be expected. If attendance at school has been under compulsion, the parent may inevitably tend to blame the infection upon the authorities; if attendance was voluntary, there can be no attachment of blame. Thus the school board may find an escape from an awkward dilemma, an escape that is not possible if there be a complete postponement of one or two weeks, after which usual rules of attendance are enforced. Postponement until the real end of the outbreak would often result in delay until late October or even early December, a delay which is obviously not warranted nor even wanted by the public.

2. **Rural Schools.** In areas that are so rural that the children have little contact with one another except in the schools, there is occasionally some merit in closing or delaying the opening of schools, provided it is for a sufficiently long period. Nothing is gained by closing for a single week. As already pointed out, children in such schools are usually transported by school buses where they make closer contacts than in the schoolroom. Thus the daily travel of these children provides a greater risk than is experienced by urban children who come to the building on foot or by streetcar, where the contacts are chiefly with adults. Undoubtedly in such rural situations, the epidemic curve of the outbreak can sometimes be altered by school closure, but too often the effect is a prolongation of the outbreak at a somewhat lower level of intensity. Thus instead of a sharp outbreak, there may be a rather longer spacing of the cases, though in the end the total number of cases may be the same. Probably the most powerful factor in stopping a school outbreak of respiratory-spread infections is a reduction in the number of susceptibles rather than an actual interruption of spread.

3. **Boarding Schools.** These almost always represent a collection of pupils who come together from widely scattered areas and who have no contact with each other unless school is in session.[8] Unless the outbreak is

[8] To a certain degree a private day school catering to a well-to-do clientele may present the same characteristics, inasmuch as the children are often scattered at vacation resorts for the summer and would stay at such resorts and thus have no contact with one another if opening of school were delayed.

extremely widely spread, these children have been very unevenly exposed. Some may be from areas where the incidence is high while others are from sections virtually free of demonstrable cases. If the school is in an outbreak area, opening of school will bring into the area many children who otherwise would run little risk of infection. It thus increases their exposure and risk. If the school is outside of the region of the outbreak, the opening of school may serve to introduce infection not only into the area but also to a group who must now live in quite close contact with each other.

The situation of a boarding school is thus quite different from that of a public school. Opening of the former undoubtedly furthers contacts that would otherwise not occur; opening of the latter merely brings under supervision children who are already in close contact within the community. Delay in opening a boarding school may therefore be justified even though comparable delay in the opening of a public school is not. This often places the health department in the embarrassing position of apparently being more concerned with the well-to-do than with the rest of the community. Too often such charges have been leveled against it by persons who did not appreciate or understand the true differences in the situation, or who seized upon such action as a basis for demagogic attacks for political reasons.

It does not follow, however, that the closure of a boarding school after communicable disease breaks out is equally logical. If the school is closed the pupils will scatter to their homes. While they will thus have little or no contact with each other, they may well carry the infection to their homes and their communities. If children in a boarding school are to return home after known exposure to infection it should be permitted only after obtaining consent from the board of health of the community to which they are going. Closing of the school may put an end to the outbreak, if the closure is for a long enough period, but it must not be done without guarding against spread of infection to the communities to which the pupils will travel.

DISINFECTION OF SCHOOL PREMISES

Along with the demand for the closing of schools, there is commonly also an insistence upon some form of special disinfection of the premises. Formerly this included fumigation of the building but such requests are almost never heard today as the public is becoming more conscious of the needlessness and lack of value of fumigation. It has no place in the school program and is an unjustifiable waste of money.

Some attention is usually given to the pupil's desk and personal possessions. There is no need for special disinfection of the desk or its contents or of the surrounding floor, yet this practice is commonly observed. The desk and floor are frequently scrubbed with a disinfectant and all the contents burned. If the custodial staff has an impulse toward greater cleanliness, it should not be discouraged, but the liberal use of soap and water is all that is required and even this is probably of no greater importance at the time of infectious disease than at other times. Papers, handkerchiefs, pencils (which have often been in the child's mouth), and other objects soiled with respiratory secretions can be burned.

Disposition of the schoolbooks presents a more troublesome problem. Some of these will have been left in the school desk, others will be at home. Unless they have been so soiled (as with vomitus) that their further usability is impaired, there is no excuse for burning them. Yet in the panic of an outbreak there is often a demand for destruction of at least those books used by the children known to be infected. Within the past 20 years the authors have known of a small town school in which all of the books of all the children were burned just because two cases of meningococcus infection had occurred.[9] There is no evidence whatsoever that any of the pathogens encountered among school children will survive on the pages of a book long enough and in sufficient quantity to cause spread to other persons. To satisfy public opinion some schools air the books (preferably in direct sunlight) for one or two days, placing the books on end with the pages spread as widely as possible on the assumption of promoting drying. This procedure is probably of little value but at least it does not harm the books and does satisfy the demand for some sort of action. In other instances in which there is an adequate supply of extra books, those used by the infected pupil are withdrawn from circulation and not reissued until the subsequent school year. This is less dramatic but an equally satisfactory solution to a problem that actually requires no specific action.[10]

IMMUNIZATION IN THE SCHOOLS

Of all the practices used for the control of communicable diseases in the schools, this is doubtless the most effective. Of course, immunization should have been performed early in life and not delayed until the age of

[9] And then the taxpayers who had demanded the bonfire wondered why the school board asked for more money the ensuing year.

[10] Those who worry about schoolbooks as a vehicle for the spread of infections overlook the fact that the books of the carriers and missed cases are not accorded any attention and are kept in constant use as contrasted with those of the patient which are out of use during the period of isolation.

school attendance. While practices are improving in this regard, the fact remains that immunizations, and especially smallpox vaccination, are too often postponed until the child is ready to go to school. The maximum incidence of most infectious diseases of childhood still occurs in the primary school group and especially at the ages of six, seven, and eight. Consequently every effort should be made to make certain that the child entering school has been properly protected or to provide facilities for immunization as early as possible after the opening of schools. So much emphasis has been properly placed on immunization in infancy that in many places the need for continuing attention to the school child has been overlooked.

Every child coming to school should have been immunized against smallpox, diphtheria, whooping cough, and tetanus. If the child has been properly protected as an infant, all that is recommended is a revaccination for smallpox and booster doses of the other antigens. If the child has not been previously protected, immunization against all of these diseases should be made available as early in the school year as possible. Some persons question the need of starting whooping cough immunizations at school age if the child has not been earlier protected, as pertussis takes its heaviest toll in the preschool group. Yet serious infections can occur in school children, and these in turn may carry the disease home to younger siblings. While the inclusion of pertussis immunization in the school program is less important than the others, there is much to be said for it, especially since the vaccine is so commonly mixed with diphtheria and tetanus toxoids in the present-day multiple antigens. A few states require smallpox vaccination of all children as a prerequisite to school attendance (see p. 91), and in one or two there are statutes regarding immunization against diphtheria. In many of the states that do not have a state-wide law, local boards of education have made and enforced their own regulations requiring smallpox vaccination prior to school attendance.

An immunization program immediately prior to the opening of school is commonly a part of the summer roundup sponsored by the board of health, the schools, the parent-teacher association, or some other civic organization. The program within the school may be sponsored either by the board of education or the board of health. There has been considerable controversy regarding the place of the school in the immunization program. Some maintain that promotion of immunization is a function of the board of health and not of the school; others, that the school can properly and with greater facility take over this duty. It cannot be denied that the board of health is established for the express purpose of health protection and has therefore a specific duty with respect to immunization. Yet many of the children to be protected are in school, and the buildings offer convenient centers for the conduct of such clinics as are required. The decision as to sponsorship is probably less important than the fact that immunization be done properly, with a minimum of disruption of the school routine and that parents be permitted and encouraged to bring younger brothers and sisters who have not yet been protected. Other clinics are frequently so inconveniently located that immunization is too often postponed until school age if the preschool children cannot be cared for at the school clinic.

It is also important to remember that written parental request for the immunization must be secured before a child is given any sort of an injection. This is of vital importance. The physician or nurse who gives an injection on the assurance that the parent will sign the request card at a later date may become embroiled in legal complications. Therefore, no exception should be made to this rule. Careful records should be maintained—such records showing the name and address of the child, the dates of all injections, and the nature, origin, and lot number of all antigen administered. Records as to site and depth of injection also are desirable.

In former years some attempts were made to control infection (notably diphtheria and to a less degree scarlet fever) by passive immunization with an appropriate serum. This practice, recalled by many, has almost entirely disappeared. For diphtheria it is no longer necessary; for scarlet fever it was ineffective. In both cases there was the usual hazard and discomfort that attends injection of any foreign protein. Like the use of active immunization, it required parental permission. More recently attempts have been made to use sulfonamides and antibiotics for routine passive protection. Their limitations to a school situation are the same as those affecting their use under other circumstances (see p. 44). If used, parental permission must be obtained and careful records kept.

SUGGESTED READINGS

Cheeseman, E. A.: *Epidemics in Schools. An Analysis of the Data Collected during the Years 1935–1939*. Medical Research Council, Special Report Series #271. London: His Majesty's Stationery Office, 1950.

Cromwell, Gertrude E.: *The Health of the School Child*. Philadelphia: W. B. Saunders Co., 1946.

Ferrell, John A.: "Control of Communicable Diseases in the Schools," *J.A.M.A.*, 109:835–37, (Sept. 11) 1937.

Health in Schools, rev. ed. Twentieth Yearbook. Washington: American Association of School Administrators, 1951.

Hobson, F. G.: *Medical Practice in Residential Schools*. London: Oxford University Press, 1938.

School Epidemics Committee: *Epidemics in Schools. An Analysis of the Data Collected during the First Five Years of a Statistical Inquiry.* Medical Research Council, Special Report #227. London: His Majesty's Stationery Office, 1938.

Wheatley, George M.: "Communicable Disease and the School," *Am. J. Dis. Child.,* 62:1052–59, (Nov.) 1941.

Wheatley, George M., and Hallock, Grace T.: *Health Observation of School Children.* New York: McGraw-Hill Book Co., 1951.

7. Role of the Public Health Nurse

The functions of the public health nurse in a communicable disease program are the same as in any other public health nursing service, namely, nursing the sick under the physician's orders, instructing and supervising the family in the care, securing medical attention for those who have not already obtained it, and educating the community in the means of prevention and methods of care. This education is carried on, as in other services, during all home visits (especially if communicable disease is present in the community or in nearby communities), through the distribution of literature, through talks to parent and teacher groups, and through other channels of publicity. The nurse is often the deputy of the health officer and, as such, is given authority to instruct regarding the regulations established to prevent the spread of the disease. The modern health department makes very few such regulations, as increased knowledge of the methods of spread of these diseases has shown the futility of many of the former regulatory procedures. A few are important, however, such as the proper disposal of excreta from typhoid patients. The public health nurse, acting as the deputy of the health officer, may have the responsibility for making certain that such regulations of the health department are enforced. In addition to the above functions, she may be responsible for making epidemiological investigations (for details see Chap. 9). How she executes these general functions will depend upon the type of organization in which she is working, the functions of other agencies in the area, the size and type of the community, and the state and local regulations regarding communicable diseases.

As in all other types of public health nursing, the nurse must first survey the problems in her community and find out what resources she has to call upon for help. She must know the diseases common to the locality and the epidemiology of these conditions. She should know their local prevalence and seasonal occurrence, the mortality and fatality rates, and the age-specific mortality rates locally in comparison with other similar areas. A knowledge of the past history of the diseases in this community will help her to understand the public's attitude toward them. This information is essential if the nurse is to do effective teaching in the home where a case of communicable disease has already occurred or in households not yet attacked.

Such a survey will probably reveal that there has been such a striking decline in the incidence of communicable diseases in recent years that no one of the diseases ranks as a main cause of death, and that even if all of these diseases are grouped together they still fail to appear among the leading causes of mortality. In some communities the so-called "children's diseases" will be found to occur periodically in epidemic form but to be mild in character, whereas not a single case of typhoid fever or smallpox will have developed for five years or more. The tables of vital statistics will probably show deaths from cancer and heart disease heading the list. Information from other sources will show that the chronic diseases—heart disease, arthritis—keep large numbers of people in a semi-invalid state for years.

The conclusion from such a survey might be that there is no need to include communicable disease in the public health nurse's program. It is clear that the communicable disease service should no longer take a major part of her time, but study of the foregoing chapters makes it equally clear that the communicable diseases are not completely conquered and that constant vigilance must be maintained in order to preserve our present favorable situation. More effort and skill are required to keep a high proportion of the population immunized when there are few cases of disease than when there are many. The public health nurse needs a very thorough knowledge of the principles of communicable disease transmission and control in order to deal effectively with the infrequent serious outbreak.

The general outlines of the program of the board of health nurse in a city, in a small urban area, and in a county and of the visiting nurse and school nurse are discussed below. While certain features are common to all programs, the details will vary in each community; and there are as many different ways of working these out as there are health organizations.

By "board of health nurse" is meant one employed by a health department and paid by public funds; a "visiting nurse" is one employed by a private organization and paid by private funds; and a "school nurse" is one employed by the board of education. There may be any combination of these employing agencies; the nurse may be employed by all three or by only one. Regardless of her employer, her work will vary somewhat, depending upon the other nursing agencies in her community, the size of the community, and whether or not special duties are required of her by her employing agency.

The "official" public health nurse is an employee of a governmental agency, which is required by law to carry out specified duties and is empowered to take action in given circumstances (see Chap. 5). Certain of these duties may be delegated to the nurse. She may be assigned very few duties in connection with the communicable disease control program, or she may be asked to perform almost every procedure carried out by the health department in this division of its work. In fact, in certain areas in the United States, the official public health nurses even collect blood samples for examination and give injections for protection against such diseases as diphtheria, typhoid, and measles.

BOARD OF HEALTH NURSING SERVICES

Urban Areas

The board of health nurse in a large city usually carries on a "generalized" program, including all services rendered by the health department. These do not usually include any nursing care of the sick nor services to schools, as in large cities there is usually a private organization which supplies the bedside care and the school nurses serve under the board of education. During recent years there has been a trend to amalgamate the official and private organizations, thus enabling one nurse to visit the entire family. Though this movement is growing rather slowly, combination agencies exist today in over 40 communities and it is anticipated that the number will increase. The school nurses are not usually included in these combination agencies but they might well be in the future. Whether the nurse making a communicable disease visit is operating on a specialized or generalized program, she should be aware of all family health problems in the households she visits and either refer them to the proper agency or care for them herself.

The board of health nurse in the city usually visits all reported cases of certain communicable diseases specified by the health officer. In some cities she may visit all reported cases of all communicable diseases, but isolation and quarantine regulations for most communicable diseases have been so modified in the past few years that many health officers do not consider a visit from the board of health to be necessary routinely. The board of health nurse is responsible for giving instructions regarding isolation and quarantine in those houses in which she visits. She may also release the uncomplicated cases and make interim visits where there is need. Placards indicating that a house is quarantined are seldom used now, but where this requirement is still in force the board of health nurse may also placard the house on the first visit and remove the sign at the termination of the quarantine period. She is acting in this capacity as a deputy of the health officer and has the responsibility of seeing that proper observance of the control regulations is carried out to safeguard the community from the spread of infection from this household. She reports failure to obey regulations to the health officer for his action. Although she has the authority of law behind her, it has been recognized for some time that education is more effective than force in obtaining compliance with the statutes. The family that feels the board of health nurse has come to *help* and understands the reason for the regulations is much more likely to observe quarantine than is the one that feels the nurse has been sent mainly as a police officer to enforce unpleasant laws limiting the family's activities. Special effort should be made to explain the reason for the regulations and why the family should abide by them. This is sometimes very difficult when these rules are archaic and not reasonable in the light of present knowledge, but some effort should always be made to explain "why" and not merely tell the family "what" they may do.

The board of health nurse, no less than the visiting nurse, has a responsibility for seeing that every family has necessary medical and nursing care. In a large city with a multiplicity of agencies, it is especially difficult for the family of limited means to know where assistance may be obtained. The board of health nurse should be alert for cases which might benefit from nursing care and should make every effort to see that such care is obtained, if the physician in attendance is willing.

The board of health nurse in a large city is seldom called upon to give demonstration of care, as there is usually a visiting nurse association ready to do this. But if there is no bedside nursing service in the city, the board of health nurse should be equipped to demonstrate care and should seize every possible opportunity to do so. Even when such service is available, if the board of health nurse on her first visit finds the patient in need of attention and takes time to give at least partial care—referring the case to the visiting nurse association for further care—she will find that the family will receive her instructions more readily because she has done them a service in time of need.

The public health nurse is frequently responsible for taking cultures of contacts and for collecting various types of specimens. The reasons for these should be explained to the family, and, when possible and with the physician's consent, the results should be given to them. Skill is needed in taking cultures in order to ensure satisfactory specimens and to minimize discomfort to the patient. Practice under competent supervision is needed before starting this work. The nurse may also be called upon to do some epidemiological investigations (see Chap. 9).

Nurses in large cities are responsible for education of the community through home visits but usually do not have to carry on any other types of education, as special personnel take care of newspaper publicity, popular literature, radio broadcasts, and lectures to civic groups. She may, however, organize community groups or classes to study the communicable diseases. In the authors' experience, lay groups—particularly parent groups—exhibit a livelier interest in this subject than in almost any other health topic. The acute communicable diseases of childhood have been experienced by almost everyone and have been a cause of so much annoyance or worry that most people have questions regarding them and therefore are receptive to instructions. In her home visits for whatever purpose, the board of health nurse, as well as those doing visiting and school nursing, should use every chance to stress the value of immunization, especially of the preschool group, and the importance of booster doses or revaccination for certain diseases as indicated. Although most persons recognize the necessity of immunization of infants against whooping cough, diphtheria, and smallpox as a routine part of child care, there are some who do not appreciate the need of immunization against diseases they have never seen. If the public health nurse will keep herself informed of outbreaks of these diseases which have occurred in this country or even in other countries, she will find it easier to convince such parents that protection is still necessary. When immunization has been neglected, these diseases will occur and cause entirely unnecessary illness and even death. In doing this work, the nurse must remember that her task is educating the mother as to the need for immunization, not building up a clinic clientele. Neither the nurse nor the health department is concerned with the problem of how or by whom the child is immunized, provided he is effectively protected. The more children who are immunized by the family physician, the less will have to be served by the public clinics. In her eagerness to have a child immunized, the nurse must not urge that children be taken to the clinic in preference to the family physician. On the contrary, she should urge private care whenever possible and point out the services of the clinic only when these seem indicated or in response to specific inquiries.

Villages and Cities under 10,000 Population

In a small community with a visiting nurse association, a board of health nurse, and a school nurse, the service is much the same as described for the large city. More frequently in a community under ten thousand, there is only one nurse doing all types of work or, at least, rendering two services—board of health and bedside nursing, or board of health and school nursing. If she is doing school work, she must be especially careful to keep a proper balance between her communicable disease activities in the school and in the home. The most constructive, far-reaching preventive work she can do is with the teachers and the principals, for they in turn teach pupils and parents. At certain times it is advisable for the village nurse who is also doing school nursing to inspect school children for early signs of illness. This is more effective in preventing the spread of a disease when only a few cases are in the village than when the epidemic is already widespread. Whatever her program, the nurse should always allot a certain amount of time to home visiting not only to instruct regarding the care of those excluded from school and to search for suspicious cases but also to see whether the cases already diagnosed need care and, if they are not receiving it, to give such care or arrange for it. As has already been pointed out in Chapter 3, we are unable to prevent the spread of many diseases, but we can often minimize the ill effects by proper care.

The nurse in a small community is often the only full-time public health employee and therefore has greater responsibilities and more varied duties than the nurse working in a large health department. A major part of the direct health educational program usually rests upon her shoulders. As she is ordinarily working directly and closely with the health officer, she can bring to him suggestions gleaned from home visits as to the type of education or publicity most needed in the community. She may have to give talks to groups and assist in writing articles for the local newspapers or for use in school.

Rural Areas

The nurse working in a rural area small enough to allow her to render a complete family nursing service carries the same type of program as the nurse in a small village (see above). At present, however, it is the exception rather than the rule to find rural areas supplied with sufficient public health nurses to make this possible. One or two nurses commonly serve a whole county, varying in size from 400 to 4,000 square miles, with populations varying from 3,000 to 35,000. Obviously, this nurse cannot give the same kind of family nursing service as can the nurse in a city or village. The distance between patients and the travel time involved are probably the greatest factors influencing the public health nursing program in an area of this kind. In order to reduce travel time, it is customary to "zone" the county and to work in each zone during certain specified days or weeks during the month. When the nurse is in a certain area, she visits all prenatal, infant, preschool, and school health supervision cases and tuberculosis and orthopedic cases which need attention at this time. Ordinarily these cases are not emergency calls and therefore can be seen at scheduled intervals.

Obviously the acute communicable disease service presents quite a different problem. If the maximum benefit is to be obtained from the nurse's visit, it should be made immediately. Even a visit to give instruction regarding convalescent care has to be made within a few days after the report has been received or at most a week or two later, as the majority of these diseases do not last longer than one to three weeks. A nurse working in this type of rural area cannot disrupt all her plans and sacrifice her other work to visit every case of communicable disease on the same day it is reported. She may, therefore, have to plan a very different type of service from the program described for the city or village nurse. Her main emphasis in the county program should be continuous education during home visits for other services, through her visits to schools, through distribution of literature, and through talks at group meetings. Utilizing all these channels, she should strive to educate the community in the modern aspects of a communicable disease program. She must, of course, keep in close touch with the health officer (or health officers) to learn of all reported cases in the territory in which she is working. Under his direction she should visit as many of these cases as possible to demonstrate care and give instructions, basing her selection of cases on such considerations as the age group most seriously affected and the economic need.

This does not mean that the county nurse should never change her plans in the interests of the communicable disease service. There are many occasions when the health of the community will best be served by immediate attention to the communicable disease problem. The nurse, working with the health officer, should discriminate between diseases which need nursing attention and those which do not need it so much. For example, chickenpox is ordinarily a mild condition and is reported only to differentiate it from smallpox. Cases do not usually need visits from the public health nurse, as once the diagnosis has been established, the health department has accomplished its purpose. On the other hand, whooping cough and measles, which are often neglected, cause more deaths in many areas than do diphtheria and scarlet fever. Some of these deaths could probably be prevented by active immunization against whooping cough, by passive immunization of measles contacts, by preventing exposure of the young infant, and by adequate medical care of the infants and preschool children who have contracted the disease. A change of schedule is therefore worth while in order to visit a community from which a few cases of whooping cough or measles have been reported.

In such an emergency, the nurse would proceed at once to that community to concentrate upon the educational program *early* in the epidemic while time is still left to protect infants and preschool children from exposure. If there is a county health officer, her activities would be carried on under his direction; if there is a local part-time health officer, she would report to him immediately upon her entering the community, obtain the list of known cases from him, receive directions, and discuss plans with him. A visit would be made to the school not primarily to inspect the children—though this would probably be done—but to discuss the disease, its dangers, and public health aspects with the teacher or principal. During the inspection, the nurse would refresh the teacher's memory regarding the early signs and symptoms of the disease and the public health regulations. Too much time should not be spent in doing classroom inspections, as control by this means is almost impossible (see Chaps. 3 and 6). Yet, until the public has been better educated in the possibility and impossibility of controlling some of the diseases with our present knowledge, the nurse may have to make regular visits to the schools during an epidemic. These should be brief and used largely to discuss with the teacher problems which may have arisen or to obtain a list of new or suspected cases. Community psychology must always be taken into consideration, and everything possible done to allay fears and satisfy the public that all possible control measures are being taken; but one does not have to *follow* public opinion slavishly and endlessly. This opinion can gradually be changed through education and be brought into harmony with the known facts regarding the diseases.

Letters explaining the danger to infants and preschool children and emphasizing the special need for medical and nursing care for this group might be sent home to parents. Newspaper articles are frequently helpful at this time. If they contain news as well as advice, they are usually welcomed by the editors. If the nurse is able to offer any nursing care, a visit to all the physicians in the area to acquaint them with this service is sometimes very helpful.

No matter what is the nature or scope of the communicable disease program, the nurse can do her most effective teaching regarding prevention when she is visiting a family in the interests of infant and preschool health supervision. At this time she teaches the importance of immunization against diphtheria, whooping cough, and smallpox and the need for protection of this age group against whooping cough and measles. Prevention of the acute communicable diseases is one of the most important phases of infant and preschool health supervision. Like charity, it begins at home.

VISITING NURSE SERVICE

At the present time, most visiting nurse services include the care of acute communicable disease in their program. The various antibiotics have lessened the severity of many of the infections. As the visiting nurse may not be called often to care for such cases, it is important that, before going on this type of case, she review the latest information about the disease and make sure that she knows the procedures necessary to protect herself and her other patients and also those necessary for the family. (Details regarding procedures will be found in Chap. 8.)

Though the visiting nurse is not responsible for the enforcement of quarantine, she should be thoroughly familiar with these regulations, the reasons for them, and the basis for changes when they occur. She can render an invaluable service by making her instructions consistent with those of the board of health nurses and can reinforce the official instruction. Frequently the family is more ready to listen to the visiting nurse than to the representative of the board of health, because she is giving them assistance and is not considered a representative of the "law."

SCHOOL NURSING SERVICE

Whether she is employed on a full-time or a part-time basis, the school nurse is part of the education staff. Her main function is therefore educational. Her aim in the communicable disease service, as in other parts of her program, is to instruct the teachers, the parents, and the children regarding the essential facts in prevention, control, and care. They should be made aware not only of the remarkable strides medical science has made in the prevention of diseases such as typhoid, smallpox, and diphtheria, but also of the limited knowledge we have regarding prevention or control of certain other diseases such as chickenpox or poliomyelitis.

These facts can be brought to the teachers' attention [1] through group discussions, by giving them articles which explain clearly the present status of our knowledge, by sending them health bulletins or excerpts of recent articles. Individual conferences with the teachers as problems arise in the classroom often find the teacher in the most interested and receptive state. Every teacher should have available a clear, easily read chart giving

---

[1] It is assumed that the nurse knows the customary methods of procedure in initiating any program in the schools; consequently there will be no discussion here of the relationship of the school nurse to the board of education, the superintendent, principal, or teacher.

the principal facts regarding the common communicable diseases and the board of health and school regulations regarding each one. It is time well spent to explain the reasons for these regulations as the teacher will observe and apply these procedures best if she understands their basis.

The teacher is probably the best person to convey this information to the pupils, but the nurse should assist her by bringing suitable material to her attention, by answering questions, and, in short, by acting as a "consultant." In some schools the nurse is required to teach courses in health. If this is part of her job, she should have special preparation for teaching. Parents are instructed individually on the occasion of home visits and collectively in parent-teacher associations or other adult groups in the community. This work is frequently delegated to either the school or board of health nurse.

In addition to this "strictly" educational work, the school nurse frequently performs certain regulatory functions in relation to the communicable disease program. The full-time school nurse usually inspects and interviews children returning after an absence due to illness, before they are admitted to the classroom. This is done to determine whether it is safe for the child to return, both from the standpoint of the child's own health and the health of the other children. If there is a full-time physician, the readmission of children may be his function, or he may have only the doubtful cases referred to him. If the child has been under the jurisdiction of the board of health either as a communicable disease case or contact, the school will often accept the release from isolation or quarantine as proof of suitability for readmission.

Full-time school nurses usually have the added responsibility of recommending the exclusion of any child who appears to be ill. Teachers are instructed to be alert for any signs of illness and to refer these children to the nurse for further inspection. Obviously the nurse, in such situations, is able to pass judgement only on those cases that have been selected by the teacher as probably suffering from an infectious condition. Thus the nurse is in the position of confirming the teacher's suspicions. These suspicions are usually based on the signs and symptoms of a "cold" and are therefore adequate grounds for exclusion with or without confirmation by the nurse. Similar criteria will be followed in determining readmission. There is a serious doubt whether the amount of time given to these functions by the average school nurse is a worth-while expenditure of her time, however much the school administrator may appreciate the luxury of being able to refer all such cases to her.

The nurse must be careful lest the teachers become too dependent upon her for this service. Even the full-time nurse must be out of the building during part of the school day in order to make home visits, nor can she be in each building at the beginning of the morning session. During her absence, the principal and teachers must assume responsibility for excluding children who appear ill. If the nurse takes every opportunity to discuss with the teacher the cases referred by the latter, the teacher will soon build up criteria for judging whether or not a child should be excluded, and her powers of observation will be sharpened so that she will be less likely to overlook cases that should be excluded.

If there is only a part-time school nurse or a county nurse visiting the school at rare intervals, the teacher must assume responsibility both for readmitting children who have had communicable diseases and excluding those who appear ill. The communicable disease chart previously mentioned guides her in this function. The nurse can be of great assistance through intelligent, timely instruction.

Nurses who work in schools usually make classroom inspections at one time or another. The method of doing this has changed from the formal regimented type to a more informal inspection taking place at a specified time, when the children are subjected to careful scrutiny but are not lined up in a row. It is generally agreed that this inspection should be the function of the teacher and should be done as the children enter the classroom in the morning or as soon as they take their seats. The teacher must be alert *all day* for signs of illness, unusual fatigue, feverish flushed skin, unnaturally bright eyes, rash, snuffles, thick voice, cough, or general lassitude. The nurse may aid the teacher by making an inspection early in the school year at which time she points out the signs of healthy skin, eyes, and general appearance. As occasion arises, she may later point out deviations from normal.

If a communicable disease appears in the school, the nurse on a full-time basis may inspect a certain classroom every morning, but she cannot inspect the entire school fast enough to exclude suspicious cases before they have had a chance to come in contact with many other children. Therefore, even when the nurse is devoting full time to one school, the teachers must know how to recognize signs of illness and should be alert for them. If the nurse spends only part time in the school, the teacher will probably wish her to visit the school when a case of communicable disease occurs. The nurse can make the inspections at that time and show the teacher how to carry out future inspections by herself if, after taking all factors into consideration, the nurse thinks this is advisable.[2]

[2] It is of course obvious that careful medical inspections are more valuable than those by the nurse or teacher. Unfortunately they can rarely be provided. The competent and conscientious nurse or teacher can usually recognize signs of illness even though not able to make a diagnosis.

Full-time school nurses almost always visit school absentees, either all children absent for a certain length of time (three days is quite usual) or only those known to be ill. Telephone calls or reports from other members of the family who are in school often save time and travel. Too much time should not be spent in this type of home visiting, as it is not effective as a control measure and often develops into a truancy rather than a nursing visit. If done in moderation and with discretion, it is useful to the extent that cases requiring care are often discovered and instruction is given at a time of need.

If a suspicious case of communicable disease is found and no doctor is in attendance, this should of course be reported immediately to the board of health. Even if no diagnosis has been made, simple instruction regarding isolation may be given as a precautionary measure. If there is no visiting nurse association in the community, the school nurse should be prepared to demonstrate care of the sick child. The school nurse should always keep in mind that most of the common acute communicable diseases are not very dangerous for the school age child but may be very serious in the preschool age. Preschool children will eventually be school children. Anything that can be done to preserve their health will result in healthier school children. Furthermore, the school child's health is affected from day to day by what is happening within the home. The school nurse may therefore well spend a good part of her time in the home talking about the infant or preschool children, if there are any, rather than concentrating entirely on the school child. For these same reasons, if letters and literature are sent to parents during an epidemic or when one is apparently just starting, they should emphasize the dangers for the infant and preschool child and advise the parents how to minimize or prevent these risks as well as give information regarding the situation within the school. Inasmuch as preschool children are the responsibility of the board of health and not of the board of education, there should be a clear working understanding between the two agencies with regard to all contacts that the school nurse may make with children of this age group. Otherwise unfortunate misunderstandings may arise which are embarrassing to both agencies and confusing to the mother.

SUMMARY

It has been stated on numerous occasions by health officers of broad experience that the development of public health nursing constituted one of the outstanding contributions to the communicable disease control program. Regardless of the agency by which she is employed, the nurse has certain fundamental responsibilities that she can perform more effectively than can other type of personnel. As a nurse, she should seek to provide or to instruct the mother in those nursing procedures important to the patient's comfort and often to his recovery. As a health counselor in the home and school, she has an unparalleled opportunity for teaching the prevention of the communicable diseases. Because of her entree into the home and her position in the school program, she is able to uncover those cases not receiving care and can refer such cases, among which a disproportionately large number of deaths occur, to proper medical attention. No other person can contribute so much to the control of certain communicable diseases as can the nurse through her program of direct service, education, and case-finding.

SUGGESTED READINGS

Arnstein, Margaret G.: "A Program of Staff Education," *Pub. Health Nursing,* 31:502–8, (Sept.) 1939.

Cree, Margaret A.: "Present Day Views on School Nursing," *Am. J. Pub. Health,* 42:818–24, (July) 1952.

"Desirable Organization of Public Health Nursing for Family Service," *Pub. Health Nursing,* 38:387–89, (Aug.) 1946.

Freeman, Ruth B.: *Public Health Nursing Practice.* Philadelphia: W. B. Saunders Co., 1950.

8. Care of a Communicable Disease Case at Home

The care of a sick person in the home frequently taxes to the utmost the skill and resources of the family. If the disease is communicable, there is the added burden of the various procedures designed to prevent other members from contracting the infection. Every nurse, whether she is a private duty nurse caring for the patient twenty-four hours a day or a public health nurse giving at most an hour a day, wishes to give the best possible care to the patient and to prevent spread of the infection, insofar as this is possible, with the least burden to the family.

The care of a patient suffering from a communicable disease does not differ from the care of any other patient except that isolation and disinfection measures are carried out in addition to the usual procedures of bed bath, bedmaking, special treatments, and diet. As has been already pointed out, isolation procedures are of limited effectiveness in preventing the spread of many diseases. The care of the patient should therefore take precedence over the special communicable disease procedures in the public health nurse's visit. The nurse should first make certain that the patient has medical care, find out his condition and the physician's orders, and see that the family understands the general nursing care before proceeding to teach the special isolation techniques. In many cases good nursing care not only makes the patient more comfortable but may also be an important factor in preventing complications. It is not the function of this book to deal with general nursing procedures, but a few of the most important points in the care of communicable disease cases are considered in Part Two, under each disease.

Isolation technique for communicable diseases has usually been learned by both physician and nurse in the hospital. In adapting this to the home, it must be remembered that usually the other members of the household have already been exposed by the time the physician or nurse arrives. This is true especially for the acute infections spread through the respiratory tract, to a far less degree for those of the gastrointestinal tract. Therefore considerable doubt exists as to whether or not even the most careful technique can entirely prevent the further spread of many diseases. Within the hospital, on the other hand, since no one has been exposed to the patient until he enters the building, a meticulous technique will prevent the occurrence of secondary cases.

Because of this fundamental difference between the hospital and home situation, the authors do not believe it is sensible to try making the home technique the closest possible copy of hospital practice. Imitating hospital methods as accurately as home conditions allow may not achieve the desired results so effectively as a technique especially designed for the home and based on the needs of the situation found there.

It seems neither practical nor necessary to try to teach a family to observe a strictly aseptic technique in the home. When we consider how long it takes physicians and nurses to learn how to carry out such measures in the hospital, we realize that it is a rare person indeed who can learn aseptic technique in the home in an hour or two. The attendant may possibly learn the routine the public health nurse teaches her, but think of the number of things which she does during the day and which the nurse cannot foresee! She may learn to put a gown on correctly, only to break technique in a far worse way five minutes later. What reasons can one give for learning elaborate procedures? Can the nurse give reasonable assurance that through observance of such technique other members of the family will not contract the disease? This is not possible, as they have probably already been exposed and may be in the incubation period. Will such measures protect the community? We cannot say that elaborate home technique is necessary for that. It is unlikely that infection could be spread through the community by any break in technique within the house.

There is a limit to what the average person can assimilate in a given space of time. Too often the attendant who is to carry out complicated isolation procedures will, in her eagerness, neglect to provide for the comfort of the patient. With comparatively little chance of completely preventing the further spread of the disease by these techniques, it seems advisable to place the emphasis on the care of the patient and teach only simple and practical measures in relation to isolation procedures.

To approach the problem not with the thought of achieving absolute asepsis but rather with the aim of reducing the chances of infection by concentrating on the main sources of spread and attempting to cut these down as much as possible seems the more logical course of action. Attention should be first directed to the chief mode of spread, then to the next most important channel, in each case instructions being given the attendant as to methods of minimizing the spread from this source. If the attendant is able to learn and to carry out more elaborate procedures without sacrificing the welfare of the patient, one may go on to the methods that are third or fourth in importance and so on down the line. Thus in diseases transmitted through discharges from the respiratory tract, the most important means of transmission is direct contact. If other members of the family cannot be excluded from the room, there is very little point in teaching anything about hand-washing, wearing of gowns, or caring for dishes or linen. If a satisfactory method has been worked out to exclude other children from the room, one may then teach the importance of the attendant's washing her hands and disposing of the discharges, these being the next most important means of transmission. Dishes, linen, and other articles are less important because the contact with other persons is less direct, and because the usual methods of caring for these articles through washing and drying will probably eliminate most of the danger. Therefore, one would leave these until the last and perhaps give no instruction regarding their special care if one thought the mother had already reached her learning capacity. Instruction in too many details may only confuse the mother and lead to neglect of the most important matters.

In giving instructions for isolation procedures, one must consider each disease and each home situation separately just as one does in giving instructions regarding the care of the patient, though in each case certain guiding principles may be applicable. The attending physician's orders and wishes must be considered in regard to isolation procedures just as they are with respect to care. If his orders are less strict than the requirements of the board of health, this should be called to the attention of the health officer.

A definite technique is included in this book with some hesitation, as new facts about these diseases are constantly being discovered and techniques should change with new knowledge. Even the present knowledge is subject to a variety of interpretations and emphases. One cannot therefore say that the technique as outlined below is "right" and all others are "wrong." If the public health worker will test the instruction she gives against the known facts regarding that disease and the family situation she finds, she can make any technique reasonably safe.

SUGGESTIONS FOR TECHNIQUES TO BE USED IN THE CARE OF A COMMUNICABLE CASE IN THE HOME

If there is a physician in attendance or if the health officer has already visited the household, the nurse should find out what orders have been given regarding isolation just as she does regarding medication and treatment. She will follow these orders, even though they are more stringent than the health department regulations. For example, if the physician orders a disinfecting solution for a hand-wash and the department of health does not require this, the public health nurse will see that the family understands and carries out the order. If, before giving any instructions, the nurse will find out what the family already knows regarding isolation, she will save much time, will avoid irritation through telling what is already known, and will make subsequent teaching much easier, as it can be built directly on the family's knowledge. If the physician has left no orders, the nurse will, of course, follow the standing orders of her own organization. The following procedures are suggested as a basis for such standing orders.

Order of Visits

In a rural community where the nurse travels some distance between houses and spends some time in the open air, she may visit communicable disease cases at her convenience if the following technique is carried out. In a city where she has little or no time between visits, it is preferable either to make her communicable disease visits at the end of the day or to arrange her visits so that she does not go directly from a communicable disease visit to an uninfected household with small children. The nurse who is caring for diseases of streptococcal origin, such as scarlet fever or erysipelas, should not give care to cases with open wounds (surgical and postpartum). In an organization with more than one nurse, these two types of cases should be carried by different nurses. If the nurse is working alone, she should teach the care for either one of the cases to someone in the home.

The Nurse's Technique

The nurse must adhere to a strict personal technique because she is traveling from household to household, caring for all types of cases, sick and well, and she must be quite certain that there is no possibility of her spreading the disease in this manner.

1. The nurse's hat, coat, and bag should not be taken into the patient's room; or, if this is unavoidable, they should be placed as far away from the patient as possible.

2. Articles which cannot be sterilized or disinfected should not be taken from the nurse's bag into the room. If the family can supply all necessary articles for care, this is preferable.

3. A gown should be worn when caring for patients suffering from diseases classified in Groups II and III (see below). This may be left in the patient's home between visits. When the case is closed, the gown should be taken back to the office but not in the nurse's bag. If a paper gown is used, it should be burned.[1]

The Family Technique

In the technique suggested for family use in the home, the diseases have been considered in three groups: first, those which are transmitted by the respiratory tract and for which the conventional isolation procedures are of very little proved value; second, those which are transmitted by the respiratory tract and which may be partially controlled by a strict home technique; and, third, those which are transmitted by the gastrointestinal tract. The distinction between the first two groups is on the basis of what can be accomplished through isolation precautions. In the first group, such diseases as measles, pneumonia, and poliomyelitis have been included, though for very different reasons. Measles is included because it is most communicable before the rash appears, and infection of family contacts will therefore have occurred before precautions are instituted. Pneumonia and poliomyelitis are classed here because the secondary attack rate of clinical cases is so very low and, as far as can be determined, does not seem to be influenced by isolation techniques. Diphtheria and scarlet fever, formerly in Group II, have now been classed in Group I. Diphtheria was moved because the disease is so rare that it is usually not recognized until several days have elapsed. Many of the cases are quite atypical because of partial resistance due to earlier immunization. Little is accomplished by applying strict isolation precautions after all the family contacts have been thoroughly exposed. Scarlet fever has been moved to Group I because in recent years the disease has been so mild that, like diphtheria, it is often not recognized during the early febrile stage. The serious complications, such as otitis media and mastoiditis, which were still justly feared a few years ago, are so well controlled by the antibiotics that the disease hardly warrants the extreme precautions that were formerly justified.

[1] The question has been raised by many people whether a gown should be required. Attention has been called to the fact that nurses frequently render bedside care to cases later diagnosed as one of the acute communicable diseases and yet no gown is worn on the first visit because the diagnosis is not known. In order to be entirely consistent, one should either wear a gown when caring for all febrile cases or never wear a gown at all. The authors feel that it would not be practical to advise wearing a gown for all febrile cases. On the other hand, one can reduce the risk of transmitting the disease by wearing one whenever the diagnosis *is* known.

The authors realize that exceptions will be taken to the idea of less stringent technique in caring for scarlet fever and diphtheria but are aware of no studies to justify the present-day observance of precautions that seemed so logical when the diseases were more malignant. Those who so desire will retain the precautions set forth below for Group II or may arrive at their own compromise between the techniques recommended for the first two groups.

Whatever technique is observed, it should be modified to fit each home situation, as has already been indicated in this chapter. The following procedures may serve as a general guide:

Procedures for All Communicable Diseases

1. The patient should be in a room by himself or in one shared only by the person caring for him.
2. All necessary articles should be assembled before entering the patient's room so that it will not be necessary to leave the room until care has been completed.
3. The attendant should wear a large apron and use it only while caring for the patient; she should leave it in the sick room at all times.
4. The attendant should always wash her hands after touching the patient or articles used by the patient and before touching anybody or anything outside the sickroom.

Additional Procedures for Certain Diseases

Diseases in Group I

(Examples of diseases in Group I—measles, whooping cough, pneumonia)

1. Nasal discharges should be destroyed. Clean cloths or paper handkerchiefs should be used and discarded into a paper bag by the bed and burned if possible.
2. Other instructions should be the same as one would give for ordinary cleanliness in caring for a sick person. Hands should be washed with soap and hot running water, if available, each time after giving care. (It is well to demonstrate thorough hand-washing.) Dishes and linen should be thoroughly washed with soap and hot water; rinsing of dishes with boiling water constitutes an added precaution.

Diseases in Group II

(Smallpox)

In addition to the above procedures:

1. So far as possible, all articles used by the patient should be kept in the patient's room or properly treated immediately after removal, that is,

carefully washed, burned, boiled, soaked in disinfecting solution,[2] or aired, according to the type of articles.

2. Soiled linen should be soaked in soap and water immediately so that it will not be handled. It should then be washed as soon as possible. Ordinary washing and drying will suffice.

Diseases in Group III

(Examples of diseases in Group III—typhoid, dysentery)

In addition to the above procedures:

1. Waste food from the patient's meals should be burned, not put in the garbage can.
2. Before throwing bowel or urine discharges into a toilet or privy, they should be thoroughly mixed with chloride of lime in the bedpan and allowed to stand one hour; the stool should be broken up to enable the lime to get in contact with all parts.

Terminal Disinfection for All Diseases

1. The patient should be bathed and dressed in clean clothes.
2. The room should be thoroughly cleaned and aired.
   a) Hot water and soap should be used wherever possible.
   b) All other articles, such as mattresses, blankets, toys, books, and so forth, should be aired for about six hours. If any of these articles are soiled, they should, of course, be cleaned before being used again.
   c) Books should be kept out of circulation for about two to four weeks and then may be used again.

SUGGESTED READINGS

Lynch, Theresa I.: *Communicable Disease Nursing*, 2nd ed. St. Louis: C. V. Mosby Co., 1949.

MacChesney, Emma: "What Is Communicable Disease Nursing?" *Am. J. Nursing,* 40:266–72, (Mar.) 1940.

———: "Nursing Isolation Procedures and How to Establish Them," *Am. J. Nursing,* 40:378–82, (Apr.) 1940.

McCulloch, Ernest C.: *Disinfection and Sterilization.* Philadelphia: Lea & Febiger, 1945.

Pillsbury, Mary E., and Sachs, Elizabeth J.: *Nursing Care of Communicable Diseases.* Philadelphia: J. B. Lippincott Co., 1952.

Sommermyer, Lucille: "Disinfection of Oral Thermometers," *Pub. Health Nursing,* 42:561–62, (Oct.) 1952.

[2] Several disinfectants can be used for this purpose. A 2 per cent solution of tricresol (liquor cresolis saponatus) can be made by using five teaspoonfuls of the tricresol to a quart of water; 0.1 per cent bichloride of mercury by dissolving two tablets (usually 7.5 grams $HgCl_2$ per tablet) in a quart of water; or 3 per cent chlorinated lime by using two slightly rounded tablespoonfuls in a quart of water. The latter, though the least expensive, must be thoroughly rinsed out of the clothing and must not be used on colored goods, as it is a bleaching agent. The cresol solution is not expensive if purchased in bulk under its pharmacopoeial designation; the proprietary products are more costly.

9. Epidemiological Investigation of Communicable Diseases

Every case of communicable disease immediately raises several questions:

1. From whom was the infection contracted (the source)?
2. By what route did the infection spread from the source to the present victim?
3. To what other persons may the infection have been spread from the same source?
4. To whom may the present case have already transmitted the infection?
5. To whom may the present case transmit the infection unless suitable precautions are observed?
6. What can be learned from this case?

Prompt and complete answers to all of these questions are essential if effective control measures are to be carried out. These questions can be answered only by epidemiological investigation of the cases as they occur. The epidemiological service must be the support upon which all administrative control measures are based, for, without exact knowledge as to the facts concerning the occurrence of the cases, control measures cannot be carried out effectively. Just as the military officer maps his campaign on the basis of reports from the scouting force, so the disease control program rests on epidemiological investigation.

ESSENTIALS OF EPIDEMIOLOGICAL INVESTIGATION

Four factors enter into most investigations.

Knowledge of Disease Characteristics

A sound understanding of the general characteristics of the disease in question is necessary. This is of course possible only if the basic epidemiological facts regarding the usual occurrence of the disease are already known. The investigator should be acquainted with the usual reservoirs of infection, the common modes of spread, and the susceptibility of the various sections of the population. His background will be very limited if the disease is one of obscure etiology, yet he should be familiar with the few known facts as to its occurrence. Lack of familiarity with modern epidemiological concepts may lead to hasty and erroneous conclusions and to much loss of valuable time. Yet this knowledge as to usual occurrence must not blind the investigator to the possibility that factors out of the ordinary may have been operative in this particular instance.

Field Investigation

A careful field investigation should be made of each case. Only by personal investigation of the case can one hope to obtain the answers to the above questions. This requires interview of the patient if possible and of those persons who were so closely associated with the patient as to be aware of his comings and goings. If the patient is too young or too ill to be interviewed, the information supplied by associates will have to suffice, even though it is usually less reliable. All information obtained should be recorded promptly on suitable and uniform record blanks; loose scraps of paper or backs of envelopes should not be used, nor should reliance be placed on personal memory.

Laboratory Tests

Performance of such laboratory tests as will show the presence of infection is an essential part of the investigation. In only a few diseases can clinical judgment be accepted as a reasonable basis for diagnosis; at best it is fraught with personal errors, though it is our sole measure in the absence of suitable laboratory procedures. If such tests are available, they should be utilized lavishly, for in general they are the only thoroughly reliable and acceptable proof of infection, especially of carriers and subclinical cases. Field investigation may readily direct the finger of suspicion at certain individuals most likely to be the source of infection, but the laboratory is required for confirmation. However much one may suspect a certain food handler to be a typhoid carrier, proof rests upon the results of laboratory examination of suitable specimens.

To state that the laboratory is the backbone of epidemiological investigation is no exaggeration. The best field investigator, if deprived of reliable laboratory support, can usually accomplish less than an indifferent investigator supported by a competent laboratory. The latter will bring to light fewer potential sources of infection but will be able to prove those that he uncovers, while the former will too often wallow in a maze of good leads that are never clinched. It is of no use to subject a person to tests in a laboratory not competent to make the required examinations accurately. Adequate laboratory facilities must therefore be developed before attempting epidemiological field studies of communicable diseases, except for those conditions for which suitable tests are not available.[1]

Analysis and Interpretation of Findings

Analysis and interpretation of the findings of the field investigations and the laboratory tests constitute the final step. If the investigation deals with a single case, this interpretation may be relatively simple. If it involves a large number of cases, each with its various contacts, the analysis becomes increasingly complex and requires the use of statistical procedures to appraise the significance of the findings. It frequently involves the calculation of rates as a means of expressing the findings in simple language (see p. 159).

METHOD OF FIELD INVESTIGATION

The field investigation uses the case report as a point of departure.[2] We have already seen (p. 87) that this report comes from the physician or, if none is in attendance, from the householder or other person having knowledge of the case. In the latter instance, investigation of sources and contacts must be preceded by diagnosis so that we may know with what disease we are dealing. This is frequently the task of the health officer or a physician employed for this purpose by the health department. Inasmuch as investigation cannot usually begin until the health department has some knowledge of the existence of the case, speed and promptness of reporting are of utmost importance.

Equally important, however, is promptness of investigation after the case has been reported. For some cases of communicable disease, such as

[1] The above statement should not be interpreted as casting the slightest reflection upon the many excellent epidemiological investigations, such as those of Budd, Snow, and Panum, which were based upon mere recording of observed facts about the occurrence of disease. These investigators came to sound conclusions by the difficult and cumbersome method of deduction of general principles from study of cases. The essential correctness of their conclusions as borne out by later studies bears tribute to their genius. Their deductions would have been more forceful and convincing had they been substantiated by some of the laboratory tests now available but unknown in their day. In studying diseases for which tests are not yet available, we must still rely on general observations alone.

[2] If the health department maintains a bacteriological laboratory, the results of examination of specimens submitted for diagnostic purposes may often give information of a case before the official report has been received, thus permitting prompter investigation.

measles, the period of communicability is so short that, by the time the new victim has been recognized, the source is no longer communicable; yet from the same source there may be other victims who are just entering into the communicable stage and who, if not discovered, may infect others. Such contacts may also require prompt passive immunization to modify or prevent the disease. In other instances, the source is still in a communicable stage and transmitting the infection to other persons. Thus any delay in beginning the investigation may largely defeat its primary purpose, that of preventing further spread.

The field investigation starts with the interview of the case. The epidemiologist must know the incubation period in order to concentrate his attention upon the events occurring about the time when the patient contracted the infection. Similarly, he must be familiar with the period of communicability to determine those persons who may have been effectively exposed to this particular case. So far as possible the interview is carried out by interrogation of the patient, as he is obviously best acquainted with what he has done during the past few days or weeks. It must be remembered, however, that no matter how eagerly the patient may desire to cooperate in the investigation, certain errors are bound to enter. Human memory is notoriously untrustworthy. All of us fail to recall events.[3] If the patient is sufficiently ill, his memory may be inaccurate because of fever. In all cases there is the likelihood that the patient will misunderstand certain questions asked by the interviewer and that the latter in turn may misinterpret the patient's answers. Under certain circumstances the patient may even attempt to conceal essential information, as in the case of the diabetic child who contracted a salmonella infection from eating certain pastry purchased at a neighborhood store. For a long time she denied ever eating this pastry lest she be punished for breaking her dietary regimen. Similar unreliability enters into interviews with patients infected with gonorrhea or syphilis.

These elements of unreliability make it essential that all information be cross-checked as far as possible. In many instances this may be done by asking the same question in a slightly different way or even repeating it some time later in the interview. It is always advisable for the investi-

[3] The authors recall one professor of public health who contracted an intestinal infection from eating chicken salad in a college cafeteria. Until he was specifically asked about this salad, he clung to his story that he had eaten nothing in the cafeteria other than soup, pie, and milk. He forgot that on one unhappy day he had departed from his usual noon lunch and indulged in the salad. We can all test the inadequacies of our memories by trying to recall all of the possible events during the past month which might have led to typhoid infection through food, remembering at the same time that almost any article of food eaten by us during that period might have been the vehicle. See page 170.

gator to report or summarize the information in his own words so that the patient may correct any misconceptions. Information given by other members of the family or associates will serve as a check on accuracy, fill gaps in the patient's memory, and supply details that the patient could not recall. Whenever essential details are obviously lacking, as, for instance, the exact identity of a contact or the exact location of places visited on out-of-town trips, an attempt should be made to learn of persons who can supply the missing information. The investigator must always be careful to avoid leading questions which may tempt the patient to give unreliable answers.

Finally, it should be emphasized that no investigation is complete until the source of the infection has been determined. If no clue as to the source has been discovered, there remains some question that has not yet been asked. A second interview is often desirable to requestion the patient. During the interval, the investigator will have reviewed the information already obtained and may have new questions to ask; similarly, the patient may have thought over the questions asked—or may even have discussed them with the family or visitors—and have recalled items that were omitted. Too often investigations are dropped with a single interview, notation being made that the source cannot be found; yet, if the case is revisited, the solution may be readily discovered.

It must not be inferred, however, that all sources of infection will ever be found. So long as carriers, subclinical infections, and short periods of communicability exist, sources of infection will escape detection. The respiratory contacts that we make in a crowded building or streetcar are too numerous and indefinite to be discernible. We must often accept our inability to discover the source. This chance of inevitable failure should not, however, lead to a hasty acceptance of failure before a reasonable attempt has been made to discover the source.

Conversely, it should not be inferred that detailed and laborious search for sources of infection is always worth while. The time and money at the disposal of a health department are definitely limited and must be stretched to cover many problems, of which the control of communicable disease is but one. Interesting as may be the task of searching for all sources of infection, this cannot be pursued beyond a reasonable limit to the neglect of other matters of equal or even greater importance. Control of communicable diseases is only one of the duties of the health department.

The health officer must in each case decide how far he can afford to go. Obviously he will pursue his search further for a typhoid carrier or an unrecognized case of tuberculosis than he will for a missed case of diphtheria. The former remains communicable for many years and may, if undiscovered, convey the infection to countless persons, while the latter is usually infectious for only a short period of time. The potential danger of overlooking a source of typhoid, tuberculosis, or syphilis is thus far greater than that of missing a case of diphtheria. In most respiratory conditions little value exists in search beyond the close associates of the patient, as our casual respiratory contacts are so numerous that we can obviously recall but a small fraction of them. In many instances, the period of communicability is so short that the source is no longer infectious by the time the disease has developed in the first victim. Finally, it must be recognized that some diseases, such as mumps and chickenpox, are of so little real public health importance that even a casual investigation of all cases is of very questionable value. Good judgment is necessary to decide how far to go with the investigation of any particular case or disease. No arbitrary rules can be set down; decision must rest on the facilities of the health department in question, the frequency and relative importance of a particular disease within a given community, and the existence of other problems that may demand their share of the budget.

Case Histories

Field investigation is facilitated by a printed card or sheet on which the information may be entered. These record forms are of various sizes, shapes, and color and contain a large number of items or questions. So varied are the forms that one might well conclude that no one is satisfied with the form that anyone else has devised. They all, however, have place for certain essential data. These include information that will serve to identify:

1. The patient—name, age, sex, nationality, address, type of disease, occupation, and so forth.
2. The contacts—family roster, visitors (including addresses), place of employment or school, visits away from home, parties, and so forth.
3. Possible vehicles—water, milk, food, and so forth.

In preparing record forms, care should be taken to leave adequate space for entering the desired data and to make the questions clear-cut and not ambiguous. Their use will be facilitated if they are drawn up in such a manner that related topics are grouped and many of the questions so phrased that they may be answered by a "Yes" or "No" or by merely checking the proper item.

Two errors that frequently occur in the use of these record forms should be emphasized. The first is the error of being satisfied as soon as something is written in every blank on the form.[4] The purpose of the blank is to aid the investigator by reminding him of questions to be asked and to make certain that a few essential items are recorded in all cases. It is never intended that the investigator should limit his inquiry to the material on the card. No card could ever be devised that would cover all possible situations. Frequently the most important information must be entered under the general heading of "other items of interest" or "miscellaneous." The record that has merely trite answers in the usual blanks is worth little.

The other error often encountered is assuming that, because a particular blank has been filled, the question has been satisfactorily answered. No item entry is satisfactory unless it enables a third person to visualize the information. To state that a person is a "clerk" is not adequate, as it fails to tell the nature of the work at which the patient was "clerking" or the place of the "clerking." The term "factory worker" fails to tell either the name of the factory or the location of the machine within the factory. Similar caution must be used with respect to addresses. The card should enable a third person to get to the address. All too commonly it is stated that a patient stopped for a meal at a roadside restaurant on a certain highway a few miles from a certain village, when in reality this highway does not run within fifty miles of the village in question. Such information is obviously valueless, even though it does serve to fill all the blanks on the form. The investigator should always ask himself whether or not another person reading the notation on the card could actually go to the address.

Even more pernicious is the tendency to drop the questioning as soon as it can be ascertained that the patient obviously contracted the infection while out-of-town. It may be a satisfaction to the local health officer to know that the infection was not contracted locally; yet to drop the investigation at this point does not help the other community to discover the source, which may still be operative. The authors recall a local health officer who dropped the investigation of a case of typhoid when he found that the patient had been vacationing in another state for two months before becoming ill. What he failed to discover was that the sister with whom the patient had spent her vacation had now come to live with her and was a typhoid carrier. The health officer had actually interviewed the carrier but had been so satisfied to drop the investigation when he

---

[4] Every blank should, however, have some notation made in it, even though it may be inapplicable to the case in question. Unless this is done, the person who later consults the record will not know whether the omission of data was due to carelessness on the part of the investigator or is to be interpreted as a statement that the question was not applicable or the data were not available.

found an infection contracted out-of-town that he failed to discover the source of infection now within his own jurisdiction. Nothing is so dangerous as a smug sense of satisfaction that the disease was not contracted in the home town.

"Running-Down the Leads"

Any well-taken history will reveal countless leads that may be investigated, both as to source of infection and other persons who may have been exposed to the same source or the current case. Considerable judgment is needed in determining how far these leads should be pursued. Obviously it is not worth while to examine every possible lead in every case. A patient who has typhoid fever has eaten food handled by many different persons during the previous month, yet only one of these was a carrier.[5] If he has eaten meals in several large restaurants serving hundreds of patrons daily, are we to examine every food handler in all of these? If a child in a school of one thousand pupils contracts diphtheria, shall we culture every pupil in this school as well as the entire Sunday school and all the neighborhood children who used the same playground? Unless we do all of this, we may miss a possible source of infection, yet the cost of such examinations may be very large.

The funds at the disposal of a health department never permit complete investigation of all cases. It has already been pointed out that a health department must give the greatest protection to the greatest number of people from a given expenditure of money. The funds required for the complete investigation of a single case might be used in another way to give a far greater protection to the public. Just as the health officer must decide whether or not it is worth while even to obtain a careful history on certain cases, so also he must determine to what extent it is practical and efficient to investigate all of the many leads uncovered. This is frequently very difficult and introduces the possibility of differences of opinion. A complete and accurate case history is essential in helping to determine which leads seem most promising and worth while.

It must be emphasized, however, that all items of information should be duly recorded and transmitted to the proper authorities for them to decide as to investigation. If several persons ill with food poisoning give a history of eating at a certain large restaurant, further investigation of this establishment is obviously indicated. Yet this information would not have been obtainable if each of the field investigators had decided to omit the item simply because the restaurant was so large and so many people ate in it. Similarly, a definite responsibility exists on the part of any in-

[5] It is assumed that in this case the vehicle of infection was food.

vestigating agency to transmit to other health departments all possible information that concerns their respective communities. An example will illustrate the importance of this: Persons ill with typhoid in many different states gave histories of riding in a bus that stopped for meals at a particular restaurant in state X. This item of information in a single case occurring in state A, a thousand miles distant, might appear to be of little significance, as this person had obviously eaten at many other restaurants during the trip in question. Similarly, it might appear unimportant in connection with isolated cases in states B, C, or D. Yet when state X received this information from states A, B, C, and D, it would be immediately apparent that this restaurant should be investigated. If states A, B, C, and D had each decided that the information from a single case was too unimportant to transmit to state X, no investigation would have been possible. Every investigating agency has the responsibility for transmitting such information to the proper authorities, as only the latter can determine its true significance. The United States Public Health Service provides special forms which may be used for this purpose. The more common procedure is for the local authorities to notify their own state health department regarding all information affecting other communities. The state authorities deal with other local communities and with other states.

Epidemiological Studies

The investigation of a case or group of cases might be a very drab affair, even though effective as a control measure, if nothing were learned as to the epidemiology of the disease in question. All of our present knowledge of these infections has been derived through investigation; future knowledge will come the same way. The field worker has a remarkably challenging opportunity to learn new information as to the factors governing the occurrence of these diseases. He must be constantly alert for new facts and be ready to modify his concepts in accordance with them. All data gathered should be recorded with the same attempt at accuracy as measurements of the physical or chemical laboratory. Although they may appear to be of little immediate consequence, these records in their aggregate may contain a wealth of valuable data. The routine field records gathered under the distinguished direction of the late Dr. Charles V. Chapin in Providence during the early part of the twentieth century contain information which has materially altered and shaped our epidemiological concepts and control practices. Special records may at times be incorporated in the epidemiological investigation of cases, or special visits may be paid to certain types of cases. Although a health department should not neglect its regular control duties in favor of these interesting special studies, it should equally avoid the stagnation that results from neglecting the research opportunities present in some of the routine visits.

Personnel for Epidemiological Investigation

The health officer is responsible for the epidemiological investigations. On the other hand, no busy health officer, responsible for the direction of the entire health program of his community, can make personal visits to all cases in which epidemiological data are being gathered. Much of the routine information can be collected by the public health nurse in the course of her visits for instruction or bedside care. The better her understanding of the diseases, the purpose of the investigation, and the reason for each item on the record blank, the more valuable will be the information which she collects. All her data should be placed before the health officer,[6] who must then decide what further investigation, if any, is needed and what special administrative measures are indicated. In dealing with some diseases, such as gonorrhea and syphilis, the nurse may at times be more effective in obtaining essential information than is the health officer, as she is usually looked upon as one giving assistance and aid in time of need, while the health officer is too often eyed with suspicion as an agent of the law. The health officer—or in large departments the specially trained epidemiologists—must assume personal responsibility for the more difficult and complicated investigations which entail more extensive medical and bacteriological knowledge. The local health department must often turn to the state health department for assistance in such problems; and the state may even turn to the federal agency, as the larger unit is apt to have more highly specialized personnel. Through its Communicable Disease Center in Atlanta, Georgia, the United States Public Health Service is able to provide highly expert assistance in both field and laboratory investigations. Regardless of the person who makes the investigation, all personnel having any contact with the case should be constantly alert for any relevant information and should transmit it to the health officer.

THE USE OF LABORATORY TESTS

It has already been pointed out that the laboratory provides tests which serve to confirm clinical diagnoses. Only through such tests can we be certain of sources of infection. If the patient is in a hospital

---

[6] In large cities where the health department is organized in divisions, the director of the division of communicable diseases is responsible for direction and supervision of these investigations. The health officer of the average county or small city must assume personal responsibility.

equipped with an adequate laboratory, testing is relatively simple, as the specimens can be collected by trained personnel and the material incubated immediately. In field investigations, however, we must often rely on the individual or the family for the collection of the specimen and must submit it to a laboratory many miles distant. This introduces the possibility of many errors.

Collection of the Sample

The successful performance of any laboratory test begins with the selection of the material to be examined. As far as possible, the sample should be obtained by the field investigator, who can be carefully trained as to the pitfalls to be avoided. If the collection must be entrusted to a member of the family, very detailed instructions as to quantity and mode of collection must be given. It must also be remembered that unless the sample can be collected by the investigator, he cannot be certain as to its authenticity. While the vast majority of the public is honest and reliable, certain individuals do not hesitate to submit false specimens, especially if these individuals realize that they are suspected of being carriers. Unfortunately there is no way of guaranteeing the authenticity of such specimens unless they have been collected under supervision. Certain states provide for hospitalization of suspected persons so that suitable specimens may be collected.

Submission of Specimens to the Laboratory

The use of laboratories distant from the field of investigation introduces further chances of error. Microorganisms may die in transit, antibodies be destroyed, or blood be hemolyzed. In order to facilitate shipment under the most favorable circumstances, special specimen containers are usually provided. These often contain chemicals that will preserve organisms or reduce the overgrowth of other bacteria. In other instances the culture containers may contain special selective media. Such tubes are useful only if recently prepared so that the culture medium has not become dried. If used, they must be replaced regularly to maintain a supply of fresh tubes. Containers with special media are especially useful for specimens submitted to a distant laboratory. The postal authorities have facilitated shipment by providing for the pouching of such material with the first-class mail, though the specimens are carried at cheaper rates. Definite regulations exist, however, as to the construction of containers in order to guard against breakage which may damage the mail and endanger the postal clerks. All specimen containers designed for shipment through the mail should be carefully checked to ensure compliance with the postal regulations.

The submission of specimens by mail is, however, a slow process under the best of conditions. As organisms may have died in transit, negative results have even less value than is ordinarily attached to them. Often the manner of tests must be modified to meet these unfavorable conditions. In other instances the test is of such a nature that it cannot be adapted to "long-distance" performance since it requires the actual participation of the person tested. In such instances it becomes necessary to provide for bringing the laboratory and the individual more closely together. Examinations for the vegetative form of the *Entameba histolytica* are best performed at the bedside. Similarly dark-field examinations for spirochetes are best performed if the patient is brought directly to the laboratory.[7] In the investigation of some outbreaks, emergency portable laboratories have been established. In general, the smaller the gap between the patient and the laboratory, the better; but this must not be at the sacrifice of quality. Highly skilled personnel at a distant laboratory are usually more effective than unskilled technicians in small local laboratories attempting to carry on tests for which they are not equipped and with which they are not familiar. The slight loss in efficiency due to transit is more than made up by the reliance that can be placed on the findings of competent personnel.

EVALUATION OF THE DATA

The primary purpose of all epidemiological investigation of cases of communicable disease is the discovery of other persons who are infected. These persons may be the sources of the original case, the victims of the same source, or the victims of the case that occasioned the investigation. Regardless of their classification, they are all sources of potential spread to other persons as long as they are in an infectious condition. Yet the question frequently arises in actual practice whether a given person is the source of a particular case or merely another victim of a common source. If, in the investigation of typhoid fever following a banquet, one of the food handlers is found to be infected but devoid of symptoms, can we

[7] In the x-ray examination of contacts with a case of tuberculosis, the individual may either be taken to a hospital or a portable machine taken to the home or place of employment. In such instances the element of time does not enter as in the case of tests involving bacteriological cultures; yet the same consideration of skill in both the exposure of the plate and its interpretation are of great importance. Many places provide for the use of local x-ray facilities for the taking of the picture but submit the films to a distant specialist for their interpretation. Portable machines are at times used in rather highly organized programs under the direction of full-time personnel.

conclude that this person is a healthy carrier who infected the food or is a victim of the outbreak but so slightly ill as to be free of recognizable symptoms? If, in the course of an outbreak of streptococcal infection associated with a raw-milk route, a milker is found who carries the streptococci in his throat, are we to conclude that he is the source of the infection or may he not have acquired it through drinking the milk?

Obviously there is no simple or certain answer to such questions. Inasmuch as no bacteriological investigation of the person prior to the outbreak has been made, we can only guess as to whether or not he was the cause or part of the effect. We can never be absolutely certain that the infection was spread from this source, for no one saw the organisms pass into the food or other vehicle. The most we can say is that the circumstances were such that if the person in question had been infected prior to the outbreak, he could have been its source. If the person gives a history of prior and especially recent infection with this particular organism, the likelihood of being a carrier source rather than a new victim is of course greatly enhanced. Yet even under such circumstances we cannot overlook the possibility that the finding of this person's infection was merely an accident incidental to the investigation. The newer methods of typing of certain organisms will help in some of these problems but will never solve all of them.[8] The best that we can ever do is to indicate what seems to be the most likely source of the infection.

At the same time we must be cautious to avoid too hasty conclusions that a possible source is in reality the most likely source. The authors recall an instance in which a local health officer, after finding that the patient had drunk from a polluted water supply, dropped all further investigation of a case of typhoid. When the inquiry was pushed further, the patient was found to have eaten at the home of a friend whose mother was discovered to be a typhoid carrier. Under such circumstances one may well ask which was the source of infection. This is very much an academic question. Certainly had the investigation been dropped with the assumption that the infection was due to water, this carrier would have remained undiscovered and might have infected others. The important thing is to find as many sources of infection as possible lest they infect others. It is of less moment to debate whether this particular person is the source or victim of the outbreak. In either case the individual is infected and may well transmit that infection to others unless suitable precautions are observed.

---

[8] In epidemiologic studies, isolation of pneumococci, streptococci, meningococci, salmonellae, or dysentery bacilli is of very little value unless the organism is identified as to type.

Determination of Vehicle of Spread

In the investigation of certain outbreaks associated with articles of food or drink, it is frequently necessary to determine whether or not the simultaneous occurrence of several cases in association with this food is mere chance or is causally related. Frequently this may involve certain statistical procedures, for the study of which the reader is referred to a good textbook on statistical reasoning. In most instances simple logic rather than detailed statistics will suffice. Let us suppose that 10 cases of typhoid fever occur in a town of 1,000 persons. If one milk dealer supplied 90 per cent of the milk in this town, we would expect that at least 9 and possibly all 10 of the cases might occur among his customers, even if the true source of the infection was the water supply. If, however, all of them were on the route of one of the other dealers who supplied only 5 per cent of the total (50 persons), we might readily conclude that the milk supply was probably involved. If the only thing distinguishing those 50 from the 950 other inhabitants is that the former use a different milk supply, it is extremely unlikely [9] that all of the cases should have occurred among them by mere accident and not through association with the milk.

A Few Statistical Measurements of Disease

In any epidemiological study involving more than a few cases, various measurements become necessary to indicate the magnitude of the several forces of infection. The simplest type of measurement would be merely to count the number of cases and deaths due to a particular disease. While this may indicate the actual quantity of infection, it gives no impression as to the relative frequency, inasmuch as it neglects the number of persons potentially exposed, that is, the population at risk. One hundred cases of measles in a city of 1,000,000 people constitutes a small number of cases, yet the same number in a city of 10,000 population may mean a high incidence. In order to make comparisons, these data are expressed in terms of incidents per population at risk. This means converting the data into terms of rates, which are merely ratios. In the former city there were 100 cases per 1,000,000 people or a rate of 1 case per 10,000 population; in the latter, 100 cases per 10,000 population. Thus measles is 100 times as prevalent in the latter community as in the former.

The rates that are most commonly used by health departments in the course of the communicable disease control program are as follows:

Morbidity Rate. This is the number of cases of disease per unit population during a given period of time, usually expressed as cases per 100,000

[9] About one chance in 10,000,000,000,000,000.

population per year. Ordinarily morbidity rates are calculated for specific diseases, such as typhoid fever or diphtheria. These are referred to as cause-specific rates. Morbidity rates are occasionally referred to as case rates; the terms are synonymous. They indicate the incidence of the disease in question.

Mortality Rate. This represents the number of deaths per unit population during a given period of time. When we calculate the general death rate of a community, we count all the deaths from all causes during a year, usually in terms of 1,000 population. This is also referred to as the crude death rate. Often we are more interested in the death rate due to a particular disease. This is known as a cause-specific death rate and is usually calculated in terms of 100,000 population. Thus the scarlet fever mortality or death rate is the number of deaths due to scarlet fever per 100,000 population per year.

Case Fatality Rate. This represents the likelihood of dying if a person contracts a certain disease. Calculated in terms of percentage, it measures the proportion of those who develop a disease and who die of it. Thus if 1,000 persons contract typhoid fever and 100 die, the case fatality rate is 10 per cent. If in some other community only 100 cases occur yet 10 die, the case fatality rate is also 10 per cent. If both communities are of the same size, the typhoid morbidity and mortality rates of the former are ten times those of the latter, yet the case fatality rates are the same. This rate is often referred to merely as the fatality rate.

Attack Rate. This is merely another term for morbidity rate but is usually used to refer to a smaller sample of the population exposed to a greater risk than is the general population. Thus we speak of the secondary attack rate of diphtheria to refer to the incidence of the disease among those in contact with cases of diphtheria. Attack rates are usually expressed in terms of percentage.

Special Rates. Any of the above rates may be calculated in terms of special groups rather than for an entire population at risk. Thus we might calculate the death rate for diphtheria among male children three years of age. Such a rate would be referred to as a cause-, age-, and sex-specific rate.

Incidence vs. Prevalence. Considerable confusion has been created by failure to appreciate the difference in meaning of the terms "incidence" and "prevalence." Although many persons think of them as synonymous, to the epidemiologist each has a special connotation. The term "incidence" refers to the number of persons newly attacked by a particular disease within a given period of time, whereas the term "prevalence" is a measure of the number of persons who are suffering from a disease at a given moment of time. For example, in a given community there may be 100 new cases of tuberculosis discovered in a given year. These represent the incidence of tuberculosis. Yet a tuberculosis survey of that community may show 1,000 persons to be suffering from the disease; the latter represent the prevalence of tuberculosis. Conversely fifty cases of diphtheria may occur during a year in a certain city; yet the largest number known to exist on any one day of the year is eight, while during the summer the city is at times completely free of known infections. In this instance, the incidence of diphtheria is fifty cases per year but the prevalence varies from eight to zero. The incidence of chronic infections such as tuberculosis or syphilis is always less than the prevalence, whereas the incidence of acute short term infections is higher than the prevalence.

EPIDEMIOLOGICAL SURVEYS

It has already been pointed out that the purpose of the investigation of a case of communicable disease is to find other sources of infection. In some instances it seems preferable to embark upon a general community-wide program of case-finding rather than to wait for the development of infection which leads to the discovery of new sources. The survey method entails the routine examination of a large group of persons among whom infected individuals are suspected. The number of infected persons so discovered will obviously be less per hundred persons examined than in the case of intimate contacts who have had greater opportunity for acquiring or transmitting the infection. The survey method is therefore more expensive per case discovered but will reveal sources otherwise overlooked until at a later date when they infect an associate.

Selection of the group to be surveyed is important. Were money no consideration, one would examine the entire population. Since this is obviously not possible at present, selection is made on the basis of what is already known regarding the occurrence and distribution of infection. This may be on the basis of age, race, economic circumstances, or employment. If searching for tuberculosis, one would expect to find more cases per unit population in a group of adults from the economically poorer and crowded section of a city than in a group of grade school children from the wealthy class. Similarly, more cases could be expected in workers exposed to a silica hazard than among office personnel. A higher prevalence of hookworm would be found among rural agricultural workers than among urban factory employees. The worthwhileness of any survey as a means of case-finding depends on the care with which the group is selected.

In general, the survey is effective only in dealing with diseases in which the period of communicability is long and for which a suitable diagnostic test is relatively simply performed. Search for unrecognized cases of tuberculosis, syphilis, hookworm, or even for typhoid carriers may be worth while, inasmuch as the patient will remain communicable for a long period of time. Yet a survey for measles would be of little value, as those found would be noninfectious in a few days, while many of those apparently not infected at the moment may be in the most communicable stage in a few days. Unless there is a simple and reliable test, however, surveys would be prohibitively expensive.[10] The use of the tuberculin test and the x-ray makes tuberculosis surveys possible; the use of the serological examination is the foundation for syphilis surveys. In the absence of comparable tests for gonorrhea a survey is hardly practical. In some instances tests exist which are too expensive or complicated for use on large population groups but which can be applied to relatively small selected groups. For example, examination of stool specimens for amebic dysentery is too expensive to be applied to all the population or even to all food handlers but has been used for small groups of kitchen workers among whom there appeared to be a special risk or a likelihood of high infection rate.

In addition to their value in finding potential sources of infection for others, surveys have the further purpose of discovering patients who have passed the stage of communicability but if untreated might suffer later debilitating effects from their infection. While their discovery does not contribute to the reduction of spread, it serves to minimize the ultimate consequences of their disease and, therefore, to reduce the economic toll. Surveys to discover syphilis and hookworm may have this purpose in addition to their value in determining potential sources of further infection.

A third purpose of a survey is as a measure of the extent of the problem within a given community. The formulation of a control program depends on knowing where, when, and under what conditions the disease is occurring. Thus one may wish to know the extent of malarial infection to determine the need of mosquito-control measures or the relative prevalence of tuberculosis in various population groups in order to guide the development of diagnostic and treatment facilities. A case-finding survey which merely samples the community or group in question is adequate to give a measure of the disease. The cases found in the course of such a sampling survey should naturally be dealt with appropriately, but no attempt

[10] It should be emphasized that a laboratory test does not establish a diagnosis. Correct diagnosis depends upon interpretation of the tests in the light of clinical manifestations. The test is merely a convenient screen for selecting those who should be subjected to careful clinical study.

should be made to find all possible cases. Frequently cheaper and more effective control measures may be appropriate after the extent of the problem has been determined.

It should be emphasized that the survey is the most expensive form of case-finding, as it means examination of so many persons in order to find the infected. The worth-whileness of it therefore depends on the rate of infection within the group surveyed and the funds at the disposal of the health department. If the infection rate is fairly high and the disease of major economic importance, a survey may be of real value. If it is low and other more important health problems are neglected because of lack of funds, one may well question the propriety of a survey. Surveys spread more or less indiscriminately over a large population must never be used to the neglect of epidemiological case-finding methods that start from known infection and work outward to embrace the intimate contacts or to the neglect of provision of facilities to deal with cases already known.

SUGGESTED READINGS

Chapin, Charles V.: "The Science of Epidemic Diseases," *Scient. Monthly*, 26:481–93, (June) 1928. Reprinted in Papers of Charles V. Chapin: *The Principles of Epidemiology*. New York: Commonwealth Fund, 1934, pp. 172–205.

"Epidemiology," *The Commonhealth*, Vol. 20, No. 3, (July, Aug., Sept.) 1933. Boston: Massachusetts Department of Health.

Frost, Wade Hampton: "Epidemiology," in *Nelson Loose-Leaf Preventive Medicine and Public Health*. New York: Thomas Nelson & Sons, 1928, II, 163–90.

———: Papers of: *An Exposition of the Epidemiological Method,* edited by Kenneth F. Maxcy. New York: Commonwealth Fund, 1941.

Godfrey, Edward S.: "Epidemiology," in Park, William H.: *Public Health and Hygiene,* 2nd ed. Philadelphia: Lea & Febiger, 1928, pp. 239–59.

Hill, A. Bradford: *Principles of Medical Statistics,* 3rd ed. London: The Lancet, Ltd., 1945.

MacPhillips, Julia: "The Principles of Case Finding," *Ven. Dis. Inform.,* 18:315–18, (Sept.) 1937.

Savage, Sir William: *Practical Public Health Problems,* 2nd ed. London: J. & A. Churchill, Ltd., 1949, pp. 67–77, 130–60.

Smith, Dudley C., and Brumfield, William A.: "Tracing the Transmission of Syphilis," *J.A.M.A.,* 101:1955–57, (Dec. 16) 1933.

Smith, Geddes: *Plague on Us.* New York: Commonwealth Fund, 1941.

Snow, John: *On the Mode of Communication of Cholera.* London: John Churchill, 1855. Out of print. Reprinted with other papers of John Snow: *Snow on Cholera.* New York: Commonwealth Fund, 1936.

Stallybrass, C. O.: *The Principles of Epidemiology and the Process of Infection.* New York: Macmillan Co., 1931.

Walker, W. F., and Randolph, Carolina R.: *Recording of Local Health Work.* New York: Commonwealth Fund, 1935.

Part Two

10. Typhoid and Paratyphoid Fever

TYPHOID FEVER

Typhoid fever is a febrile condition, the acute stages of which usually last from a few days to several weeks. Relapses frequently occur. The causative organisms appear in the blood stream during the early stages but can rarely be found there after the second week, when the infection localizes in the lymphoid tissue of the intestine (Peyer's patches), the gallbladder, kidneys, and occasionally the bones, cartilages, and meninges. About 10 per cent of the patients die, frequently as a result of intestinal hemorrhage or perforation due to necrosis of the infected lymphoid tissue.

EPIDEMIOLOGY

Occurrence. Typhoid fever is found in all countries and climates. In the United States the highest incidence is in the South, especially in the smaller communities. Cases occur at all seasons but are most common during the summer. Though all ages may be attacked, the highest incidence is in the late teens and early twenties; cases are rare in persons over sixty. Males are somewhat more frequently infected than are females.

Etiological Agent. Typhoid fever is due to infection with the typhoid bacillus (*Salmonella typhosa*), a Gram-negative, nonsporulating, rodlike organism. The bacillus multiplies in milk and other foods that are not too acid; it may live for over a month in butter and cheese. It does not multiply in water but dies in a few weeks, and in about a week in carbonated beverages. It survives freezing but is readily destroyed by the usual disinfecting processes, including pasteurization. Typhoid bacilli can be divided into several types through the use of bacteriophage technique. Type determination is valuable in epidemiological studies, such as tracing the connection of carriers with cases or selecting the cases which, though occurring coincidentally with an outbreak in a community, may none the less be causally unrelated. Thus, if a case yields bacilli of a different type from those isolated from the majority of the patients, we may be certain that it is of different origin.

Reservoir of Infection. Man is the only species attacked by the typhoid bacillus under natural conditions. The reservoir of infection thus consists of two parts, the cases and the carriers. The former group is usually not large, depending upon the current prevalence of the disease and therefore varying greatly in size according to the community and the season of the year. Formerly the cases were much more frequent as sources of infection than they are at present.

Carriers may be divided into the convalescent and the chronic or permanent types. The dividing lines between the case and the convalescent carrier and between the convalescent and the permanent carrier are obviously not distinct and are usually determined by arbitrary decisions. The convalescent carrier stage is generally considered to begin with the final disappearance of acute symptoms—other than the residual debility—and to pass into the chronic stage one year after infection. About 2 to 4 per cent of those who have been infected become permanent carriers.[1] The percentage of those who continue to shed the organisms in convalescence decreases with the lapse of time, but after a year it is very rare for the carrier state to cease without surgical removal of the focus of infection.

The site of growth of the organisms in the permanent carrier is usually one of four places:

1. *The gallbladder* is the usual site, accounting for about 90 to 95 per cent of all carriers. There is always some inflammation of the gallbladder; stones are usually present if the carrier condition has persisted more than a year. The infection frequently involves other parts of the biliary tract, so that cure of the carrier condition, while usually accomplished through gallbladder removal, is not always obtained.

2. *Intestine.* Fecal carriers whose bile is apparently sterile may be encountered. Occasionally this is due to improper collection of the bile, but in other instances one must assume that the organisms are growing elsewhere along the intestine, possibly in the lumen of the appendix, in diverticula, or even free in the intestine.

3. *Kidney.* Chronic infection of the renal pelvis, often accompanied by the presence of stones, may result in a urinary carrier condition. Before concluding that the infection is located along the urinary tract, it is advisable to obtain a catheter specimen of urine, especially in the female.

---

[1] Most of the earlier figures of 10 per cent were based on a time period of three months after infection. The excellent studies of Havens in Alabama showed over 10 per cent after one year, but these figures have not been equaled by other observers.

4. *Fistulas.* Typhoid abscesses, usually in the rib cartilages, are among the unusual complications of the disease. In such cases the infection may burrow out to the skin, creating draining sinuses which persist until cured by operation.

Patients of all ages may become permanent carriers. The authors have encountered one as young as four years of age, who persisted as such until, at the age of nine, the gallbladder containing a large stone was removed. Although it is frequently stated that women are more apt to be carriers than are men, the sex difference is not so great as is commonly believed. Most of those discovered as sources of infection are women, because of their greater association with food handling; but, if only those who develop the carrier condition as the outcome of an observed attack are considered, the sex difference is less marked.

So dramatic have been the stories of a few carriers that it has often been assumed that all carriers are slovenly, careless persons who leave a trail of infection in their wake. The true situation is quite the opposite. Many carriers apparently never infect anyone, while others go for years without transmitting the disease. Consideration of the sequence of events leading to infection through food will explain this apparent anomaly. For infection to occur on a given day, (1) the carrier must discharge viable organisms, (2) contaminate the hands at the time of going to the toilet, (3) fail to cleanse the hands adequately, (4) handle food before the organisms have died on the hands; (5) the food must be eaten without such cooking as will destroy the infection and (6) must be eaten in adequate quantity by (7) a susceptible person. Each of these events depends largely upon chance. Thus even if the hands are contaminated with viable organisms, the bacilli may die in the several hours that elapse before the carrier handles food; or the food first handled may be that which is thoroughly cooked. The probability of any single event's happening is very variable. The probability of all events happening simultaneously is the product of the individual chances and therefore quite slight. Thus it happens that carriers have been known to work for years in a food-handling capacity without causing infection. This does not mean that a carrier can be safely employed, for there is chance of infection at any time; but it does mean that we cannot assume a person is not a carrier merely because he has handled food for years without causing infection.

Escape from the reservoir is usually with the feces or urine, depending upon the focus of infection. In the acute case, the bacilli do not appear in the discharges until about the third week of the disease. Although in urinary infections a fairly constant escape of the organisms occurs, there is some intermittency in the discharge of viable bacteria in the feces of either the case or the carrier. Some of this may be more apparent than real, because of the imperfections of laboratory tests (see p. 46). If there is a draining sinus, the organisms will be found in the discharge. There is no evidence that they may escape in the saliva or milk of the case or carrier. Thus a carrier may safely nurse her offspring but must be very cautious in the preparation of supplemental feedings.

Transmission to new hosts may be either directly or through the medium of a vehicle that becomes contaminated with the infectious discharges.

Direct transmission occurs through soiling of the hands of the new victim, the fingers conveying the bacilli to the mouth. It is seen most frequently in persons caring for cases or debilitated carriers, the hands being contaminated during the nursing attention, especially if the infection is not recognized and special precautions not observed. Immunization of all nursing and household contacts has reduced the secondary attack rate among such persons.

Indirect transmission is more common and important, being responsible for the community spread of the disease. The most important vehicles of infection are food (including shellfish), water, milk, and flies. Fomites are involved less commonly and usually only if there is also rather direct contact between the source and the victim.

1. *Food* is probably the principal vehicle under present circumstances. Food is most commonly contaminated by a missed case or carrier who is employed as a food handler and who transmits the infection to the food from his hands, accidentally soiled at the time of going to the toilet. Any food may serve as a vehicle, provided it has sufficient moisture to keep the bacteria alive for a brief period, is not too acid, and is not thoroughly heated to a high enough temperature between infection and ingestion. As food is a notoriously poor conductor of heat, temperatures that may thoroughly cook or even burn the surface may barely warm the interior and may even incubate bacteria centrally located. We have encountered infection spread by croquettes prepared by a carrier and fried in deep fat yet kept at this high temperature only long enough to brown the outer surface and not kill the bacteria in the center. The more intimately the hands of the worker come in contact with the food, the greater the opportunity of infection. Unfortunately, direct handling of food is inevitable and occurs more frequently than is ordinarily recognized.

2. *Shellfish.* Among the foods that have been important vehicles for spread of typhoid, shellfish occupy a prominent role. They are usually infected during growth or storage in polluted water, though occasionally through direct contamination by the hands of the person who opens them.

The mollusk drinks large quantities of water daily and concentrates in its gastrointestinal tract some of the organisms in the water. As the entire body is usually eaten, often without cooking, infection of the consumer readily takes place if the shellfish was infected. Typhoid fever spread by shellfish, though still occurring, is relatively rare today because of greatly improved sanitation of the industry.

3. *Water.* Formerly the principal vehicle, water was responsible for the tremendous outbreaks and widespread prevalence of typhoid during the last century. The rapid development of urban communities following the industrial revolution of the early nineteenth century created a need for public water supplies. These were usually grossly polluted, since water was not recognized as a vehicle for the spread of disease. Hence typhoid fever became more widespread when public water supplies replaced wells, for the former were almost invariably polluted whereas only a few of the wells or springs had typhoid contamination. With the recognition of the spread of disease through water, as shown by Budd and by Snow in England, and the development of methods of water purification, the number of cases spread through water began to decline during the end of the last century until the point has now been reached at which water is apparently a minor vehicle of typhoid in the United States. The remarkable decline in total typhoid incidence has been due in major part to this elimination of water-borne infection. This in turn has resulted in fewer carriers and thus fewer sources from which infection may spread by means of water or other vehicles. The number of carriers is still so large, however, that water-borne typhoid may recur if the sanitary safeguards for the water supplies are neglected. Several communities have learned this to their sorrow during recent years. Contamination of water occurs through pollution with sewage from typhoid cases or carriers. As typhoid bacilli do not multiply in water, it is virtually impossible to discover them, even in highly contaminated specimens. Consequently, any water contaminated with sewage, as shown by the presence of the colon bacillus, is potentially dangerous, as it may contain the organisms of typhoid or other intestinal infections—such as paratyphoid, cholera, or bacillary or amebic dysentery—depending upon the infections present in the communities from which the sewage is derived. Although most municipal water supplies in the United States are comparatively safe today, there is still room for their improvement. Private supplies are frequently open to contamination.

4. *Milk.* Like water, milk is less important as a vehicle today than formerly, largely because of improvements in milk sanitation, especially pasteurization. The milk is usually contaminated directly by a missed case or carrier, chiefly during the process of milking or bottling. In some in-

stances, typhoid has been spread through utensils rinsed in polluted water or even through milk watered from a polluted source. Cows do not contract typhoid fever nor do they pass typhoid bacilli in the milk even if they drink contaminated water; but, if the cow wades or lies in sewage, the surface of the udder may be contaminated and particles of infection drop into the pail at the time of milking, unless special care is observed. Typhoid bacilli are readily destroyed by pasteurization, though careless handling of the milk afterward has occasionally caused infection. Milk-borne typhoid is, therefore, confined almost exclusively to raw-milk routes and hence to rural areas and the smaller cities.

5. *Flies* may transfer typhoid bacilli from sewage to food by carrying the bacteria on their feet. In communities where there is adequate disposal of sewage, flies cannot pick up the infection and, therefore, no matter how numerous or bothersome, cannot transmit typhoid. They still present a problem in military camps, rural areas, or other places where sewage is disposed of through privies or similar primitive methods.

Entry and Incubation Period. Typhoid bacilli almost invariably enter the body through the mouth, whither they are transmitted by contaminated food or drink. The only exception is the rare instance in which infection has been introduced per rectum through rectal or enema tubes inadequately sterilized after use on a typhoid case or carrier.[2] The incubation period varies from 3 to 40 days, usually 10 to 17. In general, waterborne infection has a rather long incubation period, milk infection shorter, and food the shortest. This variability frequently makes it difficult to decide whether one case is secondary to another or possibly infected at the same time from the same source.

Susceptibility. There is no natural resistance to typhoid fever or development of resistance other than through infection or artificial or latent immunization. The latter depends upon opportunities for infection. It is quite apparent in those who have lived in close association with carriers over a period of years and, even though not artificially immunized, have escaped recognizable infection. Such contacts later resist infection which attacks others not previously in equally close association with the carrier. Thus if a carrier infection occurs within the home, the victim is usually the casual visitor or the new member of the family circle rather than one who has been in the household for several years.

There is no simple test for resistance. The Widal test is evidence of infection but does not measure resistance. Recently devised methods, based

---

[2] Mere immersion in disinfectant does not sterilize, even if the mucus has been removed with soap and water; since the solution is held out by the entrapped air, it fails to enter the inside of the tube. All such tubes should be washed and then boiled before use on another patient.

on the use of human serum to protect mice against intracranial injection of typhoid bacilli, yield satisfactory results but are not adapted to routine use.

PARATYPHOID FEVERS

These infections are due to *Salmonella paratyphi A* (*Bacillus paratyphosus A*) and *Salmonella schottmülleri* (*S. paratyphi B, Bacillus paratyphosus B*), organisms which are closely allied to the typhoid bacillus and distinguishable only by serological and fermentation reactions. The diseases frequently resemble typhoid fever so closely that they are differentiated only by laboratory tests.

Paratyphoid A is quite uncommon in this country, the incidence of cases as compared with that of typhoid and paratyphoid B being markedly less than in Europe. The infection very closely simulates typhoid fever though the case fatality rate is somewhat lower. The epidemiological aspects and the control measures are identical with those of typhoid.

Paratyphoid B is distinctly more prevalent and, because of the frequency of mild atypical cases, is more difficult to control. Infection may appear as a febrile illness resembling typhoid, though with a much lower case fatality rate, or as an acute but short-lived condition resembling so-called "food poisoning." The latter sometimes merges into the more prolonged febrile type. The incubation period may be as short as 24 hours, although usually a few days. Many of the infections are so mild that the patient fails to seek medical attention for what appears to be a transient diarrhea of one or two days' duration or merely a fleeting febrile disturbance with malaise. Routine cultures of the family contacts of such cases may show that as many as 25 per cent of the household are infected, though usually without symptoms. The acute cases continue as convalescent carriers somewhat longer than in the case of typhoid. Because of the frequency of unrecognized cases, the true incidence of infection is not known; official morbidity reports unquestionably give a gross underestimate of the true prevalence of the disease.

Control is particularly difficult as so many of the patients fail to suspect the nature of their illness and rely on self-medication (or no medication), while many who seek medical care are dismissed with prescriptions for a diarrhea, though no bacteriological tests have been made. If routine cultures were made of all cases of diarrhea, many unrecognized cases of paratyphoid B and of bacillary dysentery would be brought to light. Control measures are the same as for typhoid, though they are distinctly less effective. If vaccines are to be used for prophylaxis, one must make certain that they contain the paratyphoid components. This was formerly true when the triple vaccine was almost universally used. Today some of the vaccine is monovalent and contains neither the A nor B fraction. While there is apparently some cross-protection in the typhoid-paratyphoid group, this cannot be relied upon for protection, though it confuses the interpretation of Widal tests in many instances.

CONTROL MEASURES FOR TYPHOID AND PARATYPHOID

Control of Spread

The case of typhoid fever [3] should be sufficiently segregated to prevent the infectious discharges from reaching other persons. This means modified isolation with special attention to disinfection of feces and urine. During the acute stages, the patient is usually ill enough to require bed care; in the convalescent stages he may be ambulatory. Such convalescents are safely permitted freedom of the home and even of the community so long as they do not handle food or come in contact with other articles that may spread infection. They should in all cases be kept under supervision by the health department until bacteriological examinations of stool and urine specimens (release specimens) have shown that the patient is no longer shedding typhoid bacilli. Regulations differ as to the number of specimens required before release of the patient from official supervision. The usual minimum is three consecutive negative stool and urine specimens at a one-week interval, the first obtained not earlier than one month after the onset. Experience shows this number to be inadequate, certain carriers being overlooked on this basis. One state attempts to obtain a specimen every month for a year after infection. The longer the stools are positive after recovery, the more specimens should be required before concluding that the patient is no longer a carrier. As a carrier who is overlooked may cause serious outbreaks and, if unrecognized, may spread infection over many years, it is safer to err in requiring too many release specimens than too few.

Epidemiological investigation should be directed toward discovery of the source of the infection and other victims. In obtaining the case history, attention should be given to places where the patient has eaten during the past month. Special note should be made of the sources of delicatessen and dairy products, shellfish, and water. Stool and urine specimens should be obtained from all members of the patient's household, as well as friends and relatives who may have handled food eaten by the

---

[3] To avoid needless duplication, this discussion of control measures has been written merely in terms of typhoid. All parts of it are equally applicable to paratyphoid.

patient. The decision as to culturing of employees of restaurants and similar food-handling establishments will depend on the nature of the patient's history. All information regarding meals out-of-town should be sent to the state health department for transmission to the proper local authorities. Examination of suspected water supplies is often valuable as it may reveal the presence of sewage contamination; there is nothing to be learned from bacteriological examination of either food or milk samples.

Contacts of a case of typhoid do not require quarantine. Certain of them may, however, develop the infection, and others show a transient carrier condition. It is therefore desirable to keep all contacts out of a food-handling occupation until the maximum incubation period has elapsed since the date of last contact with the patient and until repeated stool and urine specimens have been found to be negative for typhoid bacilli. The incidence of secondary cases may be greatly reduced by prompt immunization of all family contacts.

Carriers must refrain from handling food for the consumption of others, except those members of their immediate families who have been recently immunized. This exception, while theoretically undesirable, is necessary in practice, as it is usually economically impossible for a carrier to stay out of her own kitchen. All carriers should, however, be forbidden employment in public food-handling capacities and be warned against preparing food for friends. They should be meticulous about hand-washing after going to the toilet, especially if the hands become soiled. Separate towels should be used. If these simple precautions are observed, carriers may live normal lives and be safely employed at other types of work.[4] There is no menace from money, books, and other fomites handled by carriers. Health departments should keep records of all known carriers and visit them periodically to make certain that they are observing these precautions. Carriers are often asked to sign agreements to refrain from food handling and to notify the health department of all changes of address. It is essential that all information of this character be held strictly confidential, as the public fear of a carrier is such as to result in social ostracism or loss of employment if the condition is known. While this is an unwarranted phobia, it is none the less real.

Carriers who know no occupation other than food handling [5] present serious problems, which are often met by subsidy or operation. As the subsidy usually fails to equal the wages earned prior to discovery of the carrier condition, such carriers have at times broken their agreements and

---

[4] The health department may at times have to assist the carrier in finding suitable employment.

[5] Domestic service almost always leads ultimately to some form of food handling, and farming involves dairying.

thus caused further cases. Although gallbladder removal cannot be forced upon the carrier nor be recommended indiscriminately, yet under suitable circumstances as to age, operative risk, and proved infection as shown by biliary drainage, it can be advised both to cure the carrier condition and to avoid the likelihood of later serious illness due to the infection and the stones. The chances of cure are good if the cases are properly selected, though considerable time may be needed before infection of the biliary tract disappears after operation. No such carrier should be considered cured unless observed for at least a year after operation. The minimum criteria for cure are a series of twelve consecutive negative fecal specimens obtained at intervals of one month and at least one negative bile specimen obtained a year after operation. Cure of urinary carriers has been reported through removal of kidney stones. Some communities pay the cost of operation, a practice which is much cheaper than subsidy.

As release specimens were not routinely collected in former years, there are many unrecognized carriers in the community. If these could be discovered, certain future infections might be prevented; yet discovery is difficult.[6] It is desirable, however, for a health department to locate as many of these former patients as possible and to have the nurse call upon them to arrange for the submission of specimens. If this type of program is spread out over a long period of time, it can be done without interfering with the regular work of the nurse and without prohibitive expense. It will reveal an occasional carrier. Similarly, routine cultures of all hospital patients who give a history of previous typhoid will bring to light an occasional carrier. This type of selective culturing is inexpensive and worth while, even though it will miss certain carriers who had had unrecognized infection. Routine culturing of all persons, as in food-handler examinations, is very expensive and rarely yields results commensurate with the expense involved.

Environmental Sanitation. *Specific Measures.* 1. *Disinfection.* Typhoid fever is included in Group III; the procedures outlined for that group on page 145 should be carefully followed. Disinfection of the feces and urine of the acute case should be carried out meticulously in nonsewered communities; in sewered communities it is also desirable, but, as it is not feasible for all convalescents and carriers, whose excreta go into the sewer system without disinfection, there is some excuse for

---

[6] Investigators in England have recently described an interesting method of carrier discovery through detection of typhoid bacteriophage in sewers. By analyzing samples taken from various parts of the sewer system, the presence of a carrier within a given home or group of houses can be demonstrated. Examination of individual stool specimens from each person in these houses is then needed to identify the carrier. The method is logical in theory and has apparently yielded good results, but more experience with it is needed before its true practical value can be determined.

omitting treatment of the excreta of acute cases in such circumstances. The public health nurse should teach the attendant why disinfection of the excreta is important; the nurse should also make certain that the attendant understands the importance of keeping these discharges covered and protected from flies at all times, that she knows how much disinfectant to add and how to break up the stool so the disinfectant reaches all parts of it. So far as possible, all disinfection procedures should be demonstrated by the nurse, the physician, or the health officer.

2. *Other Specific Measures.* The room should be carefully screened to keep out flies; as it makes nursing care more difficult, mosquito netting over the patient should be used only if elimination of flies is impossible. Even when netting is used, flies should be reduced to a minimum through the use of window screens or mosquito netting tacked to window frames. Insect sprays, flypapers, and poisons will also help reduce the number. If a case of typhoid develops on a milk farm, sale of milk should be stopped unless the patient is hospitalized or arrangements can be made for pasteurization away from the farm.

General Measures. 1. *Water.* The improvement of public water supplies has been the largest single factor in the decline of typhoid. So far as possible, water should be taken from sources subject to no possible sewage pollution. Certain ground waters are safe without treatment; all surface waters and some ground waters are exposed to possible pollution and must therefore be treated before use, chiefly by filtration and chlorination. Special attention must be given to the distribution system to avoid cross-connections that result in pollution of either the mains or the pipes within buildings. Many outbreaks have been traced to such connections in industrial establishments. Though the health department usually has jurisdiction over private water supplies and sewage disposal, the municipal engineer or some special board is responsible for the public systems. Private water supplies of homes, factories, camps, and roadside restaurants are more likely to be polluted than are the public supplies and have been the cause of many outbreaks; their control is more difficult and expensive and may require exercise of the health department's authority to regulate nuisances.

Proper sewage disposal is of prime importance in the protection of water supplies of homes, factories, camps, and roadside restaurants are sewage should be so disposed of or treated as to avoid or minimize the pollution of streams and lakes used for water supplies. Private sewage disposal facilities must be so planned and maintained as to avoid contamination of water supplies, especially wells. This means proper construction and location of cesspools and privies.

2. *Milk and Food*. Milk-borne infection has been reduced through improved sanitary handling to guard against the likelihood of introduction of contamination and through pasteurization to kill all pathogens that have found their way by accident into the milk in spite of the precautions. Food is more difficult to protect, as it is so varied in nature and handled intimately by so many persons. As the contamination of milk or food is usually traceable to a missed case or carrier, attempts have been made to eliminate these from such employment. No food handler should be permitted to work while sick, especially if suffering from an intestinal disturbance; yet it is difficult to discover mild cases and exclude them from work. Though discovery of carriers through routine testing of food handlers is theoretically feasible, it is very expensive per number of carriers found and has therefore been discarded by most health departments. Even if practical, it would not prevent the employment of a person suffering from a mild infection incurred between the dates of the periodic tests. Employers are frequently encouraged to provide for such tests, but the examinations are not usually required by law. Principal reliance is usually placed upon thorough cleansing of the hands. This should be done when the food handler begins work each day and after every visit to the toilet. In view of the obvious difficulties of policing such a practice under ordinary toilet arrangements, the hand-washing facilities of all food-handling establishments should be placed in plain view outside the toilets to make certain that due cleanliness is practiced at all times by all employees (see p. 204).

3. *Shellfish*. Prevention of spread through shellfish depends on sanitation in all steps of the industry. This means growing and storing the shellfish in clean water and opening them under clean conditions. The present system of certification for interstate shipment has removed most of the danger that formerly existed.

4. *Flies* may be reduced in number, though not eliminated, through destruction of the important breeding places, notably decaying animal material. It is far easier to prevent their access to feces by sewage treatment or screening of privies. Screening of houses also helps in keeping such contaminated flies from food. Residual DDT sprays should be used to eliminate flies in food-handling establishments.

Minimizing Ill Effects

There are no specific therapeutic measures that may be applied under health department direction. The discovery of chloromycetin has made available the first really effective therapeutic agent, but its use is the responsibility of the attending physician rather than of the health department. More experience is needed before knowing whether the routine use of chloromycetin during the acute stage will reduce the likelihood of developing a chronic carrier state. Even with this new drug, general medical and nursing care are important during the acute illness. Hospitalization is desirable both for the welfare of the patient and the protection of the family.

Public health nursing care should be provided if the patient stays at home and does not have full-time professional nursing care. This is designed to teach nursing care and disinfection procedures to the family and to assist in carrying out the physician's orders. Since, in former years, the patient with typhoid fever was usually sick for several weeks, the strain on the family members caring for him was great. Today the duration of fever has been greatly shortened through use of chloromycetin therapy.

The public health nurse should demonstrate nursing techniques which will contribute to the patient's comfort and recovery and should show how the care may be given with least effort by the attendant. Conservation of the patient's strength is important. Special effort must therefore be given to teaching the attendant how to administer the routine daily care with the least disturbance of the patient. This should include attention to such matters as changing the bed linen, bed baths, sponges for high fever, feeding the patient, and use of the bedpan.

If the patient is being treated with chloromycetin the nurse should be alert to notice any side effects which might be caused by the drug and report these to the physician in charge of the case. She should reassure the patient and the family about moderate side effects, such as nausea and vomiting, which are to be expected and are not cause for alarm.

The possibility that the patient may become irrational or incontinent must be kept in mind and appropriate apparatus for either condition devised. If the illness is prolonged, care must be taken to prevent bedsores, and the attendant instructed regarding the usual preventive measures. The mouth must be given special attention, as it is likely to become cracked and sore if neglected. It should be cleansed after each feeding, and the lips kept covered with a lubricant.

Diet is probably the main supportive measure in typhoid fever. The physician's orders and the patient's tastes will govern the selection of food which should in general be high caloric, nonirritating, and not gas-forming. The attendant should be given assistance in planning the nourishment for each 24-hour period so that she may follow the above general principles.

The possibilities of complications—notably, intestinal bleeding or perforation—must be thought of, especially around the third week of the disease, though they may occur at other times. The attendant should be instructed either by the physician or the nurse regarding the symptoms to be reported immediately to the physician. Any bleeding from the rectum, blood in the stools, sudden acute abdominal pain, undue restlessness, abnormal thirst, cold perspiration, or suddenly increased pulse rate or falling temperature should be reported at once. Hospital care should be strongly urged for the seriously ill patient if the physician approves.

Number of Nursing Visits. Daily visits are necessary during the acute stages if bedside care is being given. During convalescence, visits may be less frequent, according to the needs of the patient and family.

If bedside care is not furnished or if the case occurs in a rural area where the nursing service is too limited to give daily attention, the nurse should make a minimum of two visits on successive days. The first day she may demonstrate the most important procedures and the second day assist the attendant in carrying out the procedures learned the day before. (Three or four visits are commonly needed for this instruction.) After this the nurse may visit once a week, as long as the patient is ill, in order to make certain that proper precautions are being maintained and assisting with any nursing problems which may arise.

Control through Immunization

Immunization may be accomplished through injection of suitable doses of a vaccine of heat-killed bacilli.[7] Formerly the vaccine most commonly used—the triple vaccine—was a mixture of killed typhoid and paratyphoid A and B organisms. Due to the rarity of paratyphoid A in the United States and the relative rarity and mildness of paratyphoid B, these have been omitted from many of the present vaccines. This eliminates some of the constitutional reaction, due in large part to the paratyphoid B fraction.[8] Ordinarily, subcutaneous injections of 0.5, 1.0, and 1.0 cc are given at weekly intervals.[9] A booster dose of 1.0 cc subcutaneously or 0.1 cc intracutaneously may be given every three years or more frequently if a higher level of protection is desired. Annual booster doses

[7] Until recently a heat-killed vaccine was the standard antigen. Many of the current vaccines have been prepared by killing the organisms through exposure to ultraviolet irradiation.

[8] Late in 1940 the U.S. Army, which was the first to discard the paratyphoid A and B fractions in this country, returned to the use of the triple vaccine. This form of vaccine was used by both Army and Navy throughout the war, because of the risk of paratyphoid as well as typhoid fever in foreign areas. It usually contains 1,000 million killed typhoid organisms, 250 million paratyphoid A, and 250 million paratyphoid B per cubic centimeter.

[9] Recent studies have shown that intracutaneous injections of 0.1 cc are equally or even more effective.

were given by the Army during World War II. The effectiveness of immunization has been strikingly proved by the control of typhoid in military units and among medical and nursing personnel. Ramsey showed its usefulness in reducing the secondary attack rate among family contacts, in many of whom immunization was not undertaken until after exposure. These results leave no room for doubt as to the efficacy of typhoid vaccines even though the earlier vaccines were less potent than the present ones.

Immunization should be urged for all persons who are or may be in close association with typhoid cases or carriers. This includes medical, nursing, and laboratory personnel and family contacts of cases or carriers. Institutional and military groups, as well as travelers to areas where it is difficult to be absolutely certain of the water and food supplies, should also be protected. Community programs for immunization of all persons are desirable in areas where the disease is prevalent and where environmental conditions may favor spread. They have been extensively used in some parts of the South but in the northern states have not been made a part of the accepted community health program because of the lower incidence of the disease. To immunize 25,000 persons or more each year in order to prevent a single case is not worth while, yet such would be the situation in many states. The money needed for such programs would yield greater returns in other fields of public health.

It should be emphasized that typhoid vaccination is no substitute for sanitation. The immunized person should think of his vaccination as an added safeguard, not as a license to disregard the usual precautions with respect to water, food, or milk supplies. If he thinks that because of his immunization he can now eat or drink anything without regard to its sanitary history, he is due for a sad disillusionment. Similarly a community should not rely on widespread immunization to the neglect of the more fundamental program of sanitation. Typhoid immunization supplements but does not supplant sanitation.

SUMMARY

Health Department Program

Immediate attention must be given to all active cases to (1) find the source of infection, (2) prevent further spread to contacts, and (3) determine if the case becomes a carrier. Detection of carriers at the time they develop ensures against future spread. Permanent control depends on improved sanitation of water, milk, and food supplies, proper disposal of sewage, and discovery and supervision of carriers. Immunization is desirable under certain circumstances but should not be relied upon to the neglect of improved sanitation.

The **health officer** is responsible for the general direction of the typhoid control program. So far as possible, he should make the field epidemiological studies. Under his direction the **public health nurse** must make the usual calls for isolation and quarantine instruction and care of the patient, assist in the epidemiological investigation, and often follow the patient to collect the specimens for release cultures. She should report her observations of poor sanitation to the **sanitary officer,** whose duty it is to investigate and improve conditions surrounding private water and sewerage systems, milk supplies, and food-handling establishments. Both he and the health officer should work with the water and sewer officials to improve the public systems. All personnel have the duty of public education regarding the importance of safe water, proper sewage disposal, pasteurized milk, personal hygiene, and, if necessary, immunization.

SUGGESTED READINGS

American Public Health Association, Committee on Administrative Practice: "The Control of Typhoid Carriers," *Am. Pub. Health Assoc. Year Book, 1948–49,* Part II, pp. 71–74.

Anderson, Gaylord W.; Hamblen, Angeline D.; and Smith, Helen M.: "Typhoid Carriers: A Study of Their Disease Producing Potentialities over a Series of Years as Indicated by a Study of Cases," *Am. J. Pub. Health,* 26:396–405, (Apr.) 1936.

Batson, H. C.: "Typhoid Fever Prophylaxis by Active Immunization," *Pub. Health Rep.,* Suppl. 212, (Aug.) 1949.

Budd, William: *Typhoid Fever: Its Nature, Mode of Spreading, and Prevention.* Originally published in London, 1874; republished, Delta Omega Series of Public Health Classics, 1931.

Coller, Frederick A., and Forsbeck, Filip C.: "The Surgical Treatment of Chronic Biliary Typhoid Carriers," *Ann. Surg.,* 105:791–99, (May) 1937.

Cruickshank, J. C.: "Newer Methods in the Investigation of Outbreaks of Enteric Fever," *J. Roy. San. Inst.,* 70:34–38, (Jan.) 1950.

Feemster, Roy F., and Smith, Helen M.: "Laboratory Criteria of the Cure of Typhoid Carriers," *Am. J. Pub. Health,* 35:368–72, (Apr.) 1945.

Gorman, Arthur S., and Wolman, Abel: *Water-borne Outbreaks in the United States and Canada and Their Significance.* New York: American Water Works Association, 1939.

Lendon, N. C., and Mackenzie, R. D.: "Tracing a Typhoid Carrier by Sewage Examination," *Month. Bull. Min. Health & Pub. Health Lab. Serv.,* 10:23–27, (Jan.) 1951.

Longfellow, Don, and Luippold, George F.: "Typhoid Vaccine Studies: Revaccination and Duration of Immunity," *Am. J. Pub. Health,* 30:1311–17, (Nov.) 1940.

Moore, B.; Perry, E. L.; and Chard, S. T.: "A Survey by the Sewage Swab Method of Enteric Infection in an Urban Area," *J. Hyg.*, 50:137–56, (June) 1952.

Patterson, Robert U.: "Efficacy of Typhoid Prophylaxis in the United States Army," *Am. J. Pub. Health*, 25:258–69, (Mar.) 1935.

Ramsey, George H.: "What Are the Essentials of Typhoid Fever Control Today?" *Am. J. Pub. Health*, 24:355–62, (Apr.) 1934.

————: "Typhoid Fever among Household Contacts with Special Reference to Vaccination," *Am. J. Hyg.*, 21:665–78, (May) 1935.

Savage, Sir William: "Paratyphoid Fever: An Epidemiological Study," *J. Hyg.*, 42:393–410, (July) 1942.

Scott, W. M.: "The Enteric Fevers," Chapter XII of *Control of the Common Fevers*. London: The Lancet, Ltd., 1942.

Siler, J. F.; Dunham, George I.; Longfellow, Don; and Luippold, G. F.: "Immunization to Typhoid Fever," *Am. J. Hyg.*, Monograph Series No. 17, 1941.

Stebbins, Ernest L., and Reed, Elizabeth: "Carrier-Borne Typhoid Fever in New York State with Special Reference to Attack Rates among Household Contacts," *Am. J. Pub. Health*, 27:233–40, (Mar.) 1937.

11. The Dysenteries

The term "dysentery" is frequently used by the public—and at times by the medical profession—to refer to any severe diarrhea, especially if there is blood in the stool. While this has some justification etymologically, the use is unfortunate as it tends to classify together too many disease conditions of very different etiology. Better usage restricts the term to two groups of conditions, those due to the dysentery bacilli and those due to infection with certain protozoa, notably the amebae.

BACILLARY DYSENTERY

This is an acute infection of the large intestines, resulting in diarrhea, which, if sufficiently severe, may be accompanied by bleeding from the colon. The disease varies greatly in severity according to the strain of dysentery bacilli concerned and the previous condition of the victim. The usual textbook description portrays a fairly severe and frequently fatal disturbance. The vast majority of the cases encountered in the United States are very mild, presenting little more than a transient diarrhea without any blood, especially if the victim is a previously healthy adult or adolescent. Yet the same infection of a small child or debilitated adult may result fatally, with typical bloody diarrhea and at times even meningeal symptoms.

EPIDEMIOLOGY

Occurrence. Infection is found at all ages and in all parts of the world. The official morbidity and mortality figures would suggest that the disease is quite rare in the United States, yet repeated studies of sporadic cases of diarrhea in several parts of the country have shown that many of these are bacillary dysentery infections. Thus Maxcy and his associates found that 35 per cent of such cases in one county in Virginia were of this character; Hardy has found similar data for several parts of the South-

184

west. Several years earlier Smillie had shown that many of the cases of summer diarrhea in Boston were bacillary dysentery. Thus the infection is apparently far more widespread than is commonly recognized and is not declining at the same rate as is typhoid fever. Unfortunately the extensive evidence that many of the apparently simple diarrheas are unrecognized cases of bacillary dysentery has been so widely ignored, especially in clinical circles, that a large part of the medical profession seemed surprised to rediscover this well-proved fact during military service when bacillary dysentery frequently became widespread among certain units. The disease often appears in institutions, particularly those for the feeble-minded or mentally ill, where it spreads widely because of lack of cooperation on the part of the patients. Family outbreaks are frequently encountered.

Etiological Agent. Bacillary dysentery is due to infection with bacilli of the genus *Shigella*. These are nonmotile, Gram-negative bacilli somewhat allied to the typhoid bacilli. Several strains exist, distinguishable by fermentation and serological reactions. The Shiga strain (*Shigella dysenteriae*) which is most commonly found in the Orient is the most virulent but fortunately is rare in the United States. The most common strains in the United States are the *Shigella paradysenteriae* (Flexner strain) and the *Sh. sonnei*. The dysentery bacilli are relatively fragile, being less capable of survival outside of the human body than are the typhoid bacilli.

The reservoir of infection is in all instances the human being, usually an active or convalescent case. While permanent carriers have been described, they are so rare as to play little, if any, part in the spread of bacillary dysentery. Most infections are caused by the mild, unrecognized case, who considers that he has nothing more than a transient diarrhea due to "something he ate."

Escape of the organism is with the feces. The bacilli appear in the stool with the first symptoms and persist for a period ranging from a few days to a few weeks or months.

Transmission of infection is identical with that of typhoid fever (q.v.) except that the organisms are somewhat less viable outside the body. Inanimate vehicles are probably less important, though outbreaks due to water, milk, and food of many varieties have been frequently described. Most of the infections within the home and institutions appear to be spread by rather direct association with a prior case. In areas of poor sanitation, flies may play a very important role in the spread of infection. If human excreta are used as fertilizer, as is the case in many countries, uncooked vegetables and fruits may be important vehicles in the transmission of both bacillary and amebic dysentery.

Entry into the body is through the mouth.

The incubation period is about two to seven days.

Susceptibility. In the absence of satisfactory tests, our knowledge of susceptibility to bacillary dysentery is very indefinite. There is little evidence of any high degree of resistance, though adults seem to be somewhat less susceptible than are children. Infection can apparently be repeated in the same individual.

CONTROL MEASURES

Control of Spread

The case should be treated in the same manner as a case of typhoid fever (q.v.) and kept in modified isolation until three to four weeks have elapsed since the end of symptoms and until negative cultures have been obtained. The difficulty of obtaining viable bacilli in proved cases is, however, so much greater than in typhoid, especially if the specimens have to be shipped to a distant laboratory, that less reliance can be placed on negative stool cultures. It is therefore probably justifiable in this disease to insist on the arbitrary period of isolation if there is the slightest doubt of the accuracy of the laboratory results. The convalescent carrier condition does not often persist longer than three to four weeks after the cessation of symptoms. Treatment with sulfaguanidine not only hastens cure of the active disease but also hastens the disappearance of viable organisms from the intestinal tract. Hospitalization may be desirable to reduce the risk of spread to other persons within a home.

Epidemiological investigation is carried on in a manner quite comparable to that in typhoid fever. Special attention must be given to examination of contacts, and careful search made for a history of transient diarrhea. In an institutional outbreak, it is often hard to convince the employed personnel that the mild diarrheas affecting them for one or two days' duration are in any way related to the severe and often fatal cases among the debilitated patients. These mild cases, which are responsible for the spread, will not be discovered unless a special search is made for them. Particular attention must be directed to food-handling personnel. Stool specimens should be collected and examined from all suspected cases. Feemster has described a technique which depends on the identification of the dysentery bacillus bacteriophage and which will bring to light many cases of infection ordinarily missed if sole reliance were placed on culturing the organism from the stools. Blood tests are of slight value as the agglutinins are slow in appearing.

Contacts are usually not quarantined unless found infected. Owing to the high incidence of mild, unrecognized cases within a family, it is desirable, however, to insist on strict quarantine of any family contact engaged in a food-handling occupation of any character.

Environmental Sanitation. The measures used for typhoid control are equally applicable to bacillary dysentery, though the results have been less striking because of the large number of infections spread through contact with an unrecognized case. Attention to disposal of sewage and the sanitation of water, milk, and food all help in preventing the spread of infection. If a case occurs on a milk farm, sale of milk should be immediately stopped unless it is pasteurized away from the premises. Any food handler with a diarrhea should be immediately excluded from work. Control of flies in food-handling establishments is an important part of any dysentery control program. Watt has shown that intensive fly control measures will bring about a substantial reduction in incidence of infection in areas in which disposal of human feces is still inadequately safeguarded.

Disinfection. Bacillary dysentery is included in Group III; disinfection procedures outlined for that group on page 145 should be carefully followed.

Minimizing Ill Effects

As most cases of bacillary dysentery in the United States are mild, self-limited conditions even in the absence of medical care, little bedside nursing is required. Public health nursing visits in such circumstances should stress prevention of spread rather than nursing attention to the patient. The severe cases encountered in small children and in debilitated adults present quite different problems, requiring the best of hospital or home nursing care. The public health nursing care of such cases is essentially the same as that accorded acute amebic infection and is accordingly described under that heading. The advent of sulfaguanidine therapy has facilitated clinical as well as bacteriological cure.

Control through Immunization

Passive Immunization. No method of proved efficacy exists.

Active Immunization. Many attempts at protection have been made with vaccines of various types, and favorable results have been described. The same vaccines in the hands of other investigators have yielded disappointing results. The great variety of vaccines tried and the lack of uniformity of results must be interpreted as indicating that active immunization against bacillary dysentery is still far from proved. The most promising results have been achieved with antigens to protect against the Shiga strain.

AMEBIC DYSENTERY

Amebic dysentery, known also as amebiasis, is a more prolonged, chronic type of infection in which the acute diarrhea is but an episode. A large proportion of those who are infected have no symptoms or may suffer only vague intestinal discomfort punctuated by occasional attacks of diarrhea. During the acute stage the patient has a very severe diarrhea, the stools often containing little more than water mixed with mucus and often with blood. Recovery from these acute symptoms does not, however, mean recovery from the infection, as the amebae may persist in the intestines for years and cause few symptoms. In other instances, the amebae migrate to the liver, where they may cause an abscess. During the acute stage, ulcers appear in the colon, the amebae being found in the base of these ulcerated areas. The term "amebiasis" is frequently used to refer to the prolonged infection with the amebae and the term "amebic dysentery" restricted to the diarrheal episodes.

EPIDEMIOLOGY

Occurrence. Amebic dysentery is found in all parts of the world but most commonly appears in its clinically recognizable form in the tropical or subtropical zone. The outbreak in 1933 in Chicago showed, however, that the disease may become widespread in other areas and that many unrecognized infections occur throughout the United States.

Etiological Agent. This form of dysentery is due to infection with a protozoan parasite, the *Entameba histolytica*. The vegetative form of the ameba is extremely fragile, ordinarily living but a few minutes outside the human body and readily destroyed by the acidity of the stomach. The ameba may, however, form a cyst, the hard wall of which protects it from ready destruction. Such cysts will persist for long periods in water and food. They are not killed by the concentrations of chlorine commonly used in water purification. Special diatomaceous earth filters were developed by the Army during World War II for the express purpose of removing amebic cysts. Cysts do not stand high temperatures or prolonged drying. Apparently several strains of *Entameba histolytica* exist. Care must always be exercised to distinguish them from other amebae that occur in the human intestines but are not pathogenic.

The reservoir of infection is always man. Several studies have shown that from 5 to 10 per cent of the population of the United States harbor the *Entameba histolytica*, though without any symptoms. No satisfactory explanation exists for this high rate of infection in the face of such a low incidence of clinical disease.

Escape of the organism is through the feces. The form of the ameba that escapes depends on the speed of passage through the intestines. During the acute diarrhea, the vegetative forms present in the ulcers are carried out of the intestines before they have had time to develop cysts. As the diarrhea subsides, opportunity exists for the formation of cysts, which are characteristically found in the convalescent case and the carrier. As the vegetative forms are too fragile to survive outside the body and are destroyed by the acidity of the stomach, infection does not occur through contact with the acute case. The disease is spread by the convalescent case or carrier who is discharging the more resistant cyst.

Transmission of infection is through the medium of food and water, the former contaminated by the hands of the carrier, the latter by sewage containing cysts. Much difference of opinion exists as to the relative importance of food and water as vehicles of infection. Without going into the details of the argument, evidence apparently indicates that under certain conditions the principal vehicles may be food; yet under other circumstances, water. Attention must, therefore, be given to both if infection is to be prevented. Vegetables and berries grown on soil fertilized with human excreta are important vehicles of infection in some countries.

Entry of infection occurs solely via the mouth.

Susceptibility. Little is known regarding the factors conditioning susceptibility to infection. There is little evidence of immunity, such as develops in certain bacterial and virus infections, yet the majority of the persons infected with the ameba fail to show any resultant illness. It has been recognized that the pathogenicity of strains may vary and that their action on the body may be dependent upon simultaneous infection with certain other organisms. At the present time, no thoroughly satisfactory explanation exists for the low incidence of clinically recognizable disease in spite of such high prevalence of infection.

CONTROL MEASURES

Control of Spread

The case is of little menace during the acute stage, due to the fragility of the vegetative ameba. During convalescence, as cysts appear in the feces, special precautions comparable to those in dealing with a typhoid convalescent must be observed. Theoretically, these precautions should be continued until laboratory studies show the patient to be free of infection. Actually there is little justification for continuance of precautions if cure is delayed or not achieved, for the individual constitutes an insignificant addition to the already large reservoir of infection. The unfamiliarity of most laboratories with the highly technical task of identification of ameba cysts makes reliance on tests very hazardous. If specimens are collected for examination, they should be sent to a laboratory that has had special experience in this field.

Epidemiological investigation of an isolated case will yield little from the point of view of control, because of the large number of carriers in the population, but may reveal the existence of other unrecognized cases having a common origin. A prompt inquiry should, therefore, be made of all known contacts. Search should be made for unrecognized infections within the family group, especially among those who are handling food. The only reliable laboratory test for infection is the examination of stools, both by direct search for amebic cysts and by cultures.[1]

Contacts ordinarily require no quarantine restrictions. If any of the patient's family contacts are food handlers, however, they should be tested before being permitted to continue work, and, if found to be harboring the amebic cysts, should be given appropriate treatment before returning to work.

Environmental Sanitation. The importance of a safe water supply in preventing the spread of amebiasis cannot be overstressed. The 1933 Chicago outbreak showed also the danger of cross-connections in possible pollution of an otherwise safe supply. Routine food-handler examinations have been recommended but are not practical on a community-wide basis. However desirable such tests may be in theory, the technical difficulties entailed are too great, and the resultant cost of their performance too high, in comparison with the apparent magnitude of the problem in the United States. The sums required for such a program would yield greater returns if used for other public health problems of greater importance. Chief reliance must be placed on strict sanitation of all food-handling establishments. This should stress adequate provision for hand-washing and the use of these facilities before beginning work and after each visit to the toilet. In order to make possible the policing of such a requirement, these facilities should be provided not only in the toilet but also in the workroom, and the employees be required to use them in the latter, where any laxity will be observed.

Disinfection. Amebic dysentery is included in Group III; procedures outlined for the group on page 145 should be followed. Because of the relatively high resistance of the cyst as contrasted with the extreme fragility of the vegetative ameba, attention to proper feces disposal is more important during the convalescence than during the acute stages of the disease.

---

[1] The cultural technique is difficult but occasionally yields positive results that have been overlooked on direct examination of fecal smears.

Minimizing Ill Effects

In contrast to the relative mildness of the prevailing form of bacillary dysentery in the United States, amebic infection is often a prolonged, debilitating condition and frequently results fatally. This is especially so if the correct diagnosis is not established and the patient subjected to surgical procedures. The health department should provide laboratory facilities to aid in diagnosis and should encourage their use. Hospitalization is often necessary for the best care of the patient.

Public Health Nursing Care. The chronic form of the infection requires no public health nursing attention. The severe acute form of dysentery, however, is a very exhausting disease because of the frequent stools and resultant dehydration. As the patient should not ordinarily be allowed to get up to use the toilet or a commode, a bedpan must be provided and the attendant instructed as to warming it before use so that the patient will not be chilled. Complete rest is very important to conserve strength and also to decrease the danger of perforation.

The patient should be kept warm at all times. This is the foundation of nursing care of all forms of dysentery. Special care should be taken to prevent chilling of the abdomen, as this may cause increased diarrhea and discomfort; a flannel shirt or binder is helpful.

The diet will of course be ordered in considerable detail by the physician; the nurse may give the attendant suggestions of appropriate foods for the particular diet ordered. The patient is usually supposed to take large amounts of fluids because of the dehydration resulting from the frequent stools. Weak tea, barley water, and sometimes fruit juices are ordered at first. Broths strained to eliminate fats, diluted boiled milk, junkets, and custards are later added, followed by regular soft diet as convalescence proceeds. Meats and foods with cellulose are added last. Feedings should be small and given at frequent intervals. Return to regular diet should be very gradual, as relapses may occur if the return is too rapid. Resumption of normal activities should also be very gradual, as overexertion or exposure to wet or cold may also cause relapses.

Number of Nursing Visits. If the nursing organization offers bedside care, daily visits will probably be needed during the early acute stage. Frequent visits will be needed, even in the convalescent period, to prevent the patient's returning to full activity too rapidly. Patients and families need encouragement at this time, as convalescence sometimes seems so slow that the patient fears he may never be well and the family is tempted to suspect his becoming a hypochondriac. In rural areas where it is impossible to make frequent visits, at least two should be made at the onset to demonstrate care of the acutely ill patient and at least one (two, if possible) during the convalescent period.

Control through Immunization

No method of either active or passive immunization is known.

SUMMARY

Health Department Program

Both bacillary and amebic dysentery infections are of far more common occurrence than is generally recognized, the former causing many cases of transient diarrhea and the latter often appearing as a symptomless carrier condition with only an occasional acute case. The number of these unrecognized infections is so great that control through isolation and quarantine has yielded few results. As both infections may be spread through water and food contaminated either by an unrecognized case or a carrier, the most effective control measures are those of sanitation of water and food supplies.

The health officer should assume responsibility for investigation of all reported infections, with special attention to the discovery of other cases. In his contacts with the medical profession, he should stress the importance of bacteriological study of all cases of diarrhea to discover otherwise unrecognized infections which may serve as focuses for further spread. Laboratory facilities should be provided but not on a local basis unless there is adequate work to justify the employment of a full-time bacteriologist especially skilled and experienced in this field. Inaccurate laboratory work is worse than none, as it gives a false sense of security. In her home visits, the public health nurse should be constantly alert for cases of diarrhea that should be brought to medical attention—especially family outbreaks. The health officer should insist on a safe water supply and sanitary conditions in all food-handling establishments. The sanitary officer has a special responsibility for policing of the latter and should stress the provision of hand-washing facilities and their lavish use by all food handlers.

SUGGESTED READINGS

Andrews, Justin: "The Transmission of Endameba Histolytica and Amebic Disease," *South. M. J.,* 35:693–99, (July) 1942.

Craig, Charles F.: *Amebiasis and Amebic Dysentery.* Springfield, Ill.: Charles C. Thomas, Publisher, 1934.

———: *The Etiology, Diagnosis and Treatment of Amebiasis.* Baltimore: Williams & Wilkins Co., 1944.

"Epidemic Amebic Dysentery: The Chicago Outbreak of 1933," *Nat. Inst. Health Bull.*, No. 166, 1936. U. S. Public Health Service, Washington, D. C.

Faust, Ernest Carroll: "The Prevalence of Amebiasis in the Western Hemisphere," *Am. J. Trop. Med.*, 22:93–105, (Jan.) 1942.

———: "Some Modern Conceptions of Amebiasis," *Science*, 99:45–51, 69–72, (Jan. 21 and 28) 1944.

Hardy, A. V.: "The Influence of Variations in Exposure in Amebiasis: A Quantitative Study," *Am. J. Hyg.*, 25:421–29, (May) 1937.

———: "Shigellosis (Bacillary Dysentery) among Institutional Inmates," *Psychiatric Quart.*, 19:377–97, (July) 1945.

Hardy, A. V., and Watt, James: "The Acute Diarrheal Diseases," *J.A.M.A.*, 124:1173–79, (Apr. 22) 1944.

———: "Studies on the Acute Diarrheal Diseases. XVIII Epidemiology," *Pub. Health Rep.*, 63:363–78, (Mar. 19) 1948.

Lincicome, David R.; Thiede, Walter H.; and Carpenter, Elizabeth: "An Evaluation of the Influence of World War II on the Incidence of Amebiasis," *Am. J. Trop. Med.*, 30:171–79, (Mar.) 1950.

McGinnes, G. Foard; McLean, Allan L.; Spindle, Forrest; and Maxcy, Kenneth F.: "A Study of Diarrhea and Dysentery in Henrico County, Virginia," *Am. J. Hyg.*, 24:552–67, (Nov.) 1936.

Newton, Walter L.: "Water Treatment Measures in Control of Amebiasis," *Am. J. Trop. Med.*, 30:135–38, (Mar.) 1950.

Scott, W. M.: "Bacillary Dysentery," *Lancet*, 2:796–99, (Oct. 1) 1938. Published also as Chapter XIV of *Control of the Common Fevers*. London: The Lancet, Ltd., 1942.

Shiga, Kiyoshi: "The Trend of Prevention, Therapy, and Epidemiology of Dysentery Since the Discovery of Its Causative Organism," *New England J. Med.*, 215:1205–11, (Dec. 24) 1936.

Stebbins, Ernest L.: "Recent Studies of Epidemic Diarrhea and Dysentery," *South. M. J.*, 33:197–203, (Feb.) 1940.

Watt, James, and Lindsay, Dale R.: "Diarrheal Disease Control Studies. I. Effect of Fly Control in a High Morbidity Area," *Pub. Health Rep.*, 63:1319–34, (Oct. 8) 1948.

Wright, Willard H.: "The Public Health Status of Amebiasis in the United States as Revealed by Available Statistics," *Am. J. Trop. Med.*, 30:123–33, (Mar.) 1950.

12. Hookworm

Hookworm disease, known also as uncinariasis, is a chronic, debilitating condition attended with anemia, weakness, and loss of vitality, though rarely resulting in death. Infection of a large fraction of the population may so reduce the physical vigor as to interfere seriously with the economic self-sufficiency of the community. As poverty and lack of ambition due to the disease lead to even wider spread of the infection, a vicious cycle may be created, escape from which is often difficult. Hookworm,[1] like malaria and pellagra, constitutes a major obstacle to the economic well-being of any community that it may afflict.

EPIDEMIOLOGY

Occurrence. Hookworm is found throughout the tropical and subtropical areas, extending as far north as latitude 36° and as far south of the equator as latitude 30°. Essentially a disease of poverty, it is most commonly encountered in the rural areas where sanitation is inadequate. In the United States the highest incidence occurs in children but declines rapidly during the teens, though in some countries the rate remains high in adults engaged in agricultural pursuits. Although the infection rate is much lower in the United States than in former years, the disease has not yet disappeared; infection is still found in an appreciable fraction of certain populations in the rural South. The disease is more prevalent in areas where the soil is fairly moist, sandy, and covered with vegetation than in more arid or stony sections.

Etiological Agent. The disease is due to infection with the hookworm, of which two species exist—*Necator americanus* and *Ankylostoma duodenale*. The latter causes a more serious condition than does the former

[1] Infection with the hookworm, or illness due to it, is commonly referred to as "hookworm" though, strictly speaking, the word refers to the parasite and not to the effect on the body. For the sake of brevity, the term will be used here to refer to either the parasite or the illness, according to the context.

but is fortunately quite rare in the United States. The adult worms lodge in the human intestines and adhere to the intestinal mucosa by their mouth parts. Infection with less than 50 worms rarely causes symptoms. In some cases, the number of worms harbored by a single individual may be as high as 2,000 or 3,000.

Reservoir of Infection. Man constitutes the sole reservoir, as the hookworms pathogenic for him are encountered in no other species. Though any infected person may serve as a source from whom the disease may spread, the greatest danger is attached to those with the highest degree of infection, as this represents a large number of worms and therefore a large number of eggs being discharged. The adult worm lives about five years in the intestine, so that, unless special treatment is given, infectiousness persists for about this time after further exposure ceases. It must always be remembered that certain persons harbor too small a number of worms to cause symptoms yet are potential sources of the disease.

Escape from the Reservoir. Mating of the worms occurs in the human intestine, where the eggs are discharged and carried out with the feces.

Transmission. After leaving the body, the egg develops, ultimately rupturing to permit escape of the larva, a small free-living form of the worm. This passes through a series of molts or ecdyses, ultimately reaching the stage at which it is capable of reinfecting the human being. Survival of the larvae outside the body depends upon the environmental conditions. They seldom survive in the soil more than two or three months. Eggs and larvae are readily destroyed by sewage treatment procedures. They will not survive drying or much direct exposure to the sun or cold. Since they are not capable of traveling any distance, the larvae do not reach the surface of the ground if deposited in a pit privy. They are, therefore, found only in soil that has had surface pollution with infected human feces, due either to direct defecation on the ground or to escape from improperly constructed surface privies.

Entry into the body is through the intact skin. Infection is thus contracted only by persons who bring their bare skin in contact with contaminated soil. This means persons who are going barefoot (usually children), plantation workers, or other persons handling the soil. The local irritation which sometimes appears at the point of entry is referred to as "ground itch." Having invaded the body, the larva is carried by the lymphatics into the blood stream and is then carried through the heart into the lungs, where it is mechanically obstructed by the capillaries. Here it bores out into the alveolar sacs, crawls along the bronchial tree, up the trachea, and into the back of the throat, where it is swallowed or expectorated. Those larvae that are swallowed pass through the stomach into the intestines, where they develop to maturity and adhere to the intestinal wall. Thus they complete the life cycle. No multiplication of the worms occurs within the body.

Susceptibility. A person who is already infected may acquire additional infection if his skin comes in contact with contaminated soil. In hookworm areas, persons are constantly losing and adding to their infection as old worms die and new larvae penetrate. Infection does not therefore appear to increase the resistance to further invasion. It should not be assumed, however, that every larva penetrating the skin succeeds in reaching the intestines, for many die during their migrations through the body or are expectorated as they reach the pharynx. The nutrition of the body is apparently an important factor in determining the proportion of larvae that reach maturity.

CONTROL MEASURES

Control of Spread

The case requires no isolation precautions to prevent direct spread to the contacts. Special attention must, however, be given to the disposal of the feces. Disinfection of stools is not necessary nor is it practical, as the patient is almost invariably ambulatory and many of the infections are so mild that they escape detection. The only measure required is that the stools be discharged into a pit privy, cesspool, or any other form of proper sewage disposal. The patient must be cautioned against defecation on the surface of the ground and impressed with the dangers of this practice.

Epidemiological investigation of an individual case is of little value in discovering the source of infection, especially in an area where the disease is prevalent. Examination of the contacts is of considerable value in revealing infections that may be overlooked. This means examination of stool specimens for hookworm eggs. The technique involved is not difficult. Every public health laboratory in a hookworm area should be able to perform these examinations. In these areas, extensive epidemiological investigation on a community basis is often valuable. Such a study should include examination of stool specimens of all school children or of other groups in which infection is frequently found. In agricultural groups this may include all laborers. The purpose of such investigation is to learn the incidence and also the severity of the conditions. Because of the vagueness of the symptoms and the large number of persons who have subclinical infections, group surveys yield more previously undiscovered cases than do studies starting from a recognized case.

Contacts require no restriction but should be examined for infections, as multiple cases are usually found within a household. Cases so found should be given treatment.

Environmental sanitation is the most important single factor in the control of hookworm disease. If there were no contamination of the soil, the disease would disappear. Facilities for safe excreta disposal must be provided, and the population in question educated to their use. Such facilities must be provided and used at places of work in the field as well as at home. The habit of some agricultural workers of defecating in the fields without returning to the house results in spread in areas where the disease is prevalent. The infection rate among plantation workers has been lowered by provision of such facilities at convenient spots, thus reducing the degree of soil pollution. Expensive water-carriage systems are not required; a pit privy is adequate, if so constructed that there is no chance of the contents' being washed out upon the soil.

Personal protection may be acquired through avoiding contact between the soil and the skin, especially that of the feet. This means the wearing of shoes at all times. Unfortunately, this is easier said than done, as the economic circumstances of many of the hookworm victims is such that funds are not available to provide shoes for the children. It must be remembered also that malaria and pellagra often flourish in the same areas where hookworm is prevalent and thus further reduce the economic efficiency of the victim. The fieldworker has no effective protection against being infected through the hands and arms brought in contact with the soil, though gloves have been advised under some circumstances. If there were no contamination of the soil, there would be no need of protective devices.

Minimizing the Ill Effects

This is accomplished through treatment of the infected person to destroy the worms or to improve his nutrition so that he may withstand the ill effects of the infection. Complete destruction is rarely accomplished, though the number may be so reduced that little harm accrues to the patient. Reducing the number of worms will also reduce the number of eggs discharged and thus lessen the opportunity for spread. It should be remembered, however, that as long as infection persists, eggs will be discharged, even though in decreased number. It must also be remembered that the patient can be reinfected if exposure to contaminated soil continues. Many different vermifuges have been tried with variable results. The ill effects of hookworm infection can be markedly reduced by feeding the patient a well-balanced nutritious diet supplemented with iron. This may offer a method of combating the disease even where absolute prevention is not yet possible.

Control through Immunization

No method of either active or passive immunization exists.

SUMMARY

Health Department Program

Infection with hookworm comes from contact of the skin with soil contaminated with the feces of hookworm cases. As the patient is usually ambulatory and many persons may harbor infection without recognizable symptoms, little is accomplished through attention merely to recognized cases. Effective control is established only through sanitary measures for the safe disposal of all human feces. As the infection rate is highest in the rural areas and among the poorer classes, chief reliance must rest on disposal through sanitary privies, which are adequate if properly built and consistently used. Surveys to find infected persons and bring them under treatment are of value in reducing the quantity of spread and increasing the well-being of those with previously unrecognized infection. Protective clothing, especially shoes, also reduces the risk of infection. Neither treatment nor protective clothing will ever yield permanent results in the absence of sanitation.

The health officer has the task of organizing the program of rural sanitation. Because of the economic circumstances of those who need this program, public assistance must frequently be obtained to provide a suitable privy. The health officer may also direct a survey to find unrecognized cases but must provide adequate laboratory facilities if this survey is to be of value. Treatment must be provided for those in need of it. The public health nurse should constantly be alert for children showing evidences of reduced efficiency from unrecognized infection. In her home visits, she may instruct certain families as to methods of prevention of spread and assist them in obtaining a well-rounded diet rich in iron. The nurse should be ever alert for insanitary sewage-disposal facilities, which she should report to the health officer. The sanitary officer has immediate responsibility for the provision of sanitary sewage-disposal facilities. Surveys may show where such facilities are lacking and where corrections must be made. He should encourage the erection of facilities where they are lacking and supervise their construction to make certain that soil pollution cannot occur. Most state health departments in hookworm areas provide simple plans for suitable privy construction.

SUGGESTED READINGS

Andrews, Justin: "Modern Views on the Treatment and Prevention of Hookworm Disease," *Ann. Int. Med.*, 17:891–901, (Dec.) 1942.

Augustine, Donald L., and Smillie, Wilson G.: "The Relation of the Type of Soils of Alabama to the Distribution of Hookworm Disease," *Am. J. Hyg.*, 6(Suppl. No. 1):36–62, (Mar.) 1926.

Chandler, Asa C.: "A Review of Recent Work on Rate of Acquisition and Loss of Hookworms," *Am. J. Trop. Med.*, 15:357–70, (May) 1935.

Cort, William W.: "Investigations on the Control of Hookworm Disease. XXXIV. General Summary of Results," *Am. J. Hyg.*, 5:49–89, (Jan.) 1925.

Keller, A. E.; Leathers, W. S.; and Knox, J. C.: "The Present Status of Hookworm Infestation in North Carolina," *Am. J. Hyg.*, 26:437–54, (Nov.) 1937.

Leathers, W. S., and Keller, A. E.: "Investigations Concerning Hookworm Disease in Southern States, with Suggestions for Continued Control," *South. M. J.*, 29:172–78, (Feb.) 1936.

Loughlin, Elmer H., and Stoll, Norman R.: "Fomite-Borne Ancylostomiasis," *Am. J. Hyg.*, 45:191–203, (Mar.) 1947.

Rhoads, C. P.; Castle, W. B.; Payne, G. C.; and Lawson, H. A.: "Observations on the Etiology and Treatment of Anemia Associated with Hookworm Infection in Puerto Rico," *Medicine,* 13:317–75, (Sept.) 1934.

Smillie, W. G., and Augustine, D. L.: "The Effect of Varying Intensities of Hookworm Infestation upon the Development of School Children," *South. M. J.*, 19:19–28, (Jan.) 1926.

Stiles, C. W.: "Decrease of Hookworm Disease in the United States," *Pub. Health Rep.*, 45:1763–81, (Aug. 1) 1930.

13. Food Poisonings and Infections

Food poisoning, incorrectly known by the public as "ptomaine poison-ing," [1] is a general term used very loosely to refer to the ill effects caused by the eating of foods that carry with them certain foreign material patho-genic for man. The term does not include the allergic reactions occasioned in persons hypersensitive to certain proteins. Similarly, it does not generally include such specific infections as typhoid, paratyphoid, dysentery, or streptococcal diseases, even though these may be conveyed through the medium of food; nor does it include parasitic infections with trichinae or the various tapeworms.

Except in rare instances in which a poisonous substance such as arsenic oxide or sodium fluoride has been put in the food either by accident or intention, the so-called food poisonings are the result of bacterial contami-nation and might preferably be referred to as food infections. In many instances, however, the reaction in the human body is due to toxins formed in the food by the contaminating organism, no infection occurring in the body. In other instances, actual bacterial invasion occurs. Some have attempted, therefore, to classify the former group as true food poi-sonings, the latter as food infections. This appears a bit confusing, as it directs attention away from the fact that the food is in all instances the article contaminated and that the reaction in the body depends upon the capacity of the organism to produce toxins or to invade the human body. It appears preferable to refer to these conditions as "food infections," and at the same time to exclude mentally from this group infections with streptococci, typhoid, paratyphoid, dysentery, and the parasitic worms.

[1] The term is the remnant of a former theory that the eating of spoiled food led to illness, due to poisonous diamines known as ptomaines and formed in the course of the decomposition. Over twenty-five years ago, the work of Savage and others dis-proved this hypothesis by showing that the eating of mere decomposition products (the flavor of cheese and of "high" game is due to them) did not lead to illness and that cases of so-called "ptomaine poisoning" were due to infection with specific organisms or to the poisons secreted by them.

The clinical manifestations of food infection are quite variable, dependent upon the pathology. If the food contains a toxin which is quickly absorbed or is locally irritating to the stomach and upper intestine, the incubation period will be short, and nausea and vomiting will be the outstanding symptoms. If, on the other hand, the food contains viable pathogenic bacteria but no toxin, the incubation period will be longer, the lower part of the intestine being chiefly involved, and diarrhea the presenting symptom. The presence of toxins and viable pathogens gives rise to both effects, which merge imperceptibly into one another. If the toxin acts on parts of the body other than the intestine, as does the botulinus toxin, the clinical picture may be very different, depending upon the tissue affected. Aside from botulism, the case fatality of which is very high, food poisoning or infection rarely results fatally.

Diverse conditions having no relation to food infections are clinically confused with them. Notable among these are mild cases of acute carbon monoxide poisoning, resulting in severe nausea and vomiting, and a vague condition of unknown etiology that for lack of a better term goes under the unfortunate name of "intestinal grippe" or "stomach flu." Differentiation of the latter is usually based on epidemiological findings, the cases having no apparent relationship to any common article of food and spreading within a group or community in a manner comparable to that of infections of proved respiratory dissemination. Mild cases of paratyphoid and bacillary dysentery are also frequently overlooked as due to "something the patient ate," a phrase which is too often descriptive of the mode of spread but which ignores the true infectious nature of the condition. Cases of gastroenteritis due to water that is sewage-polluted are clinically indistinguishable from cases due to food infection, but the mode of spread is obviously quite different.

Although the mode of spread of the food infections is in all instances quite comparable, the epidemiology of the various forms is so different that it seems best to consider the three principal types separately and to classify them on an etiological basis.

SALMONELLA INFECTIONS

(SALMONELLOSIS)

These present themselves as a variable mixture of nausea, vomiting, diarrhea, and abdominal cramps, usually attended with fever and malaise of several days' duration. Although the outbreaks associated with a common article of food are dramatic and more commonly brought to attention of the health department, sporadic cases apparently unrelated to food are more common, especially in children living in areas where the methods of excreta disposal are still somewhat primitive.

EPIDEMIOLOGY

Etiological Agents. The *Salmonella* group of organisms contains a large and indefinite number of bacteria intermediate between the typhoid and colon bacilli. Considerable uncertainty persists as to the identity and classification of many of the salmonellae, as well as to their pathogenicity. The most important and commonly encountered are the *S. enteritidis, S. typhimurium* (*S. aertrycke*), *S. choleraesuis* (*S. suipestifer*), and *S. oranienburg.* They are nonsporulating organisms of only moderate viability outside the body but capable of considerable multiplication in favorable mediums, such as foods of a fairly bland and moist character. They are readily destroyed by pasteurization temperatures.

Reservoir of Infection. Five distinct reservoirs of infection are recognized:

1. *Human beings* suffering with, or convalescent from, the infection may harbor the bacilli in their intestines. Chronic carriers have been described.

2. *Rats and mice* show a high rate of intestinal infection, especially due to *S. typhimurium.* The pathogenicity of salmonellae for rodents led to attempts to incorporate these organisms in certain poison pastes, but unfortunately many rodents recovered and became carriers. These "culture baits" are prohibited in many places, as they increase the hazard of spread to man.

3. *Cattle and swine* may be infected during life, and the bacilli spread to the tissues before or after death. Meats from infected animals have been responsible for many outbreaks in England.

4. *Ducks* may harbor the infection, the bacilli entering the egg directly from the oviduct or penetrating the shell of the egg that has been laid in polluted soil. Many such outbreaks have been reported from Europe but few from the United States. Salmonellae have also been isolated from hen's eggs.

5. *Domestic pets.* The recent studies of Watt and his colleagues have shown that domestic pets of children infected with salmonellae have a high rate of infection with identical strains of organisms. It is not clear, however, whether the infection of the children is contracted from the pets or vice versa. Such a relationship has been particularly noticeable in instances of sporadic infections which apparently bear no relationship to food.

Escape from the Reservoir. Except as noted above, the bacilli usually escape from the infected person or animal through the intestinal tract.

Transmission of infection is usually by means of food accidentally contaminated with fecal discharges, either through the hands of the food handler or through droppings of rodents. In the case of meat and duck eggs, there is a direct involvement from the body of the infected animal. Almost any article of food sufficiently moist to keep the bacilli alive may serve as the vehicle, though salads and pastries have been most frequently involved in this country. Meat dishes have been more commonly incriminated in England. Infection of children from domestic pets is probably through contamination of the hands which carry the organisms to the mouth. The role of flies in the spread of salmonella infections is still debatable. Roaches may be of importance in transferring infection to food under some circumstances. Olson has shown that artificially infected roaches excrete organisms for several weeks and that salmonellae will remain viable in fecal pellets for several months.

Entry into the Body and Incubation Period. Entry into the body is effected through the mouth. There is some dispute as to the capacity of the salmonellae to produce toxins. Short incubation periods (three to four hours in some cases), coupled with the attendant nausea and vomiting, would suggest that some substance of poisonous character may be formed. The principal reaction is, however, an infection due to growth of the bacilli along the intestine and resulting in a diarrhea. The onset of this is from 12 to 24 hours after ingestion.

Susceptibility is high. Whatever resistance may be established in the course of infection appears to be fleeting.

CONTROL MEASURES

Control of Spread

The case should be treated in the same manner as one of typhoid and paratyphoid (see p. 174).

Epidemiological Investigation. Such procedure should be directed at the source of the infection in a manner quite comparable to the investigation of typhoid. The first step is the identification of the strain of salmonella responsible for the infection, for identification of sources and related cases cannot be established unless shown to be harboring organisms of the same type. Isolation of a salmonella that is not typed is of little epidemiological value. As cases of food-borne salmonella infection are usually recognized only in the presence of a rather explosive outbreak among many persons after a meal in common, little doubt usually exists as to the time or place of infection, though great difficulty may be experienced in determining the article of food responsible. This requires careful questioning of all persons who partook of the meal, the sick and the well alike, as great significance may be attached to the fact that persons who did not eat of the food in question escaped infection. More difficulty will be experienced if the cases are due to consumption of food sold in a retail store and contaminated prior to sale, since the infection would be scattered among persons unaware of anything in common. As the incubation period is usually fairly short, remnants of the food may be available for examination and should be submitted to the laboratory.[2] Stool cultures should be obtained from all persons who handled the food in question. Examination of rodents and of their droppings around food-handling establishments may reveal the probable source of infection. Investigation of sporadic infections should be directed toward discovery of unrecognized sources or infections among family associates and among domestic pets.

Contacts should be examined for evidence of infection and stool cultures obtained, especially if the individual is engaged in a food-handling occupation. The discovery of a salmonella in such a contact justifies immediate exclusion from food-handling duties without waiting to establish identity of the strain.

Environmental sanitation appears to offer the greatest promise of prevention of such infections. The strictest sanitation of all food-handling establishments is essential. This should include lavish provision of hand-washing facilities and strict enforcement of their use, especially after visits to the toilet (see p. 178). Active measures should be taken to eliminate rodents and roaches, and no food left so exposed that contamination with rodent droppings is possible or that roaches may find access to it.

Disinfection. The same precautions should be followed as are observed for typhoid fever.

Minimizing Ill Effects

Though distressing, the symptoms are generally mild and self-limited. Public health nursing care is not required except to instruct as to prevention of spread.

Control through Immunization

No method of active or passive immunization is known, nor would use of such be practical or justifiable in view of the rarity and mildness of such infections.

---

[2] Remnants fished out of garbage pails are of little value.

STAPHYLOCOCCAL POISONING

Recognition of this type of condition is of recent origin, dating from the work of Jordan and Dack in 1930. The incubation period is brief, usually one to three hours. The patient has severe nausea and vomiting with considerable prostration; diarrhea is of less importance than in salmonella infections. The pallor, weak pulse, and subnormal temperature are frightening to the patient and often cause severe apprehension of imminent demise, as the patient suspects a cardiac accident. The acute symptoms usually last only three or four hours, but the patient may remain in a weakened and exhausted condition for several days. In spite of the severity of the symptoms, deaths from staphylococcal poisoning are very rare. Outbreaks may occur following a common meal but more frequently among persons unconnected except through purchase of the same article from a given source.

EPIDEMIOLOGY

Etiological Agent. Certain strains of hemolytic staphylococci are capable of producing a powerful, heat-resistant enterotoxin. The production of toxin is conditioned in part by the medium on which the staphylococci grow and is favored by the presence of starches. The symptoms are due solely to the toxin which has been formed in the food prior to ingestion, for the organisms themselves are not pathogenic via the intestinal tract. Identification of those strains capable of producing this toxin is a matter of considerable technical difficulty.[3]

The reservoir of infection is not clearly recognized. In many instances hemolytic staphylococci may be found in the throat or in skin lesions of a person who handled food apparently responsible for the poisoning. The mere presence of a hemolytic staphylococcus is not proof that the person harboring the organism is the source of infection as many staphylococci are unable to produce the enterotoxin.

Escape of the Organism. In the occasional case in which throat or skin infection has been encountered, it would appear that the food has been contaminated directly by the food handler.

Transmission is via food contaminated with the specific staphylococci. The degree of toxicity varies with the number of organisms and their multiplication. Cooking may destroy the organisms and prevent further

[3] Certain streptococci may apparently produce comparable toxins and may possibly be the cause of similar conditions. Most of the outbreaks studied have been due to a staphylococcal infection.

multiplication, but boiling for 30 minutes does not completely destroy the toxin that has already been formed. Staphylococcal poisonings have been most frequently encountered in connection with custard-filled bakery products, though cases attributable to other foods such as prepared meats, salads, and milk have been described. Although outbreaks occur most commonly in the warmer months when refrigeration is more difficult and multiplication of organisms more rapid, cases occur at all seasons of the year.

Entry is with the food, absorption of the toxin occurring rapidly. The toxin is apparently not locally irritating to the gastric mucosa but produces its effect after absorption by acting on the nervous mechanism controlling vomiting.

Susceptibility. Little is known regarding variable susceptibility in man. The high attack rate in outbreaks suggests that little resistance normally exists, though in any group of volunteers who have swallowed the toxin an occasional person has failed to react.

CONTROL MEASURES

Control of Spread

The case requires no isolation precautions, merely sympathy, good care, and reassurance.

Epidemiological investigation is directed at the source of infection in the same manner as outlined above for salmonella infections. It should be emphasized that isolation of a hemolytic staphylococcus from the suspected food does not constitute proof of its etiological relationship, for staphylococci may be found frequently in foods eaten without producing any illness. Cultures isolated in connection with an outbreak should be submitted to a competent laboratory for careful identification. The investigator should be constantly alert for information as to the possible source of the staphylococci.

Contacts require no precautions, merely assurance that the condition is not communicable from person to person.

Environmental Sanitation. Without exact knowledge of the reservoir of the particular staphylococci, little of a precise nature may be done with any assurance of success. As custard-filled bakery products are so frequently involved, their sale—especially during the warm weather—has at times been discontinued by regulation or agreement. While this will reduce the likelihood of such conditions, it is no guarantee of protection, as cases may occur in the winter and other foods may be equally involved. Commercial bakeries have been forbidden in some places to use dried or broken (canned) eggs or milk powders, on the supposition that these might carry pathogenic staphylococci, but evidence of this seems scant. At most they can be no more than one of many sources. To reduce multiplication of staphylococci, custards should be kept in the refrigerator and filled into the shells immediately before sale by bakeries. Employees with skin infections should be kept from work. Aside from such measures, which may help, little of a specific nature may be recommended until more is known of the reservoir and identification of the staphylococci.

Minimizing Ill Effects

Cases merit medical care for relief of symptoms and may require supportive treatment. Although extremely distressing, staphylococcal poisoning is not dangerous, patients invariably recovering unless already severely debilitated by some other condition.

Control through Immunization

No practical method of active or passive immunization is known, nor would the incidence of staphylococcal food poisoning warrant its use.

BOTULISM

Botulism is an acute central nervous system poisoning caused by the toxin of the *Clostridium botulinum*. There are no gastrointestinal symptoms, the patient suffering from peripheral and central paralyses resulting in death through respiratory failure. The disease is most frequently encountered after eating of home-canned vegetables that are consumed without heating after removal from the jar. The disease is more common in the western part of the United States than in the East, due probably to the more agricultural character of the population and a higher degree of infection in the soil.

EPIDEMIOLOGY

Etiological Agent. The *Cl. botulinum* is a spore-forming saprophytic organism which has no apparent capacity for infection of man. Under anaerobic conditions, the spores germinate, and the vegetative form produces a powerful toxin which has a specific affinity for nerve tissue. The spores withstand ordinary boiling but are destroyed by temperatures of 120° C for ten minutes. The vegetative form will not grow or produce toxins in acid mediums, hence the comparative safety of home-canned tomatoes and fruits. As the toxin is readily destroyed by heat, it is broken up if the food is thoroughly boiled so that the heat will penetrate the entire food mass.

Reservoir of Infection. The *Cl. botulinum* is one of the few free-living organisms harmful to man. Its normal habitat is probably the soil; it has been found high up on uninhabitated slopes. Soils vary as to the extent to which they harbor botulinum spores; the highest rate is found in the West, particularly on the Pacific coast. Spores have also been found in the intestines of many species of animals.

Transmission of Infection. The spores contaminate the food at the time of its growth. Those foods that grow so near the earth as to be soiled by spattering of the rain are most likely to be involved, especially if the entire vegetable or fruit is eaten. Thus green beans are more often responsible for production of botulism than are peas, which are covered by a pod, or corn, which is well elevated above the soil. Any article of food may, however, be contaminated under certain conditions. Several years ago, a widespread outbreak traced to ripe olives left in many persons an unwarranted phobia against such articles. Commercially canned products are rarely involved in the United States today, because of the precautions taken by the industry as a result of extensive research. In most instances, poisoning is the result of eating home-canned products which were either not heated to a high enough temperature to destroy the spores by one cooking or not heated sufficiently often to permit destruction of all organisms and of toxins produced by the generation of spores between successive heatings. As boiling destroys the toxin, poisoning occurs only in connection with food eaten without thorough cooking after removal from the jar. An abnormal and slightly bitter taste is frequently, though not always, noticed in connection with such food. There is no danger in raw vegetables from the soil, as the spores themselves are harmless upon ingestion and toxins are formed only under the anaerobic conditions existing in sealed containers.

Entry and Incubation Period. Entry occurs via the intestinal tract. Minute quantities of the toxin may cause illness or death. Fatal cases have been reported from eating as much as a single bean from a contaminated jar. The incubation period is usually about 24 hours, varying from a few hours to two or three days.

Susceptibility appears to be universal, as shown by the high attack rate among those who ate food containing the toxin.

CONTROL MEASURES

Control of Spread

The Case. As the patient is suffering from a poisoning, not an infection, there is no danger of spread from the patient.

Epidemiological investigation of all cases should be carried out immediately upon diagnosis or even suspicion. First attention should be given to establishing the article of food responsible for the poisoning and the identity of other persons who may have eaten it, so that they may be given antitoxin if symptoms have not ensued and the maximum incubation period has not elapsed. The incubation period is usually so short and recognition of the correct diagnosis so delayed that most of those who are going to come down with the condition will have already sickened; but treatment may have been delayed because of uncertainty as to the diagnosis. If the food is part of a lot which has been sold to other persons (commercial products or restricted sale of home-canned products), it should be assumed that all other parts of this lot are equally contaminated. They should, therefore, be located and destroyed, and recent sales to the consumer should be traced lest the contaminated cans be opened and their contents eaten. Failure to make such a search may result in the deaths of other persons.

Contacts. No precautions need be taken if the contacts have not eaten of the same food. If they have so eaten, botulinus antitoxin should be administered at once if obtainable.

Environmental Sanitation. The spores are so widely disseminated in the soil that one must assume all soil is contaminated. Strict precautions as to temperature control and adjustment of the acidity of the food are observed by the commercial canneries to guarantee destruction of all spores. Fortunately, these measures are so well understood and carried out under such strict supervision from the industry itself that such goods are quite safe today. Eternal vigilance is, however, the price of safety. Although nothing can be done in the way of regulating home-canning, educational programs can be carried out as to the proper methods of canning. Cooking beyond the usual thermal death point of the spores must be provided to permit the heat to penetrate the food mass. The time, temperature, and pressure vary with the food in question. Even under these conditions such products should be boiled vigorously, preferably for 15 minutes, before being eaten, thus affording an added factor of safety. Fruits are usually so acid that they are not involved.

Minimizing III Effects

Antitoxin is essential to control the effects of the poisoning. This should be administered without delay, as minutes and hours are precious in this condition.

Control through Immunization

Active immunization is not practical or necessary because of the rarity of the poisoning. Persons who have eaten poisoned foods but not yet shown signs of poisoning should be given a therapeutic dose of antitoxin.

SUMMARY

Health Department Program

Food poisonings and infections result from the eating of food contaminated with certain bacteria. Although the source of this contamination is not apparent in all instances, the food is usually one which has been subjected to some sort of processing. The risk therefore varies with the sanitary care used in the handling of the food. Every measure that reduces the likelihood of introduction of contamination, from whatever source, lessens the risk of food infection. This requires the strictest policing of food-handling establishments. As inspectors cannot be present 24 hours of the day, great reliance must be placed on the cooperation of the management of these establishments in requiring strict compliance with all sanitary measures. This in turn requires education and training of personnel in the sanitary handling of foods. The educational program should be extended to apply also to homes, where much of the danger exists and where somewhat different measures are required.

Outbreaks of food poisonings and infection are not of common occurrence. In fact they may be considered as rather rare accidents, especially botulism. The latter is very apt to result fatally and therefore evokes a great deal of publicity, which alarms the population out of all proportion to the real risk. Outbreaks due to the staphylococci and salmonellae are more common but rarely fatal, though they are extremely distressing when they occur. In all cases there is a tendency for the victim to wish to fix responsibility, frequently so that he may recover damages. This is a matter of purely personal concern with which the health officer should strictly avoid contact, even though he can at times hardly escape a summons as a witness to facts. If responsible for a laboratory, the health officer should avoid accepting samples of food brought in by a person who claims to have been sickened by the food in question, as such evidence is usually desired merely for the purpose of suit. Commercial laboratories are available for such work. The health department should confine itself to prevention of these conditions and investigation of outbreaks as they occur but should accept no samples that have not been collected by its own personnel.

The **health officer** is responsible for the epidemiological investigation of cases of food poisoning. He must be ready to drop everything else for this, if he expects to achieve success. The assistance of a well-qualified laboratory is essential. Through the **sanitary officer** he should provide for supervision of all food-handling establishments, with special attention to methods of cleanliness rather than to mere physical equipment and layout.

The public health nurse, especially in rural areas, should be constantly alert for dangerous practices in home-canning and, where necessary, may assume some responsibility in home instruction in this regard. The assistance of 4-H clubs and of the home visitors of the agricultural extension service is invaluable in teaching proper methods. All of the health department personnel must cooperate and assume personal responsibility in educational programs as to the cleanliness of food handling in all its phases.

SUGGESTED READINGS

Adams, H. S.: *Milk and Food Sanitation Practices.* New York: Commonwealth Fund, 1947.

Best, William H.: "Is Routine Examination and Certification of Food Handlers Worth While?" *Am. J. Pub. Health* 27:1003-6, (Oct.) 1937.

Dack, G. M.: *Food Poisoning,* rev. ed. Chicago: University of Chicago Press, 1949.

Dauer, C. C.: "Food and Water Borne Disease Outbreaks," *Pub. Health Rep.,* 67:1089-95, (Nov.) 1952.

Dewberry, Eliot: *Food Poisoning,* 3rd ed. London: Leonard Hill, Ltd., 1951.

Dolman, C. E.: "Bacterial Food Poisoning," *Canad. J. Pub. Health,* 34:97-111, 205-35, (Mar., May) 1943.

Dolman, C. E., and Kerr, Donna E.: "Botulism in Canada," *Canad. J. Pub. Health,* 38:48-57, (Jan.) 1947.

Edwards, P. R.; Bruner, D. W.; and Moran, Alice B.: "Further Studies on the Occurrence and Distribution of Salmonella Types in the U.S.," *J. Infect. Dis.,* 83:220-31, (Nov.-Dec.) 1948.

Feig, Milton: "Diarrhea, Dysentery, Food Poisoning, and Gastroenteritis. A Study of 926 Outbreaks and 49,879 Cases Reported to the United States Public Health Service (1945-1947)," *Am. J. Pub. Health,* 40:1372-94, (Nov.) 1950.

Felsenfeld, Oscar, and Young, Viola Mae: "A Study of Human Salmonellosis in North and South America," *Am. J. Trop. Med.,* 29:483-91, (July) 1949.

"Food Poisoning in England and Wales in 1950," *Month. Bull. Min. Health & Pub. Health Lab. Serv.,* 10:228-39, (Oct.) 1951.

Geiger, J. C.: "Food Handler Examinations: Findings on 4386 Persons, Years 1931-1936, Inclusive," *California & West. Med.,* 49:312-13, (Oct.) 1938.

Getting, Vlado: "Epidemiologic Aspects of Food-Borne Disease," *New England J. Med.,* 228:754-62, 788-96, 823-30, (June 10, 17, and 24) 1943.

Jones, E. R.: "Food Poisoning—Its Epidemiology and Bacteriology," *Brit. M. J.,* 2:106-10, (July 17) 1937.

Korff, Ferdinand A.; Taback, Mathew; and Beard, J. Howard: "A Coordinated Investigation of a Food Poisoning Outbreak," *Pub. Health Rep.,* 67:909-13, (Sept.) 1952.

Meyer, K. F.: "Newer Knowledge on Botulism and Mussel Poisoning," *Am. J. Pub. Health,* 21:762-70, (July) 1931.

————: "The Protective Measures of the State of California against Botulism," *J. Prev. Med.*, 5:261–93, (July) 1931.

Meyer, K. F., and Eddie, B.: *Fifty Years of Botulism in the United States and Canada.* San Francisco: The University of California Medical Center, July, 1950.

Olson, Theodore A., and Rueger, Myrtle E.: "Experimental Transmission of *Salmonella oranienburg* through Cockroaches," *Public Health Rep.*, 65:531–40, (Apr. 21) 1950.

Savage, Sir William: "Food Poisoning," *Brit. M. J.*, 2:584–85, 615–16, (Nov. 14 and 21), 1942.

————: "Bacterial Food Poisoning," Chap. XIII of *Control of the Common Fevers.* London: The Lancet, Ltd., 1942.

————: *Practical Public Health Problems,* 2nd ed. London: J. & A. Churchill, Ltd., 1949, pp. 130–142.

Savage, Sir William; Lovell, R.; and Scott, W. M.: "Discussion on Salmonella Infections," *Proc. Roy. Soc. Med.*, 33:357–70, (Apr.) 1940.

Watt, James, and DeCapito, Thelma: "The Frequency and Distribution of *Salmonella* Types Isolated from Man and Animals in Hidalgo County, Texas," *Am. J. Hyg.*, 51:343–52, (May) 1950.

14. Trichinosis

Trichinosis, in its clinically recognizable form, is a febrile disturbance, preceded by diarrhea and attended with severe pain and aching in the muscles. The acute stages last for one or two weeks, almost always ending in recovery but occasionally complicated by a fatal pneumonia. The typical clinical features are seen in only a very small fraction of the patients who are infected, most persons showing no symptoms or such mild ones as to escape recognition.

EPIDEMIOLOGY

Occurrence. Trichinal infection of man is extremely widespread, apparently involving as high as 15 to 20 per cent of the population of the United States. Because of lack of symptoms in all except the moderately severe cases, only a fraction of a per cent of the total infections are recognized clinically; apparently many cases that could be diagnosed escape detection because of failure to suspect the condition and to carry out the necessary tests. There is no evidence of special geographic distribution in the United States.

Etiological Agent. Trichinosis is due to infection with a roundworm known as the *Trichinella spiralis*. The adult form persists for only a short time in the intestine and is responsible for the diarrhea; the larval forms cause the usual symptoms of fever and pain through invasion and encystment in the muscles. The larvae remain alive for several years in their encysted form, though they ultimately die and are calcified. They withstand ordinary refrigeration for periods of over a month but are destroyed in 24 hours by temperatures of −18° C. Heating to 58° C kills them in a few minutes.

Reservoir of Infection. Any carnivorous animal may show infection, though hogs and rats constitute the principal reservoirs from which trichinosis may spread. Hogs are infected primarily through eating of garbage that contains scraps of uncooked pork. The former practice of feeding slaughterhouse waste (offal) was responsible for much infection. Garbage-fed hogs show a far higher incidence of infection than do those raised on grain. If grain were in reality the sole food of the latter, trichinosis would not exist among them. The feeding of the table waste on the farm and the trimmings of home slaughter may introduce and perpetuate infection within a drove of swine fed principally on grain. The eating of the carcasses of dead rats around the pigsties adds to the infection. Much dispute exists as to the relative importance of this eating of dead rats. Some maintain that it is an important and probably the principal source of infection for hogs; others think that it rarely if ever occurs. The high infection rate of rats is due to their eating of garbage and slaughterhouse scraps and to a certain degree to cannibalistic tendencies. Cats show a high incidence due to eating of rats, though this reservoir of infection is of no human importance. Similarly, man himself constitutes a tremendous reservoir of infection, but this is of no practical importance from the point of view of spread so long as we refrain from cannibalism. Other species of carnivorous animals may show infection, human cases having been reported from eating bear, seal, and walrus meat.

Escape from the reservoir occurs only by digestion of muscles containing the encysted larvae. As there is no avenue of escape of the infection during the life of the victim, there is no danger from the closest sort of association with the patient or animal, no matter how severely infected.

Transmission is via the flesh of infected animals. Man acquires the disease almost exclusively by eating raw or undercooked pork. Frequently this is in the form of sausage containing raw pork, a type of food often homemade and used quite extensively by certain racial groups in this country. Meat products that contain raw pork and that are prepared under federal inspection are treated to destroy the encysted larvae. Since other pork is subjected to no inspection for trichinosis in either federally or locally supervised slaughterhouses, one must assume that it is potentially trichinous. If this is eaten without being thoroughly cooked, infection may ensue. Although most persons make a practice of eating only cooked pork, experience shows that in reality much of the meat is not subjected to such temperatures as will destroy all trichinae.

Entry of the Infection. When the encysted larvae are liberated in the intestine through digestion of the muscle fibers in which they are embedded, they rapidly develop to adult life, mate, and produce their young. The *Trichinella spiralis* is viviparous, discharging the living embryos into the lymph spaces of the intestinal wall. As many as one thousand may be discharged from a single female. The embryos pass from the lymph to the blood stream and are carried to all parts of the body.[1] The embryos burrow from the capillaries into the muscle fibers, where they surround themselves with a protective capsule. Here they lie dormant for years and wait to be released on ingestion of the muscle. Calcification may occur, ultimately destroying the encysted larvae. The acute symptoms of trichinosis are due to invasion of the muscles by the larvae, the severity depending on the number of larvae concerned, which in turn depends on the number of encysted larvae ingested. The incubation period is about a week to ten days after ingestion of the infected meat.

Susceptibility appears to be universal. There is no evidence that subclinical infection results in any resistance against either further small doses or massive doses that will cause recognizable illness.

CONTROL MEASURES

Control of Spread

The Case. No precautions are necessary, as there is no avenue of escape for the larvae during the life of the host.

Epidemiological investigation is desirable to establish a probable source of infection. In the average sporadic case who has eaten in many places during the preceding two weeks, this may be very difficult. As all pork sold in the meat markets is potentially infected, little good will come from establishing a presumptive source of this character. Special search should be made for meat products that are eaten without further cooking, especially certain homemade sausages. If these latter are involved, it is important to destroy all remaining parts of the lot given to friends or neighbors.[2] Spread through sausages prepared in federally approved slaughterhouses is very unlikely, but local inspection is not equally stringent in most places. Hence, special attention must be given to sausages produced and distributed locally.[3]

As a part of the epidemiological investigation, it may be desirable to test other members of the household for infection and thus aid in establishing the probable source of the infection. If the disease was acquired within the home, many of these household members would be likely to show infection; if outside, only those who had had the same meals away from home as did the patient and had eaten the same things. The skin test

---

[1] If the blood is examined at this stage, the embryos may be discovered. This is of no practical diagnostic value, as there is nothing at this stage to suggest the development of infection and, therefore, to lead to a blood examination.

[2] Generosity is a commendable trait but, when expressed through the distribution of homemade sausage, has too often meant the gift of trichinosis along with the meat.

[3] Unless produced under federal inspection, such products would not be admitted to interstate commerce.

is of considerable assistance in this examination. It consists of intracutaneous injection of an extract of the trichinae: infected persons show an area of erythema appearing within five minutes and reaching its height within an hour. Although not infallible, it is of great value. In carrying out such investigations, the health officer must remember that he is interested only in finding the source to prevent further infection, not in uncovering evidence for possible lawsuits.

Contacts. No precautions are necessary.

Environmental Sanitation. The most promising and effective methods of control lie in attempts to prevent infection of hogs and to destroy infection in the pork flesh. Discontinuance of the practice of garbage feeding would be theoretically desirable but would represent a considerable wastage. Attempts are being made at present to cook the garbage sufficiently to destroy the trichinae. Such a method, if economically feasible, will effect a tremendous reduction in the incidence of infection in garbage-fed hogs. It will not, however, completely eliminate the danger from pork because of the impossibility of preventing the feeding of table scraps and the trimmings of the private slaughterhouse on farms where hogs are raised.[4] Also, it would not remove the danger of infection of hogs from eating the carcasses of rats. Such measures cannot, therefore, be considered as completely adequate for trichinosis prevention.

The heating or refrigeration of all pork that is going to be used in raw sausages is required in federally inspected plants and renders such products safe. Similar precautions should be required in all plants under local supervision but cannot be enforced in home preparations. Freezing of all pork at such temperatures and for such time as will destroy the larvae would be theoretically possible but would introduce a severe economic problem into the industry and might increase the cost of pork unnecessarily in proportion to the risk entailed. At one time, federal inspection attempted to detect trichinal infections of pork through microscopic examination of sections of the tongue and diaphragm. This has been discontinued as unreliable, so that at present no attempt is made to detect trichinal infection.

Adequate cooking in the home (and restaurant) remains the most effective safeguard against infection from pork. The old rule of the housewife to cook pork until the flesh is white and dry is a very safe practice, which, if followed, will prevent infection. The difficulty comes from the failure of certain persons to apply it, especially in restaurants. Some infections also occur from meats (such as hamburg steak) which are supposed to consist entirely of beef but with which a certain amount of pork scraps

[4] The feeding of offal is now largely discontinued.

may frequently be mixed. To reduce the risk of addition of pork, some cities require that all hamburg steak and other ground or mixed meats shall be ground freshly for each customer and in full view so that the purchaser may see what is being put in.

Minimizing Ill Effects

This is purely a problem for the attending physician, there being nothing that the board of health can do to assist.

Control through Immunization

No method of either passive or active immunization is known, nor would the incidence of clinically recognizable disease warrant its general use if it existed.

SUMMARY

Health Department Program

Until methods of preventing infection through regulation of garbage feeding or similar procedures have been proved to be of practical value, sole reliance must be placed on methods of destroying the larvae in the pork flesh. This means strict supervision of all plants preparing such products commercially and education in the home and restaurant as to the necessity of thorough cooking of all pork. The public should be taught that pork, if properly handled, is a good and nourishing food but that one must assume all of it to be potentially infected and must treat it accordingly. There is no need of so alarming the public that consumption of pork will decline, and equally no excuse for neglecting reasonable precautions on the ground that the risk is slight in view of the rarity of severe cases. Clinically recognizable disease would be widespread if the housewife were suddenly to discontinue the thorough cooking of pork.

The health officer is responsible for all epidemiological investigation of cases and the formulation of a program of supervision and public education. If his community has meat-packing plants not under federal or state supervision, he should, through his sanitary inspectors, insist upon adequate treatment of pork products to be eaten without further cooking. Supervision of most large plants is exercised by the federal Department of Agriculture, as its approval is necessary if the product is to be shipped in interstate commerce. The local board of health may well forbid the sale of sausages that have not been adequately supervised during manufacture. Attention should be given to methods of reducing the hazard of garbage feeding on both a commercial and home basis. The educational program should be carried on through proper, though not sensational, use of the newspapers, pamphlets, and instruction in the schools and the home. In the latter, use may be made of the public health nurse and of the home economics worker of the agriculture extension service.

SUGGESTED READINGS

Augustine, Donald L.: "Trichinosis: Incidence and Diagnostic Tests," *New England J. Med.*, **216**:463–66, (Mar. 18) 1937.

Beard, Rodney R.: "Incidence of Trichinella Infections in San Francisco, 1950," *J.A.M.A.*, **146**:331–34, (May 26) 1951.

Gould, Sylvester E.: *Trichinosis*. Springfield, Ill.: Charles C. Thomas, Publisher, 1945.

————: "An Effective Method for the Control of Trichinosis in the United States," *J.A.M.A.*, **129**:1251–54, (Dec. 29) 1945.

Hall, Maurice C.: "Studies on Trichinosis: IV. The Role of the Garbage-Fed Hog in the Production of Human Trichinosis," *Pub. Health Rep.*, **52**:873–86, (July 2) 1937.

————: "Studies on Trichinosis: VII. The Past and Present Status of Trichinosis in the United States, and the Indicated Control Measures," *Pub. Health Rep.*, **53**:1472–86, (Aug. 19) 1938.

Hall, Maurice C., and Collins, Benjamin J.: "Studies on Trichinosis: I. The Incidence of Trichinosis as Indicated by Post-Mortem Examination of 300 Diaphragms," *Pub. Health Rep.*, **52**:468–90, (Apr. 16) 1937.

Maxcy, Kenneth F.: "Trichinosis: An Unsolved Problem in the United States," *Am. J. M. Sc.*, **194**:444–48, (Sept.) 1937.

Riley, William A., and Scheifley, Charles H.: "Trichinosis of Man, a Common Infection," *J.A.M.A.*, **102**:1217–18, (Apr. 14) 1934.

Schwartz, Benjamin: "Trichinosis in Swine and Its Relationship to Public Health," *Smithsonian Institute, Report for 1939*, pp. 413–35.

————: "Zoological Problems Relative to Meat Inspection and Their Bearing on Public Health," *Am. J. Pub. Health*, **29**:1133–39, (Oct.) 1939.

Shookhoff, Howard B.; Birnkrant, William B.; and Greenberg, Morris: "An Outbreak of Trichinosis in New York City with Special Reference to Intradermal and Precipitin Tests," *Am. J. Pub. Health*, **36**:1403–11, (Dec.) 1946.

Wright, Willard H.: "Studies on Trichinosis: XI. The Epidemiology of *Trichinella spiralis* Infestation and Measures Indicated for the Control of Trichinosis," *Am. J. Pub. Health*, **29**:119–27, (Feb.) 1939.

Wright, Willard H.; Jacobs, Leon; and Walton, Arthur C.: "Studies on Trichinosis: XVI. Epidemiological Considerations Based on the Examinations for Trichinae of 5313 Diaphragms from 189 Hospitals in 37 States and the District of Columbia," *Pub. Health Rep.*, **59**:669–81, (May 26) 1944.

15. Undulant Fever

Undulant fever, better referred to as brucellosis, is an infection with organisms of the *Brucella* group. The clinically recognizable case usually appears as a prolonged fever with frequent remissions, accompanied by malaise and profuse sweating and sometimes complicated by involvement of the joints or urinary bladder. The physical disability may last for several months and in some cases one or two years. Cases severe enough to be clinically recognizable are, however, the exception; most infections give rise to no symptoms or little more than prolonged, low-grade fever, malaise, and sweating. Infection rarely results fatally.

EPIDEMIOLOGY

Occurrence. Human brucella infections have been recognized in all parts of the world. The prevalence of such conditions depends on the degree of association with cattle and swine and the extent to which raw milk is used. There is thus a higher incidence in rural areas than in cities— and especially among farmers, veterinarians, and slaughterhouse employees. Children are less frequently affected than are adults.

Etiological Agent. Three strains of brucella are recognized as pathogenic for man. The caprine strain, *Br. melitensis,* is normally an invader of goats but is found also in cattle and swine. It was first recognized as a cause of infection spread through goat's milk on the island of Malta; hence the disease was referred to as Malta fever. It is less commonly encountered in the United States because of the small amount of goat's milk used here, though occasionally infections have been described from the Southwest. The bovine strain, *Br. abortus,* is found chiefly in cattle, less commonly in swine. As this strain is extremely widespread throughout the United States, its relatively low pathogenicity for man is fortunate. The porcine strain, *Br. suis,* is more pathogenic for man. Unfortunately it involves not only hogs but also cattle, in which it causes contagious abortion (Bang's disease) as does the bovine strain. The brucella organisms do not form spores. Though fairly resistant and capable of prolonged survival outside the body, they are destroyed by pasteurization. They will survive at least a month in certain dairy products though the exact importance of butter and cheese as vehicles is uncertain.

The reservoir of infection consists of cattle, swine, and goats, depending on the several strains. The incidence of infection is high, the disease being found in all parts of the United States and often involving 10 to 15 per cent of the cattle within an area. Some herds show almost 100 per cent infection. It was estimated in 1949 that about 5 per cent of the adult female cattle in the United States were infected, that 20 per cent of the herds were involved and that from 1 to 3 per cent of all swine were infected. So far as is known, man never serves as a source of infection. Brucella infections of horses, sheep, and dogs have been described but appear to be of little or no importance in transmission to man.

Escape from the reservoir may occur through several channels. The milk may be contaminated through an inflammation of the udder; the organisms are most prevalent in the milk shortly after calving. As only a small fraction of the infected animals discharge the brucellae in the milk at any one period, a herd may show a high incidence of infection, yet few, if any, organisms in the milk. Yet at a later test of milk from the same herd, the organisms may be readily found. It is safe to assume that any infected animal is potentially a spreader. The bacteria may be found in abundance in the lochial secretion as well as in the placenta of an infected animal. They are also found in the tissues, from which they are released mechanically at the time of slaughter or dressing of the meat. The organisms have been found in the urine and feces of the human case, though they have apparently never given rise to further infection.

Transmission occurs either by direct contact with the infected tissues or through the medium of milk or milk products. Persons who come in contact with animals may acquire an infection directly. This group includes farmers and veterinarians, the latter being especially exposed through manual extraction of retained placentae. Slaughterhouse employees who are handling the tissues of infected cattle and hogs are also infected through direct contact. Milk is the only important vehicle of indirect infection; it has been responsible for many outbreaks and a countless number of sporadic infections. The importance of dairy products made from unpasteurized milk or cream, such as butter and cheese, is problematical, though the demonstrated survival of brucellae in such products indicates the possible danger. Laboratory workers are frequently infected through handling cultures or infected animals. Respiratory spread, through inhalation of contaminated dust or droplets, is possible.

Entry of the organisms is effected through either the gastrointestinal tract or breaks in the skin. Although the latter route is well proved and may explain many of the contact infections of farmers, veterinarians, and slaughterhouse employees, there is always doubt in such cases as to whether infection entered through such breaks or was unconsciously transferred to the mouth via the fingernails which became contaminated through handling infected animals or carcasses.

Susceptibility. Little is known of an exact nature regarding susceptibility and resistance to brucella infection. It appears certain that many subclinical infections occur. Heathman reported that 55 per cent of 1,096 slaughterhouse employees showed positive skin tests, which may be taken as evidence of past infection. Jordan found a positive agglutination test among 45 per cent of a group of 120 veterinarians, while Weisman found evidence of infection in 15 per cent of a sanatorium group using raw milk from an infected herd and King found 13 per cent in a similar group. None of these persons had recognizable brucellosis, and only a rare individual had a history suggestive of infection. This would suggest that man possesses a relatively high level of resistance to infection and that only rarely is the dose sufficiently large and virulent to overcome such resistance. This is probably due in large part to latent immunization with small doses of organisms of low virulence, possibly the bovine strain. As only a small fraction of the infected animals are shedding organisms at any one time, there is usually a large dilution in the mixed milk of a herd, thus reducing the dose. The relative scarcity of cases among children in spite of their large consumption of milk suggests that certain autarceologic factors of resistance are present.

Several methods of testing for recent infection have been described. These include the agglutination test, a skin test for allergy to the brucella, and the opsonocytophagic test. The exact relationship between these tests and resistance is not fully established.

CONTROL MEASURES

Control of Spread

The case requires no isolation precautions. As the organisms have been proved to be in the feces and urine, reasonable care should be observed in the disposal of these, though infection has not been observed to spread from person to person, not even to a nursing attendant, in spite of the large number of unrecognized, subclinical cases. Release cultures are not required, nor is there any restriction regarding return to work when the patient is physically fit.

Epidemiological investigation should be directed to finding the source of infection. If the patient's occupation entails the handling of cattle or swine or their tissues, one can only presume that this was the most likely source of infection. Obviously, one can never identify the animal or carcass responsible for the spread, unless the patient be a farmer whose sole contact has been with his own herd. Special inquiries should be made regarding raw-milk consumption, and, if possible, search made for cases among other consumers of the same supply. Blood or milk testing of the cattle on a milk farm will yield only presumptive evidence as to the source of the infection.

Contacts require no quarantine precautions. In case of suspected milk-borne spread, they may be tested for evidence of subclinical infection.

Environmental Sanitation. So long as the infection of cattle persists, the only effective method of preventing spread through milk is by pasteurization. The wearing of rubber gloves by veterinarians and slaughterhouse employees may reduce the risk of contact infection for this group.

Disinfection. No disinfection procedures are necessary.

Elimination of infection from cattle constitutes the only real protection of man, as this would prevent contact infection (except from hog carcasses), whereas pasteurization prevents only milk-borne spread. Attempts have been made to eradicate the disease in cattle. These have been prompted principally by the desire to avoid the economic loss to cattle breeders and dairymen, for whom contagious abortion in cattle represents one of the most serious economic problems. Infected cattle eat as much as do noninfected, yet frequently fail to carry their calves to term.

Control through testing and slaughter has been attempted and is yielding good results in some cases. Infection is detected by blood testing,[1] and all cattle found infected are slaughtered as potential spreaders of the disease. Unfortunately, contagious abortion spreads more readily among cattle than does bovine tuberculosis, so that greater difficulty has been experienced in keeping a herd clean. The infection rate is so high and the incidence of reactors found on repeated tests is also so high that the cost of indemnity would be even larger than was required for the federal-state programs for bovine tuberculosis elimination. Unfortunately, also, the industry has often sought to minimize the hazard of spread through milk and at times has even denied any human health problem. In this attitude

---

[1] The ring test, applied to whole milk samples, has been shown to be a very reliable and simple screening device in the detection of herds or individual animals which should be subjected to the more cumbersome blood test.

it has rejected one of the most potent arguments that could be advanced for the appropriation of indemnity funds. The certified milk industry requires that all herds be free of contagious abortion; similar requirements have been attempted for certain other grades of milk in some states.

Due to the practical difficulty of eradicating the infection through slaughter, many attempts have been made to immunize cattle, it being assumed that a cow infected with an organism of low virulence would be resistant to the severe and aborting form of the disease. Numerous vaccines have been described, some of which appear to reduce the incidence of abortion. Unfortunately, however, the use of a living vaccine is attended with a risk that a certain number of the animals may shed the organisms in the milk. No proof exists that these organisms are equally attenuated for human beings, so that vaccination may constitute an added hazard to the milk consumer unless the milk is pasteurized. There is, then, every reason for the health officer to oppose the use of a living vaccine, unless all milk from such herds is pasteurized before sale. More recently, the Federal Bureau of Animal Industry has urged calfhood vaccination with an attenuated strain (strain 19) in the hope that infection with an attenuated organism prior to the development of the udder would reduce the risk of subsequent transmission through milk. While there are still uncertainties and differences of opinion regarding the exact value of this vaccine, there is little doubt that its use does reduce the infection rate in animals. It is to be thought of as a valuable adjunct to other control measures, especially useful in reducing the disease rate in heavily infected herds. If pasteurization can be provided, it would seem that a consumer was adequately protected and that the use of such vaccines for their economic value could be justified.

Minimizing Ill Effects

A health department can do nothing to assist the physician in the treatment of undulant fever. Diagnostic facilities may, however, be afforded through the laboratory; these include the performance of blood cultures and agglutination tests.

Public Health Nursing Care. As the patient is likely to be confined to bed for long periods, it is especially important that someone in the household learn to give good nursing care. Elaborate techniques are usually not required. During the acute stages, the profuse sweats with accompanying unpleasant odors make frequent baths necessary. The attendant should be carefully instructed in doing this quickly, easily, and in such a manner that the patient is refreshed and rested by the bath. Ordinarily hot water and soap are the only things needed, but sometimes, if the odor of perspiration is particularly strong, soda in the water is helpful. If the patient's joints are painful, the attendant should be shown how to handle and support the affected parts and how to apply oil of wintergreen, if that is ordered. The patient whose gums are bleeding should not be allowed to use a toothbrush but should rinse the mouth after each meal.

Usually the physician wishes fluids to be forced during the stage of high fever and profuse sweats. The public health nurse can, as always, assist the attendant by suggesting various fluids, and by showing how to keep account of the amount consumed. In the period of remission, the patient is apt to be weak and depressed. The public health nurse may have an important role in explaining to the family that this depression is part of the disease and in providing occupational therapy to relieve the depression.

Number of Nursing Visits. The course of this disease is so variable, though usually long, that it is difficult even to estimate how many nursing visits may be needed. After the family has learned to give care, an occasional visit by the nurse may be helpful to give encouragement, to suggest possible amusements or occupations for the patient, and to see whether any help can be given to facilitate the nursing care.

Control through Immunization

No method of active or passive immunization is known, nor would the use of such, except in a selected group exposed to occupational hazards, appear to be justified in view of the low incidence of debilitating infection. Attempts to immunize cattle have been considered above.

SUMMARY

Health Department Program

The most effective method of protecting the general community against brucellosis is by pasteurization of all milk, as this is the only medium by which infection is widely spread. Protection of farmers, veterinarians, and slaughterhouse employees is extremely difficult—if not impossible—at the present time, though strict personal cleanliness and protection of the hands against undue direct contact with animal tissues will give some help. Eradication of the disease in cattle, either by slaughtering or by the use of a safe, yet effective, vaccine, affords the greatest promise of prevention of this group of occupational infections. Of these two methods, the former—in spite of its imperfections—is at present the method of choice, though the expense entailed has limited its general use, and adequate funds for indemnity are not available.

The **health officer** is responsible for safeguarding the milk supply of his community, and should insist on universal pasteurization at the earliest date possible. Until that time, he should point out the hazard of raw milk and urge the use of pasteurized. He should work with the group of occupational exposures to help reduce the incidence of such infection. The board of health should insist that milk from vaccinated cattle not be sold unless pasteurized. Through the home visits of the **public health nurse,** mothers may be urged to use pasteurized milk or, if it is not obtainable, to resort to home pasteurization. The **sanitary officer** should exercise close supervision over pasteurization plants and assist the milk producers in every way possible to eliminate infection from their herds.

SUGGESTED READINGS

Dalrymple-Champneys, Sir Weldon: "Undulant Fever: A Neglected Problem," *Lancet,* 1:429–35, 477–85, (Mar. 11 and 18) 1950.

Evans, Alice C.: "Brucellosis in the United States," *Am. J. Pub. Health,* 37:139–51, (Feb.) 1947.

Feig, Milton: "Some Epidemiological Aspects of Brucellosis in the Midwest," *Am. J. Pub. Health,* 42:1253–66, (Oct.) 1952.

Fleming, D. S., and Roepke, M. H.: "Relation of Human and Bovine Brucellosis in Minnesota," *Pub. Health Rep.,* 64:1044–51, (Aug. 19) 1949.

Gershenfeld, Louis, and Butts, Donald, C. A.: "A Survey of Undulant Fever and Bang's Disease in the United States," *Am. J. M. Sc.,* 194:678–84, (Nov.) 1937.

Gould, S. E., and Huddleson, I. F.: "Diagnostic Methods in Undulant Fever (Brucellosis) with Results of a Survey of 8124 Persons," *J.A.M.A.,* 109:1971–74, (Dec. 11) 1937.

Hardy, A. V.; Jordan, C. F.; and Borts, I. H.: "Undulant Fever: Further Epidemiologic and Clinical Observations in Iowa," *J.A.M.A.,* 107:599–64, (Aug. 22) 1936.

Heathman, Lucy S.: "A Survey of Workers in Packing Plants for Evidence of Brucella Infection," *J. Infect. Dis.,* 55:243–65, 1934.

Huddelson, I. Forest: *Brucellosis in Man and Animals,* rev. ed. New York: Commonwealth Fund, 1943.

———: "The Relation of Brucellosis to Human Welfare," *Ann. New York Acad. Sci.,* 48:415–28, (Apr. 10) 1947.

Jordan, Carl F., and Borts, Irving H.: "Brucellosis and Infection Caused by Three Species of Brucella," *Am. J. Med.,* 2:156–67, (Feb.) 1947.

McCullough, Norman B.; Eisele, C. Wesley; and Pavelchek, Emma: "Survey of Brucellosis in Slaughtered Hogs," *Pub. Health Rep.,* 66:205–8, (Feb. 16) 1951.

Magoffin, Robert L.; Kabler, Paul; Spink, Wesley W.; and Fleming, Dean: "An Epidemiologic Study of Brucellosis in Minnesota," *Pub. Health Rep.,* 64:1021–43, (Aug. 19) 1949.

Offut, Andrew C.: "Brucellosis—Another Battle to Win," *Pub. Health Nursing*, 44:535–57, (Oct.) 1952.

Spink, W. W., *et al.*: "Control and Eradication of Brucellosis in Animals. Report No. 1 of the National Research Council Committee on Public Health Aspects of Brucellosis," *J.A.M.A.*, 141:326–29, (Oct. 1) 1949.

Third Inter-American Congress on Brucellosis, November 6–10, 1950. Washington: National Research Council, 1952.

16. Hepatitis

Hepatitis means inflammation of the liver. The term refers, therefore, to any condition causing such inflammation. In recent years, however, special attention has been directed toward two types due to virus infection. Hepatitis manifests itself as a febrile disturbance with a rather abrupt onset. After a few days, bile appears in the urine, the patient becomes jaundiced and the stools are clay-colored. The symptoms persist for several weeks—occasionally months—and tend to recur. Many mild cases occur without recognizable jaundice but with demonstrable evidence of bile excretion in the urine. The disease is extremely disabling because of the severity of the acute stage and the persistence of symptoms. The case fatality rate is less than 1 per cent but some of those who recover have permanent liver damage.

INFECTIOUS HEPATITIS

(INFECTIOUS OR EPIDEMIC JAUNDICE)

Occurrence. This disease has been known for many years, though its viral origin was not recognized until recently. It has appeared as isolated cases (usually diagnosed as acute catarrhal jaundice) or outbreaks spread throughout the community. Even more common have been the outbreaks within special groups such as a military force, an institution, or a school or summer camp. During World War I it plagued the military forces in Europe. In World War II the infection was widespread in Africa, Europe, and the Pacific, attacking Allied and Axis forces alike. At times it was so prevalent as to impair military efficiency, involving as high as 35 to 45 per cent of a given unit over a three-month period. Infection was common in the civil population though the attack rates were lower. More recently it has affected the United Nations armies in Korea. In the United States, infectious hepatitis appears as circumscribed outbreaks in institutional groups or as isolated and apparently unrelated infections. It has been noted with increasing frequency in recent years, but this may mean better recognition and not necessarily an actual increase. Unrecognized infection is obviously widespread as blood tests show evidence of past infection in as high as 35 per cent of the population. Infectious hepatitis must, therefore, be thought of as a very common infection which is mild in most instances but, for reasons still not clear, severe in a few persons.

Etiologic Agent. Infectious hepatitis is caused by a fairly resistant virus (IH virus). In milk the virus is not destroyed by pasteurization and in water it withstands exposure of 30 minutes to one part of chlorine per million.[1] It is not easily destroyed by alcohol or other chemical disinfectants in the concentrations ordinarily employed.

Reservoir of Infection. So far as is currently known, infectious hepatitis is a disease only of man. Unrecognized cases certainly outnumber those that are so ill as to be brought to medical attention and recognition. There is no evidence of permanent carriers.

Escape from the Reservoir. The virus can be recovered from the feces readily during the acute stage and possibly for several weeks after subsidence of symptoms. It is likewise found in the stools of mild non-icteric cases that are diagnosable only through demonstration of bile in the urine. The virus has not been found in the urine. Most attempts to demonstrate it in washings of the nasopharynx have been unsuccessful. The virus is present in the blood stream during the pre-icteric and acute stages and escapes from the body if blood is withdrawn.

Transmission is usually by personal association. Fecal-oral spread is probably the most common. In this, contamination of the hands may well be an important factor responsible for the majority of the sporadic cases. The food handler who has an unrecognized infection can thus transfer virus to food or milk. Water that is sewage-contaminated may also serve as a vehicle. As the virus is not destroyed either by chlorination or pasteurization, there is a special risk of spread through milk or water. Infection may likewise occur through transfusion from a person in an early stage of the disease. Several outbreaks have been traced to spread by inadequately sterilized syringes previously contaminated with blood containing the virus. The occurrence of certain cases and outbreaks suggests transmission through the respiratory tract, but the presence of the virus in the nasopharynx has never been demonstrated. Until its presence in the nose or throat can be shown, the possibility of respiratory spread must remain uncertain.

Entry and Incubation Period. Entry is through the mouth in most cases. In case of transmission through transfusion or syringes the virus is injected through the skin into the blood stream or subcutaneous tissue.

[1] The usual chlorine residual is about 0.1 to 0.2 parts per million.

The incubation period is usually from 20 to 25 days though as short as 8 to 9 days and as long as 35.

Susceptibility is apparently universal. The frequency of relapses suggests that a high level of acquired resistance is not established even though second attacks are rare. Infection with homologous serum hepatitis does not confer resistance to infectious hepatitis.

CONTROL MEASURES

Control of Spread

The Case. Since hepatitis is usually not a reportable disease, the health department is usually unaware of the case and therefore not in a position to require any specific isolation procedures. Isolation of the case from the first week of the disease is usually recommended as there is uncertainty as to possible respiratory spread in the early stages. If the patient is a food handler, he should not return to work until the end of the second or third week after recovery. The exact duration of the period of fecal excretion is not certain as there is no practical test that can be used to determine this in each case. Exclusion from food handling for a period of two or three weeks after recovery appears warranted in view of the known presence of the virus in the stools during the acute and early convalescent stages.

Epidemiological investigation of sporadic cases is quite unfruitful as the individual has so many human contacts and there is no practical means of identifying a source of infection. Furthermore, the individual from whom the infection was acquired may no longer be shedding virus so that little practical value would result from his discovery, even if such were possible. A series of related cases or an explosive outbreak warrants careful investigation as such inquiry may reveal conditions which should be corrected to prevent further spread. In such cases, special thought should be given to the possibility of spread through water, milk, or food or through use of inadequately cleansed syringes.

Contacts. Quarantine of contacts is not warranted. If such contacts are food handlers, urine examination to detect mild unrecognized cases might be justified to reduce the risk of spread through the medium of food. Certainly the health department would be warranted in barring such persons from food handling for two or three weeks.

Environmental Sanitation. No specific measures are of known efficacy, but all measures of personal and community sanitation will help to reduce spread. In military units, camps, and institutions special attention should be given to water supplies and food sanitation. The development of a case in such a group should be the signal for special scrutiny of such procedures, as recognized cases may occur and constitute a serious hazard if there are sanitary defects. Special attention should be given to hand-washing procedures among food handlers and nursing attendants and to procedures for disinfection of syringes. Except in sewered communities, special consideration should also be given to excreta disposal and to fly control.

Disinfection. Infectious hepatitis is included in group III; procedures outlined for that group on page 145 should be followed. Unfortunately, however, little is known about the effects of different disinfectants upon hepatitis virus so that too much reliance cannot be placed upon stool disinfection. As there is a possibility of respiratory spread, all nose and throat discharges should be collected and burned.

Minimizing Ill Effects

The health department has no role in the treatment of the patients as there is no drug of specific value.

Public Health Nursing Care. Since most severe cases will be hospitalized the public health nurse will probably be called upon most often to give convalescent care. This is extremely important as relapses occur frequently if patients get fatigued by attempting to return to full activity too quickly. Usually persons who have had hepatitis are kept on restricted activity for several months. This may range from a requirement of regular rest periods to a limitation on extra job activities. Diet is also a major factor in restoring complete health. The limitations set by the physician should therefore be followed strictly. As knowledge of the disease is still limited, therapeutic regimens differ widely. The public health nurse should obtain from the physician or hospital (if there is no private physician) specific orders regarding activity allowed, rest periods, diet, and drugs (such as aspirin or sleeping pills) that are permitted or forbidden. This long "convalescent" period is so difficult for many persons to accept that the nurse can render a great service by reassuring them, encouraging them to adhere to their physician's orders, and helping them devise ways and means of fitting their special needs into the family routines.

Occasionally an acute case of hepatitis will be cared for at home. General nursing care is directed mainly to alleviation of discomfort. The patient often has high fever. His skin may be dry and require special care to allay itching. The mouth should receive special attention to prevent sores. The patient is usually nauseated and has no desire to eat. Much ingenuity is needed in the selection and preparation of foods which will meet the requirements of the diet ordered and be palatable to the patient. Small and frequent feedings are usually preferable. The public health nurse can help the person in charge of the home to plan these feedings so that six or seven "meals" a day can be produced with a minimum of effort. The physician usually orders a high fluid intake, 3,000 cc a day. The attendant will have to spend much time and use great skill to achieve this. Patients with hepatitis feel so miserable that they are often depressed. The nurse can help the family in understanding this reaction and exercising the necessary patience.

Number of Nursing Visits. The acute case of hepatitis should have daily nursing visits until the acute symptoms have subsided. Thereafter visits once or twice a week will assist the patient and family to adhere to the limitations that are necessary in the ensuing weeks. If daily visits are not possible, at least two visits should be made on successive days to work out care and diet instructions with the attendant.

If the case has returned from the hospital the nurse should make two visits about a week apart and thereafter at suitable intervals if she thinks the patient and family need her support. In some cases these would continue until the physician removes all restrictions.

Control through Immunization

Passive immunization through injection of large doses of gamma globulin is of proved efficacy but is of limited value as it is so temporary. For those exposed to a known risk of infection moderate doses of gamma globulin will provide sufficient passive resistance to guard against severe involvement, but not enough to preclude a mild infection which leaves the individual with an active and more durable resistance. Gamma globulin has been so used to protect nurses and children in institutions where cases were occurring. Its use is also warranted in military units in which there are cases of hepatitis. Doses as low as 0.01 cc per pound of body weight appear to be effective, though larger doses have usually been used. The gamma globulin is given intramuscularly, never intravenously.

Active Immunization. No effective vaccine is known.

SERUM HEPATITIS
(HOMOLOGOUS SERUM JAUNDICE)

Serum hepatitis is clinically indistinguishable from infectious hepatitis. Differentiation is based on its relationship to prior transfusion or injection of blood derivatives, but even this distinction is not always clear as infectious hepatitis can also follow such injections.

Occurrence. The occasional development of jaundice as a sequel to blood transfusion has been known for many years, but the infectious nature of this condition has been recognized only recently. The extensive use of blood transfusions or injections of plasma or whole blood following surgical operations or serious injuries has resulted in more cases of hepatitis and caused more attention to be directed to it. An extensive outbreak followed yellow fever vaccination of the U.S. Army during the early part of World War II and was attributed to the human blood serum used in the preparation of a certain lot of yellow fever vaccine. Over 50,000 cases of jaundice were recorded in this outbreak. Many cases developed during the war years as a sequel to the administration of blood plasma or whole blood to the wounded.[2] Many isolated cases and minor outbreaks have been reported in recent years.

Etiological Agent. Serum hepatitis is due to infection with a virus (SH virus) that is apparently closely related to, yet distinct from, the virus of infectious hepatitis (IH virus). The SH virus is quite resistant to heat, (withstanding 56° C for 30 minutes). At room temperature it stays alive for over a year if desiccated and will survive for several years if frozen. Exposure to 2537 Ångström units of ultraviolet irradiation for 45 minutes will inactivate it in serum.

Reservoir of Infection. Serum hepatitis is a disease only of man. The virus is found in the blood stream for many weeks before the onset of symptoms and throughout the icteric phase. Evidence of permanent carriers is not clear, but one should assume that the virus may be present in the blood for many months or even two to three years after infection. Those who have hepatitis should therefore be avoided as blood donors. Unrecognized cases occur, so there is no absolute assurance of avoiding the disease even if those with a history of hepatitis are rejected as donors.

Escape from Reservoir. So far as is currently known, there is no natural portal of escape of the SH virus from the body. Escape is in all cases through blood drawn directly from circulation. The virus has not been found in the stool as is the case with the virus of infectious hepatitis.

Transmission is always through the medium of blood transfusion or injection of blood derivatives. Several outbreaks appear to have been traced to syringes, needles, or tubing used in intravenous medication, especially of arsenicals in syphilis clinics where several patients have received injections from a large syringe or reservoir containing arsphenamine solution.[3] The backflow of blood when the needle is inserted into the vein

[2] The blood was of tremendous lifesaving value but unfortunately some samples had been drawn from donors with unsuspected hepatitis and consequently conveyed the infection to the recipient.

[3] The replacement of arsenicals by penicillin in the treatment of syphilis has reduced this hazard. Malaria has also been transmitted in this way and by the use of inadequately disinfected syringes by morphine addicts who thus pass the plasmodium from one to another.

results in contamination of the syringe or tubing with resultant transfer of infection to subsequent patients. There is no evidence of spread by association or contact with a case.

Entry and Incubation Period. The virus enters only through its injection into the blood stream or tissues. Attempts to transmit the disease through feeding of blood serum known to contain the virus have been unsuccessful. The incubation period is long, varying from two to six months and averaging about three months.

Susceptibility is high. About 5 to 10 per cent of those receiving the injection of blood derivatives containing virus develop recognizable infection. Second attacks can occur. Prior infection with infectious hepatitis does not confer resistance.

CONTROL MEASURES

Control of Spread

The Case. No isolation measures are needed.

Epidemiological investigation should be directed at discovering the source of infection and the errors of procedure that resulted in the spread of the disease. If the individual has had a single direct transfusion and no blood derivatives, the source of infection is quite obvious. The growing use of multiple injections of blood from blood banks makes tracing of the source more difficult. Search for others who have been affected may help reveal the source of the infection. In case the patient has received blood derivatives, discovery of the source is usually impossible as the blood of so many donors has been pooled before the separation of plasma or fractionation of the proteins. In such cases attention should be given to the procedures used in preparation of the derivatives to discover errors in the process that permitted the virus to escape destruction.

Contacts. No quarantine measures are required.

Environmental Sanitation. No measures are of value as serum hepatitis may spread under the cleanest of conditions. Neither concurrent nor terminal disinfection procedures are required.

Supervision of donors and blood derivatives is the key to the prevention of serum hepatitis and is also of importance in the prevention of spread of certain cases of infectious hepatitis. No person with a history of jaundice should be used as a donor, for the duration of viremia is not known. Unquestionably, the risk of spread diminishes with the lapse of time since infection. Hence persons who have had jaundice several years prior might be used if necessary, but, if possible, they should be avoided to reduce all risk to a minimum. Similarly it is desirable to avoid using persons who have received transfusions or injections of blood derivatives during the preceding year or who have recently been exposed to infectious hepatitis. Similar rules should govern the selection of those whose blood is to be used in preparation of blood derivatives, such as plasma or serum albumin or gamma globulin. Since the blood of one infected donor may contaminate an entire pool of blood, these pools should be kept as small as possible consistent with efficiency and economy of processing. In this way an error in selection or technique will result in a minimum of spread.

Ultraviolet irradiation of plasma or gamma globulin provides an adequate safeguard against infection. The virus of serum hepatitis is destroyed by 45 minutes exposure to 2,537 Ångström units of irradiation. Owing to the number of mild unrecognized cases of serum hepatitis and infectious hepatitis and the occurrence of the SH virus in the blood stream for several weeks or months prior to the onset of symptoms, all blood that is processed should be subjected to such disinfection procedure. Irradiation does not, however, give absolute protection as several outbreaks have been described due to blood products that had been so treated. These probably indicate the need for better methods of irradiation and do not invalidate the basic idea of using ultraviolet light for virus inactivation.

Special attention must be given to syringes, needles, and tubing used in tranfusion, drawing of blood, or for intravenous injections. As the virus of both infectious hepatitis (IH) and serum hepatitis (SH) are quite heat resistant, such equipment must be thoroughly boiled or autoclaved after each use.

Minimizing Ill Effects

There is nothing that the health department can do to help in the medical treatment of the case of serum hepatitis.

Public Health Nursing Care. The nursing care of serum hepatitis is essentially the same as that of infectious hepatitis (see p. 230). The only essential difference is that in the case of infectious hepatitis the virus is known to escape in the stools so special precautions must be observed to protect the nurse against acquiring infection. By way of contrast the virus of serum hepatitis is not known to escape in either stools or urine and no precautions are needed.

Number of Nursing Visits. (See p. 231.)

Control through Immunization

There is no known method of either active or passive immunization Gamma globulin, though effective against infectious hepatitis, is without value in prevention of serum hepatitis.

SUMMARY

Health Department Program

Infectious and serum hepatitis, though clinically indistinguishable in individual cases, are caused by different viruses neither of which confers protection against the other. Infectious hepatitis is usually spread through defects in personal or community sanitation whereby virus that escapes in the feces from active and convalescent cases finds its way into the mouth of another person. Transmission may be by soiled hands which convey the virus to the hands or food of other persons or by way of sewage-contaminated water. Serum hepatitis and some cases of infectious hepatitis are spread through blood transfusion from infected persons or through injections of blood derivatives prepared from the blood of such persons. Prevention of infectious hepatitis depends on improved sanitation. Serum hepatitis can be avoided by careful attention to proper procedures for transfusion and for the preparation of blood derivatives designed for human injection.

The **health officer** should be prepared to make a careful epidemiological investigation of all cases of hepatitis. If cases develop in institutions or in special groups of persons, special search should be made for sanitary defects that have led to spread. Cases of serum hepatitis should be investigated to determine the source of infection or lots of blood derivatives that are obviously contaminated with the SH virus. As the latter usually are articles of interstate commerce, all information so obtained should be relayed promptly to the U.S. Public Health Service. The health department should be prepared to advise with local hospitals regarding donor procedures and, if necessary, to establish regulations regarding blood banks. The **sanitary officer** should be alert for defects in water and food sanitation, especially the employment of food handlers ill with or exposed to infectious hepatitis. The **public health nurse** should be prepared to offer bedside care to nonhospitalized cases and should be alert for unrecognized cases that should be referred to medical attention.

SUGGESTED READINGS

Brightman, I. Jay, and Korns, Robert F.: "Homologous Serum Jaundice in Recipients of Pooled Plasma," *J.A.M.A.*, 135:268–72 (Oct. 4) 1947.

Capps, Richard B.; Bennett, Alfred M.; and Stokes, Joseph, Jr.: "Endemic Infectious Hepatitis in an Infants' Orphanage. I. Epidemiologic Studies in Student Nurses," *Arch. Int. Med.*, 89:6–23, (Jan.) 1952.

Capps, Richard B.; Sborov, Victor; and Schieffley, Charles S.: "A Syringe-Transmitted Epidemic of Infectious Hepatitis," *J.A.M.A.*, 136:819–24, (Mar. 20) 1948.

Capps, Richard B., and Stokes, Joseph, Jr.: "Epidemiology of Infectious Hepatitis and Problems of Prevention and Control," *J.A.M.A.*, 149:557–61, (June 7) 1952.

Farquhar, John D.; Stokes, Joseph, Jr.; and Schrack, W. D., Jr.: "Epidemic of Viral Hepatitis Apparently Spread by Drinking Water and by Contact," *J.A.M.A.*, 149:991–93, (July 12) 1952.

Gauld, Ross L.: "Field Studies Relating to Immunity in Infectious Hepatitis and Homologous Serum Jaundice," *Am. J. Pub. Health*, 37:400–406, (Apr.) 1947.

Havens, W. Paul, Jr.: "Infectious Hepatitis," *Medicine*, 27:279–326, (Sept.) 1948.

James, George; Korns, Robert F.; and Wright, Arthur W.: "Homologous Serum Jaundice Associated with Use of Irradiated Plasma," *J.A.M.A.*, 144:228–29, (Sept. 16) 1950.

Kaufman, Gustav G.; Sborov, Victor M.; and Havens, W. Paul: "Outbreak of Infectious Hepatitis Presumably Food-Borne," *J.A.M.A.*, 149:993–95, (July 12) 1952.

MacCallum, F. O.; McFarlan, A. M.; Miles, J. A. R.; Pollock, M. R.; and Wilson, C.: *Infective Hepatitis: Studies in East Anglia during the Period 1943–47*. Medical Research Council, Special Report Series #273. London: His Majesty's Stationery Office, 1951.

McNee, Sir John: "Infective Hepatitis: A Problem of World Health," *Brit. M. J.*, 1:1367–71, (June 28) 1952.

Neefe, John R.: "Viral Hepatitis. A Consideration of Certain Aspects of Current Importance to the Practicing Physician," *New England J. Med.*, 240:445–48, (Mar. 24) 1949.

"The Outbreak of Jaundice in the Army," Circular Letter No. 95, Office of the Surgeon General, War Department, August 31, 1942. Printed also in *J.A.M.A.*, 120:51–53, (Sept. 5) 1942; and in *Mil. Surgeon*, 91:386–93, (Oct.) 1942.

Pickles, William Norman: *Epidemiology in Country Practice*. Baltimore: Williams & Wilkins, Co., 1939, pp. 59–86.

Scheinberg, Herbert; Kinney, Thomas D.; and Janeway, Charles A.: "Homologous Serum Jaundice," *J.A.M.A.*, 134:841–48, (July 5) 1947.

Stokes, Joseph, Jr.; Blanchard, Mercer; Neefe, John R.; Gellis, Sydney S.; and Wade, George R.: "Methods of Protection against Homologous Serum Hepatitis. I. Studies on the Protective Value of Gamma Globulin in Homologous Serum Hepatitis SH Virus," *J.A.M.A.*, 138:336–43, (Oct. 2) 1948.

Stokes, Joseph, Jr.; Farquhar, John A.; Drake, Miles E.; Capps, Richard B.; Ward, Charles S., Jr.; and Kitts, Albert W.: "Infectious Hepatitis. Length of Protection by Immune Serum Globulin (Gamma Globulin) during Epidemics," *J.A.M.A.*, 147:714–19, (Oct. 20) 1951.

17. Diphtheria

Diphtheria is an acute disease characterized by a local infection and a general toxemia. The local inflammation always involves an epithelial surface, usually the throat (tonsils or larynx), nose, or a wound. It is accompanied by edema and usually by the formation of a membrane, which may obstruct breathing if located in the larynx. The diphtheria bacilli present in the local process excrete a soluble exotoxin, which is carried throughout the body by the blood stream and may combine with nerve and muscle tissue to cause paralysis of the heart and peripheral muscles. Many mild cases show nothing more than a slightly sore throat or a nasal discharge. The early symptoms of even the severe cases are not striking. The onset is insidious, and the temperature not high. The toxemia is frequently out of proportion to the severity of the local manifestations. Death occurs in 5 to 7 per cent of all cases; it is due to either respiratory obstruction or cardiac paralysis.

EPIDEMIOLOGY

Occurrence. Diphtheria is a disease of the temperate and subtropical zones. In the United States it was formerly more prevalent in the North but is more common today in the South. This does not mean an actual increase in the latter area but rather a more rapid decline in incidence in the former than in the latter. The disease is not usually encountered in the tropics, though the organisms are present. Skin infections are encountered more commonly in the subtropical than in the temperate zones. The highest incidence of diphtheria is found in school children, a group which accounts for one-half to two-thirds of the cases. The preschool group, however, accounts for over half of the deaths, due to a higher case fatality rate at this age. Diphtheria is present at all seasons but reaches its peak in the late fall or early winter.

In former years, diphtheria was much more prevalent than at present and constituted one of the principal causes of death among children above the age of infancy. Today it has declined to a point of relatively minor importance and is actually a rare disease in many communities in the United States. The decrease is unquestionably due in part to unexplained natural causes and in part to the use of present-day methods of prevention and treatment.

Etiological Agent. Diphtheria is due to infection with the diphtheria bacillus (*Corynebacterium diphtheriae*), a Gram-positive organism of distinctive shape and staining properties. The bacillus does not form spores and is readily destroyed by usual disinfecting processes. Diphtheria bacilli are usually divided into two groups, the virulent and avirulent, according to their capacity to produce toxin. As infection with the avirulent bacilli is of no public health significance,[1] it is important to determine virulence in cases of suspected carriers. Recent studies have shown that numerous strains of diphtheria bacilli exist, notably the *gravis* and the *mitis,* as well as several intermediate strains. Infection with the *gravis* strain has been reported by some workers as more severe, often attended with fatality rates as high as 15 to 20 per cent, whereas *mitis* infections are supposedly mild, with less than 1 per cent of deaths. Other investigators have failed to confirm these differences. Although the *gravis* strains were originally reported from Europe, they have been found during recent years in various parts of the United States. As most of our knowledge of diphtheria is based on studies in which no differentiation was made between *gravis* and *mitis* strains, it is apparent that future studies based on such distinctions may require some modification of our ideas regarding the epidemiology of the disease, provided the differences in the strains are really significant.

Reservoir of Infection. Diphtheria is a disease of man; there is no satisfactory evidence that other animals are naturally infected. The source of all infections is a case or carrier, the latter constituting the ultimate reservoir responsible for the perpetuation of the disease within a community. Contact with a case is, however, more likely to result in infection than is equal contact with a carrier.

Most diphtheria patients harbor the organisms for about two or three weeks, though a small percentage continues as convalescent carriers for several additional weeks or months. In rare instances, the carrier condition persists a year or more. The percentage of patients found to be carriers at various intervals after onset of the illness is shown in Table 1.

The diphtheria carrier harbors the organisms in the nose or throat, where the bacilli grow in diseased lymphoid tissue, usually the tonsils,·

---

[1] There is evidence to suggest that the avirulent strains may be significant, however, in latent immunization. See Dudley, May, and O'Flynn.

adenoids, or nasal polyps. Many chronic nasal carriers show the presence of foreign bodies, but the condition disappears upon removal of the object. Although a seemingly unlimited number of chemical and physical agents has been used in attempts to cure the carrier condition, nothing has been consistently successful except surgical removal of diseased lymphoid tissue. Penicillin therapy is effective in the cure of many carriers; its trial is indicated before resort to surgical procedures. Before attempting surgical cure, it is essential, however, to test the organisms for virulence and to determine the exact site of the infection.

TABLE 1

PERCENTAGE OF PATIENTS CARRYING DIPHTHERIA BACILLI AT VARIOUS PERIODS AFTER ONSET *

Calculated from Data of Hartley and Martin † on Study of 457 Adult Patients

Days after Onset	Number Carrying	% Carrying
5	392	86
10	302	66
15	232	51
20	194	42
25	156	34
30	118	26
35	92	20
40	70	15
45	52	11
50	41	9

* This study is merely representative of many made on this topic. The data are not strictly applicable to children.

† Hartley, P., and Martin, C. J.: *Proc. Roy. Soc. Med.*, **13** (Sect. of Epidemiol. and State Med.): 277–89, 1919–20.

Many diphtheria carriers develop their condition without known exposure to infection but by contact with an unrecognized case or other carrier. The incidence of carriers in the community is quite variable. Studies made thirty to forty years ago showed that from 1 to 3 per cent of the population might be virulent carriers. Today the figure is usually smaller, commonly less than 0.1 per cent. Although most carriers are immune, occasional carriers are susceptible (Schick positive). No general agreement exists as to whether immunization of a group increases or decreases the carrier rate, other factors being equal. There is no evidence that the extensive community immunization programs have brought about an increased carrier rate in the civil population, nor is there proof that the frequently reported decline in carrier rate is due to immunization.

Escape from the reservoir is through the nose and throat secretions. The bacilli are not constantly found in all cultures from the nose and throat of proved carriers, a circumstance due either to a true intermittency of escape of the organisms or to the fallibility of our bacteriological procedures. The organisms occur in the local exudate and discharges of cases of wound diphtheria.

Transmission is usually directly from the source to the new victim, the latter inhaling the infected droplets exhaled or coughed out by the case or carrier. Spread is therefore favored by all factors that bring people together, notably crowding. Indirect spread through fomites is theoretically possible, as the bacilli may live for some time outside the body, but is probably a very insignificant factor in the total spread of the disease. Milk-borne infection has been encountered, due either to direct contamination of the milk by a case or carrier or to a temporary infection of the cow's udder secondary to an infection of the milker. In these latter cases, there is a diphtheritic membrane along the abraded teat or milk duct.

Entry and Incubation Period. Diphtheria bacilli enter the body through the nose or mouth, except in the occasional instances of wound infections, which are due to direct contamination. As the infective process is always local, there is no invasion of the tissues other than a superficial necrosis; the bacilli are not found in the blood stream. The incubation period ranges from two to seven days, usually three to five.

Susceptibility is usually determined by either the Schick test or by titration of the circulating antitoxin. *The Schick test* depends upon the response of the body to the injection of a measured amount of toxin. Toxin in the amount of 1/50 MLD, usually diluted to 0.1 cc, is injected into the skin of the flexor surface of the upper half of the right forearm. At the same time, a control test, consisting of an equivalent amount of heated toxin, is injected into the corresponding area of the left arm or at a lower level of the right arm. The control test is used to distinguish between a reaction due to the toxin and one due to the diphtheria bacillus protein mixed with the toxin (or the proteins of the broth on which the diphtheria bacilli have been grown), since the toxin in the control injection has been destroyed by the heating. The Schick test is read in three to four days. A typical positive reaction to the toxin is characterized by redness and edema over an area of 1 to 2 cm in diameter; the edema reaches its height on the third to fourth day and is often followed by some scaling, leaving a reddish or brownish area that may persist for several days or weeks. The reaction to the protein is more fleeting and accompanied by less edema, though often larger in area. As shown in Table 2, the interpretation depends on the relationship between the two reactions. If there is a reaction to the toxin but none to the control, the test is considered "positive," indicating susceptibility to the toxin but no sensitivity to the protein. If the individual is both susceptible to the toxin and sensitive to the protein, reactions will appear at both sites, but the toxin injection will cause a larger area of redness and edema, as it consisted of both toxin and protein, whereas the control injection was merely protein. Such a reaction is labeled as a combined test and, like the positive, indicates susceptibility to diphtheria. A negative reaction, manifested by lack of response to either test, and a pseudo reaction, manifested by equal areas on both arms, indicate lack of susceptibility to diphtheria. The latter, however, shows sensitivity to the protein.

TABLE 2

INTERPRETATIONS OF SCHICK TEST

Reading	Toxin	Control	Interpretation
POSITIVE	+	−	Susceptible to toxin, **not** sensitive to protein
COMBINED	+ +	+	Susceptible to toxin **and** sensitive to protein
NEGATIVE	−	−	Not susceptible to toxin **nor** sensitive to protein
PSEUDO	+	+	Not susceptible to toxin **but** sensitive to protein

The control injection and reading are integral parts of the Schick test; without them little reliance can be placed on the results. Instead of using a control injection of heated toxin, it is possible to use a dilute toxoid solution (the Moloney test), inasmuch as the toxoid is relatively rich in protein. As those who are sensitive to the protein are likely to react somewhat more severely to the subsequent toxoid injection than are others, the use of a toxoid solution for the control is very logical.

The results of Schick tests and of titrations of circulating antitoxin [2] have yielded very definite information about diphtheria resistance. The newborn infant is not susceptible. This resistance disappears at about six to eight months of age but then increases slowly with age because of processes of latent immunization (see Chap. 2, Fig. IV, p. 40). The level of resistance varies with the age, economic circumstances, and other opportunities for exposure to sources of infection. Many of the data quoted as to the percentage of children who are Schick negative at a given age were

[2] This requires the drawing of a sample of blood in which the amount of free antitoxin is determined either by titration on guinea pigs or by the flocculation reaction.

obtained in the most congested cities several years ago, when diphtheria cases and carriers were more prevalent than they are today. These data thus suggest a higher level of resistance than is currently found. At present it is not uncommon, even in the larger cities, to find as many as 50 per cent of the children still susceptible at the age of ten to twelve. Over half of the students entering the University of Minnesota are Schick positive. It is impossible, however, to set any figure of susceptibility that will apply everywhere; communities vary, and the economic groups within a single community also vary. The same community may show varying percentages of susceptibility over a period of years, dependent upon the prevalence of diphtheria.

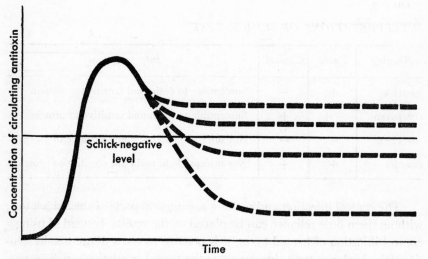

Fig. VII. *Diphtheria antitoxin in blood after toxoid immunization.*

The effective resistance of a child to diphtheria cannot be measured, however, solely in terms of circulating antitoxin. Many persons, especially those who have been artificially immunized, may show a low antitoxin titer yet have the capacity of producing large quantities of antitoxin in response to a small antigenic stimulus. These persons may therefore have a greater effective resistance than might be inferred from the tests.

The response to artificial immunization depends on the type of antigen, its strength, the number of injections and their spacing, as well as the level of resistance that existed prior to injection of antigen. The concentration of circulating antitoxin increases rapidly in response to injections and reaches a peak which is maintained for three to four months but then declines to a much lower level (Fig. VII). Individuals and groups vary as to the level to which this will fall. It is thus apparent that a child who was Schick negative one to four months after injection might be Schick positive a year later. Unfortunately this is true in so many instances that Schick tests performed during this peak of the antitoxin rise give no indication as to the probable status at the end of a year. Retests should not be relied upon if performed earlier than one year after immunization. Under present conditions of low incidence of diphtheria, immunity gained through immunization is lost even after this first year in so many instances that most persons recommend that the Schick test be redone prior to entry to school or that a booster dose be administered.

CONTROL MEASURES

Control of Spread

The Case. The diphtheria patient should be immediately segregated. Isolation should continue until two or preferably three consecutive cultures from both nose and throat have been found to be negative for diphtheria bacilli. The cultures should be obtained at intervals of at least 24 hours. The board of health frequently reserves the right to have the last culture taken by its representative. Great care must be exercised to make certain that the culture is actually taken from the tonsils, pharynx, and nasal mucosa, not merely the back of the tongue or the nares. Failure to observe this precaution may result in overlooking a carrier condition. Virulence tests should be performed if the patient continues as a carrier after a reasonable period. If the organisms are proved virulent, penicillin therapy may be tried; if this fails, consideration should be given to surgical measures to cure the carrier condition.

Routine **epidemiological investigation** is directed primarily to discovery of carriers among the patient's associates. Cultures should be obtained from all family contacts. Wholesale culturing of all school contacts was practiced quite extensively in former years, chiefly in the hope of finding the source of infection. The practice has been practically abandoned at present, as the results are not commensurate with the costs. Because of the ease of spread of respiratory infections, little success can be expected in tracing sources, except in those instances in which the disease was acquired from contact with a known case. The data of Doull and Lara on the greater infectiousness of cases as compared with that of carriers indicate the greater importance of searching for mild unrecognized cases among the contacts than of searching for carriers. All school contacts may therefore be examined for unrecognized illnesses, with particular attention given to nasal infection.

Family contacts should be quarantined according to immunity status and cultural findings. A susceptible child should be quarantined for a week since last exposure and until two consecutive nose and throat cultures which are negative have been obtained. An immune contact may be released as soon as two negative cultures have been obtained after association with the patient has ceased. In determining susceptibility, it is usually assumed that all children are susceptible unless proved Schick negative or artificially immunized. Contacts who have previously been immunized should be given 0.5 cc of fluid toxoid as a booster dose as their resistance may have declined below the protective level. If the patient is hospitalized, the contacts may remain at home; if not, it is safer to send the child contacts to a relative, provided the latter can keep them segregated until the end of the quarantine period and has no children. Adult contacts who are not proved carriers are usually subjected to little or no quarantine, provided they are not engaged in food handling or occupations that bring them in contact with children. In case of infection on a milk farm, sale of milk should be stopped until arrangements can be made for pasteurizing away from the farm.

Carriers, if found and proved to be harboring virulent organisms, should be subjected to the same restrictions (except hospitalization) as cases.

Environmental Sanitation. As fomites play little part in the spread of diphtheria, no attention need be given to these other than the usual procedures of disinfection incidental to the nursing care.

Disinfection. Diphtheria is included in Group I; procedures outlined for this group on page 144 should be followed. Diphtheria was formerly included in Group II but this no longer seems necessary.

Minimizing Ill Effects

Diagnosis and Treatment. As toxin which has combined with nerve or muscle tissue is beyond the reach of antitoxin, it is important to make a diagnosis early if serum is to have its maximum effect. Health departments usually provide laboratory service to facilitate early diagnosis on the basis of nose and throat cultures. It is important that the examination be made promptly and that the results, if positive, be reported by telephone or telegraph. It is not, however, desirable to sacrifice accuracy for speed through providing too many local laboratories manned by personnel unfamiliar with diphtheria bacilli. In suspicious cases, antitoxin should be given even before laboratory results are obtained. The antitoxin is usually furnished by the health department. Although home care is possible, transfer to a hospital is preferable, especially if there is laryngeal involvement which may require intubation or tracheotomy.

Public Health Nursing Care. The incidence of diphtheria has fallen so sharply that the public health nurse may rarely see a case. It is therefore particularly important that, when cases occur in her community, she review manifestations of this disease and refresh herself regarding nursing care. She must be constantly alert for unsuspected cases that are overlooked by the parents because diphtheria is equally unknown to them. A sore throat with an exudate should always arouse suspicion and be brought to medical attention.

When a case of diphtheria does occur it still requires the same meticulous nursing care as formerly. Most cases will be hospitalized if such facilities are available, but in some areas cases may be kept at home. The most important thing for the nurse to keep in mind in giving and teaching care of the diphtheria case is the necessity for complete bed rest. Ordinarily the physician wishes the patient to lie flat in bed and make no exertion whatsoever, thus putting as little strain on the heart as possible, for, as has been pointed out, myocarditis is not an uncommon complication. This means that the patient should be fed and should not be disturbed more than necessary and that all nursing procedures should be performed in such a manner as to require the minimum exertion on the part of the patient. A patient with myocardial involvement must be kept absolutely quiet in bed. As this complication often appears quite late and after the patient has began to feel quite well, there is often difficulty in keeping him quiet. The nurse may be helpful in suggesting amusements. Paralyzed muscles must be rested and afforded appropriate support.

The nose and mouth should be kept clean and lubricated, but the mouth and throat should not be swabbed as this may cause bleeding. If steam inhalations are ordered, the nurse should demonstrate the making of a croup tent and should be certain that the attendant knows how to place the steam kettle to avoid its upsetting or burning the patient. If an ice collar is ordered, the nurse should demonstrate how to fill, cover, and apply it. As the throat is often very sore, foods which are easily swallowed should be suggested. Often semisolid foods, such as custard, can be swallowed more easily than liquids.

Number of Nursing Visits. Daily nursing visits are advisable in most instances if bedside care is being furnished. If this is not possible, the number of visits will depend somewhat on whether or not the nurse is responsible for taking release cultures. A minimum of three visits should be made in all cases, two at the onset—on consecutive days if possible—to instruct the family and one at the termination of the disease to give instructions regarding cleaning and release. The nurse who is responsible for release cultures must, of course, visit until all required cultures have been reported negative and the family is released.

Control through Immunization

Passive immunization with antitoxin was formerly used extensively for family contacts. While effective, it is little used at present except in those instances in which the contacts cannot be kept under observation. If they can be watched daily, it is better to wait until the earliest symptoms develop and then administer massive therapeutic doses. Inasmuch as the secondary attack rate among children under fifteen is usually less than 15 per cent, even if both patient and contacts remain at home, it is hardly worth while to risk serum sensitization of all, so long as they can be observed and given adequate treatment on the first sign of illness. The extensive use of active immunization has also reduced the need for passive protection, though usually, if one child in a family is not immunized, the others are equally unprotected. If, however, the contacts have been immunized, they should be given booster doses of fluid toxoid.

Active immunization of all susceptibles is the most effective measure in diphtheria control. Several antigens have been used, each of which has its advantages and disadvantages. The original toxin-antitoxin (TAT), given in three 1.0-cc doses at one-week intervals, has been replaced by the more effective toxoid, which has the added advantage of being free of all serum. The horse serum fraction of the toxin-antitoxin (less than 1/20,000 of one part) was too small to induce anaphylactic reactions but could produce some sensitivity. Toxoid, though free of serum, contains more diphtheria protein and may, therefore, cause severe reactions in older children and adults who are sensitive to the protein. Soluble toxoid should be given in three doses of 0.5, 1.0, and 1.0 cc at intervals of three weeks. If this interval is not administratively practical, it may be shortened to one week without too great loss of immunizing value. Although many attempts have been made to use only two doses of soluble toxoid, the results have been uniformly disappointing and the method has fallen into disrepute.

The newer alum-precipitated toxoid (APT) was originally proposed as a "one-shot" method, it being assumed that the slower absorption of the insoluble precipitate would provide a prolonged stimulation. The early reports were extremely flattering, as they were based on retests during the first three to four months before the level of antitoxin had fallen. Later studies showed that the resistance following one dose of APT is inferior to that of three doses of soluble toxoid when tested at one- or two-year intervals after immunization. Two doses of APT give the highest level of resistance. The alum toxoid does, however, produce more severe local reactions with occasional sterile abscesses. (These are distinctly less common at present than when APT was first used, but they have not been entirely eliminated.) In Table 3 are shown the results of the Michigan studies comparing the several antigens.

TABLE 3

COMPARISON OF ANTITOXIN RESPONSE TO DIFFERENT ANTIGENS *
(All cases had less than 0.001 unit antitoxin prior to injection.)

Antigens	4 Months		12 Months		24 Months		36 Months	
	No. in Group	% with 0.001 or more AT	No. in Group	% with 0.001 or more AT	No. in Group	% with 0.001 or more AT	No. in Group	% with 0.001 or more AT
2 FLUID TOXOID	259	67.5	244	56.1	185	51.3	117	46.1
1 ALUM-PPT. TOXOID	415	92.0	416	86.7	420	80.4	357	71.1
3 FLUID TOXOID	448	95.3	437	91.1	198	89.4	50	94.0
2 ALUM-PPT. TOXOID	336	100.0	321	99.4	212	98.5	12	100.0

* Report of Volk and Bunney to the Committee on Administrative Practice of the American Public Health Association, Oct. 7, 1940.

During the past five years multiple antigens have largely replaced the APT, especially in private practice. The alum toxoid is mixed with either tetanus toxoid or pertussis vaccine or with both (triple antigen). These multiple antigens have the advantage of conferring protection against more than one disease, but with a reduced total number of injections. Combining one antigen with another does not reduce the effectiveness of either. The only disadvantage is the slight increase in reactions but this is not significant. Triple antigen (diphtheria, pertussis, and tetanus—referred to as DPT) is rapidly becoming the antigen of choice. Since the pertussis component requires three injections, use of the triple antigen also means that the patient receives three injections containing diphtheria toxoid, with resultant higher, and possibly more lasting, protection than comes from the two injections of straight APT formerly used.

Unfortunately, many persons have attempted to establish standard immunization procedures which purport to be applicable to all situations. No such standard is possible, as the selection of antigen must depend on local circumstances. Thus, in a southern rural area where the population is so sparsely settled that it is difficult to bring the children together for more than one injection and where higher rates of tuberculosis, typhoid, hookworm, and syphilis make it possible to assign to diphtheria control only a small fraction of an already overstrained budget, the use of a single injection of APT might be logical, though its use would mean sacrificing the simultaneous protection against whooping cough and tetanus. Yet in a northern city where the children can be brought together easily for three injections, where hookworm does not exist, and where the tuberculosis, typhoid, and syphilis problems are less severe, funds may be available for the more effective, even though more cumbersome, three doses of triple antigen. Each antigen has its peculiar advantages and disadvantages which must be carefully weighed, and the proper one selected for a given situation.

Immunization should be given during the last half of the first year of life, usually around six to eight months. It is obviously unsound to wait until the child reaches school before immunizing, as over half of the deaths occur before school age. Yet in emphasizing the importance of preschool immunization, one must not forget that the child reaching school un-immunized must be protected, as about two-thirds of the diphtheria cases occur in the school age group and as it is the school child who takes infection home to younger brothers and sisters. Too many communities in their enthusiasm for preschool immunization have overlooked the child who arrives at school unprotected. Obviously, if all the preschool group were immunized, there would be little need of concern for the school children; yet experience shows that in few, if any, communities, has the preschool group been so adequately immunized as to justify ignoring the older children who have not been protected.

In former years immunization in the preschool period conferred a resistance adequate to protect the child throughout school life. This is not true today as the striking decline in the incidence of diphtheria and the prevalence of carriers has removed the stimuli that formerly helped to maintain the high level of resistance established through artificial immunization. As a consequence, the child who is today immunized in infancy requires reimmunization through use of booster doses. In private practice such a booster dose is commonly given within a year as the initial injections are given very early in life (usually at three to four months) and are therefore somewhat less lasting in effect. In public health clinics the injections are usually begun somewhat later (about six to seven months of age) after the antibody-production mechanism is better developed, and a more lasting effect is obtained. In such instances booster injections are usually delayed until school age. In either case, the child entering school should receive a booster injection, as the resistance will probably have fallen to the level of susceptibility and the risk of developing diphtheria will have increased through more frequent exposures to other children. A booster dose is also recommended for contacts who have previously been immunized. For this purpose the fluid toxoid is preferable to the precipitated as its action is quicker.

Ideally, every child should be immunized, yet this is rarely achieved except in institutions. In general, the immunization program should be pushed actively until at least half of the children in all age groups have been protected. As the time and labor required to increase the percentage of immunization much above this level rise rapidly per unit number of children protected (law of diminishing returns), it may well be questioned whether or not a health department is justified in spending large sums to reach a little higher percentage of the child population. It must be remembered that diphtheria prevention is only one part of the community health program. Thus in a given community, the money and energy required to increase the number of immunized children from 60 to 65 per cent might yield greater returns in some other part of the health program. In our enthusiasm to control diphtheria, a proper sense of relative values may easily be lost.

Immunization is usually carried on without preliminary Schick testing, as most young children are susceptible. Schick testing is slow, subject to some errors, and introduces an additional visit to the physician or clinic. The occasional Schick-negative child who may receive injections he did not need is not harmed and, in fact, benefits from an added resistance. Schick testing may be carried out after immunization to find the occasional child who did not respond adequately and is still susceptible. While this is highly desirable in private practice, it is little used on a community basis as the results are not commensurate with the costs. The money spent to find the occasional child in need of further injections would yield greater returns in reaching children not yet protected. At times, however, it is desirable to test a small sample of the immunized group to make certain that the antigen used was adequate.

Every reasonable effort should be made to persuade parents to have their children immunized by the family physician as a part of their regular medical care. Unfortunately, a still substantial proportion of the children fail to obtain protection in this way. Clinics must often be provided for these by the board of health. Use of the Vim-Forsbeck immunization syringe will facilitate the work. Though the details of operation will vary with the community, clinics should be so located as to be convenient to the group to be immunized and should reach both school and preschool children. Only those children whose parents have signed a request for immunization should be given the injections. Complete records showing the name, age, and address of the child as well as the date of injection, type, and lot number of antigen should be kept. In some communities the health department, rather than conducting clinics, has paid the physicians for immunization in their private offices. Except in very small communities, this method is unnecessarily expensive and appears to the authors to be unsound in principle as well as questionable in efficacy.

SUMMARY

Health Department Program

Active immunization is the only method that has been effective in the prevention of diphtheria. Isolation and quarantine protect certain individuals who might otherwise be infected; but, because of missed cases and carriers, such measures fail to control the disease on a community-wide basis. Search for sources of infection discloses certain infected individuals but is more expensive than effective when applied to persons other than immediate contacts. Environmental sanitation yields few results, as it fails to affect the spread of respiratory droplets. Laboratory facilities for diagnosis, and the provision of serum and hospitalization, are valuable in reducing the deaths among those contracting the disease but do not affect the general incidence of diphtheria. Experience shows, however, that if the majority of the children of both school and preschool age are immunized with an effective antigen, diphtheria declines in incidence to a sporadic rather than an epidemic disease; in some such communities it has become a rare condition. Immunization yields prolonged protection, but only if the program is continued from year to year to reach new arrivals in the community. Booster injections must be given in order to maintain a high level of protection among the immunized. If a community is well immunized, there is no need for expenditure of large sums to find and control carriers.

The health officer is responsible for the planning and direction of the control program with special emphasis upon the promotion of immunization. With the board of health he must lay out a plan whereby immunization is made available, either through the family physician or a clinic, to all children regardless of financial status. In most communities he will be responsible for the conduct of the clinics. The promotion of this program requires the active cooperation of the school authorities through education of children and parents and use of school buildings for the operation of clinics. General publicity programs should be conducted by the health officer, but the most important educational contact in the furtherance of immunization is the home visits of the **public health nurse.** Her records should show which children in her district have and have not been protected. If diphtheria cases occur, she must make the usual home visits to demonstrate bedside care and home isolation and to obtain the necessary epidemiological information. In some cases she must obtain the cultures of family contacts and later the release cultures. The **sanitary officer** plays little active part in this program except when infection occurs on a milk farm; but, as a part of the health department, he should be alert for opportunities to point out the value of immunization.

SUGGESTED READINGS

Bell, J. A.: "Diphtheria Immunization. Use of an Alum-Precipitated Mixture of Pertussis Vaccine and Diphtheria Toxoid," *J.A.M.A.*, **137**:1009–16, (July 17) 1948.

Bixby, E. W.: "The Effectiveness of Penicillin in the Treatment of Nasopharyngeal Diphtheria," *Am. J. M. Sc.*, **215**:509–13, (May) 1948.

diSant'Agnese, Paul A.: "Simultaneous Immunization of New-Born Infants against Diphtheria, Tetanus, and Pertussis," *Am. J. Pub. Health*, **40**:674–80, (June) 1950.

Doull, James A., and Lara, Hilario: "The Epidemiological Importance of Diphtheria Carriers," *Am. J. Hyg.*, **5**:508–29, (July) 1925.

Dudley, Sheldon F.; May, Percival M.; and O'Flynn, Joseph A.: *Active Immunization against Diphtheria, Its Effect on the Distribution of Antitoxic Immunity and Case and Carrier Infection.* Medical Research Council, Special Report Series, #195. London: His Majesty's Stationery Office, 1934.

Fraser, Donald T.: "Diphtheria Toxoid: A Review," *Canad. Pub. Health J.*, **30**:469–78, (Oct.) 1939.

Getting, Vlado A.: "Some Epidemiological Considerations of Diphtheria," *New England J. Med.*, **223**:717–21, (Oct. 31) 1940.

Godfrey, Edward S., Jr.: "Study in the Epidemiology of Diphtheria in Relation to the Active Immunization of Certain Age Groups," *Am. J. Pub. Health*, **22**:237–56, (Mar.) 1932.

Harries, E. H. R.: "Diphtheria," *Lancet*, **1**:45–48, (Jan. 7) 1939. Published also as Chapter I of *Control of the Common Fevers.* London: The Lancet, Ltd., 1942.

Hartley, Percival, *et al.*: *A Study of Diphtheria in Two Areas of Great Britain.* Medical Research Council, Special Report Series, #272. London: His Majesty's Stationery Office, 1950.

Lewis, J. Tudor: *The Principles and Practice of Diphtheria Immunization.* London: Oxford University Press, 1941.

McKinnon, N. E.: "Diphtheria Prevented," Chapter IA of *Control of the Common Fevers.* London: The Lancet, Ltd., 1942.

Merkel, A. Erin: "An Outbreak of Diphtheria in Medford, Ore., 1949," *Am. J. Pub. Health,* 41:522–27, (May) 1951.

Russell, W. T.: *The Epidemiology of Diphtheria during the Last Forty Years.* Medical Research Council, Special Report Series, #247. London: His Majesty's Stationery Office, 1943.

Sauer, Louis W., and Tucker, Winston H.: "Simultaneous Immunization of Young Children against Diphtheria, Tetanus, and Pertussis," *Am. J. Pub. Health,* 40:681–85, (June) 1950.

Shepard, W. P.: "Obstacles in the No-Diphtheria Path," *Am. J. Pub. Health,* 23:547–54, (June) 1933.

Top, Franklin H.: "Present Recommendations Concerning Treatment and Prophylaxis of Diphtheria," *Am. J. Pub. Health,* 37:549–54, (May) 1947.

Volk, V. K.: "Safety and Effectiveness of Multiple Antigen Preparations in a Group of Free-Living Children," *Am. J. Pub. Health,* 39:1299–1313, (Oct.) 1949.

18. Hemolytic Streptococcal Infections

Although in former years the hemolytic streptococcal infections were divided into several clinically distinguishable types, the present tendency is to think of these as a group, many of which merge imperceptibly into one another. The antigenic interrelationships between the many strains of hemolytic streptococci are not clear; yet apparently all of those which are pathogenic for human beings possess certain infecting capacities but differ widely in their ability to produce toxins. On the other hand, resistance to the infection does not parallel antitoxic resistance. It is generally agreed that we are not dealing with readily separated disease entities but rather with a group of conditions which vary in their clinical manifestations according to the strain of organism involved and according to the level of resistance of the individual attacked. Under such circumstances, two persons infected with the same organism may show quite different reactions. While the authors adhere strongly to this concept, to discuss "scarlet fever" as a separate disease seemed preferable, inasmuch as it is so treated by most health departments at present, though a few have wisely substituted the term "hemolytic streptococcal infections" to refer to all those cases formerly reported as scarlet fever, septic sore throat, and streptococcal tonsillitis.

SCARLET FEVER

Scarlet fever, in its clinically recognizable form, is characterized by a focus of infection and a diffuse rash that fades on pressure, except at points where petechial hemorrhages have developed. The focus of infection is usually the throat but may be the uterus (puerperal scarlet fever) or an open wound (surgical scarlet fever). The infection may spread from its original site and result in secondary focuses, which are usually in the nasal sinuses, middle ears, or mastoids, less commonly in the lungs, meninges, or blood stream. The causative organism gives off a soluble toxin, which

253

is distributed throughout the body by the blood stream and is responsible for the rash and much of the fever and malaise. As many persons have a high resistance to the toxin but little to the infecting organisms, cases of scarlet fever without rash are of common occurrence, though usually not diagnosable on purely clinical grounds. Although complications are quite common, the case fatality rate in the United States is at present less than 1 per cent.

EPIDEMIOLOGY

Occurrence. A disease of the temperate zones, scarlet fever reaches its highest incidence in northern United States and Europe and disappears in clinically recognizable form as the equator is approached. Though present at all seasons of year, it reaches its peak in the late winter. The disease runs in quite definite cycles: the incidence in a given community is high for two or three years and then drops to a much lower level for an equal number of years, only to recur at its former high rate. In former years a much more malignant form existed in the United States and Western Europe, but this has been largely replaced by the present mild form. Although the reasons for this change are not clearly understood, the present mildness of the infection is probably only temporary, as mild scarlet fever has prevailed in former years only to be followed by recurrences of severe infection. Within recent years a malignant scarlet fever has prevailed in the Balkans and Eastern Europe with case fatality rates as high as 10 to 20 per cent. The occasional use of the term "scarlatina" to refer to the mild form of the disease is unfortunate and without justification, as it implies an essential difference in identity, a difference which does not exist.

Etiological Agent. Scarlet fever is due to infection with a Group A hemolytic streptococcus capable of producing an erythrogenic (rash-producing) toxin. Although some persons have maintained that only a few scarlet fever strains existed, it is generally agreed at present that many hemolytic streptococci are capable of producing the infection. As they may differ greatly in their ability to form toxin, the clinical manifestations may be quite variable. Furthermore, the clinical picture depends as much upon the patient's resistance as upon the infecting organisms. A patient with high resistance to toxin may show merely a sore throat without rash, whereas another with less antitoxic resistance may have a fairly severe typical case of scarlet fever. These do not necessarily represent infection with different organisms but rather different immunological responses to the same organism. Not all hemolytic streptococci are, however, pathogenic for man.[1] Studies based on the work of Lancefield and of Griffith have shown that the strains pathogenic for man can be divided into groups and types. The epidemiological manifestations of infection with the different types may be quite variable. The variations in severity of scarlet fever may be attributable in part at least to the predominance of certain strains of streptococci. In the Rumanian outbreak of a few years ago, two forms of the disease existed coincidentally in the country, a severe form due to infection with one type of organism and a mild form due to a variety of other types. The hemolytic streptococci pathogenic for man are Gram-positive, nonsporulating organisms, which are readily destroyed by the usual disinfecting processes.

Reservoir of Infection. As scarlet fever is a disease only of man, all cases are attributable to infection from another case or carrier. Mild unrecognized cases and infections without a rash are of such frequent occurrence as to constitute major sources of spread. The case is of greater significance as a source of infection than is the healthy carrier, probably because more organisms are discharged. The duration of the infectious period usually varies from a few days to several weeks, though certain cases remain infectious for months. Cases complicated by rhinitis, sinusitis, cervical adenitis, or otitis media harbor the organisms longer than do simple, uncomplicated cases and therefore require longer periods of isolation.

Escape of Organisms. As the infecting case or carrier usually shows involvement of the upper respiratory tract, the organisms in such instances leave the body along with the nose and throat secretions. The organisms may also be found in the drainage from other infected areas, such as the middle ear, uterus, or wounds. Although the number of organisms in this type of drainage is large, such cases are less likely to spread infection to associates than are those in which escape is effected through the respiratory passages. This is probably due to the fact that (1) no adequate dressing can be applied to catch the respiratory discharges; (2) the respiratory function cannot be interrupted; (3) slight differences from normal are less obvious in the respiratory tract and are therefore often overlooked; and (4) the respiratory discharges are driven from the body through the propulsive force of the lungs. The studies of Hamburger and his associates have shown that the patient suffering from involvement of the nasal sinuses discharges a larger number of organisms than does the patient

---

[1] Certain strains not pathogenic for man may even survive the temperature of pasteurization. Their presence in milk should not be interpreted as indicating inadequacy of pasteurization.

with mere throat involvement. There is no evidence that the hemolytic streptococci leave the body with the skin desquamation or that the duration of the infectious period is in any way related to the skin condition, as was formerly supposed.

Transmission of infection is usually by direct respiratory association between source and victim and is, therefore, conditioned by opportunities for exposure. Indirect transmission through inanimate objects is responsible for a very minor part of the spread. Fomites are relatively unimportant, except in the case of puerperal and surgical infections, in which the fomites are of major significance in bringing organisms into proximity with an open wound. Milk serves at times as an important vehicle. In such instances, the udder of the cow is usually infected, secondary to infection of the milker. Milk or other foods can be contaminated directly by an infected handler. As the organisms may multiply in both milk and food, the doses so transmitted may be quite large. Spread through water does not occur, nor is there any evidence that insects serve as vectors.

Entry and Incubation Period. Entry of infection is by way of the respiratory tract or through open wounds. The role of diseased tonsils in facilitating the invasion of hemolytic streptococci is still undetermined. The incubation period is one to seven days, usually about three.

Susceptibility. Just as the disease process consists of two parts, the infecting and the toxic, so also is the resistance composed of the anti-infective and antitoxic elements.

Anti-infective resistance is difficult to measure. Clinically, however, it is apparent that this resistance is low, as individuals may be subject to repeated streptococcal infections. There is scant evidence that an attack of scarlet fever in childhood will protect a woman against puerperal streptococcal infection. Similarly, in the presence of a milk-borne outbreak of scarlet fever, the incidence of streptococcal throat infection without rash may be as high among the adults as is the incidence of clinically recognizable scarlet fever among the children.

Antitoxic resistance can be readily measured by the *Dick test*. This is performed by injecting one skin test dose (STD) of erythrogenic toxin into the skin of the flexor surface of the forearm.[2] The reaction is read in 18 to 24 hours. If the reading is delayed, the results are unreliable. A positive reaction, indicating susceptibility to the toxin, is manifested by an area of erythema of 10 or more millimeters in any diameter; edema is not

[2] Control tests are usually not performed. They are hardly worth while in a young group prior to immunization but are valuable in an adult group or those who have been immunized.

a part of the reaction. In all cases the reaction should be measured in two opposite diameters and the readings should be recorded in millimeters.[3]

Much confusion, due in large part to misunderstandings as to its basic significance, still exists regarding the reliability of the Dick test. There is no evidence of its being anything more than a measure of antitoxic resistance. If interpreted in this sense, it may be used as a measure of susceptibility to clinically recognizable scarlet fever. Its reliability in this regard is indicated by countless studies among nurses, family contacts, and children in communities where scarlet fever existed. Table 4 contains a few data extracted from a voluminous literature on this subject. It is apparent from this table that the Dick test is a very reliable measure of susceptibility to clinically recognizable scarlet fever. Within its proper sphere, it is apparently as reliable as is the Schick test in its field. Neither can be expected to be infallible, because of the variability of dosages of infecting organisms and, therefore, of toxin produced.

TABLE 4

COMPARATIVE ATTACK RATES OF CLINICALLY RECOGNIZABLE SCARLET FEVER AMONG DICK-POSITIVE NONIMMUNIZED AND DICK-NEGATIVE INDIVIDUALS

Group Studies	Dick Positives			Dick Negatives		
	Exposed	Cases	A.R.%	Exposed	Cases	A.R.%
NURSES						
Benson and Rankin	363	52	*14*	1063	5	*0.5*
Anderson and Reinhardt	234	30	*13*	1337	9	*0.7*
FAMILY CONTACTS						
Gordon	566	73	*13*	723	15	*2.0*
Toyoda	52	6	*12*	63	0	*0*
COMMUNITY EXPOSURES						
Krumbiegel	1769	226	*13*	5142	48	*0.9*

Antitoxic resistance as measured by the Dick test varies with age and economic status in a manner almost identical with that shown by the Schick test. The high level present at birth disappears during the latter half of the first year of life. The level of resistance then rises with age; the percentage found negative at any age varies according to the opportunities

[3] In some instances, especially in retesting after immunization, the test injection has consisted of 2 STD or even 5 STD. In other instances readings of 5 mm or more have been considered positive; or the diameters in two directions at right angles have been multiplied and the reaction considered positive if the product exceeds 100.

for exposure. In an urban area it is not unusual to find over 50 per cent of the children of twelve years of age still Dick positive. Family contact with a case results in change from Dick positive to Dick negative in many instances, even in the absence of recognizable infection.

CONTROL MEASURES

Control of Spread

The Case. Application of control measures depends upon diagnosis. Except where there is known exposure, a diagnosis of scarlet fever is possible only if there is an attendant rash. Control measures should, however, be applied so far as practicable to all infected persons regardless of the absence of a rash. Removal to a hospital may be desirable if the home conditions are such that the contacts cannot be effectively separated from the patient. The case is usually isolated for two or three weeks and thereafter until any discharges from the infected areas shall have ceased or been shown to be consistently free of hemolytic streptococci. Cultural methods are not practical except in dealing with such discharges. The present tendency is toward shorter isolation periods in cases free of complications.

Epidemiological investigation is aimed at discovery of other cases. It should include listing and examination of family and school associates as well as other intimate contacts. Owing to the multiplicity of respiratory contacts, the source is rarely found except in cases of known infection of close associates or in explosive outbreaks due to contaminated food or milk. A sudden increase in cases, especially if accompanied by a high incidence of sore throats among adults, should immediately suggest such spread. Inquiry regarding the milk supply should be made in all cases in order to detect the beginnings of such outbreaks. In cases of milk-borne infection, the milk should be examined for hemolytic streptococci. As in most instances there is an udder infection of one of the cows, it is necessary to examine milk samples to locate the infection. This is most simply performed by pooling the milk of every three to five cows of the suspected dairy, at the same time making certain that milk from each quarter of the udder of every cow is contained in some pool. The sample that shows hemolytic streptococci is repeated by obtaining a separate sample from each quarter of each cow that contributed to this pool. In this way it is possible to locate the infection of the cow quite readily. Veterinary examination is often of assistance, though udder infection may occur in the absence of clinically recognizable findings. If there has been direct contamination of the milk by a case or carrier, milk examination will be of no value. In all cases of milk- or food-borne infection, all milk and food handlers should have nose and throat examinations and cultures, and those showing hemolytic streptococci excluded temporarily from work. Even though detailed studies of these streptococci are not possible, it may be assumed under such circumstances that the organisms are potentially pathogenic.

Contacts. Family contacts, if children or if adults engaged in food handling or occupations bringing them into contact with children, are usually quarantined until a week has elapsed since the date of last contact with the patient. If signs of infection with or without a rash should develop during this period, the patient should be treated in the same manner as a case. The value of such quarantine is slight. School contacts should be examined and watched for unrecognized infections, and equal attention paid to infections not accompanied by a rash. Such cases should be excluded from school, though it is often difficult to convince the parents or even the attending physician that the child without the rash is probably suffering from the same condition. There is no proved value in routine nose and throat cultures in the discovery of cases or carriers among either school or family contacts, as the identification of the hemolytic streptococci found is slow and unsatisfactory. Routine cultures in schools free of scarlet fever often show as high an incidence of streptococci as do those in schools where the disease is known to exist. Cultures may, however, be somewhat helpful in dealing with the child who shows throat infection without demonstrable rash.

Attempts have been made to control the spread of scarlet fever through administration of sulfonamides to the contacts. While such a method may at times be indicated for the benefit of certain special contacts, the method is in general unsatisfactory and its use is not indicated, especially in a large group of persons. At best it produces merely a temporary drop in the streptococcus carrier rate. The risk of producing sulfonamide-resistant strains of streptococci is serious as is also the risk of untoward reactions unless the contact can be kept under careful and constant supervision. It is better to withhold sulfonamides until needed and then to administer them in therapeutically adequate dosage.

Environmental sanitation is a minor factor in the control of streptococcal infections. Strict observance of aseptic precautions in handling maternity cases and wounds will reduce the likelihood of puerperal and surgical infections. As milk and food are the only vehicles of importance in community spread, sanitation of these industries will reduce the likelihood of occasional cases or outbreaks. If a case of infection develops on a milk farm, shipment of the milk should be stopped unless pasteurized away from the premises. No person with a known streptococcal infection (scarlet fever, sore throat, wound infection) should be permitted to work around a dairy farm or plant or in a food-handling capacity. It is not practical, however, to perform routine throat cultures to detect carriers. A very sizable fraction of the population harbors hemolytic streptococci in their throats, and there is no practical method for routine identification of these organisms. Negative cultures are meaningless, as the individual who is not a carrier today may harbor the organisms a few days later. Several attempts have been made to apply routine culturing of milk handlers but such attempts have not been satisfactory. Pasteurization is a very effective protection against milk-borne streptococcal infections. Attempts to reduce spread through ultraviolet disinfection of air and through oiling of floors and of bed linen and blankets have not been successful.

Disinfection. Scarlet fever is included in Group I; procedures outlined for this group on page 144 should be followed. In former years, scarlet fever was included in Group II, but the more stringent isolation precautions are no longer warranted in view of the present mildness of the disease and the effectiveness of the antibiotics in therapy.

Minimizing Ill Effects

Until the discovery of the sulfonamides and antibiotics, the only specific form of therapy was the use of antitoxin and convalescent serum. Their action was essentially antitoxic; neither was really effective in attacking the basic infection. The sulfonamides provided the first effective means of destroying the organisms, thus attacking both the infectious and the toxic parts of the disease. Unfortunately, however, many strains of streptococci were resistant to the sulfonamides or acquired resistance so that the use of these drugs had definite limitations. They have been almost completely replaced by the antibiotics which are more effective and produce fewer reactions. Strains resistant to the antibiotics are less common than those resistant to the sulfonamides. Undue fear of the disease persists among many who remember the time when a more severe form of the disease prevailed and no specific treatment was known.

Public Health Nursing Care. Most cases of scarlet fever at present are so mild that the patient is allowed up in a week, but cases still occur which are severe enough to be confined to bed for two to three weeks. Assistance from the public health nurse is particularly needed for the latter type. The public health nurse in these cases should teach the mother how to care for the child in bed and should assist her in simplifying the necessary procedures for his daily care and for the protection of the rest of the household.

As in any case with a fever and sore throat, liquid or soft diet is usually ordered until the symptoms subside. The mother must frequently be given suggestions as to what foods may be included under these headings. She may also need help with special diets which may be ordered by the physician, especially if nephritis occurs. Because of the effectiveness of the antibiotics in the treatment of the disease, complications are much less common than formerly and are less to be feared if they occur. Yet the possibility of their occurrence cannot be ignored. The mother should be instructed regarding early symptoms of complications, such as earache, enlarged glands, rise in temperature, and cloudy or scanty urine. If any of these occur she should call the physician at once so that treatment may be instituted promptly.

Number of Nursing Visits. As soon as the case is reported a visit should be made to appraise the home situation and the need for nursing care, and to teach isolation procedures. At this time the number of additional interim visits needed can be determined. A second visit will have to be made at the end of the isolation or quarantine period if the nurse is responsible for "releasing" the case.

Control through Immunization

Passive immunization, though frequently attempted, has not yielded consistently satisfactory results. Antitoxin, when first developed by the Dicks, was often used for this purpose. Though effective as far as protection against toxic effects, its use was very limited, since it may produce serum reactions as uncomfortable as the prevailing mild form of the disease and since it frequently leaves the child sensitive to horse serum. Convalescent serum, if obtainable, is free of both these objections. Its use has been frequently recommended, though the data as to its effectiveness against anything other than the toxemia are far from conclusive. Chemoprophylaxis through the use of sulfonamides has found a limited use in protecting intimate contacts. Its use for protection of casual contacts has not yielded uniformly satisfactory results, nor can the danger of drug reactions and the creation of sulfonamide-resistant strains of streptococci be ignored. Antibiotics are more effective and their use entails less risk. Indiscriminate and routine use of either antibiotics or sulfonamides is not warranted.

Active immunization against the toxic elements of the infection is possible through injection of graduated doses of Dick toxin. The usual course of immunization consists of five injections of 500, 2,500, 10,000, 25,000, and 80,000 STD respectively, given at intervals of one week. Although retesting two weeks after the last injection has been recommended, it is preferable to wait six months to a year to avoid a false sense of security. The injections are attended with somewhat more uncomfortable reactions than follow diphtheria immunization, though dangerous or fatal reactions have never been recorded nor is there any evidence of damage to the kidneys. The reactions consist of nausea, vomiting, malaise, fever, and occasionally joint pains and a rash indistinguishable from that of scarlet fever. Reactions are less frequently encountered in children than in adults. Toxin immunization gives a very high level of protection against clinically recognizable scarlet fever but does not confer protection against streptococcal infection. This lack of equal protection to the toxic and infectious components of scarlet fever is also true of resistance acquired through natural processes of latent immunization.

Scarlet fever immunization has never been widely accepted because of the number of injections, the reactions, and the fact that it confers protection only against the toxic part of the disease. A few community programs were attempted but found so little favor that its use was limited largely to private practice, institutions, and to groups such as nurses and medical students who were exposed to a special risk. With the advent of sulfonamides and antibiotics, immunization has fallen into disuse. So long as there was no effective specific treatment for the basic infection, protection against the toxemia was logical and desirable, but the present availability of therapeutic agents which destroy the infecting organism makes special protection against the toxemia unnecessary. Until antigens can be discovered that confer a true anti-infective resistance or unless highly virulent strains of streptococci develop which are resistant to sulfonamides and antibiotics, there seems little need for widespread use of antitoxic immunization.

SEPTIC SORE THROAT

This term was originally used to refer to infection with a particular strain of hemolytic streptococcus, the *Streptococcus epidemicus*, an organism with little or no capacity to produce erythrogenic toxin. Such infections are therefore characterized by severe throat lesions, often with septic complications, but no rash. As this organism has been the cause of several dramatic milk-borne infections, some persons have supposed that it was invariably so spread. The studies of Pilot and Davis have shown, however, that sporadic infections having no relationship to milk may occur, that it may be spread by contact though the secondary case rate is low, and that healthy carriers exist.

In some instances, the term "septic sore throat" has been applied to severe sore throats of streptococcal origin, though due to other strains. Septic sore throat is merely hemolytic streptococcal infection without rash. This absence of rash may be due either to the high antitoxic resistance of the patient or to the low toxin-producing capacity of the infecting organisms. The term "septic sore throat" is therefore unfortunate and might well be dropped since all such conditions, including scarlet fever, are classified under the general rubric of "hemolytic streptococcal infections" with possible subdivisions according to the type of organism, as in the case of pneumococcal infections. Control measures should be aimed at the prevention of streptococcal infection and should not be altered by the presence or absence of the rash, which is the noncommunicable part of the disease.

SUMMARY

Health Department Program

Control of the hemolytic streptococcal infections is at present relatively ineffective because of lack of methods of identifying all sources of infection and the unavailability of a suitable antigen which can be counted on to protect against more than the toxemia. The conditions are of less importance than formerly because of their decreased severity and the availability of therapeutic agents which destroy the infecting organisms. The **health officer** can do little more than attempt to reduce the spread through isolation and quarantine procedures applied to recognized cases and through search for unrecognized cases in the schools. The **public health nurse,** through her home visits, may assist in the care of the case that cannot be removed to the hospital, and demonstrate measures to reduce the likelihood of spread within the home. At times she may assist in the examination of school children to exclude cases that may be suspected of infection. The role of the **sanitary officer** is largely confined to attention to the general condition of the milk supply, especially pasteurization, which is our only effective safeguard against milk-borne spread.

SUGGESTED READINGS

Allison, V. D.: "Streptococcal Infections," *Lancet,* 1:1067–70, (May 7) 1938. Published also as Chapter II of *Control of the Common Fevers.* London: The Lancet, Ltd., 1942.

Coburn, Alvin F., and Young, Donald C.: *The Epidemiology of Hemolytic Streptococcus.* Baltimore: Williams & Wilkins Co., 1949.

Damrosch, Douglas S.: "Chemoprophylaxis and Sulfonamide Resistant Streptococci," *J.A.M.A.,* 130:124–28, (Jan. 19) 1946.

"Epidemiology Unit Number 22: Sulfadiazine Resistant Strains of Beta Hemolytic Streptococci. Appearance during the Course of Sulfadiazine

Prophylaxis at a Large Naval Training Center," *J.A.M.A.*, 129:921–27, (Dec. 1) 1945.

Gordon, John E.: "Epidemiology of Scarlet Fever: A Clinical Approach," *J.A.M.A.*, 98:519–24, (Feb. 13) 1932.

———: "Current Epidemiological Aspects of Scarlet Fever," *New England J. Med.*, 221:1024–29, (Dec. 28) 1939.

———: "Scarlet Fever," *Lancet*, 1:511–13, 560–63, (Mar. 16 and 23) 1940. Published also as Chapter III of *Control of the Common Fevers*. London: The Lancet, Ltd., 1942.

Gordon, John E.; Badger, G. F.; Darling, George B.; and Schooten, Sarah S.: "Reaction of Familial Contacts to Scarlet Fever Infection," *Am. J. Pub. Health*, 25:531–44, (May) 1935.

Hamburger, Morton, *et al.*: "Studies on the Transmission of Hemolytic Streptococcus Infections," *J. Infect. Dis.*, 75:58–78, (July–Aug.) 1944.

Hamburger, Morton; Green, Margaret Johnson; and Hamburger, Virginia G.: "The Problem of the 'Dangerous Carrier' of Hemolytic Streptococci," *J. Infect. Dis.*, 77:68–81, 96–108, (July–Aug., Sept.–Oct.) 1945.

Hamburger, Morton, and Lemon, Henry M.: "The Problem of the Dangerous Carrier of Hemolytic Streptococci. III. The Chemotherapeutic Control of Nasal Carriers," *J.A.M.A.*, 130:836–41, (Mar. 30) 1946.

Hamburger, Morton; Lemon, Henry M.; and Platzer, Richard F.: "The Significance of Nose to Throat Carrier Ratios in the Epidemiology of Hemolytic Streptococcal Infection," *Am. J. Hyg.*, 49:140–47, (Mar.) 1949.

Maxcy, Kenneth F.: "Changing Conceptions of Scarlet Fever," *Am. J. M. Sc.*, 196:454–60, (Sept.) 1938.

Okell, C. C.: "The Role of the Haemolytic Streptococci in Infective Disease," *Lancet*, 1:761–67, 815–20, 867–73, (Apr. 9, 16, and 23) 1932.

Schwenkter, Francis F.; Janney, John H.; and Gordon, John E.: "The Epidemiology of Scarlet Fever," *Am. J. Hyg.*, 38:27–98, (July) 1943.

Stebbins, Ernest L.; Ingraham, Hollis S.; and Reed, Elizabeth A.: "Milk-Borne Streptococcic Infections," *Am. J. Pub. Health*, 27:1259–66, (Dec.) 1937.

Woods, Hilda M.: *Epidemiological Study of Scarlet Fever in England and Wales since 1900. Medical Research Council*, Special Report Series, #180. London: His Majesty's Stationery Office, 1933.

19. Rheumatic Fever

Rheumatic fever is an acute, but frequently recurring, infection of unknown etiology characterized by fever and swelling of the joints. Many mild cases pass unrecognized under the popular term of "growing pains." Chorea is closely related, though the exact nature of this relationship is not clear. Although rheumatic fever is painful and temporarily disabling, it is rarely fatal, but its sequelae in the form of damage to the heart are so common and so serious that it ranks today as one of the major infectious disease problems of childhood and early adolescent life. It is probably responsible for more invalidism and more ultimate deaths than is any other infection of school age children. Until recently, rheumatic fever has been ignored in public health programs because little was known as to its cause and no effective measures were available to prevent its development. Broadened concepts of the scope of public health have recently brought the disease to increasing official attention through recognition of the community's responsibility for the provision of facilities for the better care of children whose hearts have been damaged by rheumatic infection.

EPIDEMIOLOGY

Occurrence. Rheumatic fever is essentially a disease of temperate zones. The incidence of the acute disease and of cardiac conditions attributable to it decreases toward the tropics. In the United States there are two zones of highest incidence, the Rocky Mountain states and the North Atlantic seaboard. Although found occasionally in children under five years of age, rheumatic fever is principally a disease of children from five to fourteen years of age. The adolescent and young adult are attacked quite frequently, as was observed in certain military and naval establishments during World War II. Recurrences continue for several years after the initial infection; each recurrence may add further damage to the heart. The heart damage, manifested as endocarditis, myocarditis, and occasionally as pericarditis, is usually most apparent several years after the initial infection, causing an increasing disability in early adult life and materially shortening the expectation of life. Rheumatic fever is more common in females than in males. Its tendency to run in certain families suggests a familial susceptibility. The incidence is highest under conditions of poverty, possibly influenced by overcrowding, poor housing, and faulty nutrition. The initial attack is usually preceded by tonsillitis, scarlet fever, or some other streptococcal infection; relapses may be precipitated by these infections or by other types of respiratory disease.

Etiological Agent. The exact etiological agent is not known. For years there has been a tendency to look upon streptococci as playing either a primary or secondary role in the cause of the disease; some investigators have looked with suspicion upon the *Streptococcus viridans,* others upon *Streptococcus hemolyticus.* Opinion has also differed as to whether the streptococcus is the primary cause of the disease, or a secondary factor operating in conjunction with some unknown virus. Some investigators have thought of rheumatic fever as an allergic response of a body sensitized to certain products of the streptococcus. Although opinions as to the exact role of the streptococcus still differ widely, there is quite general agreement today that the organism is in some way causally related to the disease, that infection with it may be either a determining or a precipitating factor, and that it plays a definite role in the development of recurrences.

Reservoir of Infection. Persons infected with streptococci constitute the sole known reservoir of these organisms. As there is no conclusive evidence that certain types of streptococci are more likely to be associated with rheumatic fever than are others, there is no reason to believe that certain cases or carriers of streptococcus infection are particularly dangerous. There is likewise no evidence to suggest the existence of carriers of "rheumatic strains" of organisms or that the victim of rheumatic fever serves as an important source of infection of his associates.

Escape of Organisms. So far as is known, the factors governing the escape of these streptococci from the body are the same as those governing streptococci that do not precipitate a rheumatic infection (see p. 255).

Transmission of Infection. Rheumatic fever has the characteristics of a communicable disease to which susceptibility is fairly low; yet direct spread from patient to contact has not been demonstrated as a frequent occurrence. Overcrowding favors its development, probably because of greater degree of respiratory exchange of infection. This is frequently manifested when the disease appears in military or institutional groups living under crowded conditions; it may also be a factor in the high incidence of infection under poor and therefore crowded housing conditions.

There is no reason to suspect that modes of spread other than through respiratory association are important in the transmission of infection (see p. 256).

Entry and Incubation Period. Tonsillitis and other respiratory tract infections appear to play so definite a role in the development or recurrence of rheumatic fever that entry via the respiratory tract is assumed, but the exact portal of invasion is not clear. Studies of Kaiser and others have shown that the presence or absence of tonsils is not a determining factor in the development of rheumatic fever, as primary infections appear as frequently in tonsillectomized children as in those who retain their tonsils. It is possible that removal of tonsils from those already infected may reduce the likelihood of recurrences. The incubation period is not known, but the development of the disease two to four weeks after a preceding respiratory infection suggests this period as the time usually needed for the development of rheumatic manifestations.

Susceptibility. Susceptibility is apparently general but not uniform. The actual rheumatic fever infection rate is not high, certainly far lower than that of other infections of streptococcal origin. One must therefore assume either that there is some other etiologic agent and that the streptococcus is a mere precipitating factor or that autarceologic factors play a determining role in the development of rheumatic fever among a small fraction of the many persons infected with streptococci. Tests for streptococcal antibodies fail to show any consistent and significant results which can be interpreted as suggesting special susceptibility or resistance of certain persons. Infection with rheumatic fever obviously confers no immunity to reinfection as is shown by the frequency of relapse as a sequel to later streptococcal infection. The tendency of rheumatic fever to appear in succeeding generations of families, and particularly along the maternal side, has been interpreted as indicating an hereditary predisposition to infection. Nutrition, and particularly vitamin intake, may also be a factor in resistance to the disease. That climate may also alter the individual's susceptibility is suggested not only by the higher incidence of the disease in certain areas but also by the fact that persons who have had an attack are less liable to recurrence if moved to a more favorable climate.

CONTROL MEASURES

Control of Spread

The Case. The patient is not usually isolated even during the acute stage of the disease for evidence of direct transfer of infection is lacking. Usually both the initial infection and relapse develop a couple of weeks after some respiratory tract infection; by the time they occur the patient appears to be no longer harboring the organisms that caused these infections. Isolation at this stage of the disease would therefore be of little value.

Epidemiological Investigation. As rheumatic fever is not a reportable disease in most states, the health department is unaware of the individual infections during their acute stages. Consequently no routine epidemiological investigation can be made. Since control measures with respect to individual cases are not contemplated, such investigation would have no immediate practical value. More extensive and careful epidemiological studies would be valuable, however, in shedding light on the circumstances surrounding the development of the disease. If multiple cases develop within a group, as in an institution or military unit, the disease is often brought to official attention. Careful epidemiologic investigation of such episodes is important; it usually reveals overcrowding, a high incidence of upper respiratory tract infection, and a high streptococcal carrier rate.

Contacts. Contacts with a case of rheumatic fever are not restricted, even during the acute stage of the disease. The use of sulfadiazine to reduce the streptococcal carrier rate among contacts within a group in which rheumatic fever is prevalent has been recommended, but opinions differ as to its effectiveness. It is certainly not a measure for general and indiscriminate community use.

Environmental Sanitation. No measures of demonstrable efficacy are known. The relationship of rheumatic fever to poor housing is such as to suggest that measures to improve housing may have some slight value, but housing is at most only a secondary factor in the development of the disease.

Disinfection. No special procedures of either concurrent or terminal disinfection are indicated.

Minimizing Ill Effects

In the absence of available measures to prevent the development of rheumatic fever, control measures must be directed at minimizing the damage that the disease causes. This can be accomplished either through provision of care for recognized cases to minimize the heart damage or through measures directed at the prevention of recurrences.

Case Finding. Case finding is usually carried on through the school medical service. This is directed not toward the discovery of active rheumatic fever but rather at the recognition of early cardiac damage resulting from the disease. Many cases of rheumatic fever are so mild that they are not brought to medical attention or are not recognized, but unfortunately these mild infections may cause appreciable cardiac damage. In other instances the child who recovers from the acute attack is not kept under medical care; cardiac involvement that was not detected during the febrile period may thus go unnoticed until it has progressed beyond the early stages. The periodic school medical examination, if well done, should reveal many cases of early cardiac involvement that would otherwise pass unnoticed. The present trend in the schools to replace the highly superficial and frequently perfunctory annual physical inspection by more careful medical examination every third or fourth year should reveal more cases of early cardiac involvement than have heretofore been recognized. Many health departments maintain rheumatic or cardiac registers comparable to the tuberculosis registers which have been found so useful.

Provision of Care. The child who has rheumatic fever usually requires prolonged bed care during and immediately after the acute stage in order to reduce the probability of cardiac damage. This care may have to be repeated with each recurrence of the infection. As most hospitals are planned for the treatment of acute illness and not for prolonged convalescence, this means either that special facilities for convalescent patients must be provided within the community or that the patient must be cared for at home. The former is preferable as the highest incidence of rheumatic fever is found in those homes which are least able to provide for prolonged bed rest. Unfortunately, however, most communities have a serious lack of suitable facilities for convalescent care of all types and particularly for children with incipient heart disease. A few communities constitute notable exceptions in that they have set aside a certain number of hospital beds for this specific purpose. In other communities the public health nurse has a special duty of assisting in the task of providing suitable home care. Bed care means not only the usual medical and nursing attention; it may require provision of special educational facilities through visiting teachers or special teachers assigned to "heart hospitals."

The community's responsibility does not cease with the provision of hospital facilities. "Rheumatic children" who have passed the stage of initial invalidism require continuing supervision. Many communities provide for this through the medium of cardiac clinics and special educational facilities. The cardiac clinics usually operate on a consulting basis, though accepting some patients without referral from a physician. Ideally the clinic should be a place to which the physician can refer his patient for expert diagnosis and consultation; the case is returned to him with a full report of the findings and recommendations for treatment. These clinics are of special value in assisting the physician in the diagnosis of borderline cases and the evolution of a program of activity suited to the capacities of the individual child. Overcaution through needless invalidism and curtailment of activities may be as disabling as undercaution which permits the child to place too severe a strain upon a weakened heart. Many communities make further provision for "cardiac classes" in which children with heart disease may obtain orderly education without the stresses and strains of usual school life. Opinions differ as to the desirability of special classes of this character, for some observers have felt that they produce a psychology of invalidism that can be avoided if the child associates with healthy children even though he is required to restrict his activities.

Prevention of Recurrences. The child who has had an attack of rheumatic fever must be supervised carefully to reduce the likelihood of recurrences. In former years this could be provided only through some sheltering of the child to guard it from exertion, exposure, and from respiratory infections if possible. The latter was usually not possible, but special care of every mild infection with somewhat prolonged bed rest was considered of value in reducing the chance that these infections would precipitate a rheumatic recurrence. Since the discovery of the sulfonamides, these have been used with apparently good results in the prevention of relapses. Many sulfonamide derivatives have been used and the dosage has been even more variable. The drug is administered in daily doses throughout the fall, winter, and spring. Recurrences are less frequent and less serious in children receiving sulfonamide prophylaxis than in untreated controls. The method is therefore of value but is one which must be used with care as the drugs are potentially toxic in the concentrations used. Children receiving sulfonamide prophylaxis must be kept under careful supervision of either a private physician or a clinic, with frequent checks to determine the earliest signs of toxic effects which may require discontinuance of the drug.

More recently penicillin has largely replaced the sulfonamides for the prevention of recurrences. The drug is given in the form of tablets of 100,000 units taken three times daily (on rising, an hour before lunch, and upon retiring). The use of such daily prophylaxis over a period of five years after the acute attack has been recommended, and in at least one community the health department has made the penicillin available free or at reduced cost according to the financial status of the family. Any other member of the family who develops streptococcal infection during this period is given intensive treatment. Even if penicillin is not being used routinely, it may be administered before tooth extraction or tonsillectomy, as a means of reducing the risk of a recurrence or of a streptococcal heart infection following these operations.

Public Health Nursing Care. The public health nurse has a dual responsibility to the patient and to the family. She is responsible for giving or securing nursing care for the patient who remains at home, and for the patient after he returns from the hospital or convalescent home. In the absence of medical attention she is also responsible for health supervision of the family, as this disease is apt to occur in more than one member of a family.

As the child is usually confined to bed for a period of several months and needs expert nursing care, it is advisable for him to be hospitalized, but this is not always possible. If the patient stays at home he should be in a bed by himself in a separate room or in a room shared only with the necessary attendant. As rheumatic fever is a disease of long duration, rearrangement of rooms is worth while to give the patient as bright and airy a room as possible. He should have as few visitors as possible, and no one with an upper respiratory tract infection should go near him. These isolation procedures are to protect the patient from exposure to other infections.

Though classical migratory polyarthritis occurs in a comparatively small proportion of the cases, the public health nurse should inquire about such symptoms and, if they are present, should assist the family to make the patient as comfortable as possible. Cradles to support the weight of the blankets may be helpful. If the physician orders hot packs or other forms of heat for the painful joints, the public health nurse should demonstrate their application. She should make sure that the attendant understands how to give any medications which may be ordered.

It is very important to see that the patient eats a well-balanced diet. As the rheumatic fever patient seldom has much appetite, the nurse can make an important contribution to his care by suggesting foods which may tempt his appetite and ways of making this food attractive. The patient should keep good body alignment while in bed and should have a firm mattress and a footboard to keep the blankets off his feet. He should be encouraged to move about to prevent the development of stiffness. This phase of the care is very important; consultation with an orthopedic nurse is often helpful.

During the convalescent stage while the patient is still in bed, the public health nurse can assist the mother in keeping the child occupied and entertained. A visiting teacher should be provided as soon as the physician approves. During convalescence, the physician may want the child to have exercises to prevent stiffness and loss of muscle tone as much as possible. After the child is out of bed he may resume normal activity gradually. His exercise should *not* be restricted, once he has regained his strength, *unless the physician specifically orders it*. Children with heart damage of varying degrees can often lead completely normal lives. They should be encouraged to do so subject only to the limitations put upon them by the physician.

The public health nurse, especially the one who works in schools, has an important part to play in interpreting the physician's statements and orders in relation to heart damage. Many children in the past, either because of overanxious parents or because they themselves became over-concerned about their cardiac condition, have become semi-invalids need-lessly. If the nurse notes extreme emotionalism or maladjustment in parents or child, she should bring these matters to the attention of the physician and with his approval may seek help from the social worker attached to the rheumatic fever clinic (if such exists), or from other com-munity resources. If the child has cardiac damage severe enough to restrict his activities, the nurse should acquaint the family with the community agencies which can help him to get a normal education and to live as normal a social life as possible within his physical limitations. The patient who is later ready to start a job can be referred profitably to a vocational guidance service for counseling and training.

The public health program for rheumatic fever is often compared to the tuberculosis program. The public health nurse can follow many of the principles and practices she uses in this service. General health supervision of the whole family is important in order to maintain optimum health. The child who has rheumatic fever should continue to sleep alone if this can be arranged.

Although any child with a suspected streptococcus infection should be put to bed, it is especially important that prompt attention be given to signs of illness in the child who has had rheumatic fever. He should be confined to bed for even a mild sore throat or elevation of temperature.

If there is a community program for the prevention of recurrent attacks of rheumatic fever by the prophylactic administration of the sulfonamides, the public health nurse may be responsible for periodic home follow-up to see that the drug is being taken regularly and to keep a watch for any reactions.

Number of Public Health Nursing Visits. During the acute stage the public health nurse should visit every day to give care. Practical nurses, if available, can give this care after the first two or three visits by the pub-lic health nurse. If it is impossible to give daily care, at least two visits on successive days should be made to establish care routines. A third visit should be made about a week later to answer questions which may have arisen; after that, once a month if possible, until the child is back in school. After the child has returned to school, either the school nurse or the board of health nurse should continue to give supervision to the child and the family, basing the number of visits on much the same criteria as one would with a tuberculous family.

Control through Immunization

No method of either active or passive immunization is known. Chemoprophylaxis for protection of contacts has been tried but with uncertain results, for the secondary attack rate after known exposure is low. The risk of relapse can, however, be reduced through routine administration of sulfonamides or penicillin to rheumatic fever patients during the winter months (see above).

SUMMARY

A health department program for control of rheumatic fever is directed at case-finding and provision of facilities for the best possible care of those children who have experienced potential or actual cardiac damage. Cardiac clinics, preferably operated on a consultation basis, have been found most useful. If such facilities are not otherwise available, the health department should take the necessary steps to provide this type of service for the community. The exact form of the service will depend on the pattern of general medical and social services already available. Convalescent hospital facilities must be provided locally or be available in some other community which serves this area. Follow-up of rheumatic children, and especially those with known heart damage, is essential to keep them under proper medical supervision. Closest cooperation with the medical society is essential to the planning and conduct of the program.

The **health officer** is responsible for the institution and direction of the program. In collaboration with the school physician he should determine the extent of the local problem, the availability of local facilities for diagnosis and care, the supplemental facilities required and the measures to provide for the use of these facilities by the patients in need of them. In collaboration with the medical society and the social agencies, he must evolve a plan for provision of needed facilities either on a local basis or through utilization of services available on an area or state-wide basis. The **school physician** must be alert so that evidences of early cardiac damage will be detected at the time of the routine physical examination. The **public health nurse** through her home visits may assist in the care of the case during the acute stage and assist in case-finding through alertness for symptoms of rheumatic fever and follow-up of familial contacts. Through school and home supervision she can assist the child and the family in their understanding of the disease and of any cardiac damage resulting from it. When indicated, she utilizes all available resources for the care and education of the child.

SUGGESTED READINGS

Bland, Edward F., and Jones, T. Duckett: "The Natural History of Rheumatic Fever: A 20-Year Perspective," *Ann. Int. Med.*, 37:1006–26, (Nov.) 1952.

Coburn, Alvin F., and Young, Donald C.: *The Epidemiology of Hemolytic Streptococcus.* Baltimore: Williams & Wilkins Co., 1949.

Gauld, Ross L., and Read, Frances E. M.: "Studies of Rheumatic Disease. III. Familial Association and Aggregation in Rheumatic Disease," *J. Clin. Investigation,* 19:393–98, (Mar.) 1940.

Glover, J. Alison: "Rheumatic Fever," Chapter VI of *Control of the Common Fevers.* London: The Lancet, Ltd., 1942.

Houser, Harold B., and Eckhardt, George C.: "Recent Developments in the Prevention of Rheumatic Fever," *Ann. Int. Med.,* 37:1035–43, (Nov.) 1952.

Kohn, Kate H.; Milzer, Albert; and MacLean, Helen: "Oral Penicillin Prophylaxis of Recurrences of Rheumatic Fever," *J.A.M.A.,* 142:20–25, (Jan. 7) 1950.

Massell, Benedict F.; Dow, James W.; and Jones, T. Duckett: "Orally Administered Penicillin in Patients with Rheumatic Fever," *J.A.M.A.,* 138:1030–36, (Dec. 4) 1948.

Massell, Benedict F.; Sturgis, George P.; Knoblock, Joseph D.; Streeper, Richard B.; Hall, Thomas N.; and Norcross, Pliny: "Prevention of Rheumatic Fever by Prompt Penicillin Therapy of Hemolytic Streptococcal Respiratory Infections," *J.A.M.A.,* 146:1469–74, (Aug. 18) 1951.

Olson, Helen G.: "Nutrition in Rheumatic Fever," *Pub. Health Nursing,* 42:146–49, (Mar.) 1950.

Parker, Mary E.: "Public Health Nursing in Rheumatic Fever," *Am. J. Pub. Health,* 38:1085–86, (Aug.) 1948.

Paul, John R.: "The Epidemiology of Rheumatic Fever," *Am. J. Pub. Health,* 31:611–18, (June) 1941.

———: *Rheumatic Fever in New Haven.* Lancaster, Pa.: Science Press, 1941.

———: *The Epidemiology of Rheumatic Fever and Some of Its Public Health Aspects,* 2nd ed. American Heart Association, New York, 1943.

Rutstein, David D.: "The Rheumatic Fever Community Program," *Am. J. Pub. Health,* 38:1082–84, (Aug.) 1948.

Sadler, Sabra S.: "Nursing the Child with Rheumatic Fever," *Pub. Health Nursing,* 41:489–94, (Sept.) 1949.

Sadler, Sabra S., and Seibel, Elizabeth: "The Child with Active Rheumatic Fever and Her Nursing Care," *Am. J. Nursing,* 46:170–75, (Mar.) 1946.

Smith, Mary Alice; Fried, Anton R.; Morris, Ernest M.; Robbins, Lewis C.; and Zukel, William J.: "Rheumatic Fever Prophylaxis. A Community Program through the Private Physician," *J.A.M.A.,* 149:636–39, (June 14) 1952.

Swift, Homer F.: "Public Health Aspect of Rheumatic Heart Disease; Incidence and Measures for Control," *J.A.M.A.,* 115:1509–18, (Nov. 2) 1940.

Waksman, Byron H.: "The Etiology of Rheumatic Fever," *Medicine,* 28:143–200, (May) 1949.

Wilcox, Elizabeth: "Rheumatic Fever—Diagnosis, Prognosis, Treatment and Nursing Care," *Am. J. Nursing,* 45:94–99, (Feb.) 1945.

Wilson, May G.: *Rheumatic Fever.* New York: Commonwealth Fund, 1940.

Wilson, May G.; Schweitzer, Morton D.; and Lubschez, Rose: "The Familial Epidemiology of Rheumatic Fever: Genetic and Epidemiologic Studies," *J. Ped.,* 22:468–92, 581–611, (Apr., May) 1943.

20. Whooping Cough

Whooping cough, known also as pertussis, is an acute infection of the respiratory tract. It begins as an ordinary cough (tracheobronchitis) which, in a typical case, becomes increasingly severe and, after the second week, is attended by paroxysms of coughing, which end in a characteristic whoop as the breath is drawn in. Vomiting may follow a spasm. Many cases fail to whoop and others show only a very mild cough, clinically indistinguishable from those of other etiology. The cough may last for several weeks and occasionally two or three months. Pertussis in small children is frequently complicated by bronchopneumonia, which may result fatally. The case fatality rate for all ages is less than 1 per cent, but may be as high as 25 per cent in infants.

EPIDEMIOLOGY

Occurrence. Whooping cough is one of the most important causes of death in small children and at present outranks all other infectious diseases except pneumonia.[1] Over 70 per cent of the deaths occur during the first year of life and over 90 per cent during the first three years. The cases show a somewhat older age distribution and reach their peak in incidence during the latter part of the preschool period. The death rate from pertussis has declined strikingly during the past few decades. As recently as 1920 the rate in the United States was 12.5 per 100,000 population. By 1935 it was 3.7, and in 1949 only 0.5. Whooping cough is found in all parts of the world. Though present at all seasons of the year, it reaches its peak in the winter.

Etiological Agent. Whooping cough is due to infection with the *Hemophilus pertussis,* frequently referred to as the Bordet-Gengou bacillus, a Gram-negative organism quickly destroyed by the usual disinfect-

---

[1] In addition to the deaths officially credited to whooping cough, many others listed as bronchopneumonia are in reality secondary to unrecognized whooping cough.

ing procedures. The organisms are most readily recovered by "cough plate" technique. This consists in making the child cough directly upon a Petri dish containing a special culture medium. In using such plates, it is important to obtain a deep and fairly severe cough. Ordinary "clearing of the throat" is not adequate. For satisfactory results, the medium must be freshly prepared and the plates examined by bacteriologists well skilled and experienced in this special work. Owing to the difficulty of the technique and the expense entailed in having a supply of fresh medium constantly present, the routine use of "cough plates" for diagnosis has not been developed by public health laboratories in a manner comparable to the cultural methods for some other infections. Favorable results have been described from the use of postnasal cultures.

The reservoir of infection is in all instances previous cases of the disease. There is no evidence that healthy carriers exist. It must be remembered, however, that many and possibly the majority of the cases show a very mild cough unattended by "whooping." These "missed cases" constitute a most important part of the reservoir in that they escape detection and circulate freely in the community.

TABLE 5

PERCENTAGE OF PATIENTS YIELDING POSITIVE H. PERTUSSIS CULTURES ACCORDING TO STAGE OF ILLNESS *

Observer	First Week %	Second Week %	Third Week %	Fourth Week %
Chievitz and Meyer (1916)	89	73	33	33
Madsen (1924)	75	57	61	45
Gardner and Leslie (1932)	75	67	75	25
Miller (1933)	78	66	43	50
Kristensen (1933)	65	58	52	40
Kendrick and Eldering (1935)	78	64	62	32
Silverthorne and Fraser (1935)	98	79	20	18
Straker and Westwater (1937)	86	84	71	50

* The data of different observers are not strictly comparable because of slight variations in counting of weeks. The data agree, however in showing the progressive decline of positive results.

Escape of the organism from the infected person is through the secretion of the upper respiratory tract. As shown in Table 5, the organisms are more readily found in the early weeks of the disease and especially during the preparoxysmal period. This means that isolation and quarantine procedures, which are usually not instituted until the child "whoops," are of little value in preventing spread, as most of the damage has been done before the diagnosis is made.

Transmission is by direct spread through respiratory and salivary contacts. There is no evidence that fomites or food are important in the spread of whooping cough. Crowding and close association with the patient facilitate spread.

Entry and Incubation Period. Entry of the organisms is through the respiratory tract. The incubation period is about 7 to 16 days, usually 10.

Susceptibility appears to be universal until the individual has been actively infected. There is no evidence of any resistance at birth, as in certain other diseases. Consequently, cases of whooping cough appear during the first month of life, and the bulk of the deaths during the first year. Nor is there definite evidence of latent immunization, as in scarlet fever and diphtheria. Owing to the high level of susceptibility, attack rates of approximately 90 per cent occur in family contacts who have not previously had the disease. Similarly, the absence of carriers means that persons living in isolated areas show no resistance if the disease has been absent from that locality for a period of years. There is no satisfactory skin test for susceptibility. Complement fixation tests yield some evidence as to recent infection.

CONTROL MEASURES

Control of Spread

The case of whooping cough should be segregated under modified isolation techniques until three weeks after the appearance of the paroxysmal cough. Special attention should be paid to suspicious cases of pertussis even though definite diagnosis has not yet been established. Any child who shows an increasingly severe cough and in whom the cough is worse at night or a child who shows coughing spells followed by vomiting merits isolation precautions even though the characteristic "whoop" has not yet developed. Cough plates are of little practical value in release from isolation. Transfer to a hospital is undesirable if reasonable care can be provided at home, as there is a greater risk of contracting pneumonia in a hospital, where there are so many acutely ill patients. Even at home, special precautions should be taken to avoid exposure of the patient to other persons, especially those with colds, to reduce the likelihood of pneumonia. As the patient was most infectious during the prodromal stage, isolation will do little to reduce spread within the family but will help to protect the patient from complications. This is most important in younger children, especially infants, for whom whooping cough complicated by pneumonia is one of the most serious of all infections. Because of the seriousness of the disease under such conditions, it is advisable to consider any severe cough, especially during known prevalence of pertussis, as a possible whooping cough and to institute isolation precautions.

Epidemiological investigation yields little in actual control because of the large number of unrecognized mild infections. A record should be made of known intimate contacts so that these may be observed and segregated at the first suggestion of a respiratory tract infection consistent with early whooping cough and so that medical and nursing care may be made available. If whooping cough is present in a schoolroom, any beginning cold or cough among other children in the room should be considered as suspicious, and the child excluded pending observation. Routine inspection of the children and exclusion of those with beginning colds is desirable. No attention need be given to food or fomites in the routine investigation, nor are cultures obtained. If facilities for cough plate examination are available, their use on contacts with early coughs or colds will facilitate early diagnosis.

Family contacts have usually been so thoroughly exposed during the prodromal period of the original case that almost all susceptibles will probably develop the infection. Special precautions should be observed to segregate any infant, as this child may at times have escaped exposure and infection will be especially dangerous. All child contacts who have not had whooping cough are usually quarantined for ten days from date of last exposure, though there is little evidence that this is really effective. If not quarantined, such contacts should at least be kept away from babies and small children, especially at the end of the normal incubation period and if they develop any cough. Contacts who have had the disease require no quarantine, as healthy carriers do not exist. All child contacts who have previously been immunized should be given a booster dose of pertussis vaccine (see p. 282). As rapid effect is desired, use of saline-suspended vaccine is indicated in such instances. Adult contacts are usually subjected to no restraint, as they have usually had whooping cough even though they have been unaware of it. In rural areas this is less true, so that here adult contacts may require observation and subsequent restriction if symptoms suggestive of whooping cough develop. This is especially important in schoolteachers and others having contacts with children. Isolation and quarantine procedures accomplish so little on a community-wide basis that the present tendency is to make them as liberal as possible and to concentrate attention upon the prevention of complications. Laboratory procedures are of no proved value in determining quarantine periods.

Environmental sanitation plays no specific part in control of whooping cough.

Disinfection. Pertussis is included in Group I; procedures outlined for that group on page 144 should be followed.

Minimizing Ill Effects

The seriousness of pertussis is due not to the primary infection but to the complicating pneumonia. The best possible medical and nursing attention must therefore be given to all cases and especially to the younger children. Whooping cough is usually introduced into a family by a child of school age. The epidemiological investigation of this case reveals the younger children who will probably be the next victims and for whom medical and nursing care is especially necessary. If the family is financially unable to secure medical aid, this should be provided by the health department. Nursing care should be demonstrated and frequently given by the public health nurse. A few visits to render such care will do more to reduce infant deaths than a large number of routine visits to well babies. Special attention must be given in homes where economic conditions are poor. Hyperimmune serum, if administered in adequate quantity, apparently has a limited therapeutic value and is therefore valuable in severe cases in small children. The health department should be prepared to furnish this serum in selected cases. Its production can be undertaken only in laboratories equipped for work with human blood. Whooping cough vaccine is of no value for treatment. Favorable results have been reported following the use of antibiotics, notably aureomycin.

Public Health Nursing Care. Because most children with whooping cough are not confined to bed, many public health nurses assume that instruction regarding nursing care is unnecessary. This is true to some extent only if the patient is of school age or older, as usually these patients are not confined to bed and complications are not frequent. Even in fairly severe cases with vomiting, they can usually afford to lose food and even to lose weight without seriously impairing their health.

Whooping cough in an infant or preschool child is, however, a serious condition. Although severe cases in this age group are less common than formerly, they still occur frequently enough to require public health nursing attention to all infants who have contracted whooping cough or been intimately exposed to it. Medical attention should be secured as soon as possible, not only because general medical attention is important but also because the physician may wish to administer antibiotics. Even with medical treatment expert nursing care is essential.

General Care. Nursing instruction is focused on the prevention of bronchial pneumonia and the maintenance of body weight and general resistance. The infant should be isolated from all persons except the one caring for him. Strict isolation of the preschool child is more difficult, but every effort should be made to reduce the number of contacts, especially to avoid anyone having a respiratory infection. The mother will appreciate the reason for isolation if she is told of the importance of reducing exposure to possible infection from outside sources.

It is important to reduce the coughing spasms as much as possible, as they are very exhausting and as the vomiting, which often follows, may cause impairment of nutrition. Since fresh air, if it is not too cold, and sunshine are beneficial, the patient should be out of doors as much as possible. In winter this is not usually advisable, as cold air makes a child cough more easily. As physicians often order steam inhalations for infants, the nurse must be prepared to demonstrate the croup tent. Violent exercise or excitement such as laughing or crying should be avoided, as it may induce a coughing spasm.

The patient needs help and reassurance during a coughing spasm yet must not be tempted to cough because of the attention he gets. The mother must try to steer a middle course between too much sympathy and not enough assistance. She should be instructed to pick up the infant when he coughs, thus reducing the danger of inhalation of mucus and giving him support and reassurance. An older child can often prevent a spasm if he makes a conscious effort to do so. He should be encouraged not to cough and be praised for these efforts.

If bronchopneumonia develops, the usual care of pneumonia should be given.

Diet. Special attention to the diet is needed if the child is vomiting after the paroxysms of coughing, lest there be undue loss of weight. Diet is so important in the infant that no advice should be given without the physician's orders. He may wish to change the formula; if so, the nurse may demonstrate the new formula to the mother. In any case, if the infant is vomiting, the mother should be instructed to make up a few extra bottles in the morning for the extra feedings which are to be given after vomiting. It may be explained to the mother that as the paroxysms usually come at intervals of about two or three hours, it is important to feed the infant directly after vomiting, but first to allow him five or ten minutes to quiet down. As the next coughing spasm will probably not occur for two to three hours, most of the food will be digested before the next vomiting spell. If the mother understands this, she can appreciate the importance of feeding at once rather than waiting an hour or more. The baby should, of course, be raised to expel gas after each feeding.

The same attention to diet is important for the preschool child, though probably no special diet will be ordered. Very hot or very cold foods (such as hot soup or ice cream) and those highly seasoned are to be avoided as they have a tendency to induce coughing spasms. Likewise, such foods as nuts and crackers should be avoided. Solids and semisolids are better at mealtime with small amounts of liquids; liquids should be given between meals.

Number of Nursing Visits. Infants may need daily nursing care. Preschool children, if not confined to bed, usually do not need such frequent visits. If regular bedside care cannot be given, at least two successive visits immediately upon receiving the report of the case should be made to infants and preschool children to demonstrate care and instruct the mother, and one additional visit six or seven weeks after onset to assist in convalescent and postconvalescent well-child care. In general, except for the initial instructional visit to explain isolation and quarantine restrictions, there is no need of visits to school children, unless there are younger children in the family.

Control through Immunization

Passive immunization by hyperimmune serum is an extremely effective method of protecting the small child known to have been exposed to whooping cough. It is prepared from the blood of persons whose antibody level has been raised to an abnormally high titer by frequent and recent injections of whooping cough vaccine. The serum is usually given in doses of 10 to 20 cc depending on the age of the child; the injection should be repeated in five to seven days if the exposure is intimate and continuous. If given promptly after exposure, hyperimmune serum will probably prevent infection; if given late in the incubation period it will reduce the severity of the disease. The serum is so expensive to produce and the supply is so limited that its routine administration to all contacts cannot be recommended. Its use should, in general, be restricted to children under three years of age and especially to infants; older children who are in poor physical condition may properly be given the serum if known to have been intimately exposed. As the protection from this serum is mere passive immunity, the effect usually lasts only two or three weeks. Gamma globulin cannot be used as it contains too low a content of pertussis antibodies. Placental extract is likewise ineffective as the newborn baby has no resistance to whooping cough comparable to that for measles.

Active Immunization. The antigen most commonly used consists of an emulsion of heat-killed organisms in either a fluid or alum-precipitated form. Three injections are given about a month apart. Reactions are relatively mild. An alum-precipitated vaccine has largely replaced the original Sauer vaccine. It is most commonly administered in the form of a multiple antigen, mixed with either diphtheria toxoid or with both diphtheria and tetanus toxoids. In this form it is administered in three injections at intervals of one month. The reactions are little more severe than following the individual injections, and the protection obtained is as high if not higher. Since the baby has no resistance to pertussis at birth, immunization should be started as soon as the infant is able to respond to the vaccine and produce antibodies. As the antibody-production mechanism is not well developed at birth, immunization is not highly effective until about six months of age. On the other hand a large number of pertussis deaths occur during the first six months of life. In selecting the age at which immunization is to be started, a compromise must therefore be made between the need for the protection and the limited ability of the small baby to produce antibodies.

In private practice, immunization is usually begun at about three months of age to obtain the benefits of the earliest possible protection. As the protection so obtained is not as lasting as is the resistance produced later in life, booster doses are recommended a year later and again at school age. Immunization so early in life is ideal but depends upon the ability to get the child back for a booster dose at the end of a year. In public clinics there is less assurance of being able to reach the child again until school age. Under such circumstances the initial immunization can well be postponed to the age of six months, thus sacrificing three months of protection in favor of a more lasting resistance.

Whooping cough vaccine is not one of the best antigens but does confer a very satisfactory level of protection. Even though some reviewers have properly pointed out certain respects in which the evidence is inconclusive, there have been too many favorable reports to permit serious question that pertussis vaccine confers a very considerable degree of protection. The reports of Sauer, Kendrick, Singer-Brooks, Bell, and others indicate definitely lower attack rates among the immunized than among the nonimmunized. The cases in the immunized children are milder than in the nonimmunized group. Yet even the most favorable reports indicate that immunization against whooping cough is not as effective as is immunization against diphtheria or smallpox if performed with appropriate antigens. For example, the studies of Kendrick (Table 6) show an appreciable attack rate among immunized children brought in contact with known infection.

Few reports of the results of community-wide immunization programs are yet available, but those of Sauer and Tucker in Evanston strongly suggest that whooping cough can be controlled in this way. Pertussis vaccination should be as standard a procedure in well-baby clinics as is diphtheria immunization. The use of the combined diphtheria-pertussis-tetanus antigen permits simultaneous immunization against all three diseases without increasing the number of injections. Owing to the large number of deaths during the first three months of life, it is apparent that, even if the vaccine is extremely effective, its use at the age of three to six months will fail to reach a large part of the group most in need of protection. As the baby is usually exposed by an older brother or sister, immunization of the latter, if effective, may reduce the likelihood of bringing the disease into the home, as healthy carriers do not exist. Inasmuch as the most favorable reports show, however, an appreciable number of failures of protection against exposure within the home, it is apparent that immunization in its present form can be only a partial solution to the whooping cough problem. There is still need for special care and protection of the young child, as it is in the first two years of life that most of the deaths occur.

TABLE 6

PROTECTIVE VALUE OF WHOOPING COUGH VACCINE
(Adapted from report of Kendrick and Eldering)

Group Studied	Immunized Group	Nonimmunized Group
Person-years at risk	2268	2307
Attacks	52	348
Annual attack rate	2.3%	15.1%
Persons exposed to family contact	83	160
Attacks	29	143
Attack rate	35%	89%

Recent literature contains a few reports of untoward reactions following pertussis vaccines. Encephalitic reactions attended by convulsions have been described but apparently are quite rare. Certain studies of severe reactions to poliomyelitis contracted within a month after immunization have contained the suggestion that such reactions might have a special relationship to pertussis vaccine. Other studies, while confirming the general phenomenon, fail to suggest any greater connection with pertussis vaccine. These reports, while indicating need for greater research, do not contraindicate the widespread use of pertussis vaccine.

SUMMARY

Health Department Program

Whooping cough, though neglected by many health departments, presents one of the most serious of the acute communicable disease problems since it is responsible for more deaths than measles, diphtheria, scarlet fever, poliomyelitis, or typhoid fever. As death is due to a complicating pneumonia, attention must be directed not simply to whooping cough control but also to the prevention of complications. Because of the existence of so many mild, unrecognized cases and the high infectiousness during the prodromal stage, little success has attended the use of isolation and quarantine procedures in preventing spread. Much can, however, be done to prevent death by furnishing adequate medical and nursing care and by education of the public as to the importance and danger of whooping cough in the first three years of life. Active immunization is apparently of personal value, affords some protection against infection, and reduces the severity of subsequent cases. The health department should promote immunization with whooping cough vaccine as a routine part of infant care with the same insistence that it advocates diphtheria immunization. If the community provides immunization in public clinics or well-baby conferences, whooping cough immunization should be made a part of the program.

The **health officer** is responsible for the institution of isolation and quarantine procedures and the promotion of immunization. In conjunction with the school authorities, he can arrange for inspection of school children to detect early suspected cases in the schools, especially in rooms where infection is known to exist. He should formulate a definite plan of community education regarding whooping cough and reach especially the homes where economic conditions are poor and there are children under three. Such a program may be organized in the same manner as that for measles (p. 293). The **public health nurse** should encourage active immunization against whooping cough. She should also carry on educational visits prior to the outbreak, pointing out the seriousness of the disease for the younger children and their need of care. Cases should be visited to make certain that care is provided for younger children. The nurse can frequently render bedside nursing care under the supervision of the physician, especially in cases where home conditions demand it and in which removal to the hospital is not desirable. Nursing visits to whooping cough patients should take precedence over all routine visits.

SUGGESTED READINGS

Bell, Joseph A.: "Current Status of Immunization Procedures. Pertussis," *Am. J. Pub. Health,* **38**:478–80, (Apr.) 1948.
———: "Pertussis Immunization," *J.A.M.A.,* **137**:1276–81, (Aug. 7) 1948.
Butler, William: "Whooping Cough and Measles. An Epidemiological Concurrence and Contrast," *Proc. Roy. Soc. Med.* (Sect. Epid. & State Med.), **40**:384–98, (May) 1947.

Cruickshank, Robert: "Whooping-Cough or Pertussis," *Lancet*, 2:33–37, (July 2) 1938. Published also as Chapter VII of *Control of the Common Fevers*. London: The Lancet, Ltd., 1942.

diSant'Agnese, Paul A.: "Simultaneous Immunization of New-Born Infants against Diphtheria, Tetanus, and Pertussis," *Am. J. Pub. Health*, 40:674–80, (June) 1950.

Emerson, Haven: "Measles and Whooping Cough: Incidence, Fatality and Death Rates in Thirty-two Cities of the United States, in Relation to Administrative Procedures Intended for Their Control—1924–1933," Supp. to *Am. J. Pub. Health*, Vol. 27, (June) 1937.

————: "Essential Problems in Pertussis," *Am. J. Pub. Health*, 29:337–40, (Apr.) 1939.

Felton, Harriet M.: "The Status of Passive Immunization and Treatment in Pertussis by the Use of Human Hyperimmune Serum. Report of the Council on Pharmacy and Chemistry of the American Medical Association," *J.A.M.A.*, 128:26–28, (May 5) 1945.

Godfrey, Edward S., Jr.: "Epidemiology of Whooping Cough," *New York State J. Med.*, 28:1410–15, (Dec. 1) 1928.

Gordon, John E., and Hood, Robert I.: "Whooping Cough and Its Epidemiological Anomalies," *Am. J. M. Sc.*, 222:333–61, (Sept.) 1951.

Kendrick, Pearl L.: "Secondary Familial Attack Rates from Pertussis in Vaccinated and Unvaccinated Children," *Am. J. Hyg.*, 32:A:89–91, (Nov.) 1940.

Medical Research Council: "The Prevention of Whooping Cough by Vaccination," *Brit. M. J.*, 1:1463–71, (June 30) 1951.

Sauer, Louis W.; Tucker, Winston H.; and Markley, Eva: "Immunity Responses to Mixtures of Diphtheria Toxoid and Pertussis Vaccine," *J.A.M.A.*, 125:949–52, (Aug. 5) 1944.

Singer-Brooks, Charlotte: "Pertussis Prophylaxis: A Controlled Study," *J.A.M.A.*, 114:1734–40, (May 4) 1940.

21. Measles

An acute infection of a few days' duration, measles is characterized by fever, rash, and symptoms referable to the upper respiratory tract. The eruption is preceded by about two days of coryza, during which stage grayish specks (Koplik's spots) may be found on the inner surfaces of the cheeks. A cough frequently occurs during the later stages. Middle ear infection and pneumonia, less commonly encephalitis, constitute the chief complications, pneumonia being responsible for most of the deaths attributable to measles. Less than one-tenth of a per cent of those contracting measles die of it; the case fatality rate in small children and in adults is much higher than in children of school age.

EPIDEMIOLOGY

Occurrence. Measles is found in all races and climates. It usually appears in epidemic waves which last from a few weeks to three or four months, depending on the size of the community. These waves are usually two or three years apart in urban communities, but in rural areas they appear quite irregularly, depending upon the chance introduction of infection into the community. Though measles may occur at all seasons of the year and though local outbreaks beginning in the fall may reach their peak in the late fall or early winter, the disease usually is most prevalent in early spring and disappears rapidly with the advent of summer. Because of the universal susceptibility of those not previously attacked, the age distribution of cases varies with the opportunities for exposure. In congested areas, most children have been infected by ten years of age, many before five, whereas in rural areas many cases occur among adolescents and young adults. Measles presents a very real problem in army camps where boys from rural areas are brought together. When the disease invaded the Faroe Islands after an absence of sixty-five years, it attacked almost all of those born in the interim, adults as readily as children. In the United

States over half of the measles deaths occur in children under the age of three, and two-thirds under the age of five. The death rate has declined strikingly during recent years. In 1920 it was 8.8 per 100,000 population; by 1935 it had fallen to 3.1, and by 1949 to only 0.6.

Etiological Agent. Measles is caused by a virus. The complicating otitis and pneumonia are due to secondary bacterial infections, principally streptococci and pneumococci.

The reservoir of infection consists solely of active cases of measles. There is no evidence that healthy or convalescent carriers exist or that other animals are infected under natural conditions.

Escape from the reservoir is effected through the respiratory secretions, especially during the prodromal stage, when the patient appears to have little more than a coryza. Although some have suggested that communicability ceases by the time the rash appears, this would appear to be too sweeping a generalization. Yet it contains an element of truth, inasmuch as most of the spread occurs during this prodromal period before the appearance of the characteristic eruption by which the diagnosis is usually made. By the time the rash has disappeared, communicability has certainly ceased even though the case may be complicated by otitis or pneumonia.

Transmission is by direct droplet contact and hence favored by crowding. There is no evidence that fomites are significant in spreading measles or that water, food, milk, or flies are capable of transmitting the disease.

Entry and Incubation Period. Entry into the new host is by the respiratory passages. The incubation period varies from 8 to 21 days, usually 10 to 14. In calculating dates of exposure, it should be remembered that the rash appears on the third day of the illness, so that if there has been constant association with the patient, first exposure probably occurred two or three days prior to the onset of the rash.

Susceptibility. The newborn infant has a temporary resistance only if the mother has had measles. This resistance at birth disappears by six months of age and does not reappear until the child has had an attack of measles. There is no evidence of latent immunization through repeated infection with doses too small to cause clinically recognizable symptoms. This may be described as an "all-or-none effect": the child remains highly susceptible until infected and then suddenly acquires a high level of protection. Although this resistance may occasionally disappear, as shown by a second attack of measles, the protection derived from one attack is reasonably lasting even in the absence of reinforcement through exposure to cases. This was demonstrated in the Faroe Islands by the scarcity of cases among those who had been attacked sixty-five years earlier but who had never been exposed in the interim. Except in rural areas, adults are rarely attacked at the time of infection of their children.

The proportion of children who have had measles and are therefore resistant to it varies with the opportunities for exposure. The percentage immune at a given age of life is greater in the urban than in the rural areas and is higher in the congested, economically poorer areas than among the well-to-do. There is no method of testing the resistance of an individual to measles, all conclusions on this subject being based solely on epidemiological observation.

CONTROL MEASURES

Control of Spread

The case should, so far as practicable, be isolated for a period of five to seven days after the onset of the rash. While theoretically this isolation is designed to prevent spread to others, in reality it serves more to protect the patient against secondary infection which may lead to pneumonia. Special care should therefore be taken to avoid exposing the patient to persons who have colds or other respiratory tract infections. If the home conditions are satisfactory, isolation is best carried out there rather than in a hospital where the number of contacts and thus the risk of pneumonia may be increased. A rigid isolation technique in the home is, however, of little value in reducing the secondary attack rate, as the siblings have usually been thoroughly exposed during the prodromal stage before the appearance of the rash. Experience shows that primary cases are followed by infection of 90 to 100 per cent of the susceptible siblings.

Epidemiological investigation directed to finding the source of infection is of little value in control, as the period of communicability in measles is so short that the source, even if discovered, is no longer infectious. Such investigations may, however, reveal other persons who were similarly exposed and who may therefore be infected simultaneously. The principal value of epidemiological inquiry is the discovery of those persons, especially preschool children, who have been exposed to the patient. This permits passive immunization or modification if desired and also permits their quarantine during the period of probable communicability. The epidemiological history should therefore list the close contacts made by the patient during the three days prior to the onset of the rash and since its appearance.

Contacts may be divided into two groups, the immune and the susceptible, separation being based solely on a history of a prior attack. No consideration need be given to the immune contacts, as carriers do not exist and second attacks are rare. Quarantine of the susceptible family contact until fourteen days have elapsed from last exposure is of little practical value, even though it is theoretically desirable and is required by some boards of health. It has consistently failed to stop the course of an epidemic, as it does not reach the large number of contacts who have been exposed outside the family. There is much to be said for the practice of some communities in abandoning all quarantine and concentrating upon the problem of reducing the severity of the infection in the younger age groups. Other communities have hesitated to give up quarantine but have attempted to shorten the school loss incident to it by applying restrictions only at the end of the probable incubation period. Under such a plan, the contact attends school for seven to ten days after initial exposure and is then excluded for a week. While administratively somewhat cumbersome, this reduces school absences without increasing the risk of spread. Within the home, every effort should be made to separate the contacts from the patient, thus reducing the risk of complications.

Environmental sanitation is not effective in the control of measles as inanimate objects play little or no part in its spread. When measles invades institutions or other crowded groups, reduction in crowding may be effective in lessening the incidence of complicating pneumonia.

Disinfection. No special procedures are required. Measles is included in Group I; procedures outlined for that group on page 144 may be followed.

Minimizing Ill Effects

Prevention of ill effects is at present our most important control measure in measles, for, while it will not reduce the incidence of the disease, it will definitely reduce the number of deaths. Use of sera for passive immunization or modification of the disease in contacts is described below. Many physicians routinely administer antibiotics to patients with measles. This will not alter the measles but will reduce the risk of a complicating pneumonia. Good medical and nursing care will also do much to reduce the likelihood and severity of complications. As most children of school age do well even in the absence of medical and nursing care, the seriousness of measles is often overlooked by the public; hence, the secondary case in the small child is largely neglected on the assumption that it will be no different from the case in the older sibling. This unfortunately means that pneumonia may have developed before the mother seeks medical assistance. Whenever a health department representative visits a home where a case of measles has been reported, special attention should be paid to the siblings under three. The mother should be impressed with the importance of good medical and nursing care for such children when they contract the infection, and the desirability of passive immunization or modification through injection of suitable antibodies should be pointed out to her (see p. 292). This instruction should be followed by a visit at the time when secondary cases are expected to make certain that care is being given. Bedside care by a visiting nurse may be of great value in such cases and can be rendered without any danger of spread of infection to other persons for whom she may care.

Public Health Nursing Care. Good nursing care is desirable for all measles patients but especially important for those of preschool age. The child should be kept in bed, and other persons, except the mother or attendant, should be kept away from him. Under no circumstances should persons with respiratory tract infections come in contact with the patient. The mother should be warned not to put all the children who have measles in the same bed or near each other, as this increases the incidence of complications. The physician's orders regarding light and ventilation should be followed and interpreted to the mother. The patient's eyes should be protected from glare, as they are apt to be inflamed, but the room should not be darkened without physician's orders.

The child should be protected from drafts and chilling because of the danger of pneumonia. If the room is cool and it is difficult to keep the child under the covers, a sleeping suit or warm pajamas and stockings may be suggested. Special care should be taken when giving the bed bath not to allow the child to be chilled; the mother may be shown or told how to do this safely. When sponges for reduction of temperature are ordered, lukewarm water 90–95° F should be used. If the child is not very sick, the nurse may have to use all her ingenuity in assisting the mother to devise ways of keeping the child occupied in bed.

The nurse should warn the mother that any rise in temperature, persistence of fever, earache, increase or return of cough, or other unusual symptom occurring about the seventh or eighth day after the rash appears should be reported to the physician at once, as it may be the first symptom of pneumonia or otitis media.

Preschool children often need special care after recovery from measles to build up their general health and resistance. The nurse should visit to instruct regarding extra rest periods, adequate diet, air and sunshine, and the importance of medical supervision until the child has completely regained his strength and vigor.

Number of Nursing Visits. If bedside care is to be furnished, daily visits should be made as long as necessary. Otherwise, there should be at least two visits, one at the onset to give initial instruction and the second about ten days later to stress convalescent care and at the same time to watch for subsequent cases, especially in preschool children.

Control through Immunization

Passive Immunization. Complete passive immunization or partial protection to achieve a modification of the disease may be obtained through use of human sera or placental extracts. (See Chap. 3 for discussion of these agents and their use.) Gamma globulin (human immune serum globulin) is at present the antibody of choice. To secure modification of measles in a child under seven, 0.1 to 1 cc is administered intramuscularly (*never* intravenously), and 2.0 to 3.5 cc for older children. For prevention the doses are 1.5 to 2.0 cc and 5 to 7 cc respectively. As complete passive immunization lasts only two to four weeks and then leaves the child as susceptible as formerly, it is used only for those for whom even a mild attack would be an undue risk—as in the case of children recovering from some other illness or otherwise debilitated. It is also valuable in preventing spread in institutional groups. Modification is based on the principle of giving a child who has been effectively exposed only enough antibodies to confer a partial protection with a resulting milder form of the disease. Modified cases have a longer incubation period, less extensive rash, and fewer complications but apparently acquire as lasting a protection as do typical infections. Modification is therefore desirable in the small child whose physical condition permits him to stand a mild attack without undue risk. It is usually preferable to permit this mild and immunizing infection than to run the risk of a later severe attack due to an unrecognized exposure. Use of passive immunity or modification is of course possible only if the child has had a known exposure. Its chief use is therefore in dealing with family contacts, especially those under three or five years of age. So far as possible, these should be given some form of protection, the choice depending upon the attending physician. Where no physician is in attendance, health departments may provide such protection for the younger group.

Active Immunization. No method of proved value is yet available.

SUMMARY

Health Department Programs

Isolation and quarantine measures are of little value in preventing the spread of measles because of the high communicability and the ease of spread during the prodromal period. Protection of small children from older ones who are developing colds will, however, reduce the spread to the younger group, in which most of the deaths occur. In the absence of means of active immunization, the disease cannot be effectively prevented but can be reduced in severity among the younger contacts by use of complete or partial passive immunization. Use of antibiotics and provision of adequate medical and nursing care of all cases, especially those under three or five years of age, are important in reducing the risk of death from complicating pneumonia.

The **health officer** is responsible for the organization of a program of community and professional education regarding the importance of measles in the preschool group and the possibility of protecting small children through use of suitable antibodies. He is also responsible for provision of these antibodies for modification or passive protection, and for the creation of facilities to administer them when needed in homes lacking medical care. Rather than diffusing his efforts through the entire community, his program should be concentrated upon those few homes with children under the ages of three or five and especially in the economically poorer sections of the community, as it is here that most of the deaths occur. This is best effected thorugh a listing of all children under three or five years of age, this listing being based on birth certificates and kept up to date by extraction of deaths, removals, and those who are known to have measles and by addition of children whom the nurses find to have moved into their districts.

Besides the mailing of pamphlet material to homes on the above list, the educational program should consist of visits by the **public health nurses,** especially in the homes where, because of crowding and a large number of susceptible children, the risk is greatest. The main purpose of such visits should be to instruct the mother regarding the importance of measles to a preschool child, to inform her regarding the possibility of passive protection and facilities to obtain this protection, and especially to guard against the often encountered practice of deliberately exposing the baby and small children in order to "get it over with" at one session. It is doubtful whether visiting the homes of all reported cases of measles is a good use of the public health nurse's time. She should, where possible, visit the homes of infants and preschool children reported to have measles and those homes in which children of this age group are known to be in household contact with a reported case of measles. Visits to these latter homes are more important as medical attention is frequently not obtained until the small child is quite ill. If the nurse cannot convince the family to obtain medical care, the board of health should arrange for passive immunization or modification in the younger children. The nurse may also assist in bedside care if the attending physician so desires and may report to the health officer cases lacking medical care—cases who, because of home conditions and lack of medical care, should be transferred to a hospital. Routine hospitalization is, however, not desirable. Observance of a program as above outlined to prevent deaths, even if not cases, will do far more to control measles than will expensive and indiscriminate campaigns of isolating and placarding.

SUGGESTED READINGS

Brincker, J. A. H.: "A Historical, Epidemiological and Aetiological Study of Measles (Morbilli; Rubeola)," *Proc. Roy. Soc. Med.,* 31:807–28, (Feb. 25) 1938.

Butler, William: "Whooping Cough and Measles. An Epidemiological Concurrence and Contrast," *Proc. Roy. Soc. Med.* (Sect. Epid. & State Med.), 40:384–98, (May) 1947.

Godfrey, Edward S., Jr.: "The Administrative Control of Measles," *Am. J. Pub. Health,* 16:571–77, (June) 1926.

———: "Measles in Institutions for Children," *J. Prev. Med.* 2:1–33, 251–72, (Jan., May) 1928.

Greenberg, Morris: "Gamma Globulin in Measles Prophylaxis," *Pub. Health Nursing,* 38:282–84, (June) 1946.

Gunn, William: "Measles," *Lancet,* 2:795–99, (April 2) 1938. Published also as Chapter VIII of *Control of the Common Fevers.* London: The Lancet, Ltd., 1942.

Medical Research Council: "Gamma Globulin in the Prevention of Measles," *Lancet,* 2:732–36, (Dec. 9) 1950.

Panum, Peter L.: "Observations Made during the Epidemic of Measles on the Faroe Islands in the Year 1846." A translation from the Danish. Delta Omega Society, 1940. Another translation appears in *M. Classics,* 3:803–86, (May) 1939.

Perkins, J. E.; Bahlke, Anne M.; and Silverman, Hilda F.: "Effect of Ultra-Violet Irradiation of Classrooms on Spread of Measles in Large Rural Central Schools," *Am. J. Pub. Health,* 37:529–37, (May) 1947.

Report of the Council on Pharmacy and Chemistry of the American Medical Association: "Human Immune Serum Globulin," *J.A.M.A.,* 131:972, (July 20) 1946.

Ruhland, George C., and Silverman, A. Clement: "What Can We Do about Measles?" *Am. J. Pub. Health,* 18:131–39, (Feb.) 1928.

Top, Franklin H.: "Measles in Detroit: I. Factors Influencing the Secondary Attack Rate among Susceptibles at Risk," *Am. J. Pub. Health,* 28:935–43, (Aug.) 1938.

22. Chickenpox, German Measles, and Mumps

These three diseases, often referred to as the minor infections of childhood, may be conveniently considered together, as their etiology, mode of spread, and general epidemiological aspects are quite similar. The general public health measures observed are also very comparable as to detail and lack of effectiveness.

These diseases are truly minor conditions in that they are almost devoid of serious consequences. Only rarely do they lead to death or to severe complications. Although they are reportable and isolation precautions are usually observed, they merit far less consideration than is given to the common cold or to "grippe," neither of which is reportable nor isolated, yet either of which may be complicated by a fatal pneumonia. The ineffectiveness of control measures is attested by the widespread character of the diseases and by the high proportion of adults who have been infected. From the point of view of the community, there would appear to be little excuse for public health attention to either chickenpox or German measles were it not for the possible confusion of the former with smallpox, of the latter with scarlet fever, and the risk of congenital defects in the child born of a mother who had German measles during the early months of pregnancy. Mumps merits attention only because of the occasional involvement of the gonads.

All three conditions are apparently due to filterable viruses which enter and leave the body through the nose and throat. The infections spread from person to person through droplets or possibly by air transmission over a limited distance. The virus of chickenpox is also carried in the skin lesions; that of mumps finds its way into the mouth, in part at least, through the saliva from the infected glands. Infection is apparently always due to contact with a previous case, there being no laboratory or epidemiological evidence to suggest carriers. Except during the first few months of life, susceptibility appears to be universal until after an attack of the disease. In the case of mumps, there is also some evidence to suggest a local resistance in the salivary glands. There is no method of active immunization against chickenpox or German measles. Recent studies have developed a promising mumps vaccine which may have limited use.

Control measures are usually limited to reporting of cases and isolation until the end of the period of communicability. Theoretically, all susceptible contacts (those without a known history of infection) should be quarantined until the expiration of the maximum incubation period; practically, this is unwarranted because of the mildness of the condition, especially in view of the school time that would be lost through strict enforcement of this requirement. Furthermore, the conditions are so mild that medical attention is frequently not obtained and the cases are therefore not reported. In view of these facts, many health departments today limit their control to exclusion of the acute case from school for the duration of the illness and omit all placarding, routine epidemiological investigation, quarantine of contacts, or other control measures. In view of the fact that all health departments are faced with far more serious problems that make demands upon budgets, which are always inadequate, it seems hardly worth while to spend large sums for attempted control of chickenpox, German measles, or mumps, which are of so minor practical importance.

CHICKENPOX (VARICELLA)

SPECIAL MEASURES

The incubation period is two to three weeks, most commonly about 17 days. The patient is usually kept in isolation until the skin lesions have healed, though exception may reasonably be made for those scabs that are the result of scratching rather than the eruption. Although it is not worth while to make an epidemiological investigation of all cases, some health departments investigate all cases in adults, to make certain that mild attacks of smallpox are not being confused with chickenpox. In areas where smallpox is infrequent, the beginnings of outbreaks have been frequently overlooked because of errors in diagnosis. It would seem worth while, then, for the health department to investigate a small fraction of the cases whenever chickenpox begins to increase in the community.

Public health nursing care is not rendered routinely as the disease is mild, rarely has complications, and is so often not reported. Except in rare instances, one visit suffices to leave with the mother necessary instructions as to nursing care.

During the acute stage when the child has a fever, he should remain in bed; the usual care for any morbidity case is indicated. Itching may be very annoying, often leading to severe scratching with resultant local infections and scars. So far as possible, the child should be kept from scratching by relieving the itching and by keeping him occupied. Small children may have to wear mittens or elbow cuffs. If the physician approves, the child should have a daily warm bath to which bran may be added to allay the itching and from which the soap may be omitted, or the child may be sponged with soda bicarbonate water. Linen, cotton, or any other smooth, cool material next to the skin is less irritating than wool or other rough material. Olive oil is soothing in the late stages; it also softens the scabs and helps them to drop off. If the pocks should become infected, medical care should be obtained at once. Chickenpox is included under Group I (see p. 144); disinfection procedures outlined for that group in Chapter 8 should be followed.

GERMAN MEASLES (RUBELLA)

SPECIAL MEASURES

This disease has no relationship to measles, in spite of the name. The incubation period is 14 to 21 days, usually about 16. Isolation is commonly required only for the duration of the fever and the rash. The character of the rash is such that clinical differentiation between rubella and scarlet fever is at times difficult; confusion with measles also occurs. If scarlet fever is known to be prevalent, investigation of cases of reported rubella is often worth while, especially when occurring in families living on milk farms or in other situations where the hazard of a missed case of scarlet fever is great—as in the instance of a food-handler's family or of a teacher or other person having contacts with children. German measles cases ordinarily need no nursing visits. In fact, the child has usually recovered by the time the case comes to the attention of the health department. Confinement to bed during the febrile stage is all that is ordinarily necessary.

During recent years, rubella has acquired increased public health importance through recognition of the fact that many children whose mothers had the infection during the first three months of pregnancy show evidence of congenital defects.[1] The defect most commonly encountered is

[1] There is some evidence to suggest that damage to the fetus may occur even in the absence of recognizable reinfection in a woman who had previously had German measles. Because of the potential seriousness for the fetus, any woman in the early months of pregnancy should be warned to avoid contact with cases of rubella even though she may apparently be immune as a result of a previous infection.

congenital cataract; deafness and cardiac malformations have also been described. These are apparently due to the fact that the virus passed through the placenta, infecting the fetus in utero and thus causing certain developmental defects. The frequency with which such malformations occur as a sequel to infection of the mother in early pregnancy is still not determined. Some investigators have expressed the belief that German measles in the first three months of pregnancy constitutes a sufficiently great risk of defects in the offspring to constitute an indication for therapeutic abortion. Others have challenged this suggestion on both scientific and moral grounds. The present data are not adequate to permit an estimate of the magnitude of the risk. There is no evidence to suggest that rubella infection in the latter half of pregnancy will cause defects in the offspring.

Because of this risk, a woman in the early stages of pregnancy should be carefully shielded against possible exposure to rubella, especially when the disease is prevalent. There is no conclusive evidence that gamma globulin will protect her after exposure has occurred. As there is no resistance to rubella without actual infection, some have suggested that a girl in her teens should be deliberately exposed to the disease in the hope that she would contract it and thus be resistant in future years. If there is ever a situation in which deliberate exposure to a disease is warranted, this would appear to be it, though there is still grave doubt as to its justification. Certainly there is little to be gained from shielding a girl from infection which would give her a resistance later in life when she is in the childbearing age and the infection is potentially so dangerous for the fetus.

MUMPS (EPIDEMIC PAROTITIS)

SPECIAL MEASURES

This disease derives its sole importance from the discomfort it causes and the occasional orchitis or oöphoritis after the age of puberty. In military units mumps has been a problem because of its ready communicability and the high incidence of complications. The importance of these complications as a cause of sterility is still debatable. The incubation period is about three weeks. The period of infectiousness and, therefore, of usual isolation lasts until all swelling has ceased.

A vaccine of apparent effectiveness has been prepared recently and is now available for general use. On the basis of present data, there is no reason to doubt either the effectiveness or safety of this vaccine. The extent to which it will be used remains in doubt. At the moment it would appear to have its greatest potential usefulness in dealing with a group of males above the age of puberty and exposed to a risk of mumps. Such groups are found in boys' schools and military units. In private practice it may find value in any boy who reaches puberty without having had mumps.

Nursing visits are ordinarily not necessary to children who have mumps before puberty. If the nurse visits in a home where there is a case of mumps, she may give advice regarding diet. Mild, bland, semisolid foods are easier to swallow than anything spicy, sour, or otherwise likely to cause salivation. The patient should stay in bed until acute symptoms have subsided. The patient (especially the male patient) who develops mumps after puberty should stay quietly in bed until complete recovery, to minimize possibility of gonadal involvement. If this develops, the physician's orders should be obtained, and the attendant assisted in carrying them out.

SUGGESTED READINGS

German Measles

Aycock, W. Lloyd, and Ingalls, Theodore H.: "Maternal Disease as a Principle in the Epidemiology of Congenital Anomalies, with a Review of Rubella," *Am. J. M. Sc.,* 212:366–79, (Sept.) 1946.

Conte, W. R.; McCammon, C. S.; and Christie, Amos: "Congenital Defects Following Maternal Rubella," *Am. J. Dis. Child,* 70:301–6, (Nov.–Dec.) 1945.

Fox, Max J., and Bortin, Mortimer M.: "Rubella in Pregnancy Causing Malformations in Newborn," *J.A.M.A.,* 130:568–69, (Mar. 2) 1946.

Korns, Robert F.: "Prophylaxis of German Measles with Immune Serum Globulin," *J. Infect. Dis.,* 90:183–89, (Mar.–Apr.) 1952.

Logan, W. P. D.: "Incidence of Congenital Malformations and Their Relation to Virus Infection during Pregnancy," *Brit. M. J.,* 2:641–45, (Sept. 15) 1951.

Ober, R. E.; Horton, R. J. M.; and Feemster, Roy F.: "Congenital Defects in a Year of Epidemic Rubella," *Am. J. Pub. Health,* 37:1328–33, (Oct.) 1947.

Swan, Charles, and Tostevin, A. L.: "Congenital Abnormalities in Infants Following Infectious Diseases during Pregnancy, with Special Reference to Rubella. A Third Series of Cases," *M. J. Australia,* 1:646–59, (May 11) 1946.

Mumps

Bahlke, Anne M.; Silverman, Hilda Freeman; and Ingraham, Hollis S.: "Effect of Ultra-Violet Irradiation of Classrooms on Spread of Mumps and Chickenpox in Large Rural Central Schools," *Am. J. Pub. Health,* 39:1321–30, (Oct.) 1949.

Gordon, John E., and Heeren, R. H.: "The Epidemiology of Mumps," *Am. J. M. Sc.,* 200:412–28, (Sept.) 1940.

Gordon, John E., and Kilham, Lawrence: "Ten Years in the Epidemiology of Mumps," *Am. J. M. Sc.*, **218**:338–59, (Sept.) 1949.

Habel, Karl: "Vaccination of Human Beings against Mumps," *Am. J. Hyg.*, **54**:295–311, 312–18, (Nov.) 1951.

Henle, Gertrude, *et al.*: "Studies on the Prevention of Mumps," *J. Immunol.*, **66**:535–49, 551–60, 561–77, 579–94, (May) 1951.

McGuinness, Aims C., and Gall, Edward A.: "Mumps at Army Camps in 1943," *War Med.*, **5**:95–104, (Feb.) 1944.

Wessellhoeft, Conrad: "Mumps," *New England J. Med.*, **226**:530–34, (Mar. 26) 1942.

23. Smallpox

Smallpox is an acute infectious condition characterized by fever, malaise, and a generalized eruption. The eruption is located in the layers of the skin and progresses through the stage of papules to vesicles and pustules. In the typical case, the lesions on any given part of the body surface are all in the same stage of development, and the face and extremities tend to be more severely affected than is the trunk. In severe cases, the eruption may be confluent and hemorrhagic. The disease appears in two forms—malignant smallpox or variola major, which is often hemorrhagic and attended with a case fatality rate as high as 25 per cent, and mild smallpox (referred to also as variola minor, alastrim, Kaffirpox, and other terms), very rarely resulting fatally. A disfiguring pitting of the skin and often blindness due to involvement of the cornea may follow infection with the malignant type but are less common in the benign form.

EPIDEMIOLOGY

Occurrence. Smallpox was formerly one of the most dreaded scourges. At times it killed as many as 10 per cent of a population in a single year and disrupted the social and economic life of whatever community it attacked. As susceptibility was universal, isolated communities suffered tremendous mortality when infection was introduced from without. In crowded areas smallpox had an age distribution comparable to that now found for measles.

Malignant smallpox is still common in India and the Orient but does not at present occur in the United States. The last extensive outbreak in this country occurred in 1924–25 when the disease caused many deaths in the Midwest, notably in Colorado, Michigan, Minnesota, Missouri, and certain parts of Canada. A few cases were introduced into the West Coast from the Orient during the winter of 1945–46, but the disease did not spread widely. During recent years there have been several circumscribed outbreaks in England due to the introduction of malignant infection from other countries. The mild form was quite common in the United States during the two decades 1920–40, occurring in all parts of the country but with fewest cases on the North Atlantic seaboard where many states have compulsory vaccination laws. During the past five years even the mild form has been very rare, but there is no assurance that the country will continue to enjoy its comparative freedom from smallpox. To assume so would be to ignore the lessons of history. The continued occurrence of the mild form to the virtual exclusion of the malignant has been interpreted by some as indicating a permanent change in the character of the disease. Such an assumption has also no basis in fact and overlooks the point that in former centuries periods of mild infection were often interspersed with the severe form. The outbreak of malignant infection in 1924–25 was ample evidence of the fallacy of assuming a permanent change in character.

The incidence of the disease within a community depends on the extent to which vaccination is practiced. Where vaccination is compulsory, smallpox is rare; where it is neglected, the disease is most prevalent. Table 7 shows the incidence of the disease in a few states in relation to their vaccination laws.[1]

TABLE 7

INCIDENCE OF SMALLPOX IN RELATION TO VACCINATION LAWS
Annual Rate per 100,000 Population, 1933–37

Compulsory Vaccination		No Compulsion	
Massachusetts	0	California	8.0
Pennsylvania	0	Minnesota	13.1
Rhode Island	0	Missouri	13.2
Maryland	0.02	Wisconsin	19.4
New Hampshire	0.08	Kansas	22.6
District of Columbia	0.14	Iowa	25.0
New York	0.3	Washington	37.1
		Montana	92.9

Etiological Agent. Smallpox is caused by a virus, of which there are at least two strains—one causing the malignant, and one the benign, form of the disease. Although some writers have speculated about possible change of one type into the other, the best evidence would suggest that they are permanently distinct, the severe infection always giving rise to

[1] Although the antivaccinationists claim that smallpox is a filth disease and controllable by sanitation, the chambers of commerce of these states with high rates hardly agree to this suggestion—i.e., that they are so many times dirtier than are their sister states which require vaccination and have low rates.

severe, and the mild to mild. Passage of the smallpox virus through the bovine species results in a permanent attenuation to the virus of cowpox or vaccinia. The virus is readily destroyed by heat but will withstand prolonged drying if in the scab of smallpox lesions.

The reservoir of infection is always a human being who is ill with, or convalescing from, smallpox. Although temporary carriers have been suggested in the spread of the malignant infection, the evidence for these is not convincing. Certainly carriers play little if any part in the spread of smallpox. The possibility of their existence is ignored in the usual regulations which impose no restriction on the immune contacts. No species other than man is infected under natural conditions.

Escape from the reservoir is through the nose and throat secretions and the material in the skin lesions. During the prodromal stage, the patient has malaise and fever, suggestive of a grippe or influenza-like condition. The rash does not appear until the third day; yet during this pre-eruptive period, the patient is in the most communicable stage. The virus persists in the skin lesions after it has disappeared from the nose and throat, so that the period of communicability cannot be considered ended until all of the lesions have healed and scabs and crusts been removed.

Transmission is through close respiratory contacts, namely, droplet infection. It is thus favored by crowding. There is no evidence that fomites, insects, or food are of importance though smallpox may be transmitted through scabs in soiled linen; transmission through milk or water does not occur. The risk of air-borne transmission was once considered important but later relegated to the rank of disproved theory. The recent work of Wells raises the interesting hypothesis of the possibility of air-borne spread over very short distances, as, for example, within a hospital ward; but it gives no excuse for reviving the old theory which envisioned spread from home to home via the air. This now discarded theory was at one time so well accepted that smallpox hospitals ("pesthouses") were located on the edge of the community far from other habitations.[2]

Entry of the organism is via the respiratory tract. A much modified and milder form of the disease results if the virus is artificially introduced via a break in the skin. This latter was the basis for the use of protection through inoculation, which preceded the discovery of vaccination.

[2] On a bitter, winter day in 1932 one of the authors found in a city of 25,000 population the board of health treating a suspected case of smallpox in a flimsy, frame shack several miles out of town and located in an inaccessible field about a half mile from human habitation. The prejudices of a former generation die slowly and may result in the perpetration of acts of inhumanity under the pretext of guarding the public health. The pesthouse of former days was usually located on the side of town away from the prevailing wind so that the infection would be blown away from the community—and toward the neighboring town.

The incubation period is about eight to ten days.

Susceptibility is universal unless a person has had smallpox or been successfully vaccinated. There is no evidence of latent immunization through unrecognized subclinical infection, though protection may come from a mild case which was missed or diagnosed as chickenpox or other skin eruption. The individual who has not had smallpox and yet fails to react to vaccination is far rarer than is commonly supposed. Most persons of wide experience even deny his existence.

CONTROL MEASURES

Control of Spread

The case should be isolated until two weeks after the onset of the illness and until all skin lesions are healed and the crusts removed. The usual case may be cared for in either the home or hospital; all cases of malignant smallpox should be hospitalized because of the need for constant nursing care. Special and separate hospital facilities are not required, provided aseptic nursing technique is followed and other patients are vaccinated. Many hospitals have shown that, by adherence to this simple precaution, cases of smallpox may be accepted along with other infections without danger of spread to other patients.

Epidemiological investigation should be directed to finding the source and other victims. Special inquiry should be made of all persons with whom the victim has had close contact, including family members, relations, school and business associates, and other acquaintances seen by the patient during the previous two weeks. Such persons should all be located and questioned as to recent illness. Careful and repeated questioning will reveal the source of infection in a large percentage of the cases but not in all; the present form of smallpox is at times so mild that the patient may remain ambulatory, thus exposing persons through an unrecollected, casual contact. Discovery of a source of infection should always be followed by an inquiry as to other persons to whom the disease may have been spread.

Contacts. All of those in close association with the patient since two days prior to the onset of the illness should be considered potentially exposed. Quarantine depends upon their immunity status. If the contact has had smallpox or been successfully vaccinated, no restrictions are necessary, as healthy carriers do not exist. If, however, the contact has had neither smallpox nor vaccination, he should be isolated for two weeks from last association with the patient or until a vaccination has passed its peak and begun to subside. All contacts, whether immune or susceptible, should be vaccinated—the susceptible, because of the almost certainty of infection otherwise; and the immune, because of the possibility that the protection from a previous vaccination may have disappeared either in whole or in part. The latter is extremely unlikely if vaccination has been performed during the past few years, but revaccination should be insisted upon if quarantine is to be waived, lest an occasional case occur. No special precautions are required for food handlers.

Environmental Sanitation. No method of community sanitation has any demonstrable influence on the occurrence of smallpox. The disease may be rampant in the cleanest city if the inhabitants are unvaccinated and may be kept out of the dirtiest by vaccination.

Disinfection. Smallpox is included in Group II; procedures outlined for this group on page 144 should be strictly followed. All nose and throat discharges should be destroyed immediately, and the crusts and scabs burned as they are removed. As the virus is present in the lesions, special attention must be paid to the linen. This should be put into a clean pillowcase in the sick room and carried in that to the washtub, where it should be disinfected or boiled. The linen should be handled as little as possible until after disinfection. Terminal disinfection should be carefully and thoroughly done.

Minimizing Ill Effects

No specific therapy is known; treatment is symptomatic and supportive. Hospitalization is desirable if infection is severe, as the hospital affords better nursing care.

Public Health Nursing Care. If the patient has a mild case with few pocks and little rise in temperature, the nursing care is the same as for chickenpox (see p. 297). The case with higher fever and extensive lesions requires additional nursing attention.

General Care. The room should be kept at an even temperature with no drafts, and special precautions observed to prevent chilling, as pneumonia is a not infrequent complication. Most of the nursing procedures are directed to allaying the itching and making the patient as comfortable as possible. The itching may be almost unbearable, leading to severe scratching, which may, in turn, produce secondary infections. The physician's orders must, of course, be obtained, but usually there will be no objection to sponging the patient with water containing soda; soap should be omitted as it is irritating. The attendant should be taught to pat, instead of rub, the skin dry after a bath. Oil sometimes relieves the itching after scabs have formed and also helps to soften the scabs. The itching and irritation may be so severe that relief is obtained by supporting the bed clothes on cradles, thus keeping them entirely off the body. No wool or other irritating material should be close to the skin.

If there are lesions in the mouth, a toothbrush cannot be used, but the patient should rinse his mouth frequently with a suitable wash, such as salt and water or soda and water. Eating and drinking are less difficult and food a little more acceptable if the mouth is clean and fresh. If the eyes are inflamed and discharging, they should be bathed with plain water or boric acid solution according to the physician's order. This procedure should be demonstrated to the nursing attendant.

Diet. The patient needs a high caloric diet. Fruit juice made with lactose is one way of obtaining a large number of calories in small bulk and easily swallowed.

Number of Nursing Visits. Daily visits are desirable if bedside care is given. If this is not possible, at least two visits at the onset will be needed to demonstrate care and disinfection procedures. About a week later it is helpful to make another visit, and one should certainly be made during early convalescence.

Control through Immunization

Passive Immunization. No method has proved to be effective, though little work has been done with convalescent serum or gamma globulin.

Active Immunization. Vaccination against smallpox is a well-established method of proved efficacy and safety. It is our oldest method of active artificial immunization. The principle was discovered by Edward Jenner in 1796, though the methods now employed are quite different from the Jennerian vaccination and are a great improvement over it.

Vaccination uses the living virus of cowpox (vaccinia), which is a permanently attenuated smallpox virus. The vaccine principally used at present is prepared from the skin of calves and has been carefully treated and tested to exclude any possible harmful contaminants that were at times found in the vaccines of the last century.[3] During recent years, vaccine virus has been grown on the chick embryo and on special media in test tubes. Such virus produces characteristic "takes" but appears to confer a less lasting resistance. Unless vaccine virus is kept cold, it will lose its potency. It is usually distributed in capillary tubes.

[3] The original Jennerian method was direct arm to arm vaccination, a method which persisted until the latter part of the nineteenth century but has now disappeared. With it went the risk of transmission of infections such as syphilis from the donor to the recipient; this possibility cannot exist at present, as syphilis does not affect calves.

The arm of the person to be vaccinated should be cleansed with soap and water and then with acetone. Ether is too inflammable, while medicated alcohol and various skin disinfectants, such as iodine, leave on the skin a residue which inactivates the vaccine. A drop of vaccine is placed on the outer surface of the upper arm [4] and pressure exerted by a needle held parallel to the surface of the skin. When pressure is exerted, the skin springs over the point of the needle and is slightly pricked as the needle is lifted. Pressure is exerted 20 to 30 times, with the point kept within an area of about an eighth of an inch in diameter. If vaccination is properly performed, there is no pain or bleeding. A somewhat older method consists of making one or two short linear scratches through the drop of vaccine and at the same time trying to avoid scratching deeply enough to cause bleeding. The old method of scarification is no longer necessary and has been almost universally discarded. No dressing is either necessary or desirable, the scab that forms being superior to any dressing and less dangerous. If mechanical protection seems necessary to avoid breaking the pustule at the height of the reaction, a gauze pad may be attached to the overlying clothing.

In the typical vaccination of a previously susceptible person, nothing is seen for the first two days. A papule appears about the third day, develops to a vesicle by the sixth or seventh, and to a pustule by the tenth to the twelfth. As the pustule dries, a crust forms and ultimately drops off, leaving a small scar. The area around the vaccination may be inflamed during the height of the reaction and the regional lymph nodes enlarged and tender. A variable degree of fever and malaise may also occur, especially in older persons who have remained quite active. Constitutional reactions are least in small children and infants.

If a person has been previously vaccinated, the reaction upon revaccination may be of three types. If the previously acquired resistance has been completely lost, there will be a repetition of the same type of reaction originally encountered, a primary take. A partial loss of resistance will be manifested by an accelerated reaction, in which the papule appears in about 36 to 48 hours and progresses to the vesicular stage in about half the usual time but usually dries up without development of the pustule. An immediate reaction, shown by merely a papule which may develop in 8 to 24 hours and persist for one to two weeks, indicates a high level of residual

---

[4] Many parents wish their daughters to be vaccinated on the leg in order to avoid noticeable scars. If vaccination is done before the child walks, this will result in no more severe reaction. In persons who are walking, a somewhat more severe general reaction can be expected, as it is impossible to spare the leg in the same manner as one may the arm.

immunity.[5] Between these three types of reaction all intermediate grades may be encountered, depending upon the level of resistance that persists from the previous vaccination. Whatever the reaction, revaccination enhances the resistance and is therefore of benefit to the individual. *The absence of a reaction does not indicate immunity; on the contrary, it indicates that the vaccination was not properly performed and should therefore be repeated.*

TABLE 8

INCIDENCE OF SMALLPOX IN RELATION TO PRIOR
VACCINATION EXPERIENCE *
Fitchburg, Mass., 1932

Vaccination Status	No. of Persons	No. of Cases of Smallpox	Case Rate per 100,000 Population
Unvaccinated	5,457	57	1,048
Vaccinated over 40 years prior	4,926	3	60
Vaccinated during past 40 years	29,558	None	None

* Feemster, Roy F.; Anderson, Gaylord W.; Burns, Robert F.; and DeWolfe, Henry M.: "The Recent Smallpox Outbreak in Fitchburg," *New England J. Med.*, 207:82–87, (July 14) 1932.

Vaccination should be performed during the first year of life. Protection is thus acquired earlier and reactions are at a minimum. Furthermore, complications due to secondary infection from scratching of the site of vaccination or to the very rare postvaccinal encephalitis are less apt to occur than in later years. It is usually recommended that the child should be revaccinated when entering school. Evidence of successful vaccination is usually required for international travel. Citizens of the United States re-entering the country from abroad must have certificates showing successful vaccination within the preceding three years. Like any other immunity, the duration and degree of protection is quite variable. Smallpox vaccination does not confer absolute immunity against infection in every

[5] Recent studies have shown that a reaction indistinguishable from the immune reaction may result from the use of heated and therefore dead vaccine in a person who has previously been successfully vaccinated. While this may properly raise some doubt as to the interpretation of an immediate reaction in an individual case, administratively we have no alternative other than to consider such reactions as indicating immunity. To reduce the resultant risk of error, emphasis must be placed upon adequate refrigeration of the virus to preserve its potency and upon proper technique in the performance of the vaccination.

case, especially against malignant strains. Cases of smallpox have occurred in a few instances shortly after vaccination, whereas in other instances the protection has lasted over 40 years. Table 8 shows the high degree of protection afforded against mild smallpox in the Fitchburg, Massachusetts, outbreak in 1932.

The effectiveness of vaccination in preventing smallpox is proved by countless studies, of which the above is but one example. As a result, some states provide for vaccination as a prerequisite to school attendance, while a few others permit the local community to decide upon the need or desirability of compulsion. Other states make no provision for such, while four [6] have gone to the point of forbidding the adoption of any rule or law requiring vaccination for school attendance. Table 9 quoted from Woodward and Feemster shows the incidence of smallpox over one decade in states from these four groups.

TABLE 9

INCIDENCE OF SMALLPOX IN RELATION TO VACCINATION LAWS, 1919–28

Vaccination Compulsory (9 states)	6.6 per 100,000
Optional with Local Authorities (6 states)	51.3
No Compulsion or Local Option (29 states)	66.7
Compulsion Prohibited (4 states)	115.2

No discussion of smallpox vaccination would be complete without mention of the antivaccinationists, a group of persons who actively oppose the practice and usually include opposition to the use of all sera and vaccines. The motives back of these groups are of several types, including religious objections, distrust of medical science, adherence to medical cults, and opposition to what appears to be infringement of personal liberty. However much one may differ with the ideas of such groups, one must respect their sincerity of purpose as long as the information they publish is correct and not deliberately misleading. Unfortunately this is not always so. In general, however, it reflects a very superficial understanding, as evidenced by the free interchange that they make in their use of such terms as "antitoxin," "toxin," "toxoid," "serum," and "vaccine." Such misinformation serves only to mislead the public. The antivaccination groups are usually animated with a crusading zeal that could accomplish much good if directed toward a worthy cause. While they influence a small number of persons and may therefore embarrass a public health program,

---

[6] The antivaccinationists refer to these (Arizona, Minnesota, North Dakota, and Utah) as "Gold-Star States." During World War II, a gold star on a "service flag" indicated a death in line of duty.

their total influence is usually not large, and they are accorded the lack of popular confidence and respect that their arguments warrant. Nothing is accomplished by public controversy with them. Far greater good comes from quiet and dignified public and personal education.

SUMMARY

Health Department Program

Effective control of smallpox depends upon one factor—vaccination. Wherever this method has been tried, it has been found effective; but where it has been neglected, smallpox has continued to flourish. Isolation and quarantine procedures are relatively ineffective because of the spread during the prodromal stage and the existence of mild cases that escape recognition. Environmental sanitation does not affect the incidence of smallpox. Thus no method can be used by a health department to protect those who will not protect themselves. Those who are vaccinated do not need to fear smallpox, as they are effectively protected against infection. This is, therefore, a disease in which the individual can protect himself, even in the face of inadequate public health work. The community program should consist essentially of promotion of vaccination through education, distribution of vaccine, and the provision of facilities for vaccination. Laws compelling vaccination are useful adjuncts since they bring about protection of so high a fraction of the population that the disease cannot spread. Essentially, however, they serve to protect those who otherwise would fail to be vaccinated either because of neglect or because of ignorance; the intelligent need no compulsion.

The health officer is responsible for the enforcement of isolation and quarantine procedures and epidemiological investigation of all cases. He should give his greatest attention, however, to the promotion of vaccination and use all legitimate methods of influencing public opinion. Provision should be made each year so that those who cannot obtain private medical care may be vaccinated. In the face of an outbreak of smallpox, special clinics may be held for this purpose. The public health nurse should seize every opportunity to emphasize the need for vaccination. If bedside care is included in the nursing program, she may reasonably give care to cases in the home. She must always be alert for cases of unrecognized smallpox that are not obtaining medical aid, especially those that the family considers to be chickenpox and too mild to warrant calling a physician. The school authorities should be alert for cases in the school, especially among those absent because of undiagnosed illness attended with an eruption. The importance of vaccination should be stressed in the health education program in the classroom, and every legitimate means used to encourage the children to be vaccinated if this is not compulsory. The sanitary officer can contribute little more than a good example through vaccination of himself and family, at the same time pointing out the importance of such a procedure whenever suitable opportunities are afforded in the course of his regular work.

SUGGESTED READINGS

Armstrong, Charles: "The Role of the Vaccination Dressing in the Production of Postvaccinal Tetanus," *Pub. Health Rep.*, 44:1871–84, (Aug. 2) 1929.

Benenson, Abram S.: "Immediate (So-called 'Immune') Reaction to Smallpox Vaccination," *J.A.M.A.*, 143:1238–40, (Aug. 5) 1950.

Chapin, Charles V., and Smith, Joseph: "Permanency of the Mild Type of Smallpox," *J. Prev. Med.*, 6:273–320, (July) 1932.

Collins, Selwyn D.: "History and Frequency of Smallpox Vaccinations and Cases in 9000 Families, Based on Nation-wide Periodic Canvasses, 1928–31," *Pub. Health Rep.*, 51:443–79, (Apr. 17) 1936.

Dearing, W. Palmer, and Rosenau, M. J.: "Duration of Immunity Following Vaccination against Smallpox," *J.A.M.A.*, 102:1998–2000, (June 16) 1934.

Downie, A. W.: "Infection and Immunity in Smallpox," *Lancet,* 1:419–22, (Feb. 24) 1951.

Greenberg, Morris: "Complications of Vaccination against Smallpox," *Am. J. Dis. Child,* 76:492–502, (Nov.) 1948.

Leake, J. P.: *Questions and Answers on Smallpox Vaccination.* U.S. Public Health Service, Special Report #1137, Washington, D.C., 1939.

Palmquist, Emil E.: "The 1946 Smallpox Experience in Seattle," *Canad. J. Pub. Health,* 38:213–18, (May) 1947.

Russell, Frederick F.: *The Epidemiology and Control of Variola. Harvard School of Public Health Symposium on Virus and Rickettsial Diseases.* Cambridge: Harvard University Press, 1940, pp. 176–200.

Weinstein, Israel: "An Outbreak of Smallpox in New York City," *Am. J. Pub. Health,* 37:1376–84, (Nov.) 1947.

White, Benjamin: *Smallpox and Vaccination.* Cambridge: Harvard University Press, 1925.

Woodward, S. B., and Feemster, Roy F.: "The Relation of Smallpox Morbidity to Vaccination Laws," *New England J. Med.,* 208:317–18, (Feb. 9) 1933.

24. Poliomyelitis

(In preparing this section on poliomyelitis, the authors have been fully aware of the fact that there are many differences of opinion regarding the epidemiology of the disease. Lack of a suitable experimental animal has made it necessary that students of poliomyelitis rely largely on deductions from field observations supplemented by laboratory studies of very small samples. Consequently, most of our theories regarding the epidemiology of poliomyelitis have been drawn by inference and often are little more than hypotheses. The authors have presented here the hypothesis that appears to them to be most consistent with observed facts as to the occurrence of the disease. Further research will serve to corroborate, disprove, or modify this hypothesis. The student should carefully maintain an open mind to this as to all other problems.)

Poliomyelitis is an acute systemic infection which, in its recognizable form, appears as an involvement of the central nervous system and often results in a variable degree of permanent paralysis. Three types of cases are usually recognized: the abortive, the preparalytic (or nonparalytic), and the paralytic. The first represents those in which there is no clinical evidence of central nervous system involvement. The diagnosis in such cases is very indefinite and based usually on presumption, though occasionally confirmed by isolation of the virus.[1] The preparalytic group is made up of those cases in which there is evidence of central nervous system involvement, as shown by spinal fluid examination, but no detectable paralysis. Some of these will later develop paralysis while others will not. The paralytic cases are those in which definite loss of muscular power occurs, in some instances resulting in complete loss of function of muscles or groups of muscles. The legs are more commonly involved than are the arms. In all of those cases which survive there is some return of muscle power, though the degree of recovery cannot be predicted exactly in any case. Death from poliomyelitis is attributed to respiratory paralysis, due

---

[1] The recent discovery of the Coxsackie virus, which causes conditions clinically indistinguishable from nonparalytic poliomyelitis, has created justifiable suspicion that some of the cases diagnosed and reported as poliomyelitis are due to this other virus.

either to involvement of the respiratory center in the bulbar cases or to loss of function of the muscles of respiration. The true case fatality rate is not accurately known because of the changing adequacy of our diagnostic methods. Varying somewhat from epidemic to epidemic, about 10 to 25 per cent of the paralytic cases result fatally.

EPIDEMIOLOGY

Occurrence. Poliomyelitis is apparently not a new condition, though serious attention has been focused upon it only during the past fifty years. The official statistics give a misleading impression that the disease is becoming more prevalent though less severe.[2] This is due to the fact that in the early years only the paralytic cases were counted. Today we can recognize many of the preparalytic and surmise as to some of the abortive. It is thus apparent that cases ignored in former years are being reported and are thereby giving a distorted picture of increased prevalence. As deaths occur only in the paralytic group, the case fatality rate is apparently falling, because of a more nearly complete reporting of cases. Outbreaks vary with respect to the severity of the infection and case fatality rate, due possibly to variations in virulence of the strains of virus that are involved. There are good reasons for believing that poliomyelitis infection is about as prevalent as measles, though only a fraction of the cases are recognizable with our present diagnostic methods.

In its recognizable form, poliomyelitis is principally a disease of the temperate zone, though it is found in the tropics as well as in the arctic regions. The reported cases usually reach their peak in the late summer and early fall; outbreaks have, however, occurred at all seasons of year.[3] Infection spreads over an area in a wavelike manner, very comparable to the spread of measles. Thus it spreads in concentric waves from its focus of origin, much like the ripples created by a stone dropped into a quiet pond. In those areas where the disease begins early, it ends early; and where it begins late, it ends late. This wavelike spread is detectable if the cases within a state or even a large city are studied by areas. Under such

[2] In spite of newspaper reports to the contrary, the year 1916 remains as the worst recorded outbreak in the United States, 27,363 cases and 7,179 deaths. It is true that more cases were reported in 1949, 1950 and 1952 respectively—but this does not prove that any of these was the worst or biggest polio year ever recorded in this country. To form a valid comparison the reader must remember that in 1916 the population of the country was smaller, only the paralytic cases were counted, and the disease was reportable in only 27 of the states. Other years of serious outbreaks in the United States were 1907, 1909, 1910, 1921, 1927, 1931, 1937, and 1946.

[3] A very serious outbreak with high attack and case fatality rates occurred on the west coast of Hudson Bay in the winter of 1948–49. This was not the first time that winter outbreaks have been described.

circumstances, the disease is found to spread in wavelike character from its focus: it is on the increase in some areas while at the same time it is on the decline in those first involved. There is no evidence that the termination of an outbreak bears any relationship to a frost or other sudden change in weather.

Poliomyelitis shows an age distribution comparable to that of measles, the greatest number of cases occurring around the ages of five to seven, though with a certain number in adults. Recent years have seen a shift in age distribution so that proportionately more cases are being recognized in the older age group. A similar shift has also occurred with respect to diphtheria and scarlet fever. Rural areas show a higher proportion of older cases than do urban.

Etiological Agent. Poliomyelitis is due to the action of a neurotropic filterable virus. At least three distinct strains exist. The relationship between these is not clear, but there is no evidence that one strain confers immunity against either of the others. The virus is fairly resistant to chemicals and will persist for several weeks in sewage. It is readily destroyed by heat. Until recently, research has been definitely limited, since the only species other than man known to be susceptible to the virus were certain monkeys. The studies of Armstrong, showing the susceptibility of the cotton rat to the Lansing strain and the possibility of transferring infection from the rat to the white mouse, have made much progress possible, but conclusions as to the one strain are not necessarily applicable to the others. The recent development of tissue culture techniques has opened a new field of poliomyelitis research.

The reservoir of infection is in all cases an infected person, there being no present evidence to suggest that under natural conditions other species harbor the virus. The relative roles of cases and carriers is problematical. It is conventionally stated that infection is spread primarily through carriers. The rapidly accumulating evidence regarding the large number of abortive cases would raise serious doubt as to the relative importance of a true carrier and the abortive case, though the practical distinction between the two is largely an academic question.[4]

[4] The authors are of the opinion that spread is primarily from the abortive case and not from true carriers using the latter term to refer to persons who, having been previously infected with the virus and recovering therefrom, are harboring the virus again at a later date. The only practical importance of the differentiation is in the possible administrative control of contacts. From analogy with other virus diseases in which infection is always detectable, such as measles, smallpox, and chickenpox, one may question the role of a true carrier in the spread of infection. There is no evidence as yet to prove that the reported "carriers" from whom the virus has been isolated were truly carriers rather than abortive cases undergoing their first real experience with the virus but manifesting no detectable evidence of this interaction between virus and the body.

The escape of the virus from the body of the infected person is through the secretions of the respiratory tract and through the feces. The virus is found in the respiratory tract for a few days prior to onset and about the first five days of the disease. In the feces it is found in even greater quantity throughout the disease and often for many weeks after recovery. The relative importance of these two portals of escape is still problematical. The communicability of poliomyelitis in the early stages when the virus is escaping from the respiratory tract has been demonstrated repeatedly. There is no comparable evidence to suggest communicability in the late stages when the virus escapes only in the feces. The epidemiology of poliomyelitis is more consistent with that of a disease in which the effective escape is through the respiratory tract than through the intestines.

Transmission of the disease appears to occur chiefly through association with an infected person. Opinions differ as to whether this association is respiratory or fecal. The authors are of the opinion that the bulk of evidence is in support of the hypothesis of respiratory spread as the important means of dissemination. The wavelike character of its spread within an area is consistent with such a method and is not consistent with dissemination through other channels. Multiple cases may occur within a family or institution. If search is made for abortive cases, these will be found far more frequently than is ordinarily recognized. Nursing attendants have been infected by their patients. Some investigators have suggested the possibility of spread through food. Though this cannot be denied as a possibility, the wavelike spread cannot be explained if this is the principal method. At least three outbreaks have been reported in which it seems possible that raw milk has served as a vehicle.[5] Milk is, however, not an important vehicle. Many suggestions have been made that insects might serve as vectors, but the evidence for this is very inadequate. Spread through sewage-contaminated water, especially in the course of swimming, has often been suggested, and the theory has been revived with the demonstration of the virus in sewage. While this possibility cannot be denied, it is hard to believe that this is an important mode of spread. The theory would certainly not explain the general occurrence of the disease, especially the large number and wide distribution of abortive cases, nor would it explain the wavelike character of spread. The spread of poliomyelitis in urban areas does not follow water distribution systems; on the contrary there is no epidemic on record in which the mode of spread was consistent with the hypothesis of transmission through sewage-polluted water

[5] Cortland, New York; Spring Valley, New York; and Broadstairs, England. Several others have been reported in which the evidence is less suggestive.

supplies. Although recognizing the possibility or even the probability that occasional cases of poliomyelitis have been spread by water, food, or insects, the authors adhere to the belief that respiratory transmission is the only mechanism responsible for the mass spread of the infection through a community or a large area.

Entry and Incubation Period. The bulk of evidence would suggest that the virus is taken in through the nose and mouth, but there is still room for much doubt as to its subsequent avenue of penetration. Undoubtedly the virus can enter through the nerve fibers from the upper part of the nasal vault and work backward toward the central nervous system through the olfactory nerve. The high proportion of bulbar cases among persons who have had a tonsillectomy suggests spread along nerve fibers. There is also experimental evidence to indicate entry along the intestinal tract and even through breaks in the skin. Possibly several channels of entry exist, and the character of the infection may even be conditioned by the avenue of entry in the individual case. Recent studies have suggested that, in at least some cases, there is a period of viremia before localization in the nervous system. The incubation period is about 7 to 14 days.

Susceptibility is apparently dependent upon two factors: (1) previous experience with, and reaction to, the virus resulting in a specific resistance and (2) physiological variations conditioning a person's response to the virus. The latter are referred to as the autarceologic factors.

Specific response to the virus is manifested by the presence of antibodies inhibiting its action. These antiviral properties are found in babies born of mothers having similar properties, in most persons who have recovered from poliomyelitis, and in the majority of the adult population. The percentage of persons whose blood contains such antibodies increases with age; at a given age a higher percentage of the urban population possesses them than does a comparable rural population. The distribution of persons with antiviral properties is consistent with the hypothesis that such properties have developed in response to infection with the virus, even though this infection may have escaped recognition. Although each of the strains of virus evokes the production of distinct antibodies, most adults show antibodies for all three strains. This is interpreted as indicating prior infection with each of the strains, as the antibodies from one strain do not confer protection against the other strains. It is therefore presumed that those persons who have a second attack of poliomyelitis are infected with a strain different from that which caused the first infection.

The autarceologic components of susceptibility and resistance include those physiological factors conditioning the response of the individual to infection with the virus. Early investigators showed that the paralytic form of the disease was more frequent in children of a certain physiological type. More recent studies have shown that the endocrine balance is somewhat different in those who have had paralytic responses than in a normal control group. Aycock has also shown that the paralytic disease shows a remarkably high incidence in certain families, a large proportion of all cases giving a history of similar attacks in relatives. This familial association can in no way be explained as contact infection. It suggests that the autarceologic factor may in some degree be a hereditary trait. Many reasons exist for believing that within an individual it may vary from one season of the year to another, there being a higher susceptibility to the paralytic form of the disease during summer months.[6]

There is also a higher attack rate among pregnant women than among those of the same age and degree of exposure but not pregnant. Recent studies have shown that children who have received antigen injections during the month prior to onset of infection develop a more severe form of the disease than do those who have not received such injections and that the paralysis tends to involve the extremity into which the injection was given. Similarly there is evidence that unusual fatigue may be a factor favoring a paralytic response to the virus and conditioning the location of the paralysis. The exact mechanisms by which these factors operate is not clear, but there can be no doubt that the body's reaction to the virus is conditioned in part by nonspecific factors unrelated to the presence of antibodies.

If these hypotheses as to autarceologic susceptibility are correct (and they are at least in accord with the facts as to the occurrence of the disease), one may consider poliomyelitis as an infection which occurs at all seasons of the year but which appears in paralytic form principally during the warmer months. The apparent anomalies of failure to spread into an area which is apparently susceptible can be explained on the hypothesis that the virus had spread in a nonparalytic form of infection during recent months and had thus immunized a large enough fraction of the population to prevent a new epidemic.[7] Such a hypothesis envisions poliomyelitis as a disease which spreads in a manner very comparable to measles, the sole distinction being that virtually all of the measles cases are recognizable while only a small portion of the poliomyelitis infections are detected.

---

[6] Proved instances of seasonal fluctuations in physiological function include variations in the concentration of circulating diphtheria antitoxin, iodine content of the thyroid, and acidity of the stomach.

[7] Gear in South Africa has described "silent outbreaks"—a large number of abortive infections from which virus could be isolated but no case of clinically recognizable paralytic involvement.

CONTROL MEASURES

Control of Spread

The case is usually kept in strict isolation for about one week from the onset. The number of abortive cases is, however, so large that this isolation probably accomplishes little, if anything, from the point of view of community spread. In general, cases should be removed to a hospital if possible. Although most multiple cases within a family suggest a common exposure, strict isolation of the patient, if left at home, is desirable to reduce the risk of spread to siblings. There is no demonstrable value in prolonged isolation during the convalescence. No present laboratory tests are of practical value in determining the duration of the isolation period of the individual case.

Routine **epidemiological investigation** is of little demonstrable value as a control measure, as it rarely yields any evidence as to the source of infection. Yet from the standpoint of possibly shedding further light upon the epidemiology of the infection, it is of great value. In such investigations, special attention should be paid to contacts who have mild febrile disturbances, as some of these are cases of abortive poliomyelitis. The investigator should always be alert for unusual groupings of cases as, for example, in association with a milk route or contact at a party, and for cases following tonsillectomy, associated with pregnancy or following immunization. It is also highly desirable to inquire in detail regarding relatives, including distant relatives, who have had known poliomyelitis or crippling of unknown etiology but possibly consistent with poliomyelitis.

Contacts are usually quarantined for a period of about two weeks. If true carriers as distinguished from abortive cases do not exist, there would seem to be little value in quarantining adults, as most of them show evidence of prior infection. Strict quarantine of child contacts might appear reasonable, in view of the large number of abortive cases at this age. If isolation and quarantine are of any value in this disease, they should be applied especially to children who are showing mild disturbances consistent with abortive poliomyelitis. If any one of the family contacts complains of fever, headache, digestive disorder, or mild respiratory disease, he should be put to bed and the physician called at once. Symptoms such as these in contacts of a known case are often the first evidence of poliomyelitis; certain abortive cases show nothing more.

General Control Measures. School closure, as well as closure of moving picture theaters, Sunday schools, and other similar groups, is frequently attempted in response to popular demand that "something be done." Although tried repeatedly, it is of no proved value, never altering the usual curve of the epidemic; nor has the disease been more prevalent or persistent in those communities with the courage to resist such demands. If a child is already in the infected area, he is as safe in school as in neighborhood contacts and often safer, as during the greater part of the day the children are seated at desks regularly spaced from one another. For psychological reasons it seems desirable to permit parents to keep their children out of school during a poliomyelitis "epidemic." Experience shows that after the first week or two of hysteria most of the children drift back to school. Little is to be gained from moving out of an infected area, though it seems desirable to stay away if already outside. It should be pointed out that the risk of contracting poliomyelitis while driving through an infected area is negligible and far less than the risk of an automobile accident.

Tonsillectomies, unless of an emergency nature, should not be performed during an outbreak; some hospitals discourage tonsillectomies during the poliomyelitis season. Since immunization is an elective procedure, it can well be postponed until after the end of the outbreak. In postponing such immunizations, care should be taken that the public does not conclude that immunization is in itself dangerous and that parents be discouraged from protecting their children. The increased susceptibility to a paralytic involvement does not last more than a month after antigen injections. Those who have been immunized more than a month prior to infection have no more severe involvement than do those who have never been immunized. It would be most unfortunate if fear of poliomyelitis were to result in an actual decrease in the number of children immunized against diphtheria, pertussis, smallpox, and tetanus. Excessive and unusual fatigue is likewise to be avoided, but this does not mean that the child should be so restrained as to interfere with normal summer activity. Poliomyelitis phobia is a real hazard in children subjected to excessive restrictions.

Environmental sanitation is of no proved value. Closure of bathing beaches is often urged and may have some remote theoretical basis due to the demonstration of virus in sewage; but experience fails to show any relationship between the spread of poliomyelitis and the use of such beaches. No methods of insect control have been shown to be of value. Pasteurization serves as a safeguard against the rare milk-borne spread. No special methods of disinfection of the home or schoolroom are required.

Disinfection. Poliomyelitis belongs in Group I; procedures outlined for this group (see p. 144) should be followed. In some areas, health departments have required or recommended the disinfection of the stools inasmuch as the virus can be found in the feces. Under such circumstances procedures for Group III (see p. 145) should also be followed.

Minimizing Ill Effects

The principal attention in the case of poliomyelitis should be directed at (1) prevention of deaths and (2) prevention or lessening of residual paralysis. Convalescent serum was at one time extensively used for treatment and was frequently distributed by health departments. It is devoid of proved therapeutic value, even if used in the preparalytic stage. Respirators are of proved value in certain cases of paralysis of the chest and diaphragm. They are also used in bulbar cases which have undergone tracheotomy and are receiving oxygen therapy. The health department should have full knowledge of the location of respirators and may even provide such to be prepared for a possible emergency. In general, they are needed only in the centers of hospitalization.

Although the subject of much controversy, the Kenny methods have been quite generally accepted to a varying degree in the treatment of both the acute stage of the disease and the residual paralyses. Stripped of all their controversial aspects, these methods consist of use of hot packs on the affected muscles and a painstaking system of muscle re-education. Braces and other mechanical apparatus find less use than formerly so long as some progress toward recovery continues. While there are still legitimate grounds for argument regarding the theory underlying the Kenny methods, there can be little doubt that a distinct contribution has been made to the treatment of paralysis resulting from poliomyelitis infection.

Proper care of poliomyelitis in the acute stage requires hospitalization, preferably in a hospital receiving a large number of cases and therefore staffed with personnel especially trained to care for this disease. Such personnel can be provided in any large hospital. Small hospitals receiving only occasional cases cannot be expected to maintain the necessary staff and should therefore be encouraged to send all but the mildest cases to a larger, suitably staffed hospital. Such staff should include adequately trained physiotherapists. During a serious outbreak, the health department of a city that serves as the medical center for any considerable area should attempt to provide additional emergency hospital facilities for the inevitable influx of cases. These facilities must include provision for diagnosis before admission to the hospital, extra hospital beds during both acute and convalescent phases of the disease, recruitment of extra nurses and physiotherapists, and establishment of clinics and home visiting to serve the paralyzed cases treated on an outpatient basis. The local chapters of the American Red Cross have often assumed responsibility for recruitment of nurses and physiotherapists to meet the emergency needs of communities suffering from serious outbreaks.

During the acute stage and in early convalescence, attention is directed toward the prevention of contractures. Bedside nursing is of great value in cases cared for at home and may be furnished by the public health nurse. After all tenderness has disappeared, the problem becomes one of orthopedic treatment of the paralyses. Increasing use is being made of physiotherapists. Many health departments provide diagnostic and treatment clinic facilities for those children who are not adequately cared for by other agencies. Funds for this work are available through the local chapter of the National Foundation for Infantile Paralysis and through federal grants for crippled children.

Public Health Nursing Care. Although most paralytic cases of poliomyelitis are hospitalized, some will remain at home, and when there is a shortage of hospital beds some will be sent home still in need of nursing care. Therefore the public health nurse should be able to give and demonstrate nursing care of poliomyelitis. Most physicians are now using hot packs in the treatment of the acute and early convalescent stages. The public health nurse should be thoroughly familiar with the method of applying hot packs and with the local resources for obtaining the necessary materials. As the hot packs have to be applied frequently during the 24 hours, the attendant must be taught how to carry out the procedure. The public health nurse should demonstrate and have the attendant assist her. If necessary the attendant should practice outside the patient's room on another member of the family until the nurse is certain that the attendant knows how to apply the pack properly so that it will not burn the patient but will be as hot as required and will not fatigue the patient unduly.

The nurse should see that there is a board under the mattress, that the bed has a footboard, and that there is space for the patient's feet between the end of the mattress and the footboard. The public health nurse should instruct the attendant how to turn the patient, giving support to the joints and avoiding touching the bellies of the muscles. At this time, she can emphasize the importance of all instructions regarding nursing care designed to avoid the aggravation of spasm, such as making certain that the attendant's hands are always warm when handling the patient, that the bedpan is warm, and that the room is well ventilated but warm and not drafty. The attendant should be taught not to fuss over the patient, that it is important to handle him as little as possible. It is not easy for most mothers to refrain from constantly touching a sick child and "making him comfortable." The *Guide for Parents* [8] is an extremely helpful pamphlet which should be used to supplement and reinforce the public health nurse's instructions. The nurse may mark the paragraphs which need special emphasis in a particular home.

Whether the patient remains at home or is hospitalized during the acute stage, he needs close supervision during convalescence. Even cases which have no apparent residual paralysis should be watched, as not infrequently weakness of a muscle may be present though unrecognized and fatigue will bring about partial loss of function and possible later deformity. Sometimes patients are ordered hot baths after the packs are discontinued, and the public health nurse should make certain that these are being given. She should visit frequently during the first weeks the patient is allowed up or is home from the hospital, in order to assist the patient or mother in carrying out the physician's instructions regarding the gradual resumption of activity and the continuation of extra rest periods.

If there is an orthopedic nurse in the area, she may take all or part of the responsibilities described here but if there is an epidemic of any size the generalized nurse will probably have to teach the administration of hot packs and supervise their application. She will also probably have to supervise the nonparalytic case during early convalescence, leaving the orthopedic nurse free to care for the paralytic case.

The public health nurse has a further important function in relation to cases with residual paralysis. In some areas the specially trained orthopedic nurse under the physician's direction supervises their home care, but in many parts of the country this service is quite limited; the trend is toward increasing responsibility of the generalized nurse for the care of orthopedic cases. The public health nurse must be ready to help the mother carry out any procedures, such as exercises, that the physician prescribes to be done at home. She should see that braces are worn when and as ordered. She may need to encourage the family and help them to see that great improvement results if treatments are followed faithfully, even though the process is slow and often discouraging. The nurse often has a real task in maintaining the patient's confidence in the attending physician or clinic. This phase of nursing in a poliomyelitis case is as important as the care during the acute stages.

Number of Nursing Visits. Hospitalization of all cases of poliomyelitis during the acute stage is desirable but there are situations in which this cannot be provided. The public health nurse has a special responsibil-

---

[8] Prepared by the Joint Orthopedic Nursing Advisory Service and available through the National Foundation for Infantile Paralysis, 120 Broadway, New York 5, N. Y.

ity for assisting with these cases unless full-time private duty nursing is available. If bedside care is provided, daily visits are necessary until the acute stage has passed and the child is completely recovered or is under orthopedic care. If daily bedside care cannot be provided, at least two visits on successive days should be made to teach and supervise the application of hot packs. In many communities private duty nurses have learned the hot pack method or volunteers have been specially trained; these may be provided through health department funds or through funds made available by the National Foundation for Infantile Paralysis. The public health nurse should always visit again two to three weeks after onset to make certain that aftercare is secured if needed. During the years that follow, the nurse will visit as often as required to accomplish the desired results—continuance of treatment.

Control through Immunization

Passive immunization through use of convalescent serum is theoretically possible, yet in practice is of very little value. Recently, attempts have been made to give a partial protection through injections of gamma globulin during an outbreak. The theory of this is that the protection so established will be enough to prevent paralysis of those who will inevitably be exposed and infected during the next few weeks but will not be so great as to prevent mild nonparalyzing infection of the individual who has been effectively exposed. Thus the exposed person will escape paralysis but become actively immune as a result of the mild modified infection —a case of passive-active immunization. The preliminary reports suggest that this method is effective for a few weeks in reducing paralysis; more time is needed to determine the degree to which active immunity develops. Even if the method is effective, the problem of obtaining an adequate supply of gamma globulin will be very difficult of solution.

Active Immunization. At present no vaccine has been demonstrated to be both effective and safe. Recent reports of vaccine studies are encouraging but still inconclusive.

SUMMARY

Health Department Program

The present methods for the control of poliomyelitis have yielded few if any results, because of the large number of unrecognizable infections which spread the virus through the community. Little can be expected of isolation and quarantine procedures. Prevention through vaccine is not yet proved to be both effective and safe. Attempts to prevent paralysis through injections of gamma globulin to those exposed to infection have yielded encouraging results, but there are serious doubts as to the practical value of the method due to the problem of obtaining an adequate supply of gamma globulin. No measure of environmental control is of proved value in preventing spread. The community program must, therefore, be directed toward prevention of ill effects, namely, death and crippling. The most important part of this program is that for the orthopedic care of those with a residual paralysis.

The **health officer** is responsible for the institution of such immediate control measures as may be decided upon, even though these may do little more than satisfy the public demand that "something be done." While he should not permit himself to be swept away by the popular hysteria, he must be prepared to make reasonable concessions that will satisfy the public demands, even though he may know such concessions are generally useless. Unless he is prepared to meet the public halfway, some other health officer who is less competent but who keeps the public satisfied will be found. Special attention should be given to the provision of adequate orthopedic care for all paralyzed cases. This must begin with the acute case, even though the bulk of the work will be carried on in later months or years. Full use should be made of the facilities offered through the state program for crippled children. The **public health nurse** may render valuable nursing assistance to those cases cared for at home during the acute stage. During the period of orthopedic care, she may aid by making certain that the directions of the physician or clinic are followed and that the mother does not get discouraged through what appears to be slow progress. The nurse trained in physiotherapy may render special care in the program of corrective exercises between visits to the physician or clinic.

SUGGESTED READINGS

Anderson, Gaylord W., and Skaar, Audrey E.: "Poliomyelitis Occurring after Antigen Injections," *Pediatrics*, 7:741–59, (June) 1951.

Aycock, W. Lloyd: "Nature of Autarceologic Susceptibility to Poliomyelitis," *Am. J. Pub. Health*, 27:575–82, (June) 1937.

———: "Tonsillectomy and Poliomyelitis. I. Epidemiologic Considerations," *Medicine*, 21:68–94, (Feb.) 1942.

———: "Familial Aggregations in Poliomyelitis," *Am. J. M. Sc.*, 203:452–65, (Mar.) 1942.

Aycock, W. Lloyd, and Kessel, John F.: "The Infectious Period of Poliomyelitis and Virus Detection," *Am. J. M. Sc.*, 205:454–65, (Mar.) 1943.

Bodian, David: "Pathogenesis of Poliomyelitis," *Am. J. Pub. Health*, 42:1388–1402, (Nov.) 1952.

Dalldorf, Gilbert: "The Coxsackie Viruses," *Am. J. Pub. Health*, 40:1508–11, (Dec.) 1950.

Dalldorf, Gilbert, and Gifford, Rebecca: "Clinical and Epidemiological Observations of Coxsackie-Virus Infection," *New England J. Med.,* 244: 868–73, (June 7) 1951.

Davis, Coralynn: "Meeting an Epidemic of Infantile Paralysis," *Pub. Health Nursing,* 36:332–35, (July) 1944.

Garber, Miles D., Jr.: "Some Emotional Aspects of Poliomyelitis," *Pub. Health Nursing,* 44:341–44, (June) 1952.

Greteman, T. J.: "Nursing Care of Acute Poliomyelitis," *Am. J. Nursing,* 44:929–33, (Oct.) 1944.

Hammon, William McD.; Coriell, Lewis L.; Wehrle, Paul F.; and Stokes, Joseph, Jr.: "Evaluation of Red Cross Gamma Globulin as a Prophylactic Agent for Poliomyelitis," *J.A.M.A.,* 151:1271–85, (Apr. 11) 1953.

Horstmann, Dorothy M.: "Acute Poliomyelitis. Relation of Physical Activity at the Time of Onset to the Course of the Disease," *J.A.M.A.,* 142:236–41, (Jan. 28) 1950.

International Committee for the Study of Infantile Paralysis: *Poliomyelitis.* Baltimore: Williams & Wilkins Co., 1932.

Joint Orthopedic Nursing Advisory Service: *A Guide for Nurses in the Nursing Care of Patients with Infantile Paralysis.* The National Foundation for Infantile Paralysis, New York, 1945.

Kumm, Henry W.: "Recent Additions to Knowledge of Poliomyelitis," *J.A.M.A.,* 150:1179–81, (Nov. 22) 1952.

Lavinder, C. H.; Freeman, A. W.; and Frost, W. H.: *Epidemiological Studies of Poliomyelitis in New York City and the Northeastern United States during the Year 1916.* U.S. Govt. Rep., Treasury Dept.; Pub. Health Bull. No. 91, U.S. Public Health Service. Washington, 1918.

Maxcy, Kenneth F.: "Hypothetical Relationship of Water Supplies to Poliomyelitis," *Am. J. Pub. Health,* 33:41–45, (Jan.) 1943.

McCloskey, Bertram P.: "Residual Paralysis after Poliomyelitis following Recent Inoculation," *Lancet,* 1:1187–89, (June 14) 1952.

Pearson, Harold E., and Rendtorff, Robert C.: "Studies on the Distribution of Poliomyelitis Virus," *Am. J. Hyg.,* 41:164–87, (Mar.) 1945.

Peart, A. F. W.: "An Outbreak of Poliomyelitis in Canadian Eskimos in Wintertime," *Canad. J. Pub. Health,* 40:405–17, (Oct.) 1949.

Perkins, James E.: "The Epidemiology of Poliomyelitis," *New York State J. Med.,* 45:159–68, (Jan. 15) 1945.

Pohl, John F.: "The Kenny Treatment of Anterior Poliomyelitis (Infantile Paralysis)," *J.A.M.A.,* 118:1428–33, (Apr. 25) 1942.

"Recommended Practices for the Control of Poliomyelitis," *Am. J. Pub. Health,* 39:1249–52, (Sept.) 1949.

Stevenson, Jessie L.: "Public Health Nursing in the 1943 Polio Epidemic," *Pub. Health Nursing,* 36:336–39, (July) 1944.

Stimson, Philip M.: "Home Care of Patients with Acute Poliomyelitis," *J.A.M.A.,* 149:719–21, (June 21) 1952.

Top, Franklin H.: "Occurrence of Poliomyelitis in Relation to Tonsillectomies at Various Intervals," *J.A.M.A.,* 150:534–38, (Oct. 11) 1952.

Weaver, Harry M.: "Epidemic Poliomyelitis," *New England J. Med.* 243: 1019–24, (Dec. 28) 1950.

25. Meningococcus Meningitis

Infection with the meningococcus results characteristically in a meningitis, hence the frequently used term "epidemic cerebrospinal meningitis" to refer to such conditions. Septicemia occurs in the early stages of the illness and is often manifested by an eruption due to petechial areas in the skin. This rash has given rise to the term "spotted fever." Death may be caused by the septicemia, fulminating cases resulting fatally in less than 24 hours, even before localization in the meninges. In other instances, after a prolonged period of meningitic inflammation, death occurs as a result of either the inflammation or obstruction of the normal flow of cerebrospinal fluid. In small children, this occlusion may result in hydrocephalus which causes death even though the infection has been overcome. Blindness and deafness are the principal complications of cases that recover. The case fatality rate of untreated cases may be as high as 25 to 50 per cent, varying somewhat with different strains of the meningococcus. The therapeutic use of sulfonamides and antibiotics has been so successful that the fatality rate has been strikingly reduced and the disease has lost much of its former public health importance.

EPIDEMIOLOGY

Occurrence. Meningococcic infections are found in all parts of the world and reach their greatest prevalence during the winter and early spring. In spite of widespread distribution of the organisms, clinical disease is of rare occurrence in the civil population, the annual morbidity rate rarely rising above 3 or 4 per 100,000, even during periods of high prevalence. In crowded and confined populations, such as military barracks, prisons, and other institutions, the attack rate may rise many times higher, and the disease may constitute a serious public health problem. Extensive outbreaks attended with high case fatality rates have often occurred among the native tribes of Africa.

326

Etiological Agent. Infection is due to the meningococcus (*Neisseria intracellularis*), a Gram-negative organism, which dies very readily when separated from the human body. It is so fragile that considerable difficulty is encountered in its cultivation, and special precautions must be observed in transmitting throat cultures to the laboratory. The most satisfactory method is that of direct plating at the bedside and of transporting the cultures in a thermos jar or similar apparatus to keep them warm while en route to the laboratory. Numerous strains of meningococci have been described, though the antigenic relationships are not clearly understood. Three distinct groups are recognized; most infections in this country have been due to group I organisms.

Reservoir of Infection. Man is the sole reservoir of infection. While the disease has been observed to spread from patient to patient, healthy carriers apparently constitute the bulk of the reservoir. The number of carriers varies with the season and is greatly increased by overcrowding. Even in interepidemic periods, 2–5 per cent of a population may harbor meningococci. In crowded groups during an outbreak, as high as 40 per cent have been found infected at a given moment and 92 per cent infected at some time during a three-month period. Patients continue to harbor the organisms for variable periods during convalescence.

Escape from the reservoir is usually through the nose and throat secretions. As the organisms may be in the spinal fluid and scrapings from petechial spots, caution must be observed in handling such material.

Transmission to the new host appears to be always through direct respiratory spread of infected droplets and is therefore favored by overcrowding. The fragility of the meningococcus outside the human body makes it unlikely that fomites are ever significant in spread.

Entry of the organisms is via the respiratory tract. From the nose and throat the organisms penetrate to the blood stream, by which they are carried to the meninges.

The incubation period is usually two to seven days.

Susceptibility. Little of an exact nature is known regarding resistance. Apparently, however, it must normally be high, as shown by the low attack rate in spite of the high infection (carrier) rate. There is no test for susceptibility. The concentration of cases in childhood would suggest that under normal conditions some degree of latent immunization may develop; yet it cannot be great, as attested by the large number of adult and even fairly aged cases under crowded conditions. The effect of intercurrent respiratory infection in reducing resistance is not known. Resistance may be temporarily reduced by acute alcoholism and possibly by other debilitating conditions.

CONTROL MEASURES

Control of Spread

The case should be strictly isolated, with special attention to the disposal of respiratory secretions. Medical and nursing personnel should avoid close respiratory contact with the patient, as many have been infected while caring for cases. Hospitalization is desirable more for the benefit of the patient than for the protection of the family. The period of isolation is conventionally set at two to three weeks following subsidence of acute symptoms. Although release cultures might be theoretically desirable, experience shows that little reliance can be placed on negative results in view of the fragility of the organism and the associated technical difficulties in its discovery.

Epidemiological investigation of the sporadic case yields little information as to the source of infection, since there is a large number of carriers in the community. Studies of institutional outbreaks likewise usually fail to show the source but reveal factors of overcrowding that must be relieved to minimize further spread. Routine culturing of family and institutional contacts was at one time widely practiced in hope of finding and segregating carriers. The results so obtained are interesting as epidemiological studies but unfortunately yield very little help in control of spread. The technique is so difficult and inexact that probably as many carriers are overlooked on a single culture as are found. Unless the contacts can be individually segregated during a period of repeated culturing (an obvious impossibility), the spread that occurs between culturing will offset the benefit of recognizing a few carriers. As a result, this procedure has been largely abandoned as of no value in control of spread. Whatever control measures are applied are based on the assumption that all contacts are carriers, an exaggeration which errs on the side of safety.

Contacts. Intimate family contacts are commonly quarantined for a period of one or two weeks on the assumption that they are probably carriers. As in the case of the patient, cultures are of little practical value in terminating the quarantine period. In many places, quarantine of contacts has been abandoned, as its value has not been proved. Administration of sulfadiazine in doses of 0.5 to 2.0 gm. per day for 3 days, cures the carrier condition in a large majority of cases. With its use during World War II, group carrier rates were reduced from as high as 35 per cent to less than 5 per cent. The method is so effective and entails such a short period of sulfadiazine administration that its routine use is justified in family contacts or in institutional groups in which meningococcus infections have occurred. Although the hazards of sulfonamide prophylaxis are less with sulfadiazine than with most of its related compounds, there is a small risk of untoward reactions, sensitization, and development of resistant strains. Its indiscriminate use is therefore to be avoided.

Environmental Sanitation. General measures of sanitation, such as control of water, sewage, food, and milk, contribute nothing to the prevention of spread of meningococcus infection, nor is any other method of sanitation of value in dealing with the sporadic case in the general civil community. In controlling institutional outbreaks, measures to reduce overcrowding are of some value, as they lessen the opportunity for exchange of secretions of the respiratory tract. These measures should include spreading out of the sleeping quarters, such as spacing of beds and alternating the heads and feet of parallel rows of beds. Attention should also be directed to overcrowding in the mess hall, recreational quarters, and other places where persons congregate indoors. As far as possible, the group should be kept outdoors, but this is often impossible due to the weather and the character of the group in question. Prior to the development of sulfadiazine prophylaxis, measures to reduce overcrowding offered the only hope of controlling the spread of meningococcus infections. They should not be neglected today, even though the use of chemoprophylaxis has reduced their importance.

Disinfection. This disease is included in Group I; procedures outlined for that group on page 144 should be followed.

Minimizing Ill Effects

Until recent years, specific antimeningococcus serum offered the most promising method of treatment, though it was relatively ineffective as compared with certain other therapeutic sera. The recent introduction of the sulfonamides and antibiotics has made available new therapeutic agents that are highly specific for the meningococcus and have, therefore, almost entirely supplanted serum. Their use has brought about a marked reduction in the case fatality rate, robbing the disease of much of its former terror and public health importance.

Public Health Nursing Care. If hospitalization is not possible, every effort should be made to provide full-time graduate nursing attention, as the care of meningococcus meningitis is difficult. In some cases, since even this is not possible, the family must care for the patient with what assistance may be obtained from the public health nurse. In most cases drug therapy will alleviate the acute symptoms in such a short time that the following nursing procedures may be necessary for only a day or two.

One of the first things to do is to see that the patient is in a darkened quiet room. The attendant should be especially careful not to jar the bed or bump into furniture in the room. Noise around the house should be reduced to a minimum, as any noise may be excrutiatingly "painful" and may cause a convulsion. To accomplish this, bells may have to be muffled, rubber guards put on doors, and other noises eliminated as far as possible.

Side boards will probably be needed on the bed, as patients are often emotional; it is better to prevent an accident by using side boards early in the disease rather than to wait until the need is made apparent by the occurrence of an accident.

The physician's orders regarding diet and any treatments will of course be obtained. Fluids are usually not forced; in fact, they may be limited during the acute stages. During the convalescent stage the patient is apt to have very little appetite. As at this time he often requires a high caloric diet, ingenuity may be needed in preparing food to tempt his appetite.

Number of Nursing Visits. If the public health nurse is attempting to give bedside care, daily visits will be needed until recovery, and, if possible, two visits a day during the acute stage. If bedside care cannot be furnished, two to three visits should be made at the onset, until the attendant feels able to handle the patient. One or two visits during the convalescent stage will be needed to assist with the diet and gradual return to normal activities.

Control through Immunization

No method of proved efficacy for either passive or active immunization is available. Active immunization with a toxin from the meningococcus has been described, but the evidence as to its value is still inadequate.

SUMMARY

Health Department Program

There is no measure of proved value that will control the spread of meningococcic infection on a community-wide basis; sulfadiazine prophylaxis is effective in controlling the disease within special groups, but has not been used on a community-wide basis. The health department can do little more than carry out routine isolation and quarantine procedures for whatever slight value they may have in protection of contacts and furnish facilities for diagnosis, hospitalization, serum, and chemotherapy to reduce the risk of death in the sick patient. In the presence of institutional outbreaks every reasonable measure should be taken to reduce overcrowding. Sulfadiazine prophylaxis is indicated, but should be supplemented by measures to reduce overcrowding.

The health officer should assume responsibility for the isolation and quarantine and the epidemiological investigation. He must make certain that facilities for diagnosis and treatment are available to all. He must be prepared to withstand a hysterical demand for sensational measures of no proved value. The public health nurse may render assistance in those cases that are not hospitalized. The sanitary officer has little part in this program other than assisting in the development and carrying out of measures to reduce overcrowding in institutions, where the infection is occurring.

SUGGESTED READINGS

Aycock, W. Lloyd, and Mueller, J. Howard: "Meningococcus Carrier Rates and Meningitis Incidence," *Bact. Rev.*, 14:115–60, (June), 1950.

Banks, H. Stanley: "Cerebrospinal Fever," *Lancet*, 1:42–44, (Jan. 6) 1940. Published also as Chapter XVII of *Control of the Common Fevers*. London: The Lancet, Ltd., 1942.

Cerebrospinal Fever: Studies in the Bacteriology, Preventive Control, and Specific Treatment of Cerebrospinal Fever among the Military Forces, 1915–9. Medical Research Council, Special Report Series #50. London: His Majesty's Printing Office, 1920.

Gover, Mary, and Jackson, Glee: "Cerebrospinal Meningitis. A Chronological Record of Reported Cases and Deaths," *Pub. Health Rep.*, 61:433–50, (Mar. 29) 1946.

Hedrich, Arthur W.: "Recent Trends in Meningococcal Disease," *Pub. Health Rep.*, 67:411–20, (May) 1952.

Kuhns, Dwight M.; Nelson, Carl T.; Feldman, Harry A.; and Kuhn, L. Roland: "The Prophylactic Value of Sulfadiazine in the Control of Meningococcus Meningitis," *J.A.M.A.*, 123:335–39, (Oct. 9) 1943.

Phair, John J., and Schoenbach, Emanuel B.: "The Dynamics of Meningococcal Infection and the Effect of Chemotherapy," *Am. J. Hyg.*, 40:318–44, (Nov.) 1944.

———: "The Transmission and Control of Meningococcal Infections," *Am. J. M. Sc.*, 209:69–74, (Jan.) 1945.

Phair, John J.; Schoenbach, Emanuel B.; and Root, Charlotte M.: "Meningococcal Carrier Studies," *Am. J. Pub. Health*, 34:148–54, (Feb.) 1944.

Sartwell, Philip E., and Smith, W. Myers: "Epidemiological Notes on Meningococcal Meningitis in the Army," *Am. J. Pub. Health*, 34:40–49, (Jan.) 1944.

26. Pneumonia

Pneumonia is a pulmonary inflammation due to some invading microorganism and attended with an exudate which fills the air spaces in certain areas of the lungs. There is frequently some inflammation of the pleura. Empyema, otitis media, pericarditis, and meningitis are the principal complications. In the past, the pneumonias have been subdivided on an anatomical basis—the lobar cases represent those with complete involvement of one or more lobes or parts of a lobe, while the bronchial cases show discrete and often widely scattered areas of consolidation. While this division is still recognized clinically and in the *International Classification of Causes of Deaths*, it is being supplanted by a bacteriological classification in terms of the organisms responsible for the infection.

EPIDEMIOLOGY

Occurrence. Pneumonia in all its forms constitutes one of the principal causes of death. In many places the deaths from primary pneumonia outnumber those due to tuberculosis. In addition, pneumonia is responsible for the ultimate release of many persons suffering from various incurable conditions, such as cancer, chronic nephritis, arteriosclerosis, and even senility. It appears frequently as a complication (too often fatal) following operations or acute infections, such as influenza, measles, and whooping cough.

Pneumonia is a disease of all climates and seasons but is more frequent in winter and spring that in fall and summer. The incidence in the United States is quite variable and unexplained, some of the southern states having rates higher than the northern. Little is known of the influence of climatological factors in the occurrence of pneumonia. During the past two decades, there has been a very substantial reduction in the pneumonia mortality rate. It is probable that the chief factor in this decline is the advent of sulfonamide and antibiotic therapy, which has materially reduced the case fatality rate; some reduction in incidence of the disease has also occurred as lobar pneumonia is seen far less frequently than in former years.

Etiological Agent. Pneumonia may be caused by a large number of organisms, including bacteria, viruses, rickettsiae, fungi, and parasites. Most of the cases are due to infection with the pneumococcus. Other causative bacteria include streptococci, Friedländer's bacillus, and Pfeiffer's bacillus.[1] Pneumonia attributable to a virus (or possibly to several different viruses) has been recognized with increasing frequency during the past decade; it presents a rather clearly defined clinical entity. Although the virus etiology can be demonstrated in only a few instances, there can be no doubt that many cases of atypical pneumonia or severe coughs with fever of several days' duration are actually instances of "virus pneumonia." There is reason to believe that the infection may be occurring more frequently than in former years, though part of the apparent increase may be due merely to better recognition of the condition. Possibly such infections in a mild form would be found far more frequently that at present if routine x-rays were taken of all cases of so-called "grippe" or "flu."

The pneumococci are divided into thirty-two different types.[2] Differentiation of the pneumococci, referred to as typing, is usually made by either agglutination reactions or by the swelling of the capsule when the organism is brought in contact with specific antiserum from a rabbit immunized with the same type (Neufeld method).

TABLE 10

DISTRIBUTION OF PNEUMOCOCCI IN 3,713 ADULTS WITH PNEUMOCOCCUS LOBAR PNEUMONIA

Type		Per Cent
I		28.6
II		11.4
III		13.5
V		8.0
VII		6.5
VIII		7.7
	Total	75.7
Other types		24.3
	Grand total	100.0

Table 10, adapted from one of Heffron's, shows the distribution of the principal types in a series of 3,713 adult cases of lobar pneumonia.

[1] Tubercle bacilli may cause pneumonia, but this is generally classed as tuberculosis rather than pneumonia.

[2] There is some doubt as to the separate identity of Types XV and XXX and of Types VI and XXVI.

The distribution of these types is, however, extremely variable from place to place and from one period of time to another in the same place. In a large area one type may predominate at one time, while a month or two later a different one may be most prevalent. Localized outbreaks due to a single type have been reported. The higher types of pneumococci (types other than I, II, or III) are important as a cause of bronchopneumonia, especially those cases appearing as postinfectious, postoperative, and terminal complications. The case fatality rate of Type I infection, untreated with serum, chemotherapy, or antibiotics, is about 30 per cent, that of Type II about 40 per cent, and that of Type III about 45 per cent, though this latter is influenced by the higher percentage of older persons attacked. The rates for the other types are somewhat lower.

The reservoir of infection is always a person infected with the causative organism, either a case or a carrier.[3] Virus infections are certainly spread from patient to patient; the role of carriers is unknown. Almost everyone harbors pneumococci in the throat at some time each year. The incidence of carriers is, however, extremely variable according to the type. About 10 per cent of the family contacts of Type I or II show infection with the homologous organisms; yet the incidence of Type I or II carriers in the general population is usually less than 1 per cent. Stebbins and his associates have described a community outbreak of Type I infection in which the general incidence of organisms was as high as 17 per cent.[4] Type III carriers are as frequent in noncontacts as in contacts and may be found in as high as 10 per cent of the population. The higher types are found much more frequently, often in as high as 25 to 40 per cent of a population, though the distribution of these between the various types is quite variable. They occur so frequently in the upper respiratory tract that their significance as the cause of the postoperative, postinfectious, and terminal pneumonias is often as invaders of the lungs of the person who is already harboring them but whose resistance is suddenly depressed.

Escape of the organism is usually via the secretions of the nose and throat and is therefore facilitated by coughing and sneezing. Pneumococci are usually present in the sputum of the active case, though the patient may have difficulty in raising the sputum because of its tenacity and the pain that goes with the attending pleurisy. The discharge of an empyema or otitis media complicating a pneumococcal infection usually contains the organism in the early stage, though other contaminants may later overgrow it.

[3] Although pneumococci are fairly resistant to drying and may be found in dust, there is no evidence that this survival and possible multiplication outside the body have any public health significance.

[4] Of 32 carriers found, only 5 were among household contacts of cases.

Transmission is apparently due to direct contact via droplet infection. Virus pneumonia appears to be more readily communicable than is pneumococcal infection. The possible importance of vehicles such as food, books, bed linen, dishes, and dust has never been proved, though reasonable precautions are justified in dealing with anything soiled with sputum.

Entry and Incubation Period. Entry of the organism is via the respiratory tract, thereby causing direct involvement of the lung. Pneumococci may be found in the blood stream in a very high percentage of the early cases; their persistence here increases the danger of the disease and the likelihood of complications. The incubation period probably varies from a few hours to a few days.

Susceptibility. It used to be stated frequently that there was little resistance to the pneumococcus, as evidenced by repeated attacks in the same individual. This general statement was not based upon immunological studies backed up by typing of the disease. During an attack, antibodies develop, some of which have the property of dissolving the pneumococcus capsule so that it may be phagocytized by the white blood cells. Since these bodies do not persist, however, their absence cannot be used as a measure of susceptibility. Much attention has been given to nonspecific factors of resistance such as fatigue, exposure, and alcoholism. The present evidence would suggest that these factors may so depress the resistance that invasion of the lungs will be favored if the individual is already harboring infection. Intercurrent infections such as colds and the acute communicable diseases also favor pneumococcus invasion. Susceptibility to pneumococcal infections seems to be highest in infancy and in the aged.

Nothing is known for certain regarding resistance to virus pneumonia. Until more is known about the different strains of virus that may cause the disease, there cannot even be assurance as to the duration of resistance following an attack. In general an immediate though possibly not permanent resistance is produced. The high incidence of infections in adults suggests either that the disease is new or that there has been little if any latent immunization through unrecognized infections.

CONTROL MEASURES

Control of Spread

The case should have as little contact with other persons as possible, though isolation requirements are not generally enforced. Differences of opinion exist as to the propriety of accepting such cases on the open wards of hospitals, though general experience shows that infection of other patients rarely occurs. Special attention should, however, be paid to the disposal of sputum and to the covering of the patient's mouth and nose when he coughs. Dressings soaked with discharge from the ear or a draining empyema should be burned. If the patient is at home, contacts with other members of the family and with visitors should be restricted so far as possible.

Epidemiological investigation is of value chiefly for research purposes. Routine inquiries and cultures of contacts, while yielding interesting information regarding the epidemiology of the disease, do not assist in prevention of spread or discovery of the source of infection.

Contacts are usually not subjected to restraint.

Prevention of Pneumonia as a Complication. Special precautions should be used to protect postoperative patients and those with acute infectious diseases. Such patients should be isolated insofar as possible to avoid contracting a pneumococcal infection from a visitor or other contact, especially one who has a cold. Routine hospitalization of patients with measles, whooping cough, and influenza is inadvisable, as this often increases their exposure to persons who may be harboring other organisms. Masking of personnel coming in contact with such cases and with postoperative patients may be of value in reducing the incidence of secondary pneumonia. Administration of prophylactic doses of sulfonamides or antibiotics has been recommended for patients suffering with conditions in which pneumonia is a frequent complication.

Environmental sanitation does not appear to affect the incidence of primary pneumonias, but overcrowding may favor the development of pneumonic complications in persons exposed to measles or influenza.

Disinfection. Pneumonia is included in Group I; the procedures outlined for that group on page 144 should be followed.

Minimizing Ill Effects

Minimizing the severity of the disease constitutes at present the most promising approach to the control of all forms of pneumonia. This consists of furnishing specific treatment and general care to reduce the risk of death.

Chemotherapy. The sulfonamides and antibiotics which have been developed during recent years have completely altered the public health aspects of the pneumonia problem. These drugs have proved to be so effective in the treatment of pneumococcal and streptococcal infections that they have replaced all other therapeutic agents. The drugs have the further advantage that their administration is comparatively simple and safe and their cost within the capacity of all but a small segment of the community. Consequently the health department, which a few years ago was vitally concerned with the pneumonia problem and had laid elaborate plans for the distribution of serum and provision for typing facilities, has today a far less active concern for this type of infection and is called upon less frequently to assist in its care. If given early and in adequate quantity, the sulfonamides and antibiotics will save many lives that would have been otherwise lost. The chief drawback to their therapeutic use lies in the fact that certain strains of organisms either are or become resistant to these drugs. At times this difficulty may be circumvented by selection of a particular drug to which the organism is less resistant; this will probably be more feasible in future years as new antibiotics or sulfonamide derivatives are developed. The problem of the development of resistant strains is sufficiently serious today, however, that the indiscriminate and unnecessary use of those drugs is to be discouraged lest it result in the development of resistance on the part of the strains of organisms that are most prevalent within a particular community. As organisms acquire resistance, patients whom they infect are deprived of the potential benefit that they might otherwise gain from chemotherapy. Although the virus pneumonias are resistant to most therapeutic agents, favorable results have been reported from use of aureomycin.

Public Health Nursing Care. The antibiotics have so changed the febrile toxic phase of pneumonia that in most cases no special nursing care is needed. The public health nurse will encounter advanced cases from time to time, however, and in these instances should keep in mind the necessity for complete and absolute rest. It will then be important to teach the attendant how to do all the required procedures in such a manner that the patient will be spared unnecessary exertion. The patient should not be disturbed except for necessary nourishment, proper elimination, and the administration of treatments ordered by the physician. Turning and raising him with a minimum of effort on his part should be demonstrated; if he is resting at the time of the nurse's visit, this may be demonstrated on a member of the family. If the patient is an adult, the attendant should be shown the proper method of giving the bedpan and assisting the patient to raise himself on it. Mouth care should be demonstrated, as the lips usually become sore and cracked and herpes frequently develops. The patient should be kept comfortably warm, and the air in the sickroom fresh and cool but not cold.

The public health nurse should be sure the attendant understands the physician's instructions regarding the administration of the drugs prescribed and the collection of any specimens ordered. If the physician wishes fluid intake and output measured, the nurse should see that the attendant knows how to do this, has suitable receptacles, and is keeping satisfactory records. The patient taking aureomycin or sulfonamides often loses his appetite and does not want to take the quantity of fluid essential to avoid drug toxicity. Therefore, assistance is often needed in planning meals and suggesting fluids which may appeal. The public health nurse must be familiar with adverse reactions to chemotherapy so that she may report such effects to the attending physician.

Though the acute stage of pneumonia has been greatly shortened by chemotherapy, the convalescent stage may be long. Even the milder cases of virus pneumonia leave the patient quite weak and with an annoying cough that may persist for several weeks. The nurse has a vital role to play in assisting the patient and family in carrying out the physician's orders regarding the slow and gradual return to normal activity. She can help the patient and family understand that full energy and vigor may not return for 4 to 6 weeks after "recovery."

Number of Nursing Visits. If bedside care is to be furnished, daily visits should be made until recovery. If intensive bedside care cannot be offered, the nurse should make a visit as soon as the case is known. At this time she should see what arrangements can be made for nursing care. If a member of the family must give the care, at least two visits should be made on successive days to give demonstrations and assistance.

Control through Immunization

Passive Immunization. No effective method has been developed.

Chemoprophylaxis. Administration of sulfonamides or antibiotics is effective in the prevention of certain pneumococcal and streptococcal pneumonias, especially those which are secondary to other infections such as influenza, measles, whooping cough, or infections which occur post-operatively. This does not, however, justify the indiscriminate administration to all persons suffering from common colds or to various groups of healthy persons. Reactions are not common but occur with sufficient frequency to show that these drugs should be administered only when necessary and when the patient can be kept under constant medical care to detect the first signs of untoward effects. Indiscriminate use further enhances the risk of development of resistant strains of infectious microorganisms. Chemoprophylaxis has its place, but this is as a means of protection of carefully selected patients exposed to a serious risk of pneumonia; routine and mass use of chemoprophylaxis is potentially harmful as well as unnecessary.

Active Immunization. Numerous antigens have been tried, but the results have been disappointing.

SUMMARY

Health Department Program

Because of the large number of carriers, direct character of spread, and the absence of an effective method of producing a fairly lasting immunity, little can at present be expected of measures to prevent the development of pneumonia in the general population. Isolation may, however, be of value in an institutional or military group. Chief reliance must be placed upon measures to reduce the severity and therefore the case fatality rate. These measures include the hospitalization of patients and the provision of nursing assistance for those who are cared for at home. Antibiotics may have to be provided for those unable to obtain them otherwise. All of these measures are of proved value in the reduction of deaths. Their application on a large scale to reach the bulk of cases of pneumonia may be expected to effect a significant decline in the death rate.

The **health officer** no longer has a major concern for the care of this disease. He may need to provide antibiotics to those who cannot pay for them and to conduct epidemiological investigations if there is an unusual incidence of cases, especially in institutional groups. Arrangements for home nursing care should be made either by the board of health or in conjunction with a bedside nursing association. The **public health nurse** should be prepared not only to make instructive visits to homes where pneumonia exists, but also to render actual bedside care. Pneumonia deaths today exceed those from tuberculosis. A little more money spent on the care of cases may be cheaper in the long run than dispensing welfare aid to those rendered destitute by the death of the wage earner.

SUGGESTED READINGS

Cruickshank, Robert: "The Pneumonias," *Lancet,* **1**:1222–25, (May 27) 1939. Published also as Chapter XI of *Control of the Common Fevers.* London: The Lancet, Ltd., 1942.

Dingle, John H., and collaborators: "Primary Atypical Pneumonia, Etiology Unknown," *War Med.,* **3**:223–48, (Mar.) 1943.

Dingle, John H.; Abernethy, Theodore J.; Badger, George F.; Buddingh, G. John; Feller, A. E.; Langmuir, Alexander D.; Ruegsegger, James M.; and Wood, W. Barry, Jr.: "Primary Atypical Pneumonia, Etiology Unknown," *Am. J. Hyg.,* **39**:67–128, 197–268, 269–336, (Jan., Mar., May) 1944.

Heffron, Roderick: *Pneumonia: with Special Reference to Pneumococcus Lobar Pneumonia.* New York: Commonwealth Fund, 1939. See especially Chapters VI and VII.

Jordan, William S., Jr.: "The Infectiousness and Incubation Period of Primary Atypical Pneumonia," *Am. J. Hyg.*, 50:315–30, (Nov.) 1949.

Smillie, Wilson G.: "The Epidemiology of Lobar Pneumonia: A Study of the Prevalence of Specific Strains of Pneumococci in the Nasopharynx of Immediate Family Contacts," *J.A.M.A.*, 101:1281–86, (Oct. 21) 1933.

Smillie, Wilson G., and Jewett, Olga F.: "The Relationship of Immediate Family Contact to the Transmission of Type-Specific Pneumococci," *Am. J. Hyg.*, 32 (Sect. A) :79–88, (Nov.) 1940.

Stebbins, Ernest L.; Perkins, James E.; Rogers, Edward S.; Champlin, R. D.; and Ames, Wendell R.: "Prevalence of Pneumococcus Carriers: Specific Types in Epidemic and Non-Epidemic Areas," *Am. J. Pub. Health,* 30:349–60, (Apr.) 1940.

27. Influenza

The term influenza is used popularly—and too often clinically—to refer to a group of apparently diverse and unrelated conditions accompanied by fever, malaise, and marked prostration, with or without evidence of inflammation of the upper respiratory tract. Epidemiologically, however, the term must be restricted to infection with a particular virus, causing a condition which is clinically indistinguishable from many diseases of apparently different origin. Distinction can be made only on bacteriological grounds. In the absence of bacteriological evidence, one must remain in doubt as to the accuracy of the diagnosis. Many of the conditions which simulate influenza are referred to as "grippe," though it must be remembered that this term may also cover a multitude of unrelated conditions.[1]

EPIDEMIOLOGY

Occurrence. Influenza constitutes one of the most important of the unsolved problems of infectious disease. Appearing in recurrent waves which have swept through the world with the speed of human travel, it has been responsible for the most devastating of all modern plagues. If uncomplicated, it rarely kills; but, unfortunately, it often paves the way for the respiratory invasion of other pathogenic organisms, notably pneumococci and streptococci. Whenever influenza becomes widespread, it is accompanied by a sharp increase in the pneumonia death rate. The extent to which fatal complications may ensue appears to vary greatly in different epidemic waves. The 1918 pandemic was accompanied by a death rate which exceeded the war casualties and resulted in a high degree of popular panic. There have been numerous subsequent epidemics in which the virus was almost as widely distributed and the attack rate probably quite comparable; yet the number of deaths, though increased over normal, was

---

[1] It must also be remembered that some of these may actually be influenza, even though we are unable to isolate the virus with present methods.

so relatively small that very little public attention was accorded the disease. Today they are forgotten, though the wave of 1918 will remain in the memory of those who experienced it. There is much uncertainty as to whether such variations are due to differences in the strain of virus involved or to other factors responsible for the simultaneous spread and enhanced virulence of the secondary invaders.

Influenza is found in all parts of the world and at all seasons of year, though the highest incidence appears to occur most frequently in the winter months. The highest attack rates occur in children, though the death rate is higher in adults. The disease appears in recurrent waves, irregularly spaced. Sporadic cases occur between epidemics.

Etiological Agent. Influenza is due to a specific virus, of which several strains have been isolated. Most of the outbreaks so far studied have been due to infection with either the A or the B strain of virus. Although these have been grouped into A and B strains, several quite different A strains have been recognized. The antigenic relationship between these strains is still uncertain though it is clear that infection with one strain does not necessarily confer protection against another strain.

Reservoir of Infection. The only known source of infection is man. The possible existence of other reservoirs in which the infection may lie latent during interepidemic periods is still uncertain. The recognition of sporadic cases furnishes an adequate explanation of interepidemic survival without the need of postulating the existence of nonhuman reservoirs. Certain experimental animals can be infected, and there is good reason to believe that the virus of the 1918 epidemic has become permanently established in the hog in a modified form as one of the factors in swine influenza. The existence of antibodies in the blood of certain ferrets suggests that infection may occur in these under natural conditions.

Escape from the body is achieved through the respiratory tract, the virus being found in the secretions of the tract during the disease. Communicability probably lasts only during the acute stages.

Transmission is apparently through direct respiratory association, fomites playing little if any part.

Entry and Incubation Period. Entry into the new host occurs via the respiratory tract. The incubation period is two to three days in most instances.

Susceptibility is quite uniformly high, as shown by the high attack rate during an epidemic period. Evidence suggestive of a fairly lasting resistance has been repeatedly brought forward, as, for example, the relative immunity in 1918 of those who had been infected in the 1889 pandemic and the higher attack rate among children as compared with that among adults. All evidence of resistance must, however, be accepted cautiously, unless it takes into consideration the different strains of virus. Infection is known to be followed by the production of antibodies which are specific for the strain concerned but do not confer protection against another strain. The duration of resistance is still unknown, as the knowledge of the virus of influenza and its antibodies has all developed in the past twenty years and no strains from earlier pandemics are available for study.

CONTROL MEASURES [2]

Control of Spread

The case should be rigidly isolated, as the communicability and risk of complications are high. Home care, if available, is preferable to hospital care, as it reduces the number of contacts and avoids association with the seriously ill patients who have a complicating pneumonia. Isolation should persist only for the duration of the acute illness.

Routine **epidemiological investigation** of the case will shed little light upon the source of infection and is therefore of no value in control. There is, however, a great need for careful epidemiological study backed up by bacteriological findings.

Contacts are subjected to no quarantine precautions. They should be warned as to the likelihood of their infection and the need for good care to reduce the risk of complications if they become ill.

Environmental sanitation is of no proved value. Closing of schools, churches, theaters, swimming pools, and so forth, has been attempted. While this may reduce crowding, so many other opportunities for respiratory contacts exist that little is accomplished.

Disinfection. Influenza is included in Group I; disinfection procedures outlined for that group on page 144 should be followed.

Minimizing Ill Effects

As influenza itself does not kill but is often complicated by pneumonia which results fatally in an appreciable proportion of cases, attempts to minimize the severity of the disease should be directed toward prevention and treatment of pneumonia. The patient should be kept in bed for the duration of the acute illness and have as few contacts as possible. During the 1918 pandemic the lowest pneumonia risk was in those who could be cared for at home away from other persons, and the highest among those who had to be cared for in crowded quarters, where they were brought in

---

[2] Aside from immunization, the measures here outlined for the control of influenza are equally applicable to "grippe."

contact with patients already suffering from pneumonia or other respiratory infections. The advent of the sulfonamides and antibiotics has provided specific drugs for the treatment, and possibly the prevention, of secondary pneumonia. The low death rate that has characterized the influenza waves since the introduction of these drugs may have been due in some degree to these improved methods of treatment for pneumonia.

Public health nursing care is aimed at prevention or care of pneumonia. The nursing procedures outlined for that disease (see p. 337) are equally applicable to influenza. The patient must be kept warm and protected from contact with persons who have other respiratory tract infections. Return to normal activity should be slow and gradual.

The number of nursing visits will depend upon the condition of the patient, home situation, and amount of time that can be given to one patient. The average, uncomplicated case requires nothing more than a single instructional visit to the home; but if multiple cases develop, including infection of the mother, repeated visits may be necessary to render care. The case that is complicated by pneumonia may require daily visits. When influenza is widespread, the demands upon the nurse may be so heavy that she cannot see all cases but must select those where she knows the home conditions are poor and therefore the risk of pneumonia increased.

Control through Immunization

Recently developed vaccines, made from A and B strains of virus, have given evidence of conferring a considerably increased resistance which lasts for a few months but not from one year to the next. Persons recently given suitable vaccine have been shown to have a lower attack rate than do unvaccinated controls. As the vaccine can be given in a single injection and produces its effect in about a week, it can be administered at the first sign of an influenza wave. To be of any effect, however, it must be made from the strain of virus against which protection is sought. Type A vaccine will not protect against Type B infection, nor do the variants of Type A protect against each other. Some of the recent outbreaks appear to have been due to variants of the A strain not then included in the vaccine; in these instances the vaccine has been found ineffective. The vaccine is made from the chick embryo and can be stored for long periods of time so that accumulation of an adequate supply and its widespread use in the face of an epidemic are theoretically possible, provided it is sufficiently multivalent. Much more experience is needed before influenza vaccine can be fully evaluated. So far, the results have not warranted its general use.

Gargles, mouthwashes, and special diet are of no value in preventing infection.

SUMMARY

Health Department Program

It may just as well be confessed that, with our present knowledge, a board of health is unable to prevent the development or spread of influenza throughout a community. We know that future epidemics will occur, and yet we can neither predict the time of their appearance nor take any measure which will prevent or abort them. The recently developed vaccines appear to be of such value that immunization of a community in anticipation of an outbreak is within the realm of possibility but more evidence is needed before the procedure can be generally recommended. The recent epidemic waves have been comparatively so mild that there is reason to doubt the extent of public response to an offer of immunization. In the meantime chief reliance must be put on prevention and treatment of complicating pneumonias.

The **health officer** should advise the public of the importance of adequate care and the serious danger of attempting to "fight off" the infection while staying at work. Protection of the patient against unnecessary contacts and especially against contacts with other patients with respiratory infection should be stressed. Emphasis should also be placed upon the importance of medical care, especially of those patients who do not show signs of recovery in three or four days. To avoid hospitalization, nursing care in the home should be provided. This may require the emergency provision of bedside care through employment of extra **visiting nurses.** The importance of influenza as a cause of death may be such that, for the duration of the epidemic, routine nursing visits in the interests of child health, tuberculosis, and even many prenatal visits may be temporarily suspended and the nursing personnel diverted to home visiting and care for influenza. Hospitalization should be reserved for patients already suffering from pneumonia and a relatively small group of cases for whom home care cannot be given.

SUGGESTED READINGS

Andrewes, Christopher Howard: "Adventures among Viruses. II. Epidemic Influenza," *New England J. Med.,* 242:197–203, (Feb. 9) 1950.

Burnet, F. M., and Clark, E.: *Influenza. A Survey of the Last 50 Years in the Light of Modern Work on the Virus of Epidemic Influenza.* Melbourne: Macmillan & Co., Ltd., 1942.

Collins, Selwyn D.: "Trends and Epidemics of Influenza and Pneumonia, 1918–1951," *Pub. Health Rep.* 66:1487–1516, (Nov. 16) 1951.

Commission on Acute Respiratory Diseases: "Endemic Influenza," *Am. J. Hyg.*, 47:290–96, (May) 1948.

Commission on Influenza, U.S. Army Epidemiological Board: "A Clinical Evaluation of Vaccination against Influenza. Preliminary Report," *J.A.M.A.*, 124:982–85, (Apr. 1) 1944.

Dingle, John H.: "Influenza," *New England J. Med.*, 237:845–52, (Dec. 4) 1947.

Francis, Thomas, Jr.: "Epidemiology of Influenza," *J.A.M.A.*, 122:4–8, (May 1) 1943.

Francis, Thomas, Jr.; Salk, Jonas E.; and Brace, William M.: "The Protective Effect of Vaccination against Epidemic Influenza B," *J.A.M.A.*, 131:275–78, (May 25) 1946.

Jordan, Edwin O.: *Epidemic Influenza. A Survey.* Chicago: American Medical Association, 1927.

Salk, Jonas E.: "Use of Adjuvants in Studies on Influenza Immunization," *J.A.M.A.*, 151:1169–75, (Apr. 4) 1953.

Salk, Jonas E., and Suriano, Philip C.: "Importance of Antigenic Composition of Influenza Virus Vaccine in Protecting against the Natural Disease," *Am. J. Pub. Health,* 39:345–55, (Mar.) 1949.

Sartwell, Philip E., and Long, Arthur P.: "Army Experience with Influenza, 1946–1947," *Am. J. Hyg.*, 47:135–41, (Mar.) 1948.

Shope, Richard E.: "The Influenzas of Swine and Man," *Medicine,* 15:453–87, (Dec.) 1936.

———: "Old, Intermediate, and Contemporary Contributions to Our Knowledge of Pandemic Influenza," *Medicine,* 23:415–55, (Dec.) 1944.

28. Common Colds

The common cold is the commonest of all infectious diseases and is responsible for more loss of time than is any other illness, except possibly rheumatism. Although probably never fatal, colds contribute indirectly to the general mortality rate in paving the way for the development of other respiratory tract infections which may result fatally. Few diseases can rival the cold from the standpoint of social and economic importance, yet little is known about its etiology and epidemiology and virtually nothing about its prevention.

One of the principal obstacles to control or study is the lack of a clearly defined diagnostic criterion. When speaking of a cold, one generally refers to a catarrhal condition of the upper respiratory tract, attended with increased nasal secretion and inflammation of lymphoid tissues and frequently followed by inflammation of the nasal sinuses, larynx, trachea, and bronchi. The variable manifestations in different persons indicate the protean character of the infection. It is frequently uncertain what part of the process is due to the true cause of the cold and how much to the action of intercurrent infection by other viruses or bacteria present in the respiratory tract.

EPIDEMIOLOGY

Etiological Agent. Although many attempts have been made to classify colds on the basis of symptomatology, the clinical manifestations apparently depend on the individual and on intercurrent infection. A more satisfactory classification would appear to be on the etiological basis, when and if the exact causes of colds are discovered. Although relatively little is as yet known regarding etiology, some of the colds can be ascribed to the action of a filterable virus. That some agent communicated from person to person is involved is indicated by the freedom from colds of persons who are isolated from civilization and the reappearance of infection as soon as contact with the outside world is re-established. The existence of a virus has, however, been demonstrated in only a few instances. This does not mean that viruses are rarely involved but may be equally interpreted as evidence of the inadequacy of our present research methods and of the existence of not one but several different viruses, each of which may bring about such a clinical condition. It is probable that, in the future, classification on the etiological basis will be more exact.

Although at present the only proved cause is a virus, it has been suggested that some colds may be due to allergy or to other conditions. If this is true, it is apparent that many diverse conditions are being classified under the broad heading of "colds" and that future research will sort out the tangle.

The reservoir of infection is in all cases infected human beings suffering from an acute infection. No conclusive evidence of carriers has been advanced.

Escape of the virus appears to be by secretions of the upper respiratory tract. The patient is most infectious in the early stages and possibly in the prodromal period. The duration of communicability is not clearly known, though it would appear to be less than the duration of symptoms. This may, however, be due to the fact that much of the bronchitis and sinusitis characteristic of the later stages of the disease is due to intercurrent infection and that the virus disappears long before the complications have ceased. An analogous situation often occurs in measles.

Transmission of infection probably occurs chiefly through direct respiratory exchange of the virus-carrying droplets. The importance of fomites in transmission of the virus is a matter of much uncertainty. Some maintain that such articles as dishes and clothing may be of importance in the spread of infection and that fingers may pick up the virus for transfer to the mouth. While one cannot deny the theoretical possibility of such spread, there are usually such abundant respiratory contacts that one can only speculate as to the relative importance of spread through direct association and fomites.

Entry and Incubation Period. Entry of the virus occurs through the respiratory tract. The incubation period appears to be from one to three days in most cases.

Susceptibility. Much uncertainty exists regarding specific and nonspecific resistance to colds. Lacking exact knowledge of etiology and tests for susceptibility, one can only reason from observation. It is common knowledge that susceptibility to colds varies greatly among individuals. One person may rarely be affected while another living under comparable circumstances may suffer from repeated colds each winter season. That some specific resistance may exist is attested by the apparent resistance which so many persons experience for a few weeks after a cold. At best this appears to be of only short duration, as another cold may be contracted a few weeks later. There is no evidence of prolonged resistance such as occurs in so many virus infections.

The nonspecific factors of resistance may be of equal importance. Although a virus is apparently the one element without which infection cannot develop, many other factors may condition the response of the body to the action of the virus. It has been suggested that some of them may be of a physiological nature, such as acidity of the nasal secretions, vasomotor responses of the nasal mucosa, vitamin deficiency, and acid-base balance. Such suggestions have given rise to many methods of treating colds, such as alkaline or vitamin therapy. Although persons suffering from severe avitaminosis undoubtedly show increased susceptibility to infection, there is inadequate evidence as yet that lack of vitamins is an important factor in the development of most colds or that the use of vitamins is a rational method of prevention or therapy. Other nonspecific factors that may alter the response of the body to the cold virus include exposure, chilling, fatigue, malnutrition, and alcoholism. It is popularly supposed that some of these may be primary causes, operating in the absence of a virus, but evidence for this is quite inadequate. Possibly, however, a person may harbor the virus for a short period of time without symptoms, and invasion may be precipitated by one of these accessory factors, such as exposure or chilling. Much more research is needed before the relationship of the virus and the accessory factors is clearly understood.

CONTROL MEASURES

Control of Spread

The case should, theoretically, be isolated to avoid spread of the virus to other persons. There can be no doubt of the infectiousness of the patient during the early and acute stages, and isolation on a voluntary or compulsory basis would unquestionably reduce spread. This is, however, one instance in which few persons practice what they preach. Most colds interfere so little with a person's ability to pursue his normal course of life that boards of health make no attempt to require isolation and quarantine, and few of us practice it in our personal lives. Familiarity with the common cold leads us to underestimate its danger and to neglect treatment; yet no doubt isolation would prevent spread, and rest and good care would reduce the incidence and toll of complications.

In dealing with groups of persons, one may, however, insist on some measure of segregation. The mother should not send to school a child who is developing a cold or is in the acute stages; and, similarly, the school authorities should exclude such children from the classroom.[1] The duration of the exclusion is problematical. To keep the child from school until all traces of sinus infection or bronchial irritation have subsided would result in virtually permanent exclusion of some children. As these complications are probably not due to the action of the virus but to organisms which are part of the normal flora of the respiratory passages, it would appear reasonable for such exclusion to apply only during the acute catarrhal stage, namely, four to five days. Longer periods would defeat their own purposes through their unreasonableness and too great interference with school attendance and would not contribute measurably to prevention of spread. Even with reasonable exclusion measures, colds will occur in a school group.

Routine **epidemiological investigation** usually shows that the patient has been in contact with someone known to have been suffering from a cold. As this person is now usually beyond the period of probable communicability, little is accomplished from the standpoint of prevention of spread.

Contacts. No restrictions are applied to contacts, though they should understand that they are the next victims and that suitable precautions may be necessary at the time of their infection.

Environmental Sanitation. Any measure that reduces the degree of respiratory contact should limit the spread of colds. Due to uncertainty as to the real importance of vehicles of infection, differences of opinion exist as to the role of general sanitation in preventing spread. Those who believe that dishes constitute an important vehicle urge great attention to them in public or institutional eating places and believe that through such measures they have reduced the rate of respiratory infection, including colds. While thorough dishwashing is aesthetically desirable and dictated by common decency, and while every reasonable step leading to cleanliness should be urged at all times, it is still questionable whether dishes are of sufficient importance in the spread of colds to expect a significant reduction through these measures. Masking of all persons with colds has similarly had its ardent proponents but is equally devoid of proved value, though good in theory.

Several attempts have been made to reduce the incidence of upper respiratory tract infections, including the common cold, by disinfection of the air either by ultraviolet irradiation or by mists of aerosols. Under

---

[1] An added reason for this precaution is that measles and whooping cough may simulate a cold in their early and most communicable stages.

conditions of crowding such as are found in military barracks, some slight reduction in so-called "catarrhal fever" has been described but no absolute control established. No evidence exists that sterilization of air is effective in controlling the spread of common colds under normal conditions of community life.

Minimizing Ill Effects

This is best accomplished through rest in bed. A variety of medications has been recommended, though none is of specific value. In a large study at the University of Minnesota, Diehl and his colleagues found better results with a codeine-papaverine mixture than with other remedies. Antihistamines, though highly advertised, are of no proved value. Lacking official reporting, a board of health can do nothing to reduce severity other than general education to stress the importance of the common cold and the danger of its neglect, especially in young or debilitated persons. The public health nurse should take every opportunity to teach that persons suffering from colds should stay in bed for the first day or two if possible and should always stay in bed and have medical attention if the cold is accompanied by fever. The person who has a cold should be particularly cautioned against becoming overfatigued or getting wet and chilled, as this may lower resistance to pneumonia. Although the public health nurse will ordinarily not be asked to visit patients suffering merely from colds or mild "grippe," she frequently encounters such cases in the course of her other visits. She may give appropriate advice and instruction and should urge medical care if necessary.

Control through Immunization

Many attempts have been made to immunize against the common cold. Most of the commercially available vaccines consist of a variety of killed bacteria, on the assumption that protection is needed not simply against the virus but also against invasion by the organisms so frequently found in the upper respiratory passages, notably pneumococci, *Micrococcus catarrhalis,* streptococci, and staphylococci. Both parenteral and oral administration have been tried. Many very favorable reports have been made on the use of such vaccines when given more or less indiscriminately to persons who suffered from frequent colds. Well-controlled studies, eliminating psychic factors through the administration of a placebo to an unsuspecting control group, have shown, however, that the reduction in incidence of colds in the vaccinated group is not substantially greater than in the control group given injections of saline or capsules of milk sugar (Diehl *et al.*). While vaccines are still worth trying, they cannot be recommended with any prospect of success either in an individual case or on a group basis. One cannot ignore the fact, however, that the occasional person who suffers from repeated colds has experienced some benefit following, though possibly not due to, vaccine administration.

Numerous attempts have also been made to increase the nonspecific factors of resistance. Such measures include vitamin tablets, cold baths, exercise, special diet, and countless other procedures. None of these is of proved value in itself, though one cannot deny that the person who is in vigorous health [2] is more ready to withstand the effects of a cold than is a sickly or debilitated individual.

SUMMARY

Health Department Program

Unfortunately, no community program has been devised which is of proved effectiveness in preventing colds. General education as to personal measures of health maintenance, coupled with precautions as to care of colds and reduction of spread during the acute stage, are advisable though unmeasurable in results. The **health officer,** in conjunction with the school authorities, should insist on temporary exclusion of children during the early stages of colds and should work with the schoolteachers to aid them in this. The recognition of a running nose or a cough requires neither medical nor nursing training and may be carried out satisfactorily by a teacher who is sufficiently alert. In her home visits, the **public health nurse** should stress the importance of keeping a child with a beginning cold out of school and of protecting younger children, and especially the babies, from older brothers and sisters who have colds. She should also emphasize the danger of neglecting a cold in its early stages. The **sanitary officer** should insist on strict sanitation of all public eating establishments.

SUGGESTED READINGS

Andrewes, Christopher Howard: "Adventures among Viruses. III. The Puzzle of the Common Cold," *New England J. Med.,* 242:235–40, (Feb. 16) 1950.

Bradley, W. H.: "The Common Cold," *J. Roy. San. Inst.,* 70:1–17, (Jan.) 1950.

Browning, C. H.: "The Common Cold," Chapter IX of *Control of the Common Fevers.* London: The Lancet, Ltd., 1942.

Cowan, Donald W., and Diehl, Harold S.: "Antihistaminic Agents and Ascorbic Acid in the Early Treatment of the Common Cold," *J.A.M.A.,* 143:421–24, (June 3) 1950.

[2] This does not mean big muscles.

Cowan, Donald W.; Diehl, Harold S.; and Baker, A. B.: "Vitamins for the Prevention of Colds," *J.A.M.A.*, 120:1268–71, (Dec. 19) 1942.

Diehl, H. S.; Baker, A. B.; and Cowan, D. W.: "Cold Vaccines: A Further Evaluation," *J.A.M.A.*, 115:593–94, (Aug. 24) 1940.

Downes, Jean: "Control of Acute Respiratory Illness by Ultra-Violet Lights," *Am. J. Pub. Health*, 40:1512–20, (Dec.) 1950.

Frost, W. H., and Gover, Mary: "The Incidence and Time Distribution of Common Colds in Several Groups Kept under Continuous Observation," *Pub. Health Rep.*, 47:1815–41, (Sept. 2) 1932.

Gover, Mary; Reed, Lowell J.; and Collins, Selwyn D.: "Time Distribution of Common Colds and Its Relation to Corresponding Weather Changes," *Pub. Health Rep.*, 49:811–24, (July 13) 1934.

McConnell, W. J.: "An Experiment with Triethylene Glycol Vapor for the Control of Colds among Office Employees," *Indust. Med.*, 18:192–96, (May) 1949.

Paul, J. H., and Freese, H. L.: "An Epidemiological and Bacteriological Study of the 'Common Cold' in an Isolated Arctic Community (Spitzbergen)," *Am. J. Hyg.*, 17:517–35, (May) 1933.

Siegel, Morris; Randall, Marian G.; Hecker, Muriel D.; and Reid, Mabel: "A Study on the Value of a Mixed Bacterial 'Oral Cold Vaccine,'" *Am. J. M. Sc.*, 205:687–92, (May) 1943.

Smillie, Wilson G.: "Observations on the Epidemiology of the Common Cold," *New England J. Med.*, 223:651–54, (Oct. 24) 1940.

United States Naval Medical Research Unit No. 4: "The Use of Triethylene Glycol Vapor for Control of Acute Respiratory Diseases in Navy Recruits," *Am. J. Hyg.*, 55:215–29, (Mar.) 1952.

"Use of Vaccines for the Common Cold. Status Report of Council on Pharmacy and Chemistry and Council on Industrial Health, American Medical Association," *J.A.M.A.*, 126:895–97, (Dec. 2) 1944.

29. Tuberculosis

Tuberculosis is a destructive disease which may involve almost any part of the body but is most frequently seen in the lungs. The body responds to the infection by the production of fibrous tissue and, in some cases, by calcification, which replaces the destroyed areas. The outcome of any case depends on the tissues involved and whether or not the fibrous repair processes develop more rapidly than the necrotic action. Symptoms vary according to the areas affected. In the typical case with involvement of the lungs, there may be a profuse sputum made up of pulmonary exudate and necrotic tissue. Most persons overcome their infection without detectable symptoms, while in many others the progress of the disease is arrested after a period of illness. Although tuberculosis is one of the most important causes of death, only a small percentage of those infected actually die of it. In infants and occasionally in older persons, the disease may run an acutely fatal course, but in most persons it is a long-drawn-out, chronic condition, frequently punctuated by remissions.

Tuberculosis is usually divided into two types, the primary infection and the reinfection. The former represents the initial response of the body to the infection and is usually manifested by a localized process in the lungs (Ghon's tubercle) or in the hilar lymph nodes. In most instances—and some persons believe in all instances—this is a benign process, healing by fibrosis and often followed by calcification. It is very doubtful if in most such cases the infection is cured; rather does it seem to be arrested in its progress, though leaving viable organisms in the sclerosed area. Such patients are sensitized to the tubercle bacillus. In certain instances, the infection in patients experiencing their first exposure to tuberculosis progresses to a generalized involvement, miliary tuberculosis, usually ending with a fatal meningitis. This is interpreted by some as an unfavorable response to the primary infection, by others as a superimposed reinfection before the primary has healed.[1] The reappearance of the active disease in a person who has successfully combated the primary infection is referred to as the reinfection type. This is essentially the destructive lesion seen in adults and is the type of infection so generally though of when speaking of tuberculosis.

EPIDEMIOLOGY

Occurrence. Being carried wherever man may go, tuberculosis occurs in all parts of the world. In former centuries, isolated tribes that had not been infected were encountered; but the disease was quickly introduced after their contact with civilization and often progressed with great rapidity and high fatality under such conditions.

During the latter part of the last century, it was frequently found that almost all of the bodies coming to autopsy showed some evidence of active or healed tuberculosis. This was an era during which tuberculosis was the leading cause of death and during which little was understood as to its mode of spread. As a consequence of the lack of precautions, the only thing that stopped the spread of infection was the death of the case. Today the incidence is markedly reduced. The tuberculosis death rate is a small fraction of the former figure and gives promise of further decline to an equally small fraction of the present rate.

The extent of infection in a community varies with the degree of congestion, economic circumstances, racial composition, the facilities for segregation of active cases, and the prevalence of bovine infection spread through milk. Only a few years ago, most adults and over 50 per cent of the children were infected as shown by the tuberculin test (see p. 358); today the rate in many parts of the country may be as low as 20 per cent in young adults and 10 per cent in school children.

The mortality rate varies in response to many of the same factors. In 1910 the rate for the United States registration area was 153.8 per 100,000 population; in 1949 it was 26.3. The present rate is somewhat higher in the South than in the North. The area of the Ohio and the Tennessee river valleys shows a disproportionately high rate for reasons that have not been explained. The rate is several times higher in Negroes than in whites; much of the high rate in some states is due to the high proportion of nonwhite population.

---

[1] The argument here is largely an academic one. The fact is that many infants die of tuberculosis if they are exposed to open cases within the family. In such instances, it is impossible to determine when and how often infection occurred or when one stage of the disease merged into the other.

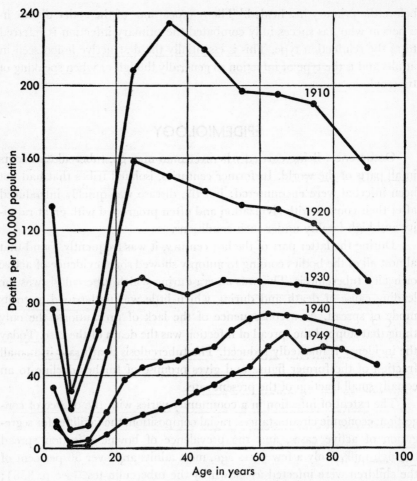

Fig. VIII. *Tuberculosis mortality rates by ages; death registration states of 1900.* (Anderson, Gaylord: "Epidemiology of Tuberculosis," *Am. Rev. Tuberc.,* 67:123–31, [February] 1953.)

During the past half century there has been not only a sharp decline in the tuberculosis death rate, but also a striking change in the age distribution of deaths (Fig. VIII). Formerly, the death rate was highest in young adult life; today it is highest after the age of forty. The sharp rise at puberty has almost disappeared from the male death rate curve, though persisting in greatly reduced degree for females. The female rate is slightly higher than the male rate during the usual period of childbearing, but after the age of forty the male rate is markedly higher. School age has always been the period of minimum death rate.

Etiological Agent. Tuberculosis is due to infection with the tubercle bacillus (*Mycobacterium tuberculosis*). Three strains are known: the human, the bovine, and the avian. The former is the one most commonly encountered in human infection, especially in cases of pulmonary tuberculosis. The bovine strain, though primarily an invader of cattle, is equally pathogenic for man, in whom it shows a predilection for other areas than the lung, especially the bones and joints. Human infections with the avian strain are very rare. The tubercle bacillus does not form spores but is more resistant to drying and other environmental factors than are most human pathogens. In sputum it may remain viable for several weeks because of the protective mucin covering. As this same mucin may protect it from the action of certain chemicals, disinfection through heat, especially burning, is the method chosen to deal with the discharges of tuberculosis cases. The bacillus is destroyed through pasteurization.

Reservoir of Infection. Tuberculosis is contracted chiefly from other persons who are infected, less commonly from cattle. The latter, which were at one time an important source—especially for the extrapulmonary type of disease—are today of minor consequence, due to the advent of pasteurization and the virtual eradication of tuberculous cattle. Infection of the primary type always represents invasion of the organisms from some external source; the reinfection type may be of either endogenous or exogenous origin. Endogenous reinfection represents a reactivation of the primary process with destruction of the fibrous tissues that have walled off the previously infected area. This permits escape of the tubercle bacilli and their dissemination to other areas, usually in the lung by direct spread from one air sac to another. Occasionally spread occurs by the blood stream, thereby resulting in involvement of distant organs. Exogenous reinfection represents the entry of new organisms and the development of a new disease process. As the body is already allergic to the tubercle bacilli, the type of response is different from that which is seen in the primary infection.

Much uncertainty exists regarding the relative importance of exogenous and endogenous reinfection. Two different schools of thought have developed, one of which believes that the reinfection type is usually of endogenous origin, the other that it is chiefly exogenous. The evidence for each is so strong that one must accept the idea that both forms are possible, though it is not certain which occurs the more frequently. In an individual case it must depend on opportunities for re-exposure and the body response to its primary infection. Endogenous reinfection can obviously occur in the absence of further exposure; exogenous implies exposure and therefore requires contact with an open case. In areas in which the tuberculosis infection rate is low, the majority of the reinfections may well be of endogenous origin. On the other hand, in areas in which the rate is high and in which there is a large number of open cases as shown by a high tuberculosis mortality rate, there can be no doubt that the exogenous source is the more important. The relative frequency of endogenous and of exogenous reinfections must depend upon the amount of active infection in the community and therefore the risk of exposure.

The existence of tuberculous infection and, therefore, the size of the potential reservoir may be discovered by means of the tuberculin test. This test depends upon the fact that, in the presence of infection, the body acquires a sensitivity to the proteins of the tubercle bacillus and consequently reacts in a characteristic manner at the time of their subsequent introduction. The test is usually performed by introducing into the skin either an extract of the tubercle bacillus, referred to as old tuberculin (usually abbreviated to O.T. or merely tuberculin), or a purified protein derivative (P.P.D.) [2] made through growth of the tubercle bacilli on a special synthetic medium. If the body is sensitive, a raised, edematous, and reddened area will appear in two to three days at the site of the test but will gradually disappear. A positive test is evidence of infection but does not indicate whether the process is active or quiescent. Further study of the patient, including x-ray examination, is necessary to determine the status of the infection.

Three forms of the tuberculin test are commonly employed. (1) The Mantoux test, which is used most extensively in this country, depends on the intradermal injection of the test material. In most instances a dose of 0.1 cc of a 1/10,000 dilution of tuberculin (0.01 mg) is used. Those who fail to react are retested with a dose of 0.1 mg, while those who still fail to react are given 1 mg. The majority of the reactors are detected on the first test. It is generally desirable to start with the weaker dilutions as some persons who are infected show rather severe local and constitutional reactions to the larger doses. (2) The von Pirquet modification is a scratch test, whereby a somewhat less accurately measured amount of the material is inserted into the skin. It has the advantage of simplicity and avoidance of retesting those who fail to react to the weaker dilutions, but it fails to reveal a small, yet significant, group of reactors. (3) The patch test (Vollmer test) depends upon the absorption of tuberculin or P.P.D. into the skin. The test material is contained in a small tape that is strapped to the skin. The method has the advantage of simplicity and avoidance of use of needles or scarifiers but lacks the precision of the Mantoux test, for the amount that may be absorbed will vary with different persons, depending upon the character of the epidermis.

The sensitivity on which the tuberculin test is based develops as a result of the primary infection and apparently disappears if the bacilli are destroyed in the process of combating this early invasion. The test is therefore

[2] One milligram of P.P.D. is approximately equivalent to 100 mg of O.T.

used to detect infection, though it gives no measure of the activity of the process. It was formerly used extensively in case-finding programs as a screen to pick out those who required x-ray examinations and is still used as a measure of the extent of infection (though not necessarily of clinically recognizable disease) within a community. With the development of improved and simplified x-ray techniques, and especially the photofluorograph, tuberculin testing has been almost entirely discarded as a screening technique.

Escape of the organisms depends on the location of the active lesion within the body. In the pulmonary case it occurs with the sputum. The organisms may leave through the urine if there is involvement of the kidney; through the feces if the intestine is affected; and through draining sinuses if these connect with areas of local involvement such as abscesses. A person who is discharging viable organisms is referred to as an "open case." Infection and spread are not synonymous. If the involvement of the lung has not yet developed to the point at which the necrosis has broken through to an air sac, organisms will not escape. When this necrotic area of infection ruptures into an air passage, the bacilli may appear in the sputum.[3] As it is usually impossible to determine when these minute areas rupture and the case becomes a spreader, it is commonly assumed that any patient who shows evidence of active progression of the disease is at least a potential spreader.

Escape of the organisms from the infected cow is through the sputum, manure, or milk. Many tuberculous cattle show pulmonary involvement, with resultant sputum. Some of this escapes through the mouth, but much more passes through the intestine and is discharged with the manure. About 2 per cent of the cattle slaughtered under the federal tuberculosis testing program showed active lesions in the udder with resultant discharge of bacilli in the milk. Although many infected cattle are not shedding the organisms at a particular time, one must assume that any infected cow is potentially a spreader.

Transmission of infection is usually by direct respiratory contact through the medium of infected droplets. Although in former years much attention was given to the possibility of spread through fomites, there is little evidence to show that they have much significance as contrasted with the great spread through respiratory association. Being contaminated either within the udder or by particles of manure, milk may serve as an important vehicle of bovine infection. The latter type of contamination is especially likely to occur if the cow, while lying in the field or barnyard,

---

[3] Similarly, the patient with a tuberculous abscess does not discharge the bacilli until the infection has burrowed its way through to the skin.

soils the outer surface of the udder and if the minute particles of manure drop into the pail at the time of milking. Proper cleansing of the udder before milking will reduce this risk. The importance of the contamination of other foods by an open case is a matter of conjecture. Viable bacilli may unquestionably be so spread, though it may be difficult to show that the number of infections so contracted is significant as compared with the risk from respiratory contact with the food handlers.

Entry and Incubation Period. Entry into the new host may be through either the respiratory or the intestinal tract. Because of the indefinite character of the early lesion, the incubation period is not clearly determinable in any single case, though it is known that a person may become sensitive to tuberculin within three weeks after exposure to an open case. One may conclude that the development of the initial lesion requires only a few days or weeks.

Susceptibility. Great uncertainty and difference of opinion exist regarding susceptibility and resistance to tuberculosis. It is generally agreed that all persons are susceptible to infection and that no high level of resistance develops comparable to that against diphtheria, measles, or certain other infections. Some maintain, however, that a person who has had a primary infection, as shown by a positive tuberculin test, is more resistant to active pulmonary involvement than is a person who has never been infected and has, therefore, a negative test. The opposite school of thought believes that the person who has had a primary infection and, therefore, a positive test is more susceptible to reinfection. In favor of the former belief may be cited the following evidence: (1) experimental animals who have had a primary infection are more resistant to reinfection than are those never previously exposed to tubercle bacilli; and (2) nurses and medical students who have had a primary infection (positive tuberculin test) are less likely to develop active tuberculosis than are those who have not (negative test).

In support of the hypothesis that prior infection results in increased susceptibility are the facts that: (1) children who are tuberculin positive are more likely to develop active tuberculosis and die of it than are children who are tuberculin negative; and (2) the death rate from tuberculosis is disproportionately high in the older age groups which show the highest incidence of prior tuberculosis infection.

In the opinion of the authors, these two schools of thought are not as incompatible with one another as many persons would believe. The apparent differences appear to rest more in the opportunities for exposure to reinfection than in personal resistance. A person who has a primary infection can obviously be reinfected from either endogenous or exogenous sources, whereas the tuberculin-negative individual is exposed only to exogenous risks. It is thus true that the former has two sources of danger as compared to only one for the latter. In the absence of sources of exogenous infection, the only person who can develop the dangerous and often fatal reinfection type is the one who has previously acquired a primary infection as manifested by a positive tuberculin test. The higher incidence of reinfection in children who are tuberculin positive is, however, to be explained not so much on differences in susceptibility as on the basis of a higher degree of exposure. The very fact that those children have become infected shows that they have greater exposure to open cases of tuberculosis than have children who are tuberculin negative. Thus their subsequent breakdown is a measure not so much of resistance as of exposure. On the other hand, studies of persons exposed to equal degrees of infection, such as nurses or medical students working in a hospital or patients in mental disease hospitals in which there is inadequate segregation of open cases, show that the tuberculin-positive group is less likely to develop active tuberculosis than is the tuberculin-negative group. It seems fair to conclude therefore that: (1) If no exposure to infection exists, a person whose tuberculin test is positive may develop reinfection, while one whose test is negative cannot. (2) If equal exposure to infection exists, a person whose tuberculin test is positive is less likely to develop active tuberculosis than is one whose test is negative. (3) If the risk of exposure is great, the partial resistance that comes from a primary infection may be more significant and important than the risk of endogenous reinfection, and the primary infection therefore serves as a protective asset against exogenous reinfection. (4) If the risk of exposure is small, the prior infection constitutes a liability as a source of endogenous reinfection.

Aside from factors of sensitivity to the tubercle bacillus, many nonspecific factors enter into resistance to tuberculosis. During puberty and early adult life, there is a rapid increase in the reinfection type among persons who had their primary infection in childhood. This would suggest certain autarceologic factors, possibly of an endocrine nature. Fatigue and malnutrition appear also to affect resistance and conduce to breakdown of the person whose infection has become quiescent.

CONTROL MEASURES

Control of Spread

The Case. Any person with active tuberculosis should be considered potentially infectious, even though the organisms cannot be demonstrated in the sputum or other discharges. The patient should be segregated insofar as possible from other persons except the essential medical and nursing personnel, thus reducing opportunity of spreading infection. Ideally, every active case should be cared for in a hospital or a sanatorium and thus reduce the risk of exposing the family. In practice, this is often not possible because of lack of hospital facilities or the unwillingness or financial inability of the patient to undergo long hospitalization and separation from the family.[4]

Most states provide for some form of public assistance for persons in need of hospitalization and give aid to the family during the absence of the wage earner. It must be remembered, however, that even with such aid the economic circumstances of the family will be reduced. If the patient is a war veteran or ex-service man, contact should be made with the Veterans Administration for assistance in providing hospitalization.

If hospitalization is not possible or if it must be deferred until a vacancy occurs, provision for home care must be made. Under such circumstances the assistance of the public health nurse in giving home care and instruction is invaluable. Yet it must be remembered that the longer hospitalization is delayed the less the chance that the patient can be persuaded to consent to removal from the home.

Surgical procedures for removal of part of an infected lung or collapsing it to facilitate healing are being used to an increasing extent. In addition to benefiting the patient, they have the further advantage of reducing the amount of sputum and, therefore, the discharge of viable organisms. An open case may become a closed one under such treatment. Many patients on whom collapse therapy has been started may be safely discharged from a sanatorium to continue treatment at home and may return to the outpatient department or a clinic for reinjection of air into the pleural sac. In some instances, collapse therapy has been conducted entirely on an ambulatory basis, thus avoiding hospitalization yet keeping the patient noninfectious. Many believe that hospitalization and collapse therapy have been just as valuable (and some think more valuable) in reducing spread as in caring for the patient. Unfortunately, however, they have not attained their maximum potential value, as over three-fourths of all patients reaching such institutions are in the advanced or moderately advanced stages and have therefore spread a great deal of infection before their condition is recognized and proper precautions taken. This means that more active case-finding measures are imperative.

---

[4] In some states, hospitalization may be mandatory, yet health departments often hesitate to use compulsion lest other patients defer diagnosis and care for fear of removal from the home. Persuasion is always better than compulsion, though the latter must be used in selected cases.

Epidemiological Investigation. Every case of tuberculosis, as of any other communicable disease, immediately raises three questions: (1) from whom has the patient contracted the infection, (2) to whom has the patient given the infection, and (3) who else has been infected from the same source? Every case merits careful and intensive epidemiological investigation from these points of view. This means examination of all contacts by using the tuberculin test to determine the presence of infection and the x-ray and physical examination as a measure of activity of the disease. The highest incidence of infection and of active cases will be found in the immediate family circle. Some studies have shown as many as 20 per cent of the household contacts have an active process sufficiently advanced to merit hospitalization at the time the first case in the family comes to official attention. First attention should consequently be directed to the household contacts. After these have been examined, the less intimate contacts, including more distant relatives, school and business associates, and other persons in more or less close association with the patient, should be examined. The less intimate the contact, the lower the incidence of infection that will be found and, therefore, the less return for the money and energy expended. Particular attention should be paid to the contacts over forty years of age as this is the group in which the highest rate of infection will be found.

The nature of the examination will vary with the type of association and the results of the initial test. All contacts should be given a tuberculin test and x-ray examination. If the latter suggests active infection, further clinical study is required—usually repeated examinations at suitable intervals. For a period of several years, especially during adolescence and early adult life, all reactors should be subjected to periodic examination by x-ray for evidence of development of an active process. The number of infected child contacts whose infection, once quiescent, flares into activity is so low that little value accrues from annual x-rays before the age of 15. Contacts who are found to be tuberculin negative should be retested at suitable intervals to detect evidence of infection.

Case-finding Surveys. The high proportion (60 to 80 per cent) of advanced cases among patients reaching sanatoria is evidence of the fact that most tuberculosis is overlooked in its early stages, thus reducing the chances of cure and favoring spread. Therefore, a need exists for an extensive and systematic program of finding cases in their early stages. Surveys have been used extensively for this purpose.

Surveys are usually performed by x-ray examination of all who volunteer. For many years, testing by use of x-rays was too expensive for mass programs, but development of the small-sized photofluorograph has made available a screening device which is rapid, economical, and of acceptable accuracy. All those who are found to have suspicious shadows are referred to their family physician or to a clinic for re-examination by the conventional 14 by 17 film. In a community program, only those 15 years of age or over are usually examined. In former years, screening was done by use of the tuberculin test with x-ray examination of those who reacted positively, and emphasis was placed on children of school age. This type of program has almost entirely disappeared. Tuberculin testing was cumbersome and not too well accepted as it involved intradermal injection; the x-ray is far more readily accepted by the public. Emphasis has also been shifted away from children toward the adult group and especially those over 40 years of age. Special attention has been given to industrial groups, as these so commonly yield an appreciable number of previously unrecognized infections.

If testing of school children is to be carried on, it should be offered as late as possible in school life yet not so late as to miss a sizable group that drop out of school before completion of the normal course. This means testing about the middle of the high school period. Such tests are incomplete, however, unless some attempt is made to find the source of infection of children who show positive reactions. In some communities testing of all children entering school has been attempted, with examination of the family contacts of all reactors. Varying degrees of success have been reported from such programs. Routine examination of college students either by tuberculin testing or x-ray has revealed active cases who might otherwise spread infection within the institution. Similarly, routine x-ray examination of all patients entering a general hospital reveals a certain number of previously unsuspected infections. Besides benefiting the patient, such discovery reduces the risk of exposure of the nursing attendants. Where facilities exist, routine fluoroscopy will quickly bring to light the majority of infected cases.

Opinions differ as to the value of community-wide surveys. Undoubtedly cases are found that would have gone undetected in the absence of a survey. The discovery of these makes earlier treatment possible and also reduces the likelihood of spread to associates. Even if hospitalization facilities are lacking ambulatory collapse therapy favors cure and minimizes the risk of spread and epidemiologic follow-up may lead to unsuspected sources of infection. Thus there is unquestioned value from such surveys even if few cases are found.

On the other hand, the health department must remember it is always operating under very limited financial resources and that tuberculosis is only one of its many problems. The department may well question whether the large amount of money needed for the survey and the necessary follow-up will yield bigger returns in this program or in dealing with some other problem of equal or greater importance. If the infection rate is high, as in an industrial group or one subjected to overcrowding, poverty, and neglect, such surveys will yield a fairly high return of previously unrecognized cases. In other groups, such as school children in a community in which the infection rate is low, the yield is often so low that there may be serious doubt as to the value of a survey. At best, surveys detect only those cases that are diagnosable at the moment. Active disease can develop within a year among persons who were negative during the survey. Surveys should be used only to supplement and never to supplant other methods of case-finding and only if the necessary funds can be made available without neglecting other parts of the public health program. In too many communities, wholesale testing of school children has been promoted even though family contacts have been largely neglected and facilities are lacking for hospitalization or care of the cases already known. It would seem that the money spent on wholesale testing under such conditions might yield better results if directed toward the contacts and provision of care for the known cases.

Diagnostic Facilities. Adequate diagnostic facilities are indispensable to any case-finding program. Many communities provide for clinics, to which any person suspecting tuberculosis in himself may go for examination. In other instances, the health department clinics are operated on a consultation basis, whereby the family physician refers suspected cases to the clinic for examination by a specialist who has x-ray facilities. Some of these clinics are connected with a local or state tuberculosis sanatorium, either as outpatient departments or as traveling clinics making periodic visits to areas where adequate facilities might otherwise be lacking. In the latter instances, the necessary x-ray films may be taken with a portable machine, or the equipment of a local hospital may be utilized. Laboratory facilities should also be available for bacteriological examination of sputum and other discharges.

Contacts. No quarantine precautions are required. Case-finding among contacts has been considered above.

Environmental sanitation plays a relatively minor role in tuberculosis control. General measures of cleanliness, epecially around cases, will undoubtedly destroy some organisms, but the amount of infection transmitted through fomites is small compared with that spread directly from person to person. Better housing may reduce congestion and therefore the chances of spread. Improved economic circumstances are usually reflected in better nutrition. The only important environmental measures, aside from concurrent disinfection in the care of the recognized case, are those in connection with spread through milk. Tuberculin testing of cattle and destruction of reactors have brought about a virtual eradication of bovine infection, while pasteurization will control the small remaining risk of spread through milk from infected cattle or from human contamination. Elimination of the common drinking cup and sanitation of eating utensils contribute in some degree to reduce spread.

Disinfection. Procedures in Group II, page 144, should be followed.

Minimizing Ill Effects

Adequate treatment of recognized cases is one of the most important parts of any tuberculosis control program. Treatment serves two purposes: prolongation of the life of the patient and prevention of further spread through converting an open case into a closed one. In former years treatment was largely a matter of rest and nourishing diet, with medical attention to the relief of symptoms. Under such circumstances sanatoria were largely rest homes. Today treatment relies more and more on antibiotics and on surgical procedures for removal of affected portions of lungs. This means that elaborate hospital facilities must be available and that the rest-home type of sanatorium is no longer adequate (see p. 362). Preventoria and fresh air camps for children have yielded disappointingly few results for the large sums required for their maintenance.

Public health nursing care has a dual objective in all cases and especially in tuberculosis, namely, prevention of spread and promoting the comfort and general welfare of the patient. Although in diseases such as measles the latter is of chief importance, the former is the more significant in the home care of the tuberculous. Home care introduces a hazard of spread of infection to other persons, especially the family contacts. The actual nursing care of the patient is relatively simple as contrasted with the obvious difficulty of preventing spread.

The nurse must be thoroughly familiar with the reasons why home care is being used in each particular instance in preference to institutionalization. If the family is reluctant to send the patient to a sanatorium, the nurse should be prepared to point out the advantages of institutional care; if there is merely a delay while awaiting an empty bed in a hospital, she must be prepared to combat a growing feeling that home care is adequate as the family adjusts itself to the new routine of life. The nurse's first responsibility is to ascertain the wishes of the attending physician with respect to such care and to adjust her program of instruction accordingly. When institutionalization is to be urged, she may need to exercise all her understanding of human nature in dealing with the family and the patient.

The patient who remains at home should have contact with as few persons as possible. If the patient is in bed—and most patients are, in the early stages of treatment—restricting the number of persons who are allowed into the sickroom will suffice. It is especially important to keep small children out of the room. If the patient remains ambulatory or the home conditions are such that a separate room cannot be set aside for the patient, an attempt should be made to remove all children from the home until hospitalization can be arranged. All articles used by the patient should be kept separate and preferably be left in the room except when removed for cleaning. The sputum should be caught in suitable paper cups and burned.[5] The patient should be taught the importance of covering his mouth and nose whenever coughing and especially when being given nursing attention.

The patient who remains at home must usually have complete rest. The meaning of rest must be explained so that the patient and family understand that even such activities as reading, talking, and sitting up in bed are "exercise." If the patient is not allowed to go to the toilet, the public health nurse should find out whether or not the family can secure a bedpan and, if necessary, assist them in making the necessary arrangements. No special diet is usually required; the ordinary, well-balanced diet with a quart of milk a day is satisfactory. As the patient is confined to bed, he often has very little appetite. The nurse can be helpful in suggesting easily digested foods which may appeal.

Sometimes the physician orders streptomycin for the patient who is cared for at home pending admission to a sanatorium or who expects to remain at home. The nurse should be familiar with the side effects of the drug so that she may reassure the patient and his family and also so that she may know what to report to the physician. It is not uncommon that patients taking this antibiotic are nauseated, find difficulty in eating, sometimes have ringing in their ears, and may expect some dizziness. Although all of these symptoms may be expected in a mild degree, they should be reported to the physician at once if they occur. There are no nursing measures known at the present time which can alleviate these symptoms.

Number of Nursing Visits. As tuberculosis is a long, chronic disease, the nurse should plan to make periodic visits to the family. While the patient remains at home, these will be as often as needed to teach the attendant the necessary care. Subsequent visits will be necessary to encourage the patient to strict adherence to the treatment program and to assist with any nursing problems that may arise. When the patient goes to the sanatorium, it may be necessary to visit the family occasionally to assist

[5] Old paper or rags will suffice if special receptacles cannot be provided.

with general health supervision, though, if the contacts are seen regularly at clinic, it may not be important to make home visits. When the patient is about to be discharged from the sanatorium, the health department should be notified so that it can make a nursing visit to the home to assist the family in such preparations as are necessary for the return of the patient. After the return of the patient, a further visit should be made promptly to assist him and the family in adjusting to the new home situation.

Control through Immunization

Active immunization is one of the most controversial aspects of all tuberculosis control programs. About thirty years ago, Calmette and Guerin described a vaccine (BCG) made from a bovine strain of organisms that had been attenuated through prolonged culture on artificial medium. This is a living vaccine, the effectiveness of which depends upon the establishment of a localized primary infection with resultant sensitivity to the tubercle bacillus. The use of the antigen presupposes the correctness of the theory that allergy due to a primary infection confers some resistance against later exogenous reinfection. The primary infection in BCG vaccination differs from that of natural infection only in the fact that it is caused by an organism of such reduced virulence that it will neither produce a malignant primary nor serve as a source of later endogenous reinfection. While many sceptics have expressed doubts as to the permanence of the attenuation, there is a growing mass of evidence to indicate that these fears are without foundation and that the vaccine is truly harmless. Persons who, because of exposure, are almost certain to become infected may better be given their primary infection with an organism of reduced virulence than be permitted to acquire infection with one of high virulence.

Much of the current controversy centers around the question of efficacy. It is easy to find flaws in most of the reported studies; yet one cannot overlook the overwhelming weight of evidence in favor of BCG vaccine. It has been used for over a score of years in the Scandinavian countries, with consistently lower tuberculosis rates among the vaccinated than among the controls. The studies of Ferguson in Canada and of Aronson and of Palmer in the United States have amply confirmed the Scandinavian findings. At present, BCG is finding community-wide use in many parts of Europe and South America where the tuberculosis rate (and therefore the risk of natural infection) is high. The American Trudeau Society, after careful study of the evidence, agreed upon the following recommendation regarding the use of BCG vaccine:

I. BCG vaccine prepared under acceptable conditions, and administered by approved techniques to persons negative to tuberculin, can be considered harmless.

II. The degree of protection recorded following vaccination is by no means complete, nor is the duration of induced relative immunity permanent or predictable............

III. On the basis of studies reported in the literature, an appreciable reduction in the incidence of clinical tuberculosis may be anticipated when certain groups of people who are likely to develop tuberculosis because of unusual exposure, inferior resistance, or both, are vaccinated.

    (a) In the light of present knowledge, vaccination of the following more vulnerable groups is recommended, provided they do not react to adequate tuberculin tests:

        1. doctors, medical students, and nurses who are exposed to tuberculosis;

        2. all hospital and laboratory personnel whose work exposes them to contact with the bacillus of tuberculosis;

        3. individuals who are unavoidably exposed to infectious tuberculosis in the home;

        4. patients and employees in mental hospitals, prisons, and other custodial institutions in whom the incidence of tuberculosis is known to be high;

        5. children and certain adults considered to have inferior resistance and living in communities in which the tuberculosis mortality rate is unusually high.

IV. ....

V. The Society believes that, since BCG vaccination affords only incomplete rather than absolute protection, the most effective methods of controlling tuberculosis in the general population are:

    (a) further improvement of living conditions and the general health;

    (b) reduction of tuberculous infection, which can be accomplished by modern public health methods and the unremitting search among presumably healthy individuals for patients with infectious tuberculosis;

    (c) prompt and adequate medical and surgical treatment of patients with active disease;

    (d) segregation and custodial care of those not amenable to accepted forms of therapy;

    (e) adequate rehabilitation.

VI. It is to be emphasized that BCG vaccination must not be regarded as a substitute for approved hygienic measures or for public health practices designed to prevent or minimize tuberculous infection and disease. Vaccination should be regarded as only one of many procedures to be used in tuberculosis control.

VII. ....[6]

[6] *Am. Rev. Tuberc.*, **60**:681–82, (Nov.) 1949.

In the light of these recommendations and the evidence upon which they are based, more extensive use of BCG vaccine is indicated. It is administered either orally or by intradermal injection and given only to those who do not react to the tuberculin test. It must not be given to persons who are already infected as shown by a positive tuberculin test. Thus use of the vaccine is limited to those who have been tested and found to have a negative reaction, except in those instances in which the vaccine is administered to newborn infants before they have had time to acquire natural infection. It is to be further emphasized that BCG vaccine is to be thought of as a measure to supplement other control measures and never as a substitute for case-finding or procedures designed to protect persons from natural exposure. There are many situations, however, in which the conventional measures fail or cannot be adequately applied. Here, BCG apparently finds its proper use to supplement but not supplant other control practices.

SUMMARY

Health Department Program

A well-balanced community program should consist of four parts:

1. Case-finding, including (a) epidemiological investigation of all cases and deaths; (b) clinics and laboratory facilities for diagnosis of suspected cases; (c) routine follow-up of infected family contacts to detect the earliest signs of active infection; (d) routine testing of certain groups in which the infection rate is high; and (e) routine testing of other groups, provided funds are still available after satisfactory development of other parts of the control program.

2. Care of active cases, including hospitalization, provision for ambulatory collapse therapy, and home care of cases that cannot be hospitalized.

3. Routine follow-up of patients discharged from active care to make certain that the process has not become active again.

4. Rehabilitation of arrested cases so that they may be placed in a gainful occupation consistent with the regulated life generally needed by such patients.

The health officer is responsible for the general direction of the program and must assume the initiative in coordinating the various community resources to be used to this end. Under his direction, the board of health should provide for the epidemiological investigation of all cases and the periodic re-examination of arrested cases and of contacts. In the larger communities, the needed x-ray and clinical facilities may be locally available. In smaller places, it may be preferable to transport the patients to the sanatoria or suitable hospitals for examination. Traveling clinics equipped with portable x-ray machines may frequently be useful, especially if they visit the area frequently enough to avoid long delays. The plan best adapted to a community depends on local conditions, but the health officer is responsible for making certain that such facilities are available and are used. Hospitalization may be the responsibility of either the board of health or of welfare agencies, but in any case the health officer must make certain that such care is available for all patients and especially for those with numerous child contacts whom they might otherwise infect. The welfare agencies, either public or private, provide for the care of families left financially dependent by the hospitalization of the wage earner and must often care for children whose mother is hospitalized. To the public health nurse falls the task of many of the routine visits to any active cases at home, to the arrested cases, and to contacts to arrange for examination. Under the direction of the health officer, she will perform a large part of the epidemiological investigation. She must be constantly alert for cases of suspected early infection which should be referred to the physician for medical examination. Where programs of routine testing exist, she must explain the value and the purpose of such tests. The school authorities are frequently called upon to assist in such programs.

The role of the **voluntary agency** in tuberculosis control is extremely variable in different communities. Its basic purpose is that of creating public interest through education. Because of the inadequacy of most official programs, the local tuberculosis associations, which are all affiliated with the National Tuberculosis Association, have often spent large portions of their funds to carry on service programs. These include the support of nursing services, case-finding programs, preventoria, summer camps, and even direct care. Although these have served an extremely useful purpose in providing facilities that might otherwise be lacking, utilization of them should not blind the health officer or the community to the fact that many of these are governmental responsibilities and ought not to be shouldered permanently by a private agency, the primary function of which is to create interest in the problem of tuberculosis control.

SUGGESTED READINGS

Anderson, Robert J., and Palmer, Carroll E.: "BCG," *J.A.M.A.*, **143**:1048–51, (July 12) 1950.

Aronson, Joseph D.: "Protective Vaccination against Tuberculosis with Special Reference to BCG Vaccination," *Am. Rev. Tuberc.*, **58**:255–81, (Sept.) 1948.

Aronson, Joseph D., and Aronson, Charlotte Ferguson: "Appraisal of Protective Value of BCG Vaccine," *J.A.M.A.*, **149**:334–43, (May 24) 1952.

Bates, Richard C., and Davey, Winthrop N.: "Tuberculosis in Medical and Nursing Students," *Am. Rev. Tuberc.*, 63:332–38, (Mar.) 1951.

Birkhaug, Konrad: "BCG Vaccination in Scandinavia. Twenty Years of Uninterrupted Vaccination against Tuberculosis," *Am. Rev. Tuberc.*, 55: 234–49, (Mar.) 1947.

Bloom, Sophia: "Some Economic and Emotional Problems of the Tuberculosis Patient and His Family," *Pub. Health Rep.*, 63:448–55, (Apr. 2) 1948.

Bryant, Zella: "Tuberculosis Case Finding in General Hospitals," *Pub. Health Rep.*, 65:710–22, (June) 1950.

Burke, M. H.; Schenk, H. C.; and Thrash, J. A.: "Tuberculosis Studies in Muscogee County, Georgia. II. X-Ray Findings in a Community-Wide Survey and Its Coverage as Determined by a Population Survey," *Pub. Health Rep.*, 64:263–90, (Mar. 4) 1949.

Cady, Louise: "Understanding the Tuberculosis Patient," *Pub. Health Nursing*, 36:622–23, 633, (Dec.) 1944.

Chadwick, Henry D., and Pope, Alton S.: *Modern Attack on Tuberculosis*, rev. ed. New York: Commonwealth Fund, 1946.

"Community-Wide Chest X-ray Survey":

    I. Anon.: "Introduction," *Pub. Health Rep.*, 65:1277–91, (Oct. 6) 1950.

    II. Bryant, Zella, and Jones, Genevieve S.: "Nursing," *ibid.*, 65:1573–87, (Dec. 1) 1950.

    III. Bloom, Sophia: "Social Work," *ibid.*, 66:139–56, (Feb. 2) 1951.

    IV. Reisner, David, and Rikli, Arthur: "Diagnostic Clinic," *ibid.*, 66: 423–43, (Apr. 6) 1951.

    V. Pamplona, Paul A.: "The Medical Profession," *ibid.*, 66:1596–1612, (Dec. 7) 1951.

    VI. Enterline, Philip E., and Sauer, Herbert I.: "Records and Reports," *ibid.*, 66:1613–24, (Dec. 7) 1951.

Derryberry, Mayhew: "The Nurse as a Teacher of Tuberculosis to the Family," *Nat. Tuberc. A. Tr.*, pp. 236–52, 1939.

Downes, Jean: "How Tuberculosis Spreads in a Rural Community," *Am. J. Pub. Health*, 26:30–36, (Jan.) 1936.

Drolet, Godias J., and Lowell, Anthony M.: "Whither Tuberculosis. A Statistical Review of Reports from Selected American and European Communities," *Dis. of Chest*, 21:527–61, (May) 1952.

Edwards, Herbert R.: "Tuberculosis Case-Finding: Studies in Mass Surveys," Supplement to *Am. Rev. Tuberc.*, Vol. 41, (June) 1940.

Ferguson, R. G.: "BCG Vaccination in Hospitals and Sanatoria of Saskatchewan," *Am. Rev. Tuberc.*, 54:325–38, (Oct.–Nov.) 1946. See also *Canad. J. Pub. Health*, 37:435–51, (Nov.) 1946.

Flahiff, E. W.: "The Occurrence of Tuberculosis in Persons Who Failed to React to Tuberculin, and in Persons with Positive Tuberculin Reaction," *Am. J. Hyg.*, 30(Sect. B):69–74, (Sept.) 1939.

Frost, W. H.: "How Much Control of Tuberculosis?" *Am. J. Pub. Health*, 27:759–66, (Aug.) 1937.

Hayes, Edward W.: *Tuberculosis As It Comes and Goes.* Springfield, Ill.: Charles C. Thomas, Publisher, 1947.

Hetherington, H. W., and Eshleman, Fannie: *Nursing in Prevention and Control of Tuberculosis.* New York: G. P. Putnam's Sons, 1950.

Joint Tuberculosis Nursing Advisory Service: *Safer Ways in Nursing.* New York: National Tuberculosis Association, 1948.

Long, Esmond F.: "Pathogenesis of Primary and Reinfection Types of Pulmonary Tuberculosis," *New England J. Med.,* 223:656–60, (Oct. 24) 1940.

McDougall, John B.: *Tuberculosis. A Global Study in Social Pathology.* Baltimore: Williams & Wilkins Co., 1949.

Myers, J. Arthur: *Man's Greatest Victory over Tuberculosis.* Springfield, Ill.: Charles C. Thomas, Publisher, 1940.

———: *Tuberculosis among Children and Adults,* 3rd ed. Springfield, Ill.: Charles C. Thomas, Publisher, 1951.

Plunkett, Robert E.: "Case-Finding: An Evaluation of Various Techniques," *Am. Rev. Tuberc.,* 39:256–65, (Feb.) 1939.

———: "Tuberculosis Control," *J.A.M.A.,* 113:2288–92, (Dec. 23) 1939.

Pope, Alton S.: "The Role of Contact Examinations in the Control of Tuberculosis," *New England J. Med.,* 217:421–24, (Sept. 9) 1937.

Puffer, Ruth R.: *Familial Susceptibility to Tuberculosis.* Cambridge: Harvard University Press, 1944.

Schneider, Leo V., and Robins, Morton: "Tuberculosis Case-Finding Survey Program of the Veterans Administration," *Pub. Health Rep.,* 67:189–95, (Feb.) 1952.

South, Jean: *Tuberculosis Handbook for Public Health Nurses.* New York: National Tuberculosis Association, 1950.

30. Syphilis and Gonorrhea

Syphilis and gonorrhea present one of the most important and challenging of current public health problems. Their importance is derived in part from their prevalence and in part from their debilitating and crippling effects. Few diseases are more disturbing in their social and economic aspects.

Although prenatal infection with syphilis frequently kills the fetus or causes the early death of the diseased infant, early acquired syphilis rarely kills or cripples. Yet a large proportion of the cases suffer late manifestations of the disease which may shorten life, seriously impair health, reduce economic ability, and affect the entire social life of the individual and his family. Gonorrhea rarely kills but, in both its early and later stages and particularly as the result of its complications, may be seriously incapacitating.

Since most of the spread occurs through sexual contact and since promiscuous sexual relations are responsible for the ultimate perpetuation of infection in the community, gonorrhea and syphilis are commonly referred to as venereal infections. The venereal diseases also include a number of other infections commonly spread through sexual promiscuity, the more important of which are chancroid, lymphogranuloma venereum, and granuloma inguinale.[1]

Many persons have taken exception to the term "venereal," as it implies sexual excess of an improper nature. It is pointed out that a person infected by a marital partner is guilty of no immorality and that the infant congenitally infected is equally undeserving of stigma. To avoid the unpleasant connotation of the term "venereal," some persons have suggested

[1] Although these other venereal diseases are quite prevalent, particularly in the South and in the tropics, the control programs go little further than to require, in some states, that they be reported. Little is known of the epidemiology of these diseases, and effective control procedures are wanting. Further consideration of these is therefore omitted from this volume, though suitable references will be found at the end of this chapter.

the term "social" disease. This seems equally inappropriate, as nonsexual social contacts may spread respiratory diseases, which, therefore, might just as readily be referred to as "social infections." Nelson has suggested the term "genitoinfectious" to refer to this group of conditions, a term which defines the focus of at least the primary infection, bears no implication of misbehavior, and has a parallel in the terms "gastrointestinal" and "genitourinary." The word has certain advantages and had some acceptance, as indicated by its use to refer to the syphilis and gonorrhea control divisions of certain health departments. Unfortunately, however, the acceptance has not increased since the term was first suggested. On the contrary, the wartime program of the military forces made such extensive use of the term "venereal" and so popularized the use of "V.D." as an abbreviation, that the term "genitoinfectious diseases" has found decreasing acceptance.

The common association of the venereal diseases with improper sexual relations introduces an element lacking in other infections and seriously complicates the development of a control program. Although no stigma should be attached to marital or congenital infections, the association of syphilis and gonorrhea with immorality is so common, involving over half of all cases, that the public inevitably feels differently toward these diseases than it does toward measles or diphtheria. Man is by nature so suspicious and uncharitable in his attitude toward his neighbors and so enjoys a bit of salacious gossip that he automatically assumes immorality (or ponders over its possibility) in every case of syphilis or gonorrhea. It is inevitable, therefore, that the infected person will feel a sense of shame, even though undeserved, and will strive in every way possible to avoid having his infection become generally known. Serious social repercussions may result from disclosure of his infection, even to members of his immediate family. These factors complicate the problem of control, yet they must be taken into consideration if a successful program is to be developed.

The frequent association with immorality also raises the question as to the degree to which control of these diseases should be combined with, or divorced from, moral teaching. It has at times been argued that syphilis and gonorrhea were the "wages of sin" and that fear of infection was a powerful deterrent to the person tempted to transgress the accepted moral code. It has, therefore, been argued that mere control of the diseases would increase immorality through removal of this supposedly powerful deterrent force. Not only is this questionable reasoning, but such an attitude ignores the heavy economic and social toll from these diseases, a toll which is largely preventable through application of measures already known. It would appear to be little less than criminal to permit a hypothesis, that has not stood the test of time, to stand in the way of control measures of proved efficacy. The large number of innocently infected victims is too great a sacrifice to platitudinous theory.

This does not mean that the moral aspect is to be ignored or that the health department has no interest in the social hygiene program. If there were no promiscuity, syphilis and gonorrhea would quickly disappear. Any steps to improve the moral structure of society will therefore assist in the control program. The job of the health department is to prevent the spread of disease through the use of medical and public health procedures. Morals are the special problem of the church and of social and police agencies. Each group plays its part in the program, but none should attempt to usurp the functions of the others. Nor should the health department await the Utopian era when the other groups will have achieved such strict observance of the moral code that syphilis and gonorrhea cease to exist through lack of opportunity to spread.

Although the mode of spread is quite similar in syphilis and gonorrhea, certain of the clinical and epidemiological manifestations are sufficiently different to warrant separate discussion. The control programs may be considered together.

SYPHILIS

Syphilis, often referred to as "the great imitator," may attack any part of the body; in this way it simulates a wide variety of conditions. The primary lesion, known as a chancre, appears at the site of entry of the organism about three to four weeks after exposure, although the incubation period may vary from eight days to eight weeks. The typical chancre is a painless ulcer which heals spontaneously after a variable period of time. It may be mistaken for some less serious lesion or may be overlooked, especially if located in the urethra, vagina, or mouth. The secondary stage, of which a generalized rash, sore throat, malaise, and fever are the most common manifestations, appears several weeks later, though it may be so slight as to escape recognition. The mucous membranes of the mouth, genitalia, and anus are affected by the rash. The moisture and heat of these areas bring about a desquamation of the epithelium with resultant open lesions known as "mucous patches." The secondary stage also heals spontaneously though there may be recurrences during the next two or three years.

A period of so-called "latency" follows the disappearance of the secondary stage. It has been estimated that this period of apparent or actual disease inactivity may continue for the remainder of the patient's life in about half of the infected cases, even in the absence of treatment. In at least half of the untreated cases, however, late manifestations of disease activity will appear. The period of apparent latency, in these cases, may vary from a year or two to twenty or thirty years or even more.

The characteristic lesion of late syphilis is an endarteritis, but the disease activity may be quite predominantly confined to a single organ or to the cardiovascular, central nervous, or skeletal system. The heart and large blood vessels and the central nervous system are the chief victims of the later stages of the disease. Cardiovascular syphilis (including aneurysm) is apparently more common in the Negro than in whites, whereas central nervous system involvement (paresis, tabes, meningitis, or various combinations of these) is more common among whites.

Congenital infections occur within the uterus through migration of the spirochete across the placental barrier into the fetal circulation. No primary lesion occurs, the first manifestation of the disease being analogous to the secondary stage of acquired syphilis. It may result in the death of the fetus and miscarriage or abortion, in stillbirth, in the birth of an acutely diseased infant, or in the birth of an apparently healthy infant. Involvement of the bones, eyes, hearing, and central nervous system results in characteristic late manifestations of congenital syphilis which may not make their clinical appearance until many years after birth.

EPIDEMIOLOGY

Occurrence. Syphilis is found in all parts of the world having contact with civilization. In primitive peoples, syphilis and civilization have often gone hand in hand. Numerous estimates have been made as to the prevalence of the disease in the United States, but generalization seems hazardous. Of the second million registrants examined in 1941 under the Selective Service Law, 4.89 per cent were found to be syphilitic. On the basis of one-day surveys in communities totaling 29,000,000 people, Usilton estimated that about 500,000 fresh infections came to medical attention each year. There is reason to believe that the total number of new cases may be at least double this number.

The prevalence of syphilis varies greatly with the racial and social composition of the community. The disease is generally more common in the colored than in the white races; the prevalence within an area therefore depends in part upon the ratio of Negroes to whites. Syphilis infection was found in 1.7 per cent of the whites among the second million selective service registrants and in 24.5 per cent of the colored. The prevalence of infection in the rural areas was only slightly lower than in the urban. A higher rate of infection is found in the economically poorer groups, but no class of society is devoid of syphilis. There is considerable evidence to suggest that the disease is declining in prevalence in certain foreign countries and in at least some parts of the United States.

Official morbidity reports suggest that syphilis is distributed among the sexes in the ratio of about three males to two females, but there is some reason [2] to believe that the prevalence is more nearly equal than these figures indicate. Approximately 75 per cent of the infections are acquired between the ages of 15 and 35 years, the peak being in the 25–30 year group in males and a year or two earlier in females. Congenital infections account for about 5 per cent of the total.

The incidence rose sharply at the end of World War I but declined steadily during the subsequent two decades. The outbreak of World War II found the infection rate at a record low level. There was a very appreciable wartime rise, but at no time did the incidence reach the rates of the prior war. Since 1945 the rate has further declined and at present is apparently at the lowest level ever recorded. There are probably many reasons for this decline; effective case-finding and treatment are undoubtedly important factors but certainly not the only ones.

Etiological Agent. Syphilis is due to the *Spirochaeta pallida* (*Treponema pallidum*). It is a very fragile organism, sensitive to drying and changes in temperature and incapable of prolonged survival or multiplication outside the human body. It is highly specific for man.

Reservoir of Infection. Syphilis is usually spread from persons who have an infection of less than three or four years' duration and who have open, early lesions or are suffering an infectious relapse. Under certain conditions patients may be infectious in the latent stage, even in the absence of detectable open lesions. There is still debate over whether the seminal fluid is infectious during latency, though the male, if untreated or inadequately treated, seems to be able to transmit syphilis by intercourse as long as ten years after infection. Syphilis in any stage is potentially communicable from the mother to the fetus within the uterus. Similarly, the disease may be transmitted by transfusion in the complete absence of external lesions. In all such instances, communicability apparently decreases with the age of the infection. Although there are no true, healthy carriers, the signs of early syphilis are so frequently missed and so many patients are potentially infectious through relapse after inadequate treatment that the disease is often spread by apparently healthy persons, many of whom think themselves cured. The prostitute who has not yet become infectious or who has a late, noncommunicable infection may harbor the organisms

[2] Results of premarital blood testing.

in the vagina, where they were deposited by a recent customer, and may thus infect a subsequent client. Congenital infections are rarely if ever communicable after the first year or two of life, when open, early lesions may be present.

Escape from the Reservoir. Syphilis furnishes an excellent example of the difference between infection and communicability. Although infection may persist for years, even for the lifetime of the patient, and be active throughout this time as manifested by the development of cardiovascular or central nervous system lesions, the period of communicability is relatively short, usually not over two to five years. This is due to the fact that, although the spirochete is multiplying and active in the body, it finds no mode of escape. The open lesions of the primary and secondary stages, and of early infectious relapse, contain innumerable spirochetes. These are predominantly upon those mucous surfaces which come into contact with other mucous surfaces during sexual intercourse or kissing. If seminal fluid carries the spirochete during latency, it also offers a mode of escape which would make intercourse dangerous even though open lesions are absent. Spirochetes may shower into the blood stream during periods of disease activity for many years, thus providing an occasional avenue of escape to a fetus or to the recipient of a blood transfusion. It has never been satisfactorily demonstrated, however, that the organisms are liberated with the discharges of late surface lesions other than on mucous surfaces. The more common skin lesions of late syphilis are usually considered not to be dangerous to others.

Transmission of infection is by direct physical contact with the open lesion, except by the rarest of accidents. This contact is usually through sexual intercourse or kissing, though physicians, dentists, and nurses have been infected on the hands through contact with unsuspected lesions. Infection via drinking cups and towels is theoretically conceivable, if these have been contaminated by open lesions and are brought almost immediately afterward into contact with the lips or skin of another person, the moisture of the article keeping the spirochete alive for a few minutes. This is apparently of very rare occurrence. There is no evidence that food or fomites, such as toilet seats and clothing, serve to spread syphilis, even though it is theoretically conceivable that under extraordinary circumstances this might occur. The fetus within the uterus is infected through transplacental transmission of the spirochete from the blood stream of the infected mother.

Entry of the spirochete is through the skin or mucosa in acquired syphilis and directly into the blood stream in congenital and transfusion infection. Differences of opinion exist as to the ability of the spirochete to penetrate unbroken skin, but it is generally conceded that an intact mucosa is no barrier to penetration. The organisms are distributed over the body, at first by way of the lymphatics and subsequently by the blood stream, within a very few hours after inoculation. Local chemical prophylaxis is less effective every hour after exposure and entirely ineffective after ten or twelve hours.

Susceptibility. There is no natural immunity to syphilis nor development of latent immunization without frank and detectable disease. The disease is, however, by no means so virulent today as it was some centuries ago, when the early stages frequently caused death and when the late forms of the disease caused extensive and horrible damage to both skin and bones. As long as the patient has syphilis, a new infection cannot be acquired, except that superinfection is possible before, and for a few days after, the appearance of the chancre. What is known as "cure" may be clinical and serological rather than biological, since reinfection of persons who are "cured" after the disease has become well established has never been satisfactorily proved. If cure is achieved shortly after the appearance of the chancre, however, subsequent reinfection is quite possible. In this latter case, cure may be biological in the sense that every spirochete has been killed. Whatever the cause of the resistance to reinfection, it has not been possible to take advantage of it for the artificial production of active or passive immunity.

GONORRHEA

Gonorrhea is an infection of the submucosa of certain areas of the genitourinary tract. Gonococcal infection may also involve certain mucosal areas and subserous tissues in other parts of the body, notably in the joints, rectum, and eyes. As the organism must penetrate the mucosa in order to reach the submucous tissues in which it can survive, infection is confined very largely to areas covered with epithelium of a single layer of cells or of the transitional type; stratified forms of mucous membrane are quite resistant to penetration. Genitourinary tract infection involves the urethra, prostate, vesicles, and epididymis in the male and involves the urethra, labia minora, cervix, endometrium, endosalpinx, and pelvic peritoneum in the female. Once implanted upon an accessible surface, the infection extends horizontally and penetrates perpendicularly until all the susceptible areas have been reached.

In the male, gonorrhea begins as an acute, purulent discharge from the anterior urethra. Unless infection is promptly checked, it extends to the posterior urethra, where it involves the prostate and usually the seminal vesicles, and may spread to the epididymis. As the acute stages subside, the discharge lessens and eventually disappears, although the prostate and other glands may harbor infection for months.

In the female, the urethra and cervix are usually infected at the same time, and involvement of the paraurethral and vulvovaginal glands follows promptly. During some subsequent menstrual period, the infection may extend through the uterus to the tubes and pelvic peritoneum. Although the resulting salpingitis and peritonitis are rarely fatal, they may cause extensive damage to the tubes, ovaries, and pelvic contents with resultant serious debility in future years. A substantial proportion of gynecological operations is necessitated by the aftereffects of gonococcal infection. Gonorrhea in the female is often complicated by an asymptomatic proctitis, due to direct spread of the discharge over the perineum to the anus.

Arthritis is the most frequent extragenital complication in both sexes; endocarditis and meningitis are rare. Gonococcal conjunctivitis in adults is usually secondary to the genitourinary infection. In infants it is usually the primary infection.

Infection in the female prior to puberty causes gonococcal vulvovaginitis, which differs from adult infection in that the epithelium of the vulva and vagina have not yet become stratified. It is extremely persistent but, since the child does not menstruate, extension to the uterus and pelvic cavity is relatively rare. Proctitis is a common complication and, in infants, seems to lead to arthritis in many cases. Cultural studies of vulvovaginal infections in children have shown that many (perhaps half) are not gonococcal in origin but caused by other members of the same group of Gram-negative diplococci which are common inhabitants of the upper respiratory tract. It is especially important that a diagnosis of gonorrhea in small girls should be substantiated by adequate cultural confirmation.

EPIDEMIOLOGY

Occurrence. Although no reliable figures are available, there are good grounds for believing that gonorrhea is one of the most prevalent of the acute infectious diseases. On the basis of one-day studies, Usilton estimated that over 1,000,000 fresh infections were medically recognized each year in the United States. These same studies showed that 500,000 cases are under medical care at all times. No one knows the number of cases that rely on self-medication or drugstore therapy, though the studies of the American Social Hygiene Association would suggest as numerous a group as that which seeks reputable medical attention. The Army found that the incidence of gonorrhea is about ten times that of syphilis. During the interwar period the incidence of gonorrhea showed no decline comparable to that of syphilis, possibly because of lack of suitable therapeutic agents. Since World War II, there has apparently been a substantial decline, attributed by many to the advent of the sulfonamides and antibiotics which have made rapid cures possible, thus reducing the size of the effective reservoir. Like syphilis, gonorrhea is most commonly acquired in early adult life, and infection is more common in the Negro than in whites.

Etiological Agent. Gonorrhea is due to the gonococcus (*Neisseria gonorrheae*), a very fragile, Gram-negative organism. Like the spirochete of syphilis, it does not withstand drying but dies almost immediately on escape from the body. Only in the past few years has it been possible to cultivate it readily in the laboratory.

Reservoir of Infection. Man is the only species known to be infected by the gonococcus. As long as gonococci are present in any area, the secretions or discharge from which can reach susceptible tissues of another person, the disease continues to be communicable.

Escape from the reservoir is through the secretions or discharges from the infected areas. Viable gonococci persist in the secretions of the prostate, cervix, and female accessory genital glands, long after the disappearance of symptoms or of signs detectable by physical examination. The male usually spreads the disease during the incubation stage, before infection is obvious, or in the late stages when the symptoms have subsided to the point where he thinks he is cured. Since many females have no suspicion of infection and since the signs and symptoms are not so characteristic as in the male, there is often little or no abstinence from intercourse unless the patient is incapacitated by an acute pelvic infection. In some women the disease seems to be particularly infectious just prior to, during, or immediately after, the menstrual period. Examination to determine cure must therefore be made at various stages of the menstrual cycle.

Transfer of infection to the adult genitourinary system is always through sexual contact; indirect transfer is so rare as to be negligible. Although adult eye infections are usually caused by direct transfer of infectious material from the genitalia to the eye, via the patient's own fingers, a physician or a nurse may develop ophthalmia from pus spattered into the eye during the examination or treatment of a patient. Gonococcal ophthalmia neonatorum is acquired during birth, through contact of the eyes with the infectious maternal discharges. How some of the later infections in infants occur is not clear.

Gonococcal vulvovaginitis in girls before puberty is probably acquired through some form of sexual contact. Careful bacteriological studies show that most of those cases of vulvovaginitis for which sources cannot be found in the home or in sexual contacts are probably nongonococcal. Among those with any considerable experience with this form of the disease, there is little acceptance of the old hypothesis that infection may be acquired from a toilet seat. Rectal thermometers have been the means of spreading infection within an institution. In such instances, the thermometer becomes contaminated through use on a girl who has an overlooked infection but who still has the rectal involvement almost invariably accompanying the vulvovaginitis. If there has been any carelessness in the cleaning of the thermometer, infection may be transferred almost directly from the rectum of one child to that of another in a hospital ward or nursery. The disease then becomes recognized through its extension from the rectum to the vulva in females or through the occurrence of gonococcal arthritis in either sex, particularly in infants.

Entry of Gonococcus. Infection usually begins in the anterior urethra and spreads to other areas with which it is in direct communication. Conjunctival involvement is due to direct introduction of the gonococcus into the conjunctival sac from outside the body. Infection of the rectum may occur either by spread over the perineal body to the anus or may be carried into the rectum by rectal thermometers or tubes or through sexual perversion.

Susceptibility. There is no evidence of either natural or acquired resistance to gonococcal infection. Repeated attacks may occur in the same person.

CONTROL OF SYPHILIS AND GONORRHEA

Because of the mode of spread and the popular stigma attached to infection with syphilis or gonorrhea, the administrative approach to these diseases must be somewhat altered from that conventionally followed for other infections. The patient is not anxious and usually not willing to have his condition made known to his friends, who will accord him scorn and neglect rather than the sympathy that goes with most illnesses. He will frequently prefer to take his chance without treatment or with makeshift therapy over the drugstore counter than run the risk of having his family, neighbors, or associates learn of his infection. It is therefore necessary to preserve the utmost secrecy with respect to the patient's condition, lest he and future patients be tempted to go without the treatment which is so essential to prevent further spread. The confidential nature of all information as to cases of syphilis or gonorrhea must be kept constantly in mind. The importance of this has been recognized by certain state laws that forbid any person having access to such records from divulging their contents, except to those who, because of their official duties, are entitled to such information (and the list of such persons is extremely short).

Reporting

Although most infectious diseases are reported to the health department by name, age, and address of the patient, a modified form of reporting is frequently provided for gonorrhea and syphilis in order to prevent too easy identification of each patient. In many states a special blank with a key number is used: the physician keeps the stub showing the name of the patient associated with a given number and sends to the health department only a blank bearing the number and essential epidemiological information. Some states use the Danish system of initials and date of birth, thus reducing the likelihood of duplication of reports if the patient visits several physicians or clinics. Reports are made directly to the state health department in some states, in others to the local board of health. The latter system entails an added deterrent to adequate reporting as many physicians hesitate to obtain a local reputation for treating too many cases of this character lest other patients hesitate to come to them.

This anonymous type of reporting is used for most cases, but provision is made for reporting the name and address of certain patients who, in the opinion of the attending physician or clinic, constitute special menaces from the point of view of spread. Such persons include those who have discontinued treatment and may therefore lapse into an infectious stage and those whose occupation is such as to render their continued employment hazardous to others. This latter group includes nursemaids and others whose occupation brings them into close contact with the bodies of others, especially children, but it need not include food handlers (see p. 379). Provision is also made for reporting the names and addresses of all persons who have been named by patients as the probable source of their infections or as contacts to whom the infection may have been spread.

Some persons have advocated the reporting of all cases by name and address in the same manner as for other communicable diseases. This is being tried in some places and is reported locally to be successful. It is so impossible to obtain a true measure of the incidence of gonorrhea or syphilis and, therefore, of the adequacy of any reporting system, that one may reserve judgment as to the success of such a plan. If, however, under such a system patients are driven to seek self-medication or to patronize the charlatan in preference to having their identity made known, more harm will be done than can be offset by the benefit from identification of a few cases. Such reporting may also encourage the use of aliases and false addresses by the patient, thus defeating the very purpose for which the system was adopted. The authors remain unconvinced as to the desirability of attempting complete reporting by name and address.

In order that cases of gonococcal ophthalmia neonatorum may be discovered and put under treatment promptly, some states require that all babies whose eyes show an abnormal redness or discharge during the first two weeks of life shall be reported to the local board of health. Responsibility for such a report rests upon any person who has care of the infant. The risk of blindness from a neglected gonococcal ophthalmia is so great that to err in reporting too many cases which ultimately turn out not to be of gonococcal origin is better than to withhold action until the etiology is proved. In her home visits for postnatal care, the public health nurse should be constantly alert for abnormal conditions of the eyes—conditions that may be the beginning of an ophthalmia. Even in the absence of specific laws, she should report all such cases to the attending physician or to the board of health if no physician is in attendance. In the latter circumstance, the board of health has a moral and, in some states, a legal responsibility for furnishing medical attention necessary to establish the diagnosis and render proper care.

Control of Spread

The case is usually not subjected to isolation precautions. Although some enthusiasts have urged that all infected patients should be segregated for the duration of the communicable stage, a moment's thought will show that such a threat would drive most of the cases under cover and thus, by denying themselves adequate treatment, such cases would tend to prolong their own infection and increase spread. Although the board of health has the right to isolate patients with syphilis or gonorrhea, in the same manner as those with measles, and occasionally may exercise this right, such power should be reserved for the rare situation in which all other measures have failed and usually only for the vicious individual who absolutely refuses to observe any reasonable self-restraint or precautions. Threat of isolation and quarantine may be of value in convincing certain patients of the need for continuing treatment. There is no justification for excluding a congenitally syphilitic child from school attendance. In fact there is no reason why the teacher should even know of the child's infection. So common are popular misconceptions regarding syphilis that the teacher may unconsciously tend to shun the child whom she knows to be infected.

Adequate treatment of the infected and infectious patients constitutes the most effective method of preventing spread and offers the key to the control of both syphilis and gonorrhea. As long as the patient with syphilis is receiving adequate treatment, there will rarely be open lesions, and communicability will cease even though the disease is far from cured. Open lesions ordinarily heal within a few days of the administration of suitable treatment. If the patient continues under treatment, it is thus possible to establish what Parran has described as a "chemical quarantine"—keeping the patient noninfectious and therefore unable to spread the disease without actually segregating him from society. Such treatment has the added personal advantage that it contributes toward cure. The advent of penicillin has made available a drug which will cure many infections within a small fraction of the time formerly required, thus not only rendering the patient quickly noncommunicable but also reducing the risk of subsequent unrecognized relapse to the communicable state. Unfortunately all cases of syphilis do not respond equally well to the drug; the best results have been obtained through its use on early infections.

Until recent years there was no therapeutic agent for gonorrhea comparable to the arsenicals for syphilis, so that little progress was made in control. The introduction of the sulfonamide derivatives made available a drug which not only brought about a rapid cessation of symptoms and of communicability but also effected a cure in a high proportion of cases in a relatively short period of time. Unfortunately sulfonamide-resistant strains of gonococci are encountered or even developed. Consequently sulfonamide therapy does not produce as high a proportion of cures today as it did when first introduced, nor does the drug show comparable efficacy in all areas. The more recent introduction of penicillin has made available a drug which is more effective and quicker in its action, less devoid of undesirable side effects, and less limited through the development of resistant strains of gonococci. It possesses the further advantage that the newer forms prepared in beeswax and peanut oil can be administered in a single therapeutic dose. It has therefore almost entirely supplanted the sulfonamides in the treatment of gonorrhea.

The sulfonamides and penicillin, used for self-medication, actually cure a reasonable number of infections. Although self-medication is to be decried and discouraged, one cannot close his eyes to the fact that it has occurred for years and still occurs, and further that it will continue to occur in the future in spite of legal and educational attempts to curb it. Before the advent of sulfonamides, self-medication did not cure; on the contrary it often prolonged the stage of communicability. With sulfonamides and penicillin the hazard to the individual is increased, owing to the risk of drug reactions, but there is at least the possibility of cure of those who take the drug in adequate quantity. Though proper medical treatment is desirable and should be urged for all patients with gonorrhea, self-medication under present circumstances is less of a public menace than it was in the period before sulfonamides.

Control of syphilis and gonorrhea through treatment of the infectious patient requires attention to three factors: (1) case-finding; (2) provision of facilities for treatment; and (3) follow-up of patients to keep them under treatment at least as long as they are potentially infectious. Case-finding programs will be discussed below under the heading of epidemiological investigation, as it is through this method that most of the early and infectious cases will be found.

Treatment facilities. The treatment of venereal disease was formerly very expensive. When based on the use of arsenicals and bismuth on an ambulatory basis, treatment of syphilis extended over a period of not less than one and a half years, with visits averaging about once a week. Intensive arsenotherapy, as carried out in a "rapid treatment center," involved a definite hazard and required hospitalization under the direction of a skilled medical and nursing staff. The treatment of gonorrhea was nonspecific but involved repeated visits for irrigations and local application of medicaments. Such treatments often extended over many months. Thus the proper care of either gonorrhea or syphilis was expensive and often beyond the financial resources of the patient. Unfortunately the incidence of infection is highest in the economic and age groups least able to afford treatment. Even the young person from the well-to-do family might hesitate to seek hospitalization or request funds for prolonged medical care lest by doing so the infection be revealed to the parents.

When penicillin was first tried, hospitalization of the patient was necessary as injections were required every three or four hours to maintain the requisite concentration in the blood stream. Cost of treatment was therefore still high, and patients tended to seek care in out-of-town hospitals where there was less risk that the nature of their illness would become known in the community. The advent of the slowly absorbed preparations of penicillin have greatly altered the problem of treatment. The development of procaine penicillin G and benzathine penicillin G has permitted the spacing of injections from intervals of 12 hours to more than two weeks. There is even evidence that a single injection may suffice to cure many cases of gonorrhea. Not only is the number of injections thus reduced, but hospitalization becomes unnecessary so that the patient may remain ambulatory and continue at his normal occupation. Thus treatment by the private physician comes within the financial reach of a higher proportion of the patients, and the cost of treatment of those who still seek clinic care is materially reduced. Yet there is still a need for clinics, for experience shows that unless the community makes some provision for treatment at reduced or public expense, many persons who are in need of it will receive inadequate care, will attempt self-medication with remedies obtained at the drugstore (too often recommended by the clerk), or will fall into the hands of the unscrupulous charlatan, who will promise short-cuts to cure but who will discharge the patient in an asymptomatic yet infectious condition as soon as the money is exhausted.

Any of these alternatives is undesirable, not only from the point of view of depriving the patient of his best chance of cure, but also from the standpoint of the public, as inadequate treatment means continued spread from patients who are still infectious. It is essential, therefore, that the board of health make provisions for free or reduced-cost treatment of those who might otherwise not obtain adequate care.

In large cities ambulatory treatment can best be offered in clinics, where large numbers of patients can be treated at a minimum cost. These clinics serve the dual purpose of diagnostic facilities and treatment centers. Such clinics must, however, be run in a spirit of help and sympathy for the patients, not as a factory assembly line designed to perform a definite operation on a piece of animate machinery. Patients will not seek or continue treatment in any clinic in which they are not accorded courteous and friendly care. The success of a clinic is to be measured not by the number of injections given but by the percentage of the patients who continue the treatment to its logical end. Such clinics should be staffed with competent physicians, nurses, and social workers and be provided with modern treatment and laboratory facilities. Insofar as possible, they should be part of a large general clinic, as many patients hesitate to be seen entering a separate clinic that is labeled as being designed for patients with gonorrhea or syphilis. Association with other types of clinics makes available the various consultation services which are often so valuable for proper treatment.

In rural areas and in the small cities, the problem of furnishing diagnosis and ambulatory treatment is much more difficult. Physicians skilled in the care of syphilis and gonorrhea are less readily available and clinics are frequently impractical. In the South it has been possible to conduct clinics more freely and in much smaller communities than in the North because the Negro, who constitutes so large a proportion of the problem, is less reluctant to attend a clinic where he will be recognized by his friends. The traveling clinic has been found of real value in some parts of the South, especially when the treatment of syphilis and gonorrhea is combined with prenatal and child health services. In the North, however, clinics have not been found practical outside the large city. Patients living in rural areas or small cities must obtain their treatment from local physicians, except in those communities so close to large centers that travel to and from a clinic is possible and at times more economical. The local practitioner who furnishes treatment should, of course, be suitably paid for the care given. As this will inevitably be at a higher rate than the cost of clinic care, the problem of treatment in rural areas and small cities is a more costly one than in the large urban centers if equal care is to be given.

Reliance upon local general practitioners, who cannot be expected to be so well versed in the care of syphilis and gonorrhea as the specialist in urban clinics, introduces a problem as to competence of medical care. In many instances, it may be desirable to arrange for periodic visits of the patient to a clinic or specialist who will advise the physician of necessary modification in treatment. The state of Minnesota has provided for assistance by mail, the services of a special consultant being retained to advise physicians as to problems of care. The advent of penicillin therapy, while shortening the duration of treatment, has introduced so many new problems that consultation service for the general practitioner is more important than ever before.

The cost of free treatment should be paid out of public funds, for treatment of these diseases is as essential in preventing spread as is isolation in the control of smallpox or diphtheria. It is not fair to expect charitable hospitals to provide for such care out of their limited funds. Insofar as possible, payments should be arranged without revealing the identity of the patient to the disbursing agency.[3] The state of Massachusetts provides for payment of all such bills by the state, rather than the local board of health, thus reducing the risk of local knowledge as to the patient's infection. Under this plan the vouchers carry only the number of patients treated and treatment given, though the state reserves the right to examine original records as a check against possible abuse of funds. Necessary travel to and from a clinic is considered an essential part of treatment and is furnished if necessary.

In most states, suitable drugs are supplied for treatment of syphilis and gonorrhea. These are distributed to clinics and physicians, though at times their use is limited to patients who cannot afford their purchase.

Follow-up of Cases. Prior to the advent of sulfonamides and penicillin the task of the follow-up worker was particularly important because of the long period of treatment required for cure. In both gonorrhea and

[3] The authors recall one instance in which the name of the patient was revealed to eleven officials and clerks in a community of 15,000 population before the bill was paid. It will occasion no surprise to add that knowledge of the patient's infection became quite generally spread throughout the town or that subsequent patients hesitated to utilize the clinic which had submitted the bill which revealed the identity of the patient treated.

syphilis, the acute stage in the untreated or inadequately treated patient is followed by a period in which the patient is free of signs or symptoms of infection yet is still in a communicable or potentially communicable condition. With older methods of treatment this period ranged from a few months to several years. During this period the patient might believe that he was actually cured and, often suspecting that the physician was urging further visits merely for the sake of the fees, would discontinue treatment. He failed to realize that lapse of treatment of syphilis might result in a return of infectiousness and reduce the likelihood of ultimate cure or that he might still spread gonorrhea even though free of symptoms. It was essential, therefore, that throughout the treatment the patient be impressed with the need for continuing such treatment long after the apparent disappearance of the disease and that provision be made for following patients who, in spite of these warnings, failed to continue under treatment. This was the task of the follow-up service.

The newer methods of treatment have materially shortened the period of latent communicability for they have brought about rapid cures in a high proportion of the cases. Whenever such methods are used with successful results the task of the follow-up worker is materially simplified. Yet the need for follow-up service remains. The newer drugs are not perfect; failures to establish a lasting cure occur, and such patients remain in a communicable or potentially communicable condition. It is highly important, therefore, that patients who respond well to treatment be retained under supervision even after the cessation of treatment and be brought back for re-examination at suitable intervals to make certain that a cure has actually been established. Such patients must also be informed that infection once cured does not confer any resistance against reinfection. There is little evidence that acquisition of a venereal disease materially alters a person's subsequent sexual habits. These persons must therefore be impressed with the importance of prompt treatment if reinfection occurs. The task of the follow-up worker has thus been somewhat altered but it remains an essential component of the venereal disease control program. Fortunately the follow-up duties require less time than formerly, thus releasing more time for tracing of contacts or for other public health duties.

The organization of the follow-up service will depend upon the local situation. In large clinics, full-time trained personnel may be employed and become highly efficient in this field. In small communities and rural areas, it becomes necessary either to utilize existing personnel employed primarily for other work or to provide for such follow-up service by having full-time workers who are employed by the state or some comparable unit of government larger than the local community and who therefore serve a large territory. The latter arrangement gives a higher quality of performance but is more expensive, and the workers may lose much of their efficiency through becoming known locally for association with this type of case. Entrusting this work to personnel who carry it merely as one of many public health duties sacrifices something in quality. But this loss may be more than offset by a better understanding of the community and its problems and by an ability to work with persons contacted in other parts of the public health program. There are valid arguments for both forms of organization; it is impossible to generalize so as to cover all situations.

Differences of opinion similarly exist as to whether the follow-up work should be performed by the public health nurse, medical social worker, or special investigator. Too often the argument degenerates into little more than a labor union jurisdictional dispute. In general, the background of the nurse would appear to equip her somewhat better for this type of work; but the individual, her training, and her tact are of far greater importance than the professional group to which she belongs. Competence and incompetence are shared by all groups alike. There are jobs for everyone. Remembering always that the control of syphilis and gonorrhea is a legal responsibility of the health department, the intelligent health officer will utilize whichever person appears most competent in a given situation. Often none of these is suitable for a particular situation, and the health officer will have to do his share of the follow-up work.

The follow-up of clinic patients is relatively easy, for their identity is fairly well known,[4] and very simple arrangements suffice to determine when a patient lapses treatment. Those under the care of private physicians are more difficult to follow, as machinery is lacking for discovering the patient's failure to continue treatment. This has been one of the arguments advanced by those who would have all cases reported by name and address. Health departments should be prepared to follow cases at the request of the physician, who should be encouraged to report them promptly. Some health departments have provided such follow-up service on a special confidential basis, whereby all the records remain in the physician's office and the worker merely reports that she has followed so many cases for so many physicians with certain results. Under whatever plan the service is organized and whatever group of patients it may serve,

---

[4] False names and addresses are frequently given. One clinic checks on this by mailing a pamphlet on measles or some comparable "harmless" subject to each new patient, and at the same time using an envelope with a post-office-box return address. Incorrect names and addresses are quickly discovered and correction made at the time of the next visit.

the follow-up worker must understand that it is her duty to induce the patient to continue with therapy. Whether the patient returns to the original source of treatment or seeks other care is of no consequence to the health department so long as adequate treatment is received. Checking is usually necessary to make certain that the patient does actually return for further treatment; no reliance can be placed upon promises to do so. The follow-up of syphilis in the early stages should be carried on without delay to reduce the likelihood of further spread. Visits in connection with late or latent syphilis may be left to convenience or, except in pregnancy, even omitted if funds are scarce, as they contribute far less to control of the disease.

Epidemiological Investigation. The purpose of this is to find the source and victims of the patient's infection so that they may be brought under treatment and thus avoid spread to other persons. As in typhoid or tuberculosis, the active case is the starting point for all such investigations. This means interview of the patient to learn of all persons with whom sexual relation has been had since a definite period prior to the onset of the disease. In the case of syphilis this period should be about eight weeks prior to the appearance of the chancre, in the case of gonorrhea two weeks prior to the onset of the discharge in the male. As some women are unaware of gonococcal infection until the onset of pelvic involvement and as this latter may be delayed over several menstrual periods, a longer time must be covered in searching for the source of infection of the female. In obtaining this information, it is important to stress to the patient that it will be used only to bring these persons under treatment for their own and others' benefit. If the patient's confidence can be secured, the identity of a large proportion of the contacts can be learned. After this information has been obtained, these persons must be located and an attempt made to have them examined by either the clinic or a competent physician. Suitable laboratory tests are essential to this examination.

This locating of contacts may be performed by the same personnel as is engaged in the follow-up of lapsed cases. The interview of the contact requires a great deal of tact and patience, and the worker must be prepared for many rebuffs. It is the most valuable single step in case-finding and control, as it brings to light cases that are in their most infectious stage and that otherwise might escape detection. Table 11, adapted from a study of Clark and Sargent in Buffalo, shows what may be accomplished in case-finding. While some have wished that more useful information might be found in those instances in which failures were experienced, the successes are to be numbered in the 143 cases of infectious or potentially infectious syphilis that were found and would have been neglected had there been no such investigation. One may only speculate as to how many future infections were avoided by bringing these patients under treatment. Each one of them must, of course, be further investigated as to other contacts. Careful and competent epidemiological investigation will bring to light more cases of infectious syphilis and gonorrhea than will be found by any other method or combination of methods.

TABLE 11

CASES OF SYPHILIS FOUND ON EPIDEMIOLOGICAL
INVESTIGATION OF 431 CASES

(After Clark and Sargent) *

Group Studies	Cases Found in Antecedent Contacts	Cases Found in Subsequent Contacts	Total
Infectious syphilis	66	43	109
Presumably noninfectious syphilis	32	2	34
Syphilis (status as to infectivity unknown)	17	10	27
TOTAL	115	55	170

* No investigation made of certain cases, as 61 declined to give information or denied antecedent contact and 301 declined to give information or denied subsequent contact.

Case-finding programs, other than by epidemiological investigation of known infections, are based on routine examination of all members of a particular group or section of society. These surveys have been extensively developed for syphilis but never for gonorrhea, due to the absence of a suitable and simple laboratory test comparable to the serological test for syphilis.[5] Routine blood testing has been applied to institutional and industrial groups, to volunteers on a community-wide basis, and to all admissions to certain hospitals and more recently has been made mandatory in some states for all marriage-license applicants and for all cases of pregnancy under medical care. The blood test must be thought of merely as a screening device. Positive serology is not proof of syphilis infection nor does negative serology exclude the presence of the disease. Much has been learned in recent years regarding the role of other infections or other antigenic stimuli in causing temporarily false positive reactions; caution must therefore be used to guard against the assumption

[5] Although this is commonly referred to as the Wassermann test in honor of the discoverer of the original test, most of the tests now in use are vastly different and properly go under different designations. The term "serological test" covers all of them, regardless of type or discoverer.

that the patient is syphilitic on the basis of a single blood test without other evidence. Conversely, patients in the incubation stage or with early primary lesions have negative blood tests. Surveys based on blood testing (and no other method of surveying is available) merely select those patients who should be subjected to careful clinical study and additional testing to determine whether or not syphilis is actually present. Undoubtedly, such wholesale tests bring to light some previously unrecognized infections, yet it is often questionable whether the yield is commensurate with the cost. Too many of the cases so found are those late infections that have passed the stage of probable communicability. Mass testing would have to be repeated every three to six months if it were to catch the openly infectious cases; this is obviously impractical. It would appear unwise to place reliance on such measures to the neglect of the more difficult, yet more worth-while, epidemiological methods, which uncover principally the early and most infectious cases. Much bitter dispute has arisen as to the value of the legislation for premarital tests. The authors can neither share the boundless enthusiasm of many of the proponents nor the bitter objection of the opposition but are convinced that such a measure is at best only a minor item in a far broader program. There is serious danger that too much reliance will be placed on such legislation to the neglect of facilities for epidemiological investigation, treatment, and follow-up.

Diagnostic facilities are essential to any program of case-finding. These should include provision for the performance of serological tests for syphilis (and possibly gonorrhea) and for examination and culture of secretions in gonorrhea. Dark-field facilities are also important for the early diagnosis of syphilis, but these tests are more readily performed by a skilled worker in the clinic than by a distant laboratory. All of these are technical procedures of considerable difficulty and require greater competence than is to be found in small, local health department or hospital laboratories.

Medical supervision of prostitutes has been attempted by some health departments. The method has generally failed to affect the incidence of syphilis or gonorrhea, nor does it seem logical for one governmental agency to assist in the conduct of an illegal activity which another department (the police department) is commissioned to suppress.

Environmental sanitation plays little if any part in the control of syphilis or gonorrhea. Prohibiting the use of the common drinking cup and towel is of some value in reducing a slight risk of syphilis. There is no value in routine examination of food handlers, as they do not spread either disease through the food. Even if they did, such periodic tests would bring to light the old, chronic infections, which are least dangerous, and would overlook the early infections, which are the only ones possessing even a theoretical possibility of spread. In children's hospital wards, individual rectal thermometers should be provided.

Minimizing Ill Effects

This is accomplished only by treatment of the infected patients. The importance of this in the communicable or potentially communicable stage has already been pointed out as the most valuable measure of control. When given in the later stages, treatment does not serve to lessen spread but merely to prevent further damage to the patient. As many of these patients with syphilis will otherwise suffer further physical impairment, including heart disease and insanity, and will, with their dependents, become public charges, it would appear wise to give some consideration to their care even after the stage of communicability has ceased. Unfortunately, however, in too many syphilis clinics the emphasis is placed on treating this group to the neglect of finding early cases and of bringing the latter under treatment. Emphasis on the early cases would appear to be a more farsighted policy, as it will serve to reduce spread and thus lessen the problem for the future. In a well-balanced program both groups should be given proper attention.

Difficulty is experienced in some states through a legal provision that treatment in the infectious stage is the responsibility of the board of health, while, after that stage, treatment is a welfare duty with all the attendant difficulty of investigating economic status and frequently of publishing names of persons receiving such aid. There might be some sense to this division of financial responsibility if it were possible to determine when potential communicability ceases. Actually, it cannot be done. Communicability through nonsexual contact ceases long before danger of spread through intercourse, and the syphilitic mother may infect her baby within the uterus even after she has ceased to be infectious for her husband. It would seem more logical that all treatment of syphilis and gonorrhea, in whatever stage, be made a financial responsibility of the board of health.

Public Health Nursing Care. The usual case of syphilis or gonorrhea requires no public health nursing care, as the patient is not confined to bed, nor does he ordinarily receive any treatment at home. The public health nurse will have an important part to play in keeping patients under treatment and supervision the necessary length of time after treatment has been completed (see p. 389). In addition to these responsibilities she may from time to time have occasion to give care to two forms of gonorrheal infection, namely, gonorrheal vulvovaginitis and gonococcal ophthalmia neonatorum.

Vulvovaginitis. The purpose of the visit is to assist the mother in carrying out whatever treatment may have been prescribed by the physician and to instruct her in measures to reduce the risk of spread to the child's sisters. The infected child must be furnished a separate bed. All articles soiled by the discharge should be thoroughly cleansed before use by another person. Because of the ease with which the gonococcus is destroyed, elaborate disinfection procedures are not required; usual cleansing measures are adequate.

Ophthalmia Neonatorum. Although this disease occurs rarely now, when it does occur it should be treated as an emergency by the public health nurse. Every minute that care is delayed increases the possibility of the formation of corneal ulcers and eventual blindness. Because of the necessity for quick action, health department policies or standing orders should be clearly worked out and thoroughly familiar to the public health nurse so that she will know what she may do if she finds a newborn with purulent discharge of the eyes. If medical care has not been obtained, the public health nurse should not leave the patient until the physician arrives or the infant reaches the hospital. In most cases standing orders will direct her to obtain hospital care at once if other medical care is not immediately available. If the infant is kept at home, full-time graduate nurse care should be obtained if at all possible. This will be needed until the discharge has cleared, which under modern therapy usually takes place quite quickly, often within 24 hours. If graduate nursing care is not obtainable, the public health nurse should stay herself or be very certain that someone in the household knows how to administer the treatment prescribed by the physician. It is essential to teach the attendant the importance of strict isolation technique in addition to the treatment requirements. She must learn the importance of adhering to the technique to avoid infecting the infant's other eye and to prevent infecting her own eyes. It is a very unusual attendant or mother who can learn all of this in one lesson. Hospital care is therefore far superior to home care. If, however, the public health nurse is responsible for home nursing care, she should obtain precise instruction from the physician regarding the administration of the drug ordered for local or parenteral use.

In addition to rendering personal care the nurse should:

1. Show the attendant how to follow the physician's orders in every detail with scrupulous exactness.

2. Demonstrate and then assist the attendant with instillation of medication until reasonably certain that the instructions will be faithfully carried out.

3. Instruct the attendant to treat the eye gently. It is very easy to injure an infant's eye through rough handling.

4. Instruct the attendant to use each compress or pledget only once and then discard in a paper bag and burn. All objects that are contaminated by discharges from the eye should be burned, boiled, or otherwise disinfected.

5. Show the attendant how to care for the infected eye without contamination of the other.

6. Instruct the attendant not to touch her own eyes or face and always to wash her hands thoroughly with soap and hot water after giving care to the infant.

It is important to keep the infant in the best possible general health, and his feedings should not be neglected because of the demands of the treatment.

The public health nurse should give close health supervision to the infant after recovery. She should be certain that he is seen by a physician six months after recovery from the infection, as scar tissue may form slowly and therefore not be detectable until some time after the end of the acute phase. If there is any loss of vision, the public health nurse should follow the case as she would any handicapped child, assisting the family to get needed care and referring it to appropriate agencies for special assistance.

Measures of Personal Protection

Increasing Resistance. There is no method of either active or passive immunization, nor reason to suspect that such will be developed.

Specific Prophylaxis. Many attempts have been made to kill the spirochete or gonococcus on the tissues before invasion or inflammation has occurred. This depends on the use of suitable chemical preparations after sexual exposure. For this purpose intraurethral instillations of protein silver or sulfonamide preparations, and local applications of mercurous chloride (calomel) ointment have been extensively used. Recently d-sorbitol and 8-hydroxyquinoline have replaced the silver salts and the sulfonamides. Success has also been reported from the oral use of sulfonamides and of penicillin for the prevention of gonorrhea. The former, though effective, is too dangerous for general use and combines all the disadvantages of sulfonamide chemoprophylaxis (see p. 44). Penicillin is also effective and less hazardous, but its extensive use cannot be recommended because of occasional adverse reactions and the risk of development of resistant strains of organisms.

Although chemoprophylactic measures have been attended with considerable success in certain instances if applied promptly and vigorously, their use has not been attended with practical success except under military discipline. Their rather striking success in the United States Army and Navy in 1917 and 1918 led to the attempt to popularize such methods and even to establish public clinics for this purpose. Nothing indicates their success under conditions of civil life. The use of the condom at the time of intercourse unquestionably reduces the risk of infection.

Prophylaxis of gonococcal ophthalmia neonatorum through the use of drops of 1 percent solution of silver nitrate (the Crédé method) in the newborn baby's eyes is of proved value. The results of this procedure have been striking in reducing blindness from this cause. Drops containing penicillin have been recommended as equally effective and devoid of the irritating effect of silver nitrate. More evidence is needed, however, before they can be recommended as superior. In the meantime, state laws quite generally prescribe the use of silver nitrate.

SUMMARY

Health Department Program

Adequate treatment of all cases to render them noninfectious is the foundation upon which all successful programs for the control of gonorrhea and syphilis are based. If "chemical quarantine" can be applied, the infection will not spread, regardless of public morals. This means the development of methods for finding cases early in the disease, the provision of suitable facilities for treatment, the epidemiological investigation of all cases, and follow-up services to make certain that treatment is continued until beyond the danger of possible relapse to infectiousness. If funds are adequate, attention should be given to treatment of the late chronic infections in order to reduce the economic toll due to the physical breakdown of such cases. This should not, however, replace adequate epidemiological investigation, which will bring the early cases to light at their time of maximum communicability and danger. Community-wide surveys are of less value than the epidemiological method.

Experience shows that measures entailing the friendly cooperation of the patient are more effective than is the exercise of the police power of the board of health. Although the board has undoubted authority to enforce drastic regulations, such measures may defeat their own purpose by driving infectious cases under cover and consequently deterring them from receiving the treatment necessary to keep them noncommunicable. Similarly, the utmost respect must be accorded the desire of the patient to keep his infection secret, lest fear of his identification also serve as a deterrent to treatment. Failure to observe these two essentials may doom a program to failure at the outset.

The **health officer,** acting as the agent of the board of health, is responsible for the direction of the program. He should make certain that treatment is denied to no one, regardless of financial status, and should strive to make it of such general availability and of such a quality that patients will not be tempted to seek out the charlatan or to experiment with self-medication. He should provide for epidemiological investigation and follow-up of all cases and at the same time should remember that insofar as possible this should be carried out by personnel associated with the treating agency, even though the cost may have to be defrayed by the health department. He must be prepared to do some of this work personally. Provision must be made for laboratory diagnostic assistance and the distribution of suitable specific drugs to clinics and physicians if necessary. Much of the follow-up and epidemiological investigation may be delegated to the **public health nurse,** especially in the smaller communities, where employment of special personnel for this work is not possible and where the nurse, through previous visits, is well acquainted with the individual and family problems.

Assistance of the schools, social agencies, and community organizations should be enlisted in the development of suitable programs of general education regarding syphilis and gonorrhea, about which the public has until recently been kept grossly ignorant. Full use should be made of the assistance of **social hygiene societies,** of which the American Social Hygiene Association is a good example. Although the health department may endorse sex education, instruction in morals, and programs for community social life and activities which will keep the young people better occupied and less likely to succumb to the temptation of sexual irregularities, it should not assume a responsibility for these. The social hygiene program is concerned with those conditions—such as prostitution, the misuse and abuse of sex, promiscuity, and family discord—which reflect unhealthy and unhappy male and female relationships and tend to disrupt and destroy the family. This is basically a broad social program for which the health department could not assume responsibility without going far afield from its function of protecting the community against disease. The health department should support the social hygiene program as a measure for ultimate disease prevention, but it ought not to become involved in controversy over moral and religious issues. Its basic function is that of preventing disease.

SUGGESTED READINGS

Allen, James H., and Barrere, Luciano E.: "Prophylaxis of Gonorrheal Ophthalmia of the Newborn," *J.A.M.A.*, 141:522–26, (Oct. 22) 1949.

Babione, Robert W.: "Ratio of Gonorrhea to Syphilis as Occurring in the United States Navy," *Am. J. Syph.*, 33:243–62, (May) 1949.

Bauer, Theodore J., and Shortal, Hazel: "Prevention of Congenital Syphilis," *Pub. Health Nursing*, 42:81–83, (Feb.) 1950.

Beerman, Herman; Ingraham, Norman R.; and Stokes, John H.: "Lymphogranuloma Venereum," *Am. J. M. Sc.*, 197:575–87, (Apr.) 1939.

Berengarten, Sidney: "When Nurses Interview Patients," *Am. J. Nursing*, 50:13–15, (Jan.) 1950.

Brown, W. G., and Nichols, W. B.: "Epidemiologic Procedures as a Case-Finding Mechanism in Syphilis Control," *Canad. J. Pub. Health*, 39:123–30, (Apr.) 1948.

Bulla, A. C.; Wakefield, F.; and Hunt, M. E.: "Case Finding of Early Syphilis by the Public Health Nurse," *Ven. Dis. Inform.*, 32:122–29, (May) 1951.

Clark, Charles Walter: "Notes on the Epidemiology of Granuloma Inguinale," *J. Ven. Dis. Inform.*, 28:189–94, (Sept.) 1947.

Clark, E. Gurney: "The Epidemiology of Syphilis, with Particular Reference to Contact Investigation," *Am. J. Med.*, 5:655–69, (Nov.) 1948.

Clark, William T., and Sargent, Clealand A.: "Investigation of Early Syphilis," *Am. J. Pub. Health*, 28:807–12, (July) 1938.

Cohn, Alfred; Steer, Arthur; and Adler, Eleanor L.: "Gonococcal Vaginitis: A Preliminary Report on One Year's Work," *Ven. Dis. Inform.*, 21:208–20, (July) 1940.

Committee on Medical Research and the United States Public Health Service: "The Treatment of Early Syphilis with Penicillin," *J.A.M.A.*, 131:265–71, (May 25) 1946.

"Control of Syphilis and Gonorrhea in the Scandinavian Countries and Great Britain: A Report of the New York City Commission," *Am. J. Syph.*, 20 (Suppl.):7–63, (July) 1936.

Cutler, John C.: "Venereal Disease Now—and Looking into the Future," *Pub. Health Nursing*, 44:613–19, (Nov.) 1952.

D'Aunoy, Rigney, and Hamm, Emmerich von: "Venereal Lymphogranuloma," *Arch. Path.*, 27:1032–82, (June) 1939.

Eisenberg, H.; Plotke, F.; and Baker, A. H.: "Asexual Syphilis in Children," *Ven. Dis. Inform.*, 30:7–14, (Jan.) 1949.

Gillis, Eugene A.: "Gonorrhea Control during the Decade of World War II," *Am. J. Syph.*, 32:99–105, (Mar.) 1948.

Heller, J. R., Jr.: "The Adequate Treatment of Gonorrhea," *J.A.M.A.*, 131:1480–82, (Aug. 31) 1946.

Iskrant, A. P., and Kahn, H. A.: "Status of Contact Examination: An Evaluation of Data from State and Local Health Areas," *Ven. Dis. Inform.*, 29:7–12, (Jan.) 1948.

Kiesselbach, M. R.: "Is Gonorrhea Control a Public Health Function?" *Am. J. Syph.*, 33:80–85, (Jan.) 1949.

MacPhillips, Julia: "The Principles of Case Finding," *Ven. Dis. Inform.*, 18:315–18, (Sept.) 1937.

Moore, Joseph Earle: "An Evaluation of Public Health Measures in the Control of Syphilis," *Am. J. Syph.*, 35:101–34, (Mar.) 1951. See also *Lancet*, 1:699–711, (Mar. 31) 1951.

Morris, Evangeline Hall: *Public Health Nursing in Syphilis and Gonorrhea.* Philadelphia: W. B. Saunders Co., 1946.

Munson, William L.: "Epidemiology of Syphilis and Gonorrhea," *Am. J. Pub. Health*, 23:797–808, (Aug.) 1933.

Nursing in Venereal Disease Control—A Suggested Guide. Washington, D.C.: United States Public Health Service, Publication 198, 1952.

Parran, Thomas: *Shadow on the Land.* New York: Reynal & Hitchcock, 1937.

Pelouze, P. S.: *Gonorrhea in the Male and Female,* 3rd ed. Philadelphia: W. B. Saunders Co., 1939. See especially pp. 407–67.

"Postwar Venereal Disease Control," *Ven. Dis. Inform.*, Supp. No. 20, 1944.

Results of Serological Blood Tests for Syphilis on Selective Service Registrants, Based on the Second Million Reports Received during the Period April 16, 1941, to August 31, 1941, for Registrants Examined in Accordance with the Selective Training and Service Act of 1940. Washington: Federal Security Agency, U.S. Public Health Service, October, 1942.

Russell, Albert E.: "Syphilis Case Finding in Industry," *J.A.M.A.*, 114:1321–24, (Apr. 6) 1940.

Simpson, W. G., and Murphy, Virginia: "Needed—Better Preparation for Venereal Disease Nursing," *Am. J. Nursing*, 51:586–87, (Sept.) 1951.

Sklar, Benson H., and Schuman, Leonard M.: "Special Contact Investigation of the Patients of Private Physicians," *J. Ven. Dis. Inform.*, 31:286–90, (Nov.) 1950.

Steiger, Howard P., and Taylor, Jane Barbara: "Venereal Disease Interviewing," *Ven. Dis. Inform.*, 28:55–60, (Apr.) 1947.

Stokes, John H.: *Dermatology and Venereology,* 4th ed. Philadelphia: W. B. Saunders Co., 1948.

Sullivan, Maurice: "Chancroid," *Am. J. Syph.*, 24:482–521, (July) 1940.

Tobey, James A.: *Public Health Law,* 3rd ed. New York: Commonwealth Fund, 1947, pp. 162–80.

Van Slyke, C. J., and Heller, J. R., Jr.: "Treatment of Gonorrhea by a Single Intramuscular Injection of Penicillin-oil-beeswax. A Coöperative Study of 1000 Cases," *Ven. Dis. Inform.*, 26:98–105, (May) 1945.

Vonderlehr, R. A., and Heller, J. R., Jr.: *The Control of Venereal Diseases.* New York: Reynal & Hitchcock, 1946.

Wright, John J., "Venereal Disease Control," *J.A.M.A.*, 147:1408–11, (Dec. 8) 1951.

Wright, John J., and Sheps, Cecil G.: "Reports of the North Carolina Syphilis Studies. I. An Evaluation of Case-Finding Measures in Syphilis Control," *J. Ven. Dis. Inform.*, 30:35–52, (Feb.) 1949.

———: "Reports of the North Carolina Syphilis Studies. II. An Evaluation of Case-Finding Measures in Multiple Episodes of Infectious Syphilis," *ibid.*, 30:187–94, (July) 1949.

————: "Reports of the North Carolina Syphilis Studies. III. An Evaluation of Case-Finding Measures in the Control of Gonorrhea," *ibid.*, 30:211–17, (Aug.) 1949.

Wright, John J.; Sheps, Cecil G.; and Gifford, Alice E.: "Reports of the North Carolina Syphilis Studies. IV. Some Problems in the Evaluation of Venereal Disease Education," *ibid.*, 31:126–33, (May) 1950.

Wright, John J.; Sheps, Cecil G.; and Gifford, Alice E.: "Reports of the North Carolina Syphilis Studies. V. "Indices in the Measurement of Congenital Syphilis," *Am. J. Syph.*, 35:225–33, (May) 1951.

31. Rabies

Rabies (hydrophobia) is an acute infection of the brain due to a specific virus. Clinically, the disease is attended by hyperexcitability which ends in fatal paralysis. In the dog, the stage of excitement causes the so-called furious rabies, during which the animal may run great distances and snap at whatever it encounters. As the infection progresses, paralysis and ultimately death ensue. In some instances, the disease passes directly to the paralytic form without the period of excitability, thus producing the so-called "dumb rabies" of dogs. The salivation and drooling, coupled with apparent aversion to water, are due to paralysis of the muscles of swallowing. Rabies is always fatal in man and almost invariably so in animals, though very rare instances of recovery have been reported.

EPIDEMIOLOGY

Occurrence. Although rabies is most commonly encountered in dogs, it may involve any mammal. Wolves, foxes, skunks, and cats are frequently affected, and the disease may be found in cattle, horses, or swine if they are attacked by a rabid dog. As it spreads only by the bite of the infected animal, it will obviously be found most prevalent among carnivorous species and only by accident among the herbivorous. Contrary to popular belief, rabies reaches its maximum incidence in the spring rather than in summer, although bites by nonrabid dogs are more frequent during the summer.

Rabies may occur in all parts of the world. Due to rigid quarantine requirements, it has never been introduced into Australia or the Hawaiian Islands and has been eliminated from the British Isles. It is found in all parts of the United States, the prevalence varying somewhat according to the strictness of enforcing regulations as to restraint of dogs and elimination of stray animals. The disease occurs in cycles within any given area, periods of high incidence alternating with periods of virtual absence, regardless of control measures.

Etiological Agent. Rabies is due to a filterable virus.

Reservoir of Infection. Dogs constitute the principal reservoir from which the disease spreads to man and to other animals. Other members of the canine family, such as wolves and foxes, may be infected under wild conditions. During recent years special attention has been directed to skunks as an important reservoir of rabies in wild animals.

Escape from the reservoir occurs only via the saliva. The virus has been shown to be in the saliva of dogs as long as a week prior to the onset of symptoms; this fact explains the need for keeping under observation any dog that has inflicted a bite, even though the dog appears well at the time of the accident. The virus has been found in the human salivary glands, though this would appear to be unusual. No cases have ever been reported from contact with human saliva.

Transmission of the virus occurs through direct physical contact with the infected animal. There is no evidence that fomites, even though contaminated with saliva, help spread the disease or that rabies has ever been contracted through eating the meat or milk of infected animals.

Entry and Incubation Period. Entry of the virus occurs by introduction of the infected saliva into a break in the skin. Usually this is through a bite, whereby the virus is virtually injected into the wound. If contaminated by saliva, scratches from animals also open up avenues for entry. In occasional instances, the virus enters through apparently unbroken skin which has become soiled with the saliva, as by the dog's lapping of the skin or by the person's putting his hand in the dog's mouth. This latter type of exposure may occur when the dog's owner misinterprets the inability to swallow actually due to a beginning paralysis of the muscles of deglutition and attempts to dislodge a bone on which he believes the dog is choking. There is some doubt as to whether the entry of the virus in such contact cases is due to passage through the intact skin or through minute unrecognized breaks. Minute abrasions are so common on a person's skin, especially the hands, that it is safest to assume their existence in any instance of actual contact with the saliva of the rabid dog.

The amount of virus entering through any wound varies with the size of the abrasion and the thickness and character of clothing through which the bite occurred. Large tearing wounds, opening up large numbers of nerve fibers, are more dangerous than the puncture type. If the bite is through heavy woolen clothing of a very fine weave, the teeth will be wiped free of most of the saliva before they penetrate the skin. Lighter clothing, such as stockings, affords very little protection. Bites on the bare skin are the most dangerous because of the complete absence of any "wiping" of the teeth.

After the virus is introduced into the body, it travels to the brain via the nerve trunks rather than by the blood stream. For this reason, the incubation period may be extremely variable and depends upon the location of the bite. Bites on the hands and feet result in a fairly long period because of the length of the nerve trunks, whereas those on the head may be followed by rabies in a much shorter interval. Incubation periods of two to three weeks have been described following head wounds, while in bites on the extremities the periods are more commonly three to six weeks. Periods as long as six months have been reported. The incubation period in the dog is somewhat shorter, usually two to three weeks, probably because of the fact that most dogbites result in wounds around the head. No inflammatory signs or symptoms due to rabies develop at the site of the wound.

Susceptibility. All mammals are apparently susceptible; there is no apparent development of resistance other than through active immunization. This does not mean, however, that everyone bitten by a rabid dog will develop rabies. On the contrary, it is estimated that rabies will ensue in not over 15 to 20 per cent of the cases even in the absence of immunization. Yet the invariably fatal outcome of the disease, if it does develop, must lead one to urge immunization rather than to rely on this "four-out-of-five" chance of not being afflicted. A one-out-of-five chance of dying is enough to warrant heroic measures in any situation.

CONTROL MEASURES

Control of Spread

The Case. Although no instance of spread from human being to human being has been reported, it is desirable that aseptic nursing care be observed and that special precautions be used to avoid contact with the saliva. This means that all nursing attendants should wear rubber gloves.

Epidemiological investigation is of critical importance. In the prevention of human cases, the investigation begins at the time of the injury or exposure. Every dogbite should raise the question as to possible rabies, and the offending animal should be observed for an appropriate period (seven to fourteen days) to make certain that it does not show signs of rabies. As the virus may occur in the saliva for as long as a week prior to symptoms, this period of observation is essential, regardless of the condition of the animal at the time of biting. In most instances, the biting is ascribed to an accident and not associated with rabies; but the high risk of disease and its invariably fatal outcome justify observation of the dog in every instance. At least one state requires the reporting of all animal bites to the board of health so that an attempt may be made to locate the animal and observe it for a suitable period. Under no circumstances should a dog that has inflicted a bite be destroyed until the end of the observation period. The pathological tests by which the diagnosis is made in the animal depend upon structural changes in the brain—changes which do not appear until the disease is well developed. Immediate destruction of the dog may therefore delay correct diagnosis and require resorting to the slower method of inoculation of the brain material into rabbits or mice. Even if the dog shows signs of rabies, it is best not to destroy it immediately, providing it can be caught and tied up safely. If the dog dies during the observation period, the head should be removed and forwarded to the laboratory for examination of the brain.

Epidemiological investigation should also include search for other persons and animals bitten by, or exposed to, the animal in question. The former must be found for the sake of protective vaccination; the latter, in order that they may be restrained until the end of the incubation period, usually two to three months. A six-month quarantine is even better as incubation periods as long as six months have been recorded. There is often difficulty in providing for so long a period of restraint.

Contacts. Family contacts of a case need take no precautions.

Prevention of Spread in Animals. The best proved and most effective measure for prevention of spread is control of animals, principally dogs. It has been amply demonstrated that rabies will not spread if dogs are subjected to restraint or muzzling. This means the enactment and enforcement of ordinances by the board of health, bureau of livestock disease control, local governing body, or whatever governmental bureau has the appropriate power. Such ordinances should provide for restraint or muzzling for at least three months and must often be renewed for a second period. To be effective, they must cover not only the area in which rabies is known to exist but an area of not less than twenty miles in all directions from such a focus. Restraint is often preferable to muzzling, inasmuch as the dog may tear off a muzzle and as a muzzled dog is too often helpless if attacked by one not muzzled. If such ordinances are enforced on an area basis, effective control can be established. In practice, however, enforcement is rarely achieved because of lack of popular support. If the power of restraint is vested in the local rather than the state government, it is very rare that any restrictions will be enacted merely because rabies exists in a neighboring community, nor will they be well enforced by the local authorities of a community not yet infected. Apparently it is human nature to wait until the danger is at hand before taking effective measures. For this reason, restraint measures have yielded poorer results under the prevailing American form of government than in some European countries. Restraining ordinances are frequently objected to by farmers who use the animals for herding purposes or as watchdogs and by dog lovers and sportsmen who think that such restrictions interfere with personal liberty and the best welfare of the dogs.[1] Because of the many difficulties in enforcing an effective restraint order, many communities are today placing an increasing degree of reliance upon immunization of dogs (see below).

Minimizing Ill Effects

At present, nothing is known that can be done to avoid the inevitably fatal outcome if rabies develops in the human being. Good medical and nursing care can merely relieve the suffering.

Control through Immunization

Passive Immunization. Recent studies have shown the possibility of developing a serum from animals highly immunized against rabies. If this serum is injected into an infected animal, there is a prolongation of the incubation period. There is thus the possibility that if this serum is given to cases in which a short incubation period is expected following bites around the head or neck, the onset of the disease may be postponed long enough to permit active immunization through use of vaccine. Studies are now under way to determine whether the results obtained in animals are applicable to human beings. If successful, the method should materially reduce the risk associated with bites around the head.

Active immunization is the only proved and efficacious method of protecting the person bitten by, or intimately exposed to, a rabid animal. Cauterization of the wound by fuming nitric acid (iodine, mercury preparations, and coal tar disinfectants do not cauterize) has long been recommended, but recent studies by Shaughnessy and his colleagues have raised questions as to its true efficiency. Even if effective, reliance must not be placed on cautery to the neglect of vaccination. The vaccine most commonly used in recent years has been a phenolized virus, often referred to as the Semple vaccine. Increasing use is being made of a vaccine prepared through ultraviolet irradiation of the virus. Rabies vaccine is given in 14 to 21 equal doses a day apart; if treatment has been delayed at the start, two doses may be given on each of the first three or four days. As the exact dosage required is not known, 14 doses are usually recommended in the case of the average bite in which the incubation period can be expected

---

[1] The neighbor who owns a garden is heartily in favor of restraint, as is also the person who has been recently bitten. The authors recall a dog that by a well-placed bite converted a city councilman to the desirability of a restraint ordinance.

to be fairly long, and 21 doses if the bite is around the head or there are severe multiple lacerations. No uniformity of opinion exists, however, as to the need for more than 14 doses. The injections are given subcutaneously, usually on the abdomen, and are spread over as large an area as possible because of local soreness.

In rare instances, the administration of antirabies vaccine results in a paralysis which may involve one or more extremities or all parts of the body below a certain segment of the spinal cord (transverse myelitis). The frequency of such paralysis is open to doubt. Greenwood, from a study of the results of Pasteur institutes in other countries, concluded that they occurred about once in 5,800 cases and were fatal once in 23,000 persons treated. Experience in this country would suggest that this is a definite underestimate of the frequency. As paralysis appears to occur most frequently following undue exertion, the patient who is receiving vaccine should pursue a reasonably quiet life, though this does not mean bed care or invalidism. Children are somewhat less frequently affected than are adults.

Decision as to the need or desirability of antirabies vaccine in any case depends on the balance between the risk of contracting rabies on the one hand and the risk of a paralytic reaction on the other. In certain situations —as, for example, a bite by an animal known to be rabid—the risk of rabies is unquestionably greater than that of paralysis. Vaccine is therefore indicated. In other situations—as, for example, a bite by an unknown dog in an area where rabies has not appeared for years—one may conceivably feel that the risk of the vaccine is greater than the risk of rabies and therefore withhold treatment. Obviously no rule can be set up to cover all cases, as different persons will evaluate the relative risks differently and therefore advise differently in a given situation. In general, it is safer to err on the side of treatment, yet there is no justification for giving the vaccine indiscriminately to everyone who has had only casual contact with a dog developing rabies. As the incubation period is long, ample time exists to observe the dog responsible for the biting, except in the case of face and head bites. In these latter instances, if rabies infection exists in the area, it may be advisable to start treatment pending observation. The following general recommendations, prepared by the Massachusetts Department of Public Health, would appear to cover most situations and to leave ample latitude for personal judgment, which must be conditioned by knowledge of the prevalence of rabies in the area in question.

1. Treatment imperative:
    Persons bitten by or intimately exposed to the saliva of
      a) A clinically rabid animal.

b) An animal the head of which was found positive for rabies on laboratory examination.

c) An animal the head of which was found suspicious for rabies on laboratory examination.

2. Treatment advised in the following instances unless the circumstances surrounding the bite are such that in the opinion of the attending physician there is no possibility of rabies in the individual case:

a) Persons bitten on the head should be treated at once regardless of the condition of the dog. Treatment may be discontinued at end of seven days provided dog is still well and is kept under observation for seven additional days; treatment to be resumed if dog shows signs of rabies during this period.

b) Persons bitten by or intimately exposed to the saliva of

(1) An animal the head of which was in such condition on reaching the laboratory that it could not be examined and was therefore classified as unsatisfactory.

(2) A lost animal, that is, an animal which could not be restrained for a clinical observation period of fourteen days or the head of which could not be submitted for laboratory examination.

(3) An animal which was killed without being held for examination and without subsequent examination of the head.

The duration of resistance is so short that vaccination is best repeated if a second exposure occurs later than six months after immunization.

Immunization of dogs has now passed beyond the experimental stage and should be looked upon as a measure of proved value. Laboratory studies and field trials have given ample evidence of its worth. The vaccine is given as an annual subcutaneous injection of a phenol-treated or chloroform-treated virus emulsion. There is a cumulative effect from year to year. Vaccination of dogs must be considered as a supplement to restraint rather than as a substitute. Restraint orders are often ineffective due to unwillingness of the community to adopt and enforce sufficiently drastic measures. Even if enforced, they leave no permanent effect on the community, inasmuch as a rabid dog may run into and infect the community the day after the orders are lifted. Similarly they confer no protection against the reservoir in wild animals. On the other hand, vaccination, even if not perfect, does confer a prolonged protection, thus reducing the risk of reintroduction of the disease. It is therefore a highly valuable adjunct to restraint measures; in areas where such measures cannot be enforced, it furnishes a high degree of primary protection. Some communities require it as a prerequisite to licensing while others have required restraint of nonvaccinated animals. Army regulations require the annual vaccination of dogs kept on military posts. There is much to be said for such measures.

SUMMARY

Health Department Program

The control of rabies depends upon prevention of spread among dogs. Prevention of spread is achieved by elimination of stray dogs, restraint or muzzling, and immunization. Lack of effective control of the disease in animals necessitates active immunization of persons exposed to infection. This is not carried out on a general or community basis but is reserved for those persons who have been bitten by, or intimately exposed to, a dog known to be, or reasonably suspected of being, rabid.

The **health officer** should be prepared to carry out the necessary epidemiological investigation to apprehend the animal responsible for the biting and to keep it under observation for a long enough time to tell the attending physician and the family whether or not the dog was in an infectious stage at the time of the biting or the injury. This may require the active cooperation and assistance of whatever governmental agency is responsible for the control of diseases in domestic animals. The board of health should make certain that laboratory facilities are available for examination of the brains of suspected animals, though this is usually better entrusted to a central laboratory. The board of health frequently furnishes the vaccine and may even give the injections or pay for their administration. The health officer should urge all dog owners to provide for annual antirabies immunization of their animals and may well recommend to the board of health that it provide clinics to facilitate immunization. In the presence of rabies he should advise strict restraint ordinances, exempting only dogs vaccinated within the past year. Enforcement of all restraint orders is usually left to the police department. The **public health nurse** may frequently be called upon to explain to a mother the need for vaccination in cases in which it is indicated but the family is reluctant to permit it. She and the **sanitary officer** should be constantly alert for neglected cases of dogbites that should be investigated. Constant educational work must be carried on to stress the value of dog immunization and the importance of not destroying a dog that has inflicted a bite but rather of keeping the dog under observation for the required time period.

SUGGESTED READINGS

"Control of Rabies," *J.A.M.A.*, **135**:770–71, (Nov. 22) 1947.
Greenwood, Major: "Tenth Report of Data on Antirabies Treatments Supplied by Pasteur Institutes," *Bull. Health Organ., League of Nations.*, **12**:301–64, 1945–1946.

Johnson, Harald N.: "Experimental and Field Studies of Canine Rabies Vaccination," *Proc. 49th Annual Meeting, U.S. Livestock San. A.,* 99–107, (Dec.) 1945.

———: "Rabies," *Ann. New York Acad. Sc.,* 48:361–83, (Apr. 10) 1947.

Kelser, Raymond A.: *The Epidemiology and Prophylaxis of Rabies. Harvard School of Public Health Symposium on Virus and Rickettsial Diseases.* Cambridge: Harvard University Press, 1940, pp. 642–60.

Koprowski, Hilary, and Cox, Herald R.: "Recent Developments in the Prophylaxis of Rabies," *Am. J. Pub. Health,* 41:1483–89, (Dec.) 1951.

Korns, Robert F., and Zeissig, A.: "Dog, Fox, and Cattle Rabies in New York State—Evaluation of Vaccination in Dogs," *Am. J. Pub. Health,* 38:50–65, (Jan.) 1948.

National Research Council, Subcommittee on Rabies: "Rabies and Its Control," *J. Am. Vet. M. A.,* 108:293–302, (May) 1946.

New York Academy of Medicine, Committee on Public Relations: "Control of Rabies," *Pub. Health Rep.,* 62:1215–37, (Aug. 22) 1947.

Pait, Charles F., and Pearson, Harold E.: "Rabies Vaccine Encephalomyelitis in Relation to the Incidence of Animal Rabies in Los Angeles," *Am. J. Pub. Health,* 39:875–77, (July) 1949.

"Rabies: Some Current Problems and Recent Improvements in Measures for Its Control," *Ann. Int. Med.,* 34:517–23, (Feb.) 1951.

Sellers, T. F.: "Rabies, Physician's Dilemma," *Am. J. Trop. Med.,* 28:453–56, (May) 1948.

Shaughnessy, Howard J., and Zichis, Joseph: "Prevention of Experimental Rabies Treatment of Wounds Contaminated by Rabies Virus with Fuming Nitric Acid, Soap Solution, Sulfanilamide, or Tincture of Iodine," *J.A.M.A.,* 123:528–33, (Oct. 30) 1943.

Steele, James H., and Tierkel, Ernest S.: "Rabies Problems and Control," *Pub. Health Rep.,* 64:785–96, (June 24) 1949.

World Health Organization, Expert Committee on Rabies: "Report on First Session," *World Health Organization, Tech. Rep. Series No. 28,* Nov. 1950.

32. Tetanus

Tetanus, popularly known as lockjaw, is an acute irritation of the nervous system due to a poison secreted by a specific microorganism. The organisms multiply at the site of a wound through which they enter the body, but they do not cause any local irritation at this point. The soluble exotoxin which they produce is carried to the central nervous system by the blood stream. The case fatality rate may be as high as 50 per cent.

EPIDEMIOLOGY

Occurrence. Tetanus is a rare disease under ordinary conditions of civil life. It is more common in rural agricultural areas than in the modern city. The risk of infection is great among those wounded in war, especially if the fighting has been carried on over fields that have been heavily manured in past years. In some countries neonatal tetanus is encountered due to contamination of the stump of the umbilical cord.

Etiological Agent. The disease is due to the *Clostridium tetani,* an anaerobic, Gram-positive, spore-forming organism, capable of producing a powerful neurotropic toxin. Although the vegetative form is quite fragile, the spores are highly resistant and persist for several years in the soil. They are destroyed by several minutes of boiling as well as by the stronger chemical disinfectants but are highly resistant to drying. The spores germinate in the body only if the oxygen tension is lower than normal. Thus they are more dangerous if introduced into deep puncture wounds than into superficial abrasions or into wounds having considerable necrosis.

Reservoir of Infection. Tetanus spores may be found as normal inhabitants of the intestinal tract of horses, chickens, and other animals. They may similarly pass through the human intestine without causing illness. The soil of barnyards and of fields fertilized with manure is highly contaminated. The extensive replacement of the horse by the automobile has reduced, though not eliminated, the risk of infection from the dirt of city streets.

Escape of the organism from the body of the animal carrier is via the feces. The organisms do not normally escape from the patient suffering from tetanus unless the wound has a drainage due to infection by other organisms.

Transmission to New Host, Entry, and Incubation Period. Transmission and entry of the organisms occur through the introduction of spore-bearing soil into wounds. Rare cases of postoperative tetanus have been traced to improper sterilization of surgical gut or of dressings. Cases have occurred following vaccination. These are due to contamination of the reaction site by the hands of the child tempted to scratch because of the itching. Dressings favor the development of tetanus spores if they are introduced following vaccination. The organisms do not spread from the point of introduction but multiply and produce their toxin at the site of entry. The incubation period is usually about 7 to 14 days. The shorter the period, the less favorable the prognosis.

Susceptibility. Human beings are universally susceptible.

CONTROL MEASURES

Control of Spread

The Case. No isolation precautions are required. If there is drainage from the wound, such drainage should be collected and destroyed.

Epidemiological investigation will usually reveal a very obvious wound through which the infection was introduced The investigator should be constantly alert for the rare instances of neonatal, postvaccinal, and postoperative infections, as such cases represent carelessness which should be discovered to prevent recurrences.

The contacts with the patient need neither restraint nor protection.

Environmental sanitation is of little value in view of the widespread use of manure for fertilizing purposes. Prohibition of such use might be of theoretical value but, considering the rarity of tetanus, would obviously be unwarranted.

Minimizing Ill Effects

Treatment with specific antitoxin and penicillin is the most effective form of therapy. The board of health may assist by providing serum to those otherwise unable to afford it.

Control through Immunization

Passive Immunization. Prior to the recent development of active immunization with toxoid, passive immunization was the only effective method of tetanus prevention. Although the number of actively immunized persons is increasing, it is still so small that passive immunization of those suffering puncture wounds is the method most commonly used. As infection is almost invariably preceded by a wound of such severity and character as to come to the attention of the victim and frequently to bring him to medical care, ample opportunity exists for giving this protection to those few persons in need of it. Administration of 500 to 3,000 units of antitoxin is recommended in connection with deep wounds that have been contaminated with soil, especially manured soil. Many hospitals and physicians administer antitoxin routinely to all such accident cases. During World War I, it was given to all wounded soldiers, with the result that tetanus was of very rare occurrence as contrasted with its high incidence in prior wars. As it is impossible to know for certain whether tetanus spores have entered a wound and as the risk of death is around 50 per cent if the disease develops, it is safer to err on the side of too lavish treatment than to risk infection. It does not follow that every cut or scratch requires antitetanic treatments, but in case of doubt it is better, again, to err on the side of caution. Passive immunity lasts about two to three weeks.

Active immunization with tetanus toxoid, either in fluid or alum-precipitated form, affords a remarkably high degree of protection. The toxoid is given either alone or in conjunction with other antigens. During World War II, the soluble toxoid was used by the Army, and the alum-precipitated toxoid by the Navy. At the outset of the war, these preparations were relatively untested as to clinical efficacy in man. Their routine use in the Armed Forces demonstrated that tetanus immunization is one of the most effective of present-day immunizing procedures, for tetanus was virtually unknown in both services, whereas nonimmunized troops of other nations suffered severely from it as a sequel to war wounds. One year after completion of immunization a booster dose is given; a subsequent booster dose is indicated (though possibly not required) whenever the individual receives a wound that entails a serious risk of tetanus. Routine immunization is indicated for all military units. The incidence of tetanus in the civil population is not high enough to warrant routine antitetanus immunization if this requires a separate course of injections. Fortunately, tetanus toxoid can be mixed with diphtheria toxoid and pertussis vaccine without reducing the efficacy of any of the three antigens. Multiple antigens are rapidly replacing the use of separate antigens in pediatric practice and in public clinics for small children. The result is that an increasingly large proportion of the children being immunized against diphtheria and whooping cough are simultaneously receiving tetanus toxoid. Such children, if later suffering a wound that requires antitetanus treatment, should be given a booster dose of tetanus toxoid, a procedure which brings about a rapid increase in circulating antitoxin without any risk of serum reactions from the horse protein contained in the antitoxin used for passive immunization.

SUMMARY

Health Department Program

Tetanus is so rare and the mode of infection so personal that little if anything can or need be done by a board of health to meet this problem. The public should be informed of the danger of certain types of wounds so that competent medical attention may be obtained for the administration of antitoxin or a booster dose of toxoid if advisable. Good obstetric service will prevent the occasional case of neonatal tetanus. The risk of postvaccinal infection will be greatly reduced by vaccination in infancy rather than at the age of entering school, when the child is active and the hands are usually so soiled that infection, if present, may be introduced into the wound by scratching. The provision of antitoxin for those cases of tetanus otherwise unable to afford it is desirable. Active immunization is so well proved that it can be recommended, but the infection rate is so low that special community campaigns for general immunization can hardly be advocated as a worth-while public health measure. Multiple antigens containing tetanus toxoid should, however, be urged or furnished for use in pediatric practice and in all immunization programs of both preschool and school age groups. Immunization is essential for troops and is to be strongly urged for farmers and children living on farms, for it is among this group that the infection rate is the highest; its use for other children is becoming deservedly more popular in pediatric practice.

SUGGESTED READINGS

Bensted, H. J.: "Immunization against Bacterial Toxins," *Lancet,* 2:788–89, (Dec. 21) 1940.

Bergey, D. H.; Brown, Claude P.; and Etris, S.: "Immunization against Tetanus with Alum-Precipitated Tetanus Toxoid," *Am. J. Pub. Health,* 29: 334–36, (Apr.) 1939.

Bigler, John A.: "Tetanus Immunization," *Am. J. Dis. Child.,* 81:226–32, (Feb.) 1951.

diSant'Agnese, Paul A.: "Simultaneous Immunization of New-Born Infants against Diphtheria, Tetanus, and Pertussis," *Am. J. Pub. Health*, 40:674–80, (June) 1950.

Gold, Herman: "Active Immunization against Tetanus," *Ann. Int. Med.*, 13:768–82, (Nov.) 1939.

Hayden, R., and Hall, W. W.: "Active Immunization against Tetanus Using Alum-Precipitated Tetanus Toxoid," *U.S. Navy M. Bull.*, 36:524–35, (Oct.) 1938.

Long, Arthur P.: "Tetanus Toxoid, Its Use in the United States Army," *Am. J. Pub. Health*, 33:53–57, (Jan.) 1943.

Long, Arthur P., and Sartwell, Philip E.: "Tetanus in the United States Army in World War II," *Bull. U.S. Army Med. Dept.*, 7:371–85, (Apr.) 1947.

Zinsser, Hans; Enders, John F.; and Fothergill, LeRoy D.: *Immunity: Principles and Applications in Medicine and Public Health.* New York: Macmillan Co., 1940, pp. 553–69.

33. Impetigo, Pediculosis, Scabies, and Ringworm

The communicable skin infections of childhood—impetigo, pediculosis, scabies, and ringworm—constitute a group of conditions which are usually of relatively minor importance to the individual affected but are often among the most troublesome problems confronting a health department. These conditions rarely incapacitate the victim and may interfere very little with his normal activities, though, if severe, they may be extremely unpleasant and uncomfortable. They may affect all ages but usually become public health problems only when they appear in groups of children in schools, camps, or institutions.[1]

IMPETIGO CONTAGIOSA

A purulent infection of the superficial layers of the skin, impetigo is disfiguring and offensive in appearance but rarely serious, except when it occurs in newborn infants. The lesions most commonly involve the exposed surfaces, especially the face and arms, but may occur anywhere and spread from one part of the body to another. It is more frequent in children living in conditions of poor personal sanitation, though it appears under the best hygienic circumstances. If unchecked, the disease may spread quite widely through a school, camp, or institutional group; it occasionally invades the nursery of maternity hospitals, where it persists and spreads in a very stubborn fashion.

[1] It should be pointed out that widespread infestation with body lice may make possible the spread of epidemics of typhus or relapsing fever if these infections are introduced into the community. Under such circumstances, pediculosis may constitute a major public health problem.

EPIDEMIOLOGY

Etiological Agent. Impetigo is due to infection with either a staphylococcus or a streptococcus.

Reservoir of Infection. Although staphylococci and streptococci may be found normally on the skin and in the throats of many persons, infection is most commonly contracted from association with another case.

Escape of organisms is with the serum and pus that exude from the skin lesions.

Transmission of infection is usually through direct physical contact with a person already infected or through an article, most commonly a towel, used by such a person. The moisture in towels or clothing permits the survival of the organisms for a reasonable period of time after contamination. Although health departments frequently receive complaints of individuals who claim to have contracted impetigo while they were swimming at certain beaches or pools, infection in such instances is apparently spread through personal association rather than through the water. In fact, there is no evidence that water is itself of any importance. The patient who already has impetigo may reinfect himself on other parts of the body through scratching.

Entry and Incubation Period. Establishment of the initial lesion is probably favored by any slight break in the outer layers of the skin. From this point the disease spreads to surrounding areas by direct extension. The incubation period is usually from two to five days.

Susceptibility. There is no evidence of any true resistance to impetigo. The same individual may suffer repeated attacks. Many persons believe that malnutrition favors its development, as may also a diet too rich in carbohydrates.

CONTROL MEASURES

Control of Spread

The Case. Although theoretically the case should be isolated until all lesions have disappeared, this is utterly impossible in practice, except for cases in certain institutions and in nurseries. Since the child with impetigo is usually not incapacitated, he circulates freely. The schools attempt, insofar as possible, to exclude such cases because of danger of spread to other children. Mustard has pointed out very frankly that in many cases exclusion because of impetigo (or for pediculosis, scabies, or ringworm) is almost welcomed by the family as it frees the child temporarily for farm or plantation chores. Certainly, exclusion does not guarantee medical care of the lesions,[2] which will remain communicable until cured. Therefore much is to be said for Mustard's contention that in many cases it is better to let the child continue at school and to arrange for proper treatments which would be neglected at home. Just as proper treatment of syphilis serves to reduce spread, so also treatment of impetigo is a means of protecting the associates. It may therefore be justified as a preventive measure under public health auspices in situations where the child would otherwise go without care. It must be recognized, however, that control through treatment to the neglect of sanitation is a practical expedient though not an ideal measure. When segregation is possible, as in nurseries, camps, and institutions, it reduces the risk of spread. Isolation as applied to impetigo does not mean complete segregation as for measles or smallpox but rather the avoidance of all direct physical contact with other persons or with articles used by other persons. Special attention must be given to towels, a measure not always easy in some of the poorer homes with many children.

Epidemiological investigation serves no useful purpose except for the occasional discovery of other cases in a schoolroom or family. In the presence of impetigo in a school or camp, the other children should be examined daily for lesions.

Contacts require no quarantine, though they should be watched closely for the beginning of lesions that should be treated promptly.

Environmental Sanitation. Although impetigo is most commonly encountered under conditions of poor sanitation, no measure of community cleanliness will reduce its spread other than strict supervision of public places to avoid use of common towels and similar articles brought in contact with the lesions.

Minimizing Ill Effects

Treatment is important primarily as a means of reducing spread. Although every effort should be made to have the cases brought to the attention of the family physician, the health officer should recognize the fact that this is often not done and that the child may go without treatment unless it is furnished by the health department. If the health department assumes responsibility for treatment of such cases, it will follow whatever measures are used in that community. If the physician has prescribed medication for the treatment of the lesions, the public health nurse may be of great assistance in helping the family to apply it properly. A home

[2] Nursing follow-up of all cases, whether excluded or not, is very important in many areas as it is often the only way of forcing upon the parents the need for medical care of the lesions.

visit is usually needed to demonstrate how to remove the scabs, cleanse the sores, and apply the medication. Merely telling the mother that the scab should be removed before applying an ointment is often ineffective as the mother is afraid to do this, washes the lesion in a half-hearted way for fear of hurting the child, and then applies the salve. The mother thinks she is following instructions, but still the impetigo does not clear up.

Control through Immunization

There is no method of either passive or active immunization. Some thought should be given to the problem of nutrition of the child repeatedly infected.

PEDICULOSIS

Pediculosis is infestation with lice. The *Pediculus capitis* (head louse) is found chiefly in the hair; the *Pediculus corporis* (body louse) on the body or seeking refuge in the clothes. Although any person may be accidentally infested, extensive lousiness is a sign of poor personal hygiene, chiefly lack of bathing. The incidence of infestation is a good measure of the degree of personal cleanliness of the community.

In certain countries where typhus is prevalent, human lousiness becomes a matter of major public health importance that must be combated by the strictest possible measures for disinfestation. In the United States at the present time, however, body infestations are rarely of any great consequence, though head involvement may be a matter of considerable embarrassment to school authorities or others having charge of groups of children.

The louse or its egg passes directly from person to person through close physical contact or through use of personal articles such as clothing, combs, brushes, towels, and bedding. The head louse is found in the hair; and its eggs (nits), as small grayish objects attached to the individual hairs.[3] Nits may often be found in the hair behind the ears even when not visible on other parts of the head. They must be cleared from all the hair before the child can be considered free of the infestation. The body louse and its eggs are found on the body or in the seams of clothing. Infestation of either the body or head may lead to scratching with local irritation, infections, and scars. The glands of the back of the neck are frequently enlarged in cases of head involvement.

As in the case of impetigo, exclusion from school of children who have

---

[3] Nits must not be confused with dandruff. Nits are actually attached to the hairs, dandruff loosely scattered among the hairs.

pediculosis is theoretically desirable and is required by law or regulation in many states. In this disease also, mere exclusion may accomplish little, as the disease is not self-limited and, in some homes, treatment is neglected unless the health department provides it. Families with much self-respect will obviously obtain treatment, but the problem is most severe in those in which treatment is most often neglected. The health department must, therefore, often take responsibility for delousing certain children. This can be entrusted to the nurse who will probably have to visit the home, explain carefully the necessary procedures, and possibly even carry them out.

Removal of body lice was formerly achieved through bathing, accompanied by disinfestation of the clothes; head lice were removed by soaking the hair in tincture of larkspur or a kerosene mixture, followed by thorough combing to remove the nits. Delousing thus involved cumbersome procedures which were often destructive of clothing and were of limited effectiveness unless carried out with great care. Insecticides developed during World War II provide delousing methods of greater effectiveness and far simpler application. Dusting the body, hair and clothing with a dusting powder containing 10 per cent DDT (dichlordiphenyltrichlorethane) in pyrophyllite kills all lice within a few hours. The nits are not destroyed by the dusting but the clothes (if not laundered) retain enough DDT dust to kill any lice that hatch out and to prevent any new infestation for several weeks. It is advisable to re-examine the patient for adult lice the day after dusting to make certain that the dusting was thorough. The dust is not harmful unless swallowed. Emulsions of DDT in kerosene or oil should not be used on the body or on clothing, as DDT in this form is readily absorbed in sufficient quantity to produce poisoning. As infestation of one child is frequently accompanied by similar involvement of brothers and sisters, attention must be given to the entire family lest the child be reinfested.

The control of pediculosis in a school requires a great deal of tact on the part of the public health nurse. By inspection of the children, she may discover those who are affected. It is often preferable to inform the parents by a home visit rather than through a blunt and often misunderstood written notice. As lousiness is usually a sign of poor personal cleanliness, many parents may resent a suggestion that their children are infested. The nurse may need to explain the chances of the child's acquiring the lice from association with other children out of the home and should be firm in stressing the likelihood of subsequent spread to other members of the household. If the family obtains medical care, the nurse may assist them in carrying out the prescribed measures. If they are not willing or unable to do so, she may have to demonstrate and even assist with the delousing operations herself, provided, of course, the family consents. Obtaining this permission may require great tact and persuasion on the part of the nurse.

SCABIES

Scabies is an infestation of the skin with the *Sarcoptes scabiei var. hominis*, familiarly known as the itch mite. The mite tunnels into the layers of the skin and lays its eggs at the end of the characteristic burrows. This may cause intense itching, which is quite distressing, especially at night when it may interfere with sleep. The resultant scratching may lead to scars or to secondary infection of the skin.

Scabies is encountered chiefly under conditions of crowding and poor sanitation, though it has the uncomfortable facility of showing up where least expected. During World War II many countries in which soap was scarce suffered a sharp increase in the prevalence of scabies. It appears as a health problem chiefly among school children and in military or institutional groups. When infestation of one member of a family is discovered, other members are usually found to be similarly affected.

The mites pass from one person to another by direct physical contact. As they are most active at night, spread to another person with whom the patient is sleeping is almost invariable. Clothes are less important in spread of scabies than of pediculosis, as the eggs are laid in the burrows of the skin rather than in the seams of garments, as is the habit of the body louse. Intimacy of contact is therefore the most important factor in the spread of infestation. Susceptibility is universal; involvement with scabies does not in any way hinder the acquisition of additional mites.

As in the case of impetigo and pediculosis, segregation of the case, including exclusion from school, is theoretically desirable though often impractical. Scabies is uncomfortable and offensive to the aesthetic sensibilities, but it does not incapacitate. When infestation is discovered, every reasonable effort should be made to induce the family to obtain treatment; but the health department must frequently assume responsibility for this. Repeated inunctions of sulfur ointment were formerly the standard method of treatment, but these have today been largely replaced by benzyl benzoate, commonly used in a 20 per cent emulsion, which is painted over the entire body exclusive of the head. If applied only to the obvious lesions, infestation may persist due to mites in burrows that were overlooked. Prior to being painted with benzyl benzoate, the patient should be bathed thoroughly with soap and water.

RINGWORM

"Ringworm" is a term used popularly and medically for a group of fungus infections of the skin. The parts of the body most commonly involved are the scalp, face, and feet, though the fungi concerned are somewhat different for these several areas. Involvement of the scalp or face may be quite obvious and temporarily disfiguring; infection of the feet, chiefly between the toes (athlete's foot), may be attended with few symptoms other than itching and some desquamation. More severe foot involvement may lead to vesicular lesions with extensive desquamation and cracks of the skin through which pyogenic infection may enter. The toenail is frequently involved.

During the past few years many communities in the United States have experienced an unusually high incidence of ringworm of the scalp among school children, due to infection with *Microsporum audouini*. As boys have been affected more frequently than girls and the lesions have usually begun around the back of the neck, spread through barbers' clippers, combs, and shears has been suspected. Certain studies have shown presence of the fungus on such instruments. Spread through fungus contamination of the backs of the seats in theatres has also been suspected, presumably attributable to contamination of the cushion against which the infected child has rested his head. The relative importance of these media for spread is still far from proved, nor has direct transfer through contact or through exchange of combs, brushes or other articles been excluded. If one child within a family is infected, it is common to find the brothers and sisters likewise affected. Many subclinical infections occur, demonstrable only through use of the Wood lamp, a device for producing filtered ultraviolet rays. When illuminated by such light in a dark room, the fungus glows with a characteristic fluorescence. These subclinical infections or carriers are free of demonstrable skin or scalp lesions but may be an important source of infection for other children.

Most school systems attempt to exclude a child with obvious involvement of the scalp or exposed body surfaces. Infection of the feet is so nearly universal that no attempt is made to isolate cases of athlete's foot. The management of some gymnasiums and indoor swimming pools, however, attempt to exclude persons who show active foot involvement. This yields few if any returns, as so many cases are overlooked in a more or less dormant state but are still infectious. In many gymnasiums and swimming pools, attempts to reduce the spread of foot infections have been based on the use of foot baths or wading pools in the shower room and so situated that every bather has to walk through them. Solutions of sodium hypochlorite or of thiosulfate have been used in them. Although favorable reports have appeared on the use of such solutions, most persons have felt that equally favorable results can be achieved by strict daily scrubbing of the floors with soap and disinfectant. The use of foot baths and wading pools has therefore been largely discontinued in favor of measures of cleanliness. Slippers have been used in some places to reduce contact of the bare feet with the floor, preferably paper slippers that can be discarded after one use. Probably no method that is absolutely effective has yet been devised. The best that can be done is to keep the disease in check rather than to attempt preventing the spread of an almost ubiquitous fungus.

The most effective measure for the control of ringworm is adequate treatment of the lesions. This is so much more difficult than treatment of impetigo, scabies, or pediculosis and requires so much more individualization that it should not be undertaken by the health department unless medical care for the indigent is one of the department's functions. Those who cannot provide medical care for themselves can best be referred to a suitable physician at public expense. Treatment measures for ringworm of the feet are notoriously inadequate if measured in terms of complete cure but will serve to keep the condition under control.

SUMMARY

Health Department Program

Impetigo, pediculosis, scabies, and ringworm present a group of conditions of minor consequence to the individual unless extremely severe but of considerable embarrassment to a health department because of the readiness of spread within a group of children and occasionally adults in close association with one another. As spread of these diseases is favored by overcrowding and lack of personal and home cleanliness, all measures of sanitation of the living conditions will reduce the likelihood of spread. Although exclusion of the infected from school until the condition clears up is theoretically desirable and often required by law, this procedure is frequently impractical because the infected families fail to provide treatment for what seems to them to be a matter of no great consequence. As adequate treatment to cure the condition is the most effective measure of control, the health department must often provide treatment for those who fail or refuse to obtain it on their own initiative. Under some situations, it may even be justifiable to concentrate on treatment and completely ignore exclusion measures.

The **health officer** is responsible for the institution of a suitable program to detect these conditions in the school and to decide as to the need for exclusion and treatment. He should include in his budget funds for necessary treatment unless this can be provided by the welfare agency. In conjunction with the school health service, he should arrange for routine inspection of children and institute intensive examination if cases are found within a classroom. Some of the inspections for pediculosis can be safely entrusted to the **public health nurse.** To her also can be entrusted the responsibility for supervision of some of the home treatments for those who are suffering from impetigo and scabies and who fail to reach medical care. She may also assist in carrying out the doctor's orders for ringworm. Whether or not the child is excluded, the nurse may have to make home visits to stress the importance of care for the conditions. In her home and school visits the nurse must stress personal cleanliness and, in case of recognized infection, must show the mother how to cleanse all bedding, clothing, and other personal articles. The **sanitary officer's** role is limited to supervision of public washing and bathing facilities to guard against use of common towels and other personal articles and to guarantee adequate cleansing of these places.

SUGGESTED READINGS

IMPETIGO

Cohen, Stella R.: "Common Skin Diseases in the Schools," *Pub. Health Nursing,* 30:120–24, (Feb.) 1938.
Mustard, Harry S.: *Rural Health Practice.* New York: Commonwealth Fund, 1936, pp. 234–36.
Stokes, John H.: *Dermatology and Syphilology for Nurses,* 3rd ed. Philadelphia: W. B. Saunders Co., 1940.

PEDICULOSIS

Bishopp, Fred C.: "Present Position of DDT in the Control of Insects of Medical Importance," *Am. J. Pub. Health,* 36:593–606, (June) 1946.
Buxton, P. A.: "The Louse: Present Knowledge and Future Work," *Tr. Roy. Soc. Trop. Med. & Hyg.,* 33:365–88, (Jan.) 1940.
———: *The Louse. An Account of the Lice Which Infect Man, Their Medical Importance and Control.* Baltimore: Williams & Wilkins Co., 1940.
Wheeler, Charles M.: "Control of Typhus in Italy 1943–44 by Use of DDT," *Am. J. Pub. Health,* 36:119–29, (Feb.) 1946.

SCABIES

Buxton, P. A.: "The Parasitology of Scabies," *Brit. M. J.,* 2:397–400, (Sept. 20) 1941.
Gordon, R. M., and Seaton, D. R.: "Observations on the Treatment of Scabies," *Brit. M. J.,* 1:685–87, (June 6) 1942.
Johnson, C. G.: "Recent Research and the Scabies Problem," *J. Roy. San. Inst.,* 63:29–37, (Jan.) 1943.

Johnson, C. G., and Mellanby, K.: "The Parasitology of Human Scabies," *Parasitology,* 34:285–90, (Nov.) 1942.

Mellanby, Kenneth: "The Transmission of Scabies," *Brit. M. J.,* 2:405–6, (Sept. 20) 1941.

Mellanby, Kenneth; Johnson, C. G.; and Bartley, W. C.: "The Treatment of Scabies," *Brit. M. J.,* 2:1–4, (July 4) 1942.

RINGWORM

Benedek, Tibor: "Contribution to the Epidemiology of Tinea Capitis. Tinea Capitis as a Public Health Problem in Family and School," *Urol. & Cutan. Rev.,* 47:416–32, (July) 1943.

Culbert, Robert W.; Robinson, Anna E. Ray; and Lerner, Max N.: "Study in the Reduction of Absences from School of Children with Tinea Capitis," *Am. J. Pub. Health,* 40:1089–95, (Sept.) 1950.

Schwartz, Louis; Peck, Samuel M.; Botwinick, Isadore; Leibovitz, Armand Leo; and Frasier, Elizabeth S.: "Control of Ringworm of the Scalp among School Children," *J.A.M.A.,* 132:58–62, (Sept. 14) 1946. Published in greater detail as *Public Health Bulletin 294,* United States Public Health Service, 1946.

Steves, Richard J., and Lynch, Francis W.: "Ringworm of the Scalp," *J.A.M.A.,* 133:306–9, (Feb. 1) 1947.

34. Q Fever

Q fever, an infection recognized only during the past twenty years, occurs as a febrile disturbance accompanied by pneumonic involvement. In the typical case there is an abrupt onset with malaise, headache, and fever; an unproductive cough develops in a few days. The acute symptoms are not unlike those of virus pneumonia with which many cases have doubtless been confused. Pneumonia is demonstrable by x-ray. The duration of the acute stage is usually from 7–14 days with gradual subsidence of fever. In addition to the frank recognizable cases, there is a large number of mild unrecognized infections. Diagnosis is by complement fixation test, but unfortunately this is usually not positive until the tenth to fourteenth day. Agglutination tests are positive somewhat later. The disease is rarely fatal.

EPIDEMIOLOGY

Occurrence. Originally discovered in Queensland, Australia,[1] in 1937 by Derrick, Q fever has subsequently been described from many parts of Europe, Africa, and the Western Hemisphere. In the United States, it has been reported most extensively from Texas and California, but isolated infections have been recognized in many parts of the country. Most of the naturally occurring cases have been in slaughterhouse or stockyard workers or other persons having association with or living in close proximity to cattle. Many mild unrecognized cases doubtless occur among such persons. Numerous outbreaks have developed among workers in laboratories where the disease was being studied, many of the victims having had no known contact with the organism.

[1] Contrary to usual impression, the letter "Q" in the name does not stand for Queensland. Derrick used the Q as an abbreviation for "query" owing to uncertainty as to the nature of the infection.

Etiological Agent. Q fever is due to infection with *Rickettsia bur-neti*,[2] an organism that is much more resistant to chemicals and physical forces than are most of the rickettsiae. It is quite resistant to drying. Different investigators have found conflicting results as to the ability of *R. burneti* to survive pasteurization temperature. Some have reported that not all the organisms were killed while others have found complete destruction, but with practically no margin of safety. Until further data are available, it is preferable to think of pasteurization as killing most of the organisms in contaminated milk but to recognize the possibility that a few may survive.

Reservoir of Infection. Q fever is basically a disease of animals, other than man. Most human infections are apparently due to spread from infected cows, goats, and sheep. Certain species of ticks have also been found to be infected—*Dermacentor andersoni, D. occidentalis* and *Amblyomma americanum, Otobius megnini* and *Ixodes dentatus* in the United States—but there is no evidence that they are important sources of human infection. In cattle, Q fever can occur without clinical evidence of illness, the infection being demonstrated either by complement fixation tests or by isolation of the organism from the milk. In certain herds as high as 20 per cent of the cattle have been found infected. The presence of the infection has no apparent effect on the quantity of milk produced. The infection rate in sheep may be as high as 50 per cent of an entire flock.

Escape of the Organism. Infected cattle shed the organism in the milk for long periods of time. Enormous quantities are also found in the placenta. Thus calving of infected cattle results in contamination of the soil with large numbers of organisms that are highly resistant to drying. *Rickettsia burneti* has also been found in the feces of calves feeding from infected cows. In man the organism can be found in the urine and sputum. In ticks it occurs in the lumen of the gut and consequently escapes with the feces.

Transmission. Much uncertainty exists regarding the exact modes of spread to man. Inhalation of dust contaminated with *R. burneti* is probably the most important. Contact with infected animals might explain many infections among stockyard or abattoir workers, but fails to explain the large number of cases among persons having no physical contact with animals. In the Los Angeles area, many cases developed in persons who merely lived near the milking pens where infected animals were kept. The

---

[2] The term *Coxiella burneti* is preferred by some who think of the organism as belonging to a separate genus distinct from the Rickettsiae, though closely related to them.

many cases in American troops in the Mediterranean area during World War II could not be explained on the basis of direct animal contact. Laboratory infections have occurred in persons such as secretaries whose only contact with the disease was the fact that they worked in buildings where Q fever was under study. One person was infected who merely stepped inside the building. In one instance the disease developed in a laundry worker who was handling linen from a laboratory where Q fever was being studied. The hypothesis of dust contamination finds further support from the known resistance of the organism to drying. Also of significance is the observation that injection of the rickettsiae in the experimental animal produces only a mild infection whereas inhalation causes pneumonia.

These many observations suggest that, although infection can develop though contact with infected material, inhalation of contaminated dust is probably the most important mode of transfer in the recognizable pneumonic cases. It appears to be the only possible explanation in many instances. The mechanism of the air contamination, however, is not clear. Australian investigators have suggested that in some instances the dust may be heavily contaminated with the feces of infected cattle ticks. The existence of rickettsiae in placental tissue, in milk, and in the feces of calves nursing from infected cows would explain possible modes of dust contamination around cattle yards, even in the absence of ticks.

The role of raw milk in the spread of the disease is also a matter of some uncertainty. Although the rickettsiae are present in the milk in large quantities and for long periods of time and are probably not completely destroyed by pasteurization, the circumstantial evidence to incriminate milk as an important vehicle of spread is very weak. While there can be little doubt that milk can and does serve as a vehicle of infection, the total evidence indicates that it is not the chief mode of spread of recognizable disease.[3]

Although *R. burneti* has been isolated from the sputum and urine of human cases, the risk of direct spread to other persons is so slight that many investigators have commented on the complete absence of cases among nursing attendants and other close associates. Deutsch and Peterson have, however, reported an instance of apparent infection of three persons attending a pneumonic case. More observations of this character are needed to establish the magnitude of the risk.

[3] Huebner and Bell have pointed out the high infection rate among creamery workers "exposed to large quantities of infected milk." They have suggested that occupational contact with raw milk may be a means of spread and that "the ingestion of raw milk is not necessary to account for such infections."

Entry and Incubation Period. In most cases, entry is apparently via the respiratory tract. Entry via the intestinal tract is a possibility that can be demonstrated in the laboratory animal. Blanc and his colleagues showed that injection of *R. burneti* into humans produced only febrile disturbances without lung involvement but that inhalation resulted in pneumonia. These findings coupled with the epidemiologic observations suggest that respiratory invasion is the important mode of entry in the typical pneumonic case, but that invasion through other portals may be of importance in the mild nonpneumonic infections. The incubation period is usually 14 to 16 days.

Susceptibility is universal. Infection with *R. burneti* confers a very durable resistance. Prior infection with other rickettsiae confers no protection against Q fever.

CONTROL MEASURES

Control of Spread

The case requires no special isolation or quarantine precautions as there is little evidence of spread from person to person, even though the rickettsiae have been isolated from the sputum and urine. Any sputum should, nevertheless, be burned as a precaution and care observed in the disposal of the excreta.

Epidemiological investigation is highly important to add to our limited knowledge of this disease. Special attention should be given to occupational hazards, history of contact or association with cattle or other animals, tick bites, and to the use of milk and milk products. Attempts to isolate and cultivate the rickettsiae should be limited to those laboratories prepared to guard against infection of their personnel. The most extensive studies so far conducted in the United States have been those of the U.S. Public Health Service and the California Department of Public Health. As a part of the epidemiologic investigation of a case, special inquiry and search should be made for persons suffering from vague febrile illnesses which may be unsuspected cases of Q fever.

Contacts require no restriction.

Environmental Sanitation. No effective methods of dust control around cattle have yet been developed. Laboratories handling the organisms should provide for segregation of this work and should provide for dust control and disinfection of the outgoing air. Pasteurization will reduce the risk of spread through milk even though it will apparently not destroy all the organisms.

Disinfection. Q fever is included in Group I (see p. 144).

Minimizing Ill Effects

Health departments will rarely if ever be required to help in the care of Q fever cases. The disease is a self-limited infection which is very rarely fatal. The cases that are recognized are usually hospitalized, are clinically indistinguishable from a typical pneumonia of virus origin, and require the same sort of nursing attention. Milder infections are not brought to medical attention. Both aureomycin and terramycin have been reported to be effective in therapy.

Control through Immunization

Active immunity can be produced through use of a formalinized vaccine prepared from the infected yolk sac. This vaccine has been extensively used for protection of laboratory personnel working with *R. burneti* and has apparently conferred a very satisfactory degree of protection. Its use among those exposed to an occupational hazard would appear justified.

SUMMARY

Health Department Program

Q fever is at present a disease of limited public health importance. It occurs chiefly as an occupational hazard among persons working in close association with infected cattle or among persons living in proximity to such animals. The principal mode of spread is apparently inhalation of dust contaminated with *R. burneti* through infected material from the cattle or ticks. While the organism appears in abundance in milk from infected cattle and is not always completely destroyed by pasteurization, milk is apparently a minor vehicle for spread of the disease.

Until more is known about the exact epidemiology of Q fever there is little that can be done to protect those exposed to this hazard. Ultimate prevention will apparently depend upon control of the infection in cattle, but so far no practical and effective means for its detection and eradication have been developed. The health department should insist upon milk pasteurization to reduce the risk of infection. All personnel of laboratories working with Q fever should be immunized, but immunization has not yet been extended to those exposed to infection from cattle. Public health nurses working in areas where Q fever occurs or is likely to occur should be alert for vague febrile illnesses which might be unrecognized cases.

SUGGESTED READINGS

Bell, Joseph A.; Beck, M. Dorothy; and Huebner, Robert J.: "Epidemiologic Studies of Q Fever in Southern California," *J.A.M.A.*, 142:868–72, (Mar. 25) 1950.

Commission on Acute Respiratory Diseases: "Epidemics of Q Fever among Troops Returning from Italy in the Spring of 1945," *Am. J. Hyg.*, 44:88–102, (July) 1946.

Deutsch, David L., and Peterson, E. Taylor: "Q Fever: Transmission from One Human Being to Another," *J.A.M.A.*, 143:348–50, (May 27) 1950.

Dyer, R. E., *et al.*: "Q Fever. A Symposium," *Am. J. Pub. Health*, 39:471–503, (Apr.) 1949.

Huebner, Robert J.: "Report of an Outbreak of Q Fever at the National Institute of Health," *Am. J. Pub. Health*, 37:431–40, (Apr.) 1947.

Huebner, Robert J., and Bell, Joseph A.: "Q Fever Studies in Southern California. Summary of Current Results and a Discussion of Possible Control Measures," *J.A.M.A.*, 145:301–5, (Feb. 3) 1951.

Lennette, Edwin H., and Clark, William H.: "Observations on the Epidemiology of Q Fever in Northern California," *J.A.M.A.*, 145:306–9, (Feb. 3) 1951.

Meiklejohn, Gordon, and Lennette, Edwin H.: "Q Fever in California. Observations on Vaccination of Human Beings," *Am. J. Hyg.*, 52:54–64, (July) 1950.

Oliphant, John W.; Gordon, Donald Q.; Meis, Armon; and Parker, R. R.: "Q Fever in Laundry Workers, Presumably Transmitted from Contaminated Clothing," *Am. J. Hyg.*, 49:76–82, (Jan.) 1949.

Robbins, Frederick C.; Gauld, Ross L.; and Warner, Frank B.: "Q Fever in the Mediterranean Area: Report of its Occurrence in Allied Troops. I. Epidemiology," *Am. J. Hyg.*, 44:23–50, (July) 1946.

Shepard, Charles C.: "An Outbreak of Q Fever in a Chicago Packing House," *Am. J. Hyg.*, 46:185–92, (Sept.) 1947.

Shepard, Charles C., and Huebner, Robert J.: "Q Fever in Los Angeles County," *Am. J. Pub. Health*, 38:781–88, (June) 1948.

35. Diseases Spread through Arthropods

The role of arthropods, especially insects, in the spread of infections of man and animals was first recognized in the closing years of the nineteenth century. This discovery shed the first clear light upon the epidemiology of some of our most important diseases which more than almost any others had altered the course of history and shaped the economic development of human civilization for centuries. Important as are the more common infections that spread daily from man to man through close personal association, those that are spread by insects include some of the most devastating of the old and modern plagues and pestilences, notably yellow fever, bubonic plague, typhus, and malaria.

In considering these diseases as a group, we are departing somewhat from the plan of etiological classifications so far followed. In a certain sense, these diseases have nothing in common other than a comparable mode of spread through arthropod vectors. Some of the diseases are due to bacteria, others to viruses, some to rickettsiae, and still others to protozoa. Viewed from a somewhat different standpoint, however, these diseases, with the possible exception of malaria, constitute a logical group in that they are all apparently infections of other species of animal and their appearance in man is a biological accident brought about by the arthropod. Some of them, such as tularemia and Rocky Mountain spotted fever, appear to be diseases of arthropods which the infected tick may bring to man directly. Plague and possibly typhus appear to be diseases of rodents, the insect merely bridging the gap between the rodent and man; others, such as yellow fever and African sleeping sickness, are diseases of still different species of mammals and are also spread to man by accidental insect transmission. The arthropods thus expose man to a realm of infections from which he might otherwise escape—infections which, because of their lack of long adaptation to the human body, show a high degree of virulence and are attended with a high case fatality rate.

The existence of these diseases within a given area depends upon two factors: a reservoir of infection and a suitable arthropod. The reservoir is usually furnished by infected animals or, in case of malaria, by man. Travel and commerce serve to shift infected reservoirs from one part of the world to another. Thus plague-infected rodents have been carried by ships to all corners of the globe, and the migration of malarious people has set up new foci in areas previously not infected. Yet if a suitable vector is absent from the new area, infection cannot spread, as there is no way for the causative organisms to pass from the infected to the noninfected persons.

The arthropods in general serve the triple function of effecting the escape of infection from the old host, transmitting it to a new one, and bringing about its entry into this victim. In the case of certain tick-borne diseases, it serves the added function of reservoir. Aside from the relatively rare spread through mechanical contamination of the surface of the body, the insect or tick performs its mission through its biting or sucking mechanisms. Through this process it takes out of the body of the host the infectious agents that otherwise would have no avenue of escape and would, therefore, perish within the host. It harbors the infection within its body and may even incubate it and enhance its virulence for man. Later, by biting a new host, the vector breaks through the normal protective integument of skin and implants the infection directly into the tissues.

Fortunately for man, arthropods show a remarkably high degree of specificity with respect to their ability to spread infection. Certain diseases are spread by flies, others by mosquitoes, still others by ticks, lice, or fleas. In general, one species does not share its role of vector with another. Within a given group an even higher degree of specificity is found, as, for example, the ability of certain Aëdes mosquitoes to spread yellow fever and dengue yet their inability to spread malaria, a function of the Anopheles mosquito. This specialization is carried to even further degrees when we find that only certain species of Anopheles are malaria vectors and that possibly only certain races of these species are involved. Failure to identify the exact vector spreading infection within a given locality will inevitably lead to waste and disappointment in control measures, which are obviously of no value if directed against the wrong agent.

This dependence upon a suitable vector results in a very definite geographical and often a seasonal limitation upon these several diseases, in that their occurrence is coextensive with the distribution of the corresponding vector. Many of the arthropods that serve as vectors are more numerous in the tropics and disappear as the colder temperate zones are reached. Such diseases are therefore more prevalent in the tropical areas. When they invade the colder regions, it is for short periods of time, terminated by the return of unfavorable seasonal conditions. Thus yellow fever has paid repeated excursions into the northern half of the United States but has always disappeared with the advent of cold weather, whereas in the tropics it is spread at all seasons of the year. The winter hibernation of ticks and their increased feeding in the spring cause a definite seasonal distribution of Rocky Mountain spotted fever and tularemia. Other arthropods may be found in all parts of the world, as, for example, the rat flea that spreads bubonic plague. Some, such as the louse specific for man, may be more active in the colder months when congregation of people within buildings and the wearing of heavy clothes increase the intensity of human infestation, thus causing an increased prevalence of typhus during the winter.

MODE OF SPREAD THROUGH ARTHROPODS

In serving as vectors and occasionally also as reservoirs of infection, many different mechanisms are involved in effecting the transfer.

Mechanical Transmission. In occasional instances, an insect, especially a fly, may carry infection on the external surface of the body. The best example of this type is seen in the common housefly that may contaminate its feet by walking over feces of the typhoid or dysentery case and may leave the bacilli on food over which it later walks. The fly is never infected nor does it do any biting but serves merely as a passive vehicle that has, however, independent power of locomotion. Its role is essentially the same as that of the fingers in transferring infection to food. Obviously such spread can occur only if contaminated material is carelessly left where flies can find access to it.

Passive Intestinal Harborage. Certain insects harbor infection within their intestines without suffering ill effects from it, much as horses and chickens harbor tetanus spores. Thus it was estimated that 0.5 per cent of the flies following the British troops during the Mesopotamian campaign in 1918 harbored cysts of amebic dysentery. Typhoid and dysentery bacilli may likewise pass through the intestinal tract of the fly. When such flies find access to food and leave their droppings on it, infection may readily occur. The amount of disease so spread is probably not large except under conditions of very primitive sanitation.

Mechanical Contamination of the Mouth Parts. If a sucking or biting insect should feed upon an infected person, the organisms, besides being drawn into the body of the insect, may also lodge on the mouth parts. Transmission of the disease may occur if a noninfected person is bitten before the organisms have died. This is apparently the usual method of spread of trypanosomiasis by the tsetse fly; spread of anthrax and of tularemia through this mechanism has been described. Although it is theoretically possible in many diseases, it is unlikely to occur frequently. There is no evidence that it ever occurs in such diseases as syphilis.

Infection of the Intestinal Tract of the Vectors. Some organisms are pathogenic for the insect as well as for man. The insect infected by some of these, notably plague bacilli, shows an obstruction of the gut which may result fatally. During the early stages in the rat flea, the organisms may be shed in the feces, be deposited with the feces upon the skin of a new host, and be scratched into the bite wound. As the infection in the flea progresses, there is a multiplication along the anterior end of the gut, the proventriculus, ultimately resulting in complete obstruction. Unfortunately, however, the sucking apparatus is lodged in the pharynx, anterior to the obstruction, so that the flea can still feed.[1] The blood that is sucked in at the time of biting distends the anterior part of the gut but is regurgitated into the wound as soon as sucking has stopped and before the mouth parts are withdrawn. Thus the blood contaminated by the infection of the gut is injected by this regurgitation into the wound, thereby resulting in human or rodent infection.

Biological Transfer. This term is used to refer to spread that entails a vital change in the parasite during the sojourn in the body of the vector. The insect sucks in the organisms along with a blood meal but is not able to transmit the infection until after a definite time period, during which the parasite has been changed and has migrated into the salivary glands. This period is referred to as the extrinsic incubation period. We may thus think of the life cycle of the parasitic organism as alternating between the human and the insect phase, each of which is essential to the completion of the cycle. As we are considering these problems from the selfish standpoint of man, we are wont to speak of the insect as the intermediate host. Zinsser has pointed out, however, that, from the standpoint of the insect, man is the intermediate host. In the case of parasites which have a definite sexual phase of reproduction (as, for example, malaria), biologists consider the host in which the sexual phase occurs to be the definitive host and that in which the asexual phase occurs to be the intermediary host. On such a basis, the Anopheles mosquito is the definitive host of malaria, and man the intermediate host (see p. 28).

The length of the period of extrinsic incubation is a factor of major im-

[1] Like the old man who could "chaw but not swaller."

portance in the epidemiology of an insect-borne disease. Many insects that acquire an infection through feeding on a suitable reservoir fail to survive the period of extrinsic incubation before being eaten by birds or otherwise destroyed. The longer the period, the less the probability of survival to the stage of infectiousness. The length of the period varies with the species of vector, the strain of parasite, and the climatic conditions. For example, the period is shorter in the *Anopheles gambiae* infected with *Plasmodium falciparum* (estivo-autumnal malaria) in a tropical area than it is in *A. quadrimaculatus* (the vector of malaria in the United States) infected with *Pl. vivax* in a subtropical or temperate zone. Thus a higher proportion of the former mosquitoes will survive until infectious, with resultant more extensive spread of malaria. In many areas the period of extrinsic incubation in available vectors is too long for an infection to become firmly established even though it is repeatedly reintroduced.

Coelomic Harborage. Certain arthropods harbor pathogenic organisms in the body cavity as well as in the intestines and salivary glands. Under such circumstances, the infection may escape if the insect is crushed, even though no biting or defecation has occurred. The material thus liberated may be rubbed into any wound or break of the skin. Tularemia may be carried to human beings by ticks in this manner.

ARTHROPODS AS RESERVOIRS OF INFECTION

Although arthropods do not usually transmit disease organisms from one generation to another, exception must be made for the tick and the mite which can pass certain microorganisms through their eggs to their offspring. The larvae that hatch from these eggs start life infected and carry the condition through to the adult phase, only to transmit it again through the eggs. The organisms have thus established a symbiotic relationship with the arthropod, in which they cause no symptoms. The arthropod serves, however, as a constant reservoir of infection from which spread to man may occur.

Aside from this phenomenon in the tick and the mite, the infection of an arthropod always ceases with the death of the host. In the case of many insects, this means the end of the summer season, so that infection is not carried through from one year to the next. Under such circumstances, the next season's crop of insects must become infected from some reservoir before they are able to spread disease. Such occurs with the Aëdes mosquito infected with yellow fever virus. In other instances, certain of the infected insects hibernate for the winter and survive to spread the disease again the following spring. Thus the carry-over of malaria from one season to another in certain localities may be due as much to the renewed activity of infected mosquitoes as to fresh infection of a new generation by human carriers. Fortunately, in some instances, infection may even die out in an insect before the death of the latter.

GENERAL METHODS OF CONTROL

Although the usual methods of isolation and quarantine, epidemiological investigation, case-finding, and immunization are as applicable to diseases transmitted by arthropods as to other conditions, principal attention is usually given to interrupting the spread through attack upon the vector as the weakest link in the chain. This may be accomplished in several ways.

Prevention of Infection of the Vector. It has been pointed out that a vector is of no importance unless it has a chance to acquire infection. If the reservoir can be destroyed or rendered noninfectious or if the vector can be kept away from it, disease cannot be spread. Treatment programs have been attempted to destroy infection in the reservoir, as, for example, wholesale antimalarial treatment designed to cure the patients or at least to destroy the gametocytes that will infect the mosquito. By keeping the patient noninfectious through suitable treatment, this type of measure is comparable to the "chemical quarantine" used in syphilis. Another method of preventing infection of the insect is by screening patients so that the insect cannot get at them. This method is, of course, applicable only if the reservoir consists of human beings. Its use will reduce the infection rate of insects but will never eliminate spread because of the obvious impossibility of keeping all infected human beings behind screens at all times, especially if the period of potential communicability is prolonged as in malaria. Use of insect repellent, while designed primarily for protection of the noninfected, may serve also as a means of reducing the extent to which insects acquire infection from a human host.

Destruction of vectors is the most permanent form of control, as it obviates the potential risk from reintroduction of the infection into an area and does not depend on accuracy of diagnosis or cooperation of individual patients. If no suitable vectors exist in an area, there is no danger from importation of an unsuspected case or carrier, as, for example, the migration of persons who have uncured malaria. Ideally, complete eradication of the vector might be desired, but in practice this is often not feasible. Effective control of disease spread will usually be achieved if the number of insects is reduced to a very low level, so low in fact that the chance of an insect's coming in contact with an infected person at the right time is infinitesimal. The longer the insect population is kept down, the smaller the number of infected persons in the reservoir and, consequently, the smaller the chance of the insect's becoming infected. In this way the disease may be virtually eradicated over a period of years, even though the vector has not been completely eliminated. For this reason we are accustomed to speak of insect "control" rather than "elimination," which would be much more difficult and in many cases hardly worth the extra effort.

Methods of Insect Control. Insect control can be brought about through use of one of several different methods. In actual practice, a control program is usually a combination of these several measures, though the emphasis placed on each is somewhat variable. A trained entomologist is the first essential of any program, for he has the technical knowledge to permit identification of the particular vector locally involved, to study its local breeding habits, to indicate the point of its life cycle at which it is most vulnerable to attack, and to measure the progress of the control program. The methods that are used are highly detailed; their study constitutes a technical specialty. The health officer who needs to apply them on a community-wide basis will need to refer to special texts on insect control. For the purpose of this volume, a simple grouping and brief summary will suffice.

Elimination of Breeding Places. Each arthropod has its special requirements for the laying and development of the eggs. In some cases, this may be clear pools of water near human habitation. Some require stagnant pools, others running streams; some seek sunlight, others shade; some require salt water, other cannot breed in salt water. There is thus no single measure applicable to all species. The essential method is to determine carefully the particular species involved, to become thoroughly familiar with its habits and biological needs, and then to take such measures as will eliminate the breeding places or make them unsuitable for use. This may require drainage or filling of marshes or increasing their salinity, elimination of clear pools, shading of other pools, or even increasing the sunlight on the specific breeding place. Much ingenuity may be required but must always be based on careful entomological studies.

Destruction of Larvae. In places where elimination of the breeding places is not possible, it may be simpler to allow the adults to lay their eggs and then destroy the larvae after they hatch out. This may be accomplished by poisoning the water with oil or Paris green, spraying of manure piles with oil, or introducing into the pool or stream a species of fish that feed on the larvae. The introduction of DDT (dichlorodiphenyltrichlorethane or 1 trichloro—2, 2 bis [p-chlorophenyl] ethane) during World War II has made available a larvicide that is far superior to any previously known. DDT for this purpose can be dispersed on breeding areas either in the form of a liquid spray or as a 5 to 10 per cent dust. The former is in general the more effective and the more easily applied. The amount of spray that is needed varies with different insects; certain species are so sensitive that as little as $\frac{1}{10}$ to 1 lb in $\frac{1}{2}$ to 1 gal of liquid per acre will bring about control if evenly dispersed. One part of DDT in 100 million parts of water is lethal to the larvae of certain mosquitoes. When used as a spray, it is dissolved in oil or used as an emulsion. Small areas can be covered by hand or power sprayers; large areas can be covered by spraying from airplanes. Selection of the proper form of DDT and the best method of dispersal for a particular situation requires the advice of a trained entomologist or public health engineer with special knowledge of insect control.

Destruction of Adult Vectors. This is less desirable and less permanent than control of breeding, as many of the adults may have already reproduced before they are overtaken by the destruction program. Yet this stage of the life cycle is often the most easily attacked. Examples of this method are seen in programs for delousing to control typhus and fumigation of ships to prevent the introduction of bubonic plague. In the latter, not only the insect but also the rodent that carries the flea from one place to another is destroyed.

Application of this method depends on the use of chemicals which are highly poisonous for the species to be attacked. To be useful in human habitations these chemicals must be reasonably nontoxic for man in the concentrations poisonous for insects. Prior to the advent of DDT, pyrethrum was the most suitable insecticide for this purpose, but today it has been largely supplanted by DDT which is more toxic to the insects and persists longer in the treated area. The area to be treated (usually a room or a cabin), can be disinfected by release of an aerosol, which is a suspension of fine particles of insecticide as a mist or fog. A mixture of about 3 per cent DDT and 0.4 per cent pyrethrum in a suitable oil medium is contained in a metal cylinder charged with Freon under pressure. Release of pressure by a suitable valve causes the dispersion of the chemicals as a fine mist which is lethal to all flies and mosquitoes in the room, but not lethal in this form or concentration to bedbugs and roaches. DDT dissolved in a suitable oily base and applied as a heavy spray to walls, floors, ceilings and screens will usually so poison these surfaces that the insect that alights or crawls on them during the next few months is killed. This form of DDT spray is referred to as a residual spray; 1 gal of a 5 per cent solution will cover 1,000 sq ft of surface (0.2 gm per square foot.)

Residual sprays are particularly suitable for the control of flies [2] and mosquitoes and have been highly effective in control of malaria in areas where the major vector invades human habitations. This method is particularly effective in interrupting the chain of infection by destroying the insect during the period of extrinsic incubation.

Destruction of adult arthropods on the human or animal body is readily achieved by means of thorough dusting with DDT powder (10 per cent DDT in pyrophyllite or talc). The powder can be rubbed on the body and in the hair; for large programs of delousing, a power duster is desirable, the nozzle being inserted successively into the sleeves, trouser legs (or under the skirt), around the neck, and around the waist if possible, and several strokes of the pump applied for each location. Additional DDT dust is sprayed into the hair. About 4 oz of powder per person is required for adequate treatment. This method destroys all adult lice or fleas in 6 to 20 hours. Too many persons have been disappointed in DDT because it does not have the immediate killing power of certain insecticides which in their ultimate effect are less toxic for insects. The nits are not destroyed, but DDT adheres to the clothing or hair for two or three weeks, which is long enough to kill any lice that hatch out from the nits present at the time of dusting. The patient should be checked for adult lice the day after the dusting to make certain that the dusting has been effective.

Prevention of Access of Vector to Man. This may be accomplished either by protective devices applied to the individual person or through methods of keeping the vector at a distance. The greater the area of exposed skin the greater the risk of attack by certain insects such as mosquitoes. The baring of the skin through removal of the shirt, rolling of sleeves and wearing of shorts may increase the risk of attack by mosquitoes. In highly malarious areas it may therefore be desirable to provide for complete clothing during the hours when mosquitoes bite; headnets and special mosquito gloves may even be advisable. The clothing must be heavy and loose enough so that the mosquito cannot bite through it. Heavy and closely fitting clothing may also protect against ticks which tend to crawl in under the clothes; boots are especially suitable in grass that is tick-infested. The attendant upon a patient suffering from typhus or bubonic plague may be protected against lice or fleas by the wearing of suitable coverall clothing which fits tightly around the wrist, ankles, and neck.

Insect repellents have recently found new application in personal protection. Prior to World War II, such repellents were usually crude and

---

[2] Unfortunately, some species of flies appear to have developed a tolerance to DDT.

not very effective; most of them contained oil of citronella as the essential ingredient. Repellents developed during the war were highly effective against mosquitoes, though quite specific as to their repellent qualities for different species. Most repellents contain dimethylphthalate, indalone (n-butyl mesityl oxide oxalate), or Rutgers 612 (2 ethyl 1, 3 hexanediol indol) as their effective ingredient. Impregnation of clothing with dimethylphthalate furnishes effective protection against attack by mites.

Screening of habitations is also an effective means of keeping infected arthropods at a safe distance. This screening is usually applied to an entire building or at least to certain rooms, especially to kitchens, dining rooms and sleeping quarters. The effectiveness of screening depends on its completeness, immediate repair of all breaks, and the relationship between size of holes and the size of the arthropod to be kept out. For very fine insects such as sand flies, screening of extremely fine mesh must be used, but for the average fly or mosquito 18 mesh per inch is adequate. Where screening of the sleeping quarters cannot be provided, bed nets are effective provided they are carefully tucked in and the sleeper does not roll up against them so that the mosquito may bite through the mesh.

Although the several methods of preventing spread of infection through arthropods are somewhat unrelated and attack the problem from different angles, the usual control program attempts a reasonable combination of these in so far as practicable. They all require, however, a thorough understanding of the habits, life cycle, and biological needs of the responsible vector. In any single program, special emphasis is placed on the method which yields the greatest returns from a given expenditure of money; but this should always be supplemented by other methods to the extent to which they are applicable.

SUGGESTED READINGS

Andrews, Justin M., and Simmons, S. W.: "Development in the Use of the Newer Organic Insecticides of Public Health Importance," *Am. J. Pub. Health,* **38**:613–31, (May) 1948.

Bishopp, Fred C.: "Present Position of DDT in the Control of Insects of Medical Importance," *Am. J. Pub. Health,* **36**:593–606, (June) 1946.

Getting, Vlado: "Insect Vectors of Disease," *New England J. Med.,* **232**: 315–21, 344–50, 373–78, (Mar. 15, 22, and 29) 1945.

Herms, William B.: *Medical Entomology,* 4th ed. New York: Macmillan Co., 1950.

Herms, William, and Gray, Harold F.: *Mosquito Control—Practical Methods for Abatement of Disease Vectors and Pests.* New York: Commonwealth Fund, 1940.

"Insecticides and Rodenticides, 1952. Recommendations for Use," *Pub. Health Rep.,* **67**:455–58, (May) 1952.

Jarcho, Saul: "Arthropod-Borne Diseases with Special Reference to Prevention and Control," *War Med.,* 3:447–73, 596–618, (May, June) 1943.

Olson, Theodore A.: "Place of the Entomologist in Public Health," *Am. J. Pub. Health,* 36:1031–34, (Sept.) 1946.

Simmons, James S.: *Insects as Vectors of Virus Diseases, Harvard School of Public Health Symposium on Virus and Rickettsial Diseases.* Cambridge: Harvard University Press, 1940, pp. 118–75.

Smith, Theobald: *Parasitism and Disease.* Princeton: Princeton University Press, 1934.

Stone, William S.: "The Role of DDT in Controlling Insect-Borne Diseases of Man," *J.A.M.A.,* 132:507–9, (Nov. 2) 1946.

U.S. Public Health Service: *Rat-Borne Diseases. Prevention and Control.* Atlanta, Ga.: Communicable Disease Center, Feb., 1949.

36. Diseases Spread through Arthropods (cont.)

PLAGUE, TULAREMIA, ROCKY MOUNTAIN SPOTTED FEVER, TYPHUS, AND YELLOW FEVER

It is not possible in a book of this character to discuss in detail the epidemiology and control of all diseases spread by arthropods, even though such diseases may be of major public health importance most of the time in some parts of the world and at certain times in any section. Aside from malaria, their distribution is usually so limited that they constitute real problems for only relatively small areas. In other instances, they have been brought under such effective general control that they break into major importance only when the social, economic, and political life of the community is disrupted by war and famine. Only a few salient facts about a selected group of these will be presented here. The health officer confronted with such problems should consult the large texts and references and, before undertaking a control program, should become throughly familiar not only with the disease but also with the vectors.

PLAGUE

Bubonic plague is basically a disease of rodents and invades man only when carried from the rodent host by the rat flea. Rampant during the Middle Ages, the disease several times swept over Europe, left a huge death toll, and disrupted the entire social order. Several of the great plagues of this era were due to this disease. At the end of the nineteenth century it was apparently extinct but reappeared in 1894 in Hong Kong, whither it had probably come from infected wild rodents. Being carried by the rat that infests the trading ships, it has been spread from Hong

Kong to all corners of the globe. It appeared the early part of the century in California, where it caused small outbreaks in 1919 and 1924 and sporadic infections more recently. In many parts of the world the infection is found in wild rodents (sylvatic plague) which constitute a sizable natural reservoir from which infection may spread to domestic rodents or man. The infection is entrenched in the ground squirrels of the West and is gradually spreading eastward, infected animals having been found as far east as Kansas. The infection of wild rodents in the United States is so extensive that extermination of the disease in these hosts seems improbable; rather, the disease may spread further. Constant watchfulness is thus important to prevent the outbreak of localized epidemics.

Plague is due to infection with the *Pasteurella pestis*. The disease appears in two forms, the bubonic and the pneumonic. The former is characterized by local swelling of the regional lymph nodes, the swelling being accompanied by a septicemia which may result fatally. This form is spread by the bite of the rat flea (*Xenopsylla cheopis*) infected by feeding on the rat during the septicemic stage. With the advent of either fever or death of the rat, the flea seeks another host, usually another rodent or a human being, and thus spreads the infection. As pointed out above, the flea, itself a victim of the disease, deposits infected feces on the skin or regurgitates infected blood into the wound because of obstruction of the anterior portion of the gut. As fleas have little ability to migrate far from the rat, infection of other rodents or human beings is likely to occur only in the home where the flea left its prior host. Consequently, measures to keep rats out of dwellings are extremely effective in preventing human infection.

The pneumonic form of the disease is characterized by an extensive purulent pneumonia, which is almost invariably fatal. The sputum is heavily laden with the *P. pestis*. In contrast to the bubonic form, which is spread only through the flea, the pneumonic form is highly communicable from person to person through respiratory association.

CONTROL

Bubonic plague control hinges on measures directed at the rodent rather than the flea, for it is the rat that brings the flea into the habitation of man. Ships from plague-infested ports are routinely fumigated to destroy all possible rats and their attendant fleas, thus reducing the likelihood of introducing further infection. In areas where plague occurs, special attention should be given to the construction of homes and other buildings to prevent access of rats. Ratproofing of buildings and of ships is a veritable art in itself and requires thorough acquaintance with the habits of the rat. Though expensive, it is the most durable form of plague control; all other measures are but temporary expedients. In the presence of plague, special measures are essential for destruction of all rodents within the infected areas. This involves the trapping of rats and examination of their fleas to determine the limitations of the area in which infection occurs; this in turn is followed by systematic ratproofing and rodent extermination.

The wartime development of new rodenticides and insecticides has opened new possibilities of plague control. Alphanaphthylthiourea, popularly known as ANTU, is highly toxic for rodents and comparatively nontoxic for man and other animals in the doses required for rat destruction. It is a quick-acting poison for the Norway or brown rat (*Rattus norvegicus*) but not effective for the black or roof rat (*Rattus rattus*) or for mice. It produces such a degree of bait shyness that it can rarely be used more than once a year. Sodium monofluoracetate (1080) is the most effective and fastest acting rodenticide but is so toxic for humans and other animals that it should be used only by specially trained personnel.

The most recently developed rodenticide, Warfarin (a derivative of Dicumarol), has so many advantages over all others that it is rapidly becoming the poison of choice. It does not produce the same degree of bait shyness as do the others, is toxic for all domestic rodents, and has the lowest toxicity for man and useful domestic animals. When used for roof rats, a concentration of 0.25 mg per gram of bait is indicated. For Norway rats a concentration as low as 0.05 mg per gram of bait is effective. ANTU for a quick effect and warfarin for prolonged control make a desirable combination of rodenticides. Although many types of baits have been tried, a very simple one of corn meal has been found to be satisfactory.

The advent of DDT as an insecticide has also opened a new approach to the problem of plague control. Dusting of rat-runs with DDT causes the rats to pick up on their hair enough DDT to kill fleas, thereby reducing the risk of spread of plague from rat to rat and from rat to man. While one may naturally be reluctant to do so great a favor to a rat as to free it of its fleas, the method has possibilities as a plague control measure for it is these same fleas that spread the infection from one host to another.

The case. Bubonic plague is of danger to others only through infected fleas that may leave the case.

Contacts. All persons having contact with the case should use special precautions to avoid the acquisition of a flea from the patient. Such measures include special clothing for the attendant, disinfestation of the patient's clothing, and frequent bathing. As the pneumonic case is infectious through the respiratory excretions, the strictest aseptic nursing techniques should be observed, with special precautions as to disposal of the sputum and as to masking of both patients and contacts in order to reduce the likelihood of transfer of respiratory droplets.

Vaccines for immunization against plague have been developed and accorded some use. They appear to be of some value, though reliance should not be placed upon them to the exclusion of "anti-rat" measures. Their use is certainly not justified except under conditions where, because of poverty and poor home situations, rat control is utterly impossible. Such is the case in some parts of the world.

In those areas, we may expect to see plague continue to spread and often to flare anew in fresh localities. In the United States, in spite of the large reservoir among the wild rodents, it seems improbable, in view of the more substantial character of housing, that plague will ever reach epidemic proportions. Cases will occur from time to time, but the prompt application of measures directed against the rats in the home should prevent wide spread among human beings.

TULAREMIA

This is likewise a rodent infection which may at times resemble plague and was at one time confused with it. Tularemia has, however, spread far beyond the rodent host, since it is now encountered in almost all forms of wild mammals and in some wild birds. The causative organism, *Bacterium tularense*, has recently been shown to exist in the water of certain streams in areas where the disease occurs in wild life. Tularemia is most common in the rabbits of the Midwest but is found in all parts of the country. Infection is also found in wood ticks, which pass it to succeeding generations, thus constituting a large reservoir which may conceivably be the habitat of the organism.

Infection in man is of several types but usually manifests itself as a febrile illness attended with a sore at the point of entry of the organisms and with enlargement of the regional lymph nodes. In some instances, the local manifestations may be lacking. The case fatality rate is about 5 per cent.

Man may be infected in several different ways but most commonly through handling the tissues of an infected animal. The most numerous group of cases has occurred through handling infected wild rabbits, the organisms entering through a cut or abrasion of the skin. The appearance of cases with the primary lesion in the conjunctiva suggests transfer to the eye through the contaminated hand and possibly actual penetration of the unbroken conjunctival epithelium. Special danger attends the skinning and cleaning of rabbits that were easily killed, as these are frequently the ones that were too sick to run. Tularemia is so widespread among the rabbits of the Midwest that it is safest to assume the potential infection of any rabbit and to wear gloves in handling the carcass. Wood ticks, dog ticks, and deer flies may also transmit the infection through their bites. These insects probably play a major role in the spread among wild life. Infection of laboratory workers has occurred very frequently. The disease has been contracted from water contaminated by the carcasses of infected animals, and by eating rabbits which had been inadequately cooked.

In spite of its high infectiousness among those exposed, tularemia is rarely a serious problem for a board of health. Aside from the occasional infection through ticks and deer flies, most of the cases occur in a very limited group of persons, chiefly those who indulge in rabbit hunting and who therefore handle the carcasses. Prevention of such infection is therefore a matter of education as to personal precautionary measures to be taken. Those who enter the woods in infected areas should be warned against the danger of ticks. The danger from the sale of rabbits for meat is apparently not great, though a few market employees have been infected through handling these carcasses. The usual method of cold storage cannot be depended upon to destroy the organisms.

No serious attempt has been made to eradicate the reservoir of infection which is now so widespread. The periodic drives made on rabbits in agricultural states unquestionably reduce this important part of the reservoir but never destroy it. The board of health in an area where tularemia infection is low is justified in vigorously opposing the attempts of sportsmen to import rabbits from infected areas just to obtain a more abundant supply of living targets. It is doubtful if any measure suggested to cull the infected rabbits from such a shipment is practical.

ROCKY MOUNTAIN SPOTTED FEVER

This condition, caused by a rickettsia, is at present a rather uncommon infection which constitutes a serious problem in only a few localities. The term "Rocky Mountain" is a misnomer, since cases occur as far east as the Atlantic seaboard. Most serious attention has been given to it in certain areas of the West, where it attacks the herders, and in the South

Atlantic states, where it has affected chiefly children. The disease is being recognized with increasing frequency, though this does not necessarily mean more extensive spread.

Infection is transmitted through the bites of ticks—wood ticks (*Dermacentor andersoni*) in the West and dog ticks (*Dermacentor variabilis*) in the East. This is apparently a disease of ticks that by accident is carried by them to man. The infected tick passes on its infection through the egg to its offspring. As both adult and larval stages of the ticks hibernate in the winter, infection of man does not occur at all seasons. With the advent of warm weather, both the adult ticks and the larvae enter a period of feeding which results in the spread of the infection to man. In the West the disease is most common in the spring but in the East reaches its peak in the summer.

Control of this disease through eradication of ticks seems at present like an impossible task and has never been attempted. Individuals who live in infected areas—and especially those whose occupation keeps them outdoors and in the brush—should be very careful to avoid ticks by wearing protective clothing which will keep the ticks from gaining a foothold. The body should be examined carefully twice a day for any ticks that have been picked up; these should be removed cautiously to avoid crushing the ticks and thus releasing the infectious coelomic fluid. Removal with a pair of forceps or a folded piece of paper is recommended; the hands should then be washed thoroughly. The point of attachment should be treated with a suitable disinfectant. If the tick is removed within three or four hours of its attachment to the skin, infection will probably not occur, as the organism appears to enter the wound during the latter part of the period of engorgement. A vaccine, made originally from the bodies of infected ticks but now prepared from rickettsiae grown in the yolk sac of the chick embryo and inactivated with phenol or formalin, confers a high degree of protection for a limited period. Although not recommended for the general population, its use is highly desirable among persons who are likely to be exposed to ticks. It must be repeated annually.

TYPHUS

Typhus fever is an acute infection characterized by fever and rash and caused by certain species of rickettsiae. At least three forms of the disease are recognized: louse-borne (epidemic or classic) typhus, which appears in epidemic form and is attended by a high case fatality rate; flea-borne (endemic or murine) typhus, a milder form first described by Maxcy in the southeastern United States; and mite-borne or scrub typhus (tsutsu-gamushi disease) which is widespread throughout the southwestern Pacific area and southeastern Asia but has never been found in the United States. A fourth form, usually referred to as Brill's disease, appears to be merely a recrudescence of the classic typhus after a long period of dormancy in the body of the human host. Louse-borne typhus may occur in any part of the world but is most often encountered under conditions of poverty, crowding, and famine, especially when the social order of the community is upset by war. It has frequently devastated armies and has wrought havoc among refugees and other civil populations who are the victims of war. In former times it became widespread within such groups and defied all measures of control. On the other hand, flea-borne typhus is relatively mild, rarely kills, and shows no tendency to spread widely among a population. Though found originally in the South Atlantic states, it has been recognized in many parts of the world.

The exact biological relationship between the three forms is not clearly understood. *Rickettsia prowazeki prowazeki* of the classical form and *Rickettsia prowazeki moorseri* (the murine strain) of the endemic form are closely related. Man is the apparent reservoir of the former, the rodent of the latter. However, there is reason to suspect that the rodent may also harbor the classic virus between epidemic periods. The *R. tsutsugamushi*, which causes scrub typhus, is less closely related. This organism has apparently adapted itself to the mite, in which it passes from one generation to another without causing any disease. From the mite it spreads to field rodents and to man.

Epidemic typhus is spread from man to man by the body louse, *Pedic-ulus humanus corporis*. Its transmission is therefore favored by any circumstance which increases human infestation, such as crowding and lack of bathing and of laundry facilities. The louse is as much the victim of typhus as is the human being and suffers from an infection of the in-testinal lining. Spread of the endemic form is through the rat flea, which carries the infection from rodent to rodent or from rodent to man. There is no evidence that any other vector is operative. This form of the disease is therefore found principally among persons working around food sup-plies, where rats tend to congregate. Lacking a vector which normally moves from man to man, human infection is not likely to occur in epidemic form but will rather be confined to sporadic cases having no apparent rela-tionship to one another. Scrub typhus occurs in persons who go into areas of jungle grass or underbrush infested with trombiculid mites, especially *Trombicula akamushi* and *T. deliensis*. The larvae adhere to the grass, whence they transfer to man. As the infection passes from one generation of mite to another through the egg, the larva (which feeds only once) will, if already infected, transmit the rickettsiae at the time of feeding.

CONTROL

Because of the varied method of spread, the control of the three forms is very different.

Control of epidemic typhus is essentially a problem of delousing, thus reducing the incidence of infestation to the point where infection will not spread. Typhus vaccine furnishes a remarkably high degree of protection, even in the presence of lousiness, but its use should be as a supplement to louse-control measures, not a substitute for them. Prior to the advent of DDT and vaccines, delousing was the only control measure but was cumbersome and of very limited efficacy. Present methods of DDT dusting have supplanted all prior forms of delousing. These methods (see p. 441) are highly effective and easily applied. Not only do they destroy lice already on the body but the powder that persists for about three weeks in the clothes protects the individual against the likelihood of acquiring lice from other persons. The individual who is infested or wishes to protect himself can dust his body and clothes periodically, paying particular attention to the hairy surfaces and to the seams of the clothes. In the presence of typhus, wholesale dusting of the entire civil population is a practical and effective means of control. Dusting teams must be organized and equipped with hand or power blowers to force the dust inside the clothing. Under such conditions, delousing can be carried out without the necessity of stripping and bathing, always a cumbersome procedure when applied to an entire population or even a large segment of it, and without damage to the clothing that was the inevitable result of old methods of steam sterilization.

Typhus vaccine, prepared according to the modified Cox method through growth of rickettsiae on egg yolk and treatment with formalin, is highly effective, conferring a high degree of protection. At the outset of World War II, it was new and relatively untried under field conditions in the presence of epidemics. All American military personnel in typhus areas were immunized; louse-borne typhus was virtually unknown in these troops even though occurring in the civil population and in unimmunized troops of other nationalities in the same area. Although it is difficult to determine how much of the freedom from typhus should be ascribed to the vaccine and how much to the louse-control measures, there can be no doubt that much of the protection was due to the vaccine, as DDT was not known or available during the early part of war. Typhus vaccine is administered in two injections about a week apart; booster doses are used annually in the presence of infection.

Control of Endemic Typhus. While less important, the control of the endemic type is more difficult as it entails destroying the rat or at least keeping it out of human habitation. As both the domestic rat and the field mouse are apparently infected, urban and agricultural populations are concerned. The same methods for ratproofing mentioned above under plague (p. 445) are applicable here. The continued occurrence of sporadic cases bears testimony to the imperfection of our methods as at present applied in this country. Were the disease more serious or were the domestic rat of this country widely infected with plague, more stringent application of proved methods would undoubtedly be enforced. A vaccine prepared from the murine strain of rickettsiae confers effective protection.

Control of mite-borne typhus depends on avoidance of localities known to be mite-infested and the wearing of clothing treated to be mite-repellent. The present vaccines are of no value. The mites are usually found in jungle grass, underbrush, or other forms of scrub growth. Such terrains should be avoided whenever possible in areas where the disease occurs, or should be burned over before serving as a base of habitation. Those who cannot avoid exposure may be protected through wearing of clothing impregnated with dimethylphthalate.

YELLOW FEVER

Yellow fever is an acute, highly fatal infection due to a virus. In former years it was so widespread throughout the tropics that the economic development of these areas was seriously impeded. On many occasions the disease spread northward, invading the southern United States and even reaching as far as Philadelphia, New York, and Boston. Wherever yellow fever spread, it left in its wake a high toll of death, public panic, and temporary disruption of the social and economic structure of the community.

The work of Finlay and of the Reed commission showed that yellow fever in its epidemic form was spread through the *Aëdes aegypti*. The patient is not infectious to his associates by usual human contacts but for the first three to four days of the illness has the virus in his blood, at which time it may be withdrawn by the mosquito. The mosquito becomes infectious after a period of 10 to 14 days (extrinsic incubation period) and continues to harbor and give off the virus with its bite for the duration of its life (the remainder of the current mosquito season or until it is otherwise destroyed). As the *A. aegypti* breeds in pools of clear water near human habitations, its breeding can be readily controlled by eliminating, screening, or periodic emptying of these pools, including rain barrels, tin cans, cisterns, flowerpots, vases, gutters, or any other spot where water may collect and stand near homes. The application of such measures by Gorgas in Cuba and later in the Panama Canal Zone effected an absolute control of yellow fever and gave a classic and brilliant example of controlling disease through centering attention upon the weakest link in the chain of events leading up to spread.

Following this work it was universally assumed that more extensive application of control measures would eliminate yellow fever from the earth. The day was confidently expected when "yellow jack" would be extinct. More recent investigation has shown, however, that the problem is not so simple as mere *Aëdes* control. The recrudescence of yellow fever in certain areas of South America brought to light the existence of a form of the infection which is widespread throughout the interior of the continent and Africa and is referred to as jungle yellow fever. Even more serious than the extensive distribution of infection among the natives in these areas is the occurrence of the disease in certain species of monkeys, and the evidence that under jungle conditions some other vector than the *A. aegypti* is involved. Thus, apparently, rather than being on the verge of extermination, yellow fever is more widespread than had ever been previously imagined; and the interiors of Africa and South and Central America harbor vast reservoirs of infection, whence the disease may spread outward into civilization. In fact there is good evidence that the jungle infection is spreading northward up the Central American isthmus, southward in Brazil, and has crossed into the western slope of the Andes.

The jungle form, which in the individual case is just as serious as is the classic urban type of disease, occurs in the natives of the jungle or, when seen in whites, appears largely as an occupational disease among those whose work takes them into the forest. It represents infection with the same virus but spread by a different vector. Although knowledge of the jungle vectors is still incomplete, mosquitoes of the genus *Haemagogus* are important in certain areas. Control of these mosquitoes is particularly difficult as they are found chiefly in the leafy vegetation of trees and breed among the branches, where they are relatively inaccessible to control measures. *Aëdes leucocelaenus* is also of importance in certain areas. There is good reason to believe that yellow fever is basically a disease of monkeys among which it is spread by mosquitoes that occasionally bite humans who venture into the forest and that these latter bring the infection out into civilization where it spreads to other humans through the medium of a different mosquito. Urban yellow fever thus represents a tragic escape of the virus from its normal habitat and host.

In former years the discovery of this large reservoir of infection in the jungle might have been of little concern because of the slow methods of travel and the obvious warnings that would appear on the edge of the jungle as the disease spread outward. The advent of the airplane, however, has closely connected these infected areas with the urban centers of their respective continents and of both America and Europe. Man can today travel from infected areas to distant cities in a time less than the incubation period of yellow fever (three to six days after the bite of the mosquito). Thus, apparently, there is a real danger that yellow fever may appear in parts of the world where it has been nonexistent for decades and where, accordingly, no attempt has been made to control the breeding of the *A. aegypti*. There is every reason to believe, however, that the antimosquito measures formerly so successful will continue to be effective in controlling spread within civilization, where, so far as is known, the *A. aegypti* continues as the only vector. Such measures, however, are neither applicable nor effective in the jungle, where the disease spreads through the medium of other vectors. In the meantime, control of airplane travel, including medical supervision of the passengers, elimination of breeding areas around airports, and measures to keep mosquitoes out of airplanes or to destroy those that have got in, serves to reduce the risk of spread.

Yellow fever vaccine, developed as a result of the studies of the Rockefeller Foundation, is one of the most effective of all antigens. Given in a single dose, it confers a high level of resistance for at least five years. It has been used extensively on civil populations in South America and on large military forces. The vaccine has now passed the experimental stage and should be thought of as our most valuable asset in the control of yellow fever, especially in view of the large and uncontrolled reservoir of jungle infection. Immunization is advisable and often required for all persons traveling into these areas. Many countries that are free of yellow fever require that all airline travelers who have landed in or taken off from yellow fever regions, be quarantined on arrival unless they have been immunized.

SUGGESTED READINGS

PLAGUE

Bacot, A. W., and Martin, C. J.: "Observations on the Mechanism of the Transmission of Plague by Fleas," *J. Hyg., Plague Supp. No. 3,* **13**:423–39, (Jan. 1) 1914.

Eskey, C. R., and Haas, V. H.: *Plague in the Western Part of the United States. Federal Security Agency.* U.S. Public Health Service, Public Health Bull. No. 254, 1940.

Gordon, John E., and Knies, Phillip T.: "Flea versus Rat Control in Human Plague," *Am. J. M. Sc.,* 213:362–76, (Mar.) 1947.

Humphreys, F. A., and Campbell, A. B.: "Plague, Rocky Mountain Spotted Fever, and Tularaemia Surveys in Canada," *Canad. J. Pub. Health,* 38: 124–30, (Mar.) 1947.

"Insecticides and Rodenticides, 1952. Recommendations for Use," *Pub. Health Rep.,* 67:455–58, (May) 1952.

Link, Vernon B.: "Plague," *Am. J. Trop. Med.,* 31:452–57, (July) 1951.

Meyer, K. F.: "Sylvatic Plague," *Am. J. Pub. Health,* 28:1153–64, (Oct.) 1938.

———: "The Known and the Unknown in Plague," *Am. J. Trop. Med.,* 22: 9–36, (Jan.) 1942.

———: "The Ecology of Plague," *Medicine,* 21:143–74, (May) 1942.

———: "The Prevention of Plague in the Light of Newer Knowledge," *Ann. New York Acad. Sc.,* 48:429–67, (Apr. 10) 1947.

Reugsegger, James M., and Gilchrist, Huntington: "Plague. A Survey of Recent Developments in the Prevention and Treatment of the Disease," *Am. J. Trop. Med.,* 27:683–89, (Nov.) 1947.

Wayson, N. E.: "Plague—Field Surveys in Western United States during Ten Years (1936–1945)," *Pub. Health Rep.,* 62:780–91, (May 30) 1947.

TULAREMIA

Francis, Edward: "A Summary of Present Knowledge of Tularemia," *Medicine,* 7:411–32, (Dec.) 1928.

———: "Tularemia," *Am. J. Nursing,* 34:1–5, (Jan.) 1934.

———: "Sources of Infection and Seasonal Incidence of Tularemia in Man," *Pub. Health Rep.,* 52:103–13, (Jan. 22) 1937.

ROCKY MOUNTAIN SPOTTED FEVER

Dyer, R. E.: "Typhus and Rocky Mountain Spotted Fever in the United States," *The Harvey Lectures,* 29:41–66, 1933–34. Baltimore: Williams & Wilkins Co., 1935.

Hampton, Brock C., and Eubank, Harry G.: "Rocky Mountain Spotted Fever: Geographical and Seasonal Prevalence, Case Fatality and Preventive Measures," *Pub. Health Rep.,* 53:984–90, (June 17) 1938.

Harrell, George T.: "Rocky Mountain Spotted Fever," *Medicine,* 28:333–70, (Dec.) 1949.

Parker, R. R.: "Rocky Mountain Spotted Fever," *J.A.M.A.,* 110:1185–88, 1273–78 (Apr. 9, 16) 1938.

———: "Rocky Mountain Spotted Fever. The Results of 15 Years of Prophylatic Vaccination," *Am. J. Trop. Med.,* 21:369–83, (May) 1941.

Rickettsial Diseases of Man. Washington: American Association for Advancement of Science, 1948.

TYPHUS

Blake, Francis F.; Maxcy, Kenneth F.; Sadusk, Joseph F., Jr.; Kohls, Glen M.; and Bell, E. John: "Studies on Tsutsugamushi Disease (Scrub Typhus, Mite-Borne Typhus) in New Guinea and Adjacent Islands," *Am. J. Hyg.,* 41:243–373 (May) 1945.

Dyer, R. E.: "The Rickettsial Diseases," *J.A.M.A.,* 124:1166–72, (April 22) 1944.

Ecke, R. S.; Gilliam, A. G.; Snyder, J. C.; Yeomans, A.; Zarafonetis, C. J.; and Murray, E. S.: "The Effect of Cox-Type Vaccine on Louse-Borne Typhus Fever," *Am. J. Trop. Med.,* 25:447–62, (Nov.) 1945.

Kohls, Glen M.; Armbrust, Charles A.; Irons, Edwin N.; and Philip, Cornelius B.: "Studies on Tsutsugamushi Disease (Scrub Typhus, Mite-Borne Typhus) in New Guinea and Adjacent Islands," *Am. J. Hyg.,* 41: 374–99, (May) 1945.

Maxcy, Kenneth F.: "An Epidemiological Study of Endemic Typhus (Brill's Disease) in the Southeastern United States with Special Reference to Its Mode of Transmission," *Pub. Health Rep.,* 41:2967–95, (Dec. 24) 1926.

Morlan, Harvey B.; and Hines, Virginia D.: "Evaluation of County-Wide DDT Dusting Operations in Murine Typhus Control, 1950," *Pub. Health Rep.,* 66:1052–57, (Aug. 17) 1951.

Sadusk, Joseph F., Jr.: "Typhus Fever in the United States Army Following Immunization," *J.A.M.A.,* 133:1192–99, (Apr. 19) 1947.

Soper, F. L.; Davis, W. A.; Markham, F. S.; and Riehl, L. A.: "Typhus Fever in Italy, 1943–1945, and Its Control with Louse Powder," *Am. J. Hyg.,* 45:305–34, (May) 1947.

Wheeler, Charles M.: "Control of Typhus in Italy 1943–1944 by Use of DDT," *Am. J. Pub. Health,* 36:119–29, (Feb.) 1946.

Zinsser, Hans: "Varieties of Typhus Virus and the Epidemiology of the American Form of European Typhus Fever (Brill's Disease)," *Am. J. Hyg.,* 20:513–32, (Nov.) 1934.

———: *Rats, Lice and History.* Boston: Little, Brown & Co., 1935.

———: *Epidemiology and Immunity in the Rickettsial Diseases. Harvard School of Public Health Symposium on Virus and Rickettsial Diseases.* Cambridge: Harvard University Press, 1940, pp. 872–907.

YELLOW FEVER

Anderson, Charles R., and Gast-Galvis, Augusta: "Immunity to Yellow Fever Five Years after Vaccination," *Am. J. Hyg.,* 45:302–3, (May) 1947.

Bugher, John C., and Gast-Galvis, Augusta: "The Efficacy of Vaccination in the Prevention of Yellow Fever in Colombia," *Am. J. Hyg.,* 39:58–66, (Jan.) 1944.

Courtney, K. O.: "Report on the Recent Outbreak of Yellow Fever in Panama," *Am. J. Pub. Health,* 40:417–26, (Apr.) 1950.

Dauer, C. C., and Carrera, G. M.: "Carlos Finlay's Contribution to the Epidemiology of Yellow Fever," *Yale J. Biol. & Med.,* 9:585–604, (July) 1937.

Dick, G. W. A., and Smithburn, K. C.: "Immunity to Yellow Fever Six Years after Vaccination," *Am. J. Trop. Med.*, 29:57–62, (Jan.) 1949.

Elton, Norman W.: "Sylvan Yellow Fever in Central America," *Pub. Health Rep.*, 67:426–32, (May) 1952.

———: "Yellow Fever in Panama. Historical and Contemporary," *Am. J. Trop. Med. & Hyg.*, 1:436–56, (May) 1952.

Gibson, John M.: *Physician to the World. The Life of General William C. Gorgas.* Durham: Duke University Press, 1950.

Gorgas, Marie C., and Hendrick, Burton J.: *William Crawford Gorgas, His Life and Work.* New York: Doubleday, Page & Co., 1924.

Laemmert, H. W., Jr.; de Castro Ferreira, Leoberto; and Taylor, R. M.: "An Epidemiological Study of Jungle Yellow Fever in an Endemic Area in Brazil. Part II. Investigation of Vertebrate Hosts and Arthropod Vectors," Supp. to *Am. J. Trop. Med.*, Vol. 26, November, 1946.

Soper, Fred L.: "The Newer Epidemiology of Yellow Fever," *Am. J. Pub. Health*, 27:1–14, (Jan.) 1937.

Soper, Fred L.; Wilson, D. Bruce; Lima, Servulo; and Sa Antunes, Waldemar: *The Organization of Permanent Nation-wide Anti-Aedes Aegypti Measures in Brazil.* New York: The Rockefeller Foundation, 1943.

Strode, George K., and Bugher, John C.: *Yellow Fever.* New York: McGraw-Hill Book Co., 1951.

Taylor, R. M., and Fonseca de Cunha, José: "An Epidemiological Study of Jungle Yellow Fever in an Endemic Area of Brazil." Supp. to *Am. J. Trop. Med.*, Vol. 26, November, 1946.

37. Diseases Spread through Arthropods (cont.)

ENCEPHALITIS

The term "encephalitis" implies an inflammation of the brain but gives no clue as to the cause of this irritation. The symptoms vary somewhat according to the inciting factors but are related to the brain's function of motivating impulses and thoughts. There is quite generally a fever, drowsiness or excitability, headache, mental confusion, and altered reflexes. In some instances, depending upon the degree of destruction of brain cells, permanent mental impairment may result in those who recover. The case fatality rate is high in all types of encephalitis, as vital brain centers are easily damaged.

The most satisfactory classification of the infectious encephalitides is on an etiological basis. The simplest subdivision is in terms of primary and secondary. The former consists of those cases in which inflammation is due to the action of some infectious agent directly on the brain without demonstrable preceding action elsewhere in the body. These are the cases usually referred to when speaking of encephalitis. They include encephalitis lethargica, St. Louis encephalitis, Japanese B encephalitis, equine encephalitis, African sleeping sickness, and rabies. Probably many other types exist. The secondary type includes those cases in which the brain involvement develops as a complication of a disease having its primary manifestations elsewhere in the body. These are usually of virus origin and include encephalitis due to measles and mumps and rarely occur as a complication of vaccination. The secondary encephalitides have been mentioned under the discussion of the primary conditions. Many industrial poisonings are also attended by a toxic encephalitis due to the action of the poisonous substance, notably lead and mercury.

The incidence of primary infectious encephalitis is never high. Numerically, therefore, these cases rank very low among the communicable diseases and are not major public health problems. On the other hand, the case fatality rate is extremely high, and permanent mental damage may follow certain types. In some instances, the incidence has been high over a short period of time, thus causing much public fear. The seriousness of the diseases and the very incomplete knowledge as to mode of spread and control have prompted extensive study of these conditions during recent years.

ST. LOUIS ENCEPHALITIS

This term is used to refer to a specific type of encephalitis that occurred in epidemic form around St. Louis in the late summer of 1933, though there is reason to suspect that it may have been in that part of the country for at least a year previously. Similar conditions have occurred since then in St. Louis and elsewhere, and blood neutralization tests have shown that the infection is far more common and widespread than is suggested by the clinical cases that are recognized. Infection has been found in many parts of the Western half of the United States and in other countries. The disease differs strikingly from the lethargic type, in that there are few if any residual effects in those that recover and the highest attack rate is found in adults, especially in those over fifty, whereas children are almost unaffected.

This form of encephalitis is due to a virus isolated at the time of the 1933 outbreak. The reservoir of infection and the mode of spread are still not clearly understood. The virus has been isolated on the Pacific coast from three species of mosquitoes, *Culex tarsalis, C. pipiens* and *Aëdes dorsalis*, principally the first named. Studies of the latest blood meal of these mosquitoes show that they feed predominantly on birds. Domestic fowl and several species of wild birds have also been found infected. In the laboratory many species of mosquitoes, including those mentioned above, have been found to be capable of passing infection from one bird to another. The virus has also been isolated from the chicken mite, *Dermanyssus gallinae,* and from a wild bird mite, *Liponyssus sylvarium.* Such mites have been shown to be capable of transmitting the virus to successive generations of mites through transovarian passage, as well as transmitting it from chicken to chicken.

It is thus apparent that birds, both domestic and wild, constitute a reservoir of infection which is spread from bird to bird by mosquitoes or mites. The latter conceivably constitute the ultimate reservoir from which infection is passed to birds. Human infection apparently represents a biological accident whereby mosquitoes infected from feeding on a bird happened to bite a man rather than another bird. While such an hypothesis requires much additional support and clarification, it is the explanation that is currently most consistent with known facts regarding the occurrence of the disease. The seasonal distribution of encephalitis due to the St. Louis type virus is consistent with this theory of spread by mosquitoes to humans.

EQUINE ENCEPHALITIS

This condition was first clearly recognized in horses in 1930 and in man in 1938, though suggestive evidence of its human pathogenicity had been advanced a year or two previously. In horses it appears as a very severe epidemic infection of tremendous economic importance: in 1937, over 70,000 horses were affected in the United States, and a large proportion of these died. Recurrent waves of infection have been described, but fortunately they have not been of frequent occurrence. The disease has probably been present in unrecognized form for many years.

Equine encephalitis is due to a virus, of which two distinct strains exist in the United States.[1] The western strain has been reported from every state west of the Mississippi River and as far east as Alabama and Michigan, is the less severe of the two, and may be responsible for many mild cases of human encephalitis that escape detection. There are no known mental sequelae in the person who recovers. Those human cases so far described have been dominantly in adults. A severe outbreak due to this virus occurred in Minnesota, the Dakotas, and Manitoba in 1941, causing over 2,000 human cases. The eastern strain is far more virulent; most of the recognized human cases result fatally, and the few who recover show a high degree of mental deterioration. Almost all of the cases have been in children, most of whom were under five years of age. The virus was formerly thought to be confined to the eastern slope of the Appalachians but in recent years it has been found in both Texas and Michigan. Diagnosis is established either by recognition of the virus at autopsy or by neutralization tests on recovered cases. By virus and immunological studies, these strains may be separated from one another and from the St. Louis form.

Infection with the western strain of virus is apparently far more widespread than is suggested by the number of cases that are clinically recognized. Many of these persons have had no known association with horses. The original idea that human cases were secondary to equine infection is therefore not tenable. Infection of pigeons and of pheasants was early

[1] Two other strains have been recognized in other parts of the world.

recognized; later the virus was discovered in prairie chickens and more recently in domestic fowl and wild songbirds. The rates of infection in various localities strongly suggest that there may be considerable variation in the importance of different species of host in different areas. The eastern virus has been less extensively studied but has been isolated from domestic and wild birds as well as from human cases and horses.

The mode of spread of the virus of equine encephalitis appears to resemble closely that of the St. Louis virus. Some of the earliest studies of the disease showed that certain *Aëdes* mosquitoes might serve as vectors of at least the experimental infection. The more recent studies by Hammon and his associates have shown that several species of mosquitoes may be infected in nature. The western virus has been repeatedly isolated on the Pacific coast from *Culex tarsalis* and on one or two occasions from other mosquitoes. The distribution of the virus appears to correspond roughly with that of this species of mosquito. There is therefore reason to believe that, at least in that area, this mosquito may constitute the principal vector, though other mosquitoes may serve as minor vectors. Wood ticks have been artificially infected, and the virus was found in Kansas in the cone-nosed bug (*Triatoma sanguisuga*). The role of these species as vectors is unknown. Mites have also been found to be infected and may conceivably play an important role. In fact the epidemiology of western equine encephalitis appears to be almost identical with that of St. Louis encephalitis, with *Culex tarsalis* as the principal vector of infection from birds to man. The eastern strain has been isolated from species of *Mansoni* and both strains from the chicken mite, *Dermanyssus gallinae*.

The present knowledge of equine encephalitis is obviously quite incomplete. However, evidence currently available suggests that, as in St. Louis encephalitis, birds or mites constitute the principal reservoir and that infection of man and of horses represents an accidental attack by a mosquito that normally prefers avian blood. The term "equine" is an obvious misnomer as the horse, like man, is apparently the victim of infection spread from birds by mosquitoes and is not the true reservoir.

ENCEPHALITIS LETHARGICA [2]

This condition, described by von Economo in 1917, is quite rare at the present time. During the early part of the third decade of the twentieth

[2] Although there is no evidence to suggest that encephalitis lethargica is spread by arthropods, it is included here to bring all the primary encephalitides together. The reader is warned against attaching any other significance to this grouping. Two other types of primary encephalitis spread by arthropods, Japanese B encephalitis and African sleeping sickness or trypanosomiasis, are omitted here merely because they do not occur in the United States.

century (early 1920's), it showed a markedly increased prevalence in all parts of the world but has gradually subsided to a very low level. The sudden increase about 1919 and 1920 gave rise to suspicion that it was in some way an aftermath of the 1918 influenza pandemic. Its principal seriousness comes from the fact that a very high proportion of those affected have residual disturbances of the nervous system—disturbances sometimes causing a complete loss of the higher functions of intelligence. These postencephalitic cases of Parkinsonism present an almost hopeless prognosis and may need institutional care the remainder of their lives. The tragedy is heightened through the fact that this form attacks principally children, many of whom, if they recover, are changed in a few days from normally bright youngsters to little more than vegetative existence as helpless idiots for whom there is little if any hope of improvement.

The etiological agent is unknown, though presumably a filterable virus. It is thought that man is the reservoir and that the infection is spread by carriers, since proved contact of a case with a victim is rarely discovered. In the absence of more definite knowledge, it is supposed that the virus enters and leaves through the upper respiratory tract and is transmitted by direct respiratory association. There is no reason for suspecting that vectors, especially insects, are significant. In the absence of exact knowledge as to etiology, little is known as to resistance. The small number of cases and virtual absence of infection among the known contacts suggests that susceptibility is not high.

Nothing is known about control measures. Isolation with aseptic nursing technique is usually enforced during the acute febrile stage. Inasmuch as cases occur sporadically with no known relationship to one another, it seems unlikely that any control measures will be effective until more exact knowledge is available concerning the epidemiology of the condition.

GENERAL MEASURES FOR CONTROL OF ENCEPHALITIS

In the absence of exact knowledge concerning the mode of spread of the various forms of encephalitis, little can be done for prevention. For the sake of safety, the cases should be isolated during the acute and early convalescent stages. Special precautions should be taken to protect the St. Louis and equine types of cases against access by mosquitoes. There is no evidence that special disinfection measures are required or that contacts need to be quarantined. Reasonable measures for the control of mosquitoes are indicated on the basis of proof of their role as vectors.[3] Such measures

[3] Control of the 1952 California outbreak was made difficult by the fact that *C. tarsalis* had acquired resistance to DDT and other chlorinated hydrocarbon insecticides.

should include the screening of houses and protection of animals against mosquitoes by screening of stables where horses are kept at night. Use of insect repellants is indicated for persons whose occupation is such that they cannot be protected by screening. Active immunization of horses by using a formolized virus has been attempted with promising results. The risk of human infection, except among laboratory personnel handling the virus, is so low that active immunization is not as yet indicated. Public health measures to minimize the ill effects will probably not affect the case fatality rate or the incidence of mental sequelae, but nursing aid may assist in the better care of the patient who is not hospitalized.

Public Health Nursing Care. The public health nurse will probably not often find cases of encephalitis being cared for at home except during outbreaks, which are fortunately rare. Even during outbreaks, the severe cases will probably be hospitalized.

General Care. Mild cases seen by the public health nurse when she is collecting epidemiological information may need only general nursing care such as any person with a fever requires. Information on mode of spread and allaying fears regarding the epidemic are important parts of nursing care under these circumstances.

Occasionally a severe case will remain at home, and the public health nurse will be asked to assist with care. Nursing care in these cases may be quite difficult if the patient is in either a very lethargic or excited state. In the latter case, bedboards may be needed; these can quite easily be made at home and inserted. During convalescence the patient is often unstable emotionally and may be depressed or irritable or may cry easily. The public health nurse can assist the family in an understanding of the patient's mental and emotional state.

Diet. A high caloric diet is usually ordered. The public health nurse should suggest foods which may be used and which will tempt the appetite. The patient frequently has to be fed.

Number of Nursing Visits. Visits by the public health nurse will often be required only to collect specimens or data for epidemiological purposes. If severe cases remain at home, daily visits will be needed if bedside care is to be furnished. If merely instructional aid is offered, at least two visits should be made, preferably on successive days, to demonstrate the above procedures. Visits should be made to all patients who have residual central nervous system symptoms to assist the family in handling the emotional problems.

SUMMARY

Primary encephalitis, as it is encountered at present in the United States, is due almost exclusively to infection with the St. Louis or one of the equine strains of virus. Although the reservoir and mode of spread of these infections are still not clear, there is strong evidence that the viruses are widespread among certain birds, including domestic fowl, and that spread from bird to bird and from man to man is through certain arthropods, principally the mosquito *Culex tarsalis*. Bird mites may be an important reservoir.

Most of this evidence has been acquired since the last extensive outbreak of any of these infections, so that there is no proof of the efficacy of those measures which seem indicated. In the presence of an outbreak the health officer should certainly give attention to mosquito control measures, directing his attention particularly to those species known to be capable of serving as vectors, notably members of the *Culex* and *Aedes* genera. Assistance of a trained entomologist and of a public health engineer skilled in mosquito control measures is essential. The public health nurse plays little role other than making home visits to instruct the public regarding mosquito control measures that they can apply personally.

SUGGESTED READINGS

Ayres, John C., and Feemster, Roy F.: "Public Health Aspects of the Virus Encephalitides," *New England J. Med.*, 240:966–75, (June 16) 1949.

Casey, A. E., and Broun, G. O.: "Epidemiology of St. Louis Encephalitis," *Science*, 88:450–51, (Nov. 11) 1938.

Eklund, Carl M.: "Human Encephalitis of the Western Equine Type in Minnesota in 1941: Clinical and Epidemiological Study of Serologically Positive Cases," *Am. J. Hyg.*, 43:171–93, (Mar.) 1946.

Epidemic Encephalitis: Etiology, Epidemiology, Treatment. Third Report by the Matheson Commission. New York: Columbia University Press, 1939.

Feemster, Roy F.: "Outbreak of Encephalitis in Man Due to the Eastern Virus of Equine Encephalomyelitis," *Am. J. Pub. Health*, 28:1403–10, (Dec.) 1938.

Halverson, Wilton L.; Longshore, William Allen; and Peters, Richard F.: "The 1952 Encephalitis Outbreak in California," *Pub. Health Rep.*, 68:369–77, (Apr.) 1953.

Hammon, W. McD.: "The Arthropod-Borne Virus Encephalitides," *Am. J. Trop. Med.*, 28:515–25, (July) 1948.

Hammon, W. McD., and Reeves, W. C.: "Recent Advances in the Epidemiology of the Arthropod-Borne Virus Encephalitides," *Am. J. Pub. Health*, 35:994–1004, (Oct.) 1945.

Howitt, B. F.: "Human Equine Encephalomyelitis and St. Louis Encephalitis in California, 1939–1941," *Am. J. Pub. Health,* 32:503–15, (May) 1942.

Leake, J. P.; Musson, E. K.; and Chope, H. D.: "Epidemiology of Epidemic Encephalitis, St. Louis Type," *J.A.M.A.,* 103:728–31, (Sept. 8) 1934.

MacNalty, Sir Arthur: "The Epidemiology of Encephalitis Lethargica," *Proc. Roy. Soc. Med.,* 31:1–8, (Oct. 22) 1937.

Reeves, William C.: "The Encephalitis Problem in the United States," *Am. J. Pub. Health,* 41:678–86, (June) 1951.

"Report on the St. Louis Outbreak of Encephalitis," U.S. Govt. Rep., Treasury Dept., Washington, Pub. Health Bulletin No. 214, U.S. Public Health Service, 1935.

38. Diseases Spread through Arthropods (cont.)

MALARIA

Malaria usually occurs as a febrile illness of indefinite duration and is characterized by intermittent chills and anemia. Many cases relapse after apparent recovery from the acute stages, while in others the disease assumes a chronic condition attended with considerable debility and punctuated by frequent remissions. Malaria is directly responsible for a large number of deaths in the tropics and warmer parts of the temperate zone. Of even greater importance than its killing power is the loss of strength, debility, and general impairment of well-being that characterize the chronic form, thus seriously impairing the economic and social structure of the community in which malaria becomes widespread. It has hindered the maximum economic development of the tropics and, in the opinion of many historians, was one of the factors contributing to the decline of both Grecian and Roman civilization. During World War II it was the major public health problem, often responsible for more loss of manpower than any other single cause. Until effective control measures were established, malaria was so important in the southwestern Pacific area that it jeopardized seriously the chances of military success. Since the war, application of new control measures has brought about a remarkable reduction in the incidence of malaria. Locally acquired cases have almost disappeared from the United States, and even in some of the most malarious parts of the world there has been a virtual eradication of the disease.

EPIDEMIOLOGY

Occurrence. Malaria may be found in all races and in all parts of the world except in the most extreme northern and southern latitudes. Wherever suitable *Anopheles* mosquitoes exist, malaria may occur and may, temporarily at least, become endemic. In general, the highest incidence is in the tropics and the subtropics where climatic conditions favor the multiplication of the *Anopheles* mosquitoes throughout the year.

The true incidence of malarial infection is always much higher than is suggested by the number of recognizable cases. Several methods, the most common of which are palpation of the spleen and examination of blood smears, have been used in making prevalence surveys. Whereas the spleen cannot normally be felt through the abdominal wall, in chronic malaria it is so consistently enlarged that the number of persons with palpable spleens gives a good index of the prevalence of infection in malarious districts. Reliance is placed on both the number of such cases (spleen index) and their distribution according to the apparent size of the spleen. The more severe cases may show an enlargement reaching as far as the navel, while in the milder cases the spleen is barely detectable. The method has the advantage of simplicity of performance. Inasmuch as many of the milder cases escape detection, this must be used only as a means of determining an index of the prevalence of infection, not as a means of individual case-finding. Examination of blood smears for detection of the malarial parasite is a slower method and may equally fail to reveal the milder cases in which organisms are few and therefore likely to be overlooked. It has the advantage that the cases found can be identified with certainty and classified as to type of infection, whereas enlargement of the spleen may in some cases be due to other conditions and, even if due to malaria, gives no information as to type of disease.

Etiological Agent. Malaria is due to infection with a plasmodium, three strains of which may cause the disease in man.[1] The commonest in the United States, *Plasmodium vivax,* causes tertian malaria, so named because of the regular spacing of chills every third day. The *Plasmodium malariae* is less common, causing the so-called quartan type with chills every fourth day. The *Plasmodium falciparum* causes the estivo-autumnal form, which is the most malignant and fatal type of malaria and is characterized by irregular spacing of the chills. The plasmodium of malaria is not capable of free existence outside the human being or mosquito. In man it invades the red blood cells, where it develops to maturity, this stage of the plasmodium being referred to as a trophozoite. It then ruptures its own membranes and the blood cell and breaks up into numerous young forms known as merozoites. This rupture of the cells is associated with the chill, spacing of which depends upon the time required for the development of mature trophozoites and varies with different types of plasmodia.

---

[1] A fourth form, *Plasmodium ovale,* exists but infection with this parasite is so uncommon as to be of little importance.

The merozoites that are released enter new cells, where they develop into trophozoites, and the process is repeated. The plasmodium thus multiplies in man by asexual reproduction.

The reservoir of infection consists of infected human beings who harbor the plasmodium. Coincidental with the asexual reproduction described above, certain trophozoites develop into the sexually differentiated gametocytes. In the human body, these are incapable of union and ultimately degenerate; if drawn into the body of the mosquito, they unite, leading to sexual reproduction. The mosquito cannot, however, be infected by trophozoites. Hence the active reservoir consists of those persons who have gametocytes in their blood streams, for it is only this form that can be conveyed to mosquitoes. Gametocytes are not constantly present, yet anyone infected with malaria is potentially dangerous, as they may occur at a later date. Methods of estimating the size of the potential reservoir have been mentioned above, namely, spleen index and blood-smear examinations.

Areas where suitable *Anopheles* occur may be free of malaria as long as there are no infected persons, yet the immigration of such persons may lead to a localized malaria epidemic. In this way the disease usually spreads to new localities, or a new form is introduced. As a person may harbor the infection for many years, a large proportion of the population of a malarious district may serve as foci for the spread of the disease.

Escape of the Organism. The human body furnishes no natural avenue of escape for the malaria plasmodium. Escape must therefore be considered an accident, effected by withdrawal of blood through a break in the skin. Usually this is through the bite of a mosquito. Unless both male and female gametocytes are present in the few drops of blood withdrawn, infection of the mosquito cannot occur. In rare instances, escape is effected through human withdrawal of blood for injection into another person, namely, transfusion, injection of blood for therapeutic or prophylactic purposes, or even injection for the deliberate transmission of infection in the production of therapeutic malaria for treatment of general paresis. In such instances, transfer of an adequate number of trophozoites suffices, asexual reproduction being continued in the new host.

Transmission of Infection. The Anopheles mosquito serves a triple function of effecting the escape from the reservoir, transporting the infection to another person, and injecting the organisms into this new host. As only the female bites, it alone may serve in this capacity. The gametocytes, which are drawn into the mosquito's stomach, unite and penetrate the body cavity to form an oöcyst, which, after a period of 10 to 14 days of development, breaks into sporozoites.[2] These invade the salivary glands of the mosquito, where they are ready for injection into another person upon whom the mosquito may feed. The mosquito remains infectious for the remainder of its life, which in some species may include a period of winter hibernation; thus the infection may be carried over from one season to another. In other instances, the young mosquitoes of the following season acquire the infection from a persistent human reservoir.

Although over two hundred species of *Anopheles* mosquitoes have been described, only a few of these serve as malarial vectors. The commonest of these in this country is the *A. quadrimaculatus*. A particular species may be further subdivided into varieties, of which only certain ones may be involved in the spread; thus there may be the anomalous absence of malaria from areas in which a reservoir of infection exists and a suitable vector appears to be present (anophelism without malaria—Hackett). Before attempting to develop a control program, it is important to determine what species serve as vectors in any given locality, as success can be expected only if attention is directed toward the correct species.

Entry and Incubation Period. Entry into the new host is effected through the bite of an infected mosquito, the sporozoites being injected into the blood capillaries of the skin. Once inside the body, they quickly penetrate the red blood cells to form trophozoites, thus completing the cycle of infection. The stage of asexual reproduction is then resumed. When this has developed to the point at which a sufficient number of blood cells are destroyed with each escape of merozoites, symptoms referable to this event will be noticed and the incubation period completed. The time required for the development of the disease varies according to the strain of plasmodium and the dosage of sporozoites injected by the bite of the mosquito; it is seldom longer than 14 to 18 days for *P. vivax*.

Susceptibility. All human beings appear to be susceptible. Much uncertainty exists with respect to immunity as a result of infection. Some investigators have suggested a fairly high degree of resistance against the strain in question, thus preventing reinfection. Others have interpreted some of the apparent relapses as new infections in a person who does not acquire much resistance from a prior infection. A large number of persons harbor the plasmodium for years without signs or symptoms referable to it. These persons have apparently developed a resistance that persists at least as long as the infection continues. Infection with one strain of plasmodium confers scant protection against another strain.

[2] This is an average figure for *Pl. vivax* in the United States. The extrinsic incubation period varies with the temperature, the strain of plasmodium, and the species of mosquito.

CONTROL MEASURES

Control of Spread

The case requires no isolation other than screening to prevent access of mosquitoes. Ideally, this should apply to all persons who have been infected and who continue as chronic cases (or carriers), since these serve as the source of infection for new generations of mosquitoes. If screening could be universally practiced or even if the infected persons could be kept behind screens during the evening and night when the *Anopheles* bites, infection would disappear. This would mean that in malarious districts screening would have to be applied to all persons, as infection is widespread. In actual practice, this is impossible of attainment, due to the economic conditions in many areas. In spite of the impossibility of complete control through screening, the method serves to reduce the likelihood of infection of mosquitoes and, conversely, the chance of fresh infections among human beings. It is, therefore, a useful adjunct to any control program.

Destruction of the reservoir has been frequently attempted through intensive treatment of all infected persons. Ideally, such methods should cure the infection, though they would be effective from the point of view of spread even if they merely destroyed all gametocytes as rapidly as these were produced. The effectiveness of such measures would, however, depend on their continued use until absolute cure was established, lest relapses follow their discontinuance. Many drugs have been tried for this purpose but with uncertain results. The use of both quinine and atabrine has been disappointing in that neither appears to effect a complete destruction of the plasmodia. Certain of the synthetic antimalarials developed as a result of wartime research, notably chloroquine (SN 7618) and pentaquine (SN 13,276), offered greater promise of having plasmodicidal effect adequate to destroy all infecting organisms, thus eliminating both the risk of relapse and the risk of serving as a source of infection. Unfortunately the action of chloroquine has been largely suppressive, that is, it has kept the patient free of symptoms until such time as use of the drug was discontinued. More recently, primaquine, when used in conjunction with chloroquine, has been found to be a very effective plasmodicidal agent, especially in the treatment of *Pl. vivax* infections. Current reports suggest cures in nearly all cases if administered in adequate dosages. Except in the Negro, its use is attended with a minimum of untoward reactions. Like screening, treatment of infected persons is an essential component of any control program but not to be looked on as a measure on which sole reliance can be placed to the neglect of other precautions. So far as possible, however, treatment of any recognized case should be pushed to a real cure, thus eliminating a potential source of further infection.

Epidemiological investigation of the individual case is of little value in showing the source of infection in an area where the disease is endemic. The occurrence of a sporadic case in a supposedly uninfected area should, however, be carefully investigated to determine whether or not it may have been contracted locally, thus possibly revealing a previously unsuspected source of infection. In endemic areas, epidemiological investigation on a mass basis is both valuable and essential to determine the incidence of the disease, the conditions under which it is occurring, and the species of mosquito responsible for its spread in that particular locality.

Contacts require no quarantine but should be carefully studied to determine whether they also are infected with malaria and therefore also in need of treatment.

Environmental sanitation, through elimination or reduction of mosquito breeding, is the bulwark upon which malaria control is based. Regardless of the size of the reservoir or the lack of screening, malaria will not spread in the absence of a suitable *Anopheles* vector. The basis for mosquito control programs is a clear knowledge of the vectors within a given region, their places of breeding, and their mode of life. Only after this information is at hand can one outline a rational campaign to prevent the breeding of the particular species involved. It must always be remembered that, in a given area, there exist many forms of mosquito which may be a real source of personal annoyance yet which are incapable of spreading malaria. If attention is given to a broad program of control of all forms of mosquitoes, large sums may be needlessly spent on eliminating mosquitoes with nothing more than a nuisance value. While this may be aesthetically desirable, it does not control malaria. For the latter, it is essential to concentrate on certain species, even though these may not be numerically the most prevalent.

Among the most commonly applied control measures, the following may be mentioned: (1) Suitable breeding areas should be eliminated. This may be through draining of stagnant water to combat the forms that breed in quiet pools, increasing the salt content of coastal marshes, eliminating shade for those that require protection from the sun, providing shade for those that require sunlight, and so forth. Understanding of the breeding habits and requirements may reveal factors susceptible of change through regulation of the environment. (2) Destruction of the larvae may be accomplished through spraying or dusting the breeding areas with DDT preparations, spreading of oil films, or stocking the breeding pools with fish which eat the larvae. (3) Destruction of adult mosquitoes through use of aerosols and residual DDT sprays. For the details of application of these several methods and the special indications for their use, the student is referred to the special texts on insect control.

Screening has been mentioned above as a means of keeping mosquitoes from gaining access to infected persons and thus of reducing their danger as vectors. It is of equal, if not greater, value as a means of personal protection against infection through the bite of a mosquito. Most infections are contracted in the home, as the malarial vectors are usually night fliers. Adequate screening of the home and especially of the sleeping quarters therefore reduces the likelihood of infection. In districts where the risk is great, infection may be avoided by keeping within screened areas throughout the evening and night. Adequate screening is a very difficult matter in homes in which construction is flimsy, joints are not tight, and doors so out of line that screens do not fit snugly. A high incidence of malaria may so depress the economic capacity of the community that housing is bad and adequate screening either impossible or beyond the financial capacity of the individual. When applied rigorously, it affords real personal protection. Those who cannot remain behind screens during the hours of *Anopheles* activity, should wear protective clothing or make liberal use of repellents.

Minimizing Ill Effects

For many years quinine was the only effective antimalarial. Plasmoquine and atabrine had been used to a very limited degree prior to World War II. At that time the scarcity of quinine following the Japanese seizure of the Dutch East Indies forced the use of atabrine, which was found to be superior in many respects. It also prompted an extensive search for other antimalarials. Just at the close of the war two new antimalarials, chloroquine (SN 7618) and pentaquine (SN 13,276), became available which were free of some of the undesirable features of atabrine and more effective in that they destroy the plasmodia more quickly and completely, thus reducing the risk of relapses due to uncured infections. Even more recently, primaquine, which was also a product of the war research, has been found to have distinct advantages over all other antimalarials and is rapidly becoming the drug of choice in the treatment of vivax infections.

Public Health Nursing Care. There is no special nursing care for malaria patients except the usual treatment for chills and fever. The attendant should be instructed to cover the patient warmly (if possible, with light woolen blankets), to put a covered hot-water bottle at his feet, and to give a hot drink. During the fever stage fluids are forced, and sponge baths may be ordered by the physician. Effort should be directed toward making the patient as comfortable as possible. Blankets and hot-water bags do not lessen the severity of the chill nor shorten it, but they do bring a certain amount of comfort to the patient. On the other hand sponge baths are therapeutically important and may be ordered by the physician if the temperature rises too high. The patient usually has severe headache which may need medication for relief if the cold compresses or ice bags do not help. The public health nurse should be familiar with the antimalarial drugs and their reactions.

Control through Immunization

No effective means of conferring either active or passive resistance is available.

Suppressive Therapy. Many attempts have been made to apply chemical prophylaxis in the form of regular ingestion of drugs that destroy the malaria plasmodium. The theory on which this method rests is that, if there is a constant level of such drugs in the blood stream, any organisms injected by the bite of a mosquito will be destroyed either before entry into red corpuscles or at least within a few generations of asexual reproduction, thus preventing the development of the clinical disease. Quinine was used extensively for this purpose for many years. During World War II it was replaced by atabrine, administered in doses of 0.1 gm per day. An intense yellow dye, atabrine had the disadvantage of producing a yellowish discoloration of the skin and of causing some gastrointestinal disturbances. Chloroquine has superseded both quinine and atabrine as it is devoid of the gastrointestinal and skin manifestations of atabrine and is suitable for administration in weekly rather than daily doses. Unfortunately, none of these drugs exerts a true prophylactic effect, for malaria acquired and kept dormant during the period of "prophylaxis" may appear in clinically recognizable form as soon as the drug is discontinued. Use of the term "prophylaxis" has therefore been dropped and replaced by the term "suppressive therapy," for all that is actually accomplished is to suppress the disease during the period of medication. Infection can be acquired during this period and become manifest when the patient moves to a nonmalarious area and therefore discontinues his medication. Suppressive therapy should never be used to the exclusion of other antimalarial measures. At best it is a mere expedient to avoid illness during sojourn in a malarious area.

SUMMARY

Health Department Program

The usual community program for malaria control is built around environmental sanitation, as this is the only method giving permanent results. If mosquito breeding can be either eliminated or controlled, suitable species for the spread of malaria will not exist or will at least be so uncommon that the risk will be effectively reduced. While considerable expense may be entailed in the initial elimination of breeding areas, the cost of continuing the program is usually much reduced. Where chief reliance is placed on destruction of larvae or adult mosquitoes, this work must be kept up at continuing high expense. Treatment of cases to reduce the size of the reservoir must be continued unabated year after year if the vectors are not controlled. Similarly, screening and protection through use of repellants are measures which require eternal vigilance. Elimination of breeding areas is the only control measure which has any degree of permanence and in which the gains of one year, while expensive at the outset, may be maintained undiminished at a reduced cost.

The **health officer** is responsible for general direction of the malaria program. He must personally direct the epidemiological surveys as to the incidence of infections and the conditions under which the disease is occurring locally. With the aid of a well-trained entomologist, he must determine the important local vectors so that suitable control measures may be developed. The application of these is the task of the **sanitary officer** working under the general direction of the health officer. Engineering skill and thorough knowledge of the use and limitations of the modern insecticides are essential to the development of a sound mosquito control program. Usually the assistance of special malaria control personnel from the state health department may be needed to assist the local health department's staff. The **public health nurse** should be constantly alert for cases who may be overlooked but who may require treatment, and she should instruct the family as to the need for measures of personal prophylaxis through screening and other protection from mosquitoes. All observations as to suspected cases, as well as to potential breeding areas, should be reported to the health officer so that appropriate action may be taken.

SUGGESTED READINGS

Alving, Alf S.; Arnold, John; and Robinson, Donald H.: "Mass Therapy of Subclinical Vivax Malaria with Primaquine," *J.A.M.A.,* 149:1558–62, (Aug. 23) 1952.

Andrews, Justin M.: "What's Happening to Malaria in the United States?" *Am. J. Pub. Health,* **38**:931–42, (July) 1948.

————: "Nation-Wide Malaria Eradication Projects in the Americas. I. The Eradication Program in the U.S.A.," *J. Nat. Malaria Soc.,* **10**:99–123, (June) 1951.

Boyd, Mark F. (editor): *Malariology. A Comprehensive Survey of All Aspects of This Group of Diseases from a Global Standpoint.* Philadelphia: W. B. Saunders Co., 1949, 2 vols.

Faust, Ernest Carroll; Scott, J. Allen; and Taylor, John E.: "Malaria Mortality and Morbidity in the United States for the Years 1946, 1947, and 1948," *J. Nat. Malaria Soc.,* **9**:195–204, (Sept.) 1950.

Hackett, L. W.: "Biological Factors in Malaria Control," *Am. J. Trop. Med.,* **16**:341–52, (May) 1936.

————: *Malaria in Europe.* London: Oxford University Press, 1937.

————: "Some Obscure Factors in the Epidemiology of Malaria," *Am. J. Pub. Health,* **30**:589–94, (June) 1940.

Human Malaria, with Special Reference to North America and the Caribbean Region. Publication of the American Association for the Advancement of Science. Lancaster, Pa.: Science Press, 1941.

Russell, Paul F.: "Lessons in Malariology from World War II," *Am. J. Trop. Med.,* **26**:5–13, (Jan.) 1946.

————: "Some Epidemiological Aspects of Malaria Control with Reference to DDT," *J. Nat. Malaria Soc.,* **10**:257–65, (Sept.) 1951.

————: "The Present Status of Malaria in the World," *Am. J. Trop. Med., & Hyg.,* **1**:111–23, (Jan.) 1952.

Russell, Paul F.; West, Luther S.; and Manwell, Reginald D.: *Practical Malariology.* Philadelphia: W. B. Saunders Co., 1946.

Sapero, James J.: "The Malaria Problem Today. Influence of Wartime Experience and Research," *J.A.M.A.,* **132**:623–27, (Nov. 16) 1946.

Soper, Fred L., and Wilson, D. Bruce: *Anopheles Gambiae in Brazil 1930 to 1940.* New York: The Rockefeller Foundation, 1943.

Welch, Sarah F., and Quinby, Griffith E.: "Epidemiological Appraisal of Malaria in the United States during 1951," *Am. J. Trop. Med. & Hyg.,* **1**:736–42, (Sept.) 1952.

World Health Organization, Expert Committee on Malaria: *Report on the Fourth Session.* World Health Organization, Technical Report Series No. 39, (April) 1951.

Index

Aerosols, 31, 56, 350–51
Agencies, public health
  federal. *See* Federal health agencies
  international. *See* International health agencies
  local. *See* Boards of health, local
  nonofficial. *See* Nonofficial agencies
  state. *See* State health departments
  voluntary. *See* Nonofficial agencies
Agriculture, Department of, 98, 218
Air
  disinfection of, 30–31, 56
  vehicle, role as, 30–31, 303, 350–51, 429
Airplanes
  control of, to prevent disease spread, 96, 454
  malaria spread by, 96
  yellow fever spread by, 96, 454
Alastrim, 301
Amblyomma americanum, 428
Amebiasis. *See* Dysentery, amebic
American Public Health Association, 49, 99
American Red Cross, 62, 321
American Social Hygiene Association, 105, 381, 399
American Trudeau Society, 368
Anamnestic response, 65–66
Animal Industry, Bureau of, 223
Animals, control of, 97
Animals as reservoirs of infection, 23–24, 437–38
Ankylostoma duodenale, 194
Anthrax, 27, 31, 436
Antibiotics—use in
  diphtheria, 239, 243
  gonorrhea, 44, 386–89, 397, 398
  influenza, 338, 344
  measles, 291, 338
  meningococcus meningitis, 44, 328
  pneumonia, 44, 332, 336, 337, 338
  prophylactic use, 44, 124, 261, 270, 273, 336, 338, 344, 397, 398
  Q fever, 432

rheumatic fever, 270, 273
streptococcus infections, 44, 124, 260, 261, 262, 338
syphilis, 44, 386–89
tetanus, 413
typhoid fever, 179
whooping cough, 280, 338
Antibodies, 37, 60–63
Antigens, 37, 66–71
  criteria for use, 66–68
    effectiveness, 67
    injections required, 68
    reactions, 67–68
    risk, 67
  types of, 69–71
    bacterial extracts, 70
    dead organisms, 70
    living, 69–70
    multiple, 71, 247
    nonliving, 70
    toxins, 70
    toxoids, 70
    vaccines, 70–71
Antitoxins. *See* Serum
Antivaccinationists, 302, 309–10
ANTU, 446
Armstrong, Charles, 314
Aronson, Joseph D., 368
Arthropods
  See also Fleas; Flies; Lice; Mites; Mosquitoes; Ticks
  control of
    destruction of vector, 438–39
    prevention of access to man, 441–42
    prevention of infection of arthropod, 438
  diseases spread by, 433–75. *See also* Encephalitis; Malaria; Plague; Q fever; Rocky Mountain spotted fever; Tularemia; Typhoid fever; Typhus; Yellow fever
  mode of spread by
    biological transfer of infection, 28, 436–37